The Elizabethan Club Series 5

National Portrait Gallery, London

Sir Philip Sidney ca. 1577

Young Philip Sidney

1572 - 1577

James M. Osborn

Published for the Elizabethan Club

New Haven and London, Yale University Press

1972

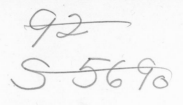

Published with assistance from the foundation
established in memory of Oliver Baty Cunningham
of the Class of 1917, Yale College.
Library of Congress catalog card number: 77-151584
International standard book number: 0-300-01443-0

Designed by John O. C. McCrillis
and set in Aldine Bembo type.
Printed in the United States of America by
The Murray Printing Company, Forge Village, Mass.

Distributed in Great Britain, Europe, and Africa by
Yale University Press, Ltd., London; in Canada by
McGill-Queen's University Press, Montreal; in Latin
America by Kaiman & Polon, Inc., New York City;
in Australasia by Australia and New Zealand Book
Co., Pty., Ltd., Artarmon, New South Wales;
in India by UBS Publishers' Distributors Pvt., Ltd.,
Delhi; in Japan by John Weatherhill, Inc., Tokyo.

In Memoriam

M-L. O.

Cor Unum, Vita Una

CONTENTS

ILLUSTRATIONS

PREFACE

This biography, occasioned by the sudden recovery of over six dozen hitherto unknown letters addressed to Philip Sidney, relates the formative years of a very remarkable young man. Special attention has been focused on Sidney as a man and as a budding leader in affairs of state, a role to which he was born and educated. Thanks to these new materials Sidney can be seen as the promising young aristocrat whose character and abilities, especially his powers of mind, astounded the experienced and learned men who came to know him.

Readers seeking a book on Sidney the Elizabethan poet should turn elsewhere, for the simple reason that it cannot be proved he wrote a single line of verse during the years here covered in new detail. On the other hand, one of the greatest surprises has been to find that earlier biographers, apparently eager to discuss the charms of the *Arcadia* and of *Astrophel and Stella*, left many stones unturned and documents unexamined. Fresh scrutiny has been highly rewarding. Further evidence about Sidney no doubt will come to light, but until it does we can be grateful for what is now available.

The new letters first dazzled my eyes early in March 1967 during a call on Mr. Peter J. Croft, Senior Manuscript Cataloguer at Sotheby's in London. He unveiled a volume listed as no. 11762 from the incredible collection of Sir Thomas Phillipps, a portion of which was to be sold on June 26. An afternoon's inspection stiffened my resolution to add the volume to the Osborn Collection at Yale, for the seventy-six letters obviously represent the most important group of manuscripts concerning a major Elizabethan poet to be offered at auction within living memory.

Eleven of the letters (one already in print) were of special Christ Church interest; they are from Canon Robert Dorsett to his former pupil, Philip Sidney, concerning his brother Robert who was then an under-graduate at the House. Mr. Croft had them removed from the volume and listed as a separate lot. Incidentally, it should be noted that many of Sidney's Continental correspondents addressed him as "Le Baron de Sidenay" after he had received that title from Charles IX of France. Because Queen Elizabeth frowned on the use of foreign titles by her subjects he remains plain Philip Sidney in the following pages. Not until 1583, six years after the central events of this book, did her Majesty dub him Sir Philip.

Inspection of the Middle Hill Catalogues, issued erratically during the nineteenth century by Sir Thomas Phillipps, yielded this meagre description of the volume:

> 11762   Letters from Foreign Correspondents to
> Sir Philip Sydney, 1574–5–6.

No previous Sidney scholar seems to have scanned the indexes of the Middle Hill Catalogues, for if any had, he would have been led to these letters. Indeed, Miss Mona Wilson is the only Sidney devotee who looked carefully enough through the original account of the Sidney family papers published by Arthur Collins in 1746 to observe that Collins had written, "Men of affairs in most parts of Christendom corresponded with him [Sidney]." Below he added a footnote: "Which appears from a Volume of Letters in all Languages, from the most learned Men of all Countries, still remaining at Penshurst."[1] This group of letters, like the Languet correspondence printed in 1633, apparently had been kept together by Sidney's secretary, Stephen Le Sieur. Who removed the present group from Penshurst cannot be determined.

The bid for the Osborn Collection succeeded in securing the first lot. After the letters to Sidney (with one from Pietro Bizari to Jean de Vulcob which Languet had enclosed in a packet to Sidney) arrived at Yale, the process of transcription and translation began. The original texts are in Latin, French, and Italian (see pp. xvii–xx below). Here I had the invaluable assistance of R. J. P. Kuin, a recent honours graduate in English at Oxford University, whose Dutch ancestry and European background gave him special advantages for the task. The Dorsett letters had been purchased by Christ Church, and the Librarian, Dr. John Mason, kindly granted permission for them to be used in the new biography.

A word should be said in passing about the miracle that so much evidence exists concerning any major Elizabethan literary figure. Shakespeare's correspondence, despite the digging of generations of bardolaters, still consists of only one letter from Richard Quiney—a letter apparently never sent to the poet. Of Spenser's letters only two he wrote and three addressed to him are preserved in originals or copies. For Ben Jonson, who enjoyed a long life and decades of fame, twenty-two letters are

---

1. *Letters and Memorials of State* (London, 1746), vol. 1, p. 99 of the introduction.

preserved, but none addressed to him. Sir Walter Ralegh, a man of action, has left 229 letters, but only one sent to him is known. Sidney's prominence as a budding statesman, as an aristocrat, and later as a famous poet made him triply venerated, so letters by him or addressed to him tended to be preserved. The recently recovered group brings the total known to approximately 117 from Sidney's own pen and 165 written to him.

Readers accustomed to nineteenth-century correspondence, gossipy letters full of personalities and personal reactions, may be unprepared for the objective, formal tone taken by Sidney's friends when writing to him. Well-bred Renaissance men wrote formal letters, the only exceptions being those between parents and siblings, or between lovers. The example of Hamlet springs to mind; he ended his letter to Ophelia with the phrase "Thine evermore, dear lady, whilst this machine is to him." Languet's letters to Sidney in Italy have many personal, avuncular passages but afterwards his style shifted:

> I do not wish to write to you so frequently, or send you idle and teasing letters, as I did formerly. Instead, I had decided to write you about public affairs and hoped that letters on this subject would not displease you, for I realized that you have an unusual desire for information on the nations with which we have some contact, and on the changes occurring there.[2]

Stimulated by the new letters, investigations have produced additional information, fresh interpretations, and unsuspected aspects of Sidney's years on the Continent, results far beyond what seemed possible at the outset. The reader who compares the chapters in this book with previous accounts of Sidney's life and experiences in Paris during the fateful summer of 1572, in Frankfurt the following winter, in Vienna, Venice, Padua, the Rhineland, and the Netherlands, will find much that is new and much that is altered from what was formerly accepted as fact. Sidney's report to the Queen and Privy Council after his sessions with William of Orange (chap. 23) has not been previously mentioned in any book on Sidney. In interpreting facts the iron yardsticks of chronology and logistics provide disciplines that never should be neglected.

All hitherto unpublished letters and documents have been included in full, but in English translation. These English versions aim to convey the

2. Languet to Sidney, June 12, 1575.

sense, and to some degree the style, of the originals, whatever the language in which they were written. Accordingly they are free translations; at times the grammar and the punctuation of the originals have been slightly altered to simplify construction while preserving the sense.

The ease of the reader has also been kept in mind by limiting the length of paragraphs, even where the author did not pause to do so. New letters have been divided into topical sections in order to avoid unrelieved pages of quotation. By giving explanatory comment in the connecting passages, the need for many footnotes has been avoided.

Similarly, the length of chapters has been limited. In this decision I was abetted by the advice of the historian J. A. Froude, advice pointed out by my colleague F. W. Hilles. In the Hilles Collection there is an autograph letter written by Froude in October 1889 to an aspiring author, Mrs. Alexander Ireland, who had sent Froude the manuscript of her life of Jane Welsh Carlyle. Froude replied, "With a chapter ended comes a pause and an opportunity for a few serious or humourous reflections of your own, with a chapter begun a new breath is taken and the reader is lifted forward. He is apt to weary when there are no resting places."

When citing documents and other sources the principle followed has been that direct quotation is preferable to paraphrase. If quotations are from English letters and documents the original spelling has been retained, even though Sidney's orthography and that of his contemporaries may temporarily slow the reader to some degree. The original texts of the new letters will appear in a separate publication for the use of scholars; further explanatory and textual notes will there be included.

Citation of sources has been specific except for the following: the new letters now in the Osborn Collection; the Dorsett-Sidney letters in the Library at Christ Church, Oxford; and eighteen letters to Sidney in the British Museum. The sources of all these letters are included in the list which appears on pages xvii–xx below. Similarly, the published letters between Sidney and Hubert Languet, which exist in several editions and translations, are cited only by date. Throughout the text Latin names have been given in their vernacular equivalents; to minimize the number of footnotes the dates of most persons mentioned will be found in their index entries. Fortunately there has been no confusion over new-style dating of letters from the Continent, since the Gregorian calendar reforms were not introduced until 1582, five years after the events in this biography.

Although, like most lovers of Sidney's poetry, I have wished for more manifestations of literary interest during his early years, writing this book has been fully rewarding. The experience has exemplified a sage comment made by one of the most enlightened critics of Elizabethan poetry which this century has produced, my late friend and colleague Tucker Brooke.

> No student of English literature need apologize for devoting a considerable part of his attention to the more personal and social aspects of Sir Philip Sidney. In three directions, to be sure, Sidney's actual achievement ranks him among the very highest of the Elizabethan writers. None but Shakespeare and Spenser produced a finer sonnet sequence. None but Ben Jonson surpassed him as a literary critic. None of the writers of his age approached his influence in the field of prose romance. Yet if *Astrophel and Stella*, the *Defense of Poesy* and the *Arcadia* had never been published, we should still have to regard Sidney as a cultural landmark.[3]

3. Tucker Brooke, *A Literary History of England* (New York, 1948), p. 472.

LETTERS TO SIDNEY HITHERTO UNPUBLISHED

(in order of citation; for page locations see index)

Date	From	Language	Source
June 5, 1573	Chastillon	French	Osborn
June 5, 1573	Laval	French	Osborn
June 5, 1573	D'Argenlieu	French	BM Add. MS. 15914, fol. 10
December 3, 1573	Vulcob	French	Osborn
December 10, 1573	Bochetel	French	Osborn
December 11, 1573	Vulcob	French	Osborn
January 2, 1574	Vulcob	French	Osborn
April 23, 1574	Vulcob	French	Osborn
May 3, 1574	Zündelin	Latin	Osborn
May 7, 1574	Zündelin	Latin	Osborn
May 10, 1574	Zündelin	Latin	Osborn
May 22, 1574	Zündelin	Latin	Osborn
May 31, 1574	Dohna	Latin	Osborn
June 20, 1574	Zündelin	Latin	Osborn
June 1, 1574	Lobbet	Latin	Osborn
July 5, 1574	Aubéry	Latin	BM Add. MS. 15914, fols. 43–44
August 27, 1574	Perrot	French	Osborn
September 6, 1574	Zündelin	Latin	Osborn
September 27, 1574	Wacker	Latin	Osborn
October 5, 1574	Lobbet	Latin	Osborn
October 9, 1574	Perrot	French	Osborn
October 28, 1574	Paull	Latin	Osborn
November 5, 1574	Zündelin	Latin	Osborn
November 26, 1574	Perrot	French	Osborn
November 27, 1574	Zündelin	Latin	Osborn
December 7, 1574	Lobbet	French	Osborn
January 6, 1575	Solms	Latin	Osborn
January 8, 1575	Perrot	French	Osborn
January 9, 1575	Zündelin	Latin	Osborn
January 30, 1575	Zündelin	Latin	Osborn
February 3, 1575	Carrafa	Italian	BM Add. MS. 15914, fol. 15

January 30, 1575	Hanau	French	BM Add. MS. 21522, fol. 138
February 20, 1575	Perrot	French	Osborn
February 27, 1575	Perrot	French	Osborn
February 24, 1575	Wacker	Latin	Osborn
March 17, 1575	Lobbet	French	Osborn
March 20, 1575	Crafftheim	Latin	BM Add. MS. 15914, fol. 17
April 6, 1575	Lobbet	French	Osborn
April 7, 1575	Lobbet	French	Osborn
April 14, 1575	de Banos	Latin	Osborn
April 16, 1575	de Banos	Latin	Osborn
June 3, 1575	Dorsett	Latin	Christ Church
June 21, 1575	Dorsett	Latin	Christ Church
May 31, 1575	Lobbet	French	Osborn
May 26, 1575	de Banos	Latin	BM Add. MS. 15914, fols. 21–22
June 30, 1575	de Banos	French	BM Add. MS. 18675, fols. 4–5
July 5, 1575	Lobbet	French	Osborn
June 20, 1575	Zündelin	Latin	Osborn
July, 1575	Möller	Latin	BM Add. MS. 15914, fols. 19–20
July 25, 1575	Lobbet	French	Osborn
August 30, 1575	Lobbet	French	Osborn
September 2, 1575	Seton	French	Osborn
September 5, 1575	Lobbet	French	Osborn
September 19, 1575	Lenormand	French	Osborn
September 19, 1575	de Banos	French	Osborn
October 15, 1575	de Tassis	Italian	Osborn
October 8, 1575	Slavata	Latin	Osborn
October 17, 1575	de Banos	French	Osborn
October 15, 1575	Dorsett	Latin	Christ Church
October 24, 1575	Dorsett	Latin	Christ Church
October 31, 1575	Dorsett	Latin	Christ Church
November 5, 1575	Dorsett	Latin	Christ Church
December 1, 1575	Dorsett	Latin	Christ Church
October 23, 1575	Zündelin	Latin	Osborn
October 22, 1575	Carrafa	Italian	BM Add. MS. 17520, fols. 4–5
October 31, 1575	Brüning	Latin	Osborn
November 5, 1575	Ursinus	Latin	Osborn

November 22, 1575	Lobbet	Latin	Osborn
November 19, 1575	Pavese	Italian	Osborn
December 1, 1575	Wacker	Latin	Osborn
December 2, 1575	Carrafa	Italian	BM Add. MS. 15914, fols. 25–26
December 4, 1575	de l'Écluse	French	BM Add. MS. 17520, fol. 6
December 27, 1575	Lobbet	French	Osborn
January 22, 1576	de Tassis	Latin	Osborn
January 5, 1576	de Banos	French	BM Add. MS. 18675, fol. 6
January 6, 1576	Paull	Latin	Osborn
January 10, 1576	Pavese	Italian	Osborn
January 23, 1576	Dorsett	Latin	Christ Church
January 28, 1576	de Banos	French	BM Add. MS. 18675, fol. 7
February 10, 1576	de Banos	French	BM Add. MS. 18675, fol. 8
February 14, 1576	Lobbet	French	Osborn
March 13, 1576	Lobbet	Latin	Osborn
March 21, 1576	Dorsett	Latin	Christ Church
March 19, 1576	de Banos	Latin	BM Add. MS. 15914, fol. 27
March 19, 1576	de l'Écluse	French	Musée National d'Histoire Naturelle, Paris
April 24, 1576	de Banos	Latin	BM Add. MS. 15914, fol. 28
May 17, 1576	Dorsett	Latin	Christ Church
Undated	Lobbet	French	Osborn
May 15, 1576	Lobbet	Latin	Osborn
May 28, 1576	de l'Écluse	French	BM Add. MS. 15914, fol. 29
June 5, 1576	Lobbet	French	Osborn
June 6, 1576	Purkircher	Latin	Osborn
June 8, 1576	de l'Écluse	French	BM Add. MS. 15914, fol. 31
June 23, 1576	Dorsett	Latin	Christ Church
October 1, 1581	Lobbet	Latin	Osborn

LETTERS FROM SIDNEY HITHERTO UNPUBLISHED

(in order of citation; for page locations see index)

Date	To	Language	Source
May 3, 1575	Hanau	Latin	Staatsarchiv Marburg/Lahn 86 Hanau 1831 no. 2
April 21, 1576	Languet	Latin	Bib. Nat. MS. Lat. 8583, fols. 32–33
March 30, 1577	Hanau	French	Staatsarchiv Marburg/Lahn 86 Hanau 1831 no. 1
April 8, 1577	de l'Écluse	French and Latin	Bayerische St. (Munich) MS. Lat. 10364, fol. 575
May 22, 1580	Denny	English	Bodleian Library

ACKNOWLEDGEMENTS

During the years spent writing this book, in my attempts to reveal new aspects of Sidney's life and friendships, especially his relations with eminent men on the Continent of Europe, I have benefited from the help and erudition of many scholars on both sides of the Atlantic Ocean. My inquiries have received generous response; though this verbal acknowledgement of courteous assistance is inadequate, it must suffice.

Like all students of Sidney's life and writings I am indebted to my predecessors, especially to Albert Feuillerat, Malcolm W. Wallace, John Buxton, William A. Ringler, Jr., and Roger Howell. Both Mr. Buxton and Mr. Ringler have extended continued help and encouragement, including reading the book in typescript. This service of friendship has also been performed by James E. Phillips, Katherine Duncan-Jones, Marcia Allentuck, Jordwin Kuhn, Dan Davin, and my colleagues René Wellek, Louis L. Martz, Stephen R. Parks, and Francis C. Coulter: to each of them I am grateful for suggestions. Elizabeth Tate kindly read the page proof and Elsie Church helped with the index.

Geoffrey Elton, J. H. Plumb, A. L. Rowse, Dame Lucy Sutherland, and R. B. Wernham have responded to historical queries. Help in illuminating Sidney's life and friendships in Italy has come from John Tedeschi of Chicago, Massimo Firpo of Turin, Gaetano Cozzi of Padua, and especially from my friend Gian Carlo Roscioni of Rome. Miss Gertraud Leitner of Vienna kindly examined for me the correspondence of Hugo Blotius. Similarly, Colin Clare and Miss Harriet Harvey Wood in London have checked and transcribed various documents. In preparing translations of the new letters Fred J. Nichols of Yale has offered his specialized knowledge of Renaissance Latin, for the niceties of which a proper dictionary does not exist. To each of them I am indebted, though blame for any lacunae or errata should be placed on my own head.

In any biographical study of Sidney his correspondence with Hubert Languet, first published in 1633, forms a main beam of the structure. In this book translations began with the English versions of Steuart A. Pears (1845) and of Charles Levy (Ph.D. dissertation, Cornell University, 1962). The latter's version, more modern in idiom, was taken as the starting point for comparison with the seventeenth-century texts, which have been ever-present at my elbow. I am grateful for Mr. Levy's generosity in permitting quotations from his translations, and look forward to his Clarendon Press edition of the Sidney correspondence in collaboration with R. J. P. Kuin of York University, Ontario. Mr. Kuin's help in this book would be difficult to exaggerate; during his two years as my research assistant at Yale he lived and breathed with Sidney during all the working week. Tom Davis has proven an able successor. The late Kingsley C. Adams supplied invaluable assistance with the illustrations, including proof that no authentic portrait of Languet exists; John Kerslake and Roy Strong also were helpful. Besides making available the Dorsett-Sidney letters, John Mason, Librarian of Christ Church, Oxford, has opened the early records of the College for my use.

Finally, like all latter-day Sidney scholars, I wish to acknowledge the fundamental debt we owe to Sidney's own secretary, Stephen Le Sieur, who filed and preserved the marvellous harvest of letters Sidney received from the eminent men on the Continent—a treasury of source information unexcelled for any major English poet before the time of paper-saving Alexander Pope a hundred and fifty years later.

ABBREVIATIONS

Unless otherwise stated, the following works were published in London.

ADB	*Allgemeine Deutsche Biographie.* Leipzig, 1875–1912.
Birch's *Bayle*	Thomas Birch, ed. *Bayle's Dictionary Historical and Critical.* 1734–41.
Bourne	H. R. Fox Bourne. *A Memoir of Sir Philip Sidney.* 1862.
Buxton	John Buxton. *Sir Philip Sidney and the English Renaissance.* 1966.
Champion	Pierre Champion. *Charles IX.* Paris, 1939.
Collins	Arthur Collins. *Letters and Memorials of State.* 1746.
Coryat	Thomas Coryat. *Crudities.* 1611.
CSPD1	*Calendar of State Papers Domestic, 1574–80.*
CSPD2	*Calendar of State Papers Domestic, 1581–90.*
CSPF1	*Calendar of State Papers Foreign, 1572–74.*
CSPF2	*Calendar of State Papers Foreign, 1575–77.*
CSPF3	*Calendar of State Papers Foreign, 1577–78.*
CSPI1	*Calendar of State Papers Ireland, 1509–73.*
CSPI2	*Calendar of State Papers Ireland, 1574–85.*
CSPR	*Calendar of State Papers Rome, 1572–80.*
CSPS1	*Calendar of State Papers Spanish, 1558–67.*
CSPS2	*Calendar of State Papers Spanish, 1568–79.*
de Thou	Jacques Auguste de Thou. *Histoire universelle depuis 1563 jusqu'en 1607.* 16 vols. 1734.
Digges	Sir Dudley Digges. *The Compleat Ambassador.* 1655.
Feuillerat	A. Feuillerat, ed. *The Prose Works of Sir Philip Sidney.* Vol. 3. Cambridge, 1963.
Geizkofler	A. Wolf, ed. *Lucas Geizkofler und seine Selbstbiographie.* Vienna, 1873.
Greville	Fulke Greville. *The Life of the Renowned Sir Philip Sidney.* 1652.
HMC Cecil	*Historical Manuscripts Commission Calendar of the Manuscripts of the Marquis of Salisbury (Cecil MSS.).*
HMC De L'Isle	*Historical Manuscripts Commission Report on the Manuscripts of Lord De L'Isle and Dudley.*
HMC Pepys	*Historical Manuscripts Commission Report on the Pepys Manuscripts.*

Howell	Roger Howell. *Sir Philip Sidney, the Shepherd Knight.* 1968.
Lettenhove	Baron Kervyn de Lettenhove. *Documents relatifs à l'histoire de la Belgique.* Brussels, 1890.
Levy	Charles Levy. "The Correspondence of Sir Philip Sidney and Hubert Languet, 1573–1576." Ph.D. dissertation, Cornell University, 1962.
Moffet	Thomas Moffet. *Nobilis, or a View of the Life and Death of a Sidney.* Edited by V. B. Heltzel and H. H. Hudson. San Marino, Calif., 1940.
Nichols	John Nichols. *Progresses of Queen Elizabeth.* 1823.
Pears	S. A. Pears. *The Correspondence of Sir Philip Sidney and Hubert Languet.* 1845.
Platzkoff	W. Platzkoff. *Frankreich und die deutschen Protestanten . . . 1570–1573. Historische Bibliotek.* Vol. 28. Munich/ Berlin, 1912.
PRO Dom. Eliz.	*Public Record Office, Domestic Correspondence, Elizabeth.*
Read	Conyers Read. *Mr. Secretary Walsingham.* Oxford, 1967.
Ringler	W. A. Ringler. *The Poems of Sir Philip Sidney.* Oxford, 1962.
Stählin	Karl Stählin. *Sir Francis Walsingham und seine Zeit.* Heidelberg, 1908.
Thuanus	J. A. de Thou. *The History of the Bloody Massacres of the Protestants in France.* English ed. 1674.
VDK	Gustav Turba. *Venetianische Depeschen vom Kaiserhofe.* Wien, 1892.
Wallace	M. Wallace. *Sir Philip Sidney.* Cambridge, 1915.
Wilson	Charles Wilson. *Queen Elizabeth and the Revolt of the Netherlands.* 1970.
Zouch	Thomas Zouch. *Memoirs of the Life and Writings of Sir Philip Sidney.* York, 1809.
Zürich Letters	H. Robinson, ed. *Zürich Letters.* Parker Society, 2d Series. Cambridge, 1845.

YOUNG PHILIP SIDNEY

1572–1577

CHAPTER 1. PROLOGUE

On May 25, 1572, Queen Elizabeth granted a licence for a seventeen-year-old boy to travel on the Continent. Addressed "to her trusty and well-beloved Philip Sidney, Esq.," it gave him permission "to go out of England into parts beyond the seas." With him he could take "three servants and four horses, etc.," and he could "remain the space of two years immediately following his departure out of the realm." The purpose of this journey was "for his attaining the knowledge of foreign languages."[1] Such expeditions by young Englishmen were then very rare. Indeed, not even one each year was permitted to risk the perils of the road and of corruption by foreign manners and religious zealots. Between 1560 and 1579 only nine sons of English peers are known to have travelled from France into Italy.[2] Because Philip Sidney was such a very unusual youth, these years of educational experience and intellectual growth deserve detailed study. Fortunately, more evidence has been preserved about Sidney than exists for any other young Englishman of his class.

Young Philip's family background gave him many advantages and some disadvantages. His father, Sir Henry Sidney, came "of ancient and allwaies well esteemed and welmatched gentry," as Philip later described the line.[3] The Sidneys were men of character; loyalty and responsible service were a family tradition. Philip's grandfather, William, achieved distinction under Henry VIII. He was knighted for his bravery in the French war and raised to Knight Banneret after Flodden Field, where he had commanded the English right wing. After his military career had ended, Sir William Sidney was chosen by the King to be tutor and steward

1. The original document is now in the library of New College, Oxford (see B. E. Juel-Jensen and John Buxton in *The Library*, n.s. 25 [1970]: 42–46). In 1746 it was at Penshurst (Collins, 1:98) but it later belonged to the great Elizabethan scholar Edmond Malone. After Malone's death in 1812 it passed with other literary papers to James Boswell the younger, and it was sold to Thorpe for £11 in the Boswell sale of May 24, 1825 (lot 3122).

2. Lawrence Stone, *The Crisis of the Aristocracy, 1558–1641* (Oxford, 1965), p. 792 (see also pp. 692–702). Sidney is excluded from these statistics because he was not, technically, the son of a peer, though of comparable status. The Grand Tour as a "journey of illumination" (Osbert Sitwell's phrase) did not become obligatory for the Englishman of taste until a century later.

3. "Defence of the Earl of Leicester," Feuillerat, 3:65.

of the infant Prince Edward, and he consequently became a member of
the Privy Council and a Knight of the Garter. He also received several
important grants of land, among them Penshurst in Kent. There he died
in 1554, nine months and twenty days before his grandson Philip was
born on November 30.[4]

William's son, Henry, thus became a boyhood companion to Edward
and one of the child-king's four gentlemen of the Privy Chamber. At
the age of ten Henry had been appointed a henchman to his godfather,
Henry VIII, and in 1541 he was thus officially designated to Edward:
"the first boy that ever he had."[5] Two of Henry's sisters, Mabell and
Elizabeth, lived in the household of Princess Mary, whose fondness for
them lasted until her death. Henry Sidney received knighthood at twenty-
one, and his influence on the boy-king prompted John Dudley, Earl of
Warwick (later Duke of Northumberland), to arrange in 1551 Sir Henry's
marriage to Lady Mary Dudley, his eldest daughter.

After the death of Edward VI (he expired in Henry's arms) Sir Henry's
career was that of a responsible public servant and administrator, whose
once-considerable estate was consumed in the service of his sovereign,
Elizabeth. Even before her accession, he had accompanied his brother-in-
law, the Earl of Sussex, to Ireland where the Earl had been appointed
Lord Deputy. During Sussex's frequent visits to England, Sir Henry
functioned in his place. In 1559 Elizabeth appointed Sir Henry Lord
President of the Marches of Wales, a post he held for the remainder of
his life. In October 1565, five months after Queen Elizabeth had invested
Sir Henry with the Order of the Garter, she commissioned him as Lord
Deputy of Ireland. Thus, except for a return to England between October
1567 and September 1568, Sir Henry was away from home during much
of Philip's adolescence.

Philip's mother, Lady Sidney, apparently continued to live at Penshurst
when she was not on duty as lady-in-waiting to the Queen. In October
1562 she nursed Elizabeth during an attack of the smallpox to which the
Queen nearly succumbed. Lady Sidney caught the dread disease, and it
disfigured her face so horribly that even the devoted Sir Henry wrote,

4. For a discussion of the time of Sidney's birth and his horoscope see appendix 1 and
my article "Mica, Mica, Parva Stella," in *TLS*, Jan. 1, 1971, pp. 17–18. Philip's horoscope
reveals that in his first year he suffered from a fever so severe that the family feared for his
survival.

5. As Sir Henry reported to Sir Francis Walsingham, Mar. 1, 1583. PRO Dom. Eliz.,
clix, no. 1, fol. 38.

"I lefte her a full faire Ladie in myne eye at least the fayerest, and when I returned I found her as fowle a ladie as the smale poxe coulde make her, which she did take by contynuall attendaunce of her Majesty's most precious person."[6] Later, when she had recovered, she avoided appearing in court unless absolutely necessary. The eight-year-old Philip also caught the disease, though he escaped excessive disfigurement (see appendix 1).

At the end of 1565, still in poor health, Lady Sidney set out with Sir Henry for Dublin. They landed in January 1566 after tempestuous weather had sunk a ship containing most of Lady Sidney's clothing, jewels, and household effects. Philip had already been at Shrewsbury school for a year. Although he was growing up in a somewhat fragmented family, the affectionate relationship of father, mother, and children is manifest in their letters and other testimony. Sir Henry's appointments, in contrast to those he had held in London, now required that he supply constant subsidies from his own pocket. At the end of his career he estimated his assets had shrunk by £30,000.[7] Queen Elizabeth, who watched her own finances like a hawk, never rewarded him with lands, licences in the customs, or other grants.

The Queen apparently failed to realize that Sir Henry was the ablest man to govern Ireland in her reign. She was even niggardly about offering to raise him to the peerage, the reward for which he had yearned during years of service and sacrifice. Finally, in 1572, she agreed to confer a barony on him—the lowest rank of the hereditary nobility—but offered no property to support the honour. Realistically, and perhaps bitterly, Lady Mary wrote from the court to Lord Burghley on May 2, requesting him "to use his endeavours that her husband may not be raised to the peerage, in consideration of their inability to maintain a higher title than they now possess."[8]

This disappointment came in the month when Philip was being furnished for his Continental expedition. Ironically, it was Lady Sidney's family, the Dudleys, whose position in England opened the gates of the courts and influence abroad—ironically because the Dudleys had such different temperaments and values from those of the solid, conscientious, unpretentious Sidneys. The Dudleys were gamblers, opportunists who played for high stakes; they were usually either on top of the game or heavy losers. With this trait they combined shrewd practicality and a

6. Ibid., fol. 37.
7. Ibid.
8. *CSPD*1, p. 442. The full text appears in Bourne, pp. 48–49.

belief in education both in books and in physical skills such as horseman-ship, swordsmanship, and dancing. The Dudleys were also personally attractive and brave in battle and in court politics. These positive qualities carried them to the heights and spread their fame throughout Europe.

The family first leapt to prominence with Philip Sidney's great-grand-father, Edmund Dudley (ca. 1462–1510). His father, a Sussex squire who served as sheriff of his county in 1485, sent Edmund to Oxford and later to Gray's Inn, thus establishing the family's traditional emphasis on education. Edmund Dudley's legal abilities attracted the notice of Henry VII who on his accession in 1485 made Dudley, then only twenty-three, a member of his Privy Council. Nine years after his first wife died Edmund turned to account the fact that an heiress had been appointed his ward by marrying her. She was Lady Elizabeth, daughter and coheiress of Edward Grey, Viscount L'Isle. Thus the Dudleys were gentry who married into the nobility.

Henry VII found Edmund Dudley's legal sharpness highly useful; it is estimated that sale of offices and arbitrary fines for which Dudley was responsible produced an income of £120,000 per year, which permitted the King to accumulate about £4,500,000 in currency and bullion before his death in 1509. But Dudley never received a title. He was widely loathed and Henry VIII upon his accession to the throne sent him to the tower. After an unsuccessful attempt to escape, he was led to the scaffold and beheaded in August 1510.

At this time his son John Dudley was eight years old. Two years later an Act of Parliament restored John's rights and repealed his attainder. A bright boy and a natural athlete, he soon attracted attention at court and in the tilt-yard. He became chief of Henry VIII's henchmen in 1537 and five years later he became Viscount L'Isle and was given life appointment as admiral. His courage and skill in the French war, during which he led the attack that captured Boulogne, attracted favourable attention. Shortly before the death of Henry VIII John Dudley was created Earl of Warwick and High Chamberlain of England. More military exploits followed. When Somerset was clapped into the Tower in October 1549, Dudley dominated the council and court of the sickly Edward VI and, his ascendency complete, he became Duke of Northumberland in 1551.

In 1553, as Edward VI's consumption grew worse, Northumberland arranged to alter the succession so that the King's cousin, Lady Jane Grey, became heir presumptive. Next, he married Lady Jane to his son Guilford

Mary Dudley, Lady Sidney

Dudley, and when Edward succumbed seven weeks later, Northumberland proclaimed Lady Jane queen. His ruthless rapacity and physical courage, however, were not enough to overcome the forces that gathered in support of the Princess Mary. He was sent to the Tower and promptly decapitated.

Despite the quick end to his daring gamble to capture the throne for the Dudley family, Northumberland unquestionably was the ablest leader in the England of his time, a fierce and inspiring soldier with an alert political awareness, an organizer and effective administrator. Ambitious to establish a famous family line, he was also a conscientious father who planned the careful education of his seven children. All of them distinguished themselves in one way or another, though Guilford, who almost became king, followed his father to the block and was thus the third of the line to lose his head on Tower Hill.

Ambrose, later Earl of Warwick, and Robert, created Earl of Leicester, were Philip Sidney's most famous uncles. In the days of Edward VI, both had been prominent at court and were intimate friends of Edward and his sister, Princess Elizabeth. Both had followed their father in his plot to put Guilford's young wife on the throne and had languished in the Tower while their father, brother, and Lady Jane were successively condemned and led out to the block. Like their brother Henry, who was killed at St. Quentin, Ambrose and Robert distinguished themselves there in 1557. Their valour prompted Queen Mary in March 1558 to exempt them and their sisters from the act of attainder. Philip Sidney was a child of three when his mother and uncles were thus cleared.

After Elizabeth succeeded to the throne her childhood friends were rewarded with honours. Ambrose, preeminent for military ability, became Master of the Ordnance in 1560, and a year later he was raised to the peerage, becoming Earl of Warwick. As Captain General in 1562, he headed the forces that captured Le Havre. There, before leading his plague-ridden survivors back to England, he suffered a leg wound from a poisoned bullet, a wound which hampered him for the rest of his very active life. In his absence he had been installed as a knight of the Order of the Garter in 1563; his brother-in-law, Sir Henry Sidney, had stood in as his deputy. In 1569 Warwick again saw active service as commander of the southern forces which crushed the rebellion of the Northern Earls and chased their followers over the border to Scotland.

Although Philip had little direct contact with Ambrose, the fact that he was not only nephew but heir presumptive to the Earl of Warwick was not overlooked by those connected with his travels in 1572.[9] Even more important, Philip was also heir presumptive to his uncle Robert, the powerful Earl of Leicester, known everywhere as the Queen's favourite. Elizabeth's and Leicester's intimacy had been so close in the years following her accession that scandalous rumours ran from the alehouses of provincial England to the courts of Europe. Clearly Leicester hoped to marry Elizabeth, and she obviously enjoyed his lovemaking, as well as the game of being wooed.[10]

Leicester knew the French would react violently to such a match. It was inimical to the claim of Mary Queen of Scots who during her brief reign as Queen of France had quartered the arms of England on her own coat of arms, thus proclaiming her right to the English crown. Hence, to get the backing of Spain, Leicester persuaded his faithful brother-in-law, Sir Henry Sidney, to approach the Spanish Ambassador with the proposition that in return for Spanish support of the marriage he and the Queen would become Catholics and revive the saying of Mass through the realm.[11]

Leicester had overlooked one fact that Elizabeth never forgot, namely that an unmarried person of eminence made opportunities for marriage serve his or her ambitions. Elizabeth, the most desirable match in Europe, encouraged suitors from the royal families of France, Sweden, Spain, Saxony, and the Holy Roman Empire, using this device to shift political alignments. On the other hand, Leicester had during his eighteenth year rushed into marriage with Amy Robsart, heiress to a modest estate far below the status he could have attained. His father, the Duke of Northumberland, acquiesced when Robert wished to marry the object of his whirlwind passion, and in the early years the pair had seemed happy enough.

In the course of time, however, Amy became a millstone and Robert visited her less and less. Tongues wagged more frequently, especially as his intimacy with the Queen increased. When, in September 1560, his wife was found dead with a broken neck at the foot of a staircase, the millstone became an albatross. His enemies cried murder, and foreign courts tittered

9. Moffet, p. 82, tells that he was "written down sole heir" to his uncles' and father's "riches and lands."

10. In her fine biography Elizabeth Jenkins concluded that Elizabeth's relationship with Leicester was "a sexual one which stopped short only of the sexual act." *Elizabeth the Great* (London, 1958), p. 99.

11. *CSPS1*, pp. 178–80. Unsupported statements from this source should be taken *cum grano salis*.

at the scandalous reports that Elizabeth's Master of the Horse (sometimes degraded to "her horse-keeper") had killed his wife to be free to marry the Queen. Elizabeth continued to enjoy his company and his advice at court and in the council, but did not create him Earl of Leicester until 1564 when she proposed him as a husband for Mary Queen of Scots, a plan that failed to mature.

Nine years later the dashing Leicester bungled again in the marriage market. In 1573 he went through a purported wedding ceremony with the widowed Lady Sheffield a matter of hours before she bore him a son, who never succeeded in proving his legitimacy. Later Leicester tried to buy Lady Sheffield's silence with an offer of £700 per year, which she angrily refused. Then in 1578 Leicester secretly married another widow, the Countess of Essex. Queen Elizabeth first heard of the event a year later from Jehan de Simier, the close friend of the Duke of Alençon, who had come to press the Duke's suit for her hand. She flew into a rage, and though she continued to use Leicester's services on the Council their relationship was never again the same.

These follies occurred some years after the events with which this chapter is concerned, yet they reveal the increasing tendency for Leicester's gambles to fail, and for the Dudley opportunism to misfire. Back in the midsummer of 1565, Mary Queen of Scots by her impetuous marriage with the baby-faced Darnley (a commoner but of the blood royal) had ended any possibility of Leicester's becoming king of Scotland and thus potential sire of future kings of England. He had then toyed once more with the possibility that Elizabeth might accept him. If the Queen of Scots could marry the object of her infatuation, why not Elizabeth? Two circumstances stood in the way, Elizabeth's own wishes and a wide circle of Leicester's enemies. This included Norfolk (England's only surviving Duke), the Earl of Sussex, and Sir Thomas Heneage (a courtier to whom Elizabeth had shown special attention).

In October 1566 Parliament met and attempted to require the Queen to settle on her successor to the crown before they would produce the revenue she had requested. Leicester foolishly joined the group in the House of Lords who supported this attempt. Elizabeth excoriated all of them, including Leicester, and forbade him and several others to enter the Presence Chamber. Three years later when the Northern Earls Westmorland and Northumberland plotted with Norfolk to overthrow Sir William Cecil and his administration of new men, they included Leicester among their targets. But Leicester responded by joining the cabal. Their plans against Cecil failed, however, when Leicester faltered and proposed to forewarn the Queen. Their objective now changed to sponsoring the marriage of Norfolk to the again-widowed Mary Stuart, and Leicester took up the leadership of the plotters. He saw a chance to put Norfolk under an obligation; for if the marriage occurred Norfolk would be just one heartbeat away from becoming king of England. When news of the plot reached Elizabeth Norfolk was sent to the Tower. Leicester managed to confess his part, and Elizabeth granted her forgiveness.

Leicester thus continued to be one of the Queen's intimates. She called him her "Eyes," and ornamented his letters with this symbol. (Burghley was her "Spirit" and the dark-skinned Walsingham her "Moor.") But the nature of their relationship had altered by 1570. Sir John Neale has well described the change: "There were no dregs of Elizabeth's old passion for Leicester left to disturb her resolution. The romance had sobered down into a sentimental friendship—a sweet memory of the past, and no more." [12] Nevertheless, Leicester still had the Queen's ear, and the world knew it. He was described as "the chick that sitteth next the henne," and Elizabeth consulted him and Burghley more than any other members of the Privy Council. When Philip Sidney went abroad he carried the prestige of the Dudleys along with the lesser weight of Sir Henry Sidney.

Besides these family connections, young Philip possessed qualities that made him loved and admired wherever he went. Graceful and athletic, attractive and responsive, he gained admiration from everyone. Even as a boy at Shrewsbury he impressed both his fellow students and his masters. The familiar description by his classmate, Sir Fulke Greville, gives a remarkable picture of Philip:

> Though I lived with him, and knew him from a child, yet I never knew him other than a man: with such staiednesse of mind, lovely, and familiar gravity, as carried grace, and reverence above greater years. His talk ever of knowledge, and his very play tending to enrich his mind: So as even his teachers found something in him to observe, and learn, above that what they had usually read, or taught. [13]

This insatiable thirst for knowledge was widely noticed; it was reported, for example, by Thomas Moffett who in later years lived in the household of Sidney's sister Mary, the Countess of Pembroke. Probably deriving his

12. Sir John Neale, *Queen Elizabeth* (London, 1934), p. 219.
13. Greville, p. 7.

information from her, Moffett wrote: "He so held letters in his affection and care that he could scarce ever sleep, still less go forth, without a book. Nor did he direct his eyes so much to the colored and gilded cover of the book as to the letters and meaning of it." Moffett added further details:

> Out of his zeal for virtue sprang all of Philip's studious interests; when, indeed, by the indulgence of his parents he was given entire liberty with regard to his learning, so that he might go to the school-room at his own time and by his own choice, yet burning with a warm, or rather a fervid, zeal for letters, he spent the largest part of the day in studies, so that scarcely was he unoccupied at breakfast, and still more rarely at luncheon. Indeed, in place of lunch and dinner he used often to imbibe sciences, liberal arts, and every kind of discipline . . . directing the whole power of his mind to the matter.[14]

These details of Sidney's precocity and application, however exaggerated, represent family tradition.

Stressing Philip's early love of books and learning, Moffett tells us that the boy found sports and games a bit tame. When called "from study to a game, from the schoolroom to sport" Philip "carried on all these things negligently, and, though he feared no one (who was of an age with him) in a game of chance or bodily strength, he foresook it for the sake of literary studies."[15] At Shrewsbury these sports were limited to running, jumping, and wrestling, as well as chess and shooting with the longbow. Wagers of up to 4d. were permitted, a sizeable sum in those days.[16] Among his recorded expenses while at Shrewsbury was the purchase of "bird bolts for to shoot at birds."[17] On one occasion Philip injured a knee so badly that he could not bend it.[18] In later years he became a very accomplished horseman, active in the tournaments.

The only letter preserved from Philip's school days is from his father with a postscript by Lady Sidney. Although rather lengthy and Polonian, Sir Henry's letter reveals the affectionate relationship between the parents in distant Ireland and their precocious twelve-year-old son.

Son Philip:
I have received two letters from you, one written in Latin, the

14. Moffet, pp. 71–72.
15. Ibid., p. 72.
16. Wallace, p. 41.
17. Ibid., p. 42.
18. Ibid., p. 48.

other in French; which I take in good part, and will you to exercise that practice of learning often; for that will stand you in most stead in that profession of life that you are born to live in. And now, since this is my first letter that ever I did write to you, I will not that it be all empty of some advices which my natural care of you provoketh me to wish you to follow, as documents to you in this your tender age.

Let your first action be the lifting up of your mind to Almighty God by hearty prayer; and feelingly digest the words you speak in prayer, with continual meditation and thinking of Him to whom you pray, and of the matter for which you pray. And use this as an ordinary act, and at an ordinary hour; whereby the time itself shall put you in remembrance to do that you are accustomed to do in that time.

Apply your study to such hours as your discreet master doth assign you, earnestly; and the time I know he will so limit as shall be both sufficient for your learning and safe for your health. And mark the sense and the matter of that you do read, as well as the words; so shall you both enrich your tongue with words and your wit with matter, and judgment will grow as years grow in you.

Be humble and obedient to your masters, for, unless you frame yourself to obey others—yea, and feel in yourself what obedience is, you shall never be able to teach others how to obey you.

Be courteous of gesture and affable to all men, with diversity of reverence according to the dignity of the person. There is nothing that winneth so much with so little cost.

Use moderate diet so as, after your meal, you may find your wit fresher and not duller, and your body more lively and not more heavy. Seldom drink wine, and yet sometimes do, lest, being enforced to drink upon the sudden, you should find yourself enflamed. Use exercise of body, yet such as is without peril to your bones or joints; it will increase your force and enlarge your breath. Delight to be cleanly as well in all parts of your body as in your garments; it shall make you grateful in each company—and otherwise loathsome.

Give yourself to be merry; for you degenerate from your father if you find not yourself most able in wit and body to do anything when you are most merry. But let your mirth be ever void of all scurrilous and biting words to any man; for a wound given by a word is oftentimes harder to be cured than that which is given by the sword.

Be you rather a hearer and bearer away of other men's talk than a beginner and procurer of speech; otherwise you shall be accounted to delight to hear yourself speak. If you hear a wise sentence or an apt phrase, commit it to your memory with respect of the circumstances when you shall speak it.

Let never oath be heard to come out of your mouth, nor word of ribaldry; so shall custom make to yourself a law against it in yourself. Be modest in each assembly, and rather be rebuked of light fellows for maidenlike shamefastness than of your sad friends for pert boldness. Think upon every word that you will speak before you utter it, and remember how nature hath ramparted up, as it were, the tongue with teeth, lips—yea, and hair without the lips, and all betokening reins and bridles for the loose use of that member.

Above all things tell no untruth; no, not in trifles. The custom of it is naughty. And let it not satisfy you that for a time the hearers take it for a truth; for after it will be known as it is to your shame. For there cannot be a greater reproach to a gentleman than to be accounted a liar.

Study and endeavour yourself to be virtuously occupied. So shall you make such a habit of well-doing in you as you shall not know how to do evil, though you would. Remember, my son, the noble blood you are descended of by your mother's side; and think that only by virtuous life and good action you may be an ornament to that illustrious family. Otherwise, through vice and sloth, you may be counted *labes generis,* one of the greatest curses that can happen to man.

Well, my little Philip, this is enough for me, and too much, I fear, for you. But if I find that this light meal of digestion nourish in anything the weak stomach of your capacity, I will, as I find the same grow stronger, feed it with other food.

Commend me most heartily unto Master Justice Corbet, old Master Onslow, and my cousin, his son. Farewell! Your mother and I send you our blessings, and Almighty God grant you His, nourish you with His fear, govern you with His grace, and make you a good servant to your prince and country!

Your loving father, so long as you live in the fear of God,

H. Sidney.[19]

19. Text from Wallace, pp. 68–69; several early transcripts of this remarkable letter exist.

Lady Mary added a sweet note of her own "on the skirts of my Lord President's letter." This postscript and Sir Henry's longer admonitions reveal a tenderness of family affection that carries across the intervening centuries. They are phrased in such simple and evident language that we can feel the flow of parental love towards the darling son, the *lumen familiae suae*. Significantly, the boy preserved the letter for the rest of his life.

Your noble, careful father hath taken pains with his own hand to give you, in this his letter, so wise, so learned and most requisite precepts for you to follow with a diligent and humble, thankful mind, as I will not withdraw your eyes from beholding and reverent honouring the same—no, not so long as to read any letter from me. And therefore, at this time, I will write unto you no other letter than this; whereby I first bless you, with my desire to God to plant in you His grace, and, secondarily, warn you to have always before the eyes of your mind these excellent counsels of my lord, your dear father, and that you fail not continually, once in four or five days, to read them over.

And for a final leave-taking for this time, see that you show yourself as a loving, obedient scholar to your good master, to govern you yet many years, and that my lord and I may hear that you profit so in your learning as thereby you may increase our loving care of you, and deserve at his hands the continuance of his great joy, to have him often witness with his own hands the hope he hath in your well-doing.

Farewell, my little Philip, and once again the Lord bless you!

Your loving mother,

Mary Sidney

Sir Henry's greetings were directed to Sir Andrew Corbett of Moreton Court, Shropshire, whose third son, Vincent, was Philip's schoolmate at Shrewsbury. Several years later when Sidney reached Venice on his travels he described Robert Corbett, the eldest son of Sir Andrew and one of his comrades there, as "my very greatest friend."[20] Richard Onslow, father of Philip's schoolmate Edward, was Recorder of London and served as Solicitor-General and Speaker of the House of Commons. During Sidney's years at Shrewsbury he made several expeditions which can be traced through the family account books. In August 1566

20. Sidney to Languet, Apr. 15, 1574.

he had been brought to Oxford from Shrewsbury to witness the ceremonies when Queen Elizabeth visited the town and University on her
summer progress. The Shrewsbury group lodged in Lincoln College.
Because his uncle, the Earl of Leicester, presided over the official reception
as Chancellor, Philip enjoyed a favoured position. Leicester was one of
the lords attending the Queen, as were Philip's two uncles by marriage,
the Earls of Sussex and Huntingdon. From Philip's horoscope, cast five
years later, we learn that he was an "oratorem . . . apud serenissimam
Principem Elizabetham," an orator before the Queen (see appendix 1).
Undoubtedly this was arranged through Leicester, to the pleasure of
Philip's family and the envy of his schoolfellows.

Little record exists of this happy trip to Oxford except in the expense
accounts kept by Philip's servant, Thomas Marshall.[21] These accounts
describe the fine clothing purchased for this occasion, the dates of arrival
and departure, and other practical details. They even record that on the
return journey Marshall gave twelve pence "by Mr. Philip's commandment to a blind harper" at Chipping Norton, where the party spent the
night at an inn.

The next year, 1567, when his parents returned from Ireland for a visit
of about eleven months, the account books show that £49 was expended
for "Mr. Philip Sidney, from Shrewsbury to London."[22] About this
time he was provided with "a rapier and dagger" (£1 9s.), shirts (£4 5s.),
a "Spanish beadstead" (16s. 4d.), and a close-stool (9s. 4d.), and the
goldsmith was paid £42 12s. "in part of two chains, the most part of
the first being lost."[23] Having their son with them may have provided
some solace to Sir Henry, who was suffering from the stone and also
from the Queen's displeasure at the situation in Ireland, a pique which
she vented on him.

It was probably during this winter that Sidney received a second
opportunity to display his precocity before the Queen. His horoscope
reveals that he appeared before Elizabeth again early in 1568, about the
time he matriculated at Christ Church. The astrologer's account of the
incident follows:

> Every member of our University of Oxford knows what wonderful
> potential was implanted in you by Nature for engaging in the noble

21. See Wallace, chap. 4.
22. *HMC De L'Isle*, 1:244.
23. Ibid., 1:243–44.

arts, and how much progress you have made, to the great admiration of your generation and the applause of all who heard you, *when you delivered an oration before her most serene Highness that was both eloquent and elegant, and this when you scarcely had passed your thirteenth year.*

In February 1568 Philip, in his fourteenth year, was sent to Oxford and enrolled in Christ Church. The following August Sir Henry stopped there to receive the M.A. degree, and carried Philip off to Wales to spend a month with him and Lady Sidney. A letter of August 10 from Cecil to Sir Henry sent "increase of all goodness to your son, my darling master Philip."[24] On September 3, Cecil mockingly chided Sir Henry for having "carried away your son and my scholar from Oxford, not only from his book but from . . . [the opportunity] to have pleasured both me and my wife."[25] Cecil's interest extended beyond mere admiration for the youth's charm and brilliance, for Sir Henry and Cecil had already discussed a match between Philip and Sir William's daughter, Anne. During the Christmas holidays Philip visited the Cecil family and Sir William mentioned in a letter dated January 6, "Your Philipp is heare in whom I take more comfort than I doo oppenly utter for avoydyng of wrong interpretation, he is wordy to be loved and so I doo love hym, as he wer myne own."[26]

Sir Henry responded by proposing the marriage, and negotiations over property settlement were carried on during the next year.[27] Meanwhile Cecil encouraged his prospective son-in-law to write to him. Three of Philip's letters to Sir William have survived. The first two, dated March 12 and July 8, 1570, are in Latin. They are basically exercises in compliment and epistolary style, skills to be mastered by a future courtier. These Latin letters reveal little of the boy's individuality; they could have been ground out by any well-trained undergraduate.

The third letter, dated February 26, fortunately reveals more. It was written for a practical reason and marks Philip's first foray into public affairs, for he was trying to influence the appointment of his tutor, Thomas Thornton, to a vacancy among the canons at Christ Church Cathedral.

24. *CSPIi*, p. 385. First noted by Bourne, p. 27.
25. *CSPIi*, p. 385.
26. *CSPIi*, p. 399.
27. The proposed settlement remains among the Cecil papers at Hatfield. *HMC Cecil*, I:415–16, 439.

Righte honorable:

I am forced for better expedition to use an unaccustomed manner of writinge unto yowe the cause proceedinge frome a reporte of sum whome neither can I judge frendlie to my selfe nor yet indifferente towardes him, from whome they seke by malise to præwente and detaine his woorthie praifermente sued for and obtained by his honorable benefactors, I meane, my singular good Lorde my Lorde of Lecestre and especiallie your selfe, by whose favor (attained by the requeste of my frendes, and his deserte towardes me, assisted by the woorthines of his lyfe and learninge) Mr Thorneton my reder hathe unto him graunted the nexte præfermente of a cannonrie in this colleage of Christechurche.

And sithence it hathe pleased God, (as I gave yow humblie to undrestande in my laste lettres) to call unto his mercie one Thomas Daie by meane whereof it restethe in your honorable favor to præsente (accordinge to your former pretence) him, aswell for whose cause as divers others I do accounte my selfe no lesse bound then I oughte.

For that it is verie constantlie reported that Mr Tobie Matthews frendes, shoulde use in his behaulfe some earneste sute, unwoorthie their callinges (because it was moved before the deathe of the incumbente, by the which it shoulde seeme they soughte rather by spite to prævente the one then honestlie to preferre the other) these are therefore moste humblie to requeste suche your wonted favor as neither your honorable benefitte may be revoked, my humble and earneste sute prævented neither the person him selfe so discredited, but that he maye withe your favor enjoye his advowson, by yowr meanes obtained, and your selfe promised.

Thus humblie commendinge my dutie unto your good opinion, my selfe preste at your commaundemente I humblie ende. Frome Oxforde this xxvi^{the} of Februarie A^o 1569[–70]

Yours in as humble sorte as

your owne

Philip Sidney

To the righte honorable Sir William Cecill Knighte her Majesties principall Secretaire &c Yeve these withe speede.[28]

---

28. Feuillerat, 3 :76–77.

Whether or not young Sidney's recommendation had any influence, Thornton was awarded the vacant stall. In any case, Thornton, who rose to become Vice-Chancellor of Oxford University, never forgot his close association with his pupil, as the inscription on his tomb testifies: "He was a sure refuge for young poor scholars of great hopes and parts, and tutor to Sir Philip Sidney when he was of Ch. Ch." [29]

Sidney's relationship with another Oxford don, probably the brilliant mathematician Thomas Allen of Trinity College, is revealed by the horoscope cast for Sidney towards the end of 1570 or in early 1571 (see appendix 1). Allen resigned his fellowship during this year because he declined to take orders. He passed the remainder of his life at Gloucester Hall, now Worcester College. Leicester extended his patronage and friendship to Allen and also to the recondite Dr. John Dee. The horoscope, addressed to Sidney, carries this testimony to the boy's intellectual powers:

> Those who taught you grammar, rhetoric, dialectics, natural philosophy, and ethics would have been able to realize without fear [of contradiction] which youths among us were the most skilled in letters and were regarded as such, because of both the renown of their names and their real merits. I myself would have got to know your natural talent, so truly open and abundant, in the study and discipline of mathematics, had not the malice of time snatched me away from you, or rather had not the unjust demands of fate kept you from me. I grieve for a youth of so much promise, designed by Nature for the study of mathematics and by birth for that of the celestial philosophy, endowed with a happy keenness of mind, godlike talents, and a spirit looking continually upwards towards whatever is furthest removed from earthly matters, who has gone so far in so many other subjects, yet they are not concerned with astrology [here] to the same extent. For I can in this place give many examples [of this zeal]: I noticed how zealous and eager your propensity for the study of the stars was when I went to visit you and there would be considerable discussion back and forth between us about astrology; I noticed then how sensibly you would discuss these matters with me; I myself am fully aware of this because I experienced greater grief in leaving [these discussions] than joy in coming to them, and from continued thought about what I gained from them. But in order that my

29. Anthony Wood, *Fasti Oxoniensis*, ed. Bliss (Oxford, 1813), col. 225.

discourse should return from wherever it has strayed to, please accept this evidence of your fortunate natural talents.

As the marriage negotiations dragged on, it gradually became clear that Cecil had developed loftier ambitions for his daughter. On February 25, 1571, the Queen had made him a peer as Baron of Burghley. Sir Henry had not been able to offer a high enough property settlement, and though Philip remained heir presumptive to both Leicester and Warwick such prospects could change quickly. One of Burghley's wards was Edward de Vere, seventeenth Earl of Oxford, who showed ability as a student of the classics and as a poet. He had also proven to be an excellent horseman, for he had recently been Champion in the tournament held in Westminster before the Queen and her court. The heir of a distinguished ancient family and possessor of a large estate, in Burghley's eyes the Earl had great advantages over Philip. Burghley's biographer, Conyers Read, summarized his attitude succinctly: "Oxford, in short . . . seemed to have everything."[30] The Queen granted permission in August 1571, and Oxford married the fifteen-year-old Anne on December 19 in Westminster Abbey before Elizabeth and a distinguished company. There is no indication of how Sidney felt. He knew that it was a matter outside his sphere of decision.

To return to Sidney's career at Oxford, it was most unusual that a boy of his rank was there at all. The investigations of Lawrence Stone show that in the decade 1570–79 only ten sons of peers matriculated at Oxford.[31] Statistics for the previous decade do not exist, but comparison with the figures for Cambridge suggest they would be lower by a third in the 1560–69 decade when Sidney entered Christ Church. True, Philip was not literally "son of a peer," though he was the grandson of a duke and the nephew of four earls, one of whom was Chancellor of the University. Little wonder that he received extraordinary attention from the Christ Church authorities. Evidence of Philip's activities and accomplishments during his Oxford years is meagre. The somewhat vague and roseate reports gathered from the Countess of Pembroke and her family by Thomas Moffet include several suggestive passages: for example, Moffett says that Philip was "crowned with the first and second laurels of the literati at Oxford." Since he did not proceed to a degree at the University, this is puzzling. Perhaps he received high honours in rhetoric and grammar,

30. Conyers Read, *Lord Burghley and Queen Elizabeth* (London, 1960), p. 127.
31. *Crisis of the Aristocracy*, p. 792.

the first of which "carried with it the insignia of a laurel wreath." [32] In both subjects Philip had undergone rigid discipline at Shrewsbury, for Dr. Moffet had written of his accomplishments while there, "to whom did he yield in reputation for and knowledge of grammar? A little later whom did he fear in the matter of rhetorical principles?" [33]

Moffet also praised Philip's ability at mathematics while at Shrewsbury, as well as his reputation for a knowledge of languages, namely Latin, French, and some Greek. Moffet attributed to the Oxford period his disdain for astrology, in contrast to his progress in "chemistry, the starry science, rival to nature." However, these attitudes apparently developed some years later when, within Philip's limited opportunities, "he himself made corrections upon various authors of scientific works, and by his methods led sundry to writing more correctly—or at least to observing more correctly." [34] Because Moffet was one of the most eminent physicians in England and a pioneer chemist and entomologist, his comments on Sidney's scientific interests cannot be disregarded lightly. Indeed, Moffet introduced a personal note in his tribute:

> The variety of opinions, the tricks of teachers, the high costs, the uncertainty of results, somewhat oppress the weakness of minds endeavouring to proceed so far, and have somewhat deterred (as I well know) me, myself. Yet so far did he have an unexhausted eagerness for complete (or rather for only the accepted) learning, that he leaped over all these obstacles at one bound; nor, diverted by any baits of friends or by the tedium of the subject matter, did he abandon the learning of a science [chemistry] so important and so pleasant. With the same alacrity he proceeded in other subjects of abstruse learning. [35]

Concerning Philip's life and habits during his Oxford years, Moffet offers a few other sidelights:

> He determined the plan of his university life not with reference to the ends of natural inclination but within the boundaries of duty and virtue; and in his eyes, his speech and his manners he presented a certain pattern of modesty and antique integrity.

32. Moffet, pp. 75, 119.
33. Ibid., p. 73.
34. Ibid., p. 75; see also appendix 1.
35. Ibid.

He did not very willingly join in conversation, whether in light or serious vein, with the reprobate. Not upon pleasures did he spend the funds provided by the kindness of his uncles and the affection of his parents, but he distributed them either frugally for his own uses or more generously for the alleviation of learned men.[36]

Philip's reputation for controlling his youthful sexual drives is also described.

Though he saw, too, that the University (once the home of temperance, thrift, chastity, and holiness) through a gradual neglect of discipline and seizure of license had fallen almost to effeminacy and debauchery, yet by no allurements could he be led astray from the antique mode of duty; and even at the first approach of puberty he checked the unbridled impulses arising from his time of life and from the custom of the place. Not by his own nature was this done, for it had made him vigorous, full-blooded, lively, ready for the sports of youth and all things after the manner of men, but by the strength of his virtue.[37]

Even though Moffet may have been gilding the lily for the benefit of Sidney's nephew, young William Herbert, his facts were basically sound. Moffet knew Sidney and perhaps served as physician to him and his wife (he discussed with Sidney his wife's "slight infertility").[38] He was also physician to Sidney's father-in-law, Sir Francis Walsingham, and lived on terms of intimacy with friends of Sidney as well as members of his family. As Dr. Moffet's learned editors state, the physician was "in a well-nigh perfect position for writing the ... biography."[39] Hence, though he embellished his subject, the solid substance beneath can be recognized. Here, then, is Moffet's account of Philip's relationship with his contemporaries and the dons at Oxford.

No one was more obliging than he, more courteous, or more agreeable to the souls of the members of the University. Nor did anyone possess such grace, facility, and affability of speech. If perchance he met on the street some learned and pious man, you would have said that nothing could have been more loving and more

36. Ibid., pp. 76–77.
37. Ibid.
38. Ibid., p. 85.
39. Ibid., p. xvi.

united than they; for not by hands alone were they joined, but even by heart's desire. He did not pour out his love rashly upon everyone, nor did he cleave in never-ceasing love to anyone not like him also in love for virtue. He very seldom rebuked his servants openly or severely, when they deviated from their duty; but, speaking by a kind of circumlocution, and, as it were, distantly, he admonished them. If they lapsed too often, he punished them with words; and those continually repeating an old offense he so frightened by masculine speech that, as if leaping from a rock or struck by the final bolt of Jove, they could not lift their eyes again.

He was never seen going to church, to the exercise ground, or to the public assembly hall (where he frequently employed himself), except as distinguished among the company of all the learned men. In their presence he maintained such a gravity, joined with modesty, that one did not know whether the spirit he had was rather elevated, sublime, and looking away from the world, or courteous, retiring, and humble. By chance (and through no fault) learning might have made him somewhat more proud, and deservedly he might have glowed with a certain self-love appropriate to exalted minds; yet, distinguished by his zeal for temperance, he used curbs upon himself and, much as he surpassed others in knowledge, to the same degree he bore himself more humbly and more modestly. On account of this singular virtue, how genuinely both the humane, learned race of academicians and the churlish, unenlightened race of townsmen loved Sidney, even as no other one! So that they seemed no more cheered by his coming than afflicted by his departure![40]

Two other items of evidence support Dr. Moffet's account. In a letter to Lady Cecil in October 1569, while the marriage negotiations were in progress, Sir Henry Sidney asked her to help keep Philip from studying too much "for I fear he will be to much given to his book, and yet I have heard of few wise fathers doubt that in their children."[41] From Philip's horoscope we learn that during the winter of 1569–70 he suffered from severe inflammation of the eyes (see appendix 1). This difficulty could have been attributed by his elders to excessive study. Philip's health appears to have been a continuing worry; when he was at Shrewsbury, Sir Henry had advised him, "Apply your study to such hours as your

40. Ibid., pp. 77–78.
41. HMC Cecil, I :439.

discreet master doth assign you, earnestly; and the time I know he will so limit as shall be both sufficient for your learning and safe for your health."

The other reference occurs in Richard Carew's *Survey of Cornwall*, written long before it was published in 1602. Carew had matriculated at Broadgates Hall, Oxford, in 1566, his eleventh year. He relates one incident which occurred while he was at Oxford as follows:

> Being a scholler in Oxford of fourteene yeeres age, and three yeeres standing, vpon a wrong conceyved opinion touching my sufficiency I was there called to dispute *ex tempore* (*impar congressus Achilli*) with the matchless Sir Ph. Sidney, in presence of the Earles Lycester, Warwick, and other great personages.[42]

Such disputations were regular exercises for undergraduates. Three times a week candidates working towards the bachelor's degree disputed before an audience of students (the only form of public examination then required). Thus the skills of the disputants were public knowledge. Disputations within the college served to measure the progress and aptitudes of the undergraduates as well as to train them for their formal appearances before University authorities. Apparently Philip had gained the reputation of being "matchless" in the college disputations at Christ Church. Probably the Sidney-Carew disputation occurred during Leicester's visit to Oxford in June 1569 when the Chancellor brought various companions with him.

Just as official records of Sidney's matriculation are lacking, so is the date of his departure. His biographers have offered various theories, the most popular being that he migrated to Cambridge for a term or two in 1571.[43] But the plain fact is that Philip suffered a serious illness in the spring of 1571, and probably spent some months in convalescence, doubtless part of the time with his family. To leave Oxford without a degree was usual among boys of noble families who would not be taking orders in the church. In April 1571 the academic activities of Oxford University came to a halt because of an epidemic. The majority of the undergraduates and dons at Christ Church would have taken refuge at

42. Richard Carew, *Survey of Cornwall* (London, 1602 ed.), fol. 102ᵛ.

43. Wallace, pp. 105–07 offered various shreds of evidence which he believed added up to conclusive proof that Sidney spent some time there. Buxton, p. 43, contributed another item. Later investigators who reject their conclusions include F. S. Boas, *Sir Philip Sidney, Representative Elizabethan* (London, 1955), pp. 21–22, and Ringler, p. xx. Howell, p. 136, terms the evidence "suggestive."

the college estates outside Wallingford, Berkshire, as they did on earlier and later occasions.

The one piece of documentary evidence available for this period fits this pattern. Among the accounts of Sir Henry Sidney's agents preserved at Penshurst are those of William Blunt for the year beginning May 31, 1571. There Blunt recorded the following items: "Expenses of Mr. Philip Sydney, in time of sickness at Reading, and other £38 11s. 6d. Necessaries for other children, £3 7s. 4d." [44] This entry proves that Philip was at Reading, was sick there, and required a large sum of money compared to the children at home. Since Blunt's accounts also include an additional round sum of £60 for Philip in this year, the seriousness of his malady seems clear. Because Reading is the first city of any size beyond Wallingford, Philip may have been moved there for better care.

Once he had fully recovered the Sidney family began to make plans to send him to the Continent to continue his education. Such planning would require much thought and preparation. A desirable opportunity opened up early in the next spring when negotiations for a peace treaty with the enemies across the Channel matured in March. The treaty was to be signed when the official parties of dignitaries could be dispatched to do so simultaneously in both France and England. Sir Henry and Leicester succeeded in arranging for Philip to cross with their old friend the head of the English delegation, Lord Admiral Edward Fiennes de Clinton, whom the Queen raised to the peerage as Earl of Lincoln to give him proper rank for his mission. Ironically, the title was bestowed on him on May 2, the very day on which Sir Henry Sidney declined his barony through Lady Sidney.

The treaty, a device to advance commerce and general amity between France and England, had been promoted by the Queen Mother of France, Catherine de Médicis, as a substitute for her earlier plan to marry her third son, the Duke of Anjou, to Elizabeth of England. The marriage plans had failed primarily because Anjou's Catholic zeal had been fanned by the Guise family (with this result in mind). After sessions which dragged on for three months between the French officials and the English commissioners headed by Sir Thomas Smith, a draft of the agreed version was signed at Blois on April 19, 1572. The official approval involved a dual ceremony; French envoys were to sign it at the English court at the same time as a parallel ceremony with English envoys took place at the French

44. *HMC De L'Isle*, 1:246.

court. In effect, the treaty was a weak defensive pact, but it did involve a pledge that each nation would not aid the enemies of the other, which actually meant that neither would join Spain in an attack on the other. Thus the Treaty of Blois was a feeble step towards preserving the balance of power in northern Europe.

Elizabeth and her government had several reasons to be pleased with the result. The fear that, if Spain could subdue the Low Countries, Philip might connive with France to invade the heretic Island Kingdom hung over England like a perpetual cloud. In France Catherine and her son, King Charles IX, seemed to be accepting the Huguenots with a tolerance which the English wished to encourage. Similarly, the Scottish civil disturbances were recognized in the Treaty, for the two signatories agreed jointly to establish Scotland under one government. Here the French attitude especially pleased the English, for the Treaty omitted any mention of Mary Stuart, her status as Queen of Scotland, her claims to the English crown, or the question of her release from custody.

Considering the plots surrounding Mary Stuart in the previous year, such terms were a welcome balm. The Florentine banker, Roberto Ridolfi, had settled in London during the reign of Catholic Mary, and soon acquired a reputation for financial reliability and acumen. Although the English Exchequer employed his services on occasion, he was subsidized by both the Spanish and French governments, while he also secretly served as papal nuncio in England. For a while Ridolfi acted as agent to combine the interests of his three paymasters in their attempts to capture the throne of England for Mary Stuart. He had been seized and questioned in October 1569, but released when no incriminating evidence could be found. A year and a half later in the spring of 1571 a messenger was apprehended at Dover with letters addressed to Mary Stuart's agent, the Bishop of Ross. The authorities subjected the courier to torture, and on the rack he revealed that Ridolfi, then on the Continent, was attempting to persuade the King of Spain and the Pope to have the Duke of Alva lead his army of six thousand men from the Low Countries to invade England simultaneously with an insurrection by Mary's followers. Their purpose was to depose (i.e. kill) Elizabeth and to crown Mary.

Ridolfi had a wagging tongue, and the outlines of the plot began to become clear. Because the letters were written in cipher it took some time to establish which English noblemen were working with Ridolfi. The Earls of Southampton and Arundel, Lord Lumley, and most important of all, Thomas Howard, Duke of Norfolk, were arrested. The Duke, then

England's sole holder of this rank, had expected to marry Mary Stuart, a weakness that had led to his downfall. He languished in the Tower as the Commons called for his head, a penalty which Elizabeth postponed while plans for the double treaty-signing ceremony slowly matured.

Even the official licences and instructions to the newly created Earl of Lincoln were postponed until Elizabeth's advisers were sure the French envoys had been dispatched. The French, in turn, stalled until the English made a definite move. On May 9 Sir Thomas Smith, who had signed the draft of the treaty three weeks before, wrote to Lord Burghley from Paris:

> I marvel my L[ord] Admiral [Lincoln] is so long before he set forward; Marshal *Montmorency* [leader of the French signatories] and *du Foix*, and all that should go with them, be ready, and attend only to hear when my L[ord] Admiral doth set forward. A man would marvel what a number of great persons both of the long and short robe [i.e. lawyers or clerics and military men], do desire to go with the Marshal and to see England, and what shift he is fain to make to cut off his train, and to shake them off that desire to go, lest he should have too many.[45]

Two weeks later Elizabeth's ambassador in Paris, Francis Walsingham, confirmed that "the last of this month the Marshal *Montmorency* will be at Bulloign with his Train, who is glad to have the commodity to pass over in her Maj. ships."[46] Walsingham had had his last interview with Montmorency two days earlier, when the Marshal had asked him to certify each of several Britons who wished to cross in his party would be accepted as persona grata on arrival. The French party had not yet reached England on June 6 when Lord Burghley reported to Walsingham that the "delay proves an unreasonable charge to great numbers to the Queens Majestie, having her offices of Houshold at Dover, and her provisions thereby lost. The Earl of *Pembroke*, Lord *Windsor*, and the Lord *Buckhurst* be at Dover with great and mighty trains: Besides, hither are come such leavies of Ladies to attend, as husbands curse the delay."[47]

Elizabeth was finally ready to act, and on May 25 she allowed Burghley to present the Earl of Lincoln with the instructions for his embassy.[48]

45. Digges, p. 201. Misdated "May 7"; Smith speaks of "yesterday the 8th of May."
46. Ibid., p. 202.
47. Ibid., p. 212.
48. Ibid., pp. 206–11.

On the same day she signed the licence for "her trusty and well-beloved Philip Sidney Esq. to go out of England into parts beyond the seas," the starting point of this biographical study. Exactly when Lord Lincoln's party left London and took ship is not known. Probably they were packed and waiting, and set out about Tuesday, May 27. Because a courier required about eight days to cross between London and Paris,[49] the larger group doubtless took about twelve days before arriving in Paris on Sunday, June 8. Since Montmorency's group were carried on English ships we may surmise that Lincoln and his train crossed in French vessels. Of one thing we may be certain: none of the English party foresaw what events the summer would bring to pass.

49. Ibid., p. 253.

CHAPTER 2

The company who attended the Earl of Lincoln on his embassy to Paris was a rather mixed assemblage of lords, gentlemen, and functionaries. In addition to Philip Sidney seventeen are known by name, all minor figures in history, and some unidentified beyond their names.[1] With servants and other attendants they must have numbered sixty or more. Because Philip had permission to travel for two years, his entourage included three servants and four horses. One of the servants was Sidney's Welsh valet-amanuensis, Griffin Madox. The other two were Harry White, one of Sir Henry Sidney's trusted servants, who was later to accompany Robert Sidney on his Continental tour,[2] and one John Fisher, otherwise unidentified.[3] Besides these servants, Sidney was accompanied by a gentleman companion, Lodowick Bryskett. The latter was actually Lodovico Bruschetto, an Italian, born about 1545 in London of Genoese parents who had come to England some ten years earlier and subsequently anglicized their name. About 1564, following a brief interval as a student at Trinity College, Cambridge, Lodowick entered the employ of Sir Henry Sidney who entrusted him with several business journeys to Italy. Because of Lodowick's known character, experience in travelling, and fluency in languages, Sir Henry chose him to accompany Philip on his Continental journey.[4]

The Earl of Lincoln's party included five noblemen, one of whom, his son Henry (ca. 1540–1616), had just acquired the courtesy title of Lord Clinton. In 1585 he succeeded as second Earl of Lincoln and served the Queen in various capacities at home and abroad. The second member of the party was Lord Clinton's cousin, Gregory Fiennes, Lord Dacre (1539–94). Camden later described him as "a man of crack'd brain," and his childless wife complained that "he was kept in undue subjection by his mother."[5] Another inconspicuous aristocrat was Francis Talbot (ca. 1550–

---

1. *HMC Cecil*, 1 : 146.

2. See *HMC De L'Isle*, 1 : 158; Wallace, pp. 208, 210; Collins, 1 : 246, 271, 272, 277, 285, 286, 299; Feuillerat, 3 : 130, 133, 313.

3. See below, p. 166.

4. H. R. Plomer and T. P. Cross, *The Life and Correspondence of Lodowick Bryskett* (Chicago, 1927), chap. 1.

5. William Camden, *History of Princess Elizabeth* (London, 1675 ed.), p. 492.

82), styled Lord Talbot, heir of George, sixth Earl of Shrewsbury. He was a distant cousin of Philip Sidney, one of whose great-grandfathers was Thomas Talbot, Viscount L'Isle (1443–71). Somewhat more eminence belongs to William, third Lord Sandys of the Vyne (d. 1623), who had been one of the Lords who had tried the Duke of Norfolk the previous January. Years later he served with the Lords during the trial of Mary Queen of Scots. At the end of the century he became implicated in the Essex revolt, as a result of which he was sent to the Tower and fined £5,000.

The fifth nobleman in the party owes his minor place in history to his youthful fellow traveller, Philip Sidney. Robert Rich of Leighs in Essex, second Baron Rich, would be forgotten if his son Robert, third Baron, had not married Lady Penelope Devereux, the Stella of Sidney's sonnets. Another young aristocrat (like Sidney, as yet without a title) was Giles Brydges (1547–94) who became third Lord Chandos the year after his return from Paris. His wife was Lady Frances Clinton, fifth daughter of the Lord High Admiral, so Brydges was another "member of the family." In later years he had the burdensome honour of entertaining Queen Elizabeth three times at his seat, Sudeley Castle in Gloucestershire, during her progresses of 1574, 1575, and 1592.

Four members of Lord Lincoln's suite were knights. Sir Arthur Champernowne, later Vice-Admiral of Devon, had been known to Lord High Admiral Clinton (now Lord Lincoln) and to Lord Burghley, who had employed him in various official capacities and continued to do so. Sir Edward Hastings (d. 1603), a younger son of Francis, second Earl of Huntingdon, and Sir Henry Borough are both shadowy figures. Sir Jerome Bowes (d. 1616), however, who accompanied Sidney again in 1577, made a name for himself a few years later. In 1583 Queen Elizabeth appointed him ambassador to the court of Ivan the Terrible in Moscow, where his bravery in defying the cruel whims of the Czar caused Ivan to commend him. The fame of his conduct was praised by Milton in his *Brief History of Moscovia* and by Pepys in his *Diary*.[6]

6. For Milton's description, see his *Moscovia* (1682 ed.), pp. 90–98. Pepys's account is dated Sept. 5, 1662, when he wrote as follows:

And among other pretty discourse, some was of Sir Jerom Bowes, Embassador from Queene Elizabeth to the Emperor of Russia—who, because some of the noblemen there would go up the stairs to the Emperor before him, he would not go up till the Emperor had ordered those two men to be dragged downstair, with their heads knocking upon every stair till they were killed. And when he was come up, they

Of the one untitled member of the entourage, Henry Middelmore, little trace remains, except that he became a Groom of the Privy Chamber. His one letter from this period available in print shows that he was well known and highly regarded by the French Huguenot leaders. Written nine days after the English party reached Paris, the letter also reveals Queen Elizabeth's good opinion of Middelmore's taste:

> Hir Majestie gave me in charge, at my leave takynge, to buy som dry thinges for hir here; but there is suche scarsitye of them throwghe defences [prohibitions] and proclamations made by the Kinge (and that lyttle that is, so greadelye bowght up for this mariage) as I feare me I shall hardly brynge home any thinge to her lykynge.[7]

By "dry thinges" Middelmore meant textiles, or "dry goods," as they became called in America.[8] The marriage he mentions is discussed further on in this chapter and in the next.

The remainder of the "Messrs." in the party were men of little consequence, though they doubtless were good swordsmen and trusted aides. Captain Shute may have been a soldier, as may Luke (or Leke) Paston. One Scudamore was possibly John (d. 1623), later M.P. for Herefordshire and Gentleman Usher to the Queen. Ralph Bowes seems to have died by 1598 when another of the name petitioned the Queen to forgive his father's debts in light of the latter's services. And finally there was Charles Arundel, whose presence on the mission raises several questions. Arundel later proved to be a Roman Catholic who in 1584 became deeply involved in the Throckmorton plot to release Mary Queen of Scots. He fled to

---

demanded his sword of him before he entered the room. He told them, if they would have his sword, they should have his boots too; and so caused his boots to be pulled off, and his night-gown and night-cap and slippers to be sent for; and made the Emperor stay till he could go in his night-dress, since he might not go as a soldier. And lastly, when the Emperor in contempt, to show his command over his subjects, did command one to leap from the window down and broke his neck in the sight of our Embassador, he replied that his mistress did set more by, and did make better use of the necks of her subjects: but said that to show what her subjects would do for her, he would, and did, fling down his gantlett before the Emperor; and challenged all the nobility there to take it up in defence of the Emperor against his Queene: for which, at this very day, the name of Sir Jerom Bowes is famous and honoured there.

7. Middelmore to Lord Burghley, June 17, 1572 (BM Cotton Vesp. F. VI, fol. 89), printed in Sir Henry Ellis, *Original Letters*, 2d ser. (London, 1827), 3:3–11.

8. *OED* lists no example of this usage before 1708.

Paris where he helped to organize Catholic refugees and at one time planned to lead an invasion of Scotland.[9] Although Burghley and Lord Lincoln may have known of Arundel's religious convictions and included him as a token Catholic to please the French, more likely he dissembled in order to serve his cause when opportunity offered.

All who accompanied Lord Lincoln had some knowledge of the recent events which were changing the political situation in Europe. Rivalry between France and Spain had resulted in a precarious balance of power which it was England's policy to maintain. (Since both Continental powers were financially embarrassed, penny-pinching Elizabeth held one advantage over these larger rivals.) The Holy Roman Emperor and other German rulers remained on the sidelines. Venice and the papal establishment were primarily worried about the Turks, who dominated the Eastern Mediterranean, threatened the coasts of Italy and Sicily, and controlled the Danube Valley up to the gates of Austria. How far did the Turk wish to extend his dominions? In southern Europe this threat haunted the commerce and even the homelands of many Christian states.

When the Turks seized Cyprus the alarmed Venetians appealed to Pope Pius V to form a Christian League against the infidel. The Pope convinced Philip II of Spain to join his own token forces and the powerful Venetian navy in a united fleet. The combined force of three hundred ships under the command of Philip's illegitimate half brother, Don John of Austria, proceeded to the Gulf of Lepanto where Ali Pasha waited with about the same number of Turkish ships. The battle on October 7, 1571 (the last great clash of oar-propelled vessels) resulted in the smashing of the Turkish navy, the slaughter of some twenty-five thousand Turks and the liberation of about fifteen thousand Christian galley slaves. When news of the victory reached western courts some weeks later it rocked them into the realization that Philip of Spain had become more than ever the most powerful man in the western world.

Before this event the English had been making halfhearted attempts to assist their fellow Protestants in the Netherlands, but now that the full might of Spanish arms could be focused there, the situation required reassessment. The French were even more alarmed. The English Ambassador, Francis Walsingham, reported from Paris to Lord Burghley on November 8:

9. Read, 2:387, 409, 417.

It is much feared by those of judgement here, that this Victory, though generallie it may grow to Christendom profitable, yet particularlie it may prove dangerous to some, in that it is likely to increase the reputation and greatness of *Spain*, which may breed some change here, and may cause the King [Charles IX] to relent over much to *Spain*; the reason of the fear is, that [the] Queen Mother [Catherine de Médicis], who directeth all things here, is of nature fearful.[10]

To the Earl of Leicester Walsingham stated that he thought England and France should now try to join together against Spain: "I think therefore no time more fit to treat of Amitie, then at this present."[11] Elizabeth became convinced that the enhanced power of Philip must be countered. Since the woman who determined policy in France, Catherine de Médicis, also agreed that an alliance would be beneficial, preliminary steps were soon under way.

Catherine had lived in France since she came from Florence in her fifteenth year (1533) to marry the future Henry II. Yet after a third of a century at the French court she remained an unscrupulous, amoral Florentine. The concept of basing policy on principle was incomprehensible to her. Duplicity, poison, the dagger, and bold-faced lies were devices of statecraft as legitimate to Catherine as they had been to her Florentine forbears. To her the object of statecraft was power. Politics and religion were the game boards on which she and her opponents (both foreign and domestic) played for high stakes. Now that Philip of Spain had acquired new strength she was forced to consolidate her position.

Catherine's character and her position behind the throne were understood in varying degrees by each of the men in Lord Lincoln's party. Similarly, from the grizzled Lord High Admiral to the beardless Philip Sidney, each had some knowledge of the political and religious divisions in France, where three great families struggled to dominate the weak Charles IX and Catherine, who had long directed all his moves. These families were the Guises, established in eastern France, the Bourbons, whose properties lay in the southwest, and the Montmorencys from central France. The Guises, led by their Duke and his uncle, the wealthy and clever Cardinal de Lorraine, held strong Roman Catholic views and before the present reign had controlled the court.

10. Digges, p. 149.
11. Ibid., p. 150.

The Bourbons ranked immediately behind Catherine's sons, the House of Valois, in succession to the crown. They were strong Huguenots and their coastal city of Rochelle stood as the western stronghold of Protestantism. On middle ground, in religion as in geography, were the Montmorencys. Many of them had been converted to Huguenot beliefs; others remained in the Roman church, though not militantly. With her sons, Catherine followed the conventions of Catholicism, but her own religious activities were minimal. She viewed the Huguenots as a rival power complex, to be used as a counterbalance to the ambitions of the Guises, but to be kept in their place. In earlier years she had encouraged their rise, but since 1567, when they had attempted to seize the King during his visit to Meux, she had realized that they were not psalm-singing idealists but a power-hungry organization. Now she watched them carefully and played them off against the Guises.

Peace at home became more necessary than ever, now that Spanish power could once again be concentrated in northern Europe. As Philip's armies in the Netherlands placed France in the potential pincer grip of Spain, Catherine sought to cement peace with the heretic English. Ambitious to add another crown to her family in the process, Catherine first tried to marry her son, the Duke of Anjou, to Elizabeth. But Elizabeth toyed with the proposal until Anjou fell under the influence of the Cardinal of Lorraine, the leader of the Guise family, and turned so ardent a Romanist that the marriage became impossible. Catherine next offered her youngest son, the Duke of Alençon, even though he was twenty years younger than Elizabeth. Again Elizabeth dallied with the idea to gain time. The watered-down Treaty of Blois, now about to be signed, proved to be the best alliance that could be negotiated.

Simultaneously, Catherine tried to unite the Protestants of France with the House of Valois. In April 1571 it was announced that her daughter, Marguerite of Valois, would be married to Henry, Prince of Navarre. The announcement was accompanied by various concessions to the Huguenots, who now rejoiced that their equality, officially achieved in the Edict of Toleration (1562), promised to become reality. This could mean an end to the bloodbaths which the Reformation and Counter-Reformation had produced in France over many decades. A bright new day for the Huguenots seemed to be dawning, for now amid general amnesty their prince of the blood would marry the sister of the King.

Politically, the leader of the Huguenots was not Henry of Navarre but the able and respected Admiral, Gaspard de Coligny. A nephew of the famous Constable de Montmorency, a military hero and far-seeing states-man, Coligny was also a sincere convert to Protestantism. His position, personal charm, and capacity for leadership won him the loyalty of Huguenots of all classes of whom the most difficult to command were the quarrelsome nobility. He defined the aim of Huguenot policy as the establishment of Protestant religion in all of France. Coligny stressed the ideological concept of loyalty to religious faith above loyalty to nation or the family. Accordingly, he looked to Protestants in England, Germany, and elsewhere as allies against the French Catholics, and he was a natural supporter of the alliance with England which was now developing.

Indeed, Coligny had favoured the alliance for more than a year but had not been in a position to do much about it.[12] His opportunity came in September 1571, when Charles IX, who had formed a very high regard for him, persuaded his mother to let him invite Coligny to court. By December Elizabeth decided to shift towards an alliance with France, and the resulting Treaty of Blois was a feather in the Admiral's cap, to the chagrin of his enemies, the Guises, who favoured Spain. Charles IX became persuaded that the time was ripe to attack the Spaniards in the Low Countries and, under the influence of Coligny, for once diverged from his mother's opinion. If England would only join with France the enterprise seemed to promise success. Coligny and Charles did not know that Elizabeth preferred the Spanish to the French in the Netherlands, for English trade had continued uninterrupted during the Spanish occupation but might wither if the French gained control. Antwerp was the centre of European trade, the great warehouse of the western world to which London served as a commercial satellite. Besides this, for over a quarter of a century its bankers had provided the chief source of English government loans.[13]

The Earl of Lincoln and his party reached Paris on Sunday, June 8. They had been welcomed on the road by the King's representative, Marshal de Cossé,[14] who then conducted them to St. Denis where a good dinner awaited them. Sidney and his fellow travellers found Paris very different from the glamorous metropolis of later centuries. Approaching the city, they saw various towers, notably those of Notre Dame (considered inferior to the cathedral at Amiens, not to name other provincial cathedrals), and

12. Ibid., p. 37.
13. Wilson, pp. 17–18.
14. *CSPF*1, p. 124.

Paris's forbidding walls, thirty feet in height, with their fourteen fortified gates. These ramparts enclosed two square miles into which were crowded about two hundred and fifty thousand people. Paris retained many characteristics of a medieval city; its tortuous and narrow streets were filled with stagnant water and filth. From the open sewers arose a putrid, perpetual stench. The traveller Thomas Coryat, whose curiosity and tireless feet carried him to Venice and back in 1608, wrote of Paris, "many of the streetes are the durtiest, and so consequently stinking of all that I euer saw in any citie in my life."[15] He was quite correct in pointing out that the Roman settlement there had been named Lutetia, derived from *lutum*, mud. In the mire walked "great aboundance of mules, which are so highly esteemed amongst them, that the Iudges and Counsellers doe vsually ride on them with their foot clothes."[16] At intervals official orders were issued to clean up the city, but they were not enforced. Predictable under these conditions, disease became endemic. Outbreaks of the plague recurred about every third year; in the severe plague of 1562 approximately one-tenth of the population died. During the 1569 epidemic of smallpox, the victims included doctors to the royal family; Marguerite de Valois barely survived, and her brother, the Duke of Alençon, became so badly disfigured that his position in the international marriage market was affected.

But Coryat also praised "the noble River Seine" and the fine buildings of "faire white freestone," limestone available from the local quarries. The age of Catherine de Médicis had seen a surge of building in the Renaissance style introduced by her husband, Henry II. The earliest theatre rose in 1548 in the rue Française, le Théatre de l'Hôtel de Bourgogne. Henry and Catherine were the first royal family to take up residence in the Louvre, which they did in 1559, the year of Henry's untimely death. Catherine herself was responsible for the Tuileries, begun in 1566. Only two bridges, the Pont-aux-Meuniers and Pont Notre Dame, spanned the Seine; construction of the Pont Neuf did not commence until 1578. Hence boatmen plied a busy trade. Little wonder that the English Ambassador, Francis Walsingham, and many aristocrats chose to live on the left bank in the Faubourg St. Germain, despite such disadvantages as lack of spring water and the hazards involved in dwelling outside the city walls.

15. Coryat, p. 21. Other details occur in Alfred Franklin's *Paris et les Parisiens au seizième siècle* (Paris, 1921).

16. Coryat, p. 30. "Footcloths" were pieces of carpet to stand on when the rider dismounted.

In 1572 Francis Walsingham was about forty years old. Long before, when he had been a Fellow Commoner at King's College, Cambridge, he had developed strong Protestant views. Afterwards he travelled on the Continent, to acquire "the rest of his learning," [17] and upon his return to England in 1552 enrolled at Gray's Inn. But when Mary Tudor mounted the throne in the summer of 1553, Walsingham packed his Protestant convictions in his luggage and returned to the Continent, where he studied law at the University of Padua. After the accession of Elizabeth, Walsingham joined the stream of religious refugees returning to England, and in 1562 he married and attained a seat in Parliament. He had early attracted the attention of Cecil, who in 1568 brought Walsingham into the Queen's service. In August 1570 Elizabeth sent him as her envoy to the French court, with the specific purpose of helping the Huguenots gain favourable terms in negotiations then under way. After he had proved himself to Elizabeth, she appointed him ambassador to France.

Among Walsingham's acquaintances in London Sidney's uncle, the Earl of Leicester, stood high. They wrote frequently, both officially and personally but, because of the difference in rank, their relationship was essentially that of allies in governmental business. Accordingly, the day after Philip's permission to travel was signed by Elizabeth, Leicester wrote a letter for his nephew to carry to Walsingham. It read:

Mr. Walsingham:

Forasmuch as my nephew, Philip Sidney, is licensed to travel, and doth presently repair to those parts with my Lord Admiral, I have thought good to commend him by these my letters friendly unto you as to one I am well assured will have a special care of him during his abode there. He is young and raw, and no doubt shall find those countries and the demeanours of the people somewhat strange unto him; and therefore your good advice and counsel shall greatly behove him for his better direction, which I do most heartily pray you to vouchsafe him, with any friendly assurance you shall think needful for him. His father and I do intend his further travel if the world be quiet and you shall think it convenient for him; otherwise we pray you we may be advertised thereof to the end the same his travel may be thereupon directed accordingly.[18]

17. Sir Robert Naunton, *Fragmenta Regalia*, ed. Arber (London, 1895), pp. 35–36.
18. Text as normalized by Wallace, p. 115; the original is BM Add. MS. 34591, fol. 503. The letter continues with other business concerning an employee whom Leicester was trying to bring to England; see Digges, pp. 212–13.

Sidney's biographers have tended to emphasize the word "raw" as meaning uncultivated or uncivilized. But the known facts about young Philip Sidney show this was far from his case. Leicester's purpose seems simply to make clear that Philip, in contrast to others in Lord Lincoln's party, was young, untravelled, and relatively inexperienced in court or official circles.[19]

The Valois had been famous for brilliant fêtes since the time of François I, and a busy round of receptions and entertainments greeted the Earl of Lincoln and his attendants. Banquets, as usual, provided the core of the official receptions and were an exotic adventure for the palates of the English. Balls and ballets varied the entertainment. Catherine had imported dancers from her native Italy and also an impresario named Baltazarini to organize her fêtes. He was soon known as Beaujoyeux.[20] The court musicians enjoyed special status under the direction of a "roi des violons." Charles IX had a notable fondness for dramatic interludes, often constructed around symbolic or allegorical situations.

A form of rivalry existed between the royal courts in England and France in entertaining visitors from across the Channel. On June 20 Burghley wrote to Walsingham,

> I have looked for some knowledge of my L[ord] Admirals arrival at *Paris*, and thereupon stayed to send away this bearer until now I hear by the French Ambassadors Letters, how my Lord and you have been feasted and entertained, which they here do give out with large speeches, but how indeed the same is warranted I know not; sure I am, that they [the French in England] have been so feasted and entreated, as none in my memory hath been greater.[21]

A few days later Burghley reported further:

> The Duke [of Montmorency] with all his train, to the number of forty, have been entertained here for their meat and drink each in their degrees, as it is to be affirmed that the like hath not been seen in any mans memory. The honour also done to him hath been such, as surely her Majesty could do no more; I mean, in her courteous usage

19. Examples of the word used in this sense are not far to seek; Lord Burghley writing to Walsingham Apr. 1, 1573 about his successor, Dr. Valentine Dale, advised him "And if in conference you find any rawness and imperfection, you do not forbear, but like a Tutor, teach him to inform." Digges, p. 347.
20. Franklin, *Paris et les Parisiens*, p. 517.
21. Digges, p. 214.

of him, in appointing sundry sorts of the Nobility of the highest sort
to attend on him, onely the difference from my Lord Admirals inter-
tertainment [sic] was, that no other Lord but my Lord of *Leicester* did
feast him, as in *France* was done; saving I did upon *Midsummer* even
feast him and all his Gentlemen with a Collation of all things I could
procure, being not flesh, to observe their manner.[22]

The awaited news from Paris did not arrive until about June 26, because
it was not written until Sir Thomas Smith, the Queen's Ambassador,
found time to report to Burghley. Sir Thomas, whose experienced hand
had moulded the Treaty of Blois, had been told to wait in Paris until the
Treaty was ratified, and the Earl of Lincoln followed his lead closely.
Smith's long report on the schedule kept by Lord Lincoln and his attendants, written on June 18, gives a day-by-day account of their activities.[23]
Since it is likely that Philip Sidney participated in these events, they
deserve detailed description.

Arriving on Sunday, June 8, the party was guided to the Louvre, the
royal residence, where rooms had been prepared for them. The King and
Queen were staying at Madrill (the Chateau de Madrid) in the Bois de
Boulogne. On Monday Lord Lincoln "thought best to rest," though we
may surmise that Sidney and most of the English explored parts of the city.
On Tuesday emissaries from the King arranged for Lord Lincoln, Sir
Thomas Smith, and Walsingham to dine with Charles IX on Friday the
thirteenth. The emissaries also agreed on the wording of the Treaty and
the time and procedure for the King's swearing of the oath. On Friday
morning, royal coaches arrived at the Louvre and carried Lord Lincoln
" & my lordes of his treyne," among whom Sidney would travel, to the
Chateau de Madrid

> about ix of the clock or x in the morning, when the King was
> scarsely risen. But as sone as he was up, my lord Admirall [Lincoln]
> was sent for, who after verie curteous & honorable enterteignment
> delivered hir Majesties letters and did his message, which was so well
> and so hartely received of the King, & with so good wordes againe
> as cowld be.

The King and his brothers there dined with the three English dignitaries
while

22. Ibid., p. 218.
23. BM Cotton Vesp. F. VI, fol. 93; printed in Ellis, *Original Letters*, 3 : 12–26.

Queen Elizabeth, with Lord Burghley and Sir Francis Walsingham

the lordes & the rest of the treyne were feastid in an other place. At night (for in France on fridaies thei do use ordenary soups [suppers]) my lord Admirall, we, & the rest of the noble & gentlemen of his treine supped in an hawle appointed for the same, adjoyning to my lords lodging, served with the Kinges men very honorably. Likewise on Saterday dynner & supper was ordered.

Sunday, June 15, was the day appointed for the simultaneous ratification of the Treaty of Blois on both sides of the Channel. The Paris ceremony received such a full description in Sir Thomas Smith's report that we can almost feel we were present with Philip Sidney and the other English attendants to the signatories.

On Sonday in the morning ther was great store of coches brought to Madrill, and as sone as the King had hard masse, he & his ij brethren & my lord Admirall in one coche, the prince Daulphin & Mr. Walsingham & I in an other coche, the noblemen & gentlemen of England in other coches provided for them, cam from Madrill to the Louvre, where in the great chamber or hawle, after that the King had shewed my lord Admirall the magnificence of his owne chambers & cabinetes, dyner was preparid, & ther dyned as before the King & his ij brethren, my lord Admirall & we ij, all vj at one table & on one side; the table was served very magnifically & all with gentlemen & tall men, which I have not sene here before accustomid; but such a presse in the hawle & so nere to the kings table, that scarcely the ministers cowld have rowme to bring the meate or the drinck to the table; this is the maner & familiarity in this contrey.

Not long after dyner my lord being retired to his chamber, he was streight sent for agayne (for in dede the King dyned very late) and so a great nomber of lords & gentlemen goeng before, the king & my lord Admirall, Monsieur & I, the duke of Alanson & Mr. Walsingham, with likewise a great nomber of noblemen & gentlemen folowing, cam to the place in the church of St. Germayne by the Louvre which was preparid for the King & his brethren to sit, where also was preparid a place for us, but to avoid all offences that might arise, we were conveyed by Monsieur Lausack [i.e. Lansac] to a side chappell in the same churche richtly tapisserid & hangid for the nones, where was also stooles & settes covered with cloth of gold preparid for my lord & us. The lordes & noblemen of England had an other preparid for them; and for the rest of the treyne a third, in which we taried untill that evensong was done, which thei that can skill of it did saie was song in very good musick. To us cam one of our religion the duke of Bullion [Bouillon, a Protestant].

When Evensong was done we were brought to the King & so in the same order as we cam to the churche, the King, & his brethren & we cam before the high alter, where the busshop of Auxerre, le grand Aumosner du Roy, holding the boke where gospells lay open, having in his left hand a paper of the forme of the othe, the which the King laying his right hand uppon the boke open, red, & so kissed the boke & then torned him to my lord Admirall, & said my lord Admirall I pray yow tell my good sister the Queene that I do not sweare this oth in wordes onely, but with myne hole hart, and do rejoise so mich thereof as eny man can, & will kepe it firmely so long as God shall geve me lief. Then they began & song Te deum.

And so while thei were singing the King retornid in the same order as he cam, and my lord Admirall & we so accompanid as before. Not only all the churche, but all the streetes where we passed so full, that skarsely the King & we cowld have rowme to go. The king both in the church & in the way, many tymes staying as it were to looke on the people, & that the people showld loke on him & us, & rejoice the more fully with him.

After the treaty-signing ceremonies it was time to relax and eat again. Sir Thomas's account of the proceedings follows:

When we cam against the Louvre, there was a coche preparid wherein the King & his brethren & my lord Admirall went from the Louvre to the Tuillery, and the prince Daulphin Mr. Walsingham & I in an other, the other lordes noblemen & gentlemen of England in other coches, or on horsback. In the garden of the said Tullierie is the Queene Mothers building, in an Alley beside a pleasaunt fontayne or conduicte; there was preparid the Kinges supper; the king led my lord Admirall to diverse partes of that garden which is large & faier, to se the deseignes of his mother, and there in a litle pavillion or open banketting howse covered with slate, the king & his ij brethren, my lord Admirall and we ij did sup, & no more.

Emonges other noblemen there was the Admirall of France & iiij brethren to the Mareshall Montmorency, the duke of Guise & Daumale, & Conte de Rez, altho of diverse faccions yet both well lokid upon of the King; they & the other noblemen of England & of Fraunce were provided for in other place.

The Englishmen observed the eminent position that Admiral Coligny held in the King's immediate circle. After the supper on Sunday Coligny rejoined the party and during the evening had almost an hour of uninterrupted talk with the King and his brother, the Duke of Anjou. Sir Thomas noticed that while some of the French were obviously pleased at this, others seemed suspicious and unhappy. Coligny then invited Lord Lincoln and the other English to supper at his house the next evening. There, on Monday, they enjoyed "a noble, magnificall, & sumptuous supper, and in so good order that no man had cawse to compleyne, but every man occasion to think that it cam of a loving, fre, & liberall hart."

The Duke of Anjou's turn came the following day, Tuesday, June 17, "at his loging over against the Louvre." He had assembled various noblemen, among them the Duke of Nevers, whom Sidney later had occasion to remember with gratitude. The company was seated according to rank, so Sidney would have been at the third table with "all the rest of the noblemen of England & Fraunce." Anjou took special pains to make the dinner and entertainment as elegant as possible:

> There was very great chere & costly, yet that was not enough; after dynner furst my lord Admiral & we were brought to here excellent musick, (as thei said, that could skill of yt) furst of the voice with virginalls, then of Voninis schole, with the voice, violls, & lutes; after that an Italian comedie, which eandid, vaulting with notable supersaltes [somersaults] & through hoopes, and last all the Antiques [antics], of carying of men one uppon another which som men call *labores Herculis*.

On Wednesday it became the responsibility of the King's youngest brother, the Duke of Alençon, to entertain the English visitors. Because his house was too small for such a crowd, especially during the heat wave in which Paris was sweltering, the Duke arranged to hold his dinner at the house of the Count de Retz. The banquet equalled in sumptuousness those that had preceded it. The "other noble men of England & Fraunce" (presumably including Sidney) were placed at the second of two long tables. Sir Thomas added, "There was there also standing other noble men & gentlemen of Fraunce whom I knew not; there was great presse &

therfore extreme heate all the dynner while." Fortunately, for the after-dinner entertainment the Duke led them "into a chamber somwhat more fresh, where we heard excellent musique both of voice & virginalls, & of voice & violls as the daie before." The Duke then explained that he had prepared a comedy and other performances but cancelled them because of the heat. As the guests departed, spouts of "damaske & fine water" rained upon the company, "and then a mad felow [blew] damaske and fine smelling powder all abowt."

Now the official entertainments were approaching an end. At the final supper party on Thursday, June 19, the Duke of Nevers served as host. His ample park allowed his guests to sup "abroad among trees as in an arbour." The following day Lord Lincoln, Sir Thomas Smith, and their attendants made a farewell visit to King Charles, his Queen, and Catherine de Médicis.[24] According to protocol the departing envoys were loaded with valuable gifts. The Earl of Lincoln received gilt plate weighing 2,800 ounces "which may be valued at 10s. the ounce, considering the work-manship, and that the silver is finer than in England."[25] Sir Thomas Smith and Francis Walsingham each received plate weighing 472 ounces, worth £236. Despite the lack of proper carriages, a problem solved only with the King's assistance, Lincoln and his train departed and by easy stages reached Boulogne. On July 5 Lord Lincoln came to court and gave Queen Elizabeth a detailed account of his successes and how well the French had entertained him.[26]

Because Sidney was staying on in Paris, he probably did not attend the departure ceremonies at court, though he had to make his own adieus to his returning English friends. He also had to find new lodgings for himself, Bryskett, Madox, his other servants, and his four horses, just where cannot be determined. At the moment, the greatest excitement in Paris centred on plans for the celebration of St. John's Eve, the traditional midsummer revels. These occurred on June 23, the day following the departure of Lord Lincoln's party.

For the edification of the court, animal fights were held in the garden of the Louvre. Bears, bulls, and even lions were baited by mastiffs and boarhounds. Bonfires blazed in squares throughout Paris and in front of the houses of those noble families having a member with the name John. Fireworks added to the excitement; while double-sized firecrackers

24. Sir Thomas Smith to Burghley, June 28, 1572. *CSPF*1, p. 139.
25. Ibid., p. 135.
26. Burghley to Walsingham, in Digges, p. 219.

exploded, rockets and double rockets arched through the sky and the roar of cannons deafened the crowds.

The climax of the festivities was to be the lighting of a huge bonfire in the Place de Grève; because the king and his entourage were to be present, special preparations had been made for this traditional ceremony. At considerable expense a tree thirty-six feet tall had been erected in the square and supported by four joists. Around it were piled over twenty cubic yards of great logs, five hundred large faggots and two hundred smaller ones, with bundles of straw. From the top of the tree a crossbar projected, at the end of which hung a bag full of live cats. To these, in honour of the King, a fox was added. A plentiful guard of archers, cross-bowmen, and harquebusiers directed by ten sergeants held back the crowds.

At last the trumpets and the fireworks ended as the Provost and five other worthies advanced from various sides with torches of yellow wax and ignited the straw. The flames leapt up the pyre and the excitement of the crowd mounted until the cats and fox dropped into the holocaust below. Sweetmeats were then distributed to all the onlookers, while distinguished guests received special boxes of delicacies. There is no record of how the English visitors reacted to this spectacle of Gallic taste. Actually, it differed from similar occasions in England (e.g. the annual celebration of Elizabeth's accession on November 17) chiefly in degree; the bonfires, bearbaiting, and other elements were common to both countries. Indeed, in all parts of northern Europe St. John's Eve was the occasion for bonfires and other forms of celebration. Even Breton mariners at sea hoisted baskets of inflammable materials to burn while hanging from the masts or yardarms. In the days immediately following the celebration, members of the court scattered to their estates in the country to escape the heat of midsummer. At the end of the week Charles IX and his intimate friends went hunting.

Despite this show of official gaiety, two clouds hung over the French court and the city of Paris. The first arose from the death of Jeanne d'Albret, Queen of Navarre, on June 9, the day after the English envoys reached Paris. The Queen had been in Paris for a few weeks to supervise plans for the marriage of her son Henry to Marguerite de Valois. Because the death of Pope Pius V had caused the head of the Guise family, the Cardinal of Lorraine, to hurry to Rome, the time was now propitious to foster the Huguenot position in the capital. Although her health had previously seemed satisfactory for a woman of forty-two, the Queen suddenly became seriously ill. Sensing the end, she made a will just before her death, five days after she was stricken. As happened so frequently in the case of highly placed personages, the Huguenots suspected poison. Examining physicians, however, found no evidence of this. They reported observing the Queen's right side to be "of extraordinary hardnesse and a great impostume,"[27] and one of her lungs was far gone in consumption.

The virile but unpolished young Henry was now King of Navarre, and after several weeks of preparation he set out with his train for Paris. In that Catholic city where no Protestant service had ever been allowed, indignation at his forthcoming marriage to the Princess Royal ran high. On June 30, in order to prevent trouble, Charles issued a royal proclamation forbidding the molestation of foreigners, Protestants, or followers of Henry of Navarre. Once this news became known, German students began to stream into Paris, fifteen hundred of them before the wedding day; they lodged wherever they were accepted.[28] On July 7 another royal edict prohibited the bearing of arms within the city, with the special injunction not to use weapons in the settlement of disputes. This precaution was in effect on July 8 when, following careful prearrangements, Henry, his attendants, and eight hundred gentlemen dressed in black arrived at the Porte St. Jacques. They were greeted by the King's brothers, the Dukes of Anjou and Alençon, who were attended by nobles and officers of the court.[29] The magnificence of the courtiers' clothing and the scarlet robes worn by the municipal officials contrasted sharply with the somber dress of the Huguenot train. Together the two groups, totaling fifteen hundred horsemen, rode past silent crowds until they reached the Louvre. Sidney, Bryskett, and Madox are not likely to have missed this spectacle. They had now been in Paris long enough to feel the undercurrent of religious hatred that ran through the Parisian masses at the sight of so many heretics.

The other cloud that hung over Paris rose in the Low Countries. The Huguenots under Coligny were convinced that the time was ripe for an attack on the Spanish forces holding Flanders. Success would result in the freeing of their fellow Protestants from the Spanish yoke, would remove the danger of France's being pinched between Spanish armies on both the

---

27. *An Historical Collection . . . France* (London, 1598), p. 247, *STC* 11275.

28. *Geizkofler*, p. 33.

29. Although the royal family usually wore mourning for a month, Charles IX doffed his black raiment after only a week in honour of the visiting Englishmen and the joy over the Treaty of Blois.

northern and southern borders, and would acquire for the French the prosperous industries and markets of Flanders. Success would be doubly certain if only the English would join the attack; in return for their support they would receive the Netherlands as their share of the spoils of war. The Spanish had been stung in April when a band of rebels called the Sea Beggars captured The Brill, an island port which commanded commerce entering the North Sea from the Rhine and other great rivers. Subsequently other vital ports fell under rebel control, conquests which later formed the foundation stone of the Dutch Republic.[30] In June when the English envoys were in Paris Admiral Coligny had taken special pains to try to convince them that now was the time to join together and chase the Spaniards out of the Low Countries forever.[31]

Coligny had succeeded in persuading Charles IX that the attack should be made now that the limited Treaty with England had become a reality. Indeed, Coligny's personal charm, sincerity, and statesmanlike grasp of foreign affairs won Charles to his viewpoint in this and some domestic matters. The Queen Mother realized that her son had escaped from her dominance and was now under the influence of Coligny, and she did not like it. Catherine could not realize, however, how deeply that influence was affecting the proposed adventure into Flanders. The rebellion there was being unofficially supported by the English, who allowed refugee Walloons to return to Flanders with money and supplies. At the end of June Sir Humphrey Gilbert had crossed to Holland with a large number of "volunteers." Elizabeth condoned this invasion, but her instructions limited their action to occupying Sluys and Flushing, to make certain that these ports did not fall into the hands of the French. Louis of Nassau, a leader in the revolt, exuded confidence that the Spaniards would be forced to retreat. Yet when the Spanish troops recaptured Valenciennes and besieged Mons, Coligny became alarmed, and persuaded Charles IX to permit the Huguenot commander, Seigneur de Genlis, to lead four thousand foot soldiers and six hundred horsemen to the relief of Mons on July 12. Protestants streamed northwards to support their fellow religionists.

But optimism and enthusiasm were no match for the professional troops of the Duke of Alva. On July 17 the forces under Genlis were routed ignominiously; one thousand were killed and six hundred captured,

30. Wilson, pp. 26–27.
31. Middelmore to Burghley, June 17, 1572, cited in n. 7.

Genlis among them. When the news reached Paris some days later the Huguenot leaders gathered in Coligny's house. Charles first considered a full-scale war against Spain, but he soon cooled down. Coligny's dream of a grand coalition against Spain collapsed, and Catherine de Médicis recovered her dominant position at court. Although the majority of the members of the Council opposed her, she regained her influence over them when they gathered early in August.[32] Meanwhile, to the chagrin of the Huguenots, survivors from Mons straggled into Paris, half-naked and in rags. The Catholic citizens, however, demonstrated their joy by holding banquets and processions.[33] After the week of luxurious living which Sidney enjoyed while Lord Lincoln and his attendants were in Paris, the grim reality of this turn of events must have come as a brutal surprise.

Sidney now had the opportunity of getting to know some of Paris' Protestant intellectuals, who seem to have welcomed him to their intimacy. Although Walsingham struggled with his official duties under the handicaps of frequent illness, inadequate staff, and an income insufficient to support his Embassy,[34] he had become well acquainted with intellectual circles in Paris, as his journal of these years shows.[35] Once Lord Lincoln's party departed and the French court fled the summer heat, Walsingham had time to meet with young Sidney, whose abilities and promising future could easily be recognized. How often and how informally they met during July and early August can not be determined, nor can we know how widely Walsingham introduced Sidney to the Protestant

32. Champion, 2:58–59.
33. *CSPF*1, no. 486.
34. Walsingham had used the presence of Lord Lincoln to demonstrate the financial restrictions under which he had to carry his important responsibilities. On the very day of Lincoln's departure he wrote Burghley a touching letter:

> It hath pleased my Lord of *Lincoln* to promise me, upon his experience had of the intollerable charges here, through the daily increase of dearth, to confer with your Lordship, in what sort he may best deal with her Majestie for increase of my diet considering otherwise that I shall not be able to hold out, my monethly charges drawing now to two hundred pounds the moneth, notwithstanding my diet is thin, my family [i.e. staff] reduced to as small a proportion as may be, and my horse being onely twelve. These things might seem unto Your Lordship altogether incredible, were there not so many Noblemen and Gentlemen to witness the same by their experience lately had of the extreme dearth here.

Digges p. 213; the original is summarized in *CSPF*1, no. 444.

35. *Journal of Sir Francis Walsingham, 1570–1583*, ed. C. T. Martin, Camden Society (London, 1870). Unfortunately its entries are terse, and none exist for 1572, except for January.

intellectuals. An introduction to any one of them would have provided an entrée for Sidney, whose mastery of French put him at ease in any conversation with an individual or among an assembly.

Whether or not the first such friend was Hubert Languet, he proved to be one of the greatest influences on Sidney's mind and future life. The son of the governor of Vitteaux, Languet had been born in Burgundy in 1528 and was raised as a Roman Catholic. His family sent him to the University of Poitiers, and when he left there in 1539 he travelled through Germany to Italy, where he attended the University of Bologna. From there he went on to the equally renowned University at Padua and received the degree of Doctor of Laws in 1548. While at Padua, a centre of progressive theology, he read *Loci Communes . . . Theologiae* by Melanchthon, the protégé of Martin Luther. Languet resolved to meet Melanchthon and journeyed to Wittenberg for that purpose. There in Saxony, "the cradle of the Reformation," he was converted to Protestantism. August, the Elector, was so impressed with his mind and understanding of European politics that he engaged Languet to be his ambassador in Paris. Except for absences during outbreaks of religious bloodshed he remained there until 1567. He then left the Elector's service and migrated to Germany, where he was involved in various theological and diplomatic meetings. In September 1570 he returned to Paris as the Elector's representative,[36] and there in the hot midsummer of 1572 he met Sidney.

Languet and Walsingham had become good friends and dining companions during January 1571, a circumstance that is not surprising since each was an ambassador of a leading Protestant state.[37] Perhaps the high point of Languet's diplomatic career came on December 23, 1570, when in the name of the Protestant rulers of the German states he presented a formal address to Charles IX and his court.[38] Besides being personally congenial, Walsingham and Languet were both strong proponents of a Protestant League against Spain, the policy of Protestant activism which Admiral Coligny also advocated. Like other Protestant leaders, Languet had rejoiced at the Treaty of Blois as an advance for their cause and a well-aimed blow at Spanish power in northern Europe.

36. Henri Chevreul, *Hubert Languet* (Paris, 1852; reprint ed., Nieuwkoop, 1967), pp. 100–06.
37. Walsingham's *Journal*, pp. 3, 8, 9, 10.
38. Published as "Harangue au roy Charles IX" in *Mémoires de l'état de France* (Paris, 1578), I:22–28.

Testimony to Languet's fresh intellect, well-stored mind, and warmth of personality abounds in the writings of his eminent friends. Joachim Camerarius, Professor of Humanities at the University of Leipzig, with whom Languet lived for a while about 1549, described him as an admirable conversationalist who, aided by a strong memory, keen analytical abilities, and a knowledge of kings, courts, and the lives of illustrious men, could talk pertinently about modern politics. Camerarius went further:

> I never heard a man, who could expound with so much prudence, certainty, plainness, evidence, and eloquence, whatever he undertook to relate; he never mistook the names of men; he was never wrong in the circumstances of time; nor did he ever confound the order and series of things and events. He had also a wonderful sagacity to discover the Characters of men, and to conjecture which way men's tempers would lead them, and what was the inclination of their minds. He judged almost with certainty of their designs, and could most wonderfully foresee the event of things.[39]

This description by Camerarius, who was about twenty years older than Languet, is matched by that of the historian Jacques Auguste de Thou, a liberal Catholic thirty-five years Languet's junior. De Thou met Languet at Baden just seven years after Sidney had come to know him; and after three days de Thou wished that they might never part. Thuanus (as he became known) was greatly

> pleased . . . with this man's eminent probity, and with his great judgment not only in the Sciences, but also in publick affairs, in which he had been ingaged all his life time, having served several Princes very faithfully: he was particularly so well acquainted with the affairs of Germany, that he could instruct the Germans themselves in the affairs of their own country.[40]

If any further evidence of Languet's gifts of intellect, literary ability, or personal charm should be required, his published correspondence with Sidney supplies it. From their first meeting Sidney considered Languet his guide, philosopher, and friend. In turn, Languet later described the impression the seventeen-year-old Sidney had made upon him: "As long as I live, I shall consider the day I first saw you a happy one: the innate

---

39. Birch's *Bayle*, 6:629, quoted from Camerarius's *Melanchthonis Vita*.
40. Birch's *Bayle*, 6:63, quoted from Thuanus's *De Vita Sua*, bk. 2.

virtue which shines forth in your face, in your discourse, and in your every action, immediately impelled me to become your friend."[41]

Besides being Ambassador of Saxony, one of the strongest and most economically important of the German states, Languet virtually directed the foreign policy of the Elector Augustus; in effect he served as both Foreign Minister and Ambassador. He managed relations with the French court and with de Schomberg (the able French agent to the German courts) with considerable freedom of action, and thus was one of the most influential diplomats in Europe.[42] In 1572 Languet had been in Dresden, but in mid-May he returned to Paris. His immediate purpose there was to effect an agreement between Augustus of Saxony and Charles IX. Charles welcomed it as another strand of the French-Protestant alliance against Spain. Unfortunately for Charles, however, August desired to limit any commitment of his financial resources, for he knew the exhausted state of the French treasury. Aside from the Palatinate, which hoped for a strong Protestant League to support the Netherlands, the German states feared involvement in a large-scale power game. Indeed, Brandenburg, Brunswick, and Hesse were basically more anti-Calvinist than anti-Catholic.

On June 25, after the English envoys had left Paris, Charles admitted Languet to an audience. He displayed deep disappointment that response from the German states to the proposed treaties seemed so halfhearted. Languet could explain the reasons behind their reluctance but could not promise meaningful support. While the English and German Protestants talked and delayed, the Huguenots faced Alva unsupported. The King and his advisers, particularly Coligny, became bitter, and this undermined the independence which Charles IX had lately displayed. It also prepared the way for Catherine to reimpose her will later that summer.

Once Lord Lincoln and his company had departed and the official receptions and banquets had ended, the focus of Sidney's interests changed. Hitherto he had been occupied with social activities; now the realities of power politics captured his attention. Sidney's abundant correspondence with Languet and other friends during the next few years reveals his deep concern with politics, the essential study for a future statesman. One factor in his concern was his close association with Walsingham, Languet, and other actors on the stage of European diplomacy. The events of the

---

41. Languet to Sidney, May 1, 1574.
42. Platzkoff, chap. 2 and passim.

next few weeks accelerated this phase of Sidney's education, but before discussing these external events, some account should be given of the other acquaintances and friends that Sidney made during his sojourn in the French capital.

One of the most remarkable intellectuals Sidney came to know was Pierre de la Ramée, commonly known as Petrus Ramus. In contrast to Languet, the intellectual man of action, Ramus, a logician and humanist, was a reformer of patterns of thinking, an activist in cerebral and educational rather than political matters. His passion for exposing errors in the thinking of other people, dead or alive, made him famous. At the same time it raised up enemies as numerous as the quills upon an aroused porcupine. This situation did not surprise him, for he did not consider the theological and philosophical establishment to be especially enlightened. When his opponents were unable to answer his arguments, they descended to the *argumentum ad hominem* and berated his arrogance, the pomposity of his eloquence, his heterodoxy, and particularly the bad manners which seemed to require him to challenge everyone's beliefs.

Doubtless, psychological factors explain Ramus's pattern of life, an oscillation between poverty and success, ignominy and fame. Born of an impoverished but noble family, he had such a passion for learning that he achieved a university career by working during the day as a college servant and studying at night. When the time came to present his thesis Ramus offered the iconoclastic proposition, "Whatever Aristotle has advanced is false."[43] He argued that Aristotelian logic is fallacious; thus the conclusions based on it are wrong. Ramus's brilliant defence of his thesis astonished the academic world and he found himself suddenly famous. The scholastics were shocked not only by the novelty and brashness of his thesis, but by its threat to Aristotelian authority, behind which they had defended themselves from all challenges. When Ramus published his arguments his enemies succeeded in getting the books banned, and he became a figure to be mocked in dramatic skits. In due course the freshness of his thinking won the popular support of students and the patronage of his former schoolfellow, the powerful Cardinal of Lorraine; in 1551 Ramus received a royal appointment as Professor of Philosophy and Eloquence at the University of Paris.

When Sidney met Ramus in 1572 the logician was fifty-seven. He had become a Huguenot and, after a journey into Germany and Switzerland

---

43. *Quaecunque ab Aristotele dicta sint falsa.*

in 1568 when he was welcomed as a celebrity, had returned to the University of Paris where his enemies had become more numerous than ever. They considered Ramus's attack on Aristotelian logic an attempt to undermine the tenets of Roman Catholic theology. The Protestants, however, embraced him with fervour. Languet and Walsingham were among his supporters and either of the two could have brought Sidney into his company. Walsingham's *Journal* records that "Monsr. Ramus came to visit me" on only one date, December 19, 1571. But this single entry does not preclude other meetings; in the following month Walsingham became ill, and he was out of circulation during the early months of 1572. After a partial recovery in April, excessive pressure of business prevented him from recording such engagements.

The best evidence of Sidney's friendship with Ramus is the dedication to Sidney by Ramus's former pupil and sometime secretary, Théophile de Banos, of the posthumous *Petri Rami Commentariorum de Religione Christiana Libri Quatuor* (Frankfurt, 1576). In his dedication de Banos states, "You not only entertained the tenderest love for our writer [i.e. Ramus] when alive, but now that he is dead, esteem and reverence him."[44] Through Ramus, Sidney met de Banos and another energetic Huguenot, Andreas Wechel, the scholar-printer. Both became his close friends, and de Banos one of his most active correspondents; he later told Sidney that Languet had described him as "the true image of the nobility."[45] De Banos recalled, "I well remember the first time I saw you, when I contemplated with wonder your unusual endowments of mind and body." Meeting Sidney reminded de Banos of Pope Gregory's words when he first saw some English boys, "Not Angles, but angels."[46]

Wechel, the son and successor of the famous Christian Wechel, was about the same age as Languet. His father's presses were praised both for

44. Wallace, p. 118. Evidence of how much impact Ramus made on Sidney's mind has never received full examination, though several writers have suggested it was substantial. Rosemond Tuve in *Elizabethan and Metaphysical Imagery* (Chicago, 1947) and Fr. Walter Ong in *Ramus: Method, and the Decay of Dialogue* (Cambridge, Mass., 1958) have argued in the affirmative. Their interpretations were challenged by George Watson in "Ramus, Miss Tuve, and the New Petromachia" (*MP* 4:259–68) and by A. J. Smith in "An Examination of Some Claims for Ramism" (*RES*, n.s., 7 [1958]:348–59). N. L. Rudenstine has concluded that the influence of Ramus on Sidney was minor, and "existed concurrently with a strong (and growing) interest in Aristotle." (*Sidney's Poetic Development* [Cambridge, Mass., 1967], pp. 299–300.) The argument offered by Howell, p. 113, is based on Sidney's acquaintance with some English Ramists and contributes little to earlier discussions.

45. Buxton, p. 60.
46. Zouch, pp. 316–17.

their technical merits and for the texts they printed so exactly as to be almost free from errors: the errata-leaf in one folio listed only two mistakes.[47] Andreas succeeded his father in 1554 and enjoyed equal success until the outbreak of the religious wars. Beginning in 1555 he published various volumes for Ramus, including his most important Protestant writings. Like many other printers Andreas Wechel became an active Protestant. This was in keeping with the times, for the Huguenots were mainly of the professional and middle classes. They associated Protestantism with open-mindedness, and thus found it conducive to new technologies and new ideas.

Printers were leaders in this development, though movable type had been first used in Europe only a hundred years earlier. The printing press exploded into prominence as a weapon in religious controversy when Martin Luther nailed his ninety-five theses to the door of the castle church in Wittenberg in 1517. During that year German printers had issued only 37 books in the vernacular; six years later in 1523 the presses groaned under the production of 498 vernacular books and pamphlets, 180 of which were written by Luther himself. A generation later the Calvinists were producing even greater quantities of literature, partly because their creed emphasized the Bible as the source of fundamental law in the state, a postulate that required never-ending definition and exposition. Religious persecution of printers led to fluid migration; between 1549 and 1557 fifty-six printers sought refuge in Geneva alone. From an economic standpoint the Protestant demand for printed material to be distributed by vendors throughout the cities and provinces proved highly rewarding to booksellers and the owners of printing presses. The importance and the profits of the communications boom explain why such able scholar-printers as Andreas Wechel and Henri Estienne of Heidelberg could risk publishing so many editions of the classics. In addition to being successful businessmen, they were active humanists; thus they counted among their friends the learned diplomat, Hubert Languet, and the promising young English aristocrat, Philip Sidney.

In consequence of Wechel's prominence as a Huguenot, during the outbreak of religious fervour in 1568 a mob attacked his business premises in Paris, burned his books, and confiscated his property. Forced to flee for his life, Wechel spent most of the next year wandering miserably through Germany and the Rhineland, but he managed to be at Frankfurt for the

47. Cf. J. F. Burana's *Aristotelis Priora Resolutoria* (London, 1539).

Easter Book Fair. When fortune and Charles IX again smiled on religious toleration, Wechel returned to Paris and in June 1571 reestablished his business. He also reopened his large house on the west side of St. Jean de Beauvais to paying guests, following the practice of the day. Protestant foreigners predominated, among them Lucas Geizkofler, who testified that Wechel loved the Germans and provided them with excellent board and lodging at minimum rates.[48] Many eminent men also lodged with Wechel, such as Dr. Felix Platter of the University of Basle. Languet regularly stayed with Wechel when in Paris.[49]

Among the visitors in Paris at this time were several people whom Sidney later knew well and corresponded with. Their friendships probably began during this memorable summer in Paris. For example, the eminent Huguenot intellectual, Philippe de Mornay, Sieur du Plessis-Marly took such a liking to Sidney that when he visited England in 1577–78 he asked Sidney to serve as godfather for his daughter.[50] Because Duplessis-Mornay was such a close friend of both Walsingham and Languet, either could have introduced Sidney to him.[51] Another of Sidney's new friends was the learned jurist Dr. Jean Lobbet (Lobetius, or Lubetius) of Strasbourg, agent at the French court for several imperial cities. Sidney later developed a lengthy correspondence with Lobbet, "an experienced and good hearted man."[52] A third friend, approximately his own age, was the German student Johann Conrad Brüning, whom Sidney knew later at Strasbourg and Padua.[53]

Writers on Sidney have speculated about which poets and literary figures, particularly those of the Pléiade group, he may have met during this summer in Paris. Such encounters seem unlikely. Sidney had still to reach his eighteenth birthday, and his known interests were political and intellectual rather than literary; there would have been no reason for him or the poets of the Pléiade to seek out one another. Those frequently at the French court, however, would include many persons whom he would meet in the ordinary course of events. For example, Gaspard de Schomberg who, though born in Germany and raised a Protestant, had become

48. *Geizkofler*, p. 34.

49. *Viri cl. Huberti Langueti Burgundi ad Joachimum Camerarium patrem et . . . filium medicum scriptae epistolae* (Gröningen, 1646), p. 138.

50. A. D. Vaudoré and P. R. Auguis, eds., *Mémoires et correspondance de Duplessis-Mornay*, 12 vols. (Paris, 1824), 1 : 117–18.

51. Ibid., p. 22.

52. *Geizkofler*, p. 56.

53. See Brüning's letter of Oct. 31, 1575 to Sidney.

a French citizen (naturalized in 1570) and the ambassador of Charles IX to the German states. Thus his career represented an inverse parallel to that of Languet, whose abilities in state affairs and personal charm he matched. De Thou, who knew him well, remarked on de Schomberg's love for men of learning, as well as his wit, prudence, masculine persuasiveness, and obliging manners. Sidney later described him to Lord Leicester as "one Shambourg . . . a gentleman whom I knew in the courte of Fraunce."[54]

The high-water mark of Sidney's reception came early in August when he was honoured by Charles himself. On August 9 the King signed a patent addressed to "le Grande Chambellan de France" by which he created the seventeen-year-old Philip Sidney a "gentilhomme ordinaire de notre chambre." The document, partly defaced but still preserved at Penshurst, justifies the creation: "considerans combien est grande la maison de Sydenay en Angleterre . . . desirans en consideracion de ce bien et faverablement traicter le Jeune S. de Sidenay."[55] On taking the necessary oath Philip became "Baron de Sidenay" which entitled him "to receive the Honours, Authorities, Wages, Rights, Hostellages, Profits and customary Emoluments thereunto appertaining, during Pleasure."[56] The reference to his youth is not without interest. Nor is the fact that the house of Sidney "and the rank it had always held near the Persons of the Kings and Queens" is mentioned, but not his Dudley ancestry. Because Elizabeth frowned on the use of foreign titles, Sidney did not use his when signing his name. Most of his Continental friends addressed him with it, however, as the newly recovered letters reveal.

Sidney's biographers have assumed that admiration for his personal attractiveness led Charles to confer this official honour. More likely Charles acted primarily from political motives in order to strengthen his relationship with the Protestant states. Support for this occurs in de Thou's Histoire. Coligny, reassuring his Protestant friends, is reported as saying,

> Qu'au reste le traité d'alliance que le Roi venoit de faire avec la Reine d'Angleterre, & celui qui se negocioit actuellement avec les princes Protestans de l'Empire, faisoient assez connôitre les dispositions favorables de ce Prince pour les Protestans, puisqu'il vouloit avoir à

54. Feuillerat, 3:79.
55. HMC De L'Isle, 1:271, no. 1572.
56. Collins, vol. 1, pp. 98–99 of "Memoirs of the Sidneys."

sa Cour un des fils de l'Electeur Palatin,[57] & un des seigneurs Anglois qui fut des plus zélés pour cette Religion, comme le comte de Leycestre, ou le baron de Burgley.[58]

The fact is that Charles did not forget Sidney's status as the nephew of the Earls of Leicester and Warwick.

If Thomas Moffet knew of the French title, he did not mention it. Nor did Sir Fulke Greville when he published *The Life of the Renowned Sir Philip Sidney*. Indeed, until the nineteenth century no book included the fact.[59] But Greville did record the favour Sidney found in the eyes of the young Henry, King of Navarre, who was just a few months his senior. According to Greville, the young Huguenot sovereign "having measured, and mastered all the spirits in his own Nation, found out this Master spirit among us, and used him like an equall in nature and so fit for friendship with a King."[60] Since Sidney never returned to France, the only opportunity to form and enjoy this friendship would have occurred between Henry's entry into Paris in July 1572, and his marriage five weeks later. Young Philip Sidney's personal attractiveness and eager mind had no doubt enhanced his welcome at court as well as among the Protestant intellectuals. So far, fortune had smiled on him.

57. Christopher, who had been invited to the wedding but was not allowed to go; see F. von Bezold, *Briefe des Pfalzgrafen Johann Casimir* (Munich, 1882) 1:68.

58. De Thou, 6:374. This statement is corroborated by Simone Goulart, who mentions "Qu'il [i.e. the King] des iroit aussi auoir de L'Angleterre, le myllord de Lycestre, & le myllord de Burgley, ou l'un d'eux, pour les festoyer & traiter, comme il désire de caresser tous les loyaux serviteurs de sa soeur la Roy d'Angleterre, en signe de vraye alliance" (*Mémoires de France*, 1:256).

59. First mentioned by Zouch, p. 40.

60. Greville, p. 36.

CHAPTER 3

During the week in which Philip became "Baron de Sidenay," the French nobility flocked back into Paris. The most important social and court event in two hundred years was to take place on Monday, August 18, when Charles IX would give his sister Marguerite de Valois in marriage to Henry of Navarre.[1] This ceremony would unite her with the man who was heir to the French crown after her brothers: Charles IX, the Duke of Anjou, and the Duke of Alençon. Special interest centred on the fact that this union would be the first mixed marriage among royalty, for it would link the Huguenot King of Navarre with the Catholic family of Valois.

The Protestants saw the marriage as an important advance in religious toleration and a soothing of the old animosities which had produced ten years of bloodshed. Moderate Catholics also welcomed it as an act of toleration which might provide a future of domestic peace and prosperity. But extreme Catholics, led by the Cardinal of Lorraine and the Duke of Guise, saw it as a capitulation to heresy, the first fruit of the diabolical influence exerted over the King by Coligny, and a threat to the Catholic Church. Nevertheless, the nobility of all three factions crowded into Paris, accompanied by their servants, bodyguards, and other attendants. Families who had members residing in Paris moved in with them. The Guises, for example, were concentrated in the cloisters of Notre Dame and St. Germain-l'Auxerrois. But the Huguenots, to whom Paris had been almost forbidden territory, were scattered about, some across the river in the Faubourg St. Germain.[2] Besides being given the title of baron, Sidney had been made a Gentleman of the King's Bedchamber, and thus he was entitled to a privileged position during the ceremonies and festivities.

Finally on Saturday, August 16, the busy preparations of the previous days were completed, the hammers of the carpenters who had erected the elevated platform in front of Notre Dame fell silent, and drapers covered the structure with cloth of gold and other elegant materials. Ordinarily, to the delight of the populace, a royal bride would mount the scaffold and walk into the cathedral through the choir to the altar. Because the

1. Michelet, *Histoire de France* (Paris, 1856), 9:380.
2. Ibid., p. 410.

groom in this wedding was a Huguenot, the actual ceremony was to take place on the open platform within full sight of the crowd, which would include many Protestants. Once the official ceremony ended, the bride and other Catholics would enter Notre Dame for the nuptial mass while Henry and his followers retired elsewhere.

The secular ceremony of betrothal was held in the Louvre on Sunday, August 17. Sidney is likely to have stood among the assembled witnesses as the bride and groom signed the marriage contract. This document set forth details of Marguerite's dowry, which Henry matched by assigning to her the revenues from various of his estates. He also placed on her finger a diamond ring worth ten thousand crowns, and gave her other jewels valued at thirty thousand crowns. After the ceremony, the assembled nobles and courtiers enjoyed a wedding supper, followed by dancing and other gaieties. By tradition a royal bride passed the night before her wedding in the bishop's palace next to Notre Dame. The King, his Queen, his mother, brothers, and sister accompanied Marguerite there, followed by the royal wedding party.

The next morning dawned hot and humid. Early in the day people began to fill the square before the ornate platform; they hung from the windows of nearby houses and crowded the rooftops. Most of the fifteen hundred German students had reserved window places, or took other vantage points. The procession had been scheduled for late morning, but the sweltering crowd was forced to wait until midafternoon before it appeared. Then finally "thither came out of the Louvre with all Royal Pomp, and most magnificent shew, the King, the Queen Mother, with the Brethren the Dukes of Anjou and Alanson, the Guises, the Colonels of the Horse, the chief Peers of the Kingdom leading along the Bride, who lodged that night in the Bishop's Palace." [3] They walked in glittering state, in costumes ornamented with gold and silver and adorned with pearls and precious stones.

Henry proceeded from the other side of the square "with the Princes of Condé and Contie his Cousins, Coligni Admiral of the Sea, Franciscus Count de la Roche-fou-cault, and a great company of the Protestant Nobles, who came together out of all Provinces of the Kingdom." [4] Their sober dress contrasted with the dazzling display of the Valois; though they had now abandoned the black they had worn in mourning

3. Thuanus, p. 7.
4. Ibid. The next three quotations come from the same source.

for Henry's mother, they came to the wedding in ordinary clothing. As a gesture of perpetual friendship the two Kings, the two royal Dukes, and the Prince of Condé wore identical suits of yellow satin embroidered with silver lace. Marguerite was appropriately resplendent in purple velvet with a shoulder cape of ermine; she wore crown jewels estimated to be worth one hundred thousand crowns.

The Cardinal of Bourbon performed the ceremony, after which Henry led his bride along the scaffold "on every side railed in to keep off the multitude," into the choir. Having placed his wife before the great altar to hear mass, "he with Coligni and Count de la Roche-fou-cault, and the other Nobles of his Retinue went into the Bishop's Palace by the contrary door." After the religious service Henry was called "into the Chore again, and kissing his new Bride before the King, Queen, and the Brethren, when they had entertained one another some little while with discourse, they returned into the Bishop's Palace, where dinner was provided." The wedding party then returned to the Louvre, where a royal supper was served to a throng of court functionaries and officials of the city government. These groups had filled the cathedral for the nuptial mass, waiting there for most of the sultry day, so only afterwards would they hear the report of the outside ceremony. When the Cardinal had asked

> whether she would take the King of *Navarre* for her husband, [she] returned no answer at all; but the King, her brother, having made her bow her head, with his hand, it was said, that she signified her consent by that action, though both before and after, when she could speak with freedom, she always declared, that to be deprived of the Duke of *Guise*, to whom she was pre-engaged, and to take his most inveterate enemy for her husband, were such things as she could never possibly be reconciled to.[5]

No doubt Sidney witnessed the open-air ceremony. The young German Lucas Geizkofler reported that various "noble Counts and gentlemen who were not Papists remained outside the cathedral, walking up and down" until the royal bride emerged.[6] This would explain how Sidney occupied himself during the nuptial mass. There is no reason to question his attend-ance at the supper party in the Louvre afterwards, where he would have witnessed the first of the extraordinary entertainments which occurred

5. E. C. Davila, *The History of the Civil Wars of France*, trans. E. Farneworth (London, 1758), 1 : 305.
6. *Geizkofler*, p. 39.

during the next four days. By this time Sidney knew of Charles's fondness for "interludes," dramatic presentations ranging from broad burlesque to allegory, subtle or otherwise. After the dancing was over, the wedding guests cleared the central hall, and the dramatic offering began. A contemporary account describes it as follows:

> The representation of three Rocks silvered over, upon which the three Brethren, the King, the Duke of Anjou, and Duke of Alanson did sit, and seven more, upon which Gods and Sea-Monsters were set, which followed, being drawn along in Coaches, and were brought through the great Hall of the Palace, which was divided by a triumphal arch in the middle, and when they made a stand, some choice Musitians recited Verses in their own Tongue, composed by the best of their Poets. And thus a great part of the night being spent in interludes, they afterwards betook themselves to their rest.[7]

In theatrical history there has never been an actor as ardent as a royal one, and the captive audience was required to remain until Charles and his thespian "brethren" were willing to let them retire. This was not until they had sat through a comedy presented by a company of Italian actors.

When the wedding guests straggled forth at one o'clock on Tuesday afternoon for an informal luncheon, Charles treated them to another of his favourite diversions, the baiting of captive animals. Lucas Geizkofler's eyewitness account describes the scene.

> The King had a Lion, a great Ox, and a Bear that had recently strangled a Swiss, brought together in a garden and set at each other. While the Germans, with many other foreigners, were watching this spectacle, the Bear (a large white one) was tied to a cart and then let loose; so that a mass of people pressed back in a panic and fell in heaps, losing their hats and cloaks in the crush, while the King and his brothers watched from a long gallery. They were much amused, and it was suspected that the bear had, by royal command, been deliberately tied carelessly to the cart, so that it might work itself loose. The Swiss guards were also suspected of having let the bear loose on *their* initiative, and then, when the crowd fell over each other in confusion, sending accomplices in who brought back many exquisite cloaks and hats, which were subsequently gambled for.[8]

7. Thuanus, p. 8.
8. *Geizkofler*, p. 40.

After the animals were disposed of, the guests convened at the Hôtel d'Anjou where Henry of Navarre offered dinner. Following his hospitality they returned to the Louvre for more dancing.

The great event scheduled for Wednesday at the palace of the Cardinal de Bourbon was another dramatic spectacle. Not only were the Valois brothers cast in prominent roles in the allegory, but so were the bridegroom and some of his close associates. Henry must have been both a good sport and a very naive young man to allow himself to be publicly displayed in the part he had to play. The scenery depicted heaven on one side of the hall and hell on the other; the chief roles were taken by the King and his brothers who occupied heaven and by Henry and some of his Huguenot friends, a group of Knights-Errant, who tried to gain admittance. They were repulsed by the Valois brethren and sent to hell. Nymphs then danced about a fountain for an hour before the Huguenots were released at their behest: the wedding guests could not have missed the significance. Their reaction was reported by de Serres: "This shew was variously interpreted, for that the assailants who were most of them Protestants, did in vain attempt to get into the seats of the blessed, and were thrust down into Hell: for so they put a mockery upon the Protestants, and others did bode that it portended some mischief."[9]

The fourth and final round of entertainment came on Thursday the twenty-first. On the previous day there had been some running at tilt, merely for knightly exercise. Now the large courtyard of the Louvre had been transformed into a tilt-yard, but for another dramatic allegory. The King, his brothers, the Duke of Guise, and his kinsman the Duke of Aumale appeared in the costume of Amazons. Opposing them were Henry and his Huguenot friends dressed as Turks in turbans and flowing robes; virtue triumphed, and the Turks were defeated. The allegory again humiliated the bridegroom and his friends; no one could fail to interpret it as the victory of the Roman church over the heretics. On this note the wedding celebrations ended, and the guests could return to their lodgings through the tense city streets.

For the next two days there is no evidence of where Sidney may have been, or what he was doing. Probably he was merely resting, for the revels of the French court could have proved exhausting even to a youth of his vitality. The French historian Jean de Serres recorded the "nightly

---

9. Jean de Serres, *The Fyrst Part of Commentaries of the Ciuil Warres of France*, trans. T. Timme (London, 1573), *STC* 22241, p. 9.

riottous sitting up," and condemned especially "the familiaritie of men and the women of the Queene mothers trayne, and so greate libertie of sporting, entertainement and talking togyther, as to foreine nations may seeme incredible, and be thought of al honest persons a matter not very conuenient for preseruation of noble yong Ladies chastitie." [10]

Tension was now mounting in the narrow streets. The populace, notorious for its Catholic zeal, found the bold self-confidence of the Huguenots difficult to accept. The Protestants from the provinces were especially irksome, for, certain of the superiority of their reformed religion and confident in their new equality, they seemed to swagger through the capital city. What at first seemed smugness began after a week to look like arrogance. Despite the royal proclamations, Catholics knew in their hearts that Huguenots were heretics damned to burn in hell. How much longer should devout members of the True Church suffer the divinely ordained structure of salvation to be challenged and even threatened?

In high places the tension almost crackled, especially in the private quarters of Catherine de Médicis and those of the King. Catherine had fought desperately to obtain the crown of Navarre for her family and now, when it was just within her grasp, a critical problem had arisen. Because Marguerite and Henry were third cousins, a papal dispensation was necessary. Catherine had to get one promptly from the new Pope, Gregory XIII, who, as the Cardinal of Lorraine made sure, would consider Henry a heretic. Four days before the wedding, realizing that the Pope would not cooperate, Catherine sent a courier to ride full speed to the governor of Lyons. He was instructed to permit no messages from Rome to leave Lyons for Paris until August 19, by which time the ceremony would be performed and the marriage consummated. On Saturday the sixteenth, Catherine and Charles assured Henry's uncle, the Cardinal de Bourbon, that a letter had arrived from Rome advising that the Pope had granted the dispensation, which would follow as soon as it could be prepared. Whether the Cardinal was merely easygoing, or perhaps felt relieved of further responsibility by the royal assurance, he acquiesced without asking to see the papal letter.

Catherine had further cause for desperation. In her eyes Coligny posed a great threat, not only to her influence over the King, but also to the

10. From the translation by T. Timme published as *Three Partes of Commentaries* (London, 1576), bk. 10, fol. 10. He complained further of the numbers of Italians at court, "since the Administration of the Realme was committed to the Queene mother, that many do commonly call it . . . a *Colonie* and some a common sinke of *Italie*."

survival of her family. He was like the camel in the Arabian parable, which, soon after being allowed to put its head in the tent, shouldered its way inside and finally occupied it entirely. Even more, Catherine feared that Coligny's policies threatened the peace of France, a delicate equilibrium which she had finally attained after a decade of striving. Specifically, she considered his support for the disastrous invasion of the Low Countries a risk that might draw Spain into a full-scale war and increase the friction between Protestants and Catholics. How to rein him in perplexed her, but she believed it must be done to preserve peace for France and the throne for the Valois.

To the Guise family, who had the additional motive of revenging the assassination of François de Guise in 1563, the solution seemed simple: liquidate Coligny. Catherine's favourite son, the sybaritic Duke of Anjou had aligned himself with the Guises and seconded this proposal. Catherine's Italian creatures, the Dukes of Retz and Nevers, advised the same action. All agreed, however, that the wedding must take place first. Although the deliberations remained secret, rumours that trouble was brewing wafted through the city. Lucas Geizkofler was warned by a fellow countryman with court connections to move out of the house of Andreas Wechel and to lodge with a priest, Monsieur Blandis, near the Église St. Hilaire. Geizkofler hesitated but his friend persisted, saying that perhaps Geizkofler would learn the reason later; he took the advice.[11] The situation was so obviously dangerous that worried Huguenots daily warned Coligny of his peril. The Admiral replied with characteristic courage and faith. He believed that the King was a man of his word. Peace between the two religious camps had now been established, and concessions were being extended. Meanwhile Charles addressed Coligny as "Father" and seemed to hang on his advice.

Actually, the Guise party had decided at least as early as June that Coligny and some other Huguenot leaders should be assassinated. There is evidence that by mid-July the Duke of Guise's mother, Madame de Nemours, had confided the plan to Catherine in hope of obtaining her assent. Other evidence shows that Catherine (though not Charles, as yet) had agreed to it during the week before the wedding. Now the conspirators began to execute their plan. On Thursday, August 21, while the mock battle between the Amazons and the Turks held the attention of

11. *Geizkofler*, p. 34. The friend was Paul von Welsperg, an Augsburg patrician and Hofmeister to the Count of Hanau, later one of Sidney's intimate friends.

the wedding guests, the Huguenot hierarchy, and the diplomatic corps,[12] the hired assassin of the Guises, one Maurevert, was secreted in a house vacated for the purpose by Madame de Nemours. The house was situated near the Louvre on the narrow Rue de Béthisy, the street Admiral Coligny customarily travelled between the palace and his living quarters. There in a room with a barred window, Maurevert placed an oversized harquebus upon a tripod, aimed it through the window, and loaded it with ball-shot. A curtain covered the window for the time being. The next day a horse would be saddled and waiting for Maurevert near the back door.

On Friday morning Coligny attended a meeting of the Royal Council called for an early hour despite the revels of the previous evening. The business promptly dispatched, Coligny followed the King to the tennis court in the Louvre and, after watching him battle the Duke of Guise across the net, left with his men to return home for luncheon. As they strolled along the accustomed route towards the house with the concealed harquebus, a petition was handed to the Admiral; he read it as he walked, slowing his pace accordingly. Suddenly, the curtain was whipped back and a shot blazed forth. Three bronze balls would have gone through his chest had not Coligny at that moment leaned forward to spit. One ball broke his left wrist and lodged in his elbow; another shattered the index finger of his right hand. As Coligny's men broke down the front door, Maurevert leapt on his horse and galloped to the Porte St. Antoine where a Guise family groom held a Spanish jennet waiting for him.

The Admiral, who had faced bullets before, said laconically, "Bad shot." Then turning to an attendant, he commanded, "Go, tell the King what has happened to me." The messenger found Charles still playing tennis with the Duke of Guise. On hearing the news his face blanched; he threw down his racquet and left the court, saying with an oath, "Shall I never find any peace?" He sent the royal surgeon who cut off Coligny's shattered finger and cleaned the wounded arm. Meanwhile the news spread through Paris. Walsingham heard it about nine that evening; his informant was the Huguenot Count of Montgomery:

> Amongst other communication he said, That as he and those of the Religion had just cause to be right sorry for the Admirals hurt, so they had no less cause to rejoyce to see the King so careful, as well

12. Walsingham and the other ambassadors were placed in window seats with the best view of the spectacle. The only exception was the Spanish Ambassador, who declined to be present. Champion, 2:75.

for the curing of the Admiral, as also for the searching out of the party that hurt him.[13]

Once the limited extent of Coligny's wounds became known, a stream of eminent friends called to express their sympathy and assuage their curiosity. Henry of Navarre, the Prince of Condé, La Rochefoucauld, and other Protestants were prominent among them. Meanwhile the Admiral had sent Téligny, his son-in-law, to the King, requesting him to come, since the Admiral wished to discuss the situation. Catherine was with the King and insisted on accompanying him, for she feared what Charles might say or do if freed from her royal apron strings. Accordingly she, Anjou, Alençon and the whole mob of court officers and lords crowded into the upper-floor bedroom, under the low ceiling of which Coligny was trying to rest in the sweltering humidity of August. When they left the Admiral finally had a chance to relax with his personal attendants and attempt to sleep.

In the room below the Protestant leaders, including Navarre and Condé, assembled. One faction urged immediate withdrawal from Paris, taking Coligny with them on a litter. Others, whose opinion prevailed, cited the King's vow, "By God's death, I protest and promise to you that I will have justice done for this outrage." Outside, the Huguenots were thronging the streets and openly carrying arms, seeking some program of action to ensure that those responsible for the attempted assassination be captured and punished. Merchants feared that fighting might erupt and closed their shops. City officials ordered the gates to be watched and harquebusiers and archers to assemble in the Place de Grève (where the great bonfire had been held two months earlier on St. John's Eve), in case rioting should break out.

On Saturday morning tension seemed to ease when the physicians announced that Coligny's wounds would not endanger his life and that he should recover the use of his arm. Visitors crowded in to congratulate him; among those from the court was Marguerite, the new Queen of Navarre. Protestants, excited by the drama of the occasion, came in droves. Even the German student-sightseers crowded into the dwelling.

> Many German scholars including Lucas Geizkofler visited him, to whom he spoke in a very friendly fashion, while consoling himself and saying that nothing had occurred or would happen to him with-

13. Walsingham to Sir Thomas Smith, Sept. 24, 1572. Digges, p. 254.

out God's special providence; that he would leave revenge to the omnipotent, omniscient and just Judge. This consolation he supported with many *argumenta* and *exempla*.[14]

Was Sidney among the Protestants who called at the house on the Rue de Béthisy to congratulate the Admiral? Considering his presence at various official gatherings during the previous weeks it seems highly probable. Indeed, Sidney's status as an eminent English Protestant recently honoured by the King made such a call almost obligatory.

Saturday morning also produced the news that Maurevert, a known professional killer, had been identified. Furthermore, the man who had supplied the Spanish jennet had been caught; he admitted being an employee of the Guises and rumour reported that the Duke of Guise was to be arrested. On hearing this Catherine lost her sangfroid; she feared for her life and the throne as she foresaw the Duke in self-defence disclosing her complicity in the plot. Ensnared by the Guises' inept management of the assassination, she now became convinced of the necessity for complete liquidation of all eminent Huguenots. Her son Anjou and the Guise leaders were gratified that she now saw the light. They had additional cause for worry, for the harquebus was known to have come from Anjou's armoury. Charles had yet to be brought in on the plan, but they were confident that the Queen Mother could handle him. Meanwhile, Charles enjoyed an early evening game of tennis with Henry and Condé, and after supper Catherine tackled him alone. His scruples melted when Catherine used the ancient excuse of aggressors: the Huguenots, she said, planned to seize Paris and the throne, so the King must slaughter them to protect himself, his family, and the Catholic religion.

All afternoon the Guise leaders had been busy organizing the royal forces and the city constabulary, stationing them at strategic places and allocating specific assignments. All boats on the Right Bank of the Seine were chained to their moorings. Historians have been able to record these steps in considerable detail, so complete was the mobilization. The plan even listed the houses where Huguenots were living: "The Undermasters of the Streates commonly called Quartermen, surveyed all the vittailing houses and Innes from house to house, and all the names of those of the Religion, together with the place of euery of their lodgings they put in bokes, and wyth speede deliuered ouer the same."[15]

14. *Geizkofler*, pp. 37–38.
15. De Serres, *Three Partes of Commentaries*, bk. 10, fol. 12.

Marcel, the Provost of the Merchants of Paris, who had links with the underworld, passed the word to the professional thieves and killers (estimated to number seven thousand) that Huguenots and their belongings were fair game. Despite the increased tension prompted by these marchings and other activities, the Protestants went unperturbed to bed, some after midnight. The soldiers and guards were not to move until the great bell at the Palais de Justice rang at dawn.

Events failed to cooperate. The King, his mother, and Anjou went through the pretence of going to bed but were up and dressed again by two o'clock, and met in a room overlooking the courtyard where the guards were assembled. The noise and clatter of arms there awakened some Protestant noblemen, who came to investigate. An altercation occurred and the guards attacked them, killing all but a few who escaped. This premature beginning required immediate action, and Catherine ordered the great bell of the Palace church, St. Germain-l'Auxerrois, to be tolled, a bell known to Parisians as "la Marie" which was never rung except on royal occasions. Other church bells joined in the alarm, lights appeared in windows, and soon shouts, screams, and shots added to the clamour.

The Duke of Guise had not waited for the tocsin. As soon as he received the royal command to kill Coligny, he rode to the Rue de Béthisy with a company of soldiers. Forcing their way in, Guise's Swiss mercenaries seized the Admiral who was kneeling in prayer, stabbed him repeatedly, and threw his body out of the window to prove to the Duke that the House of Guise was now revenged and the way open for it to dominate France. As morning dawned the lodgings of all Huguenot leaders were forced open and they were put to the sword. Charles watched from his window as the bodies of two hundred Huguenots (whom he had moved into the Louvre "for protection") were piled in a gory heap in the courtyard. By midday blood running from the gutters coloured the Seine; mangled bodies were dragged to the river banks and heaved into the stream.

Many eyewitnesses later chronicled the savagery of the massacre, though their accounts differ in detail and in estimates of the numbers killed. Because the mob got out of hand and plunder became as strong a motive as religious fanaticism, four thousand murdered seems a conservative estimate for Paris alone. Once word of the massacre reached the provincial centres (especially Lyons, Orléans, Bordeaux, Bourges, Meaux, and Troyes), blood gushed in comparable quantities there as well. By the end of a fortnight another twenty-five thousand had been slaughtered and their torn corpses thrown into the Rhône, the Loire, and other rivers, to the horror of village people downstream as the decayed flesh washed ashore.

What happened to Sidney during these days of carnage? His biographers have tended to assume that he was living at this time with Walsingham at the English Embassy on the Quai des Bernardins[16] across the river in the Faubourg St. Germain and, since he was therefore outside the city walls, was never in danger. There is no evidence, however, to support this assumption. As we have already seen, Walsingham took pains to point out that his establishment was too small and too expensive for him to cope with the requirements of his position.[17] Under these circumstances, it seems unlikely that Sidney would stay at the Embassy. Moreover, Walsingham's already too full household had been crowded even further by his wife and five-year-old daughter Frances who had come over from England to visit him. The only contemporary evidence that Sidney ever stayed in Walsingham's house occurs in a letter dated September 9 at Woodstock from five members of the Privy Council: the Lords Burghley and Leicester, and Messrs. Knowles, Croft, and Smith. It reads:

> Where we understand, that the English Gentlemen that were in *Paris* at the time of the execution of the murther, were forced to retire to your house, where they did wisely; for your care of them, we and their friends are beholding to you, and now we think good that they be advised to return home; and namely, we desire you to procure for the Lord *Wharton* and Mr. *Philip Sidney*, the Kings license and safe conduct to come thence, and so we do require you to give them true knowledge of our minds herein.[18]

Besides Philip Wharton,[19] third Baron, at least one other Englishman also found refuge with Walsingham. Timothy Bright, later a famous physician, theologian, and the inventor of the first successful method of shorthand in England, revealed in his epistle dedicatory to Sidney, who

16. De Thou, p. 408, says "Rue de Bernardins," but Stählin, 1 : 527 n., pointed out that this street was in the university sector and "Quai des Bernardins" is correct.

17. See above, chap. 2, n. 34.

18. Digges, p. 250.

19. Lord Wharton (1555–1625), son of a Catholic Privy Councillor in the reign of Mary, had been living at the Jesuit college. During the massacre an English clergyman whom Elizabeth had sent over to tutor him was murdered by the mob. Stählin, 1 : 529.

was then at the height of his reputation: "I once had the good fortune to see you, viz. during the fateful storm of the Church in France, the St. Bartholomew's Massacre (in which I was involved, and which my mind shudders to recall, and flees from in grief)."[20] Dr. Bright went on to praise Walsingham,

> whose immense and honourable kindness saved my life during those days of terror in France, when the blood of the godly was everywhere being shed by fiendish killers. But why do I say "saved *my* life"? For the most noble Francis Walsingham's house stood open, as asylum, to all those of our nation—as long as they were free from Papist superstition—who happened to be in Paris at the time. You yourself, Philip, had precisely that experience, and can thus vouch for your father-in-law's nobility. And not only to Englishmen was his house open, but to some foreigners too, who were overcome by fear and terrified by the sudden frightful slaughter.[21]

Of two other English visitors then in Paris whose names have been preserved, the first was the son of a Lady Lane, who sent £30 to Walsingham on September 12 to pay any debts and speed her son's return home.[22] The second was John Watson, Dean of Winchester, of whom more later.

With these four, Sidney and his four companions, the three Walsinghams, Walsingham's secretary Robert Beale, and the rest of the Embassy staff, about twenty people are accounted for. Walsingham's biographer, Conyers Read, confidently wrote of the "troops of terrified Englishmen who hastened from all quarters of the city to find shelter behind his doors." Again, "Each newcomer with his new tale of the horrors across the river added to their fears. Others came besides Englishmen, Germans, Dutch and one or two Huguenots who were later dragged forth again to meet their fate."[23] No evidence for these numbers is cited except Bright's dedicatory statement. Nor is other evidence offered by the cautious Dr.

---

20. *In Physicam G. A. Scribonii Animaduersiones* (Cambridge, 1584), p. ii. This book was the first one printed by the Cambridge University Press when their right was restored after half a century of prohibition.

21. Ibid., p. 10. Five years later Dr. Bright repeated his gratitude to Walsingham, citing many of the same details, in dedicating to him his *Abridgement of Foxe* (1589). Pietro Bizari wrote that Walsingham saved his life during the massacre, which suggests the possibility that he was one of the foreigners given refuge (*Senatus Populique Genuensis* [Antwerp, 1579], p. 562).

22. Sir Thomas Smith to Walsingham, in Digges, p. 252.

23. Read, 1:221.

Karl Stählin in *Sir Francis Walsingham und seine Zeit* (1908), though he does quote a dispatch dated August 31 and sent by Zuñiga, the Spanish Ambassador. Zuñiga reported that a few days earlier a mob led by a fanatic had besieged Walsingham's house. Fortunately the Duke de Nevers came by, chased them away, and stationed troops of the Royal Guard to protect the Embassy.[24] Accordingly, when Zuñiga tried to call on Walsingham, he found the English Embassy so tightly closed, locked, and barred that not even the smallest wicket gate was open.

Indeed, there is convincing evidence that Catherine de Médicis took immediate action to protect the Englishmen. She wished to assure foreign courts that the bloodshed of St. Bartholomew's was a matter of internal politics, the prevention of a coup d'état. Above all, she did not wish to upset the Treaty of Blois, and still hoped to arrange the marriage of the eighteen-year-old Duke of Alençon to Elizabeth of England. In consequence, only three Englishmen lost their lives, according to Walsingham's report; none of them was named.[25]

It seems likely that responsibility for helping the English was entrusted to the Duke de Nevers. According to a recent account of the events on that bloody Sunday,

> Nevers was riding with a number of his retainers, and four or five of the accompanying noblemen had tall bewildered-looking men riding pillion behind them: they were English noblemen whose lives had been tactfully spared by the Duke. He had driven away the mob that was besieging their house, which they intended to defend to the death. But he thought it amusing [he was a Florentine!] to keep them captive for the whole day and compel them to witness the slaughter of their co-religionists. To begin with, he took them to Rue de Béthisy early in the morning to show them Coligny's mangled body.[26]

Confirmation of Nevers's role appears in the first extant dispatch of those Walsingham wrote during the week of carnage. Earlier, fearing to commit himself on paper, he had sent a courier to make a verbal report.[27]

---

24. Stählin, 1 : 530–31; he rejects Zuñiga's statement that the mob invaded the Embassy, killed two servants, and forced Walsingham himself to hide.

25. Digges, p. 239.

26. Henri Noguères, *The Massacre of Saint Bartholomew* (New York, 1962), p. 100. (The original French edition appeared in Paris in 1959.)

27. Five months later Leicester warned Walsingham that this method resulted in leakage of information; the courier's report on the massacre was "in open talk within ten hours after we had it." Digges, pp. 322–23.

This first letter, written by Walsingham on Wednesday, August 27, was addressed to "The right Honorable Sir Thomas Smith, her Majesties's principall Secretary" and began,

> It may please your Honor to advertise her Majesty that yesterday I sent my Secretary [his brother-in-law, Robert Beale] unto Q[ueen] Mother, willing her in my name, first to render unto her and to the Kings Majesty most humble thanks for the great care it pleased them to have of my safety, and the preservation of the English Nation in this last tumult, whereof I assured them I would not fail to make honorable report unto the Queens Majesty my Mistrese.[28]

Walsingham ended with a postscript:

> The Duke of Nevers hath shewed himself much addicted to our Nation, having not spared to come and visit me in his own person, with offer of all kind of courtesie, not only to me, but also to divers of our English Gentlemen. Besides that, he did very honourably entertain three English Gentlemen, who otherwise had been in great jeopardy of their lives.[29]

The following year Walsingham also told Nevers's brother Gonzaga, the Mantuan Ambassador, that he owed his life to Nevers.[30]

From these brief references in contemporary sources, and in light of Sidney's status in Paris, several conclusions seem to be justified. First, Sidney was not staying with Walsingham when the tocsin sounded on the fateful morning of August 24. Secondly, from that morning on, Sidney and other eminent Englishmen were protected by the Duke of Nevers. Thirdly, Sidney ended up in Walsingham's house, though he may have been lodged under Nevers's roof for a short period. One other possibility, that Sidney may have been forced to ride pillion to view Coligny's mangled body and other gory scenes, is not as unlikely as it might seem at first. Who else could have been among the four or five English noblemen? Aside from Sidney, the young Lord Wharton, and the unidentified son of Lady Lane, what other Englishman entitled even to the courtesy title of

---

28. Digges, p. 238. On the same day the King wrote to Fénélon, his ambassador in London, "Le Sr. de Walsingham a esté soigneusement conservé pendant ce trouble en son logis" (B. de S. de la Mothe-Fénélon, *Correspondance diplomatique*, ed. A. Teulet, 7 vols. [Paris, 1838–40], 7 :330).

29. Digges, p. 238.

30. Stählin, 1 :531.

nobleman was in Paris at this moment? No other names occur in the voluminous literature concerning the bloodbath in Paris which horrified the Protestant world.

Sidney's friends among the Protestant intelligentsia suffered in varying ways. The Count of Hanau, disguised in poor clothing, managed to escape from Paris with a group of companions, and made his way safely back to Germany.[31] Duplessis-Mornay, wearing the clothing of a clerk, also succeeded in reaching Germany despite the horsemen stationed by the King to ambush foreigners riding out of Paris.[32] Even Languet was seized in the street by a gang of killers who were no respecters of ambassadorial dignity; he gained release only with the special aid of de Morvilliers, First Counsellor of the King.[33] Soon after, Languet visited Lucas Geizkofler, a close acquaintance at that time, and related the harrowing experience to him.[34]

Geizkofler also reported the fate of the booksellers and printers in the University quarter. He watched from a top dormer window of his lodging house as books "worth thousands of crowns" were thrown into the street and burned.[35] Unlucky owners who did not escape were slaughtered, as were their wives and children, and then hurled into the scarlet-tinted Seine. One Huguenot bookseller was suspended over a fire made from his burning merchandise. Sidney's friend Andreas Wechel, with the help and advice of his lodger Languet, saved his life but lost his valuable stock of books, his presses, and fonts of type.[36]

The learned Dr. Ramus was not so lucky. During his academic career he had made many enemies, some deliberately, and none more bitter and vengeful than Jacques Charpentier, the rector of the Collège de Boncour. In 1550 as leader of the Aristotelian conservatives, Charpentier developed a deadly hatred of Ramus for his ridicule of Aristotelian logic and the conclusions based on it. Charpentier enjoyed both a substantial private income and the favour of the Guises. Since 1550 he had fought against the cross-disciplinary teaching under Ramus at the Collège de Presles, and in 1563 he had even attempted to have Ramus assassinated. Now that the

---

31. *Geizkofler*, p. 65. One wealthy man who was unsuccessfully disguised was seized and held for ransom by two French noblemen.

32. Ibid., p. 56.

33. Charlotte de Mornay, *Histoire de la Vie de M. Philippes de Mornay* (Leiden, 1647), p. 22.

34. *Geizkofler*, p. 53.

35. Ibid., pp. 47–50.

36. Wechel recorded his gratitude for Languet's help in the dedication to his edition of Arthur Krantz's *Wandalia* (1575).

Guises were purging Paris in a flux of blood his moment of triumph had come.

Following his directions (though Charpentier discretely kept away), a gang of killers broke into the Collège de Presles but found Ramus's rooms empty. They searched the garret and other areas but did not find their quarry; on the advice of his disciples Ramus had hidden himself in a cellar in the Rue St. Jean de Beauvais. Roving bands looted the book-shop[37] above without disturbing him. After the boredom of a night in confinement Ramus thought the threat had subsided, so the following day he returned to his rooms on the fifth floor of his college. But Charpentier did not accept defeat so easily. Perhaps tipped off by an informer, he sent the band of murderers back again on Tuesday, August 26. They found the door unlocked and Ramus at prayer. After stabbing him repeatedly they threw his body down to the pavement below, where students of the Aristotelian cult assaulted his corpse and dragged his entrails through the streets.[38] Report of this nasty incident spread rapidly on the Left Bank. Walsingham and Sidney probably heard of it within hours, despite the barricaded security in which they huddled at the English Embassy.

Precisely how long Sidney and the other fugitives remained under Walsingham's roof we have no way of knowing. Walsingham himself did not venture out until Monday, September 1, when a dozen gentlemen-at-arms arrived to escort him to the Louvre. There the King explained the details of the Protestant conspiracy, and the Queen Mother followed with her version of the story. Another similar interview occurred on Friday, September 12. Meanwhile in England the Council had ended a long letter to Walsingham on September 9 with the order "we desire you to procure for the Lord *Wharton* and Mr. *Philip Sidney*, the Kings license and safe conduct to come thence. . . ."[39] Leicester wrote a personal letter with the same request on September 11, "I bid you farewel, trusting you will be a mean for my Nephew *Sidney*, that he may repair home, considering the present state there."[40] Since the time required for a messenger to cross the Channel was about eight days, Walsingham did not receive the order

---

37. Perhaps this was Andreas Wechel's second bookshop, the Pegasus, opened on this street when his business on the Rue St. Jacques expanded.

38. Charpentier's guilt was questioned by Joseph Bertrand in *Revue de Deux Mondes* 44 (1881):286–322. See also Ong, *Ramus*, pp. 29, 327.

39. Digges, p. 250, cited above.

40. Ibid., p. 252.

from the Council until September 17, an order that Sidney would have had to obey. But the Baron de Sidenay had already left Paris for Germany. With the original licence in mind, Walsingham must have arranged for a royal letter of safe-conduct to permit Sidney and his travelling companions to leave on the next leg of their journey.

CHAPTER 4

Just as Sidney, Bryskett, and the three servants were attached to a company of travellers when they crossed from London to Paris, so they joined a larger group when they set out for Germany about September 15. Their announced destination was Heidelberg, but they may well have named that university city though still uncertain about their plans. Probably some of the party were Germans, and at least two other Englishmen were with them. On such a journey at such a time safety lay in numbers, as some groups of half a dozen or so found to their regret. Very likely Sidney's party also avoided when possible the larger provincial cities to which the red plague of "bloody Bartholomew Day" had spread.

As the travellers wound up the fertile valley of the Marne into the highlands that crest in the Vosges Mountains, one of Sidney's companions became seriously ill. The travellers came to a halt when the unfortunate man died. Walsingham heard this news from a member of the party after it had reached Heidelberg, so the death probably occurred during the last week in September. On October 17 Walsingham dutifully forwarded the report to Leicester in a letter which raises more questions than it answers.

> *To the right honorable and his very good Lord, the Earl of Leicester.*
> It may please your Lordship to understand, that by certain that returned from *Frankfort* Mart, I understand that one of the Gentlemen that departed hence with intention to accompany your Mephew [*sic*] Mr. *Philip Sidney* to *Heidelberg*, died by the way at a place called *Bladin* in Lorain, who by divers conjectures I took to be the Dean of *Winchester*, who, as I advertised your Lordship by Mr. *Argall*, I employed to encounter the evill practices of your said Nephews servants. If therefore your Lordship, he now being void, shall not speedily take order in that behalf (if already it be not done) the young Gentleman your Nephew shal be in danger of a very lewd practice, which were great pitie in respect of the rare gifts that are in him. Touching news. I refer your Honor to these inclosed occurrents, and the report of this Bearer, to whom I have given order to communicate certain things unto you. And so leaving further to trouble

your Honor at this present, I most humblie take my leave. At *Paris*
the 17 of October, 1572.

Your Honours to command,

Fr. Walsingham[1]

The first question concerns "Bladin." This is now generally accepted as
referring to Blâmont, situated between Lunéville and Strasbourg. The
Dean of Winchester, John Watson (1520–84; he received the mitre in
1580), is another mystery man. Since Walsingham knew him so well, he
probably was one of the Englishmen who sought asylum in the Embassy
during the massacre. His being "employed to encounter the evill practices" of Philip's servant may well have been a charge accepted in
gratitude for Walsingham's kindnesses. What these evil practices were
can not be determined; almost anything, from lack of religious ardour
to gambling or any of the seven deadly sins, is possible. Although the
words "lewd practice" also could describe any sin, at this time the phrase
usually meant only heterodox religious or political opinions or activities.[2]
Mr. Argall was one of Leicester's employees, "that most opportune
messenger" mentioned in a letter to Sidney several years later.[3]

The letter also raises several questions that are unanswerable, the first
being the identity of the dead traveller, for Walsingham erred in thinking
him to be the Dean of Winchester. Similarly, we do not know whether or
not someone was sent to replace him. Leicester could have chosen Philip's
cousin, Thomas Coningsby,[4] who was with Sidney in Vienna the next
summer. If Leicester did select Coningsby, some time would have been
required before he could set out, so the journey may have been deferred
until the end of winter. In any case, no further references appear to
Sidney's being "in danger of a very lewd practice," whatever it may have
been.

The fact that Sidney and his companions were at Blâmont indicates that
they followed the Zorn River around the northern end of the Vosges and

<hr>

1. Digges, p. 273; there is another copy in MS. Harley 260, fol. 348[v].

2. A few examples: in June 1573 Edward Windsor sent Burghley a "lewd book," a
discourse on the government of England, suggesting that it be shown to Queen Elizabeth
and then burned (*HMC Cecil* ii, no. 136); in 1580 "certain lewd and forbidden books"
referring to Jesuitical writings (*CSPD*1, p. 688); "lewd" meaning "impious" (Birch's
Bayle, 10:107).

3. Robert Dorsett to Sidney, May 17, 1576.

4. A first cousin, being the son of Philippa, Sir Henry Sidney's sister, and Humphrey
Coningsby, treasurer to Queen Elizabeth.

down into the valley of the Rhine. The civilized comforts and Lutheran stability of Strasbourg may have induced them to linger for some days within that city's double walls of igneous stone, fortifications more formidable than the limestone walls of Paris and London. Even a short stop in Strasbourg would have impressed the travellers with the rows of trim four-story buildings and the "unmatchable"[5] spire of the Gothic cathedral, where the famous astronomical clock fifty feet high was then being constructed.

Friends of Hubert Languet among the travellers rejoiced to find him in Strasbourg.[6] On the first or second day of September he had managed to leave Paris and had come directly to Strasbourg. The City Council wished to take advantage of the presence of such an eminent witness to hear his sober account of the horrible event in Paris, for stories of the massacre, magnified in the telling, ran from house to house and from street to street. Languet accepted the invitation and on Sunday, September 21, read to the Council an account of the St. Bartholomew's Day massacre which is still preserved in the municipal archives.[7] He was careful to stress that his report was mostly secondhand ("ex relatione aliorum") for he had kept himself within doors most of the nine days after the bungled assassination attempt of August 22. He did not allude to the rough treatment he had received when he first ventured forth; it would be unknown but for Geizkofler's account of his rescue. Languet ended by drawing from the savage example of Paris the conclusion that only unified action by Protestant states could provide effective protection for freedom of worship and their very lives. The Counter-Reformation in northern Europe had taken the offensive, a reality written in rubrics of blood for all Protestants to read.

When the time came for Sidney's party to leave, they crossed the Rhine and continued along the eastern edge of the valley to Heidelberg, the capital city of the Palatinate and a centre of Calvinism. Here they may again have paused briefly and parted from some of their fellow travellers. From Heidelberg they continued north to their final destination, Frankfurt-am-Main. Once again their date of arrival is unknown, as is the address of their first lodging. Indeed, we cannot be entirely certain where Sidney

5. Coryat's adjective; he considered it "the exquisitest peece of work for a tower that ever I saw . . . one of the principall wonders of Christendome" (pp. 451–52).

6. Alkuin Hollaender, "Hubertus Languetus in Strassburg," in *Zeitschrift für die Geschichte des Oberrheins*, neue Folge, 10 (Karlsruhe, 1895) :42–56.

7. Ibid., pp. 51–55, quoted from Strasbourg City Archive AA. 707.

lived during any part of his winter in Frankfurt; his biographers have repeatedly said that he stayed in the house of Andreas Wechel, but no evidence has ever been offered for this beyond Fulke Greville's statement. All Greville's assertions about Sidney's travels during these years require checking against ascertainable facts.[8] These show that Wechel fled Paris within days of Sidney's departure, leaving his printing office and bookshop in the hands of looters. He must have brought some money with him, for on December 23 he purchased "das weisse Haus" on the Zeil, the broad central avenue where the prosperous Frankfurt book trade was concentrated.[9] Four days later Wechel officially became a citizen.[10] Doubtless his status in the international trade ensured any credit necessary for the purchase as well as sponsors for his citizenship application. Indeed, he may have leased the house with option to buy it when citizenship became a certainty.

Wherever Sidney lodged (probably with Wechel once the latter became established), Frankfurt offered a welcome contrast to the hot, tense months in Paris. The German city was also divided between the Catholics and the Lutherans. The former still worshipped in the great red sandstone Bartolomäauskirche with its three-hundred-foot spire, and monks were still ensconced in the monasteries. All other churches now held Protestant services, for Frankfurt had early welcomed the Reformation; the first Protestant sermon had been preached in 1522 in the Katherinenkirche. Despite reprisals by the Emperor Charles V and the Archbishop of Mainz, Lutheranism continued its vigorous growth: the merchants and banking houses flourished so abundantly that both parties hoped that the tranquillity would not be disturbed.

Situated in a wide fertile valley, Frankfurt had from antiquity been the market centre for sale of agricultural products and purchase of supplies. Geography also made it a crossroads of European trade routes; travellers from Dresden, Leipzig, and the east would meet those from Paris in the west, Basle in the south, and Berlin in the north. Similarly, merchants coming from the lower Rhine to Würzburg and Vienna would pass through Frankfurt and mingle with their counterparts travelling from the opposite direction. The handsome bridge, the Alte Mainbrücke, 815 feet long and resting on 14 arches, spanned the Main. The river teemed with

8. Greville (p. 9) also makes the erroneous statement that Languet accompanied Sidney "in the whole course of his three years travail."

9. Josef Benzing, *Buchdruckerlexikon des 16. Jahrhunderts* (Frankfurt, 1952), p. 57.

10. *ADB*, s.v. Wechel.

traffic passing to and from the confluence with the Rhine 24 miles to the west.

The busiest times of year for all Frankfurt citizens, especially merchants, came with the semiannual Fairs before Easter and in September. Coryat gives some idea of the spectacle which greeted both vendors and prospective buyers. He reported, "the Fayre is esteemed . . . the richest meeting of any place in Christendome." Of the goldsmiths' displays he wrote, "The wealth that I sawe here was incredible, so great, that it was vnpossible for a man to conceiue it in his minde that hath not first seene it with his bodily eies." Among the visitors he saw "many eminent and Princely persons." Men of learning thronged "the Booke-sellers streete where I saw such an infinite abundance of bookes, that . . . farre excelleth *Paules* Churchyard in London, Saint *Iames* streete in Paris, the Merceria of Venice, and . . . seemeth to be a very epitome of all the principall Libraries of Europe."[11]

The Book Fair was in fact a "second fair," held simultaneously with that of other merchants. A fairly full account of it exists in an *opusculum* by the learned Henri Estienne, a description of the Fair in 1574, a year after Sidney was there.[12] Estienne stressed that not only did the Frankfurt Book Fair assemble the finest, rarest, and most valuable printed books, but members of the whole republic of letters gathered there, an assembly unmatched since the great age of Athens.

> For one is mistaken who supposes that only the writings, and not the writers, themselves, are to be seen in this section [i.e. the book-sellers' quarter] which, I have said, could be called the Frankfort Athens. This at any rate applies to many of the writers who are still alive. Hence it comes about that an advantage can be gained from this Academy-Fair (as I have called it above) which can not be secured from mere libraries. For here all may enjoy the living voice of many honored persons, who gather here from many different academies. Here very often right in the shops of the book-sellers you can hear them discussing philosophy no less seriously than once the Socrateses and the Platos discussed it in the Lyceum. And not only the philosophers; those celebrated universities of Vienna, of Witten-berg, of Leipzig, of Heidelberg, of Strasburg, and, among other

11. Coryat, pp. 564-65
12. *Francofordiense Emporium* (Geneva, 1574). Quotations are from the English version by J. W. Thompson (Chicago, 1911), pp. 169, 171.

nations, those of Louvain, of Padua, of Oxford, of Cambridge—
these academies, I say, and many others which it would take too
long to enumerate, send to the Fair not only their philosophers, but
also poets, representatives of oratory, of history, of the mathematical
sciences, some even skilled in all these branches at once—those, in
short, who profess to compass the whole circle of knowledge, which
the Greeks call *encyclopædia*.

Thus Andreas Wechel had good reason to invest in the white house on
the Zeil and to prepare for the next spring when buyers could again flood
Frankfurt for the Fair. The situation also favoured setting up a new
printing house. To quote again Coryat's testimony: "For this city hath
so flourished ... in the art of printing, that it is not inferiour in that
respect to any city in Christendome, no not to Basil it selfe ... for the
excellency of that art." [13] The rapid growth of literacy and the reformed
religion led to a constantly increasing demand for Protestant books and
tracts, along with legal and medical volumes and the classic writings of
earlier ages.

According to the tradition which derives from Fulke Greville,[14]
Languet also passed the winter in Frankfurt, and spent much time in
Sidney's company. Late in December, however, the Elector of Saxony
sent Languet to Vienna.[15] Whatever the immediate purpose of the
expedition, once it was accomplished Languet returned to Frankfurt,
probably for the Fair, and remained there until the end of March.[16] But
Vienna was to be the centre of his activities for many years to come. Now
that the possibility of a French alliance had been tossed into the reddened
Seine along with thousands of Huguenots, Languet and August realized
that Maximilian, the tolerant Holy Roman Emperor, should be cultivated.
Moreover, the political map of Europe could be altered by the Polish
situation, for the throne had become vacant with the death of Sigismund
Augustus in July 1572. Vienna thus became the vantage point for diplomatic watchmen.

---

13. Coryat, pp. 564–65.
14. Greville, pp. 8–9.
15. Platzkoff, p. 76.
16. Languet to Camerarius, from Frankfurt, Mar. 24, 1573 (*Huberti Langueti*, p. 203).
His return route took him through Leipzig, whence two Camerarius brothers accompanied
him as far as Prague (ibid., p. 205). He reached Vienna on May 27 (Chevreul, *Languet*,
p. 117).

By the time Sidney and Languet were next together in Vienna, their special relationship of master and protégé, almost father and son, was so firmly established that the months together in Frankfurt must have contributed to its development. The "danger of a very lewd practice" which had worried Walsingham seems to have been crowded out by serious study of books recommended by Languet. There was opportunity for profitable conversation with the learned men of Frankfurt, Protestant theologians as well as booksellers and publishers, many, like Wechel, refugees from Catholic oppression. A number of English Protestants who had fled during the reign of Bloody Mary had settled and prospered there.

The primary topic among them was the Counter-Reformation's threat to all Protestant states. The sword in France had now been added to torture and the stake in Spain and the papal dominions. Possible plans to unite the German states, the Netherlands, and England hinged on whether England would take the active lead in such a Protestant League. This would require money to support men and equipment supplied by the Germans. Young Philip Sidney was second to none in his conviction that both self-preservation and the future success of the Protestant movement called for such a League. Languet in particular saw Sidney as a potential leader in this project. He had the intelligence, skill at arms, character, and desire, in addition to his status as heir presumptive to two of Elizabeth's closest advisers, Leicester and Warwick. Languet saw his opportunity to mould the young man, who became an apt pupil.

Sidney was also aware of the need for a definite program of learning and observation as he travelled from city to city and country to country. How soon he began to formulate such a program or how it advanced from book to book and from experience to experience cannot now be determined. Some years later when his "deere brother," Robert, embarked on a similar educational tour Philip's letter of advice to him revealed how carefully he had thought out what such a program should be.[17] The letter is too long to quote in full, so a few passages must suffice.

First, concerning how money should be spent in different countries: "For your countenance I would for no cause have it diminished in Germany; in Italy your greatest expence must be upon worthi men." Next Philip recommended that Robert and a travelling companion "passe good exercises betwixt yow," that is, do written exercises based on

---

17. A tattered copy of the letter to his brother is still preserved at Penshurst (Collins, 1 : 283). The text quoted here is Feuillerat's, letter xlii.

reading and observation, each man criticizing the work of the other. In any historical writing Philip stressed the importance of chronology: "your method must be to have *seriem temporum* very exactlie." After discussing differences between the methods and purposes of the Orator, the Poet, and the Discourser, Philip urged his brother to outline the contents of each book as he read it and make lists of witty words, sententious sayings, and similitudes. Similarly, worthwhile points in any military books that Robert read should be written down in a "Table of Remembrance." Concerning other studies Philip wrote:

> Now (deere Brother) take delight likewise in the mathematicalls. . . . I thinke yow understand the sphere, if yow doe, I care little for any more astronomie in yow. Arithmatick and geometry, I would wish yow well seene in, so as both in matter of nomber and measure yow might have a feeling, and active judgment . . . So yow can speake and write Latine not barbarously I never require great study in Ciceronianisme the chiefe abuse of Oxford, *Qui dum verba sectantur, res ipsas negligunt.*

These admonitions undoubtedly reflect Philip's own program inaugurated during the winter in Frankfurt and carried on whenever he was settled in a new city during the next two years. Although Robert was scarcely in peril of becoming a bookworm, Philip concluded by charging Robert not to neglect the other skills expected of a Renaissance man of his station: "Now sweete brother take a delight to keepe and increase your musick, yow will not beleive what a want I finde of it in my melancholie times." Before Buxton, writers on Sidney were strangely silent about this confession. His occasional melancholy was noted, but not the relief he found in music. Evidently Philip could not adequately assuage his melancholy by performing on an instrument, whereas Robert's training was such that he could.

On expertise in military arts, so necessary for a future courtier, Philip added these words of advice about combining practice with knowledge of theory: "At horsemanshipp when yow exercise it reade Grison Claudio, and a booke that is called La gloria del cavallo,[18] withall, that yow may

18. By "Grison" Sidney doubtless means Federico Grisone, who published *Gli Ordini di cavalcare* (Naples, 1550). Because Sidney also writes of "curing horses," Ringler has suggested that Sidney may have had in mind a book attributed to Grisone, *Scielta di Notabili Avertimenti, Pertinenti a Cavalli* (Venice, 1571). "Claudio" is less easily identifiable but could refer to Claudio Corte, *Il Cavallerizzo* (Venice, 1573). *La gloria del cavallo* is the title of a work by Pasqual Caracciolo (Venice, 1567).

joyne the th[o]rough contemplation of it with the exercise, and so shall
you profite more in a moneth then others in a year." Because in those
days a man's life could depend on his ability to defend himself, mere
fencing for points was, in Philip's opinion, a waste of time and practice.
His suggestions to Robert are those of a man who has lived with men
whose swords were weapons, not mere adjuncts to their costumes.

> When yov play at weapons I would have yow gett thick capps &
> brasers, and play out your play lustilie, for indeed tickes, & daliances
> are nothing in earnest for the time of the one & the other greatlie
> differs, and use as well the blow, as the thrust, it is good in it selfe, &
> besides exerciseth your breath and strength, and will make yow a
> strong man at the Tournei and Barriers. First in any case practize the
> single sword, & then with the dagger, let no day passe without an
> hower or two such exercise the rest studie, or conferr diligentlie, &
> so shall yow come home to my comfort and creditt.

The affectionate relationship between the two, as well as the fear that
so many suggestions might seem pompous, appear in the way Philip
concluded:

> Lord how I have babled, once againe fairewell deerest brother.
> Your most loving and carefull brother
> Philip Sidney

Because this letter contains many passages which reveal Sidney's thinking,
portions of it will be referred to in later chapters.

In the Renaissance, advice on conduct was eagerly sought and abundantly offered, as hundreds of books testify. Whether Sidney received any
written formulae of conduct we do not know for none has been preserved. Walsingham was in a special position to offer suggestions to
Sidney, for in his youth he had travelled to Italy where, as elsewhere, he
apprenticed himself to the trade of understanding courts and official
procedures, thus laying the groundwork for a successful diplomatic
career. Any advice he gave Sidney probably was similar to that he wrote
out for another young man, supposedly his nephew. It reads almost as if
it had been addressed to Sidney himself.

After an admonition to say prayers at regular hours, Walsingham
recommended a daily exercise in double translation: "you shall do well to
translate an epistle of Tully into French and out of French into Latin,

whereby you may profit in both tongues." [19] The study of ancient history should "mark how matters have passed in government of those days." Next, one's company should be carefully chosen.

> The next piece of a traveller to profit himself by is to join himself to some company, for books are but dead letters, it is the voice and conference of men that giveth them life and shall engender in you true knowledge.

> This company you have first to see that it be honest and godly: to take heed of lewd youths of wanton, dissolute dispositions and especially such as have of nature the humour of hypocrisy, for by them you shall learn no sound thing and shall discover yourself to yourself to the great peril. For your direction herein ... the advice of your friends, who shall advise you first to some one that is honest and good and by him you shall learn how to come to the conference of others, for like will to like.

Similarly, the languages to be learned should be chosen with care, with one's area of future action in mind. Of the sciences, only mathematics and cosmography are recommended.

The core of the young traveller's study, however, should be observations of men, manners, and politics.

> Especially have regard in this part to the manners and dispositions of the people, as in general, so chiefly of the nobility, gentry and learned sort and have their company as much as in safety of conscience and peace of God you may: that you see the inclination of each man which way he is bent, whether it be a marshall or Counsellor, a plain, open nature, a dissembling and counterfeit, whether he be in credit with his people, and what pension he hath from abroad, how inclining toward the neighbours bordering upon him; and for the disposition of the French gentry, whether they incline more to the Spanish or German or English, and who they are, and what account they make of Scotland, how they are affected to any of the Nobility of the realm and what they are; and so by conference of this nature you shall see whether there be the more similitude or disparity and by it you may discover much to serve yourself and commonwealth.

19. This and the following quotations come from Read, 1:18–20. The original manuscript was destroyed by fire.

Finally, three key precepts which generations of diplomats have followed to great advantage:

> You must show yourself civil and companionable to all but [reject advances]. You may not incline to any faction, to bind yourself in either party, but therein as a stranger remember the precept of the wise, "Perigrinatus non oportet esse curiosus." And acquaint yourself as well as you can with men of state—though otherwise they be not of themselves sufficient, neither for learning or other quality, that you may get out of their hands and by these means such dealings as daily pass in affairs of state and counsel of princes, whether they appertain to civil government or warlike affairs. For so you have to make your profit as well of your own sort as the other, as well of the experienced as of the learned: for these men of experience as the world calleth them will serve you as conduit pipes though themselves they have no water, these are secretaries, public notaries and agents for princes and cities, etc. In all these aforesaid and what else soever may serve for your profit, you must observe this, to put down in writing what you have learned either by sight or conference, keeping as it were a diary of all your doings.

Aside from Sidney's program of reading and study, the only two events that we know engrossed his attention in Frankfurt occurred in March 1573. The Fair began on March 11, the second Wednesday before Easter. Doubtless Sidney's wonder at the spectacle was similar to Coryat's though much less naive. The second event was a conference held about the same time officially to negotiate a treaty between the Netherlands and France. An ancillary purpose, however, was to determine who should become Archbishop-Elector of Cologne. Because the negotiations were a battle between statesmen of the Protestant and Catholic power groups, a brief explanation is required.

In 1567 when Salentin, Count of Isenberg-Grenzau, was elected to the position he stated clearly that his primary interest lay in managing his estates, not in being Archbishop. He refused orders higher than the subdiaconate and openly indicated his intention to lay down the mitre after a short interval. Accordingly, intrigues for the succession soon flourished, but no candidate satisfied the majority of the parties concerned. Then a new candidate appeared, the young Prince Ernest of Bavaria. His father energetically organized support and won the backing of the Duke of Alba and, through him, that of Philip of Spain. The Spaniards saw

Ernest as the means to ensure a solidly Catholic rule in Cologne which would buttress their control of the Netherlands. The Protestants reacted vigorously to this threat. They had interpreted the easygoing ways of Archbishop Salentin as a tendency to moderation in religious rivalry, especially since one of his reasons for wishing to abdicate was an avowed desire to marry. Without a strong candidate to oppose the Bavarian Catholic, the prospects of maintaining tolerance and tranquillity seemed dim.

A bold plan was now proposed which would allow Salentin to have the best of both situations, namely to become a married man and still keep the Archbishopric. This could be accomplished if he became a Protestant and introduced Protestants into the Chapter of his cathedral. Count Louis of the Palatinate and John of Nassau combined their influence in this ingenious attempt to capture the See of Cologne for the Protestants. They devoted the early months of 1573 to diplomatic maneuvers with Salentin and the court of France. Their plan was to offer a strong treaty of alliance between Salentin, the Nassau party in the Netherlands, and the Palatinate. The major problem would be to convince Catherine de Médicis that this move would be to the advantage of France. A conference to accomplish this purpose was arranged for March when Gaspard de Schomberg, the French Ambassador to the German states, would be in Frankfurt.

De Schomberg had been travelling on a circuit of the German courts to try to counteract the reaction against the St. Bartholomew's Day massacre. His announced purpose, however, was to line up support for Catherine's scheme to put her favourite son, Henry of Anjou, on the vacant throne of Poland. The bargaining at the Frankfurt meeting produced a draft treaty (never completed) which gave France the support of the House of Orange for this scheme. In return France was to aid, either secretly or openly, the Netherlands in their struggle against Spain as well as, possibly, supporting the project concerning the See of Cologne.

The experienced and practical diplomat de Schomberg played along with the proposals, but he knew that the Spaniards would not accept the situation which so entranced its Protestant sponsors. His purpose in spinning out the negotiations was to confine the energetic and unruly Nassau faction and ensure ultimate French control of the Netherlands. His dispatches urged Catherine to carry the treaty to a prompt conclusion. De Schomberg was so successful in deceiving the Protestants that Louis of Nassau's brother John was dispatched to Heidelberg to advocate the French case for Henry of Valois. Louis also promised to write to Elizabeth of England in support of Catherine de Médicis's proposal that Elizabeth consider marrying the Duke of Alençon (even though he was young enough to be her son), and agreed to intercede for French ambitions in central Europe with Landgrave William of Hesse.[20]

These negotiations provide the background for three letters from Sidney, the only documents extant concerning this Frankfurt period. The first, written on the Wednesday before Easter, is addressed to the Earl of Leicester.

> Ryghte honorable and my singular good Lorde and Unkle,
>
> This bearer havinge showed me the woorkes he dothe cary into Englande gave me ocasion humble to sende these few woordes unto yowr Lordeshippe, thoughe my wrytynge at this presente unto yow by an Englisshe gentleman that dothe now returne, take away any other cause of enlarginge the same. This bearer hathe promised me to lett no man see that whiche he cariethe untill he have showed them unto yowr Lordeshipp. If they may seeme unto yowr Lordeshippe unworthie of whiche I shoolde wryte unto yow, I do most humblie beseche yow to condemne therein nothinge but my ignoraunce, whiche bendinge it selfe wholie to content yow, if it do erre, I hope yowr goodness will suffer the dutifull mynde, to recompence the wante of judgement, whiche beinge all that I have at this tyme to trouble yow witheall, I will most lowlie committ yow to the Eternalls protection.
>
> From Francforde this 18th of Marche A° 1572[-3]
>
>   Yowr moste humble and moste obediente nephew
>
>   Philip Sidney
>
> To the ryghte honorable and my singular unkle, the Earle of Leçestre.[21]

The impersonal tone can be explained by several considerations. The "Englisshe gentleman" could be expected to report on Sidney's health and appearance and make other observations about him. The man may have been in Frankfurt for the Fair (perhaps a bookseller), or he may have been a traveller homeward bound. What kind of item he carried to show

---

20. Among other sources see von Bezold, *Briefe*, 1 : 104; Moriz Ritter, *Deutsche Geschichte im Zeitalter der Gegenreformation und des Dreissigjährigen Krieges (1555–1648)*, Bibliothek Deutscher Geschichte (Stuttgart, 1889), 1 : 473–75; and Platzkoff, p. 86 and n.

21. Feuillerat, 3, no. IV.

to Leicester is also mere conjecture: it may have been Sidney's observations on the changing political situation.

The second note, probably carried by the same messenger, was written on Good Friday to William Blunt, the Sidney family's banker.

> *Laus Deo.*—In Frankefurt, the 20th of Marche, 1573.
>
> On the last day of May next coming, I praye you pay by this my first bill of exchange, my second not being payed before, unto Reynolds Drelinge or the bringer hereof, one hundreth and twenty pounds sterling money current for merchandise: and is for the valew here in Frankfort by me received of Christian Rolgin for myne own use. At the day faile not, but make good payment. And so God kepe you.
>
> Your loving frende,
Philip Sidney
>
> To his very frende Mr. William Blunt, Master of the Counter in Wood-streete.[22]

Blunt's detailed accounts from May 1, 1572 to May 1, 1573 are preserved at Penshurst. They include these pertinent entries.

> For the use of Mr. Philip Sydney—his fee for half year, £40; his entertainment in France until All Hallow-tide, £100; to his man the same time, £33 6s. 8d.; Acerbo Vitello for money paid to Mr. Phillip beyond the seas, £161 15s. 0d.; to John Ponton on Mr. Philip's letter at his return from France, £7; with sundry bills for clothing, £75 10s. 0d.—£427 11s. 8d.

Somewhere in this total sum the £120 asked for in Sidney's letter was presumably included. "His man" was probably a reference to Bryskett. Similarly, John Ponton could have been the "Englisshe gentleman" who carried a letter and other things to the Earl of Leicester.[23] Ponton has not been otherwise identified, a lack of distinction he shares with Drelinge and Rolgin.

The third extant letter from Frankfurt, again addressed to Leicester, was written by Sidney on Easter Monday (March 23). After the customary compliments Sidney reported on some. of the principals who were in Frankfurt to intrigue on the situation in the See of Cologne.

---

22. Feuillerat, 3, no. V; first cited by Zouch.

23. This rate is consistent with the £6 13s. 4d. that Walsingham paid for a special messenger, Jan. 24, 1572/3 (Digges, p. 315).

I was uppon Thursdaie laste withe Counte Lodovik the prince of Oronges seconde brother, whose honorable usage was suche towardes me, and suche goodwill he seemes to beare unto your Lordeshippe, that for wante of furdre habilite, I can but wishe him, a prosperouse success to suche noble entreprises, as I dowte not he will shortely (with the help of God) put in execution. I founde one Shambourg an Allmaine withe him, a gentleman whome I knew in the cowrte of Fraunce, allways very affectionnate to the kinges service, I dowte not but that he assiaethe to drawe the Cownte to serve the kinge, but I hope he laboureth in vaine. All mens eyes are so bente to the affaires of Fraunce and Flaunders, that there is no talke here of any other contrey.

Shambourg was, of course, de Schomberg. The letter concludes with another plea for financial help. Clearly, Sidney had found that living up to his position required more money than he or his father and uncles had expected.

I have an humble requeste unto your Lordeshipp, whiche is that it will please you to thanke maister Culverwell the bearer hereof, for the courteisie he shewed unto me, in employnge his creditt for me, beinge drivne into some necessitie. Thus cravinge pardon for the continewance of my wonted manner, in vainely trobling yowr Lordeshippe I will most lowlie leave yow in his garde who ever preserve yow. Frome Francfort, this 23th of Marche 1572[-3]
            Yowr moste humble and most obedient nephew
                                            Philipp Sidney
    To the ryghte honorable and my singular good Lorde and unkle the Earle of Lecestre etc.

After these letters there is no further evidence of Sidney's life in Frankfurt. Tradition has it that he departed on his way south during May, but April seems more likely. He took the standard route up the Rhine Valley to Basle and crossed to the higher reaches of the Danube, which he then followed down to Vienna. The first stop was at Heidelberg, but there is no reason to believe that Sidney and his entourage tarried there long. The only person whom we can be certain Sidney met in Heidelberg on this visit was the learned printer, Henri Estienne. This remarkable man, who represented the third generation of a celebrated family of French printers, was now at the height of his powers. A phenomenal linguist who

could converse in nearly every European tongue, Estienne early specialized in ancient Greek. At the age of fourteen he had collated for his father
a manuscript of Dionysius of Halicarnassus, and at sixteen travelled to
Italy where he spent three years searching out and collating Greek
manuscripts. There his precocity brought him the friendship of leading
scholars in each city he visited.

The stream of editions that flowed from his erudite pen (including the
first edition of Aeschylus's *Agamemnon*) began appearing at the Estienne
presses in 1557. After his father's death in 1559 he became owner of the
family business, now located in Geneva. There he published in 1566 his
popular satire and best known work in French, *L'Apologie pour Hérodote*,
which went through twelve editions in the next sixteen years. When
Sidney encountered Estienne in Heidelberg, his magnum opus, the
Thesaurus Graecae Linguae (five volumes folio, 1572–73) was astounding
the learned world.

Like most facts in Estienne's life, the meagre details of his meetings with
Sidney come from the prefaces and dedicatory epistles in the printer's
numerous publications. Two such books were dedicated to Sidney, the
first being Estienne's edition of the Greek New Testament,[24] in which he
tells of his meetings with Sidney.

> I first chanced to see you at Heidelberg, and a little afterwards at
> Strasburg, and then again, after a long time, at Vienna; but at
> Strasburg the love which I had felt for you at Heidelberg greatly
> increased, and at Vienna the love I felt for you at Strasburg grew still
> more. Not that it is at all suprizing that my love for you should have
> grown in this way, since your gifts of mind, which had aroused it,
> seemed also to have grown.[25]

Clearly, Sidney's well-trained, eager intelligence was one of his most
attractive qualities. In the second volume Estienne dedicated to Sidney
five years later he stated that Sidney was so learned in reading Greek that
translations were superfluous for him.[26] Apparently a young aristocrat
who could read Greek, especially one from the remote island kingdom of
England, was an object of wonder.

---

24. *Novum Testamentum, Graece, cum H. Stephani praefatione & notis marginalibus* (Geneva,
1576); first mentioned by Zouch.
25. As translated by Buxton, p. 58.
26. *Herodiani Historiarum Libri VIII* (Geneva, 1581), par. ii.

Another literary figure whom Sidney probably met in Heidelberg on this visit was the humanist and poet Paul Schede, usually designated by his Latin name Melissus. Because their friendship cannot be proven before 1577, biographers have dated their acquaintance from that year, but circumstances strongly suggest that they met during Sidney's visit of 1573. Melissus, who now enjoyed the patronage of the Elector Palatine, had settled in Heidelberg in 1571.[27] Previously he had lived in Geneva, where a close friendship with Henri Estienne had developed. Another of his friends was Jean Lobbet of Strasbourg: in 1567 they had travelled together to Paris to sit at the feet of Ramus. Among the wide circle of writers, musicians, and intellectuals well known to Melissus were others from whom he and Sidney would have heard about each other. Of the two poems Melissus addressed to Sidney, the earliest was written in 1577, but it in no way indicates that their friendship began then, when Sidney revisited Heidelberg as a special ambassador of Queen Elizabeth.

When Sidney reached Strasbourg, Dr. Jean Lobbet, then Professor of Law at the University, was one of the distinguished men he saw frequently. Possibly they had met in Paris, for Lobbetius (as he signed his letters to Sidney) had been there during the wedding and the massacre.[28] Beginning with Sidney's sojourn in Strasbourg in the spring of 1573 their friendship flowered, as the newly recovered series of letters (to appear on later pages) abundantly testifies. Regrettably, the letters reveal no details of their meetings in Strasbourg beyond the fact that Sidney lodged with one Hubert de la Rose who was excessively fond of wine ("purée de Septembre"). From one of Languet's letters a year later (June 4, 1574) we learn that while in Strasbourg Sidney made a side trip to inspect the fortifications then under construction at Phalsbourg, about twenty-five miles back on the road he had already traversed from Nancy and Blâmont. Since the new fortress was being built on a plateau which stood over a thousand feet above the road, it commanded the passes of the Vosges mountains.[29]

Sidney also became well acquainted with the most eminent Strasbourger

27. Melissus participated actively in a literary club dedicated to two objects, the study of poetry and avoidance of alcoholic beverages. The club's detractors made appropriate sport of water as the inspiration of the members' muse.

28. Geizkofler mentions knowing him there and later in Strasbourg, where he benefited from Lobbet's thoughtfulness (pp. 102–03).

29. The fortress was finally completed by Vauban in 1680; now only two gateways remain.

of his generation, Johann Sturm, Rector of the Academy. His European reputation dated from his early career as a lecturer at Paris, where because "he liked what were called new opinions, he was more than once in danger."[30] He accepted an invitation to Strasbourg in 1537 and became Rector of the new school; first formalized under his direction, it soon "became the most flourishing in all Germany."[31] His educational theories greatly influenced Roger Ascham, who followed them in training his royal pupil, the Princess Elizabeth. Ascham corresponded with "my Sturmius" over a long span of years and showed Sturm's letters to Elizabeth (even after she had become Queen) who confessed being "very partial to John Sturmius." Concerning Sturm's comments on Elizabeth's possible choice of a husband in a letter of January 15, 1560, Ascham reported, "The passage concerning her marriage, I well remember, she read over three times, with an occasional sweet smile, and a very modest and bashful silence."[32] A few months later Ascham named his third son for Sturm.[33]

A Zwinglian, Sturm refused to attend sermons by extreme Lutherans; instead he spent "sermon time in playing at chess."[34] On the other hand, "His house was open day and night to all good men, and was ... the common Asylum of the Refugees ... especially in providing for the French Protestants, in which he spent his whole fortune, and chose to reduce himself and his family to poverty, rather than to desert the common cause."[35] Apparently monetary needs prompted him in 1572 at the age of sixty-five to apply for appointment as English agent in Strasbourg, following the death of the previous functionary. Burghley gained the Queen's agreement and wrote Sturm on September 15, 1572, while Elizabeth and her Council were meeting at Woodstock, still dazed by news of the carnage of St. Bartholomew's Day: "Her majesty therefore accepts, as is fitting, the homage of your duty so diligently and readily offered, and will willingly appoint you in the place of [the deceased agent] and with the same salary."[36]

30. Bayle's words, as translated in Birch's *Bayle*, 9:438.
31. Ibid., p. 439.
32. Quotations from a letter of Ascham to Sturm, preserved at Strasbourg, translated in *Zürich Letters*, pp. 64–72.
33. Ibid., p. 90.
34. Birch's *Bayle*, 9:440n., quoting Conrad Schüsselburg.
35. Birch's *Bayle*, 9:439n., quoting Melchior Adam.
36. *Zürich Letters*, p. 211, from the original at Strasbourg.

The experience and knowledge of public affairs that Sturm brought to this employment undertaken in his seventh decade were matched by some failings not unexpected in a man at this stage of life. He began well enough, and in November 1573 recommended to Queen Elizabeth one Christopher Landtschadt von Steinach as a candidate for English agent at Heidelberg.[37] Burghley acquiesced but replied, "when you again write to her majesty . . . take care to be a little more exact both in writing and reading over your letter. For there was such carelessness in both these respects, that it could neither be read by her without difficulty, nor by reason of verbal inaccuracy be sufficiently understood."[38] Later letters from Elizabeth and her ministers complain that though Sturm wrote often, they expected still more frequent reports from him. Part of these complaints may be attributed to the Queen's habit of prodding those in her employ to ever-increasing attention.

In 1573, however, Sturm had reported promptly on Sidney's visit to Strasbourg, though the documents themselves are not known to be preserved. On July 18 Burghley acknowledged them as follows:

> I received the letters, Sturmius, which you gave for the queen's majesty and myself to this servant of Philip Sidney, who will deliver this from me in return . . . I thank you very much for your kind reception of Philip Sidney, and I know that his most honoured parents will thank you a great deal more.[39]

Because letters from Strasbourg usually took about fifteen days to reach England,[40] the "servant of Philip Sidney" left with those from Sturm (and undoubtedly some from Sidney) before the end of May, about the time that Sidney departed for Basle, ninety miles up the Rhine. Did Sidney know that Sturm's cordiality was supported by a salary from the Queen? It seems doubtful, for the situation has not even been remarked on by Sidney's biographers.

Similarly, the early biographers were uncertain on the question of whether Sidney went from Strasbourg to Basle, or took the more direct route to Vienna (through Ulm, Augsburg, and Munich), until Buxton settled the matter by pointing out a reference in one of Languet's letters

37. For Sturm's recommendation see *Zürich Letters*, p. 239. He forwarded Landtschadt's application, now preserved in the Public Record Office (*CSPF1*, no. 1212). Some of Landtschadt's letters were forwarded by Sturm (*Zürich Letters*, p. 276).

38. *Zürich Letters*, p. 217. The one manuscript letter by Sturm in the Osborn Collection exhibits both failings. It is addressed to Robert Sidney and dated May 8, 1579.

39. Ibid., pp. 216–17. The messenger may have been a professional courier.

40. Ibid., p. 257.

written nine years afterwards.[41] Actually there are three letters to Sidney written shortly after his visit to Basle, two of them among the newly recovered group. These were written by two French youths, both fugitives from the religious massacre and both younger than Sidney himself, who was now only eighteen and a half. Apparently Sidney met the two prominent young refugees in Basle, though his visit was relatively short; the letters were written after he had departed for Vienna.

The first is from François, Comte de Chastillon, the sixteen-year-old son and heir of the Huguenot martyr, Admiral de Coligny. When his father was murdered he had fortunately been at the family estate, whence he was helped by a neighbour named Pont-Chartrain[42] to escape to Berne. His letter, a model of polite respectfulness, is written in French and in an excellent Italic hand and reads as follows:

> Sir:
>
> Having in this world no good that I value so highly as true and unfeigned friendship, I believe myself to have acquired the greatest treasure one could wish for when I had the good fortune to make your acquaintance beyond mere formality: and it is my hope that this may prove an excellent beginning of a perpetual and indissoluble friendship with you. For so have your virtues impressed themselves upon me that I have no desire other than to study always to be loved by you, and I am resolved to use every effort and means to retain your friendship—friendship which on my part will not fail for a little distance and space that may physically separate you from me. And as this is sent solely to reestablish myself in your favour and memory, assured as I am that your great kindness will gladly grant me this suggestion of mutual complaisance, I shall humbly salute you, and pray God to grant you,
>
> Sir, in all prosperity a happy and a long life. From Basle, this fifth of June, 1573.
>
> > Yours most humbly, and
> > obediently at your service,
> > > Chastillon

41. Buxton, p. 263. Ringler informs me that E. Flugel made the point in his edition of *Astrophil and Stella* (Halle, 1889), p. xvi, n. Buxton also cites the letter of D'Argenlieu quoted below.

42. See E. and E. Haag, *La France Protestante*, 2d ed. (Paris, 1877–78), 3 : 405. Charles IX had sent troops to arrest him and his cousin, Guy de Laval, and other members of the family, but they got away in time.

The letter bears no address and was sent after Sidney's departure from Basle to reach him at some stop on the road.

The second letter of the same day is in a similar vein and was written by Chastillon's cousin (two years his senior), Guy-Paul de Coligny, Comte de Laval.

> Sir,
>
> I send you this, if it please you, humbly to thank you for the pleasant memory which, in your account of your news and good health, you show yourself to have of me. This has been, as it always will be, most agreeable to me; and it will add to the obligations your courtesies and civilities have already laid upon me. It will do so the more, if you will add to your promised friendship and affection by continuing to send me news of you and yours, as I most fondly beseech you. For my part, in recognition of this obligation, you will find me most happy to render you any pleasure or service that it may please you to require of me.
>
> I am grieved indeed that the Sieurs de la Serree, who departed here yesterday hoping to find you at Strasbourg, will have been frustrated in their expectation: not only because of your goodwill which they had hoped to carry to England, but also because they will thus have lost the opportunity of giving you news of me, as I requested of them, and of paying my humble respects to your benevolence. This last I do now, most affectionately and with all my heart, beseeching our Eternal God,
>
> Sir, to grant you perfect health, and a long and happy life. From Basle, this fifth of June, 1573.
>
> > Your most affectionate friend and servant,
> >
> > > Laval

The third available letter is from Jean Hangest, Sieur D'Argenlieu, diplomat and later miltary commander under Condé, who appears to have been the companion of the two young exiles. It was also written on June 5.

> Sir,
>
> You have been pleased to honour my young masters by sending the gentleman who is the bearer of this letter to see them; and you have kindly obliged me by having him give me news of you. These things impel me to send you this note, most humbly to offer you any service

that could be of use to you: and this I beg you to put to the test with regard to anything in which you know I can serve you. Please also favour me with your continued benevolence, to which I humbly commend myself, praying to our good Lord, Sir, to give you good health, a long and happy life, and all good fortune on your journey. From Basle, the fifth day of June, 1573. Reliable reports from France tell us that the Queen your mistress is preparing armed intervention in France.

Your obedient and affectionate servant,
D'Argenlieu

From these three letters several inferences can be made, the first being that Sidney had written to Laval after they had last seen each other; Laval's reference to "your account of your news and good health" indicates this. Sidney's letter must have arrived on June 4 or 5. The fact that the "Sieurs de la Serree" had left Basle on June 4 (the day before Laval wrote), hoping to find Sidney at Strasbourg, confirms this. Further, Laval's letter suggests that when Laval last saw Sidney his future route had been undetermined and that he was considering retracing his way to Strasbourg, whence he would follow the relatively level road to Ulm instead of a shorter and steeper route. The Sieurs de la Serree may have been Raymond and Giraud de la Serre, but their identity is uncertain.[43] Nor are any further details known of the journey to Vienna.

43. See Henri Jougla de Morenas, *Le Grand Armorial de France* (Paris, 1949), 6:212.

CHAPTER 5

Sidney arrived in Vienna in midsummer, just about a year after his first busy weeks abroad in Paris. Vienna was a sleepy city; even its prosperous merchants, following a centuries-long pattern of living, relaxed in the country air of Baden and other surrounding altitudes. This retreat to seats in the hills was an even more universal custom among the courtiers of Maximilian II, Emperor of the venerable Holy Roman Empire. Despite the fact that the Emperor's military power had become more formal than real, his court was the hub of central European intelligence and culture, a place that no apprentice in statecraft could well afford to miss.

The Holy Roman Empire is a subject most nonspecialist readers (certainly those of the English-speaking world) are happy to dismiss with Voltaire's famous witticism, "Ce corps qui s'appelait et qui s'appelle encore le saint empire romain n'était en aucune manière ni saint, ni romain, ni empire." [1]. In Sidney's day, however, it was definitely an organization to be reckoned with. Because Sidney's life centred in Vienna off and on for the next two years, some background is desirable here so that his abundant correspondence during this period may be read in proper perspective.

Founded by Charlemagne in the ninth century, the "triple Empire" had originally been a device for dividing the administration of three great areas of Christian Europe. But now, though the Empire was formally still intact, Italy had become separated and fragmented, and Burgundy ruined by internecine warfare. Only in Germany did the Holy Roman Empire continue in some semblance of its intended form of organization. Each successive Emperor received the crown in Frankfurt, centred his court in Vienna, and administered as best he could the territories from Alsace through Moravia and Bohemia.

Although the written opinions of contemporary jurists were based on the ostensible power of the Empire, its actual weakness lay in the fact that the Emperor did not hold full jurisdiction over a single acre of territory. The power structure, such as it was, rested on four levels. The first consisted of the seven Electors, who had the power to select a

---

1. *Essai sur les moeurs et l'esprit des nations* (Geneva, 1756), LXX.

successor on the death of the Emperor. Three of the Electors were spiritual (the Archbishops of Mainz, Cologne, and Trier), and four were temporal (the Electors of Saxony, Brandenburg, the Palatinate, and Bohemia). The second level was composed of the princes of constituent states; they totalled about eighty, fifty of whom were spiritual and the others temporal.

At the third level were the imperial cities; they numbered about sixty-six and were, on the whole, free from the control of local princes. These cities had seats in the Diet and paid their taxes directly to the Empire. Finally, on the fourth level were the lower imperial nobility, a total of about two thousand. Among them were about one hundred counts or lords of other rank, about fifty prelates, and a large number of imperial knights. In a fumbling attempt to cope with common problems, each of these four levels belonged to an association.

The ancient feudal structure of the Empire provided the chief form of unity. All princedoms and positions of rank were held by grace of the Emperor. The act of tenure required each new occupant to swear an oath of loyalty to the Emperor: on the succession of a new Emperor the oath had to be renewed. The laws of the imperial cities did not become valid until they received official approval from the Emperor. Thus the Emperor's actual power was confined mostly to matters of law. He controlled all matters of vassalage and all titles to principalities and other feudal divisions. In some areas the Emperor held criminal jurisdiction, but in others his powers were concurrent with those of the "Kammergericht," or High Court. To reduce the potential (sometimes actual) conflict in this concurrent jurisdiction, in 1559 a permanent Council was created. Its function became partly political, serving as Privy Council, and partly legal, as a Supreme Court.

Each prince existed at the centre of three concentric power circles. The first was his own domain, the lands in his private possession; the second encompassed the areas over which the prince exercised feudal powers; and the third involved lands which were more or less constitutionally independent but under his civil authority. During the sixteenth century this third area was undergoing change and development in a number of crucial ways. The changes occurred as individual princedoms attempted to extend their administrative power beyond the original limitations, with the purpose of attaining the status of a viable state or nation.

The social order of the Empire consisted of four broad ranks. At the top were the imperial nobility, followed by the territorial nobility and imperial knights. The urban bourgeoisie comprised the third rank, a broad and mobile group ranging from the bankers and prosperous merchants through members of the guilds down to the unorganized artisans and humbler workers. The fourth rank consisted of peasants, only a few of whom were yeomen farming their own land. Most of the peasants were dependent on their local lords in varying degrees. The increasing prosperity of the cities led to more and intensified competition between town and country interests. Expanding commerce prompted the building of better roads and services at the same time as the needs of the princes for additional tax revenues caused them to take firmer control of their territories. Creation of more effective and efficient administration to deal with these situations accelerated the trend towards becoming "proper" states. All these developments necessitated new laws, administrative devices, and procedures, most of which required application to the Emperor for his official approval.

Constitutional reforms were also called for, and a number of them evolved or were created during the first half of the sixteenth century. In effect these reforms strengthened the position of the Electors in their relationship to the Emperor. For example, the Electors were permitted to meet without the permission of the Emperor, and he agreed not to call an Imperial Diet without the consent of the Electors. Furthermore, the Emperor was bound to consult them on matters of foreign policy, taxation, and fiefs. Certain military reforms were also instituted.

When Sidney reached Vienna in the summer of 1573, Maximilian II had been Emperor for nine years. From his father, the Emperor Ferdinand, he had inherited a belief in toleration; though a Catholic by birth and upbringing, he once told the papal nuncio "I am neither Catholic nor Protestant, but a Christian." His opinions on Protestantism were more favourable to the Lutherans than to the Calvinists, but the struggles between the two sects (who fought each other more energetically than they did the Catholics) thwarted Maximilian's desire to balance the Protestants and Catholics evenly enough throughout the Empire to permit the spread of toleration. In the perspective of history Maximilian was born too early to realize his ideals: he aspired to carry out the dictum *Da pacem patriae* (give the country peace) but came to the throne in an age of denominational intolerance and religious warfare. He lacked, moreover, the organizational or economic means to fulfil his aims and the personal energy to overcome these handicaps.

Despite his political disappointments, Maximilian presided over the cultural Renaissance that had begun to flower in Vienna under his great-grandfather, Maximilian I. Well-educated and thoroughly literate, he spoke six languages besides his native German (Latin, French, Spanish, Italian, Czech, and Hungarian). He actively encouraged music and architecture, but the advancement of learning was his special interest. Under his trusted councillor, Caspar von Nidbruck, a staff of scholars searched Europe for books and manuscripts to serve as source materials for a great history of the Christian Church. Among the manuscripts brought to Vienna were the Codex Carolinus and the Boniface Letters. Maximilian also understood the care necessary to maintain his collection properly, and in 1575 he appointed the distinguished Dutch scholar Hugo Blotius as imperial librarian to organize and properly catalogue the enriched library.[2]

Similarly, Maximilian restored the University of Vienna to eminence in scholarship and established an atmosphere of tolerance by bringing in renowned Protestants such as the famous physician Johannes Crato von Crafftheim and the pioneer botanist Charles de l'Écluse. Clusius (as he is called) guided the Emperor's interests in natural science. A magnificent horticultural garden, the Tusculum at nearby Ebersdorf, contained rare trees, shrubs, and flowers, and other exotic plants. A zoo housed strange birds and animals, including brightly coloured parrots and the first elephant in central Europe. It also held lions, tigers, bears, and wolves.[3]

Maximilian's learned friends served as members of an informal Court Academy. In addition to those mentioned above, there was the Fleming, Ogier Ghislain de Busbecq, who occupied the trusted position of tutor to the Emperor's sons. For many years Busbecq had been Ambassador to the Sublime Porte, where he had collected ancient inscriptions and coins, as well as several hundred precious manuscripts. When he came to court he brought many exotic plants, including the first lilacs and tulips seen in Christendom. In due course Sidney came to know many members of this learned circle, some of them intimately. His sponsor was Hubert Languet, who had been Ambassador from Saxony to the Emperor's court for about six months.

2. Blotius developed the concept of a centralized library system, combining the books of the University with those in the Imperial Library. Maxmilian encouraged him by saying, "any library, however well-equipped, that is not open to use, is as a candle burning beneath an upturned bowl, the light of which none can see."

3. The elephant was brought from Spain in 1552, to the amazement of gaping crowds; its "house" on the Graben stood until 1865. Records of the zoo expenditures exist in the royal accounts, including such interesting charges as "For purging of the Lions."

The link between Languet and these learned men had been forged in the white heat of religious conviction; for, like him, de l'Écluse and Crato were protégés of Melanchthon, under the influence of whose penetrating and civilized intelligence both had been converted to Protestantism. They formed an inner circle among the intellectuals at the imperial court, and kept up a far-flung network of friendships in the whole European republic of learning. Once Languet had adopted Sidney as his protégé, he tirelessly coached him in current history, politics, and morals, and went out of his way to introduce Philip to enlightened friends. They in turn accepted Languet's sponsorship of the young Englishman as a passport to be honoured and responded by recommending him to other eminent friends.

Sidney's recent biographer, John Buxton, suggests that during his 1573 stay in Vienna he may have been a fellow lodger with Clusius in the house of Dr. Johannes Aichholtz, Professor of Medicine at the University of Vienna, who served several times as Dean of the Faculty. Buxton cites Languet's reference in a subsequent letter to Sidney to the "rough old gardeners, with whom you lived last year," and he comments, "The phrase, which must allude to de l'Écluse, suggests that Sidney may have lodged with him in the house of Dr. Aichholtz . . . who was always prompt to send friendly messages to Sidney in letters written to him from Vienna."[4] Howell echoes this "strong possiblility" and adds that Dr. Aichholtz "was noted as an amateur botanist."[5] Both Buxton and Howell overlook the fact that while Sidney was in Vienna de l'Écluse was in Antwerp. He left there on September 10 and did not reach Vienna until November, after Sidney's departure.[6] They also overlook a more pointed reference in the Languet-Sidney correspondence that Sidney and his friend (later cousin by marriage) Thomas Coningsby had stayed "in aedibus Raicheli."[7] Since Coningsby left for Venice in September,[8] without Sidney, Raichel's house or inn must have been in Vienna rather than along the road to Venice. Furthermore, later that year Sidney wrote to Languet[9] about a problem he and Coningsby had encountered at Raichel's (Raichel had exacted double payment by letting each pay for both). If Raichel's establishment were not in Vienna where Languet was

4. Buxton, p. 62; he used Pears's translation of Languet to Sidney.
5. Howell, p. 144.
6. F. W. T. Hunger, *Charles de l'Écluse* (s'-Gravenhage, 1927), I : 123–24.
7. Feuillerat, vol. 3, no. VIII, dated Dec. 19, 1573.
8. Languet to Sidney, Sept. 22, 1573.
9. Languet to Sidney, Dec. 4, 1573.

living, Sidney's consulting him about the difficulty would have been out of order.

Some of the eminent men with whom Sidney came to be on friendly terms during this first residence in Vienna can be identified in the abundant correspondence of subsequent months. The most conspicuous friendship was with another intimate of Languet, the French Ambassador Jean de Vulcob, Sieur de Sassy, of a leading family of Bourges in the Auvergne.[10] An intelligent and literate man who had the satisfaction of knowing that his King recognized his diligence,[11] Vulcob was kept very busy by his official responsibilities. Although he had been at London in 1568 as secretary to Ambassador Bochetel de la Fôret[12] and stayed on briefly after the Ambassador returned, there are no ascertainable links between him and Sidney's family. The Languet-Sidney correspondence is dotted with references to him, usually the exchange of friendly messages and greetings. The newly recovered correspondence contains four letters from Vulcob to Sidney and another letter from a friend to Vulcob mentioning Sidney. Although the letters are formal in tone and confined to the subjects of the moment, they are signed "Vostre bien obeissant et affectionne serviteur et amy" or variations of this, always with the term "affectionate" to distinguish Vulcob's and Sidney's relationship.

The same term appears in the one letter from a secretary in Vulcob's embassy, Jacques Bochetel, Sieur de la Fôret.[13] This Bochetel was Vulcob's cousin and about Sidney's own age. Both his letter to Sidney and the frequent references to him in Sidney's other correspondence suggest that they shared a common outlook on activities more appropriate to nineteen-year-old youths than to the sage ambassadors of France and Saxony.

Sidney was also well acquainted with Antonio Abondio, a gifted medalist and sculptor from Riva di Trento who was already recognized for his abilities in bas-relief.[14] In 1571 he had received a payment from Maximilian as "pittore de corte," but his chief honours came in February 1574 when he was ennobled as an imperial "cameriere" and in December 1574 when he received the official status of "Kaiserlicher Majestät

10. *Grand Armorial*, 6 : 499.

11. Charles IX had thanked him through Henry of Valois on June 16, 1572 (Bibl. Nat. MS. fr. 3318, fol. 19).

12. *CSPS2*, p. 72.

13. Born Jacques Castelnau-Mauvissière, he was adopted as heir by his uncle, Jacques Bochetel. See *Dictionnaire de biographie française*, ed. J. Balteau, et al. (Paris, 1933–), 6 : 749–50.

14. See Fritz Dworschak, *Antonio Abondio, Medaglista e Ceroplasta 1538–1591* (Trento 1958).

Wachsbossierer und Conterfeter." Because of this last honour Sidney's recent biographers have assumed that an "image" Abondio made of Sidney was done in wax.[15] Considering the nature of Abondio's known work, a profile in wax with paint added to the garments seems reasonable. The Latin words in the Languet-Sidney letters ("tuae imaginis," "fecit," and "effigiem") provide no real clue. Because Sidney had a copy which he sent to Languet,[16] Abondio must have worked easily in his medium. Actually, Abondio could have portrayed Sidney in any medium from a charcoal sketch to a bronze medal. A medal, however, would have required long and expensive labour, and copies would have had the strongest chance for survival. The odds favour a wax portrait, head and shoulders in profile, since no trace of Abondio's head of Sidney has ever been found, though eagerly sought.[17]

Finally, to the people Sidney knew at Vienna in 1573 should be added Lazarus von Schwendi, famed fighter against the Turks and Commander-in-chief of the Emperor's forces in Hungary. In addition to being an able leader in the field, General von Schwendi was an articulate author and an authority on military theory and practice. That he and Sidney found each other congenial is indicated by the fact that Sidney wrote a letter to the General shortly after the former left Vienna for Italy.[18] The new letters also reveal that Sidney came to know the General's son, Hans Wilhelm von Schwendi, then studying abroad under the care of Hugo Blotius.[19]

In late August or early September Sidney made an excursion down the Danube to Bratislava (better known by its German name, Pressburg), about forty miles from Vienna in Hungary. That nation had been under Hapsburg rule since 1526, so intercourse between Bratislava and Vienna had long been frequent and easy. Whether Sidney had any motive besides the wish for a brief observation of another nation we do not know. Indeed, little is known beyond the detail found in Languet's letter

15. Languet to Sidney, Jan. 15, 1574.

16. Sidney to Languet, Feb. 4, 1574.

17. See Berta Siebeck, *Das Bild Sir Philip Sidneys* (Weimar, 1939), p. 178; and A. C. Judson, *Sidney's Appearance: A Study in Elizabethan Portraiture* (Bloomington, Ind., 1958), p. 24. In Dworschak's study of Abondio no mention of his "image" of Sidney occurs.

18. Languet to Sidney, Nov. 19, 1573.

19. Buxton (p. 59) states that Théophile de Banos, former secretary to Ramus, was also in Vienna at this time; but his source (*De Vita P. Rami . . .* , 1576) does not indicate that de Banos was there in 1573 rather than during one of Sidney's later visits.

Charles de l'Écluse

to Sidney of September 22, 1573. Because it is the first of this famous
series of deeply personal letters, it is quoted here in full.

> I thank you for having written to me from Bratislava as a token of
> your friendship, and I am pleased to hear that my introduction so
> impressed Dr. Purkircher that he showed you the courtesies which
> your virtue and manners deserve. I have seen him here and thanked
> him for this, and have proved that I owe him more than if he had done
> the same for me. But I have reason to complain about you; for I did
> not think you had so ill an opinion of me as not to confide your
> plans to me. Perhaps you feared that I would prepare an ambush for
> you along your way. When you left here you said that you would
> not be gone for more than three days. But now, like a little bird
> that has forced its way through the bars of its cage, your delight makes
> you restless, flitting hither and yon, perhaps without a thought for
> your friends; and you scarcely guard against the dangers that so
> often occur on such journeys.
>
> I do admire your noble eagerness to "observe the manners and
> cities of many men," as the poet says, for this is the best way to
> develop judgement and master our feelings; but I regret that you
> have no one to converse with along the way about various subjects,
> no one to tell you about the manners and customs of the peoples
> you visit, to introduce you to learned men, and when necessary to
> serve as an interpreter. I might perhaps have found you such a
> travelling companion, had you wished to tell me about your plan. I
> write as I do because I am anxious about you, and about the glorious
> flowering of your noble character which, I hope, will eventually
> bring forth the delightful fruits of your many virtues.
>
> I am giving this letter to Dr. Purkircher who will meet you in
> Neapolis [Wiener Neustadt] (but not that Neapolis rendered
> notorious by the Sirens' song), so that as you ride you may meditate
> on how to reply to the charges of your friends. Your comrade
> Coningsby has already made a quick passage of the Alps, for he left
> here a week ago. Farewell, and come back to us. Vienna, September
> 22, 1573.

Inferences made from this letter and a few other facts permit the following
reconstruction of this brief expedition, which Sidney apparently expected
would keep him away no longer than a journey from, say, London to
Reading and back. Whether he travelled down to Bratislava on the

Danube or by road, he probably took Bryskett, Griffin, and his horses. Otherwise this excursion to Wiener Neustadt would have been much less easily undertaken. Dr. George Purkircher[20] and Sidney obviously took to each other warmly. Purkircher's attitude is clear from Languet's testimony and from the fact that he and Sidney had agreed to meet at Wiener Neustadt at the end of September. Three years later de l'Écluse wrote Sidney that he and Purkircher had dined in Vienna and the latter "toasted you in excellent Austrian wine, saying that when he got home he would do it again, in even better Hungarian wine."[21] Fortunately, the newly recovered letters include Purkircher's letter to Sidney, which de l'Écluse had enclosed with his (see below pp. 435–38). It reveals that Sidney's letter to de l'Écluse, which had prompted the two in reply, told of Sidney's drinking a toast to Dr. Purkircher in French wine.

Quite possibly the idea of exchanging toasts began at a banquet in Bratislava to which Purkircher had taken Sidney. In his *Defence of Poesie* Sidney coupled the experience of feeling "my heart moved more than with a Trumpet" by "the old song of Percy and Douglas" with a parallel experience on his travels: "In *Hungarie* I have seene it the manner of all Feastes, and other such meetings, to have songs of their ancestors valure, which that right souldierlike nation, think one of the chiefest kindlers of brave courage." Since there is no record of Sidney's venturing into Hungary during later visits to Vienna, he must have crowded more than one carousal into his few weeks there in 1573, even allowing for poetic licence in his phrase, "all Feastes, and other such meetings."

After crossing the Danube, Sidney's route from Bratislava to Wiener Neustadt probably took him south by the Nieusiedler See. The fifteen-mile expanse of this far from picturesque lake was probably the largest body of freshwater Sidney had yet seen. Of his return to Vienna and the rest of his time there no record exists. He had only about three weeks to pack, terminate his affairs, and make farewell calls on friends before retracing the path to Wiener Neustadt. From there he proceeded through the Semmering Pass to Klagenfurt and Bad Villach, descending through the Carnio Alps to Udine and Venice. Since couriers needed about eight days to travel with letters from Vienna to Venice and Sidney's party had no reason to press, they doubtless left the banks of the Danube about

20. Aside from the Sidney correspondence very little about the learned Doctor of Bratislava is known. He died of the plague in 1577 (Languet to Sidney, Nov. 28, 1577). See also Hunger, *Charles de l'Écluse.*

21. De l'Écluse to Sidney, June 8, 1576 (BM Add. MS. 15914, fols. 29, 31).

Monday, October 26.[22] In any case, on Friday, November 6, Sidney was well enough established in Venice to call on the Venetian correspondent of the Italian merchant banker in London, Acerbo Vellutelli. Since Sidney drew on the banker for the then enormous sum of £400, it would appear that he needed money for bills he had run up in Vienna.[23] At the same time he established a credit to begin his winter in Italy.[24]

Sidney spent nearly all November and December 1573 in Venice, but he found the city less attractive and interesting than the rapturous reports of other travellers had led him to expect. Opinions differed then as now: some saw Venice as the Virgin City, the ceremony of whose betrothal to the sea was celebrated by a festival every summer, and others considered it "the Whore of the Adriatic." The rich ornamentation on the buildings dazzled the eye, but the structures were imitative and usually undistinguished. The climate was renowned as extremely healthy, yet nearly all houses discharged their sewage into the open canals. Famed as a republic, the government was actually a tightly run oligarchy, since 1296 rigorously controlled by a closed caste system. The contrast of this system with the mobility between classes in Tudor England, where landholders, military commanders, courtiers, and even prosperous merchants could rise to the nobility must have been apparent to Sidney.

The Venetians had perverted the Fourth Crusade in 1205 to sack their chief rival, the Byzantine capital city of Constantinople, thus gaining a monopoloy of Levantine trade until 1453, and had recently joined in crushing the Turkish fleet at Lepanto; but they had overextended their resources. The decline in Venetian power set in immediately, and when Sidney arrived there late in 1573 Cyprus had already been lost. Venetian control over its mainland provinces was overshadowed by Spanish dominance of the upper Po Valley; Spain, now in league with the Pope, ruled Italy. Economically the greatest blow came from the discovery of the Cape route to the Orient. Venice no longer "held the gorgeous East in fee."

22. Fynes Moryson followed this route in 1594, taking fourteen days from Vienna to Padua. *Itinerary* (London, 1617), pp. 67–68.

23. The receipt is preserved at Penshurst as Wallace first pointed out (p. 115, n. 1).

24. While Sidney was travelling from Vienna to Bratislava and then to Venice, back in England marriage negotiations were being carried on in his name with a daughter of Henry Fitzharding (1543–1613), seventh Baron Berkeley, apparently on the initiative of the Earl of Leicester (Wallace, pp. 160–61). The talks came to nothing and Sidney may never have known they were in progress.

Nevertheless, abundant evidence of the days of Venetian glory remained, most notably in the sumptuously elaborate facades of buildings. One of the most famous was St. Mark's Cathedral, adorned for centuries with the riches of the Orient including the incomparable bronze horses seized in the sack of Constantinople. Venetian painting was at its apogee; though Titian was over ninety, Tintoretto was only fifty-five, and Veronese forty-five. As an international trading centre Venice's piazzas were thronged with visitors from all countries and its shops were filled with exotic merchandise. The canals and the busy life circulating through them were unique and highly spectacular, though ten years before Sidney's arrival an edict required all the gaily coloured gondolas to be painted a uniform black.

Venice had been and continued to be the greatest pleasure-city in Christendom, renowned for its balls and masked carnivals, and notorious for the professional status of its recognized courtesans. They numbered in the thousands, and Thomas Coryat reported a few decades later "the reuenues which they pay vnto the Senate for their tolleration, doe maintaine a dozen of their galleys ... and so saue them a great charge."[25] Coryat devoted several pages of his detailed discourse to a description of this famed sorority, of which a brief sample may be quoted:

> For so infinite are the allurements of these amorous Calypsoes, that the fame of them hath drawn many from some of the remotest parts of Christendome, to contemplate their beauties, and enjoy their pleasing dalliances. And indeede such is the variety of the delicious obiects they minister to their lovers, that they want nothing tending to delight.[26]

With evident relish he goes on to describe the elegant palaces of the courtesans, their silk robes and chains of jewels, their skill at music or at conversation and "Rhetoricall tongues."

How much attention the nineteen-year-old Philip Sidney gave to these sirens (despite their rhetorical abilities) is unknown. More important to him was the fact that Venice was considered the "academy of politics." Not only did its oligarchy (alias "republic") represent the only government in any major state other than hereditary monarchy (or aristocracy), but it functioned as a centre of international diplomacy and intelligence.

25. Coryat, p. 265.
26. Ibid.

Venice was still the listening post for news of the Turk and other Oriental powers. Just as the diplomats of the twentieth century have cocked their ears for the latest news about the enigmatic Russians and the inscrutable Chinese, so in Sidney's day the intentions of the terrible Turk were the constant concern of Europeans. Equally important, Venice served as the vent through which news from Rome passed to most of the world. Hence reports from the ambassadors at Venice to their governments were a primary source of foreign intelligence. These topics appear quite often in Sidney's correspondence.

Surprisingly, twelve letters exist for the two months Sidney spent in Venice. Only three of them are new to us, but, taken with the known Languet-Sidney correspondence, they cast some light on Sidney's life and friendships and even more on the state of civilization as experienced by these Renaissance worthies. Although the difference of eight days or more between the dates when the letters were penned and when they were received places chronology on a rocking horse, the best way to treat them is to take each in order.

The earliest is addressed to Sidney on November 19 by Languet in Vienna. Because he had not yet heard from Sidney, despite their vows of *amicitia* when they parted, Languet began by chiding him (with rhetorical variations and flourishes) for neglecting his promise to write frequently. After this peroration Languet then explained a second letter which he enclosed with his own:

> I am sending you a letter from Pietro Bizari of Perugia, so that you may unceasingly contemplate its remarkable style and keep it ever before you as a model. You will see how impudently you English acted in not appreciating such great qualities or giving them the honour they deserved. You have begrudged yourselves the immortality he would have conferred upon you by his eloquence had you known how to exploit your good fortune and the opportunity of obliging so great a man.
>
> How much more wisely we Saxons acted—we showed more good sense in one hour than you in all of fifteen years. For we realized at once how we could procure his goodwill, and we seized upon the opportunity. Show me a countryman of yours about whom he has expressed such magnificent sentiments as he does about the recipient of this letter. I have pilfered it from him to gladden and delight you, so please make use of it in such a way as not to stir up a hornets' nest

or to arouse an uproar against us. Nevertheless, you may cull some flowers from it to adorn your letter if you ever write to its author, for I feel that he is worthy of being painted in his own colours.

Languet's letter appeared in his 1633 *Epistolae ad Philippum Sydnaeum*, and writers on Sidney have known about this enclosure only what Languet wrote about it. By good fortune the original letter from Bizari to Vulcob is preserved among the newly recovered correspondence. Although the letter is too long to insert here, two excerpts should be noted.[27] The first provides evidence that Bizari, an Umbrian who had become a Protestant and visited England in 1565, was a paid news-gatherer for Burghley, a fact Bizari had no reluctance about revealing to Vulcob. Bizari's position explains his letters (from Augsburg where he had settled) to Burghley, summarized in the *Calendar of State Papers Foreign* for 1573 and 1578–79. He told Vulcob, "I rejoice in the generosity of my patroness, the Queen of England, i.e. an annual pension of 100 Talers . . ."

The second excerpt concerns us more: "If the English Master Sidney has not yet left, you will do me a great favour if you will present my most humble respects to him." Languet's teasing suggestion that Sidney enter into correspondence with Bizari shows the amusement with which the diplomatic set viewed Bizari's use of such an ornate rhetorical style in the relation of journalistic subject matter, on the peddling of which the erudite historian was now dependent for his livelihood. This extravagant style was less out of place in Bizari's historical works.[28]

To return to Languet's letter of November 19 to Sidney, it concluded with an important sentence: "I have sent your letter to my lord von Schwendi, asking him to answer it, as I hope he will." The mere fact that Sidney had written to the great military man substantiates the more than casual nature of their relationship before Sidney had met the General's son, who was then travelling through Italy under the guidance of the famous Dr. Blotius. Sidney's path did not cross that of the son until a year later when he returned to Vienna.

27. A letter Bizari wrote to Burghley on the same day (Oct. 15, 1573) as he wrote this letter to Vulcob shows how such informants eked maximum mileage from their material (*CSPF1*, no. 1195). For the text of Bizari's letter to Vulcob, see "Sidney and Bizari," in *Renaissance Quarterly* 24, no. 3, where I have summarized their relationship.

28. Of these, the most recently published at the time were the *Historia della guerra fatte in Vngheria dall' inuittissimo imperatore de Christiani, contro quello de Turchi* (Lyons, 1569), and two works published in 1573: the *Cyprium Bellum inter Venetos, & Selymum Turcam gestum* (Basle, 1573), and the *Epitome Insignium Europae Historiarum* (Basle, 1573).

Languet wrote again on November 27, once more complaining that no letter had yet arrived from Sidney in the month since he had set out for Italy. The cult of *amicitia* provides a framework for Lanquet's attitude: "Yet this is one of the laws of friendship: that, as far as we can, we should relieve friends who are anxious about us of their concern and anxiety." It also shows Languet's very genuine personal admiration for Sidney.

> This lapse, however, cannot uproot or overturn my conviction of your steadfastness, although I realize that my abilities and circumstances are so modest that I possess nothing which could have made you fond of me, except perhaps this one thing: you knew that in my admiration for you I cherish the high hopes about your virtue which you inspire in all those who know you.

A week later Vulcob wrote a brief reply to a letter he had received from Sidney a few days earlier. From the distance of four centuries the attention devoted to the progress and route taken by Henry of Anjou, as yet uncrowned King of Poland, on his way to take possession of his throne, may seem excessive. The drama contemporaries saw in Henry's progress is clear in one of Bizari's letters to Lord Burghley, written late in October 1573: "Different reports as to the route which the King of Poland will take towards his kingdom, which will not be safe through Germany on account of the large sums owing by his brother to the reiters [cavalry mercenaries] and through the retention of Metz." [29] Here is Vulcob's letter translated from the original French:

> Sir,
> I shall be most happy, in reply to the letter which you were pleased to write to me on the twenty-first of last November, to be able to send you a correct account of the probable whereabouts of the King of Poland, in spite of the fact that where you are you will hear news of it as soon as we do here. He was expected at Alken (a small town in the Palatinate) all last month and, if a man I am waiting for had arrived, I believe I should be able to tell you the exact day of his passage there. As it is, I shall hope to include this in my next letter or in the one after that. In the meantime I shall use what remains of the present letter to ask you, Sir, to consider that you neither have nor will have servant or friend more attentive to your wishes than

29. *CSPF*1, p. 435, no. 1210.

myself; I most humbly present my respects to your benevolence, and
pray God to grant you,

Sir, good health and a long and happy life. From Vienna, this third
of December, 1573.

Your most obedient and affectionate servant and friend,

J. de Vulcob

The next day, December 4, Languet also wrote to Sidney, so the same
carrier may have had both letters in his pouch. Languet had finally
received a reply from Sidney (it is no longer extant) so that his im-
patience and worry were now assuaged.

But why do I take such pains to apologize, when I was planning a
still sharper letter at the moment I received the one you sent me
upon your arrival in Venice? That letter has dispelled the cloud from
my heart and has truly gladdened me with the news that you had
safely arrived at your destination and had not forgotten me. I was
also particularly pleased with your promise not to neglect any
opportunity of writing. But see that you fulfil your promise.

The letter next reveals that Languet had arranged for Sidney to meet
another Philip, the Count of Hanau who, like Sidney, was young, able,
and destined for prominence in the Protestant cause. Hanau and his
master-of-household, Paul von Welsperg, had been in Paris during the
August of 1572, but the passage below shows that Sidney had not known
them there.[30] Once acquainted, the two Philips became close friends, as
later chapters will delineate. Then only twenty, Hanau became a patron
to Languet and other Protestant intellectuals. The Sidney correspondence
is dotted with references to Hanau, his name appearing more than thirty
times.

I am glad that you have found my words about the kindness of the
Count of Hanau and his party to be true. By my letters I wanted
simply to give you the opportunity to meet men who, I believed,
love and admire excellence in any man whatever, since I had no doubt
that your behaviour would readily be able to win their favour. And
wherever you go you will not be without good men to receive you
with kindness, provided you are not untrue to yourself or change in

30. Von Welsperg had warned Lucas Geizkofler to leave the house of Andreas Wechel.
See *Geizkofler*, p. 65.

spirit. . . . I do not wish you to do anything to please me which you do not think you would find pleasant and profitable; nor do I want you to be bound by any promise you have made me, beyond your promise to be extremely careful of your health and safety, and not to follow your own desire or the talk of the people who discount the danger in which you would put yourself if you should travel to the places which we have often spoken of together. . . .

I would by no means have spent the winter here if the expectation of seeing you, or at least of conversing with you by letter from not too far away, had not detained me. I thank Master Coningsby heartily for obtaining the goodwill of your party for me by declaring that I had done him services which I never had. I should like to be able to do him a favour worthy of that kindness. Please pay him my respects, and also Master Bryskett, to whom I feel most indebted because he guided you safely to your destination. . . . I beg you not to show anyone the foolish letters I am in the habit of sending you. I write without thinking whatever my changeable moods suggest, and am satisfied if I can make you believe that nothing is dearer to me than you. Please give me your full opinion of the people to whom I gave you letters of introduction. Farewell. Vienna, December 4, 1573.

The only other point in Languet's letter that requires explanation is Sidney's "promise" to Languet. Like other travellers from northern Europe, Sidney had a strong desire to visit Rome and other cities in the Pope's dominions. But Languet realized that the mild attitude toward Protestants and their freedom of movement in Venice and the city-states of northern Italy did not exist south of the Apennines. Enough sad cases existed to show how dangerous it was for Protestants to venture into the papal territories. The Inquisition still pursued heretics with fervour and not many Protestants slipped through its nets. Fortunately, Languet warned Sidney so strongly that he kept his promise despite the glamorous adventures that beckoned beyond the southern horizon.

The first extant letter from Sidney to Languet is dated December 5. (He wrote twice earlier but neither letter is known to have been preserved.) It gives a few details about Sidney and his life in Venice.

I certainly do not say, "It is of little consequence to you to know this," for I well know how "full of anxious fear love is," but I will say this, and say it truthfully, that I came upon absolutely no one who was travelling towards Vienna. As to your implied charge that my affection for you is waning, affection which was and always will be my tribute to your surpassing virtue, I acknowledge your kindness; but I very earnestly beg you always, no matter how great the distance between us, to be sure that I am not so full of childish stupidity, womanly fickleness, or brutish ingratitude as not eagerly to seek the friendship of such a man; once having acquired it not to cultivate it; and, having cultivated it, not to show myself thankful for it. Oh, that I had skill enough in Latin, or you in English! Then you would see what a scene I would have made about those doubts of yours. Since arriving in Venice I have received two letters from you, but I am now writing you for the third time. And this is the arrangement to which I ask that we adhere, to converse by letter each week.

I shall constantly keep in mind what you say about taking risks, just as I do all your advice. But you will shortly have me with you, as I wrote you in my last letter. I have carefully read the delightful letter of Pietro Bizari of Perugia and have culled some flowers from it, which I imitated since I could not readily improve on them. I have not yet written more than once to Master de Vulcob; when I have improved my style a little, I shall do so more often. In the meantime, please pay my respects to him, and also to Master Bochetel. The French Ambassador received me very courteously; Perrot has returned to France, but his brother read the letter. Laski has gone to Poland. I have not yet been able to learn anything about Danus.

Please write to me, at long last, about yourself. And let me know when the King of Poland is to relieve France of his presence, so that it will be easier for me to prepare for my journey. Farewell. Venice, December 5, 1573.

Yours very affectionately,

Ph. Sidney

The French Ambassador, to whom Sidney had promptly presented Languet's letter of introduction, was Arnaud du Ferrier (ca. 1506–85), who had held the post for ten years. A native of Toulouse, in his youth he had studied law at Padua where he acquired an open-minded attitude, though he did not formally adopt Protestantism until his retirement to the court of Navarre.

François Perrot de Mésières (1530–ca. 1611), a Huguenot who had chosen to live in Venice, became Sidney's friend, and half a dozen of his letters to Sidney are among the recently recovered correspondence.

Perrot wrote poetry in Italian, Latin, and French and published several prose works, some of them translations.[31] He had several brothers, one of whom, Matthieu, also an ardent Protestant, was registered as a citizen of Geneva. The brother in Venice who read Sidney's letter of introduction from Languet probably was Denys; he is mentioned by name in a letter from Wolfgang Zündelin to Joachim Camerarius.[32]

Olbracht Laski (1533–97), Palatine of Sieradz and now in 1573 the head of a rich and powerful Polish family, had spent his early years at the Imperial Court in Vienna. His name appears later in the Sidney correspondence, and in 1583, when he visited England, Sidney accompanied him in a call on Dr. John Dee.[33] Languet gave Sidney an introduction to Laski in order to lay the groundwork for Sidney's projected journey to Poland.

"Danus" can now be identified as Johannes Laurentius Danus, a German medical student in Padua. He died there on August 3, 1575, and because he was a Protestant the city authorities would not let him be buried in consecrated ground. The ensuing dispute between the authorities and the German "nation" was resolved when the latter consulted its valued ex-procurator, Wolfgang Zündelin. Zündelin, part of whose reply survives, strongly—and successfully—advised his young compatriots to drop their demands, in order not to jeopardize their considerable religious liberties.[34]

31. Among Perrot's published writings are: *Aviso piaceuole dato alla Bella Italia . . .* (Munich, 1586); *Salmi di David, tradotti in lingua volgare Italiana . . .* (Geneva, 1603). For information about him see E. Picot, *Les français italianisants au xvie siècle*, 2 vols. (Paris, 1906). For an examination of their relationship see Martha W. England, "Sir Philip Sidney and François Perrot de Méssières: Their Verse Versions of the Psalms," *Bulletin of the New York Public Library*, vol. 75, no. 1 (1971), pp. 30–54; no. 2, pp. 101–10.

32. Dated Aug. 18, 1575; Zündelin-Camerarius Correspondence, vol. 1, no. 47. These two volumes of manuscripts are in the Munich State Library, Cod. lat. 10371, 10372; a microfilm of them is at Yale.

33. Wallace (p. 296) pointed out the following entries in Dr. Dee's *Diary*, ed. C. F. Smith (1909), p. 20: "May 13th, I became acquainted with Albertus Laski at 7½ at night, in the Erle of Lecester his chamber in the court at Greenwich . . . May 18th, the Prince Albertus Laski came to me at Mortlake, with only two men. He cam at affernone and tarryed supper, and after sone set . . . June 15th, abowt 5 of the clok cam the Polonian Prince Lord Albert Lasky down from Bissham, where he had lodged the night before, being returned from Oxford . . . He had in his company Lord Russell, Sir Philip Sydney, and other gentlemen: he was rowed by the Quene's men, he had the barge covered with the Quene's cloth, the Quene's trumpeters, &c. He cam of purpose to do me honor, for which God be praysed! June 19th, the Lord Albert Laski cam to me and lay at my hows all nyght."

34. See the *Acta* of the German "nation" for 1575, now in the Vatican library, shelfmark Italia II, Veneto 2, I (13) p. 183 and (15) pp. 99–101.

A fortnight later the courier from Vienna again brought two letters for Sidney. The earlier, dated December 10, came from his young French friend, Jacques Bochetel, then serving in the embassy of Jean de Vulcob. Obviously, Languet had spread the news that he had finally heard from Sidney, which prompted Bochetel to write as follows:

> Sir,—
>   Having heard from Master Languet that you had arrived at Venice in good health—for which praise be to God—I take this opportunity of writing to you; to honour the promise I made you at your departure from here, always to show you the hearty desire I have to serve you all my life.
>   But enough of this: I must tell you that our hostess was much incensed because you did not take your leave of her when you departed. Had this not been the case, I had intended to take your place during your absence, but I have not dared to visit her since. I believe, however, that by now you must have forgotten all about it, in view of the new delights you must have found over there. I wish I were with you to keep you company.
>   A Polish gentleman from the best circles in Poland stopped here, sent by the King of Poland to invite the Emperor to the coronation. His name is Martin Deobori. Since he had heard much talk of you, and especially of your excellence and courtesy, he begged me to write to you, telling you that, should you by any chance visit Poland (as we told him it was your intention to do), you must not stay in any house but his, and that he will consider this a great favour. When you stop here again you will hear more news of this— I fear only that those lovely courtesans will keep you there! But I will make an end; and, having paid my humble respects to your benevolence, will pray God,
> Sir, to keep you in perfect health, and to grant you a most long and happy life. From Vienna, Austria, this tenth of December.
>   Your most humble and affectionate servant and friend,
>   Bochetel

Neither the identity of "our hostess" nor the nature of her relationship with Sidney, a relationship to which Bochetel had aspired to succeed, can be determined. The tone of the letter suggests that Sidney and Bochetel shared a youthful interest, common to most young men, in "those lovely courtesans." The young Pole, whose name appears elsewhere as Debori and Deoderi, has also escaped identification.

The second letter, written the next day, is simply another report on Henry's progress through Germany on his way to receive the crown of Poland.

Sir,

These few words serve only to honour my promise by keeping you informed of the King of Poland's progress to his kingdom— although where you are you may well have sufficient information on the subject already. He left Nancy on the twenty-third of last month, and I have since heard by express messenger that my Lord the Elector Palatine has written to the Senate of Frankfurt-am-Main, telling them that the great King would enter his lands on the twenty-eighth of last month. This agrees with the information I mentioned previously. I imagine that he must [now] be leaving for Hessen or Thuringia.

As I do not wish to bother you with a longer letter, I here present my humble and affectionate respects to your benevolence, and pray God to grant you,

Sir, [good] health, and a long and happy life. From Vienna, this eleventh of December, 1573.

Your most humble servant and affectionate friend,

J. de Vulcob

Most of the extant correspondence from this Venetian visit is between Sidney and Languet. Because these letters are so revealing, no summary or paraphrase could be as satisfactory as the writers' own sentences. In them we feel the presence of the two personalities and share in the flow of mind between them. Hence in this chapter either Languet or Sidney will hold the pen on most of the pages.

On December 12 when Languet answered Sidney's "second letter" (now missing), he continued his rhetorical banter about the promises of friends and "the laws of friendship," examining the circumstances which justified bending promises or breaking laws. The question of whether Sidney planned to attend Henry's coronation as King of Poland had now to be settled because the date had been advanced. Concerning Deobori, Languet wrote:

> When I learned that he was a man of character I took care to make his acquaintance. This I did easily enough, and even became somewhat intimate with him: I have, I hope, made a friend. Of course I did this the more eagerly because he seems not unlike you in grace, spirit, and manners as well as in fine looks; he is not many years older than you. He has studied letters in Italy, and is particularly fond of reading history, and especially recent history. His appearance and the number of his servants show that he comes from an illustrious family.
>
> What is the purpose of all this? I shall tell you. I mentioned you to him, described both yourself and your lineage and, saying that I still hoped you would go to Cracow for the King's coronation, asked him to show you such courtesy as your virtue deserves. He was at once inspired with high regard for you, and told me, "If you can persuade him to visit me, I shall see to it that neither he nor you will regret it." You perceive that a hospitable reception has been prepared for you, and that you are being given a chance to make the acquaintance of eminent men, and I hope, to form friendships with some of them.

Mention has already been made of Sidney's lack of enthusiasm for

Venice, despite the praises heaped on it by other travellers. Languet wrote:

> I gather from your letter that the splendours of Venice have not met your expectations. Nevertheless, Italy has nothing else to compare with them; so if you disdain these, the rest will hold no charms at all for you. But you will admire the talents and sagacity of the people; they are certainly clear-sighted and clever, yet among them are many who belie the promise of their appearance, for they are wont by an excess of ostentation to corrupt their character to the point of rottenness. Even if our Germans have less versatile talents, perhaps they do not fall much short of the Italians in soundness of judgement. Yet because I have been away from Italy for so many years, these things are not for me to judge: I shall hear your opinion when you return.

If Sidney's letter should ever turn up, his comments on Venice and the Venetians would make fascinating reading. Until that occurs we can only recall Sidney's letter to his brother Robert, written in May 1578, "touching the direccion of his travayle," which reads in part:

> As for Italy I knowe not what wee have, or can have to doe with them, but to buye their scilkes and wynes, and for other provinces (excepting Venice) whose good lawes, & customes wee can hardly proporcion to our selves, because they are quite of a contrarie government, there is little there but tyranous oppression, & servile yeilding to them, that have little or noe rule over them. And for the men you shall have there, although some in deede be excellentlie lerned, yett are they all given to soe counterfeit lerning, as a man shall learne of them more false groundes of thinges, then in anie place ells that I doe knowe for from a tapster upwardes they are all discoursers. In fine certaine quallities, as Horsmanshipp, Weapons, Vauting, and such like, are better there then in those other countries, for others more sounde they doe little excell neerer places.[1]

To return to Languet's letter, the greater part consists of news about public affairs, the invasion of Lithuania by the Muscovite, the Emperor's hope for extending the truce with the Turk, the attempt of the King of Spain to bribe the Pashas, the progress of the King of Poland, the sad

---

1. Feuillerat, 3:127.

state of affairs in France, and reports on the struggle against the Spanish occupation in the Low Countries. Languet ended on a personal level:

> If I wished to please myself, I would never stop writing to you. Again I ask you not to show anyone my letters for I carelessly throw into them whatever comes to my mind, so that they contain few things that follow a coherent order; and perhaps I often repeat the same things, for I do not remember what I have previously written you. Farewell, and please pay my respects to our friends, particularly to his Excellency the Count of Hanau, if you are with him again. Vienna, the winter solstice, 1573.

Languet wrote again on December 18, beginning with the usual banter: "to jest with you, as is the custom among friends." He then launched into a discussion of Sidney's future travel plans.

> You write that I should have no doubts that you will come to the Polish Diet, because you promised me to do so. Yet I am neither pressing this promise nor suggesting that you come; for it would be difficult for you to cross the Alps a second time. Indeed, I advised you against an Italian journey when I saw winter approaching and knew that before it ended the Polish King would be crowned. I wished you to see his coronation, for you would have seen many things which you would have been glad to learn about, and I do not think that you would have regretted the trouble involved.
>
> If anyone who is eager to learn many things asked me what I particularly advised him to investigate for himself I would answer: those things which he does not think he can easily learn at second hand. Now, few—indeed, practically none—of your countrymen are so well acquainted with Polish affairs that they could give you accurate information to help you understand them.
>
> The election of this king will make the Poles better known among you English, or will at least make more people curious about them: hence, some day you might regret not having made yourself better versed in their affairs. Similarly, you would have regretted not having seen the splendour of the Polish court, which is great indeed. Moreover, you would have found much to approve in the ways of the Polish people, and perhaps have experienced greater kindness than you might find here. It is both an adornment and a pleasure to have knowledge which others lack. I see that your sailors' voyages through

the Arctic Ocean have taught your compatriots much about the Russians, the Tartars, and even the Persians, that was previously unknown to them. Such things your men of spirit recount to foreigners, to the great pleasure of themselves and their audience and, what is more, to the glory of your nation. On my travels I have seen most of the lands of Christendom, but I remember no voyage with greater pleasure than that which I made to the far north: for there I observed much that none at home could have taught me, things which I should not have believed had I learned of them from the lips of others.

Although nothing would have been a greater joy to me here than your company, I have never advised you to stay, but urged you instead to leave for Meissen and Saxony and there to await the coming of the King of Poland, meanwhile observing the customs and the way of life in those lands and making friends with men of integrity. And so you see that when I tried to dissuade you from visiting Italy, I was not thinking only of my personal preference.

I have indeed implored you to visit only those parts of Italy where you would not be in danger of any kind. I have asked you this repeatedly and spoken about it more emphatically than of anything else. But who is not grateful when a friend, who is anxious and concerned for one's welfare, behaves as a friend should, even if there be no cause for his concern and anxiety? So take care not to censure me again for my boldness: it is impelled by my exceeding love for you.

Remember that I fully respect and admire the brilliance of your lineage and all the other gifts with which nature and fortune have so kindly and generously endowed you. But remember also that as a friend my only regard is for the excelling spirit, the love of virtue, and the great integrity which you so radiantly display. For should I encounter a young man of no means whatever who resembled you in manner and spirit, most certainly I should make him my adopted son and the heir to all I possess. Nor would I consider it my business to inquire after his family.

However, I feel I shall have reaped the rich fruit of our friendship, if, before I die, I hear that you have entered into rank and power, that you are flourishing in your native land, and that you have obtained the just rewards of your signal virtue. Farewell. Vienna, December 18, 1573.

The reference to Sidney's unkind reception in Vienna is difficult to explain. Certainly the learned friends of the Languet circle were warm in their welcome, as abundant evidence testifies. On the other hand, there is no record that Sidney was invited to any functions at the Emperor's court or that he was presented to Maximilian himself during this first visit to Vienna. Aside from the lukewarm negotations fifteen years earlier over a possible marriage between Elizabeth and Maximilian or his brother Rudolph, contacts between Vienna and England were few. England seemed as distant as Ultima Thule; furthermore, it was populated by aggressive heretics. Indeed, there are no references to the existence of an English ambassador in Vienna, so distant did it seem from essential English interests.

The reference to "your sailors' voyages" is detailed enough to refer specifically to Anthony Jenkinson, whose intrepid explorations and adventures could well have inspired an epic. They took him from the Arctic mouth of the Severnaya Dvina, south and west to Moscow where Ivan the Terrible recognized his exploits and facilitated his travels south to the Caspian and into Persia. After returning via Moscow to England in 1561, his achievements were hailed by the Moscovy Company, which sent him as Captain General in charge of a second expedition to Persia, whence he returned in 1565. Again in 1571–72 Jenkinson was back in Moscow. Although he wrote extensive descriptions of his experiences and observations, none reached print before they appeared in Hakluyt's *Principal Navigations* in 1589. That Languet knew about Jenkinson's feats shows how his fame had spread by word of mouth throughout western Europe. Languet's own travels "to the far north" apparently occurred in 1551; he visited England and probably Scandinavia.

Somewhere on the road to Venice the courier carrying Languet's letter passed another travelling to Vienna with a letter from Sidney. It is highly revealing of Sidney's activities and intellectual pursuits.

> Yesterday I received your letter of December 4, in which I recognize your uncommon kindness towards me, for with one little letter I so easily banished all your suspicions. As for my plans, if it is true that the coronation will occur so soon, I cannot arrange to be there; but if it should be deferred for a month or two, then with God's help I shall surely come. For my entanglement in many affairs keeps me from being where so many and such great things are to be seen and learned. Be that as it may, in the spring I shall tour all those lands

in the company of the noble Count of Hanau, who announces that he too will leave the Italians behind and will visit Poland, Bohemia, and your own Saxony. At that time I shall see you, my dear Languet, and I shall take more delight in one conversation with you than in the magnificent magnificences of all those magnificoes.

Meanwhile I shall remain here for a fortnight, and then spend the rest of my time in Padua. I am studying the sphere and certain musical subjects. My [Latin] style I exercise only by writing to you, but of course I have already found that by writing badly all I learn is to write badly. Hence I beg you to send me some advice on how to improve my style, together with those warnings which you wrote that you have deferred until my return. I am confident that you will never be at a loss for advice, and that my faults will leave you an ample field for offering it.

I have sold all the horses, since their quality would otherwise surely not repay their expense. For your horse I received twenty crowns, which are among the many things I owe you. As for the money we paid twice over at Raichel's inn, I did not write to you about it in order to expect you do anything about it, but simply to exonerate Coningsby, whom I at first had unjustly accused. We would make ourselves a laughingstock if we were to take up the matter with our host, for those who so shamelessly accepted the money will more shamelessly deny that they did so.

When you advise me that the time is right, I shall find a gift for Master Abondio; I should gladly know what he has been doing. I should be grateful if you would send me a French translation of Plutarch's works, if it can be bought in Vienna, for I would cheerfully pay five times the price for it. You will, I imagine, be able to send it with some merchant; and in your next letter please tell me whether you own *L'Historia del Mondo* of Tarcagnota, the *Lettere de Prencipi*, *Lettere de Tredici Illustri Homini*, and *Imprese* of Girolamo Ruscelli, and *Il Stato di Vinegia* written by Contarini and Donato Giannotti, which are really choice books. Or if you should wish any others, I can easily have them delivered to you.

I have often wanted to ask you something else as well, although shyness has made me stop each time; but, as Cicero says, "a letter does not blush." I have a burning desire to possess your treatise on the Polish election, which you once saw fit to show to me. I entreat you either to send it to me, or at least to swear in your next letter that, when we meet again in Germany, you will lend your account to me; but by then you should add something else of yours, by way of interest.

Here there are many rumours, but of them these are the most bruited about: that there will be a treaty either between the Spaniard and the Turk; or again between the Venetians and the Spaniard; or between the Turk and the Queen of England, the King of Poland, and your Elector of Saxony. Don't you laugh to find us Saxons Turkizing now? I really heard these things from a man who is both knowledgeable and trustworthy. God keep you. Farewell. Venice, December 19, 1573.

Wholly yours,
Ph. Sidney

Coningsby and Bryskett pay you their respects as their chief protector and friend. I cannot find Witfelde. Laski, I hear, is in Poland, Perrot in France; all the others are excellent men and my good friends.

This remarkable letter illustrates how seriously Sidney was pursuing his studies in Venice, rather than indulging in the pleasures of the flesh or gawking, touristlike, at the "magnificorum magnificis magnificentiis," as he phrased it. (In striving for an improved Latin style he doubtless was rather pleased with this combination.) Sidney's study of the sphere found an echo in one of his later letters to his brother Robert: "I thinke yow understand the sphere, if yow doe, I care little for any more astronomie in yow."[2] Similarly Philip charged Robert, "Now sweete brother take a delight to keepe and increase your musick, you will not beleive what a want I finde of it in my melancholie times."[3] Sidney also recommended various books to Robert, among them Tarcagnota's *Delle Historie del Mondo* (1562). It is interesting that this volume and those by Ruscelli (all easily identifiable) were published in Venice in the 1560s and thus were considered current topics of discussion in Venetian circles.

Languet's "treatise on the Polish election" is not known to exist, but Sidney may have read Languet's own copy after his return to Vienna. The source of the rumours about treaties and alliances may well have been Wolfgang Zündelin, of whom more in due course. Although in reply

2. Oct. 18, 1580. Feuillerat, 3 : 132.
3. Ibid., pp. 132–33.

Languet called these reports unrealistic, within the next few years the Spanish did enter into diplomatic agreement with the Turks and the Venetians. Likewise in 1580 Elizabeth signed a treaty with the Sultan of Turkey. Of the persons mentioned by Sidney in his postscript, "Witfelde" is difficult to pin down; he may have been Griffin Whitefield, who attended Robert Sidney in 1576.[4]

Languet's next letter, dated December 24, burns with affection for Sidney; the highly personal part reads:

> Your second letter somewhat troubled me, since you seemed hurt by my reproaches. Instead, you should have understood what great affection I lavish on you and how anxious I am about your safety. But I was more disturbed that during the following week I received no letter from you at all, and in fact it is only now that the letter you wrote on the fifth of this month has been delivered. I was afraid that you wished to punish by silence the wrong you thought had been done to you, and you could hardly inflict a more severe punishment upon me.
>
> My very dear son (for now I feel free to use this name to sway you), thus far I have coveted no riches and have taken no trouble to acquire any besides the friendship of those in whom I have seen the eager desire for virtue flourishing; and I have not failed in this, for I have formed very rewarding and gratifying friendships with more than a few persons. But the love I bear you has plumbed my soul far more deeply than any before and has occupied it so totally as to claim sole governance and even tyranny there. Accordingly do not be surprised that I am distressed if I have even the slightest reason to suspect a lessening of your affection. If you had found a gem so precious that you believed your treasure and your wealth lay there, would you not justly fear a thief?
>
> I am glad that you promise once again to neglect no opportunity to write to me, and that you declare you will be diligent at it; for you say that you have received only two letters from me, but have sent me three. Yet if this is something for one to take pride in, I am now writing you for the seventh time, but have thus far received only three letters from you.
>
> You will not waste your efforts if you engage diligently in writing while you are away from home. For when you return you will not

4. See *HMC De L'Isle*, 2:269.

be granted such an opportunity at all, so unless you have achieved facility in writing you will be almost wholly deprived of the chief reward of your study and exertions, and it will be less convenient for you to cultivate the friendships which you have formed with persons abroad. Yet I imagine that, since nature has fashioned you entirely for humane pursuits, you are inclined to want those friendships to last. . . .

Master de Vulcob pays you his courteous respects and begs you to care for your health; because you wrote that you would not remain in Venice for long, he seems to be afraid of something. The French ambassador [du Ferrier], in a letter to him, gives evidence of having an excellent opinion of your character and thanks him because, as he puts it, Vulcob's letter gave him the opportunity of forming a friendship with you. As Hector says to his father, "It is a fine thing to have a much praised man praise you." Take care to thank both men and, by some kindness, to put in your debt that Camillo Cruci who looks after our letters. I beg you to pay him my respects and offer him my duty, even though he does not know me: I love all those who help you. Pay my respects to Master Bryskett and Master Coningsby.

I have written this letter in a state of drowsiness. Vienna, December 24, 1573.

The intimate relationship between Languet and his "foster son," which their comity of mind had nurtured, requires little comment. That such a full record of it has been preserved is just as remarkable as the fact that it ever occurred between two such eminent persons.

Of Camillo Cruci "who looks after our letters" no record is forthcoming in available sources. The name indicates that he was an Italian (probably a Venetian), and he seems to have run a courier service between Venice and Vienna. Whether other routes radiating from Venice were also part of his organization is not known. The evidence clearly shows that couriers usually set out on Saturdays from each end of the route. Hence, Friday was the usual day for writing letters, in order to do so with the latest news in mind, though Thursday provided more leisure. Languet followed this schedule with care, as a check of his dates against the calendar proves.[5]

Sidney next wrote Languet on Christmas Day (a Friday, of course),

---

5. See von Bezold, *Briefe*, 1:150n. As added proof he cites a letter Zündelin wrote to Camerarius Feb. 17, 1581, apologizing because he could not find time to write on Friday.

replying to Languet's letter of December 12. This supports the evidence concerning the schedule followed by Camillo Cruci's men and the way his clients adapted their correspondence to it.

> My dear Languet,
> I am writing you these few words at this time simply that you may see how scrupulously I am keeping the little pledge of great friendship to which you allude. I have nothing else to write except something which I know will please you greatly, namely, that I continue to enjoy the best of health.
> I have received the letter you wrote on the day of the winter solstice. There are a number of things in it which please me greatly, and particularly what you write about a certain young Pole, Dioberi, which surely makes me unhappier at not being able to come at this time, as I wrote you in my last letter. But if the King were taken ill for only a month, or some such thing happened, good Lord, how happily I should come flying!
> I have already taken rooms in Padua, where I shall go within the week.

Sidney's health was more than a matter of merely polite concern. Although the modern reader may think of Sidney in idealized terms as a strong young man, the skilled horseman exercising in the tilt-yard and competing before royalty in tournaments, or the soldier leading charges against the Spaniards in the Netherlands, he seems to have been actually rather delicate, suffering from a low resistance to bronchial infections and other afflictions. As a youth at Oxford he was allowed to eat meat during Lent because he was "somewhat subject to sickness."[6] Languet frequently pressed Sidney for assurance about his health, and his anxiety was based on personal observation. For example, in his letter of December 18, quoted in part earlier, Languet wrote: "I have complained several times that you wrote me nothing along the way [from Vienna to Venice] about your health. This you must attribute to my affection and anxiety, nor do I regret it." During the following year there would be several occasions for Languet to be anxious about Sidney.

Languet next wrote on New Year's Day 1574, replying to Sidney's letter of December 19. After admonishing Sidney to write regularly, Languet continued in a playful vein.

6. So the Earl of Leicester wrote Matthew Parker, Archbishop of Canterbury, on Mar. 3, 1570. See Zouch, p. 29, for the full letter.

Moreover, so that you may know what you have to expect from me, I want to apply the rule to you by which I am accustomed to pacify any friends who are ever angry with me. This rule is that I may freely jest with you, admonish you, reproach you, argue with you, or write you whatever comes to my mind. But since the very air of Padua has made a lawyer of you, you know that equity requires anyone who imposes a rule upon someone else to abide by it himself; I not only wish to submit to the rule to which I subject you, but also allow you to do whatever else you wish to me, except to hate me. I shall now and then sport with you in such letters as those which aroused you, so that you may practise epistolary versatility by refuting my complaints or in turn accusing me. This kind of exercise is thought to be most beneficial.

Next Languet turned to Sidney's request for suggestions about how to improve his Latin prose style. He recommended that Sidney use the method of double translation developed by Johann Sturm and subsequently espoused by his friend Roger Ascham in the second book of *The Scholemaster* (1570).

You ask me to tell you how you should develop your style. You will do very well, in my opinion, if you carefully read both volumes of Cicero's epistles, not only for the choiceness of his Latin, but also for the weighty matters which those epistles contain; for nowhere are the circumstances which hastened the Roman republic to its end better set forth. Many think that it is most beneficial to select some one epistle and translate it into another language. Next, putting the book aside, translate it back into Latin, and then, taking the book again, see how closely you have approached Cicero's kind of expression. But take care not to slip into the error of those who think that the *summum bonum* lies in imitating Cicero and waste their entire lives doing that.

Sidney's request for a copy of Plutarch elicited this reply:

If there were any copies of Plutarch's works for sale here, I would spare no expense to satisfy your desire. Because I see that Master de Vulcob is particularly taken with that writer, I have not dared to ask him for his own copy. But if you command this of me, I shall put off my reticence and ask him. When you begin to read Cicero's epistles, you will perhaps not wish for Plutarch.

Other personal passages in Languet's letter include the following:

> I congratulate you for devoting some study to astronomy; those who are utterly ignorant of it cannot understand geography, and those who read history without knowing geography seem to me very like men who make journeys in the dark.
>
> The things about which I wish to warn you are such that it is not safe to entrust them to a letter; and it is not your faults which give me ground for warnings, but rather your virtue, which, I hope, will very soon become so evident that most men will take notice of your acts and words. You must therefore be careful to whom you speak about your affairs. You are wrong if you imagine that you can dispel envy with virtue, since nothing provokes it more. But more on this subject when we meet.
>
> I have the habit of cheering myself from time to time by gazing at your portrait at the house of our most obliging friend, Abondio. Yet I immediately pay a penalty for this pleasure because it brings back the pain which I felt at your departure.
>
> I do not believe that I have a copy of the treatise on the Polish elections to show you, but if you are amused by trifles of this sort, I shall see to it that you receive the oration which we delivered in the name of several German princes before the King of France three years ago. Some things in it were so boldly put that during the massacre in Paris I sorely feared that this oration would be the end of me.
>
> Master de Vulcob pays you his courteous respects, and asks you to excuse him for not yet having answered your letter, because for the present he has had letters to write to France and Poland.
>
> If you love me, I beg you not to give up your habit of writing. I cannot tell you how much pleasure your letters give me. I wish you and yours a happy new year. Vienna, January 1, 1574.

A letter from Vulcob dated January 2 probably came by the same courier. It shows that Languet had kept Vulcob informed of Sidney's affairs, doubtless while sounding him out subtly on the subject of his volume of Plutarch. Vulcob's main topic, as usual, was Henry's meandering progress across Germany.

> Sir:
> I did not think I would have the time to write to you in the usual way and had begged Master Languet to send you my excuses.

However, you shall have these few words to acknowledge those which you have been pleased to send me, dated the nineteenth of last month. I do not wish to waste time in formalities, but rather to give you proof of my affectionate desire to serve you, whenever you may wish to make use of me, in both word and deed. However, I am certain that you have no doubt as to this desire, so I shall here tell you only that the King of Poland's coming to Heidleberg—to visit the Elector Palatine, who was ill—was unexpected, as he had not apprised his host of it until the day before. He arrived on Friday evening at eleven and remained until Sunday morning, leaving at ten o'clock. From there he went to Worms, where he spent the night; the next day to Oppenheim, then to Mainz on the twenty-fifth; and he should be at Frankfurt on the twentieth [of January]. Thus it will not be possible to hold the coronation until the beginning of February, so far as one can judge.

I shall not detain you with other matters for the present, except to tell you, sir, that I am most happy that M. du Ferrier—to judge by what he tells me in his letter—holds you in the esteem you deserve. And here I shall pay my humble respects to your benevolence, and pray God to grant you,

Sir, [good] health, a happy [new] year, and a long life. From Vienna, this second of January, 1574.

Your most humble and affectionate friend,

J. de Vulcob

Sidney was not able to go to Padua as early as he had expected, and so remained in Venice for about a fortnight. Hence some letters addressed to him in Padua were not received until he arrived there. Because of the time taken by Camillo the courier, Vulcob's letter reached Padua about the same day that Sidney did. Languet's next, dated January 7, found Sidney already established in his new quarters. Languet responded to Sidney's letter of December 25:

I am already reaping the sweet fruits of our friendship in seeing that you enjoy the high regard of those whom I particularly wanted you to please. I have received letters from his Excellency the Count of Hanau and from the distinguished Master von Welsperg, both of whom praise you to the skies and congratulate themselves on their friendship with you. They thank me for having been, so to speak, its cause. See to it, therefore, that you return their affection, that you maintain your reputation and mine, and that you vindicate the opinion good men have of you. Take care, too, that the sweetness of praise does not so bewitch you as to make you feel you have already arrived at the object of all virtue, or have already completed the effort to which you must devote yourself for as long as you live. For that effort has no other goal than to live one's life honourably to the end. You must therefore press on towards your destiny and, be it happy or sad, temper it with virtue.

But see how far my affection for you carries me! I am delighted that you have finally decided to move on to Padua; it is a quieter city than Venice, and fitter for study.

Paul von Welsperg served as companion and head of household to the Count of Hanau. His rank was high enough so that in the following November the Emperor Maximilian sent von Welsperg as an envoy to the Duke of Savoy, to bear his condolences on the death of the Duchess and to perform a concurrent diplomatic errand.[7]

Next, Languet touched on a matter of some sensitivity to him as an ambassador.

Before you leave there, make it your business, even with some little gift, to obligate this Camillo who sees to our letters. For I should not like the letters you write me to be sent to Ambassador du Ferrier. This is the reason: Perrot, who lives at his house (he has, I think, shown him a letter which I wrote his brother about you), has recently written me that I would oblige the ambassador if I occasionally wrote him about public affairs, saying that for this favour of mine the ambassador was prepared to show you any sort of kindness, since he realizes how great my affection is for you. I of course honour and esteem him for his virtue, and certainly acknowledge that I owe him a great deal because he received you courteously; and I would happily oblige him.

But, as you know, I am cultivating the friendship of Master de Vulcob, and he loses no opportunity to write the ambassador. Consequently, if I too wrote the ambassador, I am afraid that Vulcob would suspect that I wished to seem to know more than he, or was even writing some things which I was hiding from him, whose office it is to keep the court informed about German affairs. There

7. *VDK*, 3 : 550, under date Nov. 26, 1574.

are also other reasons which keep me from writing, reasons I need not review here, but which it would be useful for you to know later. You can occasionally tell the ambassador the things I write you about public affairs, so long as you do not tell him that you have them from me.

We may be sure that this lesson in diplomacy was not lost on Sidney.

Languet now turned to a lesson in Latin and to the recurrent theme of the forthcoming coronation in Poland.

My very dear son, I implore you to take pains to make certain changes in your pronunciation of Latin. Nothing is so difficult that you cannot achieve it with your native ability. This task will demand a little effort, but you can use the services of that very pleasant person, Delius, who will help you succeed by playing and jesting with you.

I believe that the King of Poland has already arrived in his kingdom. He crossed the Elbe just at the end of last month, and therefore you must put aside all thoughts of his coronation; if you had attended, I would have done something which, I believe, would not have displeased you, but I do not want to write of it or you will imagine that I want to cajole you. A great number of minstrels, actors, mimes, jesters, and good-for-nothings of that sort are travelling here on their way from Cracow. Farewell. Vienna, January 7, 1574.

The speed of Henry's progress to Poland is once more exaggerated by rumour as Languet's letter shows. Matthäus Delius, of Wittenberg, Saxony, belonged to a family bound closely in sympathy to Languet because of their devotion to the teacher and master of his youth, Melanchthon. Although Matthäus was about ten years Sidney's senior, they became close friends and convivial companions at Padua.

Before Languet had definite word of Sidney's arrival in Padua, he wrote again, replying to a letter which Sidney probably wrote on New Year's Day. Sidney had confessed to a fit of low spirits that he attributed to the lack of stimulating and sympathetic new friends. Furthermore, rumours circulated by wishful Romanists reported that Elizabeth had died and her hoped-for Protestant heir, James VI of Scotland, had been poisoned,[8] events which would have upset the status of Sidney's family—

8. These rumours were mentioned in passing by Languet in his letter of Dec. 24, 1573, but Sidney heard them independently in Venice.

both his father and the Dudley uncles. Languet's personal devotion to Sidney could not be more nobly stated than in this fine letter:

> I am very much troubled by the letter in which you write that you are not in very good health and are even more melancholy than usual. I beg you to take care of your health and not to devote so much time to your studies. Avoid the lagoons where you are— nothing is more unpleasant than they after one has looked at the things in the city which are worth seeing. I was surprised that you lingered so long in that unending noise and stench, especially because you write that you have not made friends with anyone whose company particularly pleases you. Hurry, then, to your friend the Count of Hanau in Padua, and to the other good men who are so extraordinarily fond of you and so eager for your company, as I wrote recently; for the Count of Hanau has written me a letter that breathes nothing but true and brotherly affection for you.
>
> Master von Welsperg is hardly less fond of you than I. Make it your business to become especially close to him, so that you can consult him more freely about your affairs. He is an honourable man, with experience in many things, and one who sees dangers from afar; and in addition he is of a very kind and temperate nature. He has decided to accompany my lord the Count to those parts of Italy which can be visited without danger, and afterwards to come here. By all means join them on this journey: no company could please you more or suit you better. But you will have to find out quickly about all the necessities of that journey, or some difficulty may thwart your plan.
>
> If there is anything I can do for you, you know how I feel about you. You are welcome to use my money, scarce as it is, as your own. If you do, I shall feel that you are doing me a kindness and truly believe that you realize how much I think of you, and how great my affection is for you. I say this because I know what often happens to people who take long journeys abroad: through their agents' carelessness, the funds sent them do not reach them in time, and they cannot make their plans as they wish.
>
> How I should like to converse with you just now! You know how dangerous it is to entrust such things to a letter: and this should also make you more cautious in your own dealings. If you see that any considerable disturbance is taking place where you are, I strongly

advise you to come back to Germany; for I do not think you would be safe in Venice or anywhere else in Italy. If you hear any more about this, please let me know; I shall answer with what information I have and give you my advice.

Have the letters which I am writing to my lord the Count and to Master von Welsperg delivered to them, and please write me diligently about your health, and care for it still more diligently. Farewell. Vienna, January 15, 1574.

Sidney pulled himself together and, with the help of the faithful Bryskett and Griffin, moved his books and chattels to Padua, twenty-five miles away from the magnificent façades of Venice, which to Sidney seemed empty and heartless. The short journey probably followed the same stages described by Montaigne when he made it in 1580, just seven years after Sidney.[9] He tells how one took a burchièllo along the canal as far as Fusina. From there one could either sail upriver to Padua on another boat (going through several water gates on the way) or ride along the dike which flanked the river. Riders had a pleasant view of rich cornfields, multitudes of shade-giving trees, vineyards, and the country houses which lined the road. Sidney's letters from the university city clearly show that the change of scenery and intellectual climate effected the necessary cure of his melancholy.

9. *Journal de voyage en Italie*, ed. C. Dédeyan (Paris, 1946), pp. 172–74. He was entertained in Venice by du Ferrier, whom he described as "somewhat scholastic in manner and speech, with little vivacity or wit." He also reported that du Ferrier leaned to Calvinism and was living virtually isolated from the suspicious Venetians.

CHAPTER 7

The importance of Padua on the intellectual map of sixteenth-century Europe is difficult to exaggerate. That this small provincial town earned such an eminence seems almost unbelievable, for it counted a population of only about five thousand souls. Of these, about fifteen hundred were students at the ancient University and perhaps another thousand were faculty, lodging-house keepers, and tradesmen dependent on the university community for their livelihood. Mere population figures are misleading, however, since the city, located within the horseshoe curves of the river Bacchiglione, served as the market centre for a wide and fertile valley. Many prosperous landowners lived in villas on the surrounding hills and visited the town for shopping and other business purposes.

The chief reason for Padua's fame was that in the whole of authoritarian, orthodox, and even totalitarian Europe, the Venetian state, of which Padua was a part, existed as an island of tolerance. Here varying religious creeds and intellectual convictions were accepted and accommodated. Students who sought a free forum for discussion, an opportunity for unshackled examination of dogmas, and an open area for the exploration of ideas flocked to Padua. Some might seek converts to their notions, but most came to learn new concepts and to exercise their minds against those of other eager intellectuals. As Coryat wrote a generation later, "more students of forraine and remote nations doe liue in Padua, then in any one vniuersity of Christendome. For hither come in many from Fraunce, high Germany, the Netherlands, England, &c. who with great desire flocke together to Padua for good letters sake, as to a fertile nursery, and sweete emporium and mart towne of learning."[1]

The high proportion of foreign students determined the structure of the university. There were two faculties, each under its own Rector: the Faculty of Arts and the Faculty of Law, the latter being the larger and more influential. Within each faculty the students were divided into two groups, ultramontanes and citramontanes. These in turn were subdivided according to "nations," or areas of origin. The citramontanes comprised twelve "nations," and the ultramontanes were made up of ten, one of

1. Coryat, pp. 154–55.

133

them being the English. Each "nation" elected a Consularius who represented them in a Senate, presided over by the Rector and a Syndicus. The assembled Consularii elected the Rector and had a voice in both policy decisions and their execution. In this process each Consularius gained experience valuable for his future career on how to function in a decision-making organization.

Among the ultramontane students there were some eccentrics, some zealots, and some scions of great families, but the many who possessed outstanding minds and qualities of leadership were the cause of Padua's fame. As at Oxford and Cambridge, young men of outstanding ability met others of equal promise and formed friendships which bridged political boundaries. Two of the most influential men in Sidney's life began their distinguished careers as students at Padua. There, while taking a doctorate in law, Languet cut his intellectual teeth and first read Melanchthon, an event that changed his life. A few years later Francis Walsingham also read law at Padua, where he had the distinction of being elected Consularius of the English "nation." Both men influenced Sidney's decision to go there, and both doubtless gave him some idea of what he would find.

There is no evidence that Sidney was formally enrolled as a student. Contemporary records have perished, but even if they had been preserved it is unlikely that Sidney's name would be found. The only known facts about his Paduan interlude are the dates of his stay in the city, the names of several friends, some indication of his reading, and his address. He rented all or part of the house of one Hercole Bolognese at the Pozzo della Vacca, as some of the newly recovered letters reveal.

Sidney arrived early in the week of January 10, and on Wednesday he received the letter Languet had written from Vienna on New Year's Day. That Friday he wrote a prompt reply, another letter brimming with devotion to his mentor.

> Now you will at last have my letter from Padua, not to give you hopes of greater fluency than you have been accustomed to in my other letters, but to let you know that I have arrived here safely and according to plan. I thought it best to send you a few words from here at once to satisfy you, and myself. In short, I have arrived, and have already visited his Excellency the Count and Baron Slavata, young men of the highest worth. While I am enjoying their extremely pleasant company, there comes before my eyes the surely

excessive affection you have shown me in taking such thought, which I so little deserve, not only for me but for my affairs and all my interests. But really you are not a man to thank for such things— more important matters occupy your mind, and, as for me, I owe you a great deal, and willingly.

Michael, Baron Slavata, was a member of a Bohemian family with strong connections at the imperial court in Vienna. References to him recur in the correspondence until 1576 when he visited England.

Next, Sidney reported how he had followed Languet's advice in his study of Latin.

> But enough of this. On the thirteenth I received your last letter, written on January 1, and it had nothing new in it. Yet it was full of tokens of your affection which continues to delight me, though I have long been aware of it. And this is the kind of letter I like best; for while I read it, I seem to see my dear Hubert himself right before me.
>
> I shall follow your advice on style in this way: first I shall translate some letter of Cicero's into French, then from French into English, and then back into Latin again by an uninterrupted process— though not by Abondio's. Perhaps I shall also improve my Italian with this exercise, for I have a translation of the *Epistles* into the vulgar tongue by the very learned Paolo Manuzio, and into French by someone else.
>
> I shall read Cicero's works diligently; but I shall also learn some things about the Greeks of which I have had only superficial knowledge for a long while. I shall find the *summum bonum* (next to eternal bliss) in the cultivation of true friendship, and here you will unquestionably hold first rank. You certainly made me laugh with that *summum bonum* of yours, for it characterized a whole species of our fellowmen.
>
> As for what you write about the copies of Plutarch, I should not want you to lay aside your natural reticence for so small a matter, and I am not so brash in attending to my own convenience as to neglect the pleasure of others, especially that of friends. Concerning Abondio in particular, I am quite worried about what to send him in return for his extraordinary kindness, but I shall attend to that in a short while. In the meantime, please wish him the best of health for me.

I accept no excuse whatsoever for your not letting me have your letter about Polish affairs, and now too the oration of yours which you mentioned in your last letter; for they must inevitably be much to my liking, since they were written by such a man as you.

By all means you must put your mind to writing some special monument to make known your admirable virtues to posterity. But more about that when we meet. There is no news here; I look forward to some from you. Farewell, and live a long life, for your own sake and for that of your friends and of all Christendom. Padua, January 15, 1574.

Yours most affectionately,
Philip Sidney

Sidney was carrying the method of double translation one step further into triple translation. (He speaks of double translation as Abondio's method, apparently alluding to the reverse process used in casting from a wax model.) Paolo Manuzio, son of the founder of the Aldine Press in Venice, edited several volumes of Cicero but does not appear to have translated Cicero into Italian. Accordingly, Ringler suggests that Sidney had in mind the older Italian edition of G. Loglio, edited by Paolo's son Aldo in 1551. French translations of Cicero's *Epistolae* had appeared in 1542 and 1566. A few years later Sidney warned his brother Robert, "So yow can speake and write Latine not barbarously I never require great study in Ciceronianisme the cheife abuse of Oxford, *Qui dum verba sectantur, res ipsas negligunt.*"[2]

Languet's next regular letter, dated Friday, January 22, continues with suggestions for Sidney's program of study. In it Languet's awareness of Sidney's introvertive temperament is manifest.

I am delighted that you have finally decided to go to Padua, where you will easily find better lodgings than in Venice and will, I hope, have pleasanter companions with whom to enjoy yourself and to converse about your studies. You have done wisely to learn the elements of astronomy, but I do not advise you to proceed further in that study because it is very difficult, and you will receive no great benefit from it in return. I do not know whether you are well advised to study geometry. It is, to be sure, an excellent study, and one particularly worthy of a liberal mind, but you must consider your

2. Feuillerat, 3:132.

position in life, and how soon you will have to tear yourself away from the leisure you have for reading. Therefore you must devote that brief time which remains to you entirely to the most necessary studies.

Now I call those things necessary which it is improper for men of high degree not to know, and which may both adorn and shield you in the future. To be sure, geometry can be of great service to a highborn man for fortifying and attacking cities, for setting up camps, and for all kinds of architecture. But surely you will need a great deal of time to learn enough to benefit from it; and I think it absurd to learn the elements of many skills for the sake of display rather than use.

Besides, since you are none too cheerful by nature, that study will make you more melancholy still: it demands vigorous application of the mind, consumes the vital and intellectual spirits, and very much weakens the body. The finer one's talents are, the more intense are one's interests, and therefore the more harmful—and, as you know, you do not have a strong constitution.

As for Greek, I do not know what to advise. Although it is an excellent study! I am afraid that you will not have enough time to persevere in it, and that the time you do devote to it will be taken from your study of Latin. Even if Latin is considered less elegant than Greek, you nevertheless have a greater need to know it. And so, as I said, I dare not give you any advice in this matter; but I do urge you to learn first the things that are most essential and suit your position in life. You already know four languages. If, in the course of amusing yourself, you learned enough German to understand it more or less you would not, in my opinion, be wasting your effort.

The knowledge most necessary for us is that of our salvation, which Holy Scripture teaches us. After this study, I consider nothing more beneficial to you than that branch of moral philosophy which teaches right and wrong. As for reading history, there is no need for me to try to convince you, since you incline towards it of your own accord, and have already made great progress in it.

But perhaps with this too lengthy letter of mine I am annoying you when you are involved in other affairs. Nevertheless I caution you to take great care for your health, and not to injure it with too much study. Nothing excessive is lasting, and a sound mind is not enough if it does not dwell in a sound body.

Since you are not at all cheerful by nature you should seek out companions in whose honourable society you can find good cheer. His Excellency the Count of Hanau, and his entire household, honour you with singular affection. I advise you to associate with them very intimately. Other good men, too, are not lacking, who will think it a kindness if you seek their friendship. So long as you are not untrue to yourself, you will find everywhere men who will be fond of you and will treat you with courtesy.

Languet's affection for Sidney gushes out in the following passage, a remarkable confession considering that Languet was ten years older than Sidney's father. Besides admiring Sidney's charm and fresh intelligence, Languet saw him as the messiah who could lead the much-desired unification of the Protestants of Europe. Languet hoped to bring together the Lutherans, the Calvinists, and the Anglicans of England, and by this means to resist the forces of Catholicism, which seemed neither to slumber nor to sleep. To this purpose Languet felt his greatest contribution could be to guide, train, and even create the future champion of the Protestant cause.

Since it is believed that the Emperor will go to Prague within two months, I begin to fear that I shall be so unfortunate as not to see you when you return to Germany; nothing more bitter could happen to me. And even if everything turns out just as I wish, and I do enjoy the sight of you again, I shall still not be permitted to enjoy it long. I foresee the pain your departure will give me, and should gladly remedy it; but no cure comes to mind, unless a portrait of you might bring me some relief. Although I have one engraved upon my heart which is always before my eyes, I ask you not to think it a burden to indulge my desire: send me your portrait, or bring it with you when you return.

I also wish to show it to those with whom I share my opinion of your character, and my hopes about your virtue. Since they believe that no one can have so many qualities of mind without bearing some visible signs of them, particularly in his face, they all greatly desire to see you. Yet I request this in such a way that you will feel free to refuse me without vexing me at all, for I should not like to ask you anything which I think would displease you.

Recently, the sight of your portrait at our friend Abondio's so moved me that on my return home I wrote the little verses I enclose, though I have not practised this kind of writing since early adolescence. I want to give you myself as a morsel for your amusement, and to say that these little verses seem to me not inappropriate, and that I therefore wish them to be inscribed on the picture which you order, if there is room enough.

Apparently Sidney did not preserve the verses with Languet's letter; they might have been rather revealing. Languet concludes briefly:

I thank Master Bryskett warmly for his kind letter, which I would have answered if only I had time; but truthfully I have been very busy, and as I write this the most excellent Dr. Andreas Paull, counsellor to his Excellency my prince, a man of superb ability and a great friend of mine, is with me. He likes you unseen, offers you his service, and pays you his respects.

Dr. Paull and Sidney did meet in due course, but apparently not until the spring of 1575 when Sidney stopped at Dresden on his return journey to England.

The following week Languet wrote on Thursday. The fact that the courier would not leave for Padua for two days seems to have affected him; the letter is one of his longest. It begins:

I am delighted that you have finally disentangled yourself from that troublesome business which kept you in Venice so long: it is better for you to live in Padua, whether you have studies or health in mind. And I hope that it will be easier for you to find companions in whose honourable society you may enjoy yourself and shake off that sometimes excessive melancholy of yours. Take care not to devote so much time to study that you neglect your health, or even injure it; or you may be like the traveller who takes great pains about his own well-being in preparing for a long journey but gives no thought for his horse.

I have recently written to you my opinion about your studies. You must think of your position in life, a position which will not let you grow grey in the study of letters—in fact, the time which remains to you for literary study is very short. So you must see to it that you do not undertake so much at once that one project interferes with another. Admittedly, there is nothing so challenging and difficult that your excellent mind cannot fathom it; yet it takes a long time to learn a diversity of subjects so well that you can benefit from them, and you will not be allowed that time when you return home, for you will then have at least to interrupt, if not wholly abandon, your studies.

Therefore learn what is most necessary for a man to know if he is to plan and live his life properly. Keep in mind that the words of the poet apply to you: "Remember to rule the nations with your sway," and so forth, and that to have observed the manners and cities of many men, as that other poet says, serves this purpose very well— and this is an activity for which you will not be so free once you return home as you will be to devote yourself to literature.

As I wrote before, I should like you to gain enough skill in German to understand what you hear and read; for you could not learn it perfectly except at the expense of much time and labour. You English conduct most of your trade with the Germans; their influence and power in Christendom are now preeminent and will doubtless increase further, thanks to our stupidity and that of their other neighbours.

I find it almost laughable that your countrymen should strive so energetically for eloquence in Italian, though from the Italians you get nothing advantageous that I know of. The Italians, however, get a great many such things from you, for which reason they should rather improve their knowledge of your language. But perhaps you are afraid that you will not be able to persuade them to take your money unless you are very fluent.

Fearing that his tone might seem monotonously moral, Languet shifts to a lighter vein. In so doing he offers the modern reader a delightful picture of himself, a man who had become what he warned Sidney not to be, one grown "grey in the study of letters."

See, my dear Sidney, what nonsense I talk to you; but since my thoughts are running in that vein, I want to add something else still more nonsensical. I do not know by what evil destiny I have recently stumbled upon two most engaging writers, one of whom writes of France, the other of England. The former is Robert Ceneau, by name, Bishop of Avranches, a very foolish and unlearned man. And the other one would think he had received great injury at my hands if I should call him English, because he again and again declares that he is Welsh, not English.

His name is Humphrey Lhuyd, and he is, if not really learned, at any rate well-read, though he occasionally makes judgements which seem to lack common sense. He so belabours poor Hector Boethius and Polydore Vergil that, even if they have committed serious errors, the medicine still appears excessive. And you are fortunate that your ancestors came from France, for he says that the Saxons from whom the English descend were nothing but pirates and robbers.

You know that the German writers have bespoiled us poor Frenchmen of the Empire, which they say was never under our control. They say that Godfrey of Bouillon's crusade was of their doing, and that the modern and ancient Greeks and Romans write nonsense when they say that the Gauls invaded Italy so many times, and that, having burned Rome, they advanced all the way to Greece and to Asia, since all those people were surely Germans. But that good Welshman is so far from being moved by our misfortunes, great as they are, that he even abuses us; for he deprives us of that notorious incendiary Brennus, whom some Germans have relinquished to us because of his sacrilege and his unhappy end, and he turns him into a Welshman.

Now let me tell you about Lhuyd's pitiable fate, or rather the divine vengeance he suffered: for I suppose that Vulcan wished to return the favour Apollo had done him in detecting his wife's adultery, and Apollo was still angry at Brennus and all his adherents for the sacrilege committed at Delphi. While I was drowsily extending my reading of the good Welshman deep into the night, it somehow happened that my candle ignited the book, and since it had not yet been bound, a good part of it was burned before I could extinguish the fire.

The accident somewhat troubled me at first; but when I came to myself I began to laugh, realizing that I was fortunate to have been deprived of an opportunity of spending time uselessly in trifles of this sort. Next I was on the point of sending you the scorched remains of my poor Welshman so that you might have your Griffin, his countryman, conduct his funeral; you would, however, solemnize it with a laugh. So, I entreat you, commission Griffin to write an epicede for him in Welsh, and send it to me.

The authors and books Languet refers to in this letter are easily identified. Robert Ceneau or Cenalis (1483–1560) published numerous theological and polemical writings including the two volume *Gallica historica* in Paris in 1557. The *Commentarioli Brittanicae descriptionis Fragmentum* of Humphrey

Llwyd or Lhuyd (1527–68), a learned Welsh physician, was published in Cologne in 1572. Languet's pages reveal the full and playful mind that made him the sought-after friend and correspondent of a wide circle of eminent men.

> Archduke Ernest is returning to us, having, as they say, aborted the mission for which his father had sent him to Bohemia. The Bohemians do not wish to negotiate with the son, but with the father, who is able not only to accept what is offered, but also to give some largess. The Emperor will therefore have to go to them, which I believe he will do about the end of March. How I wish you could come here about that time! We would go together as far as Prague, or perhaps further, and travel to all the places in Moravia and Bohemia which are worth seeing. We might while away the time along the road with conversations which you would perhaps not find unpleasant—they would certainly be most pleasant for me!
>
> But I write these things to you, and to no one else. According to reports the King of Poland has arrived at Poznan. The fifth day of next month has been set for the funeral of King Sigismund Augustus, and the tenth for the coronation of the new King. I am sending you these trifles, which will soon tire you. Farewell. My respects to our friends. Vienna, January 28, 1574.

On February 4 Sidney responded to Languet's letter of January 22 with a warm reply. The first topics concerned his course of study.

> For many reasons I was very much gratified by your last letter, which displayed nothing but the affection which so pleases me. I am delighted that you approve of my intention to stop studying astronomy. As for geometry, I really do not know what to decide. I have a burning desire to learn it, the more so because I have always had the impression that it is closely related to military science. I shall, however, pursue this study with restraint and shall gaze upon its elements only as, so to speak, through latticework.
>
> As for Greek, I should wish to absorb only enough to understand Aristotle well; for although several translations appear every day, I still suspect that they do not express the author's ideas distinctly and exactly enough, and besides, I am very much ashamed to "follow only the little brooks, and not to see the very fountainhead," as Cicero says. Of Aristotle's works, I think that one must read his

Politics in particular. This I say because you advise me to turn my mind to moral philosophy.

Of the German language, my dear Hubert, I quite despair, for it has a certain harshness about it, as you well realize—so much so that at my age I have no hope of ever mastering it, not even to the point of simple understanding. Still, to obey you I shall sometimes practise it with our friend Delius, particularly while I am toasting him.

The remainder of the letter equally reveals Sidney's affectionate response to Languet's devoted friendship and also Sidney's experience that the best cure for introvertive depression is application to an intellectual task. The following lines remind us that these letters were exercises in Latin prose style, a fact easily forgotten by readers of translated versions which may adequately transmit the subject matter but cannot duplicate the manner.

I readily confess that I am often more melancholy than either my age or my activities call for; but I have fully proved by experience that I am never less liable to moods of melancholy than while I am pitting my weak mental powers against some difficult challenge. But enough of this.

With regard to your ardent request for my portrait, I am happy because this is clear evidence of the affection for me which, to my delight, I have long noticed in you. At the same time I am sad because you hesitate to ask such slight favours of me. For even if our friendship were not true and perfect (friendship, which outshines all ordinary kindnesses as the sun does the lesser lights of heaven), I still have received such favours from you that you can demand much more than this from me as a debt. As soon as I return to Venice I shall have it done either by Paolo Veronese or by Tintoretto, who easily occupy first rank in this art.

As for the verses: though it is indeed "a proud thing to have a much praised man praise you," and they please me greatly as an undying token of your opinion about me, still I do not want to be so thoroughly immodest as to order the inscription of such laudatory proclamations about me, especially without deserving them. Therefore permit me this, and demand anything else of me. If I can (and desire will surely not be lacking), I shall satisfy you.

Please take all this, full of errors and erasures as it is, in good part,

for I have written it in haste. Farewell. Padua, February 4, 1574.
                    Your most affectionate and respectful,
                                        Philip Sidney
    In the meantime I shall gladly give you the portrait which Abondio
made, and I shall either send or bring him a gift. Again, farewell.
To the illustrious and excellent Master Hubert Languet, my master
and friend, with eternal regard. Vienna.

Languet begins his letter of February 5 by playfully chiding Sidney for
skipping a week in writing him. He then turns to further discussion of
Sidney's developing friendships as embodiments of the Ciceronian ideal
of *De Amicitia*.

    I am pleased that your letters show how eager you are to avenge the
    wrong you imagine I did you when I reproached you for having on
    one occasion failed to write your customary letter; but I was justified
    in doing this, unless by chance the man [Camillo Cruci] whom you
    usually have take care of your letters has deceived us. But listen to
    your lawyers who say that innocence, not a countercharge, is the
    proper defence against a charge, since my committing a crime does
    not acquit you of having done so. Take care, then, not to give me
    grounds a second time for accusing you of neglecting your duty to
    write; for if you do I shall treat you unmercifully and shall never
    forgive you for a fault of this kind.
    I am delighted that the friendship between you and my lord the
    Count is prospering so well, and that my lord Baron Slavata is
    making a threesome with you; he recently sent me a letter which
    gave strong evidence of his affection for you. It is praiseworthy in
    you that, as you report, you are placing your greatest happiness
    (next to the worship of God) in the cultivation of friendship with
    good men. You will never regret this, because, as the speaker in
    Cicero says, "Friendship is the salt and spice of life." Nature, in her
    bounty to you, has given you so much that you may choose as
    friends whomsoever you wish; for there will be no one of any worth
    who will not feel that you have done him a kindness in inviting him
    to be your friend.
    When you have amassed a wealth of friends, you will surely
    realize how much delight you will find in them and, indeed, how
    much assistance, should you ever be buffeted and tossed about by
    the storms of adverse fortune. Of course I pray God to avert this,

but nevertheless men of outstanding virtue are especially liable to bad fortune of this sort—because, as the old dictum goes, envy is always attendant on virtue and forever lies in wait for it.

You should indeed choose your friends primarily in your own country, so that you may go through life happily with them; if obviously worthy friends should offer themselves in other countries, you should by no means discourage them. Friends of this sort are seldom insincere, since they are not thinking of friendship's advantages. Moreover, they frequently find opportunities to oblige their friends, particularly in this unhappy age when too often we see excellent men exiled from their native land solely because they did not wish to assent to the criminal plans of factious men. In your own country you will never lack men who profess friendship, particularly when you have been elevated to high office, but many of them will be fair-weather friends only and will change their attitude towards you with your fortune. You must take great care to distinguish such friends from the true and sincere.

Next, Languet gives more advice about Sidney's study of languages, especially on how to improve his pronunciation of Latin.

Recently I wrote to you my opinion concerning your studies. I entreat you to make an effort to improve your pronunciation. Nothing will prove impossible for your excellent mind. At first you will find it somewhat of a burden, but, believe me, it will not take much time for you to reach your goal. Since few of your countrymen trouble themselves about this, you will reap all the more glory from it. Find yourself a learned man whose pronunciation you approve, and talk with him every day for half an hour in private.

At first take the pronunciation of only the letter *A* for correction, and tell your man to criticize you as often as you mispronounce it, and whenever you are corrected, you should pay him a little money, or something of the sort, as a penalty. I am sure that within five or six days you will feel that you have not wasted your efforts, and you will go on to the rest more quickly. I should perhaps not advise a man with a less receptive mind to do this; but you are able to do whatever you desire. Therefore you have no reason to throw that verse of yours up to me which says that nature always rushes back. For unless you perform the task I want you to, I shall accuse you, not innocent "nature," of wilfulness and negligence.

Scarcely two months have passed since you began to write to me, and yet in such a short time I find you have made as much progress in writing as others rarely make in a whole year. I have carefully observed you when you speak my language, but I have hardly ever detected you mispronouncing even a single syllable. I beg you, my dearest Sidney, to try this for my sake; when you have finished, not even the most malevolent critics will find anything about you to censure.

The letter concludes with current news on such topics as the Emperor Maximilian's kidney stone, the one thousand Muscovite horsemen sent to the Polish coronation to impress the western ambassadors, rumours, counter-rumours, and reports of various other diplomatic and military moves.

Sidney faithfully wrote again on Thursday, February 11, sporting with Languet's account of Humphrey Lhuyd's *Commentarioli Brittanicae* and the teasing inferences Languet based on it about the English, the Welsh, and the Saxons.

Greetings.

You certainly accord extraordinary treatment to our poor Cambro-Briton, who has brought upon himself the anger of Apollo and Vulcan for the offence which Brennus committed, but you seem somewhat lacking in generosity when you decide that the offence has not been sufficiently expiated even by fire, and also deprive him of what he claims for himself as, so to speak, his own patrimony. And where he maintains that the Saxons were pirates and robbers, you see, I readily grant him everything, strong in awareness of my French heritage.

But of course the important thing, as my affection compels me to warn you, is for you to remember that our "unknown God" is of the same land and substance, and will take amiss your arousing so much laughter at the expense of his blood brother; otherwise in his anger he may perhaps brandish his hieroglyphic monad at you like Jove's lightning bolt—for such is the wrath of heavenly spirits.

This passage contains a choice Latin pun which has escaped Sidney's editors Pears and Levy: the latter sees in it an obscure reference to a symbol of Wales, the leek. Sidney's Latin phrase "*ignotum Deum nostrum*" alludes to Dr. John Dee (Johannes Deus), who supposed himself to be of

Welsh extraction. Among Dr. Dee's impenetrable hermetic treatises was one titled *Monas Hieroglyphica*, published in 1571. Undoubtedly Sidney and Languet had joked on some previous occasion about Dee's arcane volume.

Sidney next reported Griffin Madox's supposed concern over the copy of Humphrey Lhuyd's volume burned by Languet's candle.

> Griffin has spoken many things in Master Lhuyd's memory and has given a kind of funeral oration which I solemnized with laughter. In order to efface the brand of stupidity with which you stamp the good Lhuyd, he says, among other things, that so far as Brennus is concerned, Lhuyd was wholly correct, and he proves this from Brennus's name; for in their ancient British language, Brennus meant king and was as common among them as Pharaoh or Ptolemy among the Egyptians, Arsaces in the Parthian empire, and Hubert among huntsmen. By this perhaps feeble reasoning he concludes that the celebrated robber was his countryman. Let me prevail upon you to concede this.

The rest of Sidney's letter is quite personal.

> But I have written all this in jest. Joking aside, I have a burning desire to see you, and if God answers my prayers I shall shortly be there, perhaps even before you set out on your projected journey to Prague. In the meantime, please write to me about all your affairs if you think it wise; and if you have any news, I should like you to confide it to me. In your letters I seem to see the picture of our times, so to speak, and this, like a bow which has too long been drawn tight, must either be loosened or break. Therefore please do me this service, my dear Hubert: consider me worthy of your opinions and send me what you think can safely be entrusted to a letter. Your letters delight me for many reasons, yet they can all be summed up in this one—that they are yours.
>
> We have had no news from England, except that your friend Walsingham has been appointed to join Smith in the office of Secretary and has been made a member of the Privy Council (to use our term), which is evidence enough of how highly our Queen thinks of him.
>
> Together with this letter you will receive one from the Count of Hanau and his entire household. Do answer it, for they are remark-

ably fond of you. I beg you to extend my humble wishes of good health to Master de Vulcob. I would surely write to him often if I did not realize that I have nothing to write—besides, let Perugians [i.e. Bizari] pointlessly annoy busy men. Please do not fail to extend the same kindness to that honourable youth, Bochetel.

I would write more if more came to mind; and so I shall stop, reminding you always to love me as you do. Farewell. Padua, February 11, 1574.

> Your most affectionate,
>
> Philip Sidney

Bryskett commends himself most courteously to you.

Most of Languet's next letter, dated February 13, is filled with ironic banter, which indicates that real news was lacking. Yet Languet does reveal that Sidney made plans for some sightseeing in northern Italy before his return to Vienna.

> In the meantime, you ought to tour those regions of Italy which you decided to visit, so that nothing will delay you when the time comes to leave Italy. I previously wrote that, if you experience any trouble over money, you can use the little I have as if it were yours, and I tell you this again.
>
> The bookseller Gallus, whom you know, is on his way to you, and I have given him a letter to my lord the Count. I have asked him to see you and to give you an idea of the state of things here and at Cracow, whence he has recently returned. I have also written to his Honour the French Ambassador du Ferrier to thank him for the kindness he has shown you, and for his care in letting me know that he would gladly do you several favours for my sake. I also include in the letter my reasons for not writing to him more often. Farewell. Vienna, February 13, 1574.

Languet's letter of February 19 has the usual playful beginning but soon goes into a lengthy review of news received from England. Towards the end Languet responded to Sidney's account of his program of study.

> The study of geometry and of Greek about which you write are certainly most excellent, but I am afraid that you do not have the time to pursue them. Aristotle is of course an outstanding writer, but for the most part so concise and pointed that he seems obscure even to those who have spent whole lifetimes reading him. Plutarch and

other writers of that sort seem better suited to your purposes; since you do not have much time left for studies, you should not devote any of it to those which you cannot continue, or that time will be taken from those which are most necessary.

To be sure, nothing is so difficult that your admirable mind could not fathom it if you were allowed to grow old in the study of letters; but you will immediately be called to other concerns when you return home. I fear that I shall bore you by repeating this so often, and I ask you to forgive me and not to object even if I am in the habit of jesting somewhat freely with you. This I do in order to lighten my heart, which the misfortunes of my native land have overwhelmed with weariness; for I have nothing but the memory of our friendship to cheer me. Thank you very much for your most gracious promises about your portrait.

I wish you the best of good fortune and prosperity. Vienna, February 19, 1574.

The following week, on February 26, Languet chose to write about Sidney himself, rather than to fill his paper with jests and heavy teasing.

I am already reaping the sweet fruits of my affection for you, as I have always greatly hoped to do. For I see that men, whose virtue I respect, greatly love and admire you: their letters to me, filled almost wholly with praise, show the strength of their feelings for you. To this my lord the Count adds that he finds so much benefit and pleasure in your company that, if he hoped anything could be achieved by wishes, he would wish for nothing more than that your affairs and his would always let you spend your lives together. For my part I congratulate myself on having promoted your friendship, or at least on having given you the opportunity of forming it. It is, however, the similarity of your manners, and your common pursuit of virtue, which have promoted it.

My dear boy, as long as you remain true to yourself, you will never be without good men to show you affection and courtesy. And if in early manhood your virtue bears such sweet fruit, what do you think will happen after twenty or thirty years, if you adhere steadfastly to your excellent intentions?

What you wrote about Walsingham pleases me greatly. I am delighted that a good and distinguished man, whose kindness I know from experience, has received some reward for the pains he has taken on behalf of the state. I praise the Queen for her sagacity: she cannot do better for herself and for her kingdom than to employ such men in the government. I wrote some things in my last letter about Irish affairs which I hope are not true.

After a long account of how the Dutch "whose stupidity was once proverbial" had outwitted the Spanish in a naval battle off Schakerloo, costing the Spaniards fifteen ships, Languet turned to other topics.

Perrot has written to me from Geneva, and I had sent him a letter for you. He is sorry that he has not had an opportunity to serve you. As far as I can gather from his letter, they hope there that peace will prevail in France. The King of Poland arrived at Cracow on the eighteenth of this month, and was crowned on the twenty-first. He took the customary oath, with only this added: "I shall watch over and maintain peace and tranquillity among dissident religious groups." Our fellow Frenchmen do not speak highly of the Poles' courtesy. I recently asked a certain witty gentleman who came from there while he was sick, why he had put himself in such danger. He answered that he was afraid of dying there because he believed that the path thence to heaven was anything but well-worn.

Banter about Humphrey Lhuyd's opinions of the English and the Saxons largely fills the rest of the letter. Again Languet's words reveal the ebullient personality beneath the ambassadorial mien.

I am not so contemptuous of your Welshman as you say, for if he did not have some talent he could not commit such remarkable absurdities. Furthermore, not only do I have no wish to deprive you and Griffin of your Brennus, although he is said to have been my fellow countryman (for the Senones are believed to have been from Burgundy), I will even permit you to choose a few other robbers of this sort from French history to adopt into your nation. Or rather, choose them from among the living and use them as shoots for grafting in Wales, where I believe there are many infertile trees!

I think that to this day some of Brennus's posterity must survive in Germany, for we read that Cologne Cathedral has recently been pillaged; it was the richest one in all Germany, just as the temple at Delphi was the richest in Greece. Some people value what was stolen at a hundred thousand gold pieces. But you will have to come to an agreement about your Brennus with Master Jacob, who is a Burgundian.

Finally you add a nice touch of malice to your letter, as it might be a fox's tail, to set me, or the Welshman, or perhaps both of us, at odds with my Delius, when you interpret my letter as meaning that the Welshman says all Saxons are robbers or pirates. For he is writing only of those Saxons who were the ancestors of the English; indeed, the Saxons of our age have more religious scruples and believe that they ought to obey Christ when he says, "Each of you bear the other's burden"—especially when they happen upon merchants whose purses are heavy with money. Then you go on to abuse all Huberts, although you have had no men in Germany who are fonder of you. But be on your guard against Hubert the patron saint of hunters. Erasmus says that he is fearsome because he is armed with rage and vents it upon those who despise his power.

I have paid your respects to Masters de Vulcob and Bochetel. They are very fond of you, and they send you their compliments in turn and are anxious to have you back with us. If you do them this favour, you will make me entirely happy. I ask you to pay my courteous respects to his Excellency the Count, and to the rest of my friends. I shall answer their letters when I find some free time. For I am quite overwhelmed by my duties, and yet I cannot stop chatting with you. I now have here the court courier with whom I must send answers to several persons. And I must also send so many letters to friends who will be coming to Frankfurt from various places that I shall have to spend several sleepless nights. Farewell. Vienna, February 26, 1574.

Languet did not know when he wrote this letter that Sidney had left his rooms at the Pozzo della Vacca and returned to Venice. Doubtless he felt restless after his weeks in Padua, where most of his time seems to have been devoted to study. Sidney's excuse was clear enough; he had promised to have his portrait painted for Languet, and now he had succeeded in getting the famous Paolo Veronese to undertake the commission.

CHAPTER 8

In 1574 Paolo Veronese was at the height of his powers and reputation. His huge canvases covered the walls of many churches and public buildings as well as the ceilings in the Church of St. Sebastian, St. Mark's Library, and the Sala del Gran Consiglio in the Doge's Palace. According to Paolo's biographer Antoine Orliac, "He was so much in demand that he could hardly cope with all the public and private commissions in spite of his great assiduity and prodigious facility."[1] Evidently Sidney's intermediary in Venice had successfully convinced the painter that the young Englishman was both an attractive and eager subject and also one who would pay fairly promptly, factors which have been known to influence painters in all generations.

Aside from their decorative quality and Paolo's skill in arranging space, his paintings were remarkable because of his great gift for portraiture. His murals contained dozens—in a few cases, hundreds—of figures and heads. Although the subject matter was often allegorical, many of the faces were recognizable portraits of living persons. The variety of facial expression and the brilliant flesh tones were then, as now, considered masterful. Furthermore, according to Orliac, Veronese prided himself on bringing out "the charm and attraction of his models" and "excelled at interpreting the distinction of high breeding." Similarly, he sought to bring out "subtle psychological values"[2] beyond the mere delineation of physical features. He had recently finished some of his most famous canvases, the great mural celebrating the victory at Lepanto behind the throne in the Sala del Collegio of the Doge's Palace, and "The Feast in the House of Levi" on forty feet of wall in the refectory of the Dominican monastery of St. John and St. Paul. In 1573 he had also completed the "Adoration of the Magi" in the Church of St. Sylvester.

Sidney's sitting for the master is reported rather casually at the end of a letter to Languet.

Greetings.
"You've come in the nick of time," as I believe that Terentian

1. Antoine Orliac, *Veronese*, trans. Mary Chamot (New York, 1940), p. 13.
2. Ibid., p. 25.

character, Davus, says. I was just ready to criticize you sharply, because this Friday was far advanced and I did not have the customary letter from you, when, lo and behold, it arrived; it quickly deterred me from my harsh intention and forced me, indeed, to play the part of the anxious defendant instead of the aggressive plaintiff. You bring many charges against me, but one in particular, that I made no mention in my last letter of our return—as if repetition were still needed when I had long given you assurances of this. Now, if I swerved from my decision, then it would be thoughtless of me not to inform you; but so long as I keep to it, why should I ply your ears again and again with the same old trifle?

Your affection for me is the reason you never tire of hearing about what concerns me, even slightly. Therefore you should not imagine— if you consider me grateful, that is to say, not disloyal—that I could possibly forget your affection, or relegate it to a secondary place among newer friendships. While I live I will honour nothing more highly.

The rumour that the Turk and the descendants of Mohammed have made peace has now become faint; however, it surely bodes some ill. For the Venetians are being treated quite harshly, and they will obviously be glad to accept peace on even the most adverse terms. Doubtless you have heard of the naval battle of the Gueux and their happy victory. In France they report that the Huguenots are penetrating the whole of Languedoc, Dauphine, and Provence without out opposition, and that Montmorency has tried to poison the King. *Tauta estin epicheira tyrannikēs philias.* Please do write me, my dear Hubert, if all this is true. I shall search out both your private and the public accounts of the Polish coronation.

Today Paolo Veronese started my portrait, so I must stay here for another two or three days. Farewell, and love me. Venice, February 26, 1574. I have written all this half asleep.

Yours very affectionately,
Philip Sidney

To the illustrious Master Hubert Languet, my master and friend, with eternal regard. Vienna.

The modern reader might gasp at the thought of allowing only four days for the portrait, but two points help to explain why this time would suffice. First, Paolo's facility for catching likenesses can scarcely be exaggerated. Secondly, the skill of his assistants, including his brother and a nephew, permitted them to paint the background and fabrics without Sidney's being present. Most likely Paolo did only the head and hands (assuming these were shown) and the assistants did the rest.

This portrait, which Languet received in due course, is not known to exist. It has long been one of the most sought-after objects on the list of famous missing treasures, and dozens of Sidney scholars have felt their pulses beat faster at the thought of finding the portrait somewhere in a provincial collection, perhaps labelled "An Unknown Youth." Meagre evidence suggests that in 1661 it was hanging in a collection in Frankfurt.[3] No later trace of this Frankfurt picture, which may have been some other than the Paolo Veronese, has ever been reported. Anyone who saw the rubble to which Frankfurt was reduced in World War II could not be sanguine about the portrait's survival even if knowledge of its presence there were certain.

Evidently Sidney had written Languet a letter (now missing) on or about February 18 with the news that he planned to set out for Venice, since Languet's reply of March 5 began, "Now that you are back in your Venice, looking down on us, as it were, from on high, you insult us, and take up your old refrain again, that I have unjustly accused you of neglecting me." After continuing this good-natured and rather conventional chiding for a while Languet reported the latest news and rumours.

Sidney must have voiced some discontent about his quarters in the house of Hercole Bolognese because Languet replied, "If you do not have decent lodgings in Padua, you can find some in the citadel of Milan, if you care to travel over there." This was the equivalent of saying, "Instead of complaining about the choice you made, choose again provided you accept the concomitant factors."[4] Languet then continued his personal advice to Sidney with this warning:

> The English book which you showed me here has been translated into French, and other things have been added to it by someone who tries to extenuate the charges brought against the Queen of Scotland.

3. A letter of Apr. 8, 1661 from Algernon Sidney (printed in Collins, 2:709) says, "I haue written to my Correspondent at *Frankfort*, for Sir *Phylip Sydney* his Picture." There is also a possibility that the picture might be in Antwerp since Languet died there in 1581 and his goods were sold there.

4. Bruce Bairnsfather created the classic answer to such a complaint in his World War I cartoon with the caption, "If yer knows of a better 'ole, go to it!"

I had a copy with me for several days, which, I believe, has been sent to the Emperor, and I read a good part of it. I beg and implore you, my dear Sidney, in the name of friendship, not to let anyone know that you have writings of this sort with you. I am very sorry that I did not say more about it before your departure; for this and other related reasons I am so eager to speak with you that, if it were at all possible, I would hurry to you at once.

Believe me, in monarchies virtue is more often the cause of ruin than vice for men of high rank. You do not have to look in ancient histories for examples of this; the life of Henry the Eighth alone can provide us with a good many, and, to be perfectly frank with you, your nation seems to have been most liable to these evils—though now we have stolen the palm from you. But I fear that in your country such tragedies will soon return to the stage, since there are those who are working up material for that purpose. I pray God that your virtue may prove the salvation of you and your country.

But more of these things elsewhere. I am very glad that you have decided to improve your pronunciation; for this is the only respect in which you have fallen short of great merit and congeniality—besides diligence in writing me. Do not listen to your countrymen in this matter, but rather to foreigners; it is for their sake that you have learned Latin. In fact, when you return home I advise you to hire a foreign tutor for your brothers to instruct them in letters.

You would do well to write to Master de Vulcob in the meantime. He is very fond of you. Our Abondio pays you his courteous respects. Dr. Andreas Paull, whose greetings I previously conveyed to you, has also written me recently to ask me to tell you again that he is very fond of you and very eager to serve you. Tell me at once to return these greetings in your name. Farewell. Vienna, March 5, 1574.

A week later Languet wrote again. He makes various references which indicate that after arriving in Venice Sidney wrote a second letter, which is also now missing. After the usual ironic recrimination, and the information that "I received your letter after mine had left with the courier," Languet discloses that Sidney had made a new friend.

I am glad that you have become acquainted with the illustrious Dr. Zündelin, whose learning, sagacity and integrity all his friends praise greatly. So see to it that you are often in his company and that you benefit from his friendship. A young man best develops his own judgement by being with men of this sort, so that he can hear their opinions about all kinds of things.

Wolfgang Zündelin had been born in Constance in 1539 but spent most of his adult life in Venice. He settled there about 1560 and, after serving as tutor to the young Prince Christopher Palatine, became the paid agent for various German Protestant princes. Zündelin was a learned man and he possessed a prose style then considered elegant; the combined traits led to his becoming a writer of intelligence newsletters, his chief source of income. The importance of political intelligence in statecraft had been one of the dawning realizations of the Italian Renaissance, especially among the students of Machiavelli. They recognized that successful statesmanship depended on knowing the strength and position of the opposing chessmen; hence information was an investment that could pay handsome returns.

That Sidney had learned this lesson seems evident from the advice he later gave his brother Robert, "in Italy your greatest expence must be upon worthi men, and not upon housholding."[5] Exactly what arrangements Sidney made with Zündelin we have no way of knowing, but the number and nature of the letters in the newly recovered group suggest that some definite plan had been agreed upon. Besides the series to Sidney, there are important collections of Zündelin's dispatches to the Landgrave William IV of Hesse (now in Marburg) and two volumes addressed to the Camerarius brothers (in the Bayerische Staatsbibliothek in Munich).[6]

Languet then commented on Sidney's report of the outbreak of new religious battles in France.

> The more wicked and shameful the reports from there the more readily I believe them. For I feel that souls stained by the monstrous crime of which you and I were spectators are tormented by madness and are driven to destroy themselves and others. . . . The fire which has been kindled in Christendom because of religion can be extinguished only by its destruction, since our adversaries are earnestly seeing to it that this flame will not lack fuel. . . .

5. Feuillerat, 3 :130.
6. These two volumes are nos. 21 and 22 of the "Collectio Camerariana." Unfortunately, they contain nothing about Sidney.

My dear Sidney, there is nothing I would more gladly talk about with you than these things, and I would even write about them if it were not dangerous to commit such things to a letter. These days, or rather these nights (for I have had no leisure during the day), I have read a great deal by your monk, Matthew Paris. He is often foolish, but his asides paint an excellent picture of the tyranny which the Roman popes exercised over the princes of his time. They commanded you no less haughtily, nor plundered you less greedily, than if they had conquered you in battle. I am not amazed at the magnificence of the Italian cities, since they have had for so many years diverted to them the booty of so many peoples whom the Italians' deceit, or rather their own folly, forced to bear the yoke of the Roman court.

While Sidney was in Venice for his sittings with Veronese he made a decision which poses one of the unsolved mysteries of his biography. He decided to break off his studies at Padua and make a rapid excursion across the widest part of Italy to Genoa and back, travelling south to Florence on either the trip out or the return journey. This route totalled about 570 miles, and for some reason Sidney crowded it all into a single month. The expedition would require six hours a day in the saddle for twenty-four days, assuming that progress could be made at the rate of four miles per hour and that the horses could endure this steady pace.[7] Obviously, any sightseeing or study of the cities or fortifications along the way could be only incidental. Nor would there be time to meet people other than innkeepers and ostlers.

Why, we may properly ask, would Sidney, the elegant young aristocrat and intellectual, undertake such a physically exhausting schedule? None of Sidney's biographers has faced this question or even realized the sheer grind of the expedition when crowded into approximately thirty days. Sidney's letter to Languet of about March 5 would have cleared up the enigma, but it has not survived. Only four facts exist on which any explanation can be based. The first is that Sidney was still in Padua when he wrote to Languet about March 5. Secondly, he had returned to Venice by April 9 (Good Friday), and perhaps as early as April 6. Thirdly, Genoa was clearly the chief destination of Sidney's party, but Florence was also on the itinerary, as Languet's letters show.

7. Montaigne's *Journal* reveals that seven years later his party covered approximately the same distance daily over level terrain. Mountainous roads reduced their progress to about eighteen miles per day.

The fourth fact seems inconsequential, but it provides the clue for a possible explanation of the expedition and its rapid pace. It occurs in one of Languet's letters after Sidney's return, that of April 23, in which he says, "I accept your excuse about French advice on undertaking a Ligurian journey, but you should nevertheless have written me about it." The words "de Gallico consilio" could mean various things, but the simplest and most satisfactory explanation is the following. When Sidney was in Venice in late February he saw some friends from the French Embassy, notably the Ambassador, Arnaud du Ferrier. Their conversation touched on the French courier who made regular trips across northern Italy from Venice to Genoa and back. Somehow Sidney got the idea of accompanying him, since in this way he could see the country while stopping at the inns and benefiting from the stabling facilities patronized by the courier. Hence the long journey could be kept to schedule, Sidney would have the feat to boast about, and he would have the care, advice, and companionship of an experienced professional. No other theory is more logical, or accounts so well for all the physical factors.

Languet continued to send weekly letters to Sidney even though he knew that Sidney would not receive them until his return from the Ligurian coast. In his letter of March 18, he reproached Sidney for not telling him earlier of his spur-of-the-moment decision to go on the hurried trip.

> You have such trust in me as a confidant of your plans that you wrote me you were setting out for Genoa only when you were on the point of leaving, that is, when there was no one who didn't know about it. In fact, your letter shows that you were not sure whether to write me about this venture, though it was very important for me to know about it in advance, so that during your absence I would not send any letters which would prove dangerous if they fell into other hands. And naturally I sent such letters, not only to you, but also to my lord the Count of Hanau, and to other friends of mine in his household, sealing them in the packet addressed to you; consequently, they will not receive them until you return, and it certainly would not go well with me if they should be opened by some stranger for I included several things which would not meet with everyone's approval.

One of their Viennese friends may have known of Sidney's travel plans, the Emperor's physician, Johannes Crato von Crafftheim. If so,

Languet assured Sidney that the information had not come from him. "I am surprised that Crato wrote to you as you report, because I did not mention the matter[8] to him or to anyone else. I do not know whether he learned it from our court, for he has never said a word about it to me, though I am often with him." Languet concluded by giving Sidney his benediction, "I pray to almighty God to keep you safe on your way to Genoa, and when you have profitably transacted your business, to bring you safely back to your friends. But you will certainly need to struggle through mountains that you will find rugged enough, and you will not be pleased with the behaviour of everyone you meet."

In his next weekly letter, dated March 26, Languet confessed his motives in writing regularly despite Sidney's absence: "The rough roads of Liguria are perhaps still delaying you, but I do not wish to break my habit of writing because I want to force you, despite your desire, finally to admit that I am the more conscientious correspondent. . . . I confess I owe to you the pleasure which I find in reading your letters; the greater this is, the more impatiently I desire it." In a more serious vein Languet then alluded to the brilliant career that he foresaw in Sidney's future. (The letter from Sidney to which he refers here may have been that of about March 5 or a subsequent one.)

> You warn me in your last letter not to be so anxious about some-one else's welfare that I neglect my own, since you know how deeply many of the papists hate me. My dear Sidney, I am anxious about your welfare because I am conscious of what your origins are, what your character is, with what eagerness you strive for virtue, and what progress you have already made; and I realize how much your country can expect from you if God grants you long life.

Languet then sent a lengthy review of the political news and concluded, "I have asked you several times not to show my letters to anyone at all, and I continue to ask this." Posterity can be grateful that Sidney preserved them for us to read. From Languet's next letter, dated April 1, we find that Camillo Cruci was carrying the letter just quoted along with its successor: "because Master de Vulcob was too busy to write," Languet did not send his letter immediately. Aside from this explanation, the April 1 letter is exclusively given over to current political news.

---

8. Languet's Latin here is vague: the *res* mentioned could be something other than the subject of the preceding sentence.

When Languet next wrote on April 9, he was not aware that Sidney was back in Venice. Probably Cruci had the professional good sense to know about Sidney's arrival and to deliver the letter there instead of forwarding it to Padua. It is a charming example of Languet's style, an essay on the distinctive traits of the Ligurians, the Tuscans, and the Venetians, crowded with acute insights into the characters of the three regional peoples of northern Italy. But because of Sidney's silence for several weeks Languet's delightful pages tell us nothing about Sidney himself, so no passages require quotation here.

Word of Sidney's return had still not reached Languet on Friday, April 16, when he sat down to his next letter. He began with these sentences of conventional teasing.

> I do not believe that your soul can have been so suddenly con-taminated by the ways of the peoples among whom you have been travelling that you have wholly cast aside the memory of a man who loves you more than himself, and that you begrudge him the great pleasure he will feel when he hears that you have returned safely to Padua and to those who are so fond of you. But since you write nothing about returning, you would give me cause to suppose some such thing if my overmastering affection for you allowed me to do so.

Despite this letter written on Friday, Languet wrote again on Sunday and explained his reason as follows:

> I wrote you . . . two days ago [because] I did not wish to send our friend Wacker away without giving him a letter for you. I do not think I have to commend him to you since not only do you know his virtue and learning, but he has also been most courteous to you, and much more important, he likes and respects you very much and will be most eager to serve you. And so I have no doubt that you will show him every kindness, since you are customarily very kind to everyone except me, who am incredibly tormented by longing for your letters.

"Our friend Wacker" was Johann Matthäus Wacker von Wackenfels. Born in Constance in 1550, he had studied at the universities of Strasbourg and Geneva and was now at Padua where he received his doctorate in 1575. His name appears half a dozen more times in Sidney's correspond-ence, and three letters he wrote to Sidney are among the newly recovered group. As a young man he wrote dramas in Latin, and in later life he became a diplomat and statesman.[9] Because Sidney had already left for Padua by the time Wacker reached Venice, he presumably carried the letter until he also arrived there.

To continue with Languet's letter of April 18, the remaining portion of it is taken up with news of the Emperor's court, expecially the Turkish raids against the Hungarian frontier and reports about the Spanish forces in the Netherlands. Languet ended the letter with this injunction to Sidney: "If you have not yet fulfilled your promise to me about improving your pronunciation [of Latin], I beg you to do so at long last; for it seems to me a most necessary, and a very easy thing to do."

By April 15 Sidney had rested enough from his travels to sit down and write a relaxed letter to Languet, full of leisurely banter and comments on points which Languet had made in his letters. (Sidney undoubtedly had picked these up in Padua before continuing on to Venice.) Sidney entered into ironic banter so thoroughly that at times he adopted an avuncular tone towards his sexagenarian friend. At the same time he recognized that Languet grieved over the religious bloodshed in his native France and over the struggles of the valiant Netherlanders.

Greetings.

My last word from you has worried me so greatly that I can scarcely put my mind to writing. Oh my poor Languet! Can you be wretched, you whom every man that has a spark of virtue in him loves and admires? If some personal matter were causing you this distress, by my affection for you and by our covenant of friendship, which I shall honour as long as I live, I would entreat you to let what you call your increasing age now find repose in my loyalty to you (for, although it is a poor source of physical strength, my very eagerness would still bring you some benefits) and to be assured that there is nothing of mine which is not by that token first yours.

But since I have so long recognized how great a soul you have, and I gather from your letter that you are grieving over the common cause and over your dear country, there is hardly anything left for me to say. Should I console you with my letter, and adduce far-fetched examples of other kingdoms which were once in much more

9. See the biographical article by Theodor Lindner in the *Zeitschrift des Vereins für Geschichte und Alterthum-Schlesiens* (Breslau, 1855–), 8:318. Some of Wacker's correspondence was published by G. Viermann in the *Teschen Gymnasialprogramen* (1860).

desperate straits, but afterwards not only regained their vigour but conquered the world? Neither my age nor my ability permits this. Should I be silent, or rather, pass over that part of your letter? But this would certainly be to slight a friend and to break every law of friendship. Therefore, since good manners command me both to be silent and to speak, it seems best for me to say a few words, and so to fulfill as best I can the duties, so to speak, of both a loving and a well-mannered friend.

First, then, my dear Hubert, I must advise you to talk with yourself more often about these things, and to listen to yourself more often. For you have such an admirable mind that no mortal can give you better advice than you yourself. Next, and most important, I beg you in thinking of the wounds which are now being inflicted upon the church of God to treat them individually; otherwise, as you heap troubles upon troubles, you will feel yourself too greatly overcome by ill fortune. In other words you should consider France's afflictions in themselves, and not unite as it were in a single picture your misfortunes with the ills of Flanders; in this way, it seems to me, you will discern what hopes can still be cherished among so many dangers.

I for my part (but it is perhaps likely that I am indulging a fault of my youth) have begun to lift up my heart a bit since learning that the King of Poland had relieved France of his presence and that in Guienne the Huguenots were having something of the success we had hoped for. But you look forward afar into the future and not only see all this, but discern the consequences of these events: I should therefore like you to take what I have said not as wisdom, but as evidence of my very great affection for you.

With regard to the Low Countries, I really do not see how matters could have gone better; for if that beautiful country is ablaze, we must remember that only such a great fire can drive the Spanish out, and it certainly seems more desirable to me that Saguntum should burn than that faithless Hannibal should possess such great wealth in peace.

The last part of your lamentation concerns the danger with which the Turk seems to threaten Italy; but what event is more to be desired than this? For first this will remove the rotten limb which has so long corrupted the whole body of the Christian commonwealth, and it will destroy, as you say, "the workshop in which the causes of so many misfortunes are being forged." In addition, this will force Christian princes to arise, as it were, from their deep sleep, and your Frenchmen, who are now fighting tooth and nail among themselves, to join forces and oppose the common enemy, just like quarrelsome dogs if they should see a wolf ravaging the sheepfold. But greater events will follow. I am quite sure that profligate Italy will so contaminate even the Turks themselves and entangle them in its wicked attractions that they will then fall more readily by their very own weight from such a great height; and, unless I am wrong, we shall see this in our own time.

Next Sidney adopted a surprisingly mature position in response to some dispirited remarks Languet made in his letter of March 26. The older man had remarked gloomily about his slight abilities and his lack of a useful function in life. In this mood he felt indifferent to the desires of his enemies for his death. Sidney replied:

But really it never ceases to amaze me that you imagine you can be of no use either to your government or your friends and should therefore not try to escape death. I do not wish to go into these ideas further; but this much I do confess, and will proclaim as long as I enjoy the daily rising of the sun: that I have benefited more from my acquaintance with you than from all other experiences combined during my time on the Continent.

So, enough of this. Yet in the meantime, my dear Hubert, you should not think that arrogance (which, I hope, is foreign to me) or garrulity ... but an inclination (more exactly, a heartfelt impulse) has made me decide to write these few words to you so that as far as possible I may help to relieve you of the unhappiness I sensed in your spirit. Yet all my words, I must admit, rank with those of the hog who presumed to teach wisdom to Minerva.

Sidney felt that Languet, the usually objective philosopher and detached commentator on human events and the unfolding pages of history, had sunk into subjective despair over the futility of his efforts to set things right. He tried to rally Languet out of this mood by bickering about one of Languet's own points of banter.

Now let me conclude by jesting a little. In this letter you go out of your way to assert your innocence of a certain Italian malady, that of writing excessively: an unnecessary protest. Henceforth you may wait until you do *not* write, and then make claims of your innocence. For I am well aware that you Burgundians are not keen enough to find pleasure in writing. Quite properly, you concede this merit to the Perugians when you report, in the letter enclosed with the one to me, that the number of guards at the English court had been increased, an item which surely smells of the lamp (I name him *honoris causa*) of Pietro Bizari. As Tigranes said of the army of Lucullus, there are enough of them, and more than enough, for the purpose they are intended to accomplish. But if, indeed, some new danger arises, new measures will be taken to cope with it. We do know that our Queen is making greater preparations on both land and sea than ever before, and she has ordered all the foreign Artisans as they are called (for they are nearly all Lowlanders) to leave London. This she has done to force them to return to the Netherlands and defend their own homelands. Doubtless this will benefit the Prince of Orange, for they total about twenty thousand men. Besides this news there is none except about the fleet of Biscay and descriptions of the sumptuous banquets given by the Pope; he is truly a *bon vivant*.

In the next paragraph Sidney indicates that he had stopped in Padua during Easter week before pushing on to Venice. There he saw the Count of Hanau and picked up letters from him for Languet as well as those that had accumulated while he himself was in Genoa and Florence.

With this letter I send you others from the Count of Hanau and his household; he gave them to me only last week when they were already behind schedule. Do not reply to him until I advise you, since he has already left on a tour of central Italy. Your unfairness may be seen in this, but I can say nothing further because I am bound by a promise I made to you. Remember though the formula for *a majore*.

Sidney concluded the letter by recommending to Languet two young English friends, Robert Corbett (elder brother of his Shrewsbury schoolmate Vincent Corbett of Shropshire, whom Sidney had visited at Christmastide in 1566) and Richard Shelley, Sidney's distant cousin. He also told Languet that he would return to Padua on April 19 when the spring term would be in full swing.

Within a few days two English noblemen will visit you, and since I must give them letters of introduction to you, I think it best, so to speak, to anticipate their arrival with a few words, so that you will be the better prepared to receive them with your customary kindness. The one I particularly commend to you is Master Robert Corbett by name, my very greatest friend, a man born to high estate, yet, as Buchanan says, "whose noble manners far exceed his birth." [10] He is a supporter of the true faith, and quite a military expert, but speaks only Italian.

The other is Master Richard Shelley by name, my kinsman; Robert is likewise, but the latter is as much closer in blood as the former is in friendship. He is well educated, for he is very well versed in Greek, Latin, and Italian, and he also has some acquaintance with things French; but he is very much devoted to papist superstition. As soon as they reach you, you may, if you wish, learn their claims from themselves.

Farewell, and love me as is your wont. Venice (but I shall return to Padua on Monday), April 15, 1574.

Your deeply devoted,

Philip Sidney

To the illustrious Master Hubert Languet, my friend, with the greatest respect.

While Sidney was in Venice he attended to one item of business, probably with the help and advice of his friends. The evidence exists in the official records of the Venetian Republic, the only entry there of his name. On April 29 a request was filed with the Council of Ten, of which the significant passage reads as follows:

The Illustrious Master Philip Sidney, son of the Most Illustrious Master Henry Sidney, Governor of the Province of Wales, being here in Venice, is intending to leave for Padua, where he plans to stay for some time for purposes of study. He desires neither himself nor his gentleman and three servants to be troubled for carrying arms, and therefore they request your Lordships [to issue a licence for this purpose].

---

10. Ringler (p. xxiii) identified this phrase as coming from the dedication to Buchanan's Latin paraphrase of the Psalms.

The name of his gentleman is Master Lodovico Bruschetto. His servants are:

Harrigo Vita
Grifone Appiano
Gio Fisher.[11]

Accordingly, on the following day a patent granting the requested permission was issued by the Council of Ten.[12] The application has the special importance of giving the names of Sidney's servants. Keeping in mind the propensity of contemporary Italians for Italianizing English names,[13] "Harrigo Vita" may be translated Harry White. Similarly, "Gio (Giovanni) Fisher" is clearly John Fisher. "Grifone Appiano" presents a slight problem, though Griffin Madox is obviously the man. If we reject any possibility that "bee-man" is intended, the droll Welshman appears to have given his name as "Ap Ian," meaning "son of John." This could easily be recorded as "Appiano." Besides the fact that Sidney had four attendants, the entry tells us nothing new except that Sidney's friends must have agreed that a licence was desirable. It is not unlikely that Sidney had borne arms on earlier occasions without official permission.

Two of Sidney's correspondents in Vienna wrote him on April 23. Among the newly recovered group is a brief letter from Vulcob. It is valuable chiefly because it proves that Sidney had completed his Genoa expedition and reached Venice during Easter week, for he had written Vulcob on Good Friday.

Sir,

My reply to the letter you have been pleased to write me, dated the ninth of this month, will only be to tell you that I rejoice with you in your return in good health from your "progress" (to put it in a kind of English) through Italy, and to thank you for the pleasant memory you are pleased to retain of me. I shall always be ready to serve you with all my heart in whatever way you may wish to make use of me.

11. This document is in the Venetian archives, Consiglio di Dieci, no. 78, fol. 127. It was cited but not quoted by Buxton, p. 264. For the original text of this and the patent granted on Apr. 30, see app. 2. These were supplied by the kindness of Dr. Giancarlo Roscioni of Rome and Professor Gaetano Cozzi of Padua.

12. Ibid., fol. 75. This document was reported in *Calendar of State Papers Venetian 1558–80*, no. 583, where it is mistranslated and wrongly dated Apr. 19.

13. See for example Carrafa to Sidney, Feb. 3, 1575; and Pavese to Sidney, Nov. 19, 1575.

I shall not give you any of our news as Master Languet can do so. I present my most humble and affectionate respects to your benevolence, and pray God to grant you,
Sir, good health and a happy life. From Vienna, this twenty-third of April, 1574.
Your humble servant and obedient and affectionate friend,

J. de Vulcob

Cruci also brought Sidney another fat letter from Languet who was not yet reconciled to Sidney's silence while travelling posthaste to Genoa and Florence. He appears to be answering another missing letter from Sidney, doubtless written from Venice on April 9 to accompany that written to Vulcob.

I consider that you have begrudged me the very great pleasure which you knew I would feel as soon as I learned that you had come safely back to Padua or Venice from Liguria. Or at least you took care to compound that sweetness with the bitter medicine of your reproaches. Yet, though you were unable to prevent me from being very happy at your safety, I still want to return the favour you did me. You vigorously proclaim how diligent you were in seeing to it that letters which I might write to you during your absence should not be lost, and that any which were included for my lord the Count, or for others, should be delivered to them immediately. But, my most delightful and most careful Sidney, you were not careful enough. You did not have your agent open such packets from me as seemed to contain several letters, though you know that I have never sent you letters for others without rolling them up in the packet addressed to you.

And here, too, is a choice item: your writing that I have clearly shown how poor an opinion I have of you, and how little hope I have of your performing a friend's duty in delivering letters, because I wrote Monau about it. This is how you have learned in Florence to prate, and to treat your friends harshly. First, let me warn you that you will not get away with such harsh treatment of me. Could I have written to you about this in Liguria? Nor could I write to my lord the Count, nor to anyone in his household, because I had no one to whom to entrust such a letter, since I do not take such advantage of Master de Vulcob as to entrust letters to his charge for anyone but you, for fear of abusing his kindness.

But letters for Monau I generally entrust to my old friend Crato, the imperial physician. I asked him to tell Master von Welsperg that I had written them, and that the letter was enclosed in the packet addressed to you. Do I seem to you to have sinned so grievously in doing this? Particularly since I did not know when you would return, and it was important for Master Jacob to receive my letter, because it contained a reference to some money I owed him. In fact, as a result of the ensuing delay, I could not call the Baron of Prague to account for him in this matter.

"Master Jacob" Monau (1546–1603), a former student of Joachim Camerarius first at Leipzig and later at Heidelberg and Wittenberg, had now migrated to Padua where his congenial personality and theological learning gained him admission to the circle of friends (Hanau, Slavata, Dohna, et al.) with whom Sidney associated.

The next portion of Languet's letter tells us that Sidney's recent trip to Genoa had been hurried and thus he had had no time for writing a proper letter. It also reveals, as mentioned earlier in this chapter, that the trip had been taken on the advice of French friends in Venice.

If I sometimes reproach you for negligence, it is my affection for you that prompts me, and also the pleasure I take in reading your letters. If you sent me ten a day, I would still crave more. I accept your excuse about French advice on undertaking a Ligurian journey, but you should nevertheless have written me about it. I wish you would follow the same advice in hurrying back to us. I do not want to scold you now by saying that you could have gladdened me greatly if during your journey you had only written, "I am alive and well at Florence," or "at Genoa." Nothing longer was needed.

Languet then went into a lengthy explanation of an incident in Vienna about which he had been misinformed, and he requested Sidney to pass the genuine account of it to Wacker. Finally, Languet asked Sidney to send him a pamphlet by one Camillo Capilupi who praised Charles IX highly for having carried out the St. Bartholomew's Day massacre.

I hear that a pamphlet written in Italian is being sold around secretly where you are; its title is *The Stratagem of the French King*. If you can find a copy or two, you will do Master de Vulcob and me a very great favour if you send them to us. Take care, however, to have it folded into a small packet, and entrust it to the person who customarily sees to your letters.

Please decide about your portrait as you wish. If you hoped to be here shortly, it would be unnecessary to send it ahead. But in this matter you are making haste *very* slowly. I wish you the best of good fortune and prosperity, and I congratulate you on your safe return to your friends; for while I have been writing my anger has subsided. Pay Master Bryskett, and the rest of your household, my respects. Vienna, April 23, 1574.

By the time Sidney had received this letter he was again well settled into his routine at Padua. Doubtless his quarters in the house of Hercole Bolognese seemed more comfortable after the accommodations he had had to accept during his month on the road, though after those long days in the saddle even the straw pallet in a postal-route inn would have felt welcome. Besides, the time to return to Vienna would come soon enough.

CHAPTER 9

After Sidney had been back in Padua for a week he took up regular correspondence again, and on Thursday, April 29, he wrote at least two letters. One was to his Strasbourg friend, Dr. Jean Lobbet; we know about the letter from Lobbet's reply of June 1 and from a reference quoted below. Sidney had sent a letter for Lobbet to give to another friend, Dr. Claude Aubéry, whose reply appears in Chapter 12. On the same day he also wrote Languet a letter so full of rhetorical devices and irony that it seems as stylized as the contemporary pavane and gaillard.

> I could never be persuaded that Machiavelli [in Chap. 8] was right in thinking that one must avoid too much clemency, until I discovered by experience just what he tried to prove with all his arguments. For I have calmly borne (see how mild I am!) not only wrongs but blows and wounds from you, hoping that no rigidity was so obstinate that it could not be softened by such gentleness. But my hope has been vain, and I see that not only have I not lessened, but I have aggravated the disease with this medicine, and I shall therefore not use it any longer. To speak frankly, I shall not prefer the empty appearance of clemency to salutary severity.
>
> What! Have you persuaded yourself that you can safely not only mock the Welsh, paint the wiles of the Saxons in their own colours, treat the Florentines and Ligurians as thieves and robbers, but also go so far as to threaten to punish even the English? I wish to refrain from turning my wrath, though it is just, upon the Burgundians, out of proper respect for your patron saint Hubert and for the sacred memory of that wise Charles [the Bold] of yours, whom the Swiss treated with such deference. But I should very much like to know what England has done to deserve such grave and violent criticism at your hands.

Sidney never used irony more heavily than in this allusion to the deference shown by the Swiss to Charles the Bold: they defeated three successive armies under his command and killed him at Nancy in the third battle.

Not content with this, you also challenge me to fight you on personal grounds (if by chance public considerations should not arouse me sufficiently) by revealing some of your new suspicions, the most serious of which is that I have forgotten you and am therefore neglecting my duty of writing. Really, you are a fine one! Like Geta in the *Phormio*, you are "afraid to entrust a secret to a man you have proved honest with money." But I shall discuss these things with you in person, and in a different way; for the present, I do not wish to cast off all my customary clemency, so that I may see from your next letter whether you are sorry for such a grievous fault.

Once playfulness was out of the way, Sidney reported a few items of current news, beginning with François de Noailles, Bishop of Dax, who had recently retired from his post as French Ambassador to the Sublime Porte.

Monsieur Dax has returned to Venice, and I shall try to become his friend, for he is (or so it is said) endowed with every virtue. He asserts, I hear, that the Turks are making great preparations this year: so I hope the Spanish will be more concerned about defending their own homes than attacking those of others. As a result many people have begun to doubt whether John of Austria will leave for Spain. Cosimo [the Great], Duke of Florence, has recently died, and his people mourn him deeply, but in the same state of mind as the Syracusan woman prayed that all the best would befall Dionysius the Tyrant. His successor is already diligently negotiating with the Turk to obtain free access to Greek commerce for his Tuscans. How successful he will be I do not know.

It will soon be time for me to keep my promise to return, and I do not want you to invent the charge of inconstancy against me in the future as you have done in the past. I therefore give you the entirely free option and authority to decide whether you wish me to wait until the Count of Hanau returns, or immediately to make my way to you, my dear Hubert. All I have left to say is that Master du Ferrier and Dr. Zündelin continually show me the greatest kindness.

Farewell, and if you love me, take great care to be of a calm mind. Padua, April 29, 1574.

Your most affectionate and respectful,

Philip Sidney

I beg you to wish Master de Vulcob and Bochetel the best of
health for me. Bryskett wishes you the same. I have written all this,
and another letter which I am now sending Lobbet, in a state of great
drowsiness. To the illustrious Master Hubert Languet, my friend,
with the greatest respect. Vienna.

Somewhere on the road to Vienna the courier with Sidney's letter
passed his counterpart bringing one from Languet, written on the first
of May and full of warm personal sentiments towards the young man
whom he had not seen for nearly six months.

As long as I live, I shall consider the day I first saw you a happy one:
the innate virtue which shines forth in your face, in your discourse,
and in your every action, immediately impelled me to become your
friend. And an unhoped for opportunity for this presented itself
when you arrived here. I do not know what destiny of yours brought
this about, but it was my very good fortune, and, thanks to your
kindness, I then easily accomplished that for which I had decided to
strive with all my might. When I grew closer to you, I discovered
that you had a great natural inclination to virtue, and such a burning
desire for it that I henceforth considered myself extremely fortunate
in your friendship, and the thought of you brought me my only
joy among the great misfortunes of my native land.

Now, if I ever did experience that joy, I did so most when I
received your letter yesterday. For it contains nothing but evidence
of your goodness, kindness, and uncommon benevolence towards
me, and your anxiety about my afflictions, all of which naturally
gratify me. But even more than that, your excellent mind and your
sound judgement about the greatest affairs amazes me: I would
never have believed, before I knew you, that there was so much
sagacity in young manhood. . . .

It remains for me to thank you for offering me your resources so
affectionately and freely: I would presume to use them if I did not
have sufficient means available elsewhere. I have learned to live
happily with so little that I hope I shall not be a burden to my
friends. Yet your offer is most gratifying as a token of your benevolence, and as such I consider it a great favour. But, my noble Sidney,
I seek only this one favour of you, and that is for you to come to me
safe and sound; I pray unceasingly to God for this, since He alone

can bring it to pass. For so long as you are safe and sound, then I shall feel that all is well with me too.

The state of affairs in France and the fate of the Protestant cause in the Low Countries weighed heavily upon Languet's spirit. The triumph of the Spanish forces over Prince Louis of Nassau at the battle of Mooker-heide (April 14 and 15), where both Nassau and Christopher of the Palatinate were slaughtered with four thousand Protestant soldiers, depressed Languet deeply. "What troubles me, my dear Sidney, is not my personal misfortune, which I usually endure with a strong enough spirit whenever it assails me; but public misfortune, and particularly that of my own country, affects me like a tender mother, who grieves deeply when her children are punished, even though she realizes that they have fully deserved it."

In reply to Sidney's suggestion in his letter of April 15 that if the Turks overran Italy at least the Protestants would be rid of the deceitful Italians, Languet concurred: "You are right about Italy. Whenever the Turks gain possession of it, whatever ancient virtues they still maintain will immediately disappear. Hence the rest of Christendom will benefit doubly from the destruction of Italy." This reminded Languet of the Count of Hanau's plans to travel south into the papal territories.

I do not quite understand what you mean in accusing me of injustice to you, unless you perhaps imagine that I advised my lord the Count to do what I counselled you against; but I certainly did not do that. In fact, I warned his party more than once to take care of themselves, and I wrote Master von Welsperg in particular about this. I am really surprised that he is now so ready to take risks, since I know that in these matters he not only used to be cautious and prudent, but sometimes even seemed timid. Even though my lord the Count's guardians allowed them to undertake these journeys, it does not follow from this that they were taking proper precautions. Therefore I shall continue to be anxious about them until I know that they are back with you; and for that reason I beg you to write me all the news of them you have.

I am eagerly awaiting those excellent men, so close to you in many ways, whom you mention in your letter, and I pray that I may be able to show them some kindnesses which may please you and them. Urge them, I beg you, to treat me as someone who is very eager to serve you and them.

Be well and happy; and my respects to our friends. Vienna, May 1, 1574.

Before either of these letters reached its destination, Sidney found himself deep in correspondence with Wolfgang Zündelin. During his Easter visit to Venice Sidney had apparently entered into some arrangement whereby Zündelin would send him his news reports. Sidney had then written to him from Padua, and the floodgates opened. Because Zündelin's letters are hitherto unpublished and also because they are good specimens of the free-lance intelligence reports so avidly sought in that era before other forms of new communication had been developed, they are given here in their entirety. Explanatory annotation has been kept to a minimum.

> First of all I beseech you, noble and illustrious Lord, not to believe that I have failed in my duty of writing to you out of negligence; as, of many things, none would be more honourable to me, so nothing could be more pleasant or delightful. But as your Master Bryskett had told me (which his brother later confirmed) that you would be returning to us any day now, I hoped to be able to tell you everything in person more accurately and completely than by letter. When, afterwards, the same Bryskett returned without you, saying that he would go back to you at once, I would have given him any news worth writing: I did not see any reason to cause you unnecessary trouble by tediously and uselessly repeating in writing what you would hear from him. And even most of those matters I could not have written to you without great difficulty, nor indeed did I think them worth writing until I should have received somewhat more sure and trustworthy news of them. Such are those matters of which, as you say in your letter, the English Baron has apprised you.

Although the first name of Bryskett's brother is not mentioned, it appears to have been Sebastian.[1] He was the eldest son, and since his father Antonio and his brother Lodowick were in government service, it is understandable that he too would turn his linguistic knowledge to similar use. The English Baron was Edward, third Baron Windsor of Stanwell (1532–75) whose name occurs several times in the newly

---

1. Plomer and Cross, *Lodowick Bryskett*, p. 2. For Sebastian's letters from Rome see *HMC Pepys*.

recovered letters. Lord Windsor maintained a house in Venice. He may have been an agent for Burghley, though the evidence is meagre.[2]

Zündelin now inserted a long account of the battle of Mookerheide, a summary of the various reports which had reached Venice.

> That a battle has been fought I do not doubt: I believe, however, that rumour and the Spaniards' reports have made out the Orangists' defeat to be much greater than in actual fact it was. I append the most widely circulated version of the affair, which runs as follows—
>
> Requesens had heard that the four thousand foot and six hundred horse that were on their way from France as auxiliaries to the Orangists had found their way blocked by the Archbishop of Trier, and that the Orangists were scattered hither and thither near the city of Nijmegen, wandering about without care or anxiety. So he gathered together such troops as he could, both infantry and cavalry, crossed the Meuse with great haste, and unexpectedly attacked the Orangist infantry on April 14. Of these, some say six thousand were killed, but many maintain that the number of dead was four thousand out of six thousand, and that the rest fled; among the cavalry that would have come to the infantry's aid, about seven hundred were killed. Since the rest saw that further resistance would be useless, they turned about, keeping closed ranks. Their commander, Christopher Palatine, was killed, and Count Louis escaped wounded. It is even said that one of his brothers was captured. None of this, however, is true for certain.
>
> Of the Spaniards and their allies, the Spaniards themselves admit four hundred dead, others say three thousand. These things were confirmed by a letter from Augsburg last Saturday, although the rumours had been widespread previously. A certain friend who had read a letter from the Venetian secretary at Milan to the Venetian Senate says that it was very brief, and mentioned only that Duke Christopher was dead, that six thousand foot and fifteen hundred horse were either dead or routed, and that, on the Spanish side, there were four hundred dead and about two hundred wounded. Indeed,

---

2. The Cecil papers show that in June 1573 Lord Windsor sent Queen Elizabeth an Italian "discourse of the government of England" and asked to be made a secret agent, assuring her that if accepted he "shall never be found a blab, or an utterer of matter of state, but as sure as a column of marble, for in that consisteth true nobility." *HMC Cecil*, vol. 2, no. 136.

there is such diversity of accounts that I have not yet been able to decide to my satisfaction what to believe. I shall certainly not credit what is said either in the letters of the Spaniards, who are insolently exaggerating their victories, or by the general rumour, which anyone may exaggerate at his own pleasure.

My great love for Duke Christopher makes me the more afraid for him: especially because I hear that he was wont to consider the dangers of war, not with regard to his princely dignity, but rather with the sense of duty of a common soldier; and that in the Netherlands two years ago he only most narrowly escaped the hands of the enemy, into the midst of whom he had too boldly hurled himself. Whatever may have happened, it did so by the providence of the unchanging Divine Power, and we must bear it steadfastly and in a Christian spirit. What is being said also by the Spaniards about their vast land and sea preparations against the Netherlands, I shall entrust orally to Master Bryskett, though I believe that you will already have heard it from the letters of those who supply you with news.

Zündelin's "great love for Duke Christopher" developed while he was the Duke's tutor. The battle two years previously occurred during the siege of Mons.

The next topic to which Zündelin turned was the threat to Venice of a possible alliance between the Spanish and the Turks.

There is a certain important person who considers, and all but proves, that the same Spaniard obtained a truce from the Turk. Certainly no preparations against this city can as yet be discerned from that quarter, and John of Austria, having dispatched the fleet with Sesse and Antonio in command, is now (if I remember correctly) leaving Orense for Milan, there to concentrate upon the preparations for the Dutch war: and some even say he is about to leave for the Netherlands. I believe that the former efforts of the Pope, the Spaniard, the Frenchman, and most of the Catholic princes everywhere were only halted temporarily; that the old treaties against the heretics as they call them, never abjured, have been renewed; and that from now on everything will be done with the more passion, the more abjectly they see the Lutherans, especially in Germany, conduct themselves, most of all at this time when the priests themselves do not deny that they might have been curbed by them [the Lutherans].

Mention of the Germans led Zündelin to discourse on their lack of unified help in the Protestant cause.

One who recently arrived here from Germany asserts that the Elector of Saxony is not only doing nothing to help the Dutch cause, but is actually hindering both this and many other plans in the common Protestant interest, led by a certain excessive zeal for his own interests. Another writes to me from Franconia, and tells me that he [the Elector] is doing what he pleases with the children of the late John William of Saxony, without having consulted his co-guardians, the Elector Palatine and the Elector of Brandenburg. Also, that Duke Casimir Palatine recently left him somewhat angry; he does not give the reason.[3] He reports that the Elector of Saxony is transferring his court from Dresden to I know not where, and that he has decided to divert the river to that place at insane cost and to the greatest possible detriment of the local peasantry.

That is the most essential political news: "he may rest who omits not this," etc. I hear that the Landgraves are secretly helping Orange, but very much more scantily than his need requires. Someone writes in a very recent letter from Augsburg—I had almost forgotten to mention it—that the same Augustus has imprisoned certain of his councillors and ministers because of a pamphlet, published many months ago at Leipzig, on the Lord's Supper, the ideas of which do not exactly clash with those of Calvin. Truly, the priests will have something to enjoy a quiet laugh about.

It is a long time since I had a letter from any of my friends; if anything happens, I shall let you know. This, as you see, is written in haste, and I beg of you to forgive my hurry—I was called away while I was writing it.

Zündelin ended with another reference to Lord Windsor, along with the usual compliments.

All that remains—and which I should have done at the beginning—is to thank you, not as much as I should but as well as I can, for your most kind letter to me; and though I know that all my zeal and service are unworthy of you, yet do I offer them with all my heart. Farewell, most noble Lord. From Venice, the third of May, 1574. If it is not too difficult, please give Master Bryskett my greetings.

3. This sentence is an afterthought written in the margin.

That English nobleman [Lord Windsor], whom formerly I once entertained here for a meal, has kindly brought me your letter today and, in short, shows me much goodwill for your sake.

> Yours most faithfully,
> with affection and esteem,
> Wolfgang Zündelin

The dire news in Zündelin's letter hit Sidney very hard. He immediately thought of how it would affect Languet and dash the hopes of the ardent Protestants in his circle of friends. On Friday, May 7, he sat down and wrote Languet a letter which reveals his anguish at the news.

> Although I do not doubt that from many sources, in a word, from rumour itself, you have had far better information than my letter, written here and now, can bring you, nevertheless I feel it my duty to converse with you a little by letter about so important a matter. For I have always considered friendship's greatest benefit the possibility of communing freely with a friend, that is, with one's self, about either public or personal affairs. This matter seems, so to speak, to demand that all of us who are imbued with the true faith abandon all other thoughts and devote ourselves to this one concern with all our hearts.
>
> But what is the object of this long, drawn-out preface? To make you realize that I am very, very deeply troubled. For I have heard, not from insignificant men, but from the Council of Ten itself, that Count Louis was mortally wounded, his brother taken prisoner, and he himself routed with a great loss of men, chief among them doubtless Christopher of the Palatinate and several Rhenish counts, as they are called; and that this has so greatly upset the morale of the Low Countries that unless some Christian prince quickly takes matters in hand, the rebels are apt even to surrender.
>
> For my part I hope, and hope because I wish it so, that these rumours have been falsely published to help the Spanish, for they desire no greater prize than to have the reputation of being fortunate. But be that as it may, my dearest Languet, this is certain, that our princes are sleeping too deep a sleep, and I hope that while they are, they will take care not to contract the disease in which the appearance of death is accompanied by death itself.

Sidney's statement that his news came "not from insignificant men, but from the Council of Ten itself" offers a slight puzzle. It could mean that the Council of Ten had been Zündelin's source of information, or Sidney may have had confirmation from some other friend who had received the news through official channels. That Zündelin had access to someone closely connected with the Council of Ten is not unlikely, for such connections would be of prime importance to him.

Sidney then turned to the vexing problem of the lack of zeal on the part of the Protestant princes of Germany. He echoes the letter from Zündelin, including the report that the Elector of Saxony was planning to divert the course of a river.

> I have recently seen a certain piece of writing, really quite choice (I shall send it to you if I can find it), in which the author energetically urges the princes whom he calls Catholic to execute the decisions of the Council of Trent; and he finds particular grounds for this exhortation in the disgraceful sloth of the German princes, and is confident that they can easily be crushed while some of them are engaging in drinking bouts or in absurd hunting expeditions, and others are planning to turn rivers from their courses at insane expense, and all except the Elector Palatine have resolved both to neglect the public resources and to exhaust their own.

> Good Lord! How I wish I could get to you for even one hour, for I have many things which are absolutely not to be entrusted to a letter. That will certainly happen soon. For the Count will, I hope, return soon, and once here surely will not delay our immediate departure in your direction, a thought which certainly appeases my burning desire somewhat.

The letter ends with an account of Sidney's report to Leicester about the Spanish victory, and of what Sidney had done to get the pamphlet Languet requested.

> Today I wrote to my uncle, the Earl of Leicester, and told him what great hopes the Spaniards cherish as a result of their victory. Perhaps some good will come of my writing, but if not, so far as I am concerned I would rather be blamed for being too little wise than for being too little patriotic. Believe me when I assure you, my dear Hubert, that I have never seen an impulsive woman exult more over some unexpected news than some of these Spaniards do over this event, and yet they wish to give the impression of being extraordinarily restrained. May God grant that their laughter be sardonic!

But enough of this. I have attended to the *French Stratagem*, and by Thursday two copies will have been written out for me; none are being printed because the Pope was prevailed upon by the French Ambassador's vigorous protest to forbid it. For while the pamphlet highly praised certain Italian virtues in the King, the unsophisticated Frenchman imagined that his King was being insulted rather than praised. As soon as I have the copies I shall send them to you, together with a letter to Master de Vulcob; I am not writing to him at this time both because I am very busy and because I should not want to trouble him without cause, since he is as busy as ever. Please wish him the best of health for me, and thank him very much for his kind letter. All I have left to do is to ask you to share what news you have with me, if you think it proper.

Farewell, and love me as you do. My Lodowick commends himself most courteously to you. Padua, May 7, 1574.

Your most affectionate,
Philip Sidney

To the illustrious Master Hubert Languet, my dearest friend. Vienna.

On the same day (May 7), Zündelin wrote his second letter to Sidney. More information had reached Venice about Mookerheide, so he hastily passed it along to Sidney as he probably did to various other patrons or potential patrons among his correspondents.

I expected, noble and illustrious Lord, that this messenger from the Netherlands, who arrived last night, would bring me a letter from Heidelberg that would enable me to send you some rather more accurate information concerning the battle fought on the Meuse. But in the first place I have nothing from that source, and of what I have received from the Netherlands, most is either anonymous or clearly from the same source as that which we have already received by special messengers. Secondly, up to April eighteenth (to the wonder of many) none had appeared, besides the one report of the famous victory, who could relate anything about what happened afterwards.

The anonymous news is as follows: The Orangist infantry, ordered to prepare for battle, raised their voices in seditious demands; this problem was solved by the Spaniards when they annihilated them in a well-merited defeat, although, unfortunately, together with many very courageous men. Some say that Duke Christopher Palatine was not killed but captured. Of the important men and nobles with great names, most sources report twelve captured; the Spaniards, thirty. There is a rumour that John of Nassau, Orange's brother, was killed.

Finally, there is no certainty so far as to the number of cavalry and infantry killed. Some are hopeful that Orange, intending to join up with his brother Louis who had escaped unharmed, may have led most of his garrison troops out of the Dutch cities before the battle; but in the opinion of many who have encountered the desperate tenacity of the Dutch, it has been in vain, and most of the Dutch cities, either undone by fear or terrified by the defeat of their side, will pass into Spanish hands.

The fleet of the Gueux, helped by some English ships, has captured twenty-two Spanish vessels. In Zeeland the fortifications have been rebuilt, and in all other respects the island's defence is so thoroughly prepared that it seems to have been made impregnable again. The other news from the Netherlands was, as I wrote, already known here.

About matters French: this morning a report was circulated, derived from a letter brought from Florence and dated from Lyons the twenty-seventh of April, to the effect that the French king has more closely incarcerated his brother Alençon and the others who were held at Vincennes. But all the French assert that nineteen of them were freed.

Yesterday one trustworthy correspondent told me that there are good grounds for suspecting the existence of a new mutual aid treaty between Spain, France, and the Emperor. Others will more accurately inform you of the rest of this story. Farewell, most noble Lord. V[enice], May 7, 1574.

Yours most respectfully,

W. Z.

Most of Zündelin's report is self-explanatory, but a few points call for comment. The "seditious demands" of the infantry were the usual pressures of mercenaries for back wages, reinforced by a refusal to fight further. John, the reigning Count of Nassau, was not present at the battle, but his brother Henry died there. The general fear that Dutch cities would pass into Spanish hands was well justified; 1574 was a year of crisis in the matter. But the relief of Leiden from a long siege on October 3 determined the issue and restored morale to the cities of the Netherlands. The report of the treaty proved groundless, a typical Protestant rumour.

Three days later (May 10) Zündelin again wrote to Sidney. The larger part of the letter consists of his response to one Sidney had written; the verbose language of compliment does, however, reveal a few bits of information about Sidney, including the fact that he had passed along some parts of Zündelin's reports to his uncle, the Earl of Leicester.

When I had returned home last night, noble and illustrious lord, I found your letter; as clearly yours, I may say, as if it were the visible image of your friendliness and kindness. For not only have you answered my letter in the most friendly manner but, as if you had replied less copiously to mine and thereby neglected a necessary duty, you have been pleased to apologize at length. And then, not content with this, you even thank me for writing to you. I hereby acknowledge and most warmly thank you for your benevolence and singular love for me.

At the same time I perceive that, in your wish to prove to me abundantly that friendship for me of which I was already aware, you have been pleased (pardon me, I beg of you, for speaking plainly) to depart somewhat from the way both of your dignity and of your duty. For you do me the greatest possible favour by kindly accepting my letters, or most kindly replying to them without giving yourself to apologies, or usurping the gratitude that it is for me to show. Although nothing is more welcome and pleasant to me than your letters, I do not wish you to go to any trouble in writing for my sake; nor, after this, shall I trouble you with another letter; but I shall write to you only what I believe to be both worth writing, and less well known to you from other sources.

Let me return to your letter, in which what delighted me most of all was your saying that you have written to your most illustrious uncle. Truly you could not have selected a subject worthier of either him or yourself. For you were born to the highest position in the state, and are writing concerning this state to the man who, as I have heard, holds the most profound love for your country. Moreover, he will receive what you write about the native land you share more gladly from you than he would from anyone else: more appropriately because of your intense love for England, more gladly because your letter will come to him, your uncle, from the dearest son of his sister. When you apologize for your age you are too modest: as you know, men are wise rather in heart and mind than by years and age, and there have been many youths who were wiser than old men who were themselves by no means foolish. But enough of this, lest it seem to flatter you—a thing most foreign to my nature.

What follows in your letter I can scarcely mention without a blush. For it is plain that you err through a certain excessive kindness when you decline what is the right and proper address for me to accord you, that of "patron"; and that I have transgressed so grievously, and even more through rude negligence, as to seem by my silence to approve that address ["osservandissimo suo"] which, coming from you, would be fitting for anyone rather than myself. But nothing could be further from the truth. For I understand well enough how incompatible that would be both with your dignity and with my humble position and fortune, of which none could be more aware than myself. I beg you, therefore, in future to omit that form of address, and because this is no more than proper, I even claim it as my right.

To the last part of your letter, where you surpass all kindness by most generously offering me the privilege of your hospitality, I can only reply that, though as yet I cannot properly thank you or repay you, I shall attempt never to cause you to regret your great kindness and benevolence to me.

The last part of Zündelin's letter comprises his current menu of political news. Clearly, the report of the defeat at Mookerheide was depressing ardent Protestants in all parts of Europe.

Concerning news, especially reports from the Netherlands, I intended, when letters from Augsburg had given us more trustworthy information, to write and tell you everything promptly and diligently. But they have made me far more uncertain than I was before. They contain scarcely anything that we had not heard already, nor do they have anything from sources other than letters sent from Antwerp on the seventeenth and nineteenth. However, a correspondent writes from Frankfurt (on April 20), very briefly: I believe that, as a man very friendly to the Gueux, he could not write more because of heartfelt grief. The Orangists were definitely defeated at the Meuse and routed, and fleeing horsemen arrive at Frankfurt in daily growing numbers. If this is true, we can deduce much from the scanty information.

They say that a letter from France, mentioning this defeat and dated from Paris on April 27, has been brought here only last night, so that I am not yet free to speak of this and other matters written by quite trustworthy sources. Certain Frenchmen wish to persuade the Italians that the King has released his brother and all other captives. The Italians, on the contrary, assert that it has been written to them that they [i.e. the prisoners] are not only more closely imprisoned, but some have been secretly killed. Moreover it is alleged—which is not to be wondered at with such a king who, as they say, hastens to his own downfall with oar and sail—that this same King of France, when a letter about the Orangist defeat had been sent to Lyons, acted almost triumphantly; and that he considered the defeat highly useful to him for the subsequent persecution of the Huguenots, glorying in their stubborn preference for continued war rather than the acceptance of the proffered peace conditions. As soon as I have anything more certain about matters French, I will write to you.

Here the papal legate is striving with all possible means to exercise the Inquisition in a daily more severe and cruel manner, against many Venetians, but also against some sympathizers—in order that he may subsequently find the Pope, who has been so long incensed with him, in a more propitious frame of mind.

Farewell, most noble, etc. Lord. Unless it be too difficult, I beg you most heartily to return your Lodowick's greetings. I almost forgot: a German nobleman was here with me, who was recently at Rome, and gave me the greetings of the Count of Hanau and his friends, and told me, to my very great joy, that they were safe and well, and did not intend to proceed farther, deterred by the heat. From V[enice], May 10, 1574.

Yours most faithfully,
with affection and esteem,
W. Z.

In the meantime Languet kept up his regular schedule of weekly letters to Sidney. The religious bloodshed in France and the Spanish victory over Louis of Nassau had filled him with gloom, from which Sidney's recent letter (not preserved) had lifted him temporarily. This more cheerful mood pervades his letter of May 7.

I would complain about the brevity of your letter and accept no such excuses except that your previous letter received a week ago pleased me so much that I have reread it over and over, and still have not read it enough. Certainly it was delivered to me at the right moment to relieve my intense distress, distress for which I do not believe I have ever had more just cause.

Besides the sad news from France and the Netherlands, the religious situation in Languet's adopted country of Saxony had deteriorated badly. His employer, the Elector Augustus, had issued requirements for a return to strict Lutheran tenets concerning the Eucharist, thereby ending the tolerance towards Calvinism or Philippism, as the beliefs of Languet and his fellow disciples of Melanchthon were designated. Thus the divisions in Protestant doctrine were widened at a time when unity was most desirable. Languet poured out his heart:

> The Spanish are revelling in the victory which they have recently won from Duke Palatine Christopher and Count Louis of Nassau, and they hope shortly to conquer the Prince of Orange. Although I know that this will not be so easy as they think, still I am naturally very much troubled by the disaster suffered by those for whose success I heartily prayed.
>
> Furthermore, so that I may have every reason to be wretched, almost all of the men whose friendship I have cultivated during my happy life in Germany during the last twenty years, and whose company in fact made me consider Germany my homeland (all, I say, as if caught up in a single whirlwind and overwhelmed by the violence of fortune), have been plunged into disasters in which I can give them no help whatsoever. Instead I am afraid that, as a matter of fact, some of them believe that part of the blame for those misfortunes lies with me, since that calamitous dispute about the Lord's Last Supper is given as a pretext for everything.
>
> And yet these woes have no other source than the pride and ambition of theologians who immediately conceive an unappeasable hatred for, and plot to destroy by whatever means they can, any good man who should try to recall them to moderation, or should peacefully remind them of their office, or should not subscribe to all their decrees.
>
> Twenty months ago fortune dealt me her cruellest blow in France when she snatched from me in practically a single moment all my

friends there; but cruel as this blow was, it could not satisfy her harshness to me, for in Germany she proved most hostile to the men whose virtue and benevolence had made it possible for me to endure the burdens of my long exile with some equanimity.

Therefore, just as you previously were the dearest by far of all my friends, now you are almost the only one I have left to think about with pleasure. In my sorrow and grief I find the same pleasure in reading your letters, not only because they show how fond you are of me, but because your excellent mental powers shine forth in them, and more and more they strengthen my hopes for the virtue you will attain.

Languet ended by alluding to a stock joke he shared with Sidney about the art of Genoese bankers in extracting usurious interest rates on loans to war-making but impoverished monarchs. Languet had made the charge in his letter of April 9 and Sidney had evidently offered a mock defence of this Genoese art in his reply. Under this playfulness, however, the hearts of both the venerable Languet and his nineteen-year-old protégé were heavy. Although the Protestants had their backs to the wall in France and the Netherlands, advocates of the cause struggled to maintain their objectivity. Their rhetorical jestings were a means of sustaining such necessary detachment.

CHAPTER 10

Meanwhile Languet wrote every week with the regularity of a metronome. It took about ten days for the letters to reach Sidney, and this time lag requires that we adjust our reading of them to the march of interim events. The next letter from Vienna is dated May 13. As usual it begins with teasing, this time about Sidney's supposed conversion to Italian values, specifically those delineated in chapter 18 of *The Prince*.

> I admire you for your frankness in forewarning me to beware of you, for your dreadful threats can have no other meaning. But here you do not observe the rules of your friend Machiavelli, unless perhaps fear has elicited this grandiloquence and bombast from you, and you thought that this was the way in which you could sway me from my resolve. I am surprised it did not occur to you that [we] Burgundians are of a lofty and untamed spirit, and that like the palm tree we rise up against those who would oppress us. But as it is proper for courage not to yield to the insolence of enemies, so it suits us to be susceptible to pity for those who struggle with or are threatened by disaster.
>
> Therefore I shall now put aside animosity, and assuming the role of a friend shall urge you quickly to seek some diligent man to give you careful instruction in marranism [i.e. pretended conformity], since without such knowledge it will hereafter be impossible for anyone to hope to acquire any influence in your England. For the Spanish say that they are sending John of Austria to the Low Countries, and that, once he has conquered the Gueux, he will subdue you English with the mere fear of his name, restore the Queen of Scotland to liberty, marry her, and receive the kingdoms of England and Scotland as her dowry. I wish you could now change the name of Philip, at which you are so proud that you do not spare even St. Hubert himself, into John, so as to have the name of your future prince, and thereby be provided with easier access to his favour. So I urge you to consult your canonists about this, your Delius first of all. And if this can be acccomplished by indulgences or a dispensation, or

by any other means, look to it that you spare no expense so that you can return to your family adorned with so famous a title.

Languet's jest about Sidney's Christian name plays on the ironic fact that his godfather, Philip of Spain, was now riding high on the Catholic tide which threatened to engulf both England and the Protestant centres on the Continent.

> But, joking aside, the Spanish are bursting with pride at this recent victory, and are making dire threats not only against the Gueux, but also against you [the English] and the Elector Palatine. They say that John of Austria will lead a great army of Spaniards and Italians to the Low Countries from Milan. In Germany, too, [mercenary] cavalry and infantry are being enlisted for the Spanish in great numbers, and troops are even being sought from the Swiss. Besides, a fleet is being fitted out among the Biscayans which is so strong that the Spanish believe that the Gueux, the English, and the French will not be able to bear even the sight of it. What do you say to all this? "The mountains will be in labour. . . ."
>
> I fully believe that the Spanish are contemplating peace, since they see that so far they have accomplished nothing with arms, and I believe that their bombast is designed to procure peace for them as cheaply as possible; but in this endeavour they will meet more difficulty than they imagine. It is not difficult to hire large armies, but to maintain them for any length of time, "this is the task, this the toil." They have few soldiers in the Low Countries, and yet even those are in mutiny over arrears in their pay and have thrown their officers in chains.
>
> I believe that the Pope will suffer the fate of Priam, that is, will have outlived at his death all those who had honoured him. The papist kings are taking great pains to make this happen, for they are knowingly and willingly casting themselves to destruction, in order to preserve the Pope's authority and grandeur. You little foxes have stolen away, and in fact "a woman led the action" which is all the more disgraceful and scandalous for us.

Sidney's plans to visit several places in Germany on his return journey from Padua to Vienna elicited more advice from Languet, who was well aware of Sidney's aversion to the German language.

The certain hope you now give me of your return has greatly gladdened me. I forgive you and all Englishmen whatever wrong you have ever done me, and I am almost sorry that I prophesied your coming misfortunes. It will be far more convenient for you to travel through Germany with my lord the Count [of Hanau], particularly since none of your people know German. You will therefore be better advised to wait until he returns to Germany, provided that he extricates himself before the solstice—for I fear the effect of the heat upon you, since you have a very frail constitution, and I know how eagerly, in fact, how intemperately, you consume fruit, and I therefore predict fevers and dystenteries for you if you stay where you are during the summer.

Languet concluded with this personal note.

When I read your letters or when I write to you I experience my only relief from the sorrow I have every reason to feel; so I include at random in my letters whatever comes to mind. I beg you to take this in good part, knowing that I write nothing in malice. When you have made some definite decision about leaving, I beg you to let me know, so that I shall not send any letters to your present address in vain.

Farewell; and my respects to our friends, and particularly to Master Bryskett. Vienna, May 13, 1574.

The following Friday, May 21, Languet continued in the same vein. Word had come from the Netherlands about pillaging by mutinous Spanish troops whose pay was three years in arrears. Immediately after routing the enemy at Mookerheide the soldiers broke discipline and began to loot indiscriminately.

I admire you for your virtue and goodness, my dear Sidney, in being troubled at the calamities of good men, and fearing that the victory the Spanish recently won will prove the end of those who are opposing their tyranny in the Low Countries and who are fighting for the freedom of their homeland; in my last letter I wrote you my feelings about this. And our later reports from there confirm my opinion more and more, for I see the Spanish turning war into piracy and putting their minds to treacherously plundering their allies instead of conquering their enemies.

I imagine that you have already heard how viciously they took control of Antwerp after their victory; I do not know whether the treachery or the simplicity of *el Comendador* [Requesens] is more to blame for this. For who will hereafter have confidence in him? Or what discipline will he be able to exert upon the army, after having loosed its chief bond? A soldier who is accustomed to plunder his allies will never wish to take the risk of seeking booty from an enemy. Although Alva committed many things worthy of reproof in the Low Countries, still no deed of his stands out as so infamous, and he would never have permitted such an offence against military decorum.

Now that summer weather had reached Vienna, Languet expected that Sidney would soon leave Italy and head back to Austria.

If, when you receive this letter, you are not yet ready for travel, I beg you to let me know, and also to tell me when you will arrive here at the latest, and whether you want me to wait for you here (if the Emperor should happen to leave before your arrival) or at Prague. For within the month we expect him to leave here, since we are told that several people have already been sent to Bohemia with decrees for the calling of a Diet on July 1; but because this usually is done with the agreement of the nobles of the Kingdom, and they perhaps will not agree to that day, the meeting may be deferred for a while. Please tell this to his Excellency the Count when he is back with you. Since we find the heat oppressive enough here, I do not doubt that it is uncomfortable where you are. Therefore you will be wise if you imitate the cranes and seek more suitable summer haunts.

After recounting the latest reports from Constantinople, Languet concluded with this response to Sidney's kindness in sending him two handwritten copies of the tract he had requested, "I thought that the pamphlet on *The Stratagems of the French King* was in print; otherwise I would not have troubled you about it. When you are here I shall tell you who wrote it and on what occasion, for it is not safe to entrust this to a letter." [1]

---

1. An enthusiastic but unauthorized defence of the St. Bartholomew's Day massacre by Camillo Capilupi (d. ca. 1600), entitled *Lo Stratagema di Carlo IX, re di Francia, contro gli Ugonotti, rebelli di Dio et suoi* (Rome, 1572). A French translation appeared in the same year, and a second edition in 1574.

While these letters were en route, another one had come from Wolfgang Zündelin. Dated Saturday, May 22, it retails the latest rumours
that had reached him.

> For the news you have so kindly sent me, illustrious and noble
> lord, I thank you, not as much as I should, but as well as I can. I
> have, however, little with which to repay you. A letter from
> Augsburg was delivered here, dated the fifteenth of this month,
> which gives the same news from the Netherlands which we already
> know—all taken from the same letters, written at Antwerp on the
> first and second of this month. Some write that Duke Christopher
> Palatine and Count Louis of Nassau are alive, others that they are
> dead: hence it is uncertain whom you had best believe. They add
> that Orange is at D[omburg] and is attempting to fit out a fleet, and
> that a large convoy of heavily laden ships of every sort from Saxony
> lately arrived in Holland.
>
> Recently there was a letter from Nuremberg which apparently
> indicates that correspondents from Strasbourg are writing the
> following (which to many seems unlikely): that the troops coming
> from France to Count Louis attacked Count Hannibal's infantry on
> its way to the Netherlands (the place is not mentioned) and, after
> killing a great many of them, routed the rest. A correspondent from
> Strasbourg writes on the second of this month that the Prince of
> Condé has arrived in that city with sixty horsemen; there is nothing
> more from Augsburg that I know of. It is already being said here,
> after last night's session of the senate, that both Montmorency and
> his brother Damville have been captured by the King. Any other
> news there may be among us is either not spoken about in public or
> not known.
>
> Farewell, illustrious lord: from V[enice], May 22, 1574.
> I would have come to you myself if I had not known that you were
> busy writing and in a place where it would be difficult to come and
> meet you.

Zündelin's last sentence reveals that Sidney had again returned to Venice.
Where Sidney was staying and what (aside from letters) he might have
been writing are questions to which we have no clues even for speculation.

More details about the clash in which Jacob Hannibal, Count of
Hohenems (1530–87), was attacked occur in Languet's next letter which

was written on May 28 though it did not reach Sidney until the second week in June.

> I believe you have heard that Count Hannibal von Hohenems, brother of the Cardinal of Constance, has enlisted two legions for the King of Spain, or two infantry regiments, as we say, to lead to the Low Countries. Several of the French cavalrymen who were going to join Christopher of the Palatinate, but retreated when they heard that his forces had been slaughtered, attacked Count Hannibal as he was going from Strasbourg to Saverne, killed several of his escort, and even pursued him as far as Saverne, where he fled after being twice wounded.
>
> When he entered the city, they immediately demanded that the lord bishop surrender him to them, threatening that, unless he did so immediately, they would set fire to the outlying buildings. Some say that the bishop was frightened by their threats and surrendered him, but that does not seem likely to me. This took place on the fourth of this month.

Count Hannibal, who made a career of fighting for Spain, was nearly killed in this encounter and required a long recuperation before he returned to action.[2]

In addition to this report and a long account of the mutiny of the Spanish troops in Antwerp and surrounding areas, Languet's letter had a modicum of personal comment. He explained the reason.

> Although I have not received a letter from you recently, I do not wish to break my habit of writing, for now that most of my friends have been overwhelmed by disasters of various kinds I find pleasure in almost nothing but the thought of your friendship, and I feel this pleasure most while I am writing to you or reading your letters. Because I fear that my letters may arrive at your present address after you have left there, I shall write you only such things as will not cause me to worry much about my letters falling into the hands of others. Things which require greater freedom of expression I shall reserve for your arrival.

Once again, Sidney was writing to Languet on the same day, and probably at the same hour, as the above letter was being addressed to

2. A full account of the incident will be found in Ludwig Welti's *Graf Jakob Hannibal* (Innsbruck, 1954), pp. 188–91.

him. His letter opens with skillful variations on the favourite themes of *amicitia jocique*.

Greetings.

You surely behaved quite moderately, although I exasperated you so, and I admire you for your mildness in this; doubtless you realized that, however great an error you had made, it was better to admit the offence frankly than by persisting in error to arouse the wrath of St. George. You have tried, and I approve your decision.

But, my dear Languet, what are we doing? Are we jesting in these times? Indeed, I believe that no one with normal intelligence can fail to see the result of the fierce storms which have severely shaken the whole Christian commonwealth for so many years; truly, the man who foresees the consequences of these events, and can bear them with equanimity, should, I submit, either be elected to the company of the gods, or be counted among the beasts endowed with human features, *hōs ei thērion ei theon.*

But this is the true spice, or rather, the true fruit, of friendship: when the thought of a dear friend not only proves a great relief for all one's sorrows, but also forces one to let one's soul somehow relax. Now this spiritual recreation especially consists in the decent wit inherent in and, as it were, engrafted upon the natures of some men, and wise men at that; for neither Socrates nor our More could resist jesting at their executions. Therefore let us jest.

After this Sidney passed on all the recent news and rumours that he had picked up since arriving in Venice, embellished with literary allusions and elegancies of expression.

"The land of Africa shudders and quakes with fearful unrest." Goletta and Tunis are held by the Spanish, I believe. But it is said that they are shivering badly in that great heat, although the Turk lacks galley slaves to launch a great attack this year. This is a rumour which our Queen is also circulating widely. I have told you that for a long time all English sailors have clearly been kept aboard Orange's ships.

The people here certainly say a great many things: John of Austria, as some would have it, is to set out for Flanders with a large force of Italians; as others would have it, he will be recalled to Spain; as still others would have it, he will remain in Italy. I fully believe that

Philip is using John as a Delphian knife, in order both to appear to have such a commander to send against the Turk or the Frenchman, if they should attack at all, and by John's presence to curb uprisings among the Italians, which the Spaniards are beginning to fear, and finally to keep the Flemish in order by the expectation of his arrival. I should hope that, while acting as such a *polypragmōn*, he will accomplish nothing in the long run. The Ragusans have provided Philip with forty ships for fitting out that Biscayan fleet.

The French Ambassador, de Foix, is held in great honour at Rome, an expression none too unusual, but which is particularly appropriate to him, for (as I have learned from an honourable and trustworthy man) he is being held in such a way that he cannot escape even if he wishes to.

Sidney then concluded with reports of his friends in Italy and messages to those in Vienna.

But enough of this. I believe that the Count of Hanau is already at Padua, for three days ago he was at Ferrara. I expect a letter today from my father; if it carries any news, I shall write you, but I hope I shall arrive so quickly as to outstrip my letter. But since I have not yet spoken with the Count, and have not been able to make any definite decision, I should like you to reply. If that letter arrives here after I leave, I shall carefully see to it that it is sent back to Vienna, and the files will grow still thicker.

Corbett started his journey towards Vienna yesterday, although I believe that he will be forced to leave his servant behind, who is too ill for such an effort. Please wish Master de Vulcob and my friend Bochetel the best of health. As for the French Ambassador, about whom I wrote you in an earlier letter, that was a mistake: I had not understood du Ferrier properly. Farewell. Venice, May 28, 1574.

Yours,
Philip Sidney

My friend Bryskett most humbly wishes you the best of health. Since writing the above, I have heard that the Count is safely back in Padua.

To the illustrious Master Languet, my very dear master. Vienna.

Sometime within the next week Sidney returned to Padua. Which day he chose cannot be determined, and the exact date of his return would not be of any importance except for an event that took place in the university city on the night of Monday, May 31. Earlier that day Sidney's friend Fabian, Baron and Burgrave of Dohna, wrote him from Padua a letter full of courtly compliment which indicates that Dohna thought Sidney was still in Venice. Evidently Sidney had sent Dohna the letter of a third person which Dohna was asked to return after he had perused it. (Apparently it was a specimen of elaborate prose style, possibly the letter from Bizari to Vulcob, or another similar to it.) The address reads only "To the Renowned and Noble Master Philip Sidney, Englishman, of the Illustrious family of the Earls of Warwick; Deserving of all sincere Faith, Honour and Loyalty." The letter differs from most others of the period because the most fulsome compliments occur in the middle of the text instead of at the beginning or the end.

Illustrious and noble Lord Count,

I thank you greatly, in your singular kindness and goodwill towards me, for not having hesitated to send me the letter which I received at Venice; and most earnestly I entreat you that, if by chance I should keep it here with me for longer than you had expected, you will kindly forgive me. For I have given it to your neighbour Master von Rödern and to Baron Slavata to read; nor do I think that in so doing I have offended you, especially as in the contents I see nothing that may not be safely shown to them also.

Now I ask of you nothing but that, as you have borne with me until now, so you will also in future continue to accord me your love and benevolence. In these matters I certainly will not fail, wherever I can, to place such trustworthiness as I have, and such little offices as I can perform, entirely at your service and pleasure. And if by chance physical distance should briefly divide us, I will continue, as the Lord grants me life, to honour you in your absence. I solemnly assure you that I shall do so. May God and His saints keep you safe and well for many years, for the declaring of His holy name, and to the benefit of your country. If at some time an opportunity should present itself, I should like you in one of your letters to present my best respects to Master Languet; and although I should not be entitled to ask this favour of you, your amazing kindness has quite persuaded me that in this matter you will gladly oblige me. I believe, in fact, that he already knew my name from a certain fellow countryman of mine, Tidemann Klefeld from Danzig, who is at present at the court of the Emperor. Once more, every happiness and farewell. Dated on this my birthday, May 31, 1574, at Padua.

From him who wholeheartedly honours and loves you,

Fabian, Burgrave and Baron Dhona [*sic*], Prussian

Of the persons Dohna mentions, Sidney's friend Baron Slavata has already been introduced. Melchior, Baron von Rödern (1555–1600), sixth son of Frederick, the first president of the Silesian Parliament, was another active member of the German "nation" at the University of Padua; he later became a brilliant general and ultimately Field Marshal to the Emperor. Even as a soldier he was known for his civilized interests and unaffected steadfast character. Tidemann Kleinfelt or Klefeld served as ambassador of the city of Danzig and, like his fellow citizens, was an ardent Protestant. Languet and he had much in common.

In his letter Dohna mentioned that May 31 was his birthday, so he probably spent the evening with friends. That night, to celebrate the departure of two prominent friends, Frederick von Kreckwitz and Johann Schindel of Silesia, the German "nation" held a banquet. Among the diners were Baron von Rödern, and the brothers Michael and Albert Slavata, barons of Cossumberg. Although Baron Dohna is not listed in the report of what ensued,[3] most likely he was a participant. After the banquet the guests walked together to the lodgings of the Slavata brothers. Their merriment annoyed a group of young bloods from Vicenza who in the dark mistook the company for their special adversaries, the Burgundians. They confronted the Germans with drawn swords, levelled spears, and verbal insults. The Slavatas and their friends in turn drew swords and prepared to defend themselves.

The Vicenzans soon found that the party were Germans, whom they hated almost as much as Burgundians, and began to wield their weapons in earnest. Ironically, some Frenchmen were attracted by the fray and joined in the attack. The hard-pressed Germans, despite their lack of body armour or any weapons but their swords, fiercely held their ground. At this moment Melchior von Rödern and a few companions caught up with their friends and flung themselves furiously into the middle of the fight. The Germans felt their reputation was at stake, so they fought recklessly even though several of them had been wounded. They pressed

3. This report, written by the chronicler of the German "nation," Eucharius Seefrid of Ottengen, is preserved in the *Acta* of that nation for 1574, in the Vatican Library, Italia II, Veneto 2, I, (15) pp. 181–82.

back the attack and forced the Vicenzans to flee down an alleyway. The Germans, despite the wounds of some of their best swordsmen, picked up two abandoned spears and followed the attackers to the house into which they had retreated. Stones thrown through the windows and shouted insults did not provoke the Vicenzans to return to the street, and stormy weather now persuaded the Germans also to retire.

Sidney's whereabouts on the evening of this fracas cannot be determined. We know that on the previous Friday he was still in Venice and that by June 4 he had become reestablished in Padua. Perhaps he was one of the merrymakers who ended the evening with the clash of steel on steel; perhaps he was packing his saddlebags in Venice. Wherever he was, we can be sure that Sidney was concerned at least vicariously, since he probably was involved in other incidents with the tumultuous society of "nations" at Padua. Whether Sidney and his attendants were actually involved in the May 31 clash or simply learned of it after the event, they would have appreciated their recently acquired permission to bear arms.

Sidney's letters, it should be remembered, were moulded by the Ciceronian tradition (though he carefully avoided its extremes), a tradition which did not admit the description of minor personal adventures. Although we regret that he did not leave detailed accounts of his daily triumphs, disappointments, and personal opinions in the style of later centuries, we should marvel that so much of his correspondence is preserved and be grateful for the many personal passages in his letters.

During the first few days of June Languet's letter of May 21 reached Padua. On June 4 (a Friday, as usual) Sidney replied to it.

This is the twenty-ninth letter I have received from you since arriving in Italy, my dear Languet, yet I have actually found that each succeeding letter always delights me more than the previous one. And thus I discover something which I had never believed possible: my affection for you, which I was sure could not increase, nevertheless has grown greatly during the time we have been apart. For you are the same man you were, and your excellent mind bears the same fruit. Yet, as I love you, I find that although your earlier letters brought me more pleasure than I think our gay Pietro [Bizari] took in his Hungarian history, still your most recent ones have surpassed them; I feel that, while I have indeed tasted the former, I have really drained the latter with a Saxon draught. Therefore I beg you please to repay my diligence for another few days.

The prospect of midsummer heat did not deter Sidney from planning to travel back to Vienna, since he would be able to accompany the Count of Hanau.

> For his Excellency the Count has decided not to leave within the next three weeks, and certainly, if we must expect some loss, I should prefer having a letter of yours delivered here after my departure to staying here even a few days without the joy of seeing you in what you write, particularly since I have seen to it that your letters will be sent back safely to Vienna. I am sorry indeed that the Count has, as it were, saved his journey until we could endure all the heat, which has thus far been quite mild, but will doubtless not be so then. But that is his worry. I have decided to accompany him on the journey, and I am sure that I can stand everything as well as he. I am sending you his letter, as well as those of Welsperg and Gruse, both of whom are exceedingly fond of me and you.

Paul von Welsperg, the *Hofmeister* of the Count of Hanau, has been mentioned earlier. Gruse (or Goetz) probably was another member of Hanau's household.

Sidney then carried out Baron Dohna's request for an introduction to Languet.

> In this city there is a certain noble German, the Baron and Burgrave of Dohna in Prussia. The renown of your name has made him very fond of you: he desires to become your friend, and has insistently asked me to commend him to you. Now I know that this will be as pleasant for you as for him, since, to make a long story short, he surpasses all the Germans here in every kind of virtue; but to satisfy him, I am giving him a very strong recommendation. While I was writing this, the wise and good Monau interrupted me, and he wishes you the best of health.

Because Languet had plans for a visit to Prague during the summer, Sidney had to make certain where and when they might meet on his return.

> As for your suggestion that I let you know whether I prefer to meet you in Prague or in Vienna, be assured that nothing would please me more than to see you as soon as possible, provided only that it is convenient for you. Therefore, when you think of the

Robert Sidney, Earl of Leicester

question, please remember that I am your loving friend. That is to say, I not only desire to enjoy your company soon, but also wish to take your interests wholly into account, particularly since this will make little difference; for if the Emperor is not at Vienna, the Count will immediately go to wherever he is holding court.

He ended the letter with scraps of news, banter, and greetings to friends.

> Your report about the Spanish has greatly pleased me. Nothing new is being said in Padua, except (and this is not new) that our [English] scholars are very much out of date. How gracefully you have written me that you "would not have wanted to trouble me about that pamphlet if you had not thought it was in print"! As if I would really deserve thanks for performing such wholly insignificant favours, even if I felt only ordinary affection for you. But I have had so many favours from you that I despair of ever being as thankful as they warrant, and I shall be wholly unable to return them unless God should answer my prayers too generously. Therefore stop being so eloquent, or we may perhaps stir up new quarrels, which will doubtless be more dangerous because they will be carried on at close hand.
>
> I pray you tell Master de Vulcob that I am not writing him now because I have nothing worth writing, and I do not doubt that he is in quite a troubled frame of mind; let him be sure of this, that I repay his kindness to me with a grateful heart and much affection. Commend me to my two English kinsmen, who I imagine are now with you. Do not forget Bochetel. Farewell. June 4, 1574.
>
> Your most affectionate and respectful,
> Philip Sidney

This was Sidney's last letter dated from Padua. As it explains, he lingered on for about seven weeks waiting for the Count of Hanau's convenience. Sidney spent part of this time in Venice. Any attempt to gauge the value of his Padua experience is handicapped by the fragmentary nature of the evidence. Despite all the letters during this period we know little about his actual studies. With Languet's guidance he embarked on a plan to improve his Latin style and his pronunciation of that essential language. For this purpose he read Cicero primarily. How far he persevered in Greek beyond what he had acquired at Shrewsbury and Christ Church is undetermined, though he began with the

ambition to master Aristotle's *Politics* in the original language. To some
degree he disregarded Languet's advice to read *about* the Greeks so that
he would not "grow grey in the study of letters," for in 1581 Henri
Estienne singled out his knowledge, saying that for Sidney translations of
Greek texts were unnecessary.[4] As Buxton has pointed out, he translated
at least two books of the *Rhetoric*, and in the *Arcadia* he used the *Characters*
of Theophrastus, no translation of which then existed in print. In scientific
studies Sidney acquired the elements of astronomy but was drawn more
to geometry since it was of practical value in the study of fortifications
and other military matters.

Socially Padua seems to have been quite rewarding, though there is no
record of friendships with any members of the English "nation" of
students. All his friends there were from Germany and eastern Europe.
Not surprisingly, several of them were of noble birth: the Count of
Hanau, the Barons Slavata, Dohna, and von Rödern, and others of lesser
rank including Matthäus Wacker, Jacob Monau, and Matthäus Delius
who came from well-established families. In contrast, Sidney's friends in
Venice (Zündelin excepted) were generally French or English. The number
of his Italian friends is surprisingly small. They include, however, two of
his correspondents, Cesare Pavese and Cesare Carrafa, both of them poets.[5]
Carrafa also mentions Giovanni Grimani, the Patriarch of Venice, as
being one of Sidney's acquaintances.

Sidney's aversion to the German language doubtless prompted his
German friends in Padua to converse with him in Italian, French, Latin,
or occasionally English, but he would still have picked up a good deal of
German from them, enough to answer Languet's injunction to be able to
"understand what you hear or read." Having spent the previous winter in
Frankfurt and summer in Vienna, Sidney must have acquired a passable
knowledge of German, despite his basic distaste for it.

Concerning Sidney's habits of exercise or forms of recreation during his
residence at the Pozzo della Vacca there is not a shred of evidence.
Considering his advice to Robert Sidney we might assume that Philip
exercised his horsemanship and practised with the sword; but the only
times that we can be certain that he sat on a horse were on his journeys
between Venice and Padua and on his rapid overland circuit to Genoa and
Florence.

---

4. *Herodiani Historiarum Libri VIII* (Geneva, 1581), par. ii.
5. For details about the two Cesares see the discussion of their letters to Sidney, below.

In summary, the nine-month gestation period which Sidney spent in northern Italy produced many results that enriched his career as a courtier, a potential statesman, a soldier, a humanist, and a poet. Yet the Italian chapter of his education lacked sustained discipline. He learned much but could have benefited vastly more if he had had a guide, philosopher, and friend of Languet's stature near at hand. He gained, however, from the fact that for the first time he was completely on his own, away from uncles, English officials, and even his accepted mentor, Languet. Perhaps the biggest benefits from this interlude were the depth and perspective it added to his knowledge of politics and current history. Actual observation of the luxury and commercial bustle of Venice and participation in learned conversations at Padua also added new perceptions. Although Sidney formed a low opinion of the character of the Italians, later describing them as "discoursers" (rather than doers) and their learning as often "counterfeit," he did make many new and valued friends among the Germans he met at Padua. These friendships may have been the most lasting benefit of his *Italienische Reise*.

CHAPTER 11

Whether in Padua or in Venice, letters from friends continued to reach Sidney during the remainder of his stay in Italy. The faithful Languet wrote to him every week. His letter of June 4 began with a reference to a disagreement between Sidney and the courier, Camillo Cruci. Languet urged caution:

> Take care not to arouse that hornet with whom you report you were arguing, for we need his services as long as you remain in Italy if we wish to continue enjoying the fruits of our friendship. From several of his letters to a friend of ours I perceive that he is a very foolish man; even though he has received many favours from our friend, he does not spare him. Therefore punish his wrongdoing with kindness. I am not satisfied by his promise to be more careful in the future; indeed, I should prefer him to be less so.

After some banter about Sidney's delay in returning to Vienna, Languet reported that it really made little difference, since the Emperor was not going to Prague after all but sending instead his son Rudolph, King of Hungary.[1] Languet offered more details about the fight in which Count Hannibal von Hohenems had been wounded and subsequent alarms in eastern France. These events in Lorraine reminded Languet of Sidney's 1573 excursion, described earlier, to inspect the fortifications at Phalsbourg. From this letter we learn another significant fact, that Sidney had invited Languet to visit him in England. Languet replied:

> My dear Sidney,
>   I acknowledge your extraordinary kindness and benevolence in inviting me to your country as a safe port from the many storms which have assailed me, and if my affection for you were not too great to increase, this invitation would have much augmented it. You do not have to assure me of anyone's courtesy in order to attract me to England. Nothing could more effectively entice me there than your virtue and my affection for you, if my affairs permitted

---

1. Rudolph had been delayed by a slight accident. While exercising with an iron bar which he swung about rather carelessly, he injured himself in the right calf. He had now recovered.

this; and I wish that several years ago, when I was younger, I had formed the plan which you now suggest, but my love of country made me hope that France would abandon her madness and kept me from forming sound plans. Now I regret this, but regret comes too late.

Languet concluded by recording his satisfaction that Sidney was now practising the pronunciation of Latin. "I am greatly pleased that you have decided to consult our Wacker about your pronunciation. This is the only request I asked of you; the others I have suggested in such a way as to leave them to your own judgement."

Languet's next letter, dated June 11, reveals that Robert Corbett had arrived in Vienna and had called on Languet with Sidney's letter of introduction. Corbett's companion, Sidney's cousin Richard Shelley, had not yet called. Considering that Sidney had written about their visit in his letter to Languet of April 15, they appear to have travelled at a leisurely pace.

Yesterday I received your letter from your noble Corbett, now my Corbett too because you wish it thus and because his virtue warrants it. I have discussed various things with him, and he appears to me just such a man as you described him in your letter—devout, sagacious, temperate, without pretence, and so fond of you that he could not be more so. You have deceived him by giving him expectations of me which I cannot possibly fulfil. I shall do what I can for him, and he will lack nothing which lies within my power.

I have not yet seen the other one, although I went to the house where he is lodging in order to accompany him to Master de Vulcob. Because he is closely related to you, I resolve to love and honour him. Therefore he will lack nothing which lies within my power.

Corbett also brought Languet the portrait of Sidney by Paolo Veronese; Languet's initial reaction was qualified.

Master Corbett showed me your portrait which I kept near me for several hours to feast my eyes on it. Yet this increased my longing rather than diminishing it. Instead of representing you, it seems to me to be someone resembling you; at first I thought it was your brother. Though most of your features are very well portrayed, it is far more youthful than it should be. I imagine that you looked like this at the age of twelve or thirteen.

Corbett brought Languet the news that Sidney did not wish to leave the Veneto until a letter came from his father. But Languet still feared that Sidney would attempt an expedition to Rome and fall into the clutches of the Inquisition, so he pleaded with him not to do so. Even the risks of a trip to Constantinople would be preferable to what might happen to him in the papal states.

> In the dangers which can arise on the way, and in trials and annoyances, a journey to Constantinople is far more difficult than one to Rome; but if you had it in mind to undertake it, I would not try to sway you from your purpose. For in that journey you would not have, as in one to Rome, to put your faith in danger, or your conscience (as we say) and reputation, things which we should consider dearest of all to us, and yet which are very easily injured, and are restored with difficulty. For if you should fall into the hands of those robbers, you would have either to abjure the faith which you profess, or put your life in danger.
>
> Moreover, it would be practically impossible for you to escape from their hands, since, even if you did not have to fear the treachery of those who perhaps pretend to be your friends, still your fine features would cause a great many persons to inquire about you; and, in fact, if you should happen to have the very lightest of fevers, your host, or the physician you summon, would immediately disclose this to his parish priest—for they are under orders to do that. Furthermore, what extraordinary benefit would you realize if for a few days you apprehensively toured Roman rubbish heaps? Simply that you would be able to boast that you had seen them.

In his plea Languet testifies to Sidney's intellectual brilliance, one of the young man's obvious attractions for friends and admirers of his own and later generations.

> God has bestowed mental powers on you which I do not believe have fallen to anyone else I know, and he has done so not for you to abuse them in exploring vanities at great risk, but for you to put them in the service of your country, and of all good men; since you are only the steward of this gift, you will wrong Him who conferred such a great benefit on you if you prove to have abused it.
>
> You see what happened to Master de Foix, a sagacious man and one experienced in important affairs, just because he imagined that

there was at the Roman court the polite courtesy which customarily exists even among the most barbarous peoples, although he should have realized it was the foul workshop in which, as Petrarch says, is forged whatever deceit and wickedness is strewn throughout the world.

Be careful, therefore, not to undertake anything for which you may later be sorry, and which may bring endless sorrow not only upon you, but also upon all those who feel true affection for you. I beg you to pardon this freedom of mine, and if I say anything foolish, to understand nevertheless that it comes from a heart which loves you dearly.

This letter would not have reached Sidney in Venice; he was there about June 18, when he wrote to Languet, but by June 21 he had returned to Padua, as one of the new letters shows. About ten days were required for packets to travel from Vienna to Padua, and some took a fortnight. Sidney began his letter by consoling Languet for his grief over the sad events in France and the Netherlands.

I have received your letter, my dear Hubert; and although you entrusted nothing to it which could reveal your real feelings, for fear that in my absence it might fall into other hands, nevertheless I who know you intimately recognized easily the great sorrow which you have been suffering. I have detected this from various things and especially from the fact that your style, which usually overflows in a great flood of eloquence, now glides away like a charming brook with a certain soft murmur; and although it pursues another course, it still seems to reveal openly what is "laid up deep in your heart."

I would certainly be a stranger to human nature if I did not heartily lament this misfortune of my best friend, and therefore I will not try to lighten your grief by referring to my own, for you know that I am neither inhuman nor insensible.

Sidney next responded to Languet's reports (in his letters of April 23 and May 7) on the religious restrictions imposed by the strict conservative Lutheran leaders in Saxony. Sidney's reference to Laodiceans (Rev. 3:14) would have been understood by Languet as sympathetic to his view that the Lutherans had become smug and lukewarm in their attitude towards the cause of Protestant activism.

But again and again I beg you, as I have done in previous letters, to abandon at last that ungrateful soil which you have tilled for so

many years while harvesting no fruit, or very little, and to go to
those who love you and are not Laodiceans; I should not wish you
to be deterred by the dangers which perhaps threaten our country,
for you whose mind harbours the histories of all nations know that
such crises have never brought harm to anyone in England except
great personages. But, my dear Languet, we shall discuss these
things when we meet.

An earlier invitation for Languet to come to England, to which Languet
had responded on June 4, had evidently been made in one of Sidney's
missing letters.

Important political news just received from Paris reported the death
on May 30 of Charles IX and subsequent turmoil in ruling circles.

> The day before yesterday we received definite news here which
> confirmed the rumour about the death of the French King, and also
> reported that his mother has been named Queen to manage the
> government until the King of Poland can return, while in the mean-
> time Alençon, Navarre, and Montmorency are under guard.
> Extraordinary! I really do not know what to think: that by his
> death a blow has been dealt our cause, or (as I should wish) that a
> remedy has been applied. Almighty and gracious God rules Christen-
> dom with wonderful providence in our time. They say that Mont-
> gomery has been captured by Montpensier, but I do not believe it.

Sidney was right not to believe that the Count of Montgomery had been
captured by the Duke of Montpensier whose army was near Guienne.
Montgomery had landed in Normandy where he surrendered on May 25
to Marshal Matignon with the understanding that his life would be spared;
Catherine de Médicis had him beheaded a month later.

There was also news concerning the proposed treaty between the
Turkish government and the Venetian Republic: "Tomorrow a certain
Jew, Selim's physician, will negotiate with the Venetians to establish
peace on definite terms. I shall write you when these are decided on."
The Jew was the German Rabbi Solomon Ben Nathan Ashkenazi
(ca. 1520–1602), physician not to the Sultan but to the Grand Vizier,
Mohammed Pasha, who actually held the reins of government in
Constantinople.

On the Spanish occupation of the Netherlands and the mutiny in
Antwerp Sidney made these comments.

That exceptional man, *el Comendador*, is trying to restrain the mutinous Spaniards, or at least is pretending to; and in his great haste he is giving evidence of his simplicity. I hope at all events that within a few years all nations will recognize the virtue of the Spanish: they are born slaves, and have never done anything else but change masters as if paying a debt with borrowed money. They have always belonged either to the Carthaginians, the Romans, the Vandals, the Goths, the Saracens, or the Moors. To be sure, they were invigorated not long ago by the virtue of Charles alone (and he was, indeed, a Netherlander), but since his death one can easily see what great haste they are making to return to their original state.

The Emperor Charles V had been born in Ghent and had always favoured the Low Countries, where the citizens had responded by holding him in high esteem.

Sidney's letter ends with two negative reports, but it does introduce the name of his friend and correspondent Otto, Count Solms, whose home was at Rödelheim near Frankfurt. Although Count Solms had been in England as a guest of the Earl of Rutland before Sidney left for Paris, they probably first met at Padua.

The Count of Hanau has not yet received the letter he has been expecting from the Elector Palatine. But Count Solms has recently arrived from there and declares that it will be delivered here shortly. Nor have I, for my part, received the letter which I wrote my father had sent me; for the merchant who had them has gone to Rome, but he will return within ten days.

Farewell. My courteous respects to Master de Vulcob and Bochetel. June [   ], Venice, 1574.

Yours most affectionately,
Philip Sidney

Once again Sidney was writing to Languet at the same time that Languet was scribbling a long letter to him (assuming, of course, that Sidney's letter was written on Friday, June 18). Indeed, Languet's letter of the eighteenth is one of his fullest, and it begins, as usual, with a statement of his affection for Sidney and his anticipation of a reunion.

If I wished to please myself, I would write about nothing but my affection for you; and since your virtue has occasioned it, or, rather, stands as its principal cause, my affection is growing just as much as both my friends and your letters tell me you are growing in virtue. Some of our friends have recently informed me that they hear from you and your household that you have no other reason for going back to Germany than to demonstrate your affection for me. I cannot deny, my dear Sidney, that nothing is dearer to me than you are, and that nothing could please me more than to see you; but, believe me, if I thought that by returning to Germany you would inconvenience yourself, I would try vigorously to dissuade you. And I beg you now by our friendship in no way to accede to my desires in this regard, but to make the decision about your plans which you think will best suit your interests. The pleasure which I shall take in seeing you will not last, but I fear that the sorrow which your departure will later bring me will remain much too deeply implanted in my heart, and the thought of this is already causing me anguish and torment.

Languet now shifts to another of his favourite themes, his dislike of Italian ways.

I do not want to conceal anything from you. I am not such an admirer of the Italians' wisdom that I take everything they say for an oracle, nor do I accept the reasoning of those who believe that they have ordered their lives excellently if they approximate Italian ways as closely as possible. In fact, as I recall, whatever nations have used their advice in conducting their governments have involved their countries in great disaster.

Of their crimes, I shall say nothing. But does not most praise in Italy go to those who know how to dissemble, who know how to flatter, and to insinuate themselves into the favour of powerful men in every possible way, and to adapt themselves so well to their moods that, once they have decided to serve such a man, they treat as sacred whatever his "bright yellow choler" suggests to him, and they believe that they must fight for it as for their altars and their hearths?

In fact their spirits are broken by long servitude, and they happily endure any indignities and insults, as long as they are not deprived of money and of base pleasures; and they consider themselves excellently treated if the one upon whose nod they hang looks at them from time to time with, as the poet says, closed lip.

As for me, I believe that nothing is more harmful to the intellects of free men than these arts, which soften their manly virtue and

prepare their spirits for servility. The Italians themselves have discovered to their own great misfortune that servitude is the reward
of such arts.

Why Languet felt he had to warn Sidney so firmly against Machiavellian
ideas is difficult to understand at four centuries' remove. His knowledge
of Sidney's character should have precluded such fears. But he was aware
that Sidney had not yet reached his twentieth birthday and that the
allurements of Italian ways were as great as the attractions of the scenery
and climate. The expression from Martial (*Epigrams*, XII, IV, 10), as Charles
Levy has pointed out, shows Languet's strong feelings, for in this context
the "closed lip" is that of a courtesan.

Having curled his own lip at Italian hypocrisy, Languet now took a
positive approach in the program he urged Sidney to follow.

> But does it not suit your character and your lineage better to
> cultivate piety, to preserve the faith, to have the same thing on your
> face as in your heart, to defend the good against the evil force, and to
> put the safety of your country above your life? And since these arts
> are more easily learned in Germany than in Italy, I called you back
> here, not so much for you to learn these arts as to perfect those which
> are innate in you.
>
> You remember why Schwendi urged you to go to Nuremberg,
> and since he is wiser and more skillful in military affairs than anyone
> I know, I should like nothing better than for you to have your first
> military service under him if he should lead an army while you are
> abroad. I much prefer the custom of the Germans, Poles, and Danes,
> who take care that their princes can do nothing contrary to the laws,
> to the custom of the people who, through choice or fear, have so
> enslaved themselves that they actually think it sinful even to suspect
> a prince of acting wrongly.

General von Schwendi had taken a kindly interest in Sidney during his
visit to Vienna in 1573, an interest which Sidney had followed up with a
letter after his arrival in Venice, as has been recounted. Why von
Schwendi should have suggested that Sidney go to Nuremberg is difficult
to explain. Perhaps he had plans for training a body of troops there and
offered Sidney the opportunity to participate in the program and exercises.

Actually, Languet feared that England was so unstable that a Catholic
coup d'état might very well occur there and that, as a consequence,

Sidney, whose career was so important to the Protestant cause, might even have to seek safety in exile. In that event Sidney, like his Marian predecessors, would find Germany the most satisfactory refuge. Furthermore, if Sidney were to become the leader of a pan-Protestant activist movement, the firmer his established connections with his German peers, the better.

> I advise you to tie the bond of friendship between you and my lord the Count of Hanau as firmly as possible, and to be careful to procure the goodwill of more Germans, and particularly of those in whom you see some quality of virtue shining forth. They rarely introduce pretence into a friendship; when they cultivate one they are for the most part loyal, and, what is a bond of special importance in friendship, they feel the same as you in religion; so many harsh controversies have been stirred up about religion that true friendship can hardly be established between those who disagree in this.
>
> I do not wish to prophesy ill for you, but still as I urge these things I have in mind how liable your country is to changes, and when they occur fortune vents her greatest rage against those who are most eminent and distinguished in virtue, ability, and lineage. Accordingly, if either some enemies' unjust power, or some other compulsion, should force you one day to go into exile, nowhere, in my judgement, would a more honourable and secure retreat await you than in Germany. Everyone knows that in recent years the Frenchmen of our persuasion, after being assailed by diverse calamities, have again and again experienced the Germans' kindness towards them. In fact the Germans' assistance has more than once restored them to their homeland, which they say is what the Prince of Condé now hopes for again.

News of the death of Charles IX had reached Vienna, so Languet now had special reason for urging Sidney to visit Poland. He used the occasion for another little lesson in practical statecraft.

> I wish you could convince my lord the Count that you two should travel together as far as Cracow. For we could arrange to have you presented to the King, not of Poland, but now also of France. This would, I think, serve your interests well, if you have not yet changed your plan to go to the French court before you return home. For he [Henry] would receive you the more courteously and amicably

because you had first been presented to him when he was so far from home. One should not disdain the goodwill of such great princes, whatever sort of men they are, for even those who are not good sometimes undertake, for ulterior motives, to defend those who suffer wrong.

Moreover, an acquaintance made there could give no one in your country cause for suspicion, since everyone would think that you had gone to those parts only in order to tour them. If my lord the Count should be averse to that journey, and should delay his return to Germany for one or two months, I advise you to come before he does, but to promise that you will wait for him here. In the meantime, then, you will visit Cracow and return here; you can make this whole tour by hired carriage in fifteen or sixteen days.

As Sidney expected, Languet responded favourably to the request of Baron Dohna. He also revealed that decades earlier he had known well one of Dohna's kinsmen.

What you write about my noble lord the Baron and Burgrave of Dohna pleases me very much, and since he has asked for my friendship before being prompted to do so by any service I had done him, I shall be sure to make him realize that I consider this a great favour. I beg you to pay him my respects and offer him my duty and obedience. Many years ago at Wittenberg and later at Paris I knew and even was on friendly terms with my lord Christopher of the same family, who I believe was his paternal uncle. My respects as well to Monau if he is still with you. I have not written him for a while because I gathered from a letter which he sent me a month or two ago that he had already crossed the Alps and was worshipping the nymphs which swim the limpid waves of the Rhone and Lake Geneva.

Farewell, and my respects to our friends. Vienna, June 18, 1574.

In a postscript Languet added news of Sidney's friend Robert Corbett and his kinsman Richard Shelley.

Your countrymen have not yet left here. I advised them to use hired carriages as far as Nuremberg, since they had decided to travel to Prague; but they preferred to buy horses, although I think they are already sorry that they did not follow my advice.

That this letter reached Sidney in Padua becomes clear in a letter from Zündelin. He had written from Venice after learning from Jacob Monau that Sidney had left. Dated June 20, Zündelin's letter reveals that Sidney had been staying in Venice with Lord Windsor.

> When our Jacob had told me, noble and illustrious lord Philip, that in your singular and almost excessive kindness you had several times visited my house, I was most grieved: in the first place because your trouble, which you certainly should not have undertaken, was in vain; and secondly because I was unable to enjoy and profit by your most excellent conversation, and to thank you in person. For I heard that you were enjoying the hospitality of your friend the Baron, and to seek you out in such an unfamiliar place was more than I dared. Later, when you had left there, it was impossible to discuss the same things with you by letter as face to face, and of the little that could be written there was scarcely anything of which others could not inform you more correctly and freely.

The rest of the letter is simply a digest of all the news that had come from Zündelin's wide-flung correspondents. It testifies to the problem of determining the truth of the various reports from sundry secondary sources.

> Such, for instance, is the death of our Duke Christopher Palatine, recently confirmed in letters and messages from many sources in France and in the Netherlands. Also the deaths of Louis and Henry, Counts of Nassau. The Spanish ambassador recently replied to the inquiries of a certain important gentleman that there can be no further doubt as to this. Yet neither he nor anyone else (as far as I know) can add the place where they died. A friend wrote to me, in a letter from Heidelberg dated the twenty-ninth of May, solely to tell me this: that although there are still some who give the Elector Palatine hope that Duke Christopher is still alive, yet those who seem better informed hold that he is dead.
>
> Yesterday at last a letter from Augsburg brought some more cheerful news (but this is in itself doubtful, as I hear that it is only from one source, to whom it had been written privately): that both he and Count Louis were still alive, but that they did not plan to show themselves until they had brought their troops up to full strength again. The following, however, has been confirmed by

several letters: that the news of the twenty-two Spanish ships captured by Orange near Antwerp is true; that Duke Casimir is raising three thousand cavalry for the Prince of Condé against France (no one has written to me about this); that the Saxon rulers and states have concluded some sort of mutual treaty.

Apart from this, nothing I know from Augsburg is worth writing, and I do not even know how certain these things are. From France there has been nothing for a long time now. I hear that someone has written from Nuremberg that the King of Poland attempted to flee, but was forced to terminate his journey after only two days when the Poles discovered his plan. Should there be anything more certain and detailed, I will let you know.

In concluding Zündelin thanks Sidney for the honour of his attentions.

Meanwhile I wanted to write and tell you [these] few things, and thank you as much as is in my power: not only for taking the trouble to see me here, but also for writing to me from Padua, thus deigning to give abundant proof of the love you bear me, although I already knew and perceived it. Farewell, most noble Lord, and if it is not difficult for you, I beg you most respectfully to greet your Lodowick from me. V[enice], the twentieth of June, 1574.

Yours most devotedly,
with affection and esteem,
W. Z.

The letter from Sir Henry Sidney that Philip awaited so eagerly may have arrived before he left Venice or soon after his return to Padua. His anticipation, like that of so many sons, was doubled by the fact that the letter was bringing money. Although the letter itself has not survived, the Sidney papers at Penshurst contain a receipt dated June 28, 1574 from Acerbo Vellutelli to Sir Henry Sidney.[2] Doubtless the letter also brought reports about the health and affairs of the Sidney and Dudley families as well as comments on affairs of state. But, in the absence of the actual text, speculation is fruitless.

Indeed, all we can be sure of derives from Languet's reply of June 25 to a letter written by Sidney. It revealed that Sidney definitely had given up any thought of trying to visit Rome. He complained about some

2. Wallace, p. 115, n. 1. An expenditure of £136 on June 26 to "Acerbo Vitello" is listed in *HMC De L'Isle*, 1:257.

acquaintances who had departed without making a farewell call and reported that he had introduced himself to François Perrot de Mésières, the Protestant French poet who had now returned from Switzerland to the Embassy in Venice. More importantly, Languet's reply revealed that Sidney had picked up an infection (it nearly went into pleurisy) from which he suffered a fever, a severe headache, and a craving for water. During his recovery he seems to have been content to live quietly in Padua.

While Sidney was slowly recuperating from his illness, weekly letters from Languet continued to arrive. That written on June 25 is filled with an account of the arrival in Vienna of Henry, who was now King of France and Poland. He had surreptitiously slipped away from Poland as soon as he learned that the French throne awaited his presence. Although Sidney undoubtedly read with great interest the account of Henry's entry into the imperial city, it does not require repetition here. Languet, who had been keeping Sidney's future in mind in order to pave the way for any return visit his protégé might make to the French court, had picked out the venerable François de Montmorin, First Squire to the widowed Queen (Elizabeth, daughter of Maximilian II), as Sidney's potential sponsor.

> I have recommended you to Montmorin, who is here, and I asked him to give you his friendship if you should ever return to France. He answered that wherever you may meet he would show you every friendly courtesy. Furthermore he offers you the hospitality of his house if you should not find better accommodation at court, as may often be the case. He begged me to offer you his compliments.

Languet stressed again how important he thought it was for Sidney to renew his acquaintance with Henry. "If you could have the opportunity of paying your respects to the King on his present journey, I urge you to do so. You could avail yourself of Montmorin's help. Or, if he should be away, of Bellièvre's assistance; I shall recommend you to him."[3]

Besides passing comments on conflicts in France and the Netherlands, Languet also sent the latest reports on the travels of Corbett and Shelley.

> I hope your countrymen will arrive in Prague today. I obtained a travelling companion for them, or rather a guide, who is well

---

3. Pomponne de Bellièvre (1529–1607), Chancellor of France, had been put in charge of Henry's journey to Poland by Catherine de Médicis. On the return from Cracow he functioned as Henry's advance agent. Like Languet, he was another Padua alumnus.

acquainted with the regions to which they are going. I gave them letters of introduction to friends of mine in Prague and Nuremberg who, I trust, will show them some kindness. Your Bizari at Augsburg will take pains to do them imperishable favours and so to cast reproach on your nation for its ingratitude towards him and to make you forever indebted to him; I therefore suggest that in your leisure you devise what means you can to recompense him in some way for his great kindness to you.

Finally Languet added the following postscript:

> I have sent my letter to our friend Wacker because Master de Vulcob is now very busy. I have just been told that Pibrac, battered by diverse mishaps and subjected to many outrages, arrived here yesterday evening, which delights me. Yesterday I received a letter from Lobbet, which he told me to deliver to you, and I shall obey him in this, for if I should send it to you, it would perhaps arrive at your present address after you leave.

Guy du Faur, Sire of Pibrac, another Paduan alumnus and close friend of du Ferrier, relaxed from his duties as Councillor of State by writing verse; he was also a friend of Ronsard and de Thou. Sidney had met him in Paris and he is mentioned several times in the Sidney correspondence. The mishaps and outrages were consequences of the flight from Poland which Languet had mentioned in the lengthy account of Henry's escape from Cracow. "Pibrac, an able and learned man, whose eloquence is such that I do not consider France had another to equal him, became separated in the woods from the rest of the company who were proceeding too fast for him. Those of the party now here believe he was killed by the Poles who tried to capture those fleeing, or died in some other way." Little wonder that Pibrac's arrival in Vienna caused rejoicing among his friends.

The letter from Sidney's eminent Strasbourg friend, Dr. Jean Lobbet, had been written on June 1 and was thus at least five weeks on the way. In turn, Sidney's letter of April 29 to which Lobbet was replying had reached Strasbourg after a month on the road. It had been carried by a slowly travelling friend, apparently a son of Christopher Mont (d. 1572), long an English agent at Strasbourg.

> Two days ago our friend Mont gave me your letter dated Padua the twenty-ninth of last April, noble lord Baron Sidney, which

hugely delighted me. For previously I did not know where you were and what you were doing. For, though I had heard from Master Languet and others that you are still in Padua, I thought—not hearing anything further from you—that you had departed to other towns and provinces in order to see something of Italy. This was the sole cause for my not writing to you.

Here again there was a letter within a letter, for Sidney had asked Lobbet to pass an enclosure along to a mutual friend, Claude Aubéry, physician, humanist, and sometime Rector of the Academy at Lausanne.

The letter you wrote to Aubéry the Frenchman I shall keep for him, until I know where he is now. Previously he was at Basle; but when I recently charged a friend at Basle to make inquiries about him there, my friend replied that he was unable to find out anything concerning him at Basle. I imagine, therefore, that he has departed elsewhere: but where he has gone I do not yet know. I will, however, attempt diligently to find out, and when his abode is known I will send him the letter. Meanwhile I am writing you at Master Languet's in Vienna: for the time between now and when you say you will leave Padua for Vienna seems too short for my letter to be able to reach you while still at Padua.

Dr. Lobbet realized that his chief news offering should be reports of the latest events in France. In presenting these reports he mixed together details of two separate happenings: the abortive Huguenot revolt in which the King and the Queen Mother were to be killed and which was to be led by the Duke of Alençon and Henry of Navarre; and, secondly, the arrest of the Duke's and Henry's subordinates, de la Mole and Coconnas, who had been executed on April 29. Most of the other actors in this chapter of the tragic history of France have appeared earlier.

What do you wish me to tell you about France? You can hear it all from Master Languet. Certainly all is wretched in France—the appearance both of men and of affairs there is daily more miserable. Previously there were complaints about religion, about the St. Bartholomew's Day massacre. But already some new conspiracy that exceeds all imagination has been detected, to which so many are said to be privy that it is a marvel that it could for so long have been kept secret. What this conspiracy actually comprised I do not know. It is said that the chief aims were: to expel the Italians and the Guises from the kingdom; to make the Queen Mother abdicate her position; to obtain an account of the money received nineteen years before; and to have these present heavy taxes suppressed.

As I said before, a vast number have come under suspicion: it is even said that the Duke of Alençon, the King's brother, and the King of Navarre were privy to it. The prince of Condé is fleeing to Germany. Montmorency and Cossé, the Marshals of France, are under guard in the Bastille at Paris. The same had been planned for Damville, but I hear that he has seized those that had been sent to seize him. Moreover, there are women of high birth who have been suspected on the same count.

Many men have already been executed: every day more are arrested and rounded up. Charles Count of Mansfeld has fled. It is even said that Méru the brother of Montmorency has fled: Thoré, the other brother, is with Condé. Condé is now with the Elector Palatine. Another who was there was the Count de Retz on his return from Poland. What they are doing or have done I do not know for certain. Montgomery is in lower Normandy. They say that a few days before he fought the King's troops, with some success. I do not know if this is true. La Noue is in the neighbourhood of Poitou; it is said that in a battle there he defeated Montpensier. To sum up: all is in confusion, nor can we detect an approaching issue.

Lobbet's letter ends with a report of events in the Netherlands, now old news indeed to Sidney, and the usual compliments.

In the Netherlands, Christopher Palatine and Count Louis have lost a battle against the Spaniards. Both, however, are said not only to be alive but well, and—what is more—to be regrouping their former troops, now scattered; and even to be raising new ones. But I believe they are dead. Furthermore, there are some French troops in Lorraine, who previously were raised under the auspices of the Prince of Orange: what they plan to do is not known. They are still in camp at Turckenstein.

I beg you to give Master Lodowick Bryskett my fondest and most respectful greetings. Farewell, and rest assured that I honour, love, and esteem you. From Strasbourg, the first of June, 1574.

Yours most respectfully,

Jo. Lob.

Recently your Queen has sent an ambassador extraordinary to the King of France. I do not know what his requests are.

Languet had written Sidney on the twenty-fifth but, since there was so much news, he wrote again on the following Monday, June 28, accurately analyzing the reasons why Catherine de Médicis directed Henry to return to France by the long route south to Venice and across Italy.

I wrote you three days ago about the King's departure from Poland and arrival here, but the rumour of this event has doubtless preceded my letter, and perhaps this one will be delivered to you before the other. I had written that I supposed he would not go in your direction because he could get to Lorraine by a far shorter and easier route via Austrian territory, and thus not put himself in the power of any prince besides the Emperor, in whose power he already was. But I was mistaken in my surmise, for he prefers to cross the Alps twice, to endure the heat and dust of your beloved Italy, and to arrive in his country by a long detour (although his interests demand speed), than to submit any longer to the sterner customs of the Germans. But I wish to take a kinder view of this preference, and to believe that he is planning his journey so as to see the city of Venice and to form a closer friendship with that Republic and with neighbouring princes.

Languet continued to stress the importance to Sidney of renewed acquaintance with the French King.

If the rumour of the King's arrival reaches you before your departure, you will doubtless wish to observe the pomp with which he is received by the Venetians, for I do not doubt that it will be extraordinary and very well worth seeing. I advise you to make every effort to be presented to the King, and you can accomplish this with the help either of du Ferrier, of Montmorin, of Pibrac, or of Bellièvre. You are well known to du Ferrier; Montmorin also knows and likes you, and I made appropriate mention of you to Bellièvre and Pibrac, from both of whom I have moreover experienced uncommon kindness. But you will remember that in a great milling crowd you have to be alert for your opportunity and not too bashful.

Languet's concluding paragraph reveals the very human side of the eminent humanist, who despite his learning, wisdom, and overriding purposefulness, could also enjoy looking upon the hock when it glistened in the glass.

> It would be a long story to describe how the King decamped from Poland with his party, and how courteously he has been received by the Emperor, therefore I shall postpone it until your arrival. However, if you wish, you can learn all this from those who are accompanying the King, particularly from that old friend of mine, Master de la Beurthe, who will deliver this letter to you. I have written all this hastily, with the fumes of yesterday's tippling not yet dispersed, for we are always running around in this heat, and even without being invited we sometimes drink more freely than is good for our health. Farewell. Vienna, June 28, 1574.

Despite Languet's repeated urgings that he should attend Henry III during his ceremony-crowded visit to Venice (July 18–27, 1574), so far as can be discovered Sidney did not take advantage of the opportunity. Whatever reasons prompted Sidney's decision not to attend this gala occasion, two seem highly likely. In the first place, Sidney's recuperation from his debilitating illness may have been slower than he had expected. Secondly, the recollection of the St. Bartholomew's Day massacre still seared his memory. Although Sidney had many warm friendships with French Protestants, after he left that blood-soaked land in 1572 he never again set foot on French soil.

CHAPTER 12

From the time of Sidney's recovery until his return to Vienna late in the summer his movements and activities can be followed only indirectly through the surviving letters from his friends. Languet continued to write faithfully each week in July, but he stopped when he expected Sidney's arrival. The earliest of this final series of letters is dated July 2 and begins with the correct surmise that illness had caused Sidney's lapse in writing. "I am worried that either the heat, which here we find more oppressive than usual, or excessive eating of fruit has afflicted you with one of the illnesses of which I warned you should you remain where you are now during the summer season, though I pray that I am a false prophet in this matter." Modern travellers can testify to the wisdom of Languet's advice, for the eating of unpeeled fruit in Italy still results frequently in "Nero's Revenge," though Sidney's friends probably gave it another name.

Languet had not yet heard that Sidney had abandoned thoughts of a journey to Rome, the possibility of which Corbett and Shelley had confirmed, so he sent a lengthy homily comparing Sidney's danger in such an adventure with that of a virgin who tried to slip past the sentries into a besieged city and suffered the violent loss of her chastity. Languet expected that Sidney would be in Venice "watching the Venetian pomp with which the King of France is received" when this letter reached him; he again urged Sidney to renew acquaintance with Henry III. In "such a milling mob, as I imagine you will find yourself in, you must put on a bold face. Untimely bashfulness is often the cause of losing opportunities to achieve the ends we have in mind or even to maintain our own status."

Soon after sending this letter, Languet received the one Sidney wrote about June 18 which took about a fortnight in transit from Venice. In his reply, dated July 10, Languet sent news of Corbett and Shelley in Prague, especially of the latter who was suffering from "John Huss's Revenge."

> Your countrymen have not had much success, because they did not follow my advice about hiring a carriage; they were unable to travel as fast as the guide we had obtained for them here, since their servant had loaded his horse with too heavy a pack. Furthermore

Richard suffered so badly from diarrhoea that at Prague he despaired of his life, though the illness did not seem very dangerous to the physicians, who were more apprehensive about his despondency than about the illness itself. Finally a Jesuit was brought to him, and when Richard had poured out into the man's bosom the refuse of his soul (I wish it had been that of his body too!) he felt that he would carry less of a burden to Charon's bark. I believe that he even made a will.

More mockery of Shelley's Catholic ardour occurs in Languet's prediction of the young man's probable reaction to the sight of Wittenberg, where Luther had launched the Reformation.

Afterwards, however, he began to feel better, and changing his plan of travelling to Nuremberg, he decided to take a boat down the Elbe to Hamburg, and from there to England. Doubtless he will shudder all over at the sight of Wittenberg (it is on the Elbe), should it occur to him that there the first grave wound was dealt to the Pope: an injury he has thus far tried in vain to heal with sword and fire and other unspeakable remedies, yet still he tries, at Christendom's great cost.

Languet also reported on Robert Corbett's travels and added his testimony to the problem of sending letters to friends in transit: one could not address letters *to* the recipient, but only *at* him.

Your friend Corbett will continue his journey, and will make quickly for Nuremberg from Prague. He has sent me a letter from Prague which shows his courtesy. He wrote to you too, but I am keeping the letter here for you; for if you have not changed your mind about returning to Germany, and if you have had your fill of the Venetian spectacles and the pomp with which the King of France is to be received, you will doubtless be preparing for the road, and this letter of mine will be delivered to your present address after you leave. I do not mind the loss of my trifles; however, I do not wish your friends' letters to go astray, and shall send them to you only if you destroy all our hope of your return.

After a long account of political and military matters including candidates for the Polish throne, the Turkish takeover in Moldavia, and the defection of some Spanish ships to the Prince of Orange, Languet ended with this note: "As I was about to seal this letter, yours was delivered to me. It makes me especially happy because you wrote that you have completely dropped the project of visiting Rome."

About this same time Sidney received a letter from his friend, the learned Claude Aubéry, in Basle. Because Aubéry's name is little known in books on Sidney a brief account of him may be desirable. Brevity is necessary because most of what we know about his friendship with Sidney is derived from this sole surviving letter. Four years older than Sidney, Aubéry was a Huguenot who had been educated in medicine, philosophy, and theology at Geneva. He had lived in Paris for a short while but left about 1568 because of his Protestant faith. Eventually he settled in Basle where he taught philosophy and medicine, but just when he became established there is not known. Sidney may first have met him at Basle in 1573, though the uncertainty of Aubéry's address suggests that the meeting may have been in Strasbourg, perhaps under Lobbet's roof.

Dated July 5, the letter is an answer to one which had just come into Aubéry's hands, the letter Sidney had sent in April via Lobbet. Aubéry begins by explaining the delay and continues with fulsome compliments.

> I at last received your letter, most illustrious and noble Sir, on the fourth of July. This was certainly not due to any carelessness on the part of Master Lobbet—please believe that this was how it occurred: while I, attending to my affairs, was so housebound that few as yet knew I was in Basle, he was searching (I had almost said heaven and earth) for me but could not find me anywhere.
>
> Now to turn to your letter: I am immensely grateful to you, not only because you adorn me with your praise, assist me with money, and follow me with your benevolence, but above all because you are pleased to count me among the number of your friends. Of this fact your letter to me is a living and most glittering testimony, and I am keeping it as my most cherished treasure. For it is not to please you (of whose most excellent nature, admirable wit, and highest virtues I and all who know you are aware), nor even to be loved by you, that I attach the greatest importance. For if indeed, as our friend Aristotle says, friendships are cemented by qualities held in common, and since good men are judged to have in common virtuous qualities, our friendship[1] because it is according to virtue is, in prospect,

---

1. ὅτι κατ' ἀρετή.

eternal; because virtue, as you know,[2] is eternal. I would write more
in this vein, but you know the rest. For you remember, and you can
remember—indeed, you are the son of Memory.[3] From which you
will have understood that for you ever to fade from my mind is
impossible. Indeed, let me tell you truly what happens to me almost
every moment of every hour. Whenever I think of virtue or learning
(without which I could not live for even half a day), you appear
before my mind's eye, adorned with such a multitude of virtues and
such splendour of wit that, confronted with you, all my mind can
do is mark your footsteps and follow you wherever you go in your
wanderings. Such is the magnetic power of souls.

Evidently Sidney had found Aubéry so able and attractive that he
urged him to come to England. The letter Sidney wrote from Padua in
April repeated the suggestion.

You say—as if you know the labours and griefs I have suffered—
that you have found my failure to leave for England a grievous blow:
and your very accusation is testimony of your amazing love. Believe
me, most noble Sir, to have aroused this friendship on your part is
something that moves me deeply, for I do not see how I could
possibly be worthy of you in any way. This, however, I know: that
I shall never be last in the company of those who honour and respect
you. All the noblest minds are such that they estimate services not
by their number but by the sincerity that inspired them.

It would certainly have been better had I left for England at the
time when you urged me, as I later discovered to my cost. For what
griefs have not befallen me here while those to whom I wished to
be of service did not scruple to impose on my sense of decency? But
you have wrought well in renewing my hope, which is vested in
your amazing kindness. Thus you have set me on my feet again with
your letter, which makes it clear that in great and heroic spirits—of
which you if anyone are possessed—virtue is its own reward. And
when you urge me to return, in due course, to the earlier plan I
abandoned, you show quite plainly that the abundance of your love
for me has surpassed all human bounds and attained to the level of
the gods—

2. ὅτι ἕξις.
3. μνημοσύνης υἱός.

Nevertheless, strengthened by your encouragement and impelled by your authority, I would have come to England in the spring, had I been able to find agreeable companions for my voyage. Now, however, I can find none such, nor do you mention any in your letter: perhaps I shall learn of one from the Bilbani,[4] whom I will meet when they return from the Strasbourg Fair.

In his letter to Aubéry Sidney had also mentioned that he had become well acquainted with Hartmann von Liechtenstein (1544–85), the founder of this princely house, and his younger brother Johann Septimus (1558–95) who later became a noted humanist. Their names recur in Sidney's letters from other friends. Aubéry replied, "That you are extremely fond of the Barons Liechtenstein does not surprise me, for what young nobleman would not delight in their character? I am happy, too, that you were able to enjoy each other's company in Italy."

Aubéry concluded with compliments and the promise to dedicate a book to Sidney. If he did so, the dedication has not been traced.

Finally, I would not have you think that your Aubéry has not had a reason for the labours that he has groaned under in his troubled and gloomy solitude. For it has occurred to me—and I hope this will not be unwelcome to you—to publish the fruits of my labours with a dedication to you. But of this and other matters more when we meet, D. V. May the great Lord God grant you every kind of grace, and preserve you for many years, to His greater honour and glory. Basle, July 5.

Yours, in greatest devotion to your most
illustrious and noble nature,
Claude Aubéry of Zurich

Languet's next letter, dated July 17, brought the news that Richard Shelley's intestinal virus had proved to be no laughing matter.

I was recently jesting about the illness of Master Richard, your countryman and kinsman, for I had had word that the physicians were laughing at his faintheartedness in being so frightened about an illness from which no danger threatened him. But, alas! He prophesied the danger threatening him more accurately than the physicians themselves. I learned this from the letter our friend Corbett wrote:

4. Unidentified.

Richard's health was wholly despaired of and, in fact, he was already giving up the ghost and was abandoned by the physicians.

This turn of events has caused me deep regret, since my affection for you compels me to grieve over the misfortunes of those who are close to you in any way. But I feel that another cause for compassion lies in his being snatched away from his country in the very prime of life, especially since he had cultivated his talents by the study of letters and by experience with many things.

Languet's concern about Shelley's illness camouflages the fears that haunted him about what might happen to Sidney. Shelley somehow managed to recover.[5] Although Sidney also survived the vicissitudes and viruses to which he was exposed during these years of Continental travel, he was himself "snatched away from his country in the very prime of life," and a few years after Languet himself was in his grave.

Corbett, in his loneliness, had turned to Languet as the nearest mentor for advice on his next course of action. Sidney's friendship with Languet would have created the opportunity, but Languet's character, practical wisdom, and personal warmth facilitated the sympathetic relationships that developed between him and various young men.

In his letter, Corbett shows that he is very much troubled in spirit, and no wonder! He consults me about his plans and asks whether, after the loss of his friend, he should continue his projected journey, as he hears that troops are being recruited in the regions through which he is to travel, and that everything along the Rhine and in Lorraine is most unsettled. And since he had intimated that he would not leave Prague before receiving my answer, I wrote him immediately with my advice.

Languet now turned to Sidney's reports about his decision to abandon the Roman journey and the details of his illness.

The letter in which you write that you have given up all thought of a journey to Rome has freed me from great anxiety. You know that I have sought this one thing of you in accordance with the terms of our friendship. But see that you keep your promise, for I shall

5. In 1585 he was in a different kind of trouble. See "Articles for Enquiry in the Examination of Richard Shelley, a Papist, signed by the Council, 1585," BM Lansdowne MS. XIV, fols. 176–79.

guard your letter carefully, like a debtor's promissory note, so that I can bring suit against you should you cheat me.

I was much troubled when I read in your letter that you were having severe headaches and drinking water to excess, and that you had only just avoided pleurisy. This, my dear Sidney, is what I envisaged and feared, and why I advised you to wait for your travelling companions only if they did not delay their departure beyond the solstice. But now thirty-five days have passed since the solstice, and I wonder why they are deferring the journey until August, since men are especially prone to disease in that month, and, as the poet says, it "brings on fevers and unseals the will."

If you love me, take great care of your health, and where it is concerned think of yourself and not of others. If anything worse happened to you, no one living would be more miserable than I, for I take pleasure in nothing but our friendship and my hopes for your virtue. For the ruin of my country and the misfortunes which have recently befallen my friends make my life sadder than death itself.

After comment on the situation in France and Henry III's plans to hasten back to Paris, Languet returned to the letter Sidney wrote from Venice about June 18. "I am delighted that you have introduced yourself to Master Perrot, a kind man and a very good one. Please pay my courteous respects to him, if he is still in Venice." Languet's conclusion reveals that his intimate correspondence with Sidney contrasted sharply with the commentary on affairs of state which he felt was required in letters to the Count of Hanau.

> Give my apologies to his Excellency the Count and to his household for my not writing to them, for I did not know that they would remain there so long. If they should say that I ought to have felt the same way about you, but still do not break my habit of writing you, I reply that I am little concerned about the loss of my letters to you since for the most part they contain nothing but the most trifling trifles, that is, my foolish moods which I pour out onto my page as they arise only to spatter it and to satisfy your curiosity, since you wish to have letters from me. Besides, you wrote that you had taken great care that my letters to you would not be lost, even if they should be delivered to your present address after you leave.
>
> I wish you the best of good fortune and prosperity. Vienna, July 17, 1574.

The final letter from Languet, the last one preserved of those written before Sidney's return to Vienna, is dated July 24. Because Sidney and Languet saw each other almost daily for the balance of the year, occasion to write was so rare that this letter ends their formal correspondence for the year. It begins with a flashback to recent exchanges of correspondence.

> The short letter which I last received from you deeply disturbed me because of what you wrote about your health, but the one which has just been delivered has freed me of that anxiety. I am surprised that you make no mention in it of the letter which I sent you by Master de la Beurthe, Master of Requests at the court of Navarre, who set out from here for Venice by post-horse and hoped to arrive on the third or fourth of this month. Since he had come from Poland with the King, and had promised me to tell you the whole story of the royal departure, or flight, as some call it, I did not write you anything about this.

In his latest letter, probably written about July 2 (it is missing), Sidney had rejected Languet's commendation of Pibrac, basing his views on Pibrac's justification of the St. Bartholomew's Day massacre which had been published under the title *Ornatissimi cujusdam Viri de rebus gallicis ad Stanislaum Elvidium Epistola* (Paris, 1573). In reply to Sidney, Languet explained that Pibrac had written the pamphlet under threat of death for being "soft on Protestants."

> You seem to me to be a little too hard on Pibrac. I do not usually judge men as most people do (unless they are wholly wicked, for I do not think that the vices of such men should go unmentioned). I single out what virtues they have, but whatever faults they commit either by mistake or by frailty of spirit I cloak as best I can. Pibrac is a man of such talent, such learning, and eloquence too, that I do not know whether France possesses his equal. He is extremely kind, and helps good men as best he can, and I believe that he has never been the instigator of a wicked measure.
>
> On the day when the King publicly acknowledged in the Parliament of Paris that the Admiral and his comrades had been killed by his order and decree, Pibrac delivered a splendid speech in his presence, advising him almost more freely than the times permitted, to set bounds to the massacres, while the rest were flattering the King and praising that monstrous deed.

In his house were found Cavagnes who was put to death with Briquemaut, and La Garde, professor of law at Strasbourg. This was almost his ruin, because there were many people who claimed that he should be liquidated. He was compelled to ransom his life with that letter for which you so grievously reproach him; and I by no means approve of his action, for, as the poet says:

> Although Phalaris commands you to be
> A liar, and, bringing forth the bull, prescribes perjuries,
> Consider it the greatest sin to put breath before shame,
> And for life's sake to lose the reasons for living.

Languet showed, moreoever, that he could see with an unjaundiced eye the weaknesses of the Protestants' extremism; he considered that they were overly strict in their moral stance, to their detriment.

> I am not a Stoic, and I do not believe that all faults are the same. Our party has this failing, that if an excellent man should err even in the smallest matter, they immediately class him among the wickedest of men. I am by nature and principle averse to judgements of this sort, and I know that many people criticize me for this and say that I derive it from my teacher, Melanchthon. Thus far I regret neither my teacher nor my principles, and shall not be led away from either by the criticisms of those who are naturally more captious or severe than I am.

Sidney had also expressed indignation over the precipitate departure from Padua of some friends, apparently Germans, without taking leave of him. Languet's comments testify to two of Sidney's traits: his innate sense of courtesy and the quickness of his temper when he felt he had been slighted or wronged.

> Had you been in good health, your complaints about the discourtesy of the people who left you without a farewell would have made me laugh. Perhaps you think, my dear Sidney, that men are generally endowed with your courtesy. Unless you change your mind, you will never be without people to stir your anger and to give you grounds to complain in this way. In this age I feel that those who do not actually cheat their friends do a great deal. If there should be some courtesy added besides, it must be put down to profit, as something which exceeds the bounds of everyday friendship.

From your last letter, however, you appear to have thought better of your anger, and to have let yourself be mollified, smoothing over what could not be changed. And this is a method you will have to use again and again before you arrive at my age, unless you perhaps wish to spend your life in never-ending quarrels.

Languet's letter concludes with references to friends:

I opened Lobbet's letter to you [that of June 1, quoted above] because you told me to, and also Corbett's, which is written in your language and I could therefore not understand, but I think he reports the same things about Richard [Shelley's] illness as he wrote me. Lobbet writes that he has made careful inquiry about Aubéry but has not learned anything about him. My respects to Master Perrot, whom I wish to free from concern.

When Sidney left Padua on his return journey to Vienna cannot be determined. Because he wished to travel with the Count of Hanau and his retinue he had to wait on Hanau's wishes. From the newly recovered letters one fact about their route emerges, namely that the travellers did not follow the direct road, but went north through the Alps to Ortenburg, Bavaria. Hanau had estates and a castle there, which business required him to visit at intervals. They had received an invitation to visit Joachim, Count of Ortenburg (1530–1600); undoubtedly they were invited because Hanau and he were friends, for he is otherwise unmentioned in the Sidney correspondence. A learned man and friend of scholars, Ortenburg had been converted to the Protestant faith in 1563. From then until the end of his life he was embroiled in struggles with the Duke of Bavaria who threatened both the religion and the independence of Ortenburg.

Hanau, Sidney, and their party probably took the route from Padua to Verona and then over the Brenner Pass to Innsbruck, whence they could descend the valley of the Inn to Passau. After leaving Ortenburg they most likely followed the Danube to Vienna. Undoubtedly Bryskett had this adventure through the Alps in mind, not the party's trip through the gentler mountains near Villach (which they traversed before reaching Venice), when he wrote,

> . . . and with him [Sidney] didst scale
> The craggie rocks of th'Alpes and Appenine!
> Still with the Muses sporting. . . .[6]

6. *A Pastorall Aeglogue*, printed in Spenser's *Colin Clout's Come Home Againe* (1595).

While Sidney was on the road, an interesting letter was written to him by a friend in Venice. Dated August 27, it came from François Perrot de Mésières, the literary Frenchman whose trip to Geneva had kept Sidney from actually meeting him until his last few months in Italy. Perrot began with a formal introduction, consisting mostly of compliments.

> Sir,
>
> Before your request for a letter was conveyed to me by a gentleman whom I believe to be one of your company, I did myself the honour of presuming to write of my own accord, wishing both to retain your favour and to refresh your memory of me. You will, in return, reward me beyond all measure if you use my services to the utmost, whenever you think they may be of value. I am therefore writing this for my own pleasure; I do so all the more willingly because I know it pleases you.

Because Languet had written the letter which originally brought about their meeting, Perrot alluded to him next and to Languet's influence among persons enlightened enough to follow the reformed faith. As an Italophile who felt that Languet's attitude about the lures of Italy was too strict and Calvinist, he indulged in a touch of irony.

> And perhaps I would not have been put to this trouble (if that is the word to describe the pleasant task of chatting to you a little on paper), had I been allowed to persuade you to lengthen your stay here, according to my wishes. But my enjoyment of such unusually good company was overruled by the reasons that induced you to return to Germany—that is, before you could begin to take a greater delight in things Italian than is needful for those who are brought up in the faith of God and are guided by it on their road to virtue and honour worthy of their origins, without looking back.
>
> Because, however, I have realized the great affection and the sound judgement of him who recommended this to you, I have been ready to be persuaded, and would not wrong you by advising you other-wise. I would have much to say to you on the subject: but I know that you will not lack such talk, as you are with one [Languet] who greatly loves you and has shown himself most desirous, if not jealous, of your well-being. As his vision, both in this matter and farther ahead, is sufficiently clear to make you decide for the best, I

will leave this argument: it would lead me to speak more of myself, and the reason that led me to return here and is keeping me here, than would be approved by those who know me and are not acquainted with the rest of the story.

With these preliminaries out of the way, Perrot tells of Henry III's departure from Venice. His letter indicates clearly that Sidney had not come to Venice to participate in the magnificent entertainments for the as yet uncrowned King of France.

So I shall just give you what news we have and, inter alia, what we have seen or heard, since you went away, of the voyage of our King,[7] which I attended as far as Ferrara. I shall not say more of the honours he received, as I think they have already been extensively reported: as also what happened here and at Mantua. This we have had printed in two versions,[8] and as I believe others have sent it to you, you will be able to see it for yourself: it has not shamed the Venetian Government. I shall mention only that the Pope's son[9] came to meet him, who at the banquet held at the Mount was received with the Ambassador[10] at the Royal table. They had no one at their right hand, and at their left the Princess of Urbino and Signora Leonora, the sisters of the Duke of Ferrara. The Duke of Savoy, the Duke of Ferrara, and the Duke of Urbino who had also arrived on the day before, remained standing. A report from France, however, showed displeasure with the fact that the Ambassador was following, and made it clear that the King could scarcely be pleased to have him continually at his heels. He had said that his orders were never to move from the King's side, and he fulfilled them with considerable importunity. This report made it possible to get rid of both him and

7. For details of this progress, see A. M. P. G. Nolhac and A. Solerti, *Il Viaggio in Italia di Enrico III* (Turin, 1890), and P. Champion, *Henri III, Roi de Pologne*, 2 vols. (Paris, 1943–51).

8. This could refer, as far as the Venetian reception is concerned, to either of the following: Rocco Benedetti, *Le feste e trionfi fatte dalla Sereniss. Signoria di Venetia nella felice venuta di Henrico III christianiss. re di Francia et di Polonia* (Venice, 1574); or Claudius Dorronius, *Narratio rerum memorabilium, quae propter adventum . . . Henrici III Franciae & Poloniae Regis a . . . Venetorum Republica facta sunt* (Venice, 1574). For Mantua there is *Entrata del Christianiss. re Henrico III di Francia nella citta di Mantova* (Venice, 1574).

9. Giacomo Boncompagni, Duke of Sora, sent to welcome Henry.

10. Probably Filippo Boncompagni, Cardinal of St. Sixtus, the Pope's nephew, whose errand was to persuade Henry to hurry back to France and punish the Protestants.

the other. They left the King at Ferrara, and returned to Rome via Bologna.

Perrot's report about the personalities involved in the King of France's visit indicate a fact which previously known letters have not revealed about Sidney, namely his awareness of the diplomatic actors who participated in the royal pageant.

> M. da Foix[11] was also sent there again; and he has since got part of what he wanted, having obtained confirmation of the bishopric of Toulouse. On the same day M. de Bellièvre[12] was sent to Switzerland, and M. de Lansac's son[13] to Poland; and on the evening of that same day—the last of July—the King embarked on the Po to go to Mantua. He stayed there for two days and would have stayed longer, so much did he enjoy Marmirolo,[14] but for a dispatch from France.

As a recent traveller across the top of Italy, Sidney would have been interested in the route followed by Henry and his entourage.

> Then when he was back on the Po again, he found the water so low that it took him five days to reach Cremona (where he came ashore and entered the town): so he changed his plans, left the river along which he had planned to sail as far as Turin, and returned to the road. Going via Novara and Casale, he bypassed Milan, and arrived in Turin on the fifteenth of this month. The Council has been told that he has left there and that the Queen was to leave Paris on the ninth to come and meet him. But it is not yet known which route he will take: via Lyons or, bypassing that, through Bresse and Burgundy on his way to Reims.

11. Paul de Foix (1528–84), professor of law, diplomat, and churchman. A moderate Catholic, he was Queen Catherine's favourite because of his brilliant mind and diplomatic skill. De Foix had been ambassador to Scotland and England, and in 1564 he had negotiated the treaty of Calais.

12. Pomponne de Bellièvre has already been mentioned. He had previously been ambassador to the Swiss and had been required to justify the St. Bartholomew's Day massacre to them in 1572. Afterwards he was sent by Queen Catherine as French ambassador to Poland, accompanying Henry of Valois.

13. Unidentified: the family name was Du Vivier, Counts of Lansac.

14. The villa of Marmirolo (since destroyed) was built for Federico Gonzaga, Duke of Mantua (d. 1540), by Giulio Pippi, better known as Giulio Romano (ca. 1492–1546). Romano also built the wonderful Palazzo del Té there.

Here the historical comment might be inserted that Henry's party took the route through Lyons: moreover, they ascended the Mont Cenis Pass, the lowest in the Western Alps but a formidable enterprise in those days. Little wonder that once they reached Lyons they rested there for two months.

Perrot ended his letter with a brief summary of military events on scattered fronts.

> From France there is no news. From Flanders we hear that all the Comendador's troops have been disbanded for lack of money. From Goletta we hear, via a report from Palermo dated the sixth, that the Spaniards are trying gamely to defend their new fortress, and are even making several sorties.[15] In one of those, led by Pagan Doria, the Sangiarch of Tripoli and many other Turks died. In all, the number of Turks killed since the siege is estimated at more than nine or ten thousand. Others, possibly jealous of the honour the Spaniards are reaping, are distorting this news, saying that the Turkish artillery has already destroyed all the defences at Goletta, which they attacked first, and that, on the other hand, Serbellone, the commander of the fortress, is ready to abandon it.
>
> That is all the news we have; and I shall end with my humble respects to the Count of Hanau, to your benevolence and to that of Master Languet; praying God, Sir, to protect you always. From Venice, this twenty-seventh of August, 1574.
>
> Your humble and affectionate servant,
>
> F. Perrot de Mésières
>
> Master Canaye[16] and my brother[17] present their humble respects.
> To the Baron de Sidenay, at Vienna; and in his absence to Master Languet.

About the end of August Sidney reached Vienna, for on September 2 he wrote from there to Lobbet in Strasbourg. His reunion with Languet must have been joyous for both. During the following autumn and winter

15. For the dramatic story of the Turkish capture of Tunis and its fortress Goletta, see especially Zündelin's letter of Nov. 5, 1574 in chap. 13 below.

16. Philippe de Canaye (1551–1610), sieur du Fresne, was a lawyer and diplomat who lived in Italy for some time. He was made a Councillor by Henry III and served as an envoy to England in 1586, to Switzerland in 1588, and again to England after the accession of Henry IV. A Protestant through much of his career, he later converted to Catholicism.

17. Probably Jacques Perrot.

they spent much of their time together. To facilitate their friendship Sidney took lodgings in the same house as Languet.[18] The house belonged to Dr. Michael Lingelsheim, as Languet revealed in a letter dated May 27, 1573 to Joachim Camerarius. Languet wrote "I am living here with that most excellent man, Dr. Michael Lingelsheim, who knew you in Italy and is full of affection for you."[19] Though both Sidney and Languet held to their own schedule of activities, they were able to dine together and join in conversation with Languet's wide circle of friends.

18. See Lobbet to Sidney, Oct. 5, 1574; and Languet to Sidney, June 12, 1575.

19. *Huberti Langueti*, p. 206. "Hic vivo apud optimum virum Doctorem Michaele Linghelium, qui te novit in Italia." This reference was first pointed out by J. A. van Dorsten in "Sidney and Languet," *HLQ* 29 (May, 1966):215–22.

CHAPTER 13

Of Sidney's activities during the early autumn of 1574 we have no certain details, though there is every reason to believe that he returned to his former round of daily life under Languet's guidance. Living in the same house as Languet had many advantages, not the least being access to the books on Languet's shelves; in those days books were still a rare commodity, as Sidney's Venetian correspondence has shown. Besides his reading and other studies, Sidney enjoyed conversations with the physician Crato von Crafftheim, the botanist Charles de l'Écluse, the artist Abondio, and such statesmen as Jean de Vulcob. He also returned to fencing practice and began "to learne horsemanship of Jon Pietro Pugliano." This riding master placed equestrian skill at the pinnacle of the arts, and Sidney later immortaized him in this famous passage at the opening of the *Defence of Poesie*.

He said souldiers were the noblest estate of mankind, and horsemen the noblest of souldiers. He said they were the maisters of warre, and ornaments of peace, speedie goers, and strong abiders, triumphers both in Camps and Courts: nay to so unbleeved a point he proceeded, as that no earthly thing bred such wonder to a Prince, as to be a good horseman. Skill of government was but a *Pedanteria*, in comparison, then would he adde certaine praises by telling what a peerlesse beast the horse was, the onely serviceable Courtier without flattery, the beast of most bewtie, faithfulnesse, courage, and such more, that if I had not bene a peece of a *Logician* before I came to him, I thinke he would have perswaded me to have wished my selfe a horse.

Sidney also enjoyed the company of friends of his own generation, especially Edward Wotton, who joined him in the study of equestrian art under the direction of the fastidious Maestro Pugliano. Six years older than Sidney, Wotton (later Baron Wotton) had spent several years in the Spanish colony at Naples where he developed his brilliant linguistic abilities for his subsequent career as a diplomat. Walsingham recently had assigned him to Vienna as secretary to the English embassy at the imperial court. There he and Sidney formed a close friendship which lasted until he helped to carry the pall at Sidney's funeral.

One of the first letters Sidney received after arrival in Vienna came from Wolfgang Zündelin in Venice. Dated September 6, it reveals several interesting details about Sidney's departure from Padua, including his sending Bryskett in the opposite direction to deliver letters in Venice. Presumably Bryskett, travelling alone, doubled back and rejoined the party. Zündelin's letter also provides the evidence for the visit to Ortenburg, which in turn determines the route that Hanau, Sidney, and their attendants followed from Padua to Vienna.

> The letter, noble lord Philip, which you sent me when you left Padua was delivered to me by your Lodowick; and I would have replied to it at once, had I not been uncertain of your whereabouts. For I have received nothing from any of you after you left us here, and I thought that you must have been detained longer than you had expected by Count Ortenburg, whom you had turned aside to visit. Then I received your letter, addressed to our friend Wacker and committed to my care.

The next passage contains a puzzle: a mysterious "Spanish nobleman" was going to meet with Sidney.

> As from this I guessed more or less (for he has not yet told me whence it was sent) that you had already reached Vienna, I did not wish to delay my duty of writing to you any further: especially since opportunity presented itself in the form of a man who claimed that he was going directly to you. Who he is I do not know—your English friends tell me he is a Spanish nobleman. He has told me something of his acquaintance with you; moreover, in his admittedly very brief conversation with me, he shows himself to be a man of breeding and education. I should have liked to do him some service, especially for the sake of him to whom I owe everything; but as the opportunity did not present itself he will I am sure be kind enough to regard what I should have wished to do rather than what was in my power.

This clearly is a joke of some kind. No other trace of any Spanish friend of Sidney is known; furthermore, if the friend were indeed a Spanish nobleman Zündelin would not need to be told so by Lord Windsor or other Englishmen in Venice, for his nationality would have been obvious. Quite possibly this man was Edward Wotton, en route to Vienna from the Spanish court at Naples. The Englishmen may well have enjoyed teasing the slightly pedantic German savant.

Zündelin continues in a personal vein:

> To return to your letter: I thank you—not as much as I should but as well as I can—not only for visting me before your departure, but also for so kindly having written to me when you had scarcely left us. For although it was by no means your duty but rather mine, to omit no occasion to send you my greetings: yet this token and reminder of your singular love for me is, as it should be, my greatest delight. And I hope that you with your uncommon kindness will not hesitate to grant me your favour since the hour of your unexpected departure so forestalled you that at the time it deprived me of the great pleasure of saluting you for what I believe would have been the last time in Italy. I have however followed you with all my best wishes, and will accompany you thus as long as I live; and the farther you remove yourself from us, the more ardently shall I pursue you, and finally find you though all the world lie between us.

The mention of Sidney's "unexpected departure" indicates that Sidney himself was not innocent of the discourtesy of which he had complained to Languet earlier in the summer. We are also reminded of the complaint which Bochetel reported Sidney's hostess in Vienna had made and still another which was to come from his friend Wacker.

Another habit which Sidney frequently indulged was to urge his Continental friends to visit him in England. His repeated invitations to Languet and to Claude Aubéry have already been cited, and similar hospitality was offered to Lobbet and Wacker. Later letters show that Zündelin also was invited; the concluding lines in this one suggest that Sidney had done so already or that Zündelin was angling for the offer.

> Shall I see you some time in that England of yours? And shall I find you the same as ever in your kindness and love for me, yet in that position and dignity which I believe will be yours by virtue of these singular gifts of talent and spirit with which God has adorned you? I pray that He will in His goodness be gracious to your most honourable ambitions, and will grant you those powers that will enable you to continue fearlessly along that hard and difficult way of piety and virtue. And may you succeed in attaining the goal He has set you; to the glory of His holy name, and to the advantage of the

Christian nation in which you were born and to which you are dedicated. Farewell. V[enice], the sixth of September, 1574.

Kindly greet the noble Count Hanau and your other friends from me, especially Master Languet. The bearer of this will personally tell you the news from here.

Yours most respectfully,
Wolfgang Zündelin

Zündelin's concluding words about Sidney's goal are worth comment. The latter's Protestant activist friends never lost sight of his potential leadership of a unified Protestant front against the Catholic powers. They considered him their man of destiny. For the Protestants had developed a well-founded fear of a universal Catholic conspiracy to extirpate other religions, especially Calvinism, of which the Huguenots were the French division. Queen Mary's Spanish marriage had instilled this fear in England; the Spanish-Venetian-Papal coalition that defeated the Turks at Lepanto set a pattern that could be followed elsewhere; and the papal blessing of the St. Bartholomew's Day massacre was still a bitter memory. The devious schemes of the Jesuits and other groups involved in the Counter-Reformation threatened the Lutherans as well as the Calvinists and the Church of England. Little wonder that the Protestants sought a League and leaders to inspire it.

Soon after settling in Vienna Sidney wrote to friends in Padua. One of them, Johann Matthäus Wacker von Wackenfels, whose name has occurred in several of Languet's letters, replied on September 27. His letter is preserved among the recently recovered group. Although it contains little except courtly compliments, Wacker shows the warm admiration that the German students at Padua felt towards Sidney. The letter is also interesting as an example of florid style, for Wacker displays an unselfconscious pleasure in turning out conspicuously embellished sentences.

Greetings in the Lord Jesus Christ.

May God so love me, illustrious and noble Master Sidney, that nothing more welcome and delightful can befall me than your letter, in which you have been graciously pleased to address, and in your kindness benevolently to express your affection for, your humble servant. Is Wacker truly so blessed as to receive a letter from Sidney? Am I so happy that he, to whose service I long since dedicated myself completely, should with his own hand inscribe the friendliest of letters to me? Indeed—to speak truly—when I examined the letter, and when I recognized the seals and the hand itself, yea, even though I read it through for a second time, I could scarcely bring myself to believe that it came from your Illustrious Magnificence. For what could I less expect than a letter from you?

And even if, due to your kindness, one should arrive, what content thereof had I less right to hope for than that scrupulous and oh so exquisite apology for your departure? Indeed, I thought: here, in disguise, he is reminding you, Wacker, of your duty; and in offering such scrupulous apologies he is saying what you ought to have done. For clearly—should I wish to make my confession—it was my duty not only to take my leave of you at your departure, as you mention, but also to accompany your leaving with all such sorts of service as were in my power, and to testify to the magnitude of the grief inspired in me by that departure not only with words but with weeping.

Wacker had been in Venice for the ceremonies and entertainments during the visit of Henry III, and he had just returned to Padua when he learned that Sidney and Hanau were about to depart.

But whether you speak truly or, as I am pleased to suspect, artfully, we were both indeed thwarted by the extreme confusion of events, which easily succeeded in upsetting not only the imprudent and pre-occupied, but even all the most scrupulous. When I learned of your departure I had not yet heard from our friends that you would be leaving; when I heard it I did not believe it; and when I was forced to believe it, it could not have been more unwillingly. When I returned to Padua from Venice I visited your old lodgings and our mutual friends: besides the repute of your name and the delightful and honoured memory that all retained of you, I found no one.

For my unhappy self there was no way, except by letter, to tender you my apologies, to absolve myself of a charge of negligence or pride, and finally so to take my leave of a most excellent and delight-ful friend as he deserves of me. But this was itself impeded on the one hand by a certain somewhat clownish hesitancy on my part, and on the other by the press of your affairs. For I feared both to trouble one already more than sufficiently occupied with my trifles, and also to be forced to confess my imprudence.

Thus it happened that, while on the one hand I do not wish to appear somewhat audacious in writing and overbold in excusing myself, on the other hand enough days have since elapsed which seemed not only to lift none of the grief I had incurred, but indeed with the passage of time to swell and increase it. Until at last, on September twenty-fifth, that most eagerly awaited letter of yours was delivered to me: which I not only read and reread—as we do with ordinary letters—but kissed again and again (which we reserve for the specially welcome) and stored most carefully among the rest of my dearest treasures. Not only did it enable me to breathe again: but, having thus obtained an opportunity of replying to you, I considered it a most fitting moment to put pen to paper at once and write you this letter—partly in order to defend myself to you which I believe I have done with this account, and partly in order to fulfill my duty and obligation.

Wacker's ornate compliments continue to the very end of the letter.

Indeed, I thank you most warmly—not as much as I should, but as well as I can—most honourable Master Sidney, both for this singular kindness and for your other favours to me; and I beg you, as you also promise in your letter, to yield to none in your love and regard for me: because I long ago became so attached to you that you neither have nor will easily obtain (if I may be allowed to say so) a more faithful client. And although you have not yet had the opportunity of testing this in reality, yet I hope that the time will come when I shall remove all shadow of doubt on your part; and I greatly hope that this may happen as soon as possible and with the greatest possible advantage to both of us.

Farewell. May the Lord Jesus bless your most praiseworthy ambitions, and with his spirit most mightily protect you from all harm. Amen. From Padua, Friday, September twenty-seventh in the year of the last age, 1574.

Your little servant,
Matthew Wacker of Constanz

I reverently salute the Illustrious & Noble Count Hanau; and amicably and respectfully greet the most honourable Masters Welsperg, Bryskett, and Delius; and in the first place the most renowned Master Languet, my lord, patron, and (if I may be so bold) father. The Barons Liechtenstein respectfully return your greetings.

Mention of Matthäus Delius indicates that he now was in Vienna; probably he had travelled with Hanau, Sidney, and their party from Padua.

A week or so after Wacker's letter arrived from Padua Sidney received one from Dr. Lobbet in Strasbourg. Dated October 5, it begins with comments on the contents of a letter Sidney wrote to him on September 2, thus providing a glimpse of Sidney's situation on his arrival in Vienna.

> Greetings.
>
> A week ago I received your letter (noble Master Sidney) dated the second of last month: I would willingly have replied to it on the same day as I received it, had not a tertian fever hindered my work: and as it happened that was when the fever was in its crisis. I have mentioned this at once so that you may excuse me, and not accuse me of negligence. I congratulate you on your happy return to Austria from Italy. I am glad, moreover, that at Vienna you have found men whose conversation delights you. Most of all am I pleased to hear that you are living in the same house with Master Languet. He loves and honours you greatly, as you deserve: while you on your part can learn from him many things that might be useful to you in great affairs.

Sidney's letter had conveyed greetings to various friends. The first was Christopher Mont's son who had carried a letter from Sidney in Padua to Lobbet some months earlier. Sidney's "host" in Strasbourg was the wine-loving Hubert de la Rose, mentioned in previous correspondence with Lobbet.

> I shall convey your greetings to Mont and your host in Strasbourg when my fever allows. I wish it would seek other lodgings. It would be more competently handled by some cardinal or rough abbot. But as my health is in the hands of Almighty God, I must pray him to grant me what He knows to be best for me. Aubéry is in Basle. About a month ago I sent to Master Languet the letter he wrote to you. I believe you must have received it by now. As I said before, he is still in Basle. He wrote to me on the twenty-third of last month, and sent me the medical propositions which he defended in public debate. He tells me that he has obtained the title of doctor. He also asks me (which I will do gladly), if I should hear anything about you, to let him know.

Lobbet next introduces us to a young Czech, Johannes Hájek, whom Sidney later generously took back to England so that Hájek could "study virtue," a subject which proved somewhat incompatible to his temperament.

> Master Languet has, I believe, spoken to you about the son of Doctor Thaddeus, the Emperor's physician: this boy is at present here. He is about fifteen years old, of good character, and, as far as I can determine, intelligent. He knows German, and in the study of letters he has, for his age, made sufficiently good progress.
>
> A man who recently returned here from England, and who was in London until the eighth of last month, tells me that Parliament is urgently entreating its Queen to choose a successor: he also said that the Queen would reply to these demands this month of October.
>
> Farewell, noble sir, and accept my best respects. From Strasbourg, the fifth of October, 1574.
>
> Your most respectful servant,
>
> Jo. Lobbet
>
> Lord Walsingham [*sic*] has been created Secretary of your kingdom.

Sidney also heard from his friend in Venice, François Perrot de Mésières, the literary light of the French embassy. Written in French, the language that Sidney undoubtedly employed in their correspondence, Perrot's letter is dated October 9 and dwells only on political news. Events in France especially engaged his attention.

> Sir,
>
> I have received your letter of the twenty-fourth of September, which merely by its courtesy offers me great friendship: and I shall feel greatly honoured if at any time, for this friendship's sake, I can be of service to you.
>
> As I am still here, although I did not expect to be here so long and am so, indeed, against my will, I shall not fail to send you some news from these parts, for I trust that will please you; indeed I will do so wherever I am, as long as I know that my letters can reach you.
>
> The King's arrival at Lyons on the sixth of last month quickly showed us how little sincere intention there is of making peace. From the very first day, M. de Bellegarde was proclaimed Marshal of France; and he has been given charge of the projected war in the Dauphiné with Monsieur the Dauphin. Their forces are: infantry,

four or five thousand Frenchmen and three or four thousand Piedmontese provided by the Duke of [MS torn], as well as six or seven thousand Swiss; cavalry, fifteen hundred Reiters, as well as several companies of soldiers. Their plan is to start with Poussins, Livron, and Laureol. The Marshal de Retz, on the other hand, has been sent to Provence with other troops. In the meantime, the Huguenots have seized Castres, near Toulouse. And while M. de Savoye was at Lyons with the King, Madame the Duchess died in Turin the fifteenth of last month. She had been trying hard to act as mediator, and to persuade both sides to effect a proper peace. This event caused the said Duke of Savoy to return. The Duke of Urbino has also let himself die instead of coming here: all the preparations for his stay had already been made. Since the twenty-third of August Goletta has been stormed: it was also said that the citadel had been taken on the twenty-ninth of that month, but that is now doubted.

That is all I can tell you. If M. Languet is still there—you did not mention him in your letter—he will find here my most sincere respects; and, having also presented them to yourself, I shall pray God,

Sir, to protect you always. From Venice, the ninth of [October], 1574.

Your humble and [affectionate servant,
F. Perrot de Mésières]

The events described by Perrot require little comment except to say that Roger de Bellegarde did not remain long in the favour of Henry III, but shortly afterwards was dismissed in disgrace. The royal forces converged on the three towns situated at the point where the river Drôme flows into the Rhône. Marguerite, the Duchess of Savoy, had been a patroness of learning and literature.

During this autumn in Vienna as Sidney followed his program of reading, writing, and practising his fencing and horsemanship, he doubtless listened to many discussions and debates on the topics then uppermost in the minds of all Viennese, from members of the imperial court to frequenters of the neighbourhood *Weinstube*. Sidney's friends were much concerned over the actions of the Elector Frederick of the Palatinate who had disregarded his obligations to the Emperor Maximilian by concluding a treaty with the Prince de Condé and the Montmorency family. The Elector's purpose was to win back from France the imperial dioceses of

Metz, Toul, and Verdun and to affiliate them with the fanatically Protestant Palatinate. The overly ambitious and unrealistic treaty was viewed with utmost alarm in Vienna, and proposals were even afoot to punish the Elector Frederick by deposing him at the forthcoming Diet.

On October 14 the leader of the opposition to Frederick, his cousin Count George Hans, reached Vienna and he remained there until December 2. He energetically lobbied for his cause at court and in private circles. Both Maximilian and the French Ambassador, Sidney's friend Jean de Vulcob, entertained Count Georg Hans very civilly. Maximilian, however, did not wish to let Frederick's flouting of imperial law interfere with his own program at the Diet. This centred on getting his son Rudolph elected King of the Romans as a stepping-stone to succeeding him as Emperor. For this purpose he wished to gain the vote of the Palatinate. Vulcob could be courteous to Count George Hans because he realized the Count's schemes were so wild that they could not be (and were not) taken seriously.

Sidney would have been specially interested in reports on Condé's efforts to get financial support from Elizabeth so that he could raise the troops necessary for his success against the French. Agents representing the German, Dutch, and Huguenot cause were in London in August, and in September the Palatinate sent a special envoy to Elizabeth to seek a loan. To no one's surprise where money was involved, Elizabeth procrastinated. Walsingham, ever sympathetic to any action to further a Protestant League, finally jolted her by writing, "For the love of God, madam, let not the cure of your diseased state hang any longer on deliberation." [1] Elizabeth then agreed to employ her favourite device for aiding the Huguenots; she offered them money to hire German mercenaries to fight for them. Characteristically, she cut the loan to a third of the requested amount. She agreed to send the secretary of her Embassy in Paris, Thomas Wilkes, to Heidelberg in the spring to negotiate a loan of fifty thousand crowns to the Elector Frederick.

Towards the end of September Sidney suffered another illness, though no details of it have been preserved. The fact that he felt it worth mentioning in a letter to Burghley about ten weeks after his recovery suggests that his trouble was no ordinary indisposition. Sidney's illness may have postponed the excursion to Poland which Languet had long urged him

---

1. Dated Jan. 15, 1574/5. *State Papers Scotland XXVI*, 66; listed in *Calendar of State Papers Scotland 1509–89*, p. 389.

to undertake. About October 21 he told Zündelin that he had recovered and was planning to set out on the expedition. By November 12 he was back in Vienna, as his correspondence with Perrot makes clear. Beyond these dates and the fact that the trip was disappointing, we know very little about his brief excursion to the north.

Once again the Procrustean bed of logistics makes Sidney's Polish expedition difficult to follow. Travelling from Vienna to Cracow and back would have required covering about 550 miles. The terrain was fairly flat, but the distance involved still meant close to forty miles in the saddle for each of fourteen days. If Sidney's party travelled by carriage, as Languet had recommended when the expedition was first proposed, the pace would have been even slower.[2] And if they took a full three weeks, only a third of the time could have been spent visiting friends and resting. Sidney's motives for the trip seem to have been simply to see more of central Europe and to accept proffered hospitality. Actually, Languet's earlier purpose in urging Sidney to visit Poland had ceased to exist, for after Henry of Valois had learned that the throne of France had fallen to him, he surreptitiously left Poland and the Polish nobles retired to their estates to nurse their disappointment and ponder to whom the crown should next be offered.

Although Cracow was the centre of Poland's political, cultural, and intellectual life, it could scarcely compare with the cities Sidney knew so well: Frankfurt, Vienna, Venice, or even Padua. Nor was the countryside an inspiration after what he had already seen. The hospitality of his Polish hosts undoubtedly offered every available comfort and local luxury. His principal host was probably Martin Deobori, whose invitation had been issued long before when the projected coronation of Henry of Valois seemed to promise a happy era for Poland. Since the Deobori family and the location of their estates still defy identification, the terminus of Sidney's Polish expedition cannot be fixed. Quite possibly Hanau and some of his attendants accompanied Sidney and his faithful Griffin. Languet gave him a warm letter of introduction[3] to the eminent Hungarian humanist and Greek scholar, Andreas Dudith, who served as

2. See Languet's letter of June 18, 1574. Twenty years later when Fynes Moryson made this journey on horseback it took ten days to travel between Cracow and Vienna, an average of about twenty-eight miles per day. *Itinerary*, pp. 64–66.

3. Bibl. Nat. Dupuy MS. 797, fol. 321ff., first pointed out by Pierre Costi, in *André Dudith, Humaniste Hongrois* (Paris, 1935), p. 147.

the Emperor's ambassador to Poland, and presumably Sidney passed a day or two with Dudith.

J. A. van Dorsten sees in this brief visit the origin of Sir Robert Naunton's statement two generations later that Sidney was a candidate for the throne of Poland, though thwarted by Queen Elizabeth "'out of fear to lose the jewel of her times.'"[4] Van Dorsten stressed the fact that Languet's introduction presents Sidney not as a promising student of good family but as a potential actor on the stage of power politics:

> His father is the Viceroy of Ireland, with whom, I am told, scarcely anyone among the nobility of England can compare in *virtus* and military experience.

> His mother is a sister of the Earl of Warwick and of Robert the Earl of Leicester, the most favoured at Court: since neither has children, this gentleman [i.e. Sidney] will probably be their heir.

> His father's sister is married to the Earl of Sussex, whom I think you have met here. His mother's sister is the wife of the Earl of Huntingdon, who is related to the Royal family.

> Neither nobleman has any sons: so that on this one person [i.e. Sidney] they have placed their hopes, and him they have decided to advance to honour after his return.

If Languet had regal ambitions for his English protégé he would have recognized their impracticality, for the Emperor proposed his own son, Archduke Ernest, for the vacant throne. The struggle between neighbouring powers continued for several years and occupies many pages in letters from Continental friends to Sidney.

Besides the fact that Sidney presented Languet's letter to Dudith, the only details we know about his Polish expedition are that one of the party was a young Pole of fine parts and noble family (probably Dioderi), that they covered in a short time an exhausting distance even for young men who loved the saddle, and that afterwards Sidney often told his friends how disappointing the whole jaunt had been.

On returning to his rooms in the house of Dr. Lingelsheim, Sidney received a letter from another friend whom he had met through Languet, Dr. Andreas Paull, counsellor to the Elector of Saxony. Paull, like Languet, had sat at the feet of Melanchthon. Because of Dr. Paull's skill as a diplomat and as a linguist, he enjoyed the special confidence of the

---

4. "Sidney and Languet," p. 218. Naunton's remark appears in *Fragmenta Regalia* (1641), p. 19.

Elector. Written from Dresden on October 28, his letter reveals that he and Sidney had not yet met.

> Greetings.
>
> It is indeed true what the ancients said—and of which you are in no way ignorant, most Noble and Illustrious Master Sidney—that virtue prefers to draw to herself, as objects of her love, those men in whom she already dwells. For when I was at Vienna a few months ago and spoke with that wonderful man, our friend Hubert Languet, of various matters (as we are used to do) and, inter alia, of those who in this age most excel in talents, learning, and virtues, he began to speak of you and told me of your talents and your most manifold and signal virtues; so that I gradually began to feel my heart fired by such a respect for your name that I became marvellously determined to strike up a friendship with you. For I knew how great is Languet's wisdom in the observation of character, and how accurate and happy is his judgement of men's virtues. And so I could not help urgently asking him to greet you respectfully in my name in his letters (you were then living in Italy) and to offer whatever services I could possibly perform.

Sidney, in turn, had been prompted at Languet's urging to begin the correspondence with the eminent jurist.

> However, that this indication of my esteem pleased you is more than sufficiently shown by your letter which was delivered to me on October 15, brimming with manifest signs of your talent, learning, and kindness. It so delighted me that I freely acknowledge my duty, not only to write to you in return, but most sincerely to thank you for first writing to me, and that so kindly. For there is nothing in this life so delightful to me as to obtain the goodwill of excellent and remarkable men, be it secured through their kindness or through my efforts and services.
>
> And as this has now befallen me with regard to you—and indeed through you yourself, with no previous effort or deserving of mine— you must believe me when I say that this love of mine for you, of which Languet by his speech was the mediator, has been wonderfully strengthened: at which I may truly and justly rejoice as I hear that you love me in return—you, a youth born to the highest estate, and most excellently adorned with all the gifts of nature and fortune;

you, who (and this is the most important) are laying, in this spring of your youth, the foundations for the remainder of your life, so that I may expect from you all that is highest and most splendid.

In the first place, my most noble lord, I congratulate you yourself on this: secondly, however, and most of all, England, your country and your nurse, to whom your name will bring the benefit of the greatest praise, glory, and—if I am not mistaken—happiness also. But of that I shall write more sparingly, lest you should think that I wish to flatter you. For so liberally placing yourself at my service I thank you most heartily.

I for my part cannot, to be sure, promise much in return to you, a youth favoured by fortune and lacking in nothing: consequently, however, I should like you to think that among those who honour you, esteem you, and wish you all good fortune, I in no way desire to be the last. But rather do I wish with all my heart that those things may befall you—as soon as may be—which those great virtues with which God has already so mercifully adorned you seem not only to need but indeed to demand as their right.

Languet had evidently thought that Sidney might go to Dresden on his return journey from Poland to Vienna.

The rest I shall leave until we meet. For Languet has given me considerable hope that you will be here soon, and certainly nothing more welcome could befall me; I hope that then I shall be able for a short while to drag my mind away from the cares which have occupied me excessively for some time. In the meantime, farewell, and continue to love me as you have begun. For indeed I shall repay you my debt, to wit my heart and my desire to love you in return. Farewell again. From Dresden, October 28, 1574.

Yours with the utmost respect and love,

Andreas Paull

Soon after his return Sidney received another letter from Zündelin, sent on November 5. It is the longest one in his extant correspondence, but the manuscript has become badly blackened by oxidization of the iron in the ink and some passages are almost undecipherable. The letter confirms the reports of Sidney's illness found in other correspondence of this time.

Your letter brought me much joy, most noble sir, though not unmixed with some chagrin. For what you write about your falling ill after you left us was, because of the singular love and honour I bear you, extremely distressing to me. You made me most happy, however, when farther on you wrote that you were recovered, and recovered to such an extent that, restored to your former strength and vigour, you are even leaving for foreign parts and do not shrink from travelling as far as Poland. I hope soon, with the same joy, to be able to learn from your letters that your journey has been completed according to your expectations and that you have returned to Vienna safe and sound.

Evidently Sidney was still applying himself to Latin epistolary style, the polishing of which was one function of his letters to Continental friends. Zündelin assures him that his efforts have been successful and that he could not be better situated than under Languet's tutelage.

When you apologize to me for your last letter, as being not so exquisitely and elegantly written, you do indeed show yourself to be very modest. But there was no need for apologies: certainly not to me, who have never approved that superstitious and excessive scrupulousness in the writing of letters; and I know that nothing coming from you could be anything but distinguished and resembling in delicacy your delightful spirit.

Concerning your decision to spend this winter in Vienna with that most excellent man, Hubert Languet, I do not know whether more strongly to commend your love for him, proceeding as it does from an honest love of virtue, or to praise your wisdom and prudence for preferring the intimacy of a most excellent and wise man to all else. I beg you on my part most respectfully to return his greetings and to commend me to him with that love and honour with which I respect him, as his singular talents and spiritual endowments deserve.

Zündelin then tells Sidney of his disappointment in being unable to travel to Constantinople. Quite likely he had hoped to join the party that accompanied Gilles de Noailles, who had been sent to succeed his brother, the Bishop of Dax, as ambassador. (The two companions Zündelin mentions remain unidentified.)

You will have heard something of my proposed journey to Constantinople. Had not some matters kept me here, I should have journeyed there with those best of companions, our friends B. Allevelt and Ranchin the Frenchman, that very learned youth who, as a friend of the Ferraran ambassador, is, I imagine, not unknown to you. Now I have missed an opportunity such as I doubt will ever recur. If, however, it should so chance and my affairs would permit it, I shall not fear to commence a journey more laborious than dangerous; and, although I have many other reasons for undertaking it, yet most of all am I inspired by the example of your friend Languet, who wished to see with his own eyes those things of which he had read accounts in the works of the ancients and to leave his footprints in places made famous by the memory of the deeds done there.

What shall I say in answer to the rest of your letter? My attempt to thank you is defeated by the greatness of your love for me, which seems to loom before me everywhere. I promise you, therefore, the only thing in my power: I shall attempt never to give you cause to regret such great goodwill towards me.

Zündelin now shifts to his main role, that of newsmonger. His first report concerns the siege and capture of the Spanish fortress of Goletta outside Tunis. The Turks began their attack late in July and the Spanish held out until August 23. Tunis itself fell on September 13. Rival accounts of the surrender were circulated by the Spaniards and the Italians, as Zündelin's report makes clear.[5]

> Although I know you have better sources, yet because I am used to do so and because I believe that you expect something of the kind from me, I shall give you a brief account of the news. Although the recent capture of the fortress Goletta is now an established fact, yet the accounts of it are so varied and contradictory that I cannot give you the most trustworthy versions. The Spaniards, favouring their compatriots who made up the garrison of Goletta, greatly praise their courage and constancy: saying how they, though few in number, so long repulsed so many of the enemy's assaults, killed many thousands of Turks, and although there was no longer any hope of assistance and the garrison was finally reduced to twenty-seven men, still offered resistance; and how, when finally vanquished, they preferred to surrender to fate and fortune rather than to abandon a jot of the innate courage and loyalty of their heritage.

5. The best contemporary account is found in a rare pamphlet, *Goleta. Wahrhafftige . . . beschreibung wie der Türck . . . die . . . Vestung Goleta belagert, gestürmt, endtlich erorbert und zerstöret* (Nuremberg, 1574).

The Italians, on the other hand, say that the Spaniards wished to surrender Goletta to the enemy and that about three hundred of them spontaneously gave themselves up. When the walls had been scaled, those that were left fled into their quarters. They were unable to show many wounds, and nearly all surrendered unharmed to the Turks, whose last assault not one of those brave Spaniards had had the courage to resist on the battlements. Thus, by their disgraceful crime, was lost the most impregnable fortress of the Christian world.

Of their fellow Italians, who were part of the new garrison, these Italians say that they perished by the same treachery of the Spaniards: that when there was still a possibility, not only of safety but indeed of a great victory, they vainly begged for the Spaniards' aid and assistance; that when Goletta had been lost they still offered the strongest possible resistance; and that when all had been wounded and most of them killed, the few survivors surrendered to the enemy. Their commander, Gabriele Serbelloni, having sustained many wounds, was living in fetters as a captive; while Portocarrero, the commander of Goletta, had somehow obtained a reward for his cowardice and perfidy, and was living in freedom and being treated with more kindness than was the custom of Turkish hospitality.

A few who are less biased and represent, as it were, a middle way, still assign the greater blame to the Spaniards: confirming the account of their betrayal and flight, and most of all accusing the King's ministers, who failed to aid the African cause in time with men and money as the King had ordered, and who would have greatly preferred to be idle spectators of, rather than actors in, so fatal a tragedy caused by their guilt. There was much else in the same vein which would take too long to recount here: so I shall pass on to other matters.

Both versions were partly correct. The Spanish in the main garrison fought bravely, but their compatriots who manned the outlying fort in the Estaña Channel did surrender after they learned that Goletta had fallen. The garrison at Tunis, comprised of both Italians and Spaniards, displayed great courage and tenacity behind their leader, Gabriele Serbelloni (1508–80), one of the finest commanders of his day. After his capture he was released with the help of the Pope in exchange for thirty-six Turkish officers; thus he lived to fight again in the Netherlands a few years later. Portocarrero, on the other hand, is said to have died in captivity on shipboard, depressed by grief and shame at the defeat. The Spanish government did indeed fail to aid the besieged garrison with men and money; this failure, in the face of urgent appeals, was the chief cause of the loss of the fortress.

Zündelin continued his recital of Turkish activities with an account of the returning fleet's stop at the Venetian-held island of Corfu.

Some men who arrived here five days ago by cargo boat from Corfu say that on October nineteenth a Turkish fleet came to that island, with about twelve hundred Spanish and Italian prisoners on board. Some, moreover, say that they were hit by a great storm and so first put into Goumenitsa [on the mainland]. Four days after their arrival the governor of the island, according to custom, sent gifts to the commander of the fleet [Sinan Pasha]. The latter refused to accept them and protested almost immediately that they were brought too late, and that by this the Venetians amply showed just how much they esteemed the Turkish Emperor. Three times he ordered them to be taken back whence they had been brought. Later, persuaded by one of his priests, he called back the returning envoys (who had previously protested in vain that they had been unable to come more quickly because of the storm), accepted the presents, and asked them whether the Venetians had shown themselves thereby faithful friends to the Turkish Emperor. With an unexpected reply, he suggested that this was scarcely credible; Christians and Turks could never reach complete agreement.

Then he ordered Portocarrero, who is living unfettered in considerable freedom among the Turks, and G. Serbelloni, who was chained in foot-shackles, to be brought before him, and asked them in how many days he had subdued Goletta and whether that stronghold were more impregnable than Corfu. Both replied that Goletta had been taken in twenty-six days; and Serbelloni, as the one responsible for the fortifications, said that it had also been more impregnable. Then Sinan said that it should therefore be possible to capture the stronghold of Corfu more quickly than the other, and dismissed the envoys scarcely more kindly than he had received them.

Later (I did not hear on which day), he went up to the citadel, to observe more closely what precautions the Venetians would be able to take against the Turks, staring at it fixedly until nearly past midday.

Sinan Pasha was so elated by his victory at Goletta that he thirsted for another triumph. He was abetted by a corsair (now an officer of the Turkish fleet) called "the Aga" and by another who had assumed the title "King of Fez" because he controlled that city.[6] The latter had already begun to plan the attack on King Sebastian of Portugal which led to the battle of Al Kasr in 1578 where Sebastian lost his life. (Turkish losses were, of course, much higher than they admitted.)

> When certain of the main fleet commanders had been given presents, these men were received at a banquet by the Governor of Corfu. Among them was the noble corsair Aga, and the one they call the King of Fez (some say it was his brother). When he too received a gift, he promptly took off his coat lined with lynx hides and gave it to the Governor in return. Rumour has it that the "King of Fez" is returning to the Turks at Constantinople and will ask their Emperor to send his fleet back to Africa within the next year: for just as his example routed the Spaniards from thence, he also wants to expel the Portuguese King who is behaving insolently.
>
> I did not wish to remain silent about these rumours which seem trustworthy (though confused by having been written down as they were heard), so that you would not justly accuse me of negligence because you had heard everything from others but nothing from me.
>
> As to when the Turkish fleet left Corfu, and where it has gone for the winter, I have not heard. Some say (on what grounds I know not) that they were still in Corfu on the twenty-fifth of October: others say that they were seen, having left the island (which might have been guessed) heading for Lepanto. It is said that, besides the Christian prisoners I mentioned, they have about 10,000 Africans in chains, while the Turks are said to have lost 101 men at Goletta, and fewer at the new citadel. Sinan Pasha himself was heard to say that, if the other Christians had not behaved like Spaniards, he would never have taken Goletta.

The reaction in Italy to the loss of Goletta inflamed the bad feeling already existing between the Italians and their Spanish rivals.

---

6. The North African corsairs, occasional allies of the Turks, were in the habit of taking grandiloquent and entirely unjustified titles. Barbarossa called himself "King of Algiers." For a lively and informative account of the pirates and their effect on Mediterranean operations, see E. Hamilton Currey, *Sea-Wolves of the Mediterranean* (London, 1910).

The following is being reported from Naples and Rome. The Italians and the Spaniards are still quarrelling vehemently among themselves as to whose fault it was that Goletta was so ignominiously lost. This has caused a feud between Giovanni Andrea Doria and the Marquis of Santa Cruz. In Naples, even the little songs of boys mention the names of John of Austria and of the viceroy of Naples, saying that they preferred to indulge their revolting lusts rather than aid Goletta. In Rome a medal is being struck, like a coin but of greater size, on the face of which you may see the King of Spain sitting, asleep, under a parasol; on the other side twenty-five donkeys sitting in a row, with the inscription *Consiglio di Spagna*.

Of the persons Zündelin named, Giovanni Andrea Doria (1539–1606), great-nephew of the famous admiral, was himself a noted naval commander, though his part in the battle at Lepanto remained controversial. Alvero de Bozan, Marquis de Santa Cruz (1526–88), the Spanish admiral at Lepanto, was credited with saving the Spanish fleet. With Don Juan he had taken Tunis in 1572, and he later initiated plans for the Armada in Spain's struggle against England. The Viceroy of Naples was Cardinal Granvelle. The papal medal ridiculing the Spanish King may never have progressed beyond the stage of a satiric quip; no copy is known to exist.

Other scraps of news and rumour fill the next paragraph of Zündelin's long letter. Pope Gregory's effort to organize the Christian states against the Turks was genuine, but unsuccessful.[7] Giacomo Soranzo commanded the Venetian squadron at Lepanto.

In the same letter the following is added. At Naples there have been several frightening earth tremors recently. John of Austria, as he was taking his fleet to the port of Palermo, had to contend with a great storm. The Pope is trying very hard to bring the Christian princes together in order to rouse them against the Turks. Privately it is said that this is only a pretence. He is said to be close to the conclusion of a bargain with the Venetians and the Florentine to make the former grant the latter the title of Grand Duke, which they have so far refused to do. The truth and the manner of this is guessed by many, but divulged by none. Giacomo Soranzo, who recently

7. See Ludwig Pastor, *The History of the Popes*, ed. R. F. Kerr (London, 1930), vol. 19, p. 343 and n.

was made admiral of the Venetian navy, has now been appointed ambassador to the Pope—this has increased the suspicion of some dark deed in the offing.

In Zündelin's final paragraph we learn why he may have indulged in such a python-long letter: it was being carried by a friend so no extra charges were incurred for its bulk.

> As you can see, this is written in haste—I had expected to be able to give you more, and more trustworthy, news. If there is any other news, you will hear it from the bearer of this. He is Doctor Hugo Blotius, a learned Dutchman who is a great friend of mine. He is returning to Vienna with two pupils: one is Lazarus Schwendi, the son of the Emperor's great general; the other is the son of the Hungarian vice-chancellor. I shall not recommend him to you any further, as I know how ready you always are by nature to extend the courtesies of kindness to good and learned men. Whatever service you may render him I shall be truly grateful for, at least in spirit (more tangible gratitude is impossible to me). Farewell, most noble sir; from V[enice], the fifth of November, 1574.
>
> Yours most devotedly,
with all honour and respect,
W. Z.

The learned Dutchman Dr. Hugo Blotius (de Bloote) and his pupil, the son of Sidney's friend, General von Schwendi have already been mentioned. In fact, this boy was not Lazarus but Hans Wilhelm von Schwendi, the General's only surviving son, born in 1560 to von Schwendi's first wife, Anna Bocklin. The other pupil was Johannes Listhy, son of Bishop Johannes Listhy, head of the Hungarian Chancery. The two young men had been entrusted to Dr. Blotius in 1571. On his arrival in Vienna he stayed with Bishop Listhy at his house in the Waller-strasse, near the Hungarian Chancery.

In Blotius Sidney made a new and valued friend who is frequently mentioned in letters during the next two years. Although twenty-one years older than Sidney he was still unmarried, so he could easily join the gatherings of the Languet circle. Blotius's erudition, integrity, and abilities gained him appointment the following year as Imperial Librarian. Because he was uncompromising in his opinions he made his share of enemies; fortunately, Sidney seems to have enjoyed the best side of his personality.[8]

8. The voluminous correspondence of Blotius with his annotations is preserved in the National Library at Vienna. Dr. Gertraud Leitner informs me that she has found no references in it to Sidney.

CHAPTER 14

Sidney's next few weeks were busy ones. Because Languet suffered a severe toothache, Philip had more time than usual for correspondence and other activities. One of his first duties was to write a long overdue letter to his uncle, the Earl of Leicester. Since the only text of this letter is among the Cotton manuscripts and was damaged in the regrettable fire of 1731 before the Cotton Collection came to the British Museum, portions are missing. The letter is in English and the original spelling has been preserved. It begins with a report of Maximilian's plans for the forthcoming Diet.

> Righte honorable and my singular good Lorde and unkle.
>
> Allthoughe I have at this presente little matter worthy the writinge unto yowr Lordeshippe, yet beinge newlie returned frome my poli[sh] journei, I woolde not omitt anie ocasion of humbly perfoorminge this dutie. Wherefore I hum[bly] beseeche yowr Lordeshippe to take these few lines in good parte, whiche I wryte rather to continew this [duty] I ow unto yow, then for any other thinge they may conteine in them. The Emperour as I wrate laste unto yowr Lordeshippe hathe these two yeeres continuallie pretended a journey to Prage, w[hiche] it is thoughte shall in deede be perfoormed, to the great contentacion of that kingedome, w[hiche] otherwise seemed to bende to disobedience. There it is thoute his son shall very shortlie be [made] kinge, whome likewise the Emperour seekes by all meanes possible to advance to the kinged[ome] of the Romaines, and for that purpose desyres to call an imperiall diett in Francfort, th[e city] appointed for the elections, but it is thoughte the Electours will rather chose an other [place] for this nexte ensuinge diett whiche is saide shall be sommer followinge at the fur[dest] and then there is no hope of election. Not beinge at Francfort, it is likely it sha[ll meet] at Regenspurg, where I beleve the Emperour will demaunde fur greater summes of mo[ney] then will be grawnted unto him.

Sidney then reported news of political moves by the Turks and the Catholic powers.

Thoughe the peace betwixte the Turke and him, [has] as yet as fur as it is knowne perfittlie concluded, yet it is thoughte the Turke will rat[her] proceede by sea then this waie, and as the frenche embassadour hathe writtne, mean[ethe to] visite the Popes territorie, perchaunce his conscience moveth him, to seeke the benefitt of [the] Jubile. I hope as the Spanierdes allreddy begin to speake lower, so the Popes holiness[e] will have lesse leasure to ministre suche wicked and detestable cownceills to the chris[tian] princes as hetherto he dothe.

Although news of affairs in France should have been known in England long before this letter came from Vienna, Sidney reported that the Prince of Condé had gone to Basle to join the young Comte de Chastillon,[1] son of the Admiral de Coligny, and the Admiral's daughter Louise de Coligny, later wife of William, Prince of Orange.

Owt of Frawnce yowr Lordeshippe hathe the advertisementes fu[rther] the Prince of Conde is retired to Basill where he livethe in companie withe the Ad[mirals] children, beinge frustrate of a greate hope he had conceaved of suckowr owt of Jerm[any] wherein many and wise men do impute greate faulte to the prince Casimire[2] the Cou[nte] Palatines seconde son, in so muche that to write to yowr Lordeshippe plainely, he is heavilie s[uspected] to be corrupted by the Frenche. His father certainely is as vertuous a prince as livethe, [though] he sufferethe him selfe to muche to be governed by that son. This I thoughte my dut[ie to] write as havinge hearde it in very good place and muche affectioned to the tr[ew] cawse.

Remarks on the situation in Poland conclude the letter. They contain nothing beyond general statements known in every capital of Europe, and Sidney gives none of the details he may have picked up in his brief visit to that country. Perhaps he suspected that his letter might be opened somewhere along the road to England and thus confined his remarks to harmless topics fit for prying eyes.

1. For his letter to Sidney of June 5, 1573 see chap. 4 above.

2. Johann Casimir, son of Ferdinand, the Elector Palatine, officially bore the title *Pfalzgraf bei Rhein* (Count of the Rhine Palatinate), but was often given the courtesy title "Duke," for example by Languet and Lobbet. Hence he is listed as "Duke" in many English books, including the *Calendars of State Papers* and Read's *Walsingham*. The courtesy title "Prince" was also used, and this practice was followed by Sidney's biographers Wallace, Buxton, and Howell. When quoting from any of these sources, the courtesy title employed in that volume will be retained.

The Polakes hartily repente their so fur fetcht election, beinge now in suche case [that] neither they have the kinge, nor any thinge the kinge withe so many othes had promised besides that their is lately sturred up a very dangerous Sedition, for the same c[awse] that hathe bredde suche lamentable ruines in France and Flandres. Now the [trouble] is reasonably wel appeased, but it is thoughte it will remaine so but a while.

I have no other thinge worthy the writinge at his presente to yowr Lordeshippe wherefore I humbly ceasse withe my dailie and most boundne praier, that it please the Eternall, to continew and encreace yow in all prosperitie. Frome Vienne. This 27. of Novembre. 1574.

Your Lordeshippes most . . .

Philippe Sidney.

[To] the righte honorable and my singular [good Lorde and] unkle the Earle of [Leicester].

About ten days after writing to Leicester, Sidney received two letters from Venice. One came from François Perrot, a polite reply to Sidney's letter of November 12. Writing on November 26, Perrot confined himself largely to comment on literary matters. Sidney had sent him some verses on Poland, probably satirizing conditions there; it is clear that Sidney did not write them. The Italian verses Sidney requested in return are unidentified and probably were unpublished. They may well have been some of Perrot's own Italian poems.

Sir,

I was glad to hear from your letter of the twelfth of this month that you have returned from Poland in good health, and also that you found Master Languet in better health than he has enjoyed throughout your absence. But you do not give me your impressions of that splendid country: do you want me to think that you agree with the author of the verses you sent me? Thank you so much for those; and in compliance with what you say I am sending you the Italian verses.

Sidney had also asked about the *Historiarum de regno Italiae libri quindecim* of Carlo Sigonio (1524–84). Perrot replied:

It is two months since the Sigonius book was printed, but permission has not yet been obtained to have it sold, though everything detrimental to the authorities has been extracted; they are afraid that the story alone will uncover the truth of many things they had cloaked, and of which they had hoped that the memory would be lost and consigned to eternal silence.

The book was Sigonio's major work and represented an important advance in Italian, as well as European, historiography. Frequently reprinted, the book was distinguished by its objectivity and its attention to the medieval period then suffering from neglect.

Another book mentioned by Sidney was *The Ethos of Princes*, but it cannot now be identified under that title.

> I believe I have also seen the second volume of the *Ethos of Princes*: but I will inquire further, so as to be able to tell you with more certainty as soon as possible. I have written all our news of France to Master Languet, so that there is no need to repeat it here: I know that you two are in such close touch that I would not even have come between you with this letter, had there not been this particular reason for replying to your own.

Perrot concluded with news of foreign affairs and of friends. His comments on the former are strangely muddled. To welcome Henry III, Elizabeth sent not the Duke of Norfolk (the title had been in abeyance since the beheading of Thomas Howard in 1572) but Roger, second Baron North (1530–1600), a confidant of Leicester and later a close friend of Sidney with whom he fought side by side at Zutphen. Although Lord North's mission was ostensibly to welcome Henry, its primary purpose actually was to test the sentiment of the French court towards England. The insulting manner in which he was received turned Elizabeth away from a French alliance and towards one with Spain. Perrot's account of an unidentified mission from La Rochelle is also garbled. So, too, concerning Mary Queen of Scots: after the secret marriage of Lord Charles Stuart to Elizabeth Cavendish, advisers urged Queen Elizabeth to remove Mary from the care of Lord Shrewsbury to a "securer place," but she decided the step was unnecessary.

> I do not think I have forgotten anything, except that the Duke of Norfolk has arrived on a mission from the Queen of England to welcome the King on his return. He arrived at court simultaneously with the envoys from La Rochelle, as we heard from a letter a fortnight ago. It is also said that the Queen of Scotland has been sent to a better fortified castle with a stronger guard.

I have presented your respects to the ambassador, who has asked me to convey his affectionate respects to you and to Master Languet. The same are presented by Master Zündelin, who is writing to you himself. And here I shall add my own humble respects, and pray God,

Sir, to protect you always. From Venice, this twenty-sixth of November, 1574.

Your humble and affectionate servant,
F. Perrot de Mésières

The letter from Zündelin, dated November 27, probably travelled to Vienna with the same courier. Not so lengthy as his last, it is, nevertheless, ample. The opening passage is entirely personal: the modern reader may suspect that Zündelin preferred calling Sidney "patron" instead of "friend" to avoid any possibility that his stipend might evaporate in the process.

From the letter, most noble sir, which you sent to our friend Perrot I saw with great pleasure that you have returned to Vienna safe and unharmed. I was much afraid that, scarcely recovered from your sickness, you would, through such a sudden change of air, adversely affect your newfound health and that your long and laborious journey would hardly increase your still-feeble powers, but rather weaken and destroy them. I even feared (for so solicitous is love everywhere) that, as is common, the lawlessness of this interregnum might threaten the safety of your travel, or that you might by some mischance have got entangled in this Polish business which rumour here has magnified far beyond the facts.

All this fear has now been lifted from me by your letter, in which you so kindly told [the recipient] to give me your regards and were pleased to call me your great friend: which I acknowledge with the deepest gratitude for your boundless love. However, I beg you—and this would be more fitting for you and more than sufficient honour for me—to allow me to be one of those who eagerly honour and love you as their patron. Among these I shall be second to none, strive with all in the utmost and perpetual love and honour towards you, and even hope to vanquish many. However, enough of this.

Zündelin makes full sport of the humiliation felt by Don John and the Spaniards over their loss of Goletta and Tunis.

Although Perrot will have told you about the political news here, yet I should like to add these few points. A letter from Rome, dated the twenty-first of this month, says that John of Austria is so changed by this African "victory" of his that you would scarcely recognize him; he does not, as was his custom, hold banquets; he does not ride through all the streets of the city to indulge in his talent for womanizing. Mostly he hides himself in private seclusion and (believe it or not) bewails the fate of Goletta and, what is more, of himself and the Spaniards. They have become so hated and despised among the Italians that they are spared no sort of revilement: in Naples and Rome there is hardly anyone so cowardly that he does not dare to assail them. The occasion and cause of this hatred is sought in the loss (and, moreover, the cowardly loss) of Goletta; but in the meantime—not so hateful but more dangerous—the memory was revived of the affronts perpetrated earlier by the Spaniards. Among others, a certain Neapolitan nobleman of a great family dared, before a large audience and with as many arguments as if he were addressing a court, to show and expound that the King had no longer any other remedy for the salvation of the Spaniards but to come to Italy himself and have several of his chief ministers executed by way of example.

The satirical medal reportedly struck in Rome still tickled Zündelin's fancy.

I wrote to you via Master Blotius the Dutchman that Roman satire has changed the Spanish Senate itself into so many mules of the lowest kind and, with the King (fast asleep), has published, as it were, their likenesses in the form of a large medal—that letter I believe will by now have been delivered to you.

Because the Venetians had made a separate peace with the Turks they were not obliged to defend papal territories, including the vulnerable port of Ancona. In the following account Zündelin errs in stating that the Pope's son, Giacomo Boncompagni, was to marry the sister of the Duke of Urbino; instead he married the fabulously wealthy Constanza Sforza, Countess of Santa Fiora in Tuscany.

To return to the letter from Rome, which further reports the following:
The Pope, having been warned by certain military experts that Ancona, if attacked by the Turks, would not be able to resist even

Specimen of Wolfgang Zündelin's handwriting

Al molto illustre Sig.or et padro
mio osservandiss.u il Sig.or co(n)te
Philippo Sidneio etc

Al pozzo della vacca in casa
di M. Hercole Bolognese

Padoua

their most mediocre troops, is taking measures to reinforce it. As, however, he is just as concerned about the French war as about the Turkish one, he will send four thousand Italians to France, under the command of Latino Orsini.[3] He is even contemplating the marriage of his son to the sister of Urbino, and will (with the Cardinals' consent) pay him one hundred fifty thousand gold pieces out of Peter's Treasury—that will be the gift of the apostolic see in some measure to support the wedding.

Next: great and extraordinary preparations are being made to celebrate the Jubilee Year; the golden hammer with which the sacred gate of indulgences will be opened has already been made and is estimated to have cost twenty thousand gold pieces. Rome, apparently, is already filled with pilgrims. The only fear is that the spectre of the Turk, though uninvited, may nevertheless come and also collect his share of the indulgences.

Miscellaneous other rumours and news items conclude the letter.

Finally, the following is added: the rumour is going round in all Rome that the Elector of Saxony has defected to the papal party, and though this is clearly untrue, yet the Pope has cause to be most grateful to him—it was his doing and his alone that the Lutherans and "heretics" in Germany have been increasingly divided. From the Netherlands and France there is either no news or such as may be considered less important. A letter from Naples of the twenty-second of this month says that John of Austria has decided to set sail from there to Spain, and several triremes which are to accompany him have been sent ahead to Genoa.

Of the Turkish fleet I have heard nothing except that the greater part of it has returned to Constantinople, while Uluck Ali with about seventy triremes is staying in Navirino to assist with the fortification of that place.

I hear that the Venetians are considering the fortification of Corfu. If there is anything else [you will learn it] from the letters of our friend Perrot.

Farewell, most noble sir, and give my respectful greetings to Master Languet, whose return to health gives me great pleasure. As I believe

3. Zündelin has confused the Cardinal of this name with Paolo Giordano Orsini, the commander against the Turks.

the Count of Hanau has by now left Vienna, I am not writing to him. From Venice, the twenty-seventh of November, 1574.

Yours with all honour and respect,

most faithfully,

W. Z.

All this news of military moves, real and threatened, and of political alignments provided material for a report (preserved in the Public Record Office) which Sidney addressed to Lord Burghley on December 17. How often he had previously written Burghley is uncertain, but the opening sentence makes clear that this letter was one of a series, undertaken at Burghley's express suggestion. Further, Sidney had not sent such a report since he left Italy. Because a messenger was to carry it directly to England with others (probably from some embassy) Sidney could be more specific than he had been a few weeks earlier when he wrote to Leicester. Again, Sidney's orthography is preserved.

Righte honorable and my singular good Lorde.

Since the laste I wrate unto yowr Lordeshippe, I have not had anie conveniente meanes of sendinge my scribbles, which humble office I desire to continew, rather to obay therein yowr commaunde-mente then for any thinge worthie to be advertised, they may happne to conteine in them. Now havinge oportunitie by a frende of mine, who presentlie sendes his lettres into Englande, I woolde not omitt this ocasion, beseechinge yowr Lordeshippe rather to respecte the hartie desire to please yow, then the simplenes of the contentes, better then whiche yowr Lordeshippe oughte not to expecte of me.

Beinge returned owt of Italie and detained for some time withe sicknesse in this cittie, yet coolde I not commaund my desire of seeinge Polande whiche time notwithestandinge, I mighte perchaunce have emploied in more proffitable, at leaste more pleasante voiages, frome thence beinge of late come hether, not in very good estate of boddie, I finde the affaires of this cowrte as fur as I can learne to passe in this ordre. The Emperour hathe at lengthe obtained his longe desired truice of the greate Turke for 8 yeeres, the grawnte of which he hathe undrestoode by a courrier sente by his legier embassadowr, called Charles Rym, who is now in his returne not fur hence and in his roome there is allreddie at Constantinople David Ungnad.

The latest news of the defeated commanders at Goletta had just come from Constantinople, and rumours of the fabled Prester John in Ethiopia were reported from Egypt.

> The conditions of the peace are not as yet knowne, but the emperowr is resolute to refuse no burdne, rather than enter in warr. He dothe expecte very shortlie the Turkishe embassadowr, for the confirmation of the peace, who is by nation a dutche man, borne in Bavier, the Turkes principall interpretour, named amonge them Mehemet Beck. This Cowrrier hathe broughte news from Constantinople that the Turkes navie is safe returned, whiche he will encreace the nexte yeere withe a hundred gallies for to invade Sicill. By the way Petro Portocarrero Capteine of the Gollett is deceassed. Serbellone builder and capteine but evill defendour of the new fort is come alive to a miserable captivitie.
>
> He saiethe likewise that there came to Constantinople advertisemente that the Belierbei of Egipte hathe latelie overthrowne in a very greate batteil, the Abissines subjectes to Pretre Jhon as we call him. In my simple opinion they have bene provoked by the Portugese to take this matter fur above their forces uppon them, for that the Turke by the redde sea dothe greatlie encroche uppon their Indian traffick.

Maximilian's long postponed excursion to Prague and the problems he encountered in the attempt to get his son Rudolph elected as his successor next come under Sidney's pen. The letter ends with an account of the troubles in Poland and Sidney's valediction.

> The expectation of these embassadowrs will cawse the Emperowr to delay his journey to Bohemia whiche notwithestandinge he muste necessarily ere it be longe performe they beinge very evill contente, of his so longe absence, in so muche that this yeere they have plainely refused to give certaine greate summes of money, whiche heretofore they had not denied. Besides that he muste please them for to gett his son the crowne for althoughe he do pretende hereditary succession they seeme they will not grawnte it any other waie but in manner of election. In this meane time he hathe sente the Lorde of Rosemberg a principall nobleman of Bohemia to the electours of Sax and Brandenbourg, and the Lord of Arach to the other 4 electours, of the Rhine, to consulte of an Imperiall diett, which it is not unlikely shall be this

sommer followinge, wherein if it be possible, he will perswade the election of his son to the kingedome of the Romaines as the[y] tearme it.

The Polakes havinge appeased a greate sedition in Crackow for the religion, have since deffaited twelve thowsande Tartars among whiche there were 3000 Turkes, whose returne with fur greater force they do daily loke for. It is thoughte they will chose an other kinge in May, allthoughe the Lithuaniens be holy againste it. They have made truice withe the Moscovit, who bendes his forces as they say againste the kinge of Sueden for havinge burnte a toune of his called Narva.

Thus yowr Lordeshippe may see how bolde I am uppon yowr commandement to troble yow from yowr weightie affaires, for whiche cravinge pardon and good acceptacion I humblie ceasse, beseechinge the Eternall to grawnte yow in healthe encreace of all honowr.

Frome Wien this 17th of December 1574.

Yowr Lordeshippes to commaunde.

Philippe Sidney

To the righte honorable and my singular [good Lord]e the Lorde hyghe Treasurer.

As the Christmas season came and the new year approached Sidney began to think of his return to England. He accommodated his plans to Languet's, for there would be many advantages in travelling together. The end of January seemed to be the earliest departure date convenient for both, and in order to visit close friends they plotted their route so that they would be in Frankfurt during the spring Fair. In 1575 this would begin on March 23, the second Wednesday before Easter which fell on April 3.

In the meantime Sidney kept busy with his studies, his physical exercises, his friends, and his correspondence. About Christmas he received another letter from Dr. Lobbet in Strasbourg, written on December 7. Lobbet addressed it, not care of Languet, but to Sidney at the Emperor's court. Taken with Sidney's first sentence to his *Defence of Poesie*, "When the right vertuous Edward Wotton and I were at the Emperours Court togither . . . ," the evidence indicates that during this 1574–75 visit Sidney participated more in court gatherings than he had while in Vienna in 1573.

Lobbet begins on a personal note.

Sir,

I received the letter you were pleased to write, dated the twentieth of last month, in reply to my earlier one. I was very glad to hear from yourself that you are well, though I was sorry to learn of Master Languet's indisposition. Please show him my humblest respects to his benevolence, so that at the same time he may see that I gladly excuse him, for your sake if for no other: for a toothache does not prevent a man's hand from writing. But you have set it in a larger context and shown yourself to be a good dialectician "by using an argument from the smaller to the greater":[4] saying that if he is lazy about writing even when in good health, then so much the more etc. And so the question is resolved, and the argument is basically sound. The little verse from Ovid would have been apt: *in promptu causa est* etc.[5]

What you write about the son of Doctor Thaddeus[6] I agree with, for the reasons you give. May it please the Name of God. I gather you are not too happy with your journey to Poland. Repentance will prevent you from going there again. But it is good that you have seen it. Beautiful countries and people will henceforth seem more pleasant to you. Be that as it may, Master Bochetel has refused to believe your words and wants to follow the Samaritan's example and see for himself. Let him go ahead, I do not envy him in the least.

Political news from Strasbourg follows.

The Polish ambassadors who are on their way to France stopped at Nuremberg on the nineteenth of last month: we had expected them to pass through this city, but as they have been so long I think they must have taken another route. In France things are bad, and it will take the King considerable time to establish the order he would like. Drops of St. Bartholomew's rain are still falling, and the flow is unlikely to stem itself. The Huguenots, Politiques, and Malcontents are all together, with the Marshal Damville as a sort of leader of their party: mostly in Langeudoc and Provence. It is said that the Marshal de Montmorency is to go to court to join the King and that he has been

4. Sidney appears to have been fond of this "dialectical commonplace." See his letter of Apr. 15, 1574 to Languet.

5. Ovid, *Remedia Amoris*, ll. 161–62. "Th'adult'rous Lust that did Aegistus seize, / And brought on Murder, sprang from Wanton Ease," as Nahum Tate translated the lines a century later.

6. See p. 242 above for more about young Johannes Hájek.

secretly released from the Bastille so that there would not be a public outcry. The Marshal de Cossé is under house arrest at his house in Paris. From Poitou it is said that M. de Montpensier has twice been defeated near Lusignan by M. de la Notte. The inhabitants of La Rochelle are letting no salt go through: many are incensed at this.

In Flanders things are going neither forward nor back: but the Prince of Orange's affairs seem to be going better and better. There has been endless talk of peace, but no results have as yet appeared. So, all in all, everything seems to be heading for disaster, both in France and in Flanders.

A brief summary may clarify this jumble of topics. The Polish ambassadors had been sent to inform Henry III of the decision made at the Warsaw Diet held in August: because of his flight he had forfeited the crown. In their search for a leader, the Protestant groups of France had turned to Henry de Montmorency, Count of Damville (1534–1614) who, as governor of Languedoc, had successfully followed an independent policy in alliance with the Huguenots. François, Duke of Montmorency (1530–79), was not released from the Bastille until the following April. Similarly, Artus de Cossé remained in custody until October. François de Bourbon, Duke of Montpensier (1539–92) was defeated by François de La Noue (1531–91) who had succeeded Admiral de Coligny as chief adviser to Henry of Navarre; a brilliant general, de La Noue excelled in guerilla warfare. The inland provinces in western France were dependent on the salt pans of La Rochelle, so stoppage of the salt trade would soon affect large areas. The only bright ray on the horizon seemed to be the successful relief of the siege of Leiden which had recently occurred.

Dr. Lobbet concluded his letter with a postscript.
And here I will present my most humble respects to your benevolence, and pray God, Sir, to keep you in his own. From Strasbourg, this seventh of December, 1574.
Your humble servant,
J. Lo.
Please tell Master Languet that I have sent the letter for Master du Plessis to Sedan.

Sidney had met the Huguenot leader Philippe de Mornay, Sieur du Plessis-Marly, in Paris in the summer of 1572. He was now in Sedan wooing Charlotte Arbaleste, to whom he became engaged a few months later.

January 1575 was Sidney's last month in Vienna. Clearly his long stay there, living with Languet, discoursing daily with learned friends at the imperial court, riding under the exacting eye of Maestro Pugliano, and reading through the volumes on Languet's shelves was one of the happiest periods in his life. To be young among such friends was very heaven, and the future which beckoned a youth of his abilities and status seemed a glorious sunrise. But he knew the time had come to return to England and face the opportunities and obligations which awaited him.

Three letters that reached Sidney during these last few weeks in Vienna are preserved in the newly recovered group. The first came from a friend at Padua, Otto, Count Solms. It was the first he had written to Sidney and may have been the only one. A warm letter of friendship, its chief purpose was to invite Sidney to visit the Count's ancestral home near Frankfurt on his way back to England. The Count's brother was Johann Georg (1547–1600).

Otto Count Solms wishes, Count Philip Sidney, that this year may be exceedingly fortunate and happy for you.

Greetings.

Although I was fully aware of my uncouthness in letter writing, noble Lord, and although this has hitherto somewhat deterred me from writing to you, yet my bashfulness was finally overcome by the authority of our friendship and by my singular love for you and your countrymen.

In the first place, indeed, trusting in your kindness, I do not hesitate to importune you with this letter and to offer, in sincerity and single-ness of heart, all my honour and respect. Wacker recently told me that you had decided to go to Frankfurt at the beginning of the summer, thence to return via France to your own country: and for the com-pletion of that plan I wish you all prosperity and good fortune.

I beseech you, however, that when you have visited Hanau, who lives in that part of Germany, you will also deign to visit our little home which is near Frankfurt at a distance of one Italian mile—it is called Rödelheim—and that there you will become friends with my brother also: for I can confidently promise you that in future he will never be less devoted to you than I. Admittedly you will not find there a vast and magnificent palace but one that is old and badly built; however, you will find the spirits of those that live there eager to honour you with unfeigned sincerity.

Count Solms had been in England as a guest of Edward Manners, third Earl of Rutland, sometime between 1571 and 1573, probably after meeting Lord Rutland during his visit to the Continent in 1570–71. This friendship and the memory of the sumptuous entertainment he had enjoyed at Belvoir in Leicestershire, the Manners family seat, predisposed him to favour young English aristocrats. Count Solms had been away from Padua on a visit to Rome during Sidney's last weeks there.

> If only I could honour you as the Earl of Rutland did me in England, I should certainly let no opportunity pass to discharge this debt. As, however, that is beyond my powers, I do at any rate offer you such things as may at least help me in trying to declare the cordiality of my heart, full as it is of friendship for you. I would ask you, noble lord, when you return, to give that same Earl of Rutland my most respectful greetings and to tell him of my exceedingly great devotion to him.
>
> You will forgive me for my impudence in taking the initiative of disturbing you with a letter: I would pray you, should you chance to have time, to reply—but I will not indeed exceed the bounds of modesty, even though Cicero says, "he that once transcends the borders of modesty should be well and truly shameless."
>
> Most of the news you will hear from others, and indeed I do not collect it with sufficient diligence: so I did not wish to send you any. Let me at least tell you, though, that we are well and that our Roman journey has been as successful as we had wished. We hope that you may long remain safe and unharmed. Farewell. From Padua, the sixth of January, 1575.
>
> I did not want to trouble Master Languet with my trifles: he is always occupied with more important matters. I should be most grateful, however, if you be so kind as to greet him from me.

The carrier who brought Solm's letter from Padua probably also brought Sidney two letters from Venice. The first, written on January 8, was from François Perrot; the other had been written by Zündelin on the following day. Since both touch on many of the same topics, explanation of the persons or incidents may be portioned between them.

> Sir,
>
> I have heard from Master Zündelin, who has been inquiring after the English gentleman you wrote about. At the lodgings where he

intended to stay they had word from a brother of his that he was not in Venice—but where he was his brother would not say. In a fortnight, however, he will be there: so then I will write and tell you what I can find out. I have just received your letter of the twenty-ninth of December: I am sorry not to have time to reply to it at length, but I prefer not to put it off and to write in haste rather than not to write at all.

The latest news we have here by the Lyons Post, since the last which I wrote to Master Languet a fortnight ago, is that the King is at Avignon. In the procession of penitents there he went dressed as the others, accompanied by the Cardinal of Lorraine who, a few days later, fell ill. On the fifteenth of last month the Cardinal received Extreme Unction, and rumours went round that he was dead: but he has recovered, just as have the Turkish Sultan and the Spanish King, who were thought to be dead, according to news from Constantinople and Rome, both on the same day.

M. Damville is doing very well in the field and is now not far from Avignon. There is talk of great unrest among the French nobility and of a large number of malcontents, Since the twenty-third of last month Livron has been besieged. Nevertheless some sort of peace treaty is still being discussed, but no one knows where to begin. M. de Bouillon died on the second of last month, and (so that you may know the unfortunate time we live in) correspondents say that he was so obviously poisoned that there is no doubt whatever. Before he died he made sure that his plans were well guarded and secure.

Part of this information was more than rumour; the Cardinal of Lorraine, that evil genius of the Guises, had died, as had Selim, the Turkish Emperor, but Philip of Spain survived for two decades. The death of Henri-Robert de La Marck, Duke of Bouillon, like those of other Protestant leaders, almost automatically prompted the charge of poison.

Perrot's budget of bad news was not yet exhausted.

That is all I can tell you, in haste, about my France; to which I must add that in Picardy some Reiter officers have been committing such violence (they even killed a well-known gentleman in his own house) that the nobility took matters into their own hands and practically tore one officer to pieces. From Rome there is no other news but of the opening of the Jubilee; a bad omen is seen in the fact that the Pope, striking the Holy Gate somewhat roughly, broke the handle of his hammer. Some say that a quarter of St. Paul (for the hammer is made of a statuette of St. Paul and one of St. Peter) came off and hit him so hard on his finger that it bled, causing his Holiness some pain.

I will write to you at greater leisure when I have news of that gentleman. And, presenting my humble respects to your benevolence and to Master Languet, I pray God,

Sir, always to protect you. From Venice, this eighth of January, 1575.

Your humble and affectionate servant,

F. de. Mésières

Since Zündelin's letter arrived simultaneously with Perrot's, Sidney may first have read the former's account of the Papal Jubilee when the incident of Gregory's thumb injury set superstitious tongues wagging. Zündelin began, however, on a personal note, a lengthy admonition to Sidney against overapplication to his studies to the detriment of his health.

It was most grievous to me to find what I was already pained to hear from Languet's letter to our friend Perrot—viz. that you are not in very good health—confirmed by your letter also. However, while he indicates the cause of your ill health in words—your lack of moderation in literary studies—you have shown it to me "in the flesh" by so unseasonably writing letters to me and many others. For not only do you write, but you apologize for not writing more often, as if you had neglected a bounden duty towards me. Since you cannot perform it at once, you should reserve me that favour until a more convenient time. Indeed, although I am amazed and delighted by your kindness and by your letter which is a surely unnecessary witness to it, yet a far greater delight to me is your good health and all that depends on it: the well-being not so much of yourself as of the state. But you will be able to give it neither what you choose nor what it expects from you, and you will not even be able to continue enjoying these very studies if you weaken yourself prematurely by excessive strain and labours.

I understand, indeed, how difficult it must be to restrain the noble thrust of your spirit and how improper it may perhaps be for me to set a limit to your industry; yet in the study of letters as in other things it is necessary to observe moderation, and the famous rule of the golden mean should be considered the best. I am not writing this to admonish you but am driven by my singular love and respect for you. For you have your own mentor and guide in all that you do, who is on guard in your mind and spirit: that divine reason, who nowhere suffers you to stray very far from what is fitting.

Sidney's special relationship with Languet was Zündelin's next topic.

You have, moreover, that eminent man, your friend Languet who, because he wishes and desires what is best for you and your efforts, understands better than anyone in what way you should restrain them to achieve the excellence of the highest glory. Yet it seems to me that, if you transfer your attention as often as possible from your books to the conversation of that most learned and wise man, you will learn everything more easily and more abundantly from him than from those speechless masters—even though you should have clung to their company as much as you could, day and night. They will come to you whenever you wish: but I do not know if you will always have the access to him that you have now—unless maybe you are thinking of robbing our Germany of such an ornament and blessing your England with him.

Indeed, I have no doubt that this is what you wish, and I believe that there is nothing he would rather do than spend the rest of his life with you and, so doing, remove himself as far as possible from those countrymen of ours where he would hear neither of their words nor of their deeds. Yet just as those who have once boarded a ship with others, put out to sea, and leaving the sails to the wind cannot leave, however much they wish to, and must suffer danger with the others unto the very end, so, I believe, will he, and await the outcome of this storm together with his comrades.

Like other Continental observers, Zündelin saw England not as a land of tranquillity and steady habits, but as an island whose history was steeped in blood and violence. Elizabeth's reign seemed to be a lull between political storms, a pause unlikely to last. Thus Zündelin half regretted the possibility that Languet might leave the stability of his present environment for such a dangerous place. The placid lagoons of Venice would be an even safer harbour for him.

I hope, however, that when the north winds shall at last have died down a little and he is driven into port by a milder breeze he will come and live with us rather than trust himself to your vast ocean— now somewhat placated, it is true, but at other times scarcely ever quiet. Jesting apart, I most sincerely hope that all his wishes may be fulfilled and that the best may befall him wherever he is; and if he should live with you, with whom alone he considers his life most happy, I cannot and should not grudge your felicity; if you will greet him from me with respect and love, I shall be most grateful.

More items of personal news occur in Zündelin's next paragraph. Why Sidney's chief attendant, Lodowick Bryskett, made so many journeys on his own cannot be explained with certainty; on occasion he served as a courier for Sidney, and he may have run some diplomatic errands. The reference to Bryskett's brother in Venice is the second in the Sidney correspondence. The brother was probably Sebastian (see p. 174 above) who may have been involved in both commercial and diplomatic business.[7]

Let me return to your letter. The one with it I gave to your servant to whom it was addressed, and he said that he would reply to you by this messenger. I have not seen your man Bryskett for some months now: I asked his brother several times what has become of him, but he replies that he knows nothing and is amazed that he has had no letters from him. In the last few days, however, he replied to my question that Bryskett himself will be here shortly: although I asked him, he did not add from where he would be coming. For having received, in response to my letter and with your usual and never sufficiently praised kindness, our friends Blotius and Schwendi, as Blotius himself tells me, I thank you, not as much as you deserve, but certainly as much as I can. In return for yours I cannot give such news as I should like, but only such as these times supply in plenty. This, however, more sparingly, as our friend Perrot has written to you mainly about French matters.

Zündelin now turns to kings, armies, and world events rumoured or real. Suffice it to say that Selim II died of an apoplexy on December 13, 1574.

The Turkish and the Spanish Kings, who reportedly were both dying at the same time, have both been restored to life: the condition of each, however, is still serious, I hear. Of the Turkish King's illness

7. As has already been mentioned, their father, Antonio Bruschetto, was in the service of the Queen. See his letter to Burghley of Mar. 27, 1573, *CSPF1*, item 843. Antonio died May 12, 1547.

I have heard nothing reliable, for everyone has a different version of the story. Some say that he fell into an apoplexy from a certain lack of moderation and temperance in wine and lovemaking; others say that he had an epileptic fit and that the very dangerous symptoms which have attacked him for two days have placed him in danger of suffocation. Those who assert this seem more trustworthy than those who suggest apoplexy, if reports are true that he was able to govern again afterwards.

For they say that since then Sinan Pasha returned with his fleet and was received with ample expressions of honour and greatly praised for his excellence and brave deeds, and that Uluck Ali was even more honourably received, for the King rose when he approached and warmly kissed his forehead. Next he was given many gifts—garments woven with thread of gold, a sword magnificently adorned with jewels—and he was enriched with a pension of five Turkish gold pieces daily. Some have heard it said that he was even seen in public, but none of this is reported by any very trustworthy correspondent.

The Venetian ambassadors at Constantinople, in a letter written on the twenty-seventh of November, say only one thing: that he is alive. For he has received no letter from Constantinople by that messenger.[8] Many of the Venetians seemed to be frightened by rumours of his death, lest his successor change his policy towards them.

The Venetians actually had good cause for worry, since the Grand Vizier Sokullu was preparing to launch a new expedition against them. The sudden death of Selim saved them, for, as a result, plans for the attack were abandoned.

The Spanish were having their troubles too, though the King's health was not one of them.

The Spaniards, however—like those who, struggling with misfortune, seize on anything as a hope of better luck—hoped, if not for an end to the war, yet at least for a check to it. Concerning the King of Spain it is said that he was dispirited by the bad news from Africa and the Netherlands and that his earlier perturbation of spirit subsequently made him fall ill and contract bad pains of the kidneys and intestines. Also, when he had come down from Rosas, his head (not

8. This passage is unclear.

sufficiently healthy in itself) was badly afflicted—whether this is true I do not know.

Because the Venetians had made a separate treaty with the Turks, the Spaniards and other Catholic powers tended to blame Venice for any attacks or threats the Turks made against them.

> From reliable sources I hear that the Venetian ambassador has written here that he is not yet sure in his mind what conclusions to draw from his most recent conversations with the King. Inter alia he was reproached by the King that the loss of Goletta was also the fault of the Venetians: and scarcely had he parted from the King when one of the highest-born councillors reproached him for the same thing, but very much more insolently and rudely. Yet later he was requested not to write this to Italy.
>
> Others add that the King hears all the news from Africa too late: Goletta was taken before he even knew that it was being besieged. Apparently, however, he feels so secure that, when he was first told that the Turkish fleet was approaching Africa, he replied that he was not at all afraid and that all the coastal towns were protected from danger with excellent garrisons. However, when he was subsequently told of the African defeat, he exclaimed that he had been betrayed by his ministers and fell into such grief and mourning of spirit that for several days he stayed hidden within the walls of his bedchamber and scarcely allowed anyone to see him.

The King of Spain meanwhile was vexed by the determined resistance of the Netherlanders.

> Some add to all this—but it is not confirmed by any trustworthy correspondent—that when he had heard the extremely proud demand of the Gueux and had learned of the tenacity of the other Dutchmen, he burst out saying that in that case the war must be pursued to the end, and that in extremes everything should be tried rather than submit to the insults of those rascals. However, what preparations he is making, where and why he is for a while transferring himself and his court, how much money he has sent to Italy, what was written thence to the Netherlands you will be able to hear from our friend Blotius. Part of this has now been taken care of here by exchange.

Don John of Austria, always a good subject for gossip, was now reported to have cast himself in the role of Don Juan.

John of Austria, on his way to Spain, was held up by unfavourable winds at Gibraltar until the nineteenth of December; I believe the other Hercules had marked the place with his memory! Scarcely returned to Genoa, he reverted to his natural self and attempted to relieve his piercing grief at the African defeat with the light loves of lighter women—and this so openly that he became the talk of the town. In Naples where he more recently wore his shame written high on his forehead, he seems to have been seeking cover and fleeing the light of day. Cardinal Granvelle,[9] in this one matter his companion, or rather his master, but otherwise not overly friendly towards him, now hears himself being blamed chiefly for all these calamities: but he does not care or, as I have heard, pretends not to care.

There has been no sign of the long-discussed granting of a successor and viceroy to Castile.

Zündelin now came to the incident of Gregory's thumb and other choice items.

I believe you have heard with what ceremonies the Pope led the opening of the Jubilee year, what honour he accorded our German Princes of Bavaria and Cleves, so I will leave out the rest here; you will also have heard how another person carried the hammer. It was indeed a bad omen that, when he was opening that sacred gate, the figure of St. Paul, leaping out of the handle of that same hammer, assaulted his finger and hurt him to such a degree that (so they say) the blood flowed.

How sweetly the King of France dances daily amid the ruins of his kingdom [i.e. at Avignon] you may hear from our friend Perrot, and the rest of the news about the state of Italy from our friend Blotius, as I said, to whom all such things will be written weekly. Farewell. From Venice, the ninth of January, 1575.

One who has recently come from Vallona [now Vlona] says that the soldiers there expect nothing less than the Turkish fleet from

9. Antoine Perrenot de Granvelle (1517–86), sometime adviser to Margaret of Austria in the Netherlands, had worked with Don John in preparing for the battle of Lepanto. Now just short of sixty, he must have been enjoying a special dispensation from the consequences of age if these allegations of his conduct were true.

Constantinople. There are many common and uncertain rumours that first Sardinia will be sacked and then Malta besieged; that the same fleet, on its return from Africa, is very short of soldiers and oarsmen; and that far more have died because they were unused to the sea and the heat than fell at the hands of the enemy.

Our friend Wacker who greatly honours you has himself, I believe, written to you via this messenger. [Wacker's letter is not known.]

When these letters arrived during the last week in January, Sidney had already packed most of his chattels and was paying farewell calls on various Viennese friends. Happy as he had been in the imperial capital, and much as he treasured the hours spent there with Languet and other friends, exercising the superb horses under the eye of Pugliano and devouring the contents of the books available there, the time had come to turn towards home. The chief problem Sidney had faced was that of health, but he seemed to recover from each illness with time and rest. Aside from his respiratory problems and related infections he escaped serious afflictions. For example, near the end of his stay in Vienna there was an alarming oubreak of the plague. It occurred the week before Christmas and, after subsiding, broke out again about January 22, so that the sewers and pits were ordered to be cleansed.[10]

But Sidney was plagued with a different affliction, he had run short of money. The ever-generous Languet, though a man of limited means, finally convinced Sidney that the most practical solution was for Languet to lend him his savings. Sidney was so embarrassed and felt his honour so much involved that, despite Languet's protest that it was unnecessary, he insisted the document of indebtedness be witnessed by Edward Wotton, probably in his function as Secretary of the English Embassy rather than as a friend.

The date of departure and the route had been settled some time in advance. After much procrastination the Emperor Maximilian had finally prepared his court for its progress to Prague. Languet and Sidney arranged to accompany the procession. They set out on February 7,[11] though instead of the direct route to the northwest they travelled due north to Brno. On February 22 they reached Prague.

10. See Hans Gerstinger, *Die Briefe des Johannes Sambucus* (Wien, 1968), letter 79, from Sambucus to Crato von Crafftheim, Jan. 23, 1575.
11. See *VDK*, 3:559 notes 2 and 3.

CHAPTER 15

On the journey to Prague Languet and Sidney spent several days at
Brno where they were entertained by the learned men of that city.
Prominent among them was Dr. Thomas Jordan of Cluj; a native of
Transylvania who lived in Brno from 1570 to 1586, he served as proto-
medicus (chief medical officer) of the area. Another eminent Czech was
Baron Johannes Žerotin, whose estates lay in western Moravia. Languet
had a special purpose in visiting these men at Brno, for he had long been
interested in the Moravian Church, sometimes called "the Waldensian
Brethren," as a Protestant organization. In this concern, Languet cooper-
ated with his friend Dr. Crato von Crafftheim who furthered the interests
of the Brethren at court. They considered the Moravian Church the link
that might reunite the competing branches of the Protestant Church, the
Lutherans and the Calvinists, and, they hoped, Protestants in other lands.
As a beginning, Crato and Languet encouraged the Brethren to publish
a version of their Confession in Latin and Czech.

On this visit to Brno in February 1575 Languet had a chance to visit
the Brethren at their headquarters. There is ample reason to believe that
Sidney accompanied him. Fortunately, Languet left an account of the visit
in a letter to Camerarius written on March 9, 1575. The Brethren were
in the midst of negotiations to bring the theologian Esrom Rüdinger from
Wittenberg to head their educational program. The delicate nature of
Languet's mission, to which Sidney would have been privy, is set forth
clearly in his letter.

>   I was recently in Moravia with Doctor Jordan, who took me to
> Evanăice where the Waldensian brothers have their chief Church.
> They spoke to me of our friend Esrom [Rüdinger], and made it clear
> that they greatly hoped he would come to them. Doctor Crato had
> written to them shortly before that he disapproved of their plan to
> call Esrom; for he feared that if [he] should come, our most Illustrious
> Prince would write to the Emperor about him, and that the Emperor,
> to please him, would take some harsh measure against Esrom.
>   However, when I visited them I easily relieved them of this worry,
> and especially Baron Johannes Žerotin, a man of great virtue who is

the main benefactor and patron of those Churches. This so much that
when they were still afraid to call our friend, Baron Žerotin promised
me that he would undertake [Rüdinger's] protection; and that, if
anything of the kind that Doctor Crato feared should befall him, he
[Žerotin] would tell the Emperor that he had called him [Rüdinger]
personally to be tutor to his son. For the Emperor has no right to
investigate the domestic retinue of the Moravian nobles.

By good luck it happened that during my stay in Brno, Doctor
Crato had a letter from Esrom, who said that he had been called by
Heidelberg, by Basle, and by the Waldensian brethren, and that he
most inclined to the Waldenses. But he had not had a letter from them
for some months, and feared that they had changed their minds.
When I had read the letter I said to Crato that we should have to do
something about this in Moravia, and I had no difficulty persuading
him to approve our plan. I advised him to let Baron Žerotin know at
once the inclination of Esrom; this he promised to do, and I believe
he has done it. I also wrote to Jordan, who is working diligently on
Esrom's behalf.

Esrom will come to a group of people who suit his way of life,
i.e. without pomp and circumstance, and he will experience much
kindness at their hands. Their chief preachers love him as their teacher.
The Senior [Ondřy Štefan], who is like a Superintendent, greatly
longs for his arrival, though he probably does not know his face. He
will have a most opportune friend in Doctor Jordan, an intelligent,
learned and sensible man, who can advise him on his affairs. This
much I wanted to tell you, hoping that you will be pleased.

The only other available evidence about this stop at Brno occurs in a
letter Sidney wrote after reaching Prague to thank Dr. Jordan for his
hospitality. Evidently Baron Žerotin, who had brought his ten-year-old
son Charles with him,[1] had found Sidney interesting and congenial. The
verses which Sidney sent to Dr. Jordan appear to have been some tavern-
inspired satire rather than anything of literary merit. The warmth of their
new friendship glows in Sidney's letter.

Since I must leave tomorrow, most excellent Jordan, I wished to
say farewell to you with these few words, in order to show you by this

---

1. Languet to Robert Sidney, May 24, 1579. *Langueti Epistolae* (Leyden, 1646), p. 387.
I owe this reference to Professor Otaker Odložilík.

attention, however small, that I have not forgotten the singular kindness you have shown me. Should any of your friends or dependants ever chance to be in a place where I can do something for them, I shall certainly try, to the best of my ability, to be of service in proportion to our friendship: that acquaintance of which Master Languet—who is dear to you, and whom I shall regard as a father as long as I live—was the begetter. Meanwhile I entreat you earnestly to remember me, and beg you (when you shall find it convenient) most warmly to greet from me [all] those kind gentlemen who, on your introduction, received me with such excellent companionship: but most especially that great and good man whom I shall honour all my life, the noble Baron Žerotin.

I am sending you the verses I promised: I wish the good would do some thinking, for the bibulous certainly do not. I do not know the author's name, he seems to have been a Frenchman. Yesterday there arrived here Mohammed, the Turkish ambassador; he was received with much ceremony—almost royally so, in fact: but he was accompanied by the foulest gang of his rascally compatriots that ever I saw: you would say they had been hung for several days, so like withered and wooden snakes were they. Farewell, and love me as you are wont. Prague, March 2, 1575.

Yours devotedly,
Philip Sidney

To my great friend, Doctor Jordan, District Chief physician.[2]

Sidney arrived in Prague on Tuesday, February 22, and stayed there for nine days. Languet mentions that he had an audience with the Emperor,[3] but besides this reference no trace of Sidney's activities remains. He was probably included in the official receptions given for the imperial party, and he must have joined Languet in his meetings with various friends. Edmund Campion, whom Sidney may have known at Oxford,[4] was now in his first year as Professor of Rhetoric at the Jesuit College in Prague, and it is tempting to speculate that they met during this brief visit. Although Campion and Sidney had a well-documented meeting two years later,

2. For the Latin original see Feuillerat, 3 : 102.

3. Languet to August of Saxony, Mar. 1, 1575: "The Emperor received him [Sidney] a few days ago, and showed him the greatest kindness." *Huberti Langueti Epistolae* (Leipzig, 1685), p. 75.

4. See Wallace, pp. 65, 87, 109–10, 177.

there is no evidence that they ran into each other during Sidney's short sojourn in Prague in 1575.

It does seem likely, however, that at least three letters forwarded from Vienna caught up with Sidney in Prague. One, dated January 30, came from the dutiful Zündelin in Venice; it consists largely of news and rumours. The incident of Pope Gregory's injured thumb continued to echo: wags made and circulated some kind of satirical ring to celebrate his ordeal.

> I shall be somewhat brief in writing, most noble sir, as I am not sufficiently sure that you will receive this in Vienna. For it is now some time since Languet wrote to our friend Perrot that you were preparing to depart from there. You will hear most of what is new here from Blotius. I know you will laugh at that ridiculous Roman business, mainly contrived on account of the boy: yet by it clever men hope to take advantage of the stupidity of others. If the business about the ring is true, I imagine the Pope will have been amused when he saw his picture stamped upon it, but in such a form as he would most certainly not like anyone to believe. I do not wish to recount to you what sort of omen this is interpreted to be by very many here, lest I should seem to pay a ridiculous amount of attention to what is in truth ridiculous.

The death of Selim II also continued to send ripples to the shores of Christendom.

> Since the day when the death of the Turkish Emperor was reported here and the succession of his son, we have had no letter from Constantinople. The Venetians are anxiously awaiting one and secretly preparing, as well as they can, for any eventuality. Nevertheless, as they hope for peace, that is what they are most anxious to obtain, and any mention of war they shun from their state like the plague: neither the supplications nor the execrations of the Pope are of any avail here. For the fish[5] know the anglers. It is said that although the Pope himself is very much afraid of the Turks, yet he shows it less. Certainly, as far as one can conclude from the visible evidence, he is making little or no preparations.

News from Spain followed that of the Turks, according to Zündelin's usual formula.

---

5. Zündelin here seems to use "ictus" for the Greek ἰχθύς.

The Spaniards now have some hope that this new Turkish Emperor, though he may not keep quiet this year, will at any rate not attack in such force and that, in the years to come, he will wage war by land rather than by sea. Events, I think, will soon show whether their guesses are correct. It is also being widely written and believed that the King of Spain will shortly visit Italy, in order personally to try to rectify his affairs that are in such disorder. I shall believe this when I see it. There is much that I should like to write if I were free to do so. Certainly we seem to be serving against his will one who is so bent on his own destruction.

Again in familiar order, Zündelin added reports of events in France.

The King of France, although he was most unwilling to continue the war, is thought to be unlikely to make peace. For he considers it due to his dignity to perform what he has promised the Pope. It is reported that he has arrested a certain number of nobles (some are said to be ambassadors, others their retinue) whom Damville sent to Avignon secretly to carry away Alençon, that he [the King] has interrogated them, and that one of them has already been executed. It is further said that Livron, a small town in the Dauphiné, has been vainly besieged for the third time, defeating the King's troops; and that Marshal Bellegarde himself was wounded in the foot. To this is added (I do not know by which correspondent) that the King is seriously ill; that he will be crowned King of France on the same day that he was crowned King of Poland; and that they are taking pains, at his request, to do this with a solemn rite and even greater pomp.

A certain reliable correspondent reports—though it is not written by many—that the nephew of the Cardinal of Lorraine has been made Cardinal Bishop of the Rhine by his brother Guise. I hear that the sister of the King of Aquitaine has been made a duchess. Her husband the King of Navarre and Alençon too are being closely guarded, and already the comings and goings of all their dependents are being watched. Of the death of your friend the Baron you will learn from the enclosed. Farewell, most noble sir, and I beg you most respectfully to greet Master Languet from me. January 30, 1575.

Yours most respectfully, Z.

In his conclusion Zündelin introduced a subject that would have brought a pang to Sidney's heart. "Your friend the Baron" whose death Zündelin reported was Edward, Lord Windsor who had warmly befriended Sidney in Venice. Details of this sad event were given in the letter which accompanied Zündelin's, that from Don Cesare Carrafa. A young man of literary interests who wrote poetry in Italian, Latin, and Spanish, Carrafa had become fond of Lord Windsor in Venice, as he also had of Sidney. His eminent Neapolitan family had recently had the honour of having one of their number occupy the throne of St. Peter (Paul IV, 1555–59). Through his friendship with the Catholic Lord Windsor, Don Cesare had contact with English gentlemen in Venice, including Protestants such as Sidney.

Because Carrafa's letter (in Italian) is dated February 3, Zündelin's letter must have been held for it: the docketing marks and later numeration show that it was once among the Sidney papers in England.[6] The letter conveys the depth of Carrafa's sorrow over the loss of their friend.

> Most noble Sir, and like a son to me,
> I am sorry that my first letter to your Excellency should be so full of grief and sadness that it contains naught but tears and sighs: for it is my duty to inform you of the death of my very dear friend, my Edward, Lord Windsor. It pleased the Blessed Lord to take him unto Himself after four days of a malignant fever. I say "to take him unto Himself," because it is many years since we have seen a death as holy as his. As he left the care of his remains and of his other affairs to me, I have had him buried with so much honour and ceremony that this city has never seen such a funeral. I shall see that your Excellency gets a special description of it: of the way the body was carried, of the route by which it was borne through the city, and the appearance of the church where it was buried—Saints John and Paul.

Carrafa's description of the funeral is not among the Sidney papers, but it probably included most of what Don Caesare reported to his Roman friend, Marco Antonio Colonna. The pertinent parts of that letter, dated January 22, 1575, and translated in the *Calendar of State Papers Rome*, read as follows.[7]

> We are here in great grief by reason of the death of Milord Edward Windsor, one of the chief nobles of England, beloved by all the city

6. The first and best account of Sidney's friendship with Carrafa is in Buxton, pp. 68–69, though Buxton did not realize that Carrafa was a Catholic. The original letter, written in Italian, is now in the British Museum, Add. MS. 15914, fol. 15. Later letters appear on fol. 25 in the same volume and in Add. MS. 17520, fols. 4–5.

7. *CSPR*, p. 194.

and particularly by the Patriarch [of Aquileia], by the Spanish ambassador, by the Legate, and particularly by me, who, from the day of his arrival in this city, for respect to his great virtue and religiousness, had him ever in loving protection, so that we were never seen save in company.

This death has marred all our pleasures. He was twelve days in dying; and his end was as holy as had been his life. By the testimony of the Spanish ambassador and other gentlemen it is many a year since a more blessed man has been seen. He has left his body to Mr. John Pole, and as to all else that pertained to him here his will was that the Prior of England and I do as God should inspire us, as well in beneficence to his servants as in almsgiving and in his obsequies, which have been solemnized in such a sort that it is current in the city that nothing grander has been seen.

To which matter I paid particular attention; a *chapelle ardente* was made; and I resolved that it should be borne on the bier according to the custom of Naples with a great pall, a thing not till then seen in Venice, which all deemed very meet. I followed the corpse with the train, as did also many other persons of quality. The Spanish ambassador awaited it at the church. All the English nobility here followed the corpse with their hoods on their heads according to the English custom. So I have been for the last fortnight busy serving him in life and in death.

He has left 4,000 crowns in ready money and 10,000 in jewels, silver plate, and movables. I would not omit to give your Excellency an account of the death of this lord because he was truly the most devout lord of his great name; and though he has annoyed me many a time, I have done him reverence.

The "twelve days in dying" Carrafa reported here had shrunk to four during the fortnight's interval before he wrote to Sidney. His letter continues with other details of their friend's demise.

During his illness I never left him, but served him and cheered him up, as was my duty. So you can imagine, my dear Master Philip Sidney, what grief I feel at the loss of such a dear friend. The whole city mourns him, as he was beloved by all—as you know. I share your sadness at this loss, which I know will hit you hard; and I beg you, when you are back in England, not to forget her Excellency Lady

Catherine Windsor and Lord Frederick his son, whose husband and father you loved.

Above all, remember that I am your Excellency's most affectionate servant: for this reason I beg you to let me know any command you may have and to write to me often. This will be most welcome and delightful to me. I greet you humbly and send my respects to his Excellency your father, and to all your brothers and her Excellency your mother, whom I honour. Venice, February 3, 1575.

If only I did not have to report the death of my dear friend Lord Windsor! But we should praise God for everything.

Your Excellency's most affectionate servant,

Don Cesare Carrafa

The monument over Lord Windsor's tomb has been admired by English visitors ever since the time of Thomas Coryat, who described it thus: "Againe in another corner of the Church, about the south end, there is a prety monument erected to the honour of an English Baron euen the Lord *Windsor*, Grandfather to the right Honorable *Thomas Lord Windsor* now [1609] living. At the toppe whereof there standeth a Pyramis of red marble."[8]

While he was at Prague a third letter probably reached Sidney. It was written in French by Philip, Count of Hanau, who had parted from Sidney in Vienna late in November. Business affairs were now keeping him on the move from one of his properties to another.

Sir:

I hoped very much before I left Vienna that you would return from Poland that I might again have the pleasure of your society which I prize so highly and of which your long stay has deprived me to my great regret. Nevertheless I trust, by the help of Providence, to see you again at the next Frankfurt Fair, together with Monsieur Languet, who has assured me that you will come.

I beg you also to do me the great favour of coming to spend some time at Hanau in order that we may revive and continue the friendship with which you have honoured me from the very beginning of our acquaintance, which I hope to preserve in its entirety, and of which I hope to give you proof in deeds whenever an opportunity presents itself. I have not written you sooner partly because of the tedium

8. Coryat, p. 223; he printed the epitaph, as did Buxton on pp. 264–65.

of my travels and partly because I have not been able to find any assured means of having my letters conveyed to you.

I arrived at my house of Steinau with all my suite safe and sound, thanks to God, on the first day of January, and was warmly welcomed by my subjects. I have come here to my residence at Ortenburg in order to attend to some business, and I hope within two or three days to be on the way to Dillenburg. From there I go to Heidelberg to visit the Elector Palatine, and then to Busweiler, from whence, when I have finished some business, I hope to return to Hanau as soon as possible in order to await your coming with Monsieur Languet.

I shall welcome you both as heartily as I now send you my affectionate greetings. I pray God that he may keep you in perfect health and give you a long and happy life with the complete fulfilment of your noble and virtuous aspirations. From Ortenburg Castle, this thirtieth of January, 1575.

Your affectionate friend at your service,
Philip Louis, Count of Hanau, etc.

Sidney's travel plans now required him to leave Prague on March 3 and proceed westward across Germany. Parting from Languet, who remained with the Emperor's court, was less painful than it might have been, since they would be reunited in Frankfurt a few weeks later. Sidney's route took him in a northern arc through Dresden, Leipzig, Weimar, and Eisenach. He travelled with a French friend of Lobbet, Thomas Lenormand, an intelligent and congenial man who had been at the French court and who later wrote Sidney several letters. Undoubtedly Lenormand was also a Huguenot.

By approximately March 6, Sidney was in Dresden,[9] bearing a letter of introduction from Languet to August of Saxony. Languet describes his young friend as follows:

> Most noble prince; the young man who brings your Highness this letter is an Englishman of high degree. His mother is the sister of Robert, Earl of Leicester, the most powerful man at the English court. The Emperor received him a few days ago, and showed him the greatest kindness. I learned that he was leaving, and would be crossing your domains: also that he desired, should the opportunity present itself, to greet your Highness and offer you his duty and

9. Languet to Sidney, Mar. 13: "I suppose you arrived in Dresden a week ago."

service. So I gave him this letter as an introduction to your Highness. For all his youth, he has a noble spirit, and a greater experience of affairs than his age would suggest.[10]

In Dresden Sidney finally met Dr. Andreas Paull with whom he had earlier exchanged letters. A friend of Languet and, like him, an ex-pupil of Melanchthon, Paull had studied in Italy and France. Later he became a brilliant young doctor of canon law in Speier. August of Saxony discovered him there in 1571 and made him a Counsellor in Dresden where he lived until his death. August also employed him as a special envoy, both on embassies abroad and at imperial assemblies.[11] In Dresden Sidney was also joined by Wotton, as Languet's letter of March 13 indicates; the friends went on to finish the journey together.

Perrot had written about coming from Venice, but that he did so cannot be proved. Sidney's host at Strasbourg, Hubert de la Rose, definitely visited Frankfurt at this time. Possibly the most important friendship which Sidney renewed was that with Théophile de Banos, the protégé of Ramus, whose *Commentaries* he was now preparing for the press. De Banos appears to have been introduced to Sidney in Paris by Languet, who described the young Englishman to him as "the true image of nobility."[12] Despite the assumptions of some writers that de Banos and Sidney met again in Vienna, the evidence for the Frenchman's being there at the proper time is unclear. De Banos had become minister of the Huguenot church in Frankfurt, so they may have met again during the winter of 1572–73. They did, however, become fast friends in 1575, as de Banos's dedication to Sidney of his *magnum opus* in 1576, *Petri Rami Commentariorum de Religione Christiana Libri Quatuor* and the correspondence of that year prove.

Once Sidney reached the hospitable house of Andreas Wechel he found a copious batch of letters awaiting him. This address was the only certain one he could give to friends, and the known letters among those which awaited his arrival demonstrate once again the remarkable response that this twenty-year-old youth aroused in men much his senior, men distinguished for their achievements and erudition. Some of the letters

10. Languet to August of Saxony, Mar. 1, 1575; in *Huberti Langueti Epistolae*, pp. 75–76.
11. Paull to Sidney, Jan. 6, 1576: "Whenever I think of the great kindness which you . . . showed me when you came here [i.e. Dresden], and of your wise conversation about the most exalted matters which at that time I enjoyed, I am deeply grieved that I was unable further to converse with you . . ." For the full text of this letter, see below, p. 404.
12. *De Vita P. Rami*, prefixed to *Petri Rami Commentariorum de Religione Christiana Libri Quatuor* (Frankfurt, 1576).

were written approximately a month before he opened them. Of the
three that came from Venice, the first was from his French friend Perrot
and had been written on February 20. It replies to a letter Sidney had
written from Brno and exudes anticipation of their meeting in Frankfurt.

> Sir,
>
> In reply to your letter of the ninth of this month, which I received
> the day before yesterday: I expect, with God's help, to be in the area
> you want to see by the middle or the end of April and will be delighted
> to meet you and to have a better opportunity of humbly doing you
> some service than I have had until now. However, I thank you with
> all my heart and am most grateful for the great affection which, by
> your courtesy and goodness alone, you are pleased to entertain for
> me. This affection will enlarge ever more that which I entertain for
> your virtue and merit, and will make me increasingly eager to honour
> and serve you in whatever way possible.

Next came local news, though the reported death of Charles de Gonzaga-
Clèves was an error, for he lived another twenty years.

> The Council, a few days ago, received a letter from their ambassa-
> dor in Constantinople, in which he says that, having kissed the hand
> of the new Prince, he was well received and is hopeful concerning
> the ratification of the peace treaty with that state.
>
> I believe you must have heard, on your way through Prague, of
> the death in Rome of the Prince of Clèves—the reward for his
> Odyssey—and that the Pope is not in the best of health.

Reports from France describe Damville's latest success. The Huguenot
Jacques de Crussol, Duke of Uzès (1540–94) had deserted Damville and
gone over to the King, who put him in command of the royal forces
when he went to be crowned at Rheims.

> In regard to France, the last post brought us confirmation of the
> fact that Aiguemortes has fallen to Marshal Damville without a
> blow and without a single man killed. You can imagine what an
> important capture this is, as much because of the town's citadel with
> the wealth of artillery in it as for the great salt revenue, which had
> been assigned to the army of the Duke of Uzès. This arrangement will
> now be used by the Marshal's army: and he will be able to help others
> with it also, by making salt as expensive as sugar in Lyons and that

entire province, which correspondents say he is threatening to do. The siege of Livron also has been lifted, and that army has been scattered by the garrison.

So that is the state in which the King has left the country because he wants to go and have himself crowned—and that on the very same day that he was crowned in Poland. Of that coronation, which was to take place on the thirteenth of this month, we can have no news as yet, nor of what future policies are being debated. You will hear everything at the Fair: so this is just to send you my most humble and respectful greetings, and to beg you to make use of me whenever you think I could do you some service.

Perrot ended with various items of Venetian interest. The "English gentleman" to whom Sidney sent his compliments may have been George Lewknor.

> Finally: permission has been given for the sale of Sigonius's history *De Regno Italiae*, and I think you will be able to buy one in Frankfurt. I have given your respects to Master Zündelin, who returns them, accompanied by my own, most humble and affectionate; and I pray God,
> Sir, to increase his grace towards you, and to protect you always. From Venice, this twentieth of February, 1575. I have informed the English gentleman you wrote about of your letter; and I have replied to Master Languet via Prague.
> > Your most humble and affectionate servant,
> > > Fr. de Mésières

Waiting with this letter was another from Perrot. Although written in French, it was addressed "A L'Illustre Signore, il signor Baron de Sidene, in casa de Wechel, Libraro et stampatore, In Francford." Perrot had employed a well-known Venetian bookseller to carry his first letter to Sidney, but he now seized an opportunity offered by the unknown "English gentleman."

> Sir,
> In reply to your letter of the fourth of this month, I wrote to you a week ago, sending the letter by Pietro Lungo, a bookseller who was on his way to the Frankfurt Fair, and telling you all the news we had of France and elsewhere. I am writing you this because I heard that the servant of the English gentleman you wrote to me about previ-

ously was on his way to you, and I wanted to take the opportunity of letting you know what we have since heard.

As a Frenchman, Perrot continued to give precedence to news out of France, knowing that Sidney would expect it. There are two references to the announced plan of Henry III for founding two new Orders of knights to be dangled as plums before the nobility, who were wavering in their loyalty to the royal party.

> From Turin a correspondent writing on the fifteenth of this month sends word that on the third a messenger from the King passed through there on his way from Dijon to Rome, to deal with the matter of the religious orders of new knights which the King wants to found in his realm. This messenger reported that there was very little hope of peace, however hard the Parisians were trying to achieve it, and that there was a lot of talk about the troops the Prince of Condé is raising. He is near Salins with a goodly gathering of several French lords and hopes also to get some Swiss from around Berne.
>
> The same correspondent says that the Marshal Damville, not content with his splendid capture of Aiguemortes, is still advancing without encountering much resistance. Also, that the Catholics are beginning to show themselves just as eager for popular support as the Protestants. What I wrote you about Marseilles has been supplemented by the news that its inhabitants have forced their Governor, M. de Meuillon, to withdraw into the inmost fortress, having seized the citadel and the chain of the harbour, expelled all strangers, and repudiated all taxes. And several other towns have apparently done the same, determined not to contribute a penny to the costs of such a beastly war.

This account of the affair at Marseilles had been exaggerated in the report. Actually, a group of about four dozen men, in protest against continued levying of excise taxes after the date of their expiration, broke into the customs house, threw its contents into the harbour, and occupied the building for three days until the authorities acceded to their demands.

Henry III's plans to found two Orders of knights had been the subject of the latest letter from Rome to reach Venice, along with the news that he had married Louise de Vaudémont on February 15, immediately following his coronation.

What was said in the report mentioned above has been confirmed by a letter from Rome dated the eighteenth, which says that the King intends to found in his realm these two Orders of knights: one for the land war, to go under the name of the Passion, the other, of St. Louis, for the naval war. He is asking the Pope for six hundred thousand écus as an allowance on the security of the abbeys and priories of France: he would augment this with eight hundred thousand pounds of his own for the maintaining of the said knights. At the same time he asked, giving his own consent, that the abbeys and priories be restored to their original type and discipline, and that henceforth they should only be allowed to be held by regular clergy, who must be in residence. The said knights will take an oath to defend the Catholic faith and to serve his Majesty at all times, to observe this undertaking faithfully in both articles.

Such are the marvellous remedies and plasters they want to apply to the outside of this body quite rotten within and falling to pieces; a good symptom of sickness indeed, to conceive such dreams and schemes, which will rather increase the disease than cure it. I have written to Master Languet in similar vein, so that he may judge for what a deplorable condition France is heading unless God takes a hand.

From Rome it is also written that the marriage of the King with the daughter of M. Vaudemont is held to be certain and arranged. But both of this and of the peace in the Netherlands, which according to our latest information seems assured, you will hear more trustworthy news at the place to which this letter is being sent; as also of the rumours that the Emperor's son Rudolph is to be elected King of the Romans at the forthcoming Diet.

Perrot ends the letter with news of the Turk, a reiteration of his hopes for a reunion in Frankfurt, and greetings to de Banos.

From the Orient it is said that a *chiaus* [envoy] has arrived at Ragusa, who was sent there for the exchange of the prisoners taken at Cyprus and Goletta for the Turkish prisoners now being kept at Rome. About the new Emperor himself it is said that he enjoys walking about Constantinople in shabby clothes to see and hear how things are going, so that he can reform abuses concerning the price of bread and such like.

As I wrote to you, I expect to be where you wish to go at the Fair, at the latest at the end of April; and I shall be delighted of any opportunity to be of some service to you—just as it will always and everywhere be an honour and a favour to me to receive your commands. Meanwhile I shall present my humble respects to your benevolence, and pray God, Sir, to protect you always. From Venice, this twenty-seventh of February, 1575.

Your humble and affectionate servant,

F. de Mésières

Master Banos will find here my affectionate respects to his benevolence.

The third letter addressed to Sidney in care of Wechel came from the elegant quill of Matthäus Wacker. His studied style is almost cloying in its attempt to be coy and sophisticated. At least we learn one fact about Sidney from the letter, that he still intended to return to England through Paris, where he expected to stay with Dr. Valentine Dale, the English ambassador.

It was a great token of your love for me, illustrious and noble Master Sidney, that, in what was already your second letter sent to me via our friend Languet, you were pleased so kindly and courteously to invite me to come and stay with you. But an even greater sign of your most faithful goodwill is that you did not trust to the eloquence of that most excellent man—as if it were not enough to have such a famous Chancellor—but inscribed to me with your own hand a letter brimming with kindness and courtesy. I should be less than human, most virtuous Sidney, if—whether moved by your Agamemnonian authority, or persuaded by his Nestorian sweetness of speech—I did not attempt to perform what both of you so kindly and strongly request of me.

So if it be possible I shall disengage myself and, when I am disentangled, I shall follow your advice in the arranging of my departure: to go and stay in France with the English ambassador where, if I find you there, I can decide about the crossing with you or, if you have already left, with him. Of that event, however—though before the end of the summer many and great causes might bring it about—I almost despair: however, I will do my best, so that you may know that it has not been the fault of me or my willingness if it does not satisfy your desire the first time also. Yet why do I call it yours, when I should rather call it mine?—since the delight and love awakened by the prospect of seeing you so inflame me that I believe nothing, even the immenence of the event, can in any way, indeed at all, appease my desire.

When I have come, I hope it will be easy so to make all our decisions that your commissions in no way fail to be matched by my goodwill: which, although by its weakness it may perhaps not meet your expectations, will nevertheless far exceed them in promptness and alacrity. I should prefer the event itself to be witness to this, rather than this uncouth missive. Yet even a letter may effect an exchange of spoils, until the plaintiff himself shall stand before you to be repaid. Thus I wished, briefly, to reply to your letter: whatever may happen to myself (for the fortunes of human matters are uncertain and fickle) I shall try diligently to let you know at once.

I have written a letter practically to the same effect to our friend Master Languet, adding to it—nor do I wish to omit it here—that on the sixth of February (a good omen) I received the highest title of honour in both branches of the law. Farewell my Lord and most excellent future Maecenas: and accept my respects in return. You are most kindly greeted by Otto Count Solms, who recently wrote to you—a man of great zeal and love towards you. From Padua, the twenty-fourth of February, the fourth day since I received your letter from Perrot, in the year of the last age, 1575.

With the greatest love for your Illustrious Eminence,
					Matthäus Wacker of Constanz V.I.P.

Soon after reaching Frankfurt Sidney received a letter from Languet, written on March 10, a week after they had parted in Prague. One of the most interesting items in it is that rumours reaching England about Sidney's friendship with Lord Windsor and other Catholics in Venice had caused Walsingham to write to Languet for reassurance. Languet's warning may have prompted Sidney to be specially attentive to de Banos.

Since you departed many things have occurred to me which I felt I should write to you, but as soon as I take my pen in hand and turn my thoughts towards you, my mind is so clouded with grief that everything which I have just been thinking escapes my memory. Nevertheless I shall write, confusedly, whatever occurs to me.

14 April 1575 B88 52

Expectabam, clariss.me domine, breuem tuū ad nos reditū
vt suauissimis, et doctissimis tuis sermonibus frui rursus
mihi concederetur. Licet enim epistola tua, sit absentis velutj
imago, praesentis tamen sapientia cum ex ore — percipitur,
mirabiles excitat tuj amores, et te nobilitatis ornamentis vndiq
praeditum, nobiliorem depredicat. Generis enim nobilitas qua
virtute caret ignauiae est velamen; virtuti verò coniuncta
animi et corporis est ornamentum. Equidem hac virtutis, et
sapientiae tuae recordatio effecit vt te praesentem amauerim
absentem verò amare et colere nunquam desinam. Erubescit
verò calamus cum muneris tuū tuj ευχαρισιων meditatur. Occurrit
enim non tantum philosophi Alexandrj talenta recusantis exemplu
sed illud praecipuè Beatius multò esse dare quā accipere: Verum
singularis tua in me beneuolentia iubet, vt ad gratiarum actionē
potius quam ad pudorem me comparem, hancq tuam liberalitatem
amoris erga me tuj monumentum retineo, vicissimq humilimè precor
vt amicum hunc a tuo Theophilo in perpetua obseruantia testimonium
apud te retineas. De comentarijs qd promisj prestabo, et curabo vt sub
tuis auspicys (quandoquidem ita perplacet) ad proximas nundinas excudamur.
Vale ornatissime Sidnae, et Ecclesiae Christi, Republicaeq Anglicanae, diu et
feliciter viue. Francofurti 14 Aprilis 75

Tuj obseruantissimus
Theophilus Banosius

Specimen of Théophile de Banos's handwriting

Quae nobis iniecta nuper fuit de peste suspicio, periculum nunc apertum denunciat.
illa quidem paulatim in oppido prorupit, nosq omnes minatur; quo fit vt maior
pars honi Academicorum aufugerit. Ille tuus, vt poëtae verbis vtar, omnium
iuuenculorum flosculus, et Edoüardus Mountaguus, accersiti à Dno Mountag̃
cũ Busto et duobus famulis Griffino et Hobsono, post paucos dies quos in aed
kellãwei posuerñt, in Comitatũ Northãptonieñsem profecti sunt, ibi, nisi te
velis, commoraturi, donec propitius Deus pestem ab Vrbe depulerit. Reliquꝰ
duobus Joãni et whito qui aegñt apud me, ego intra biduũ locũ mag
idoneum cõparabo, nisi tu secus statueris. Quam potui, mandat
curaui D. fowgreuelli: librũ verò, quẽ volebat, Cyrũ xenophõtis latinũ
non possũ inuenire. Nunc, ne sim longior, relatã tibi quãm amplissimã grati
de tuã perquã eximia bonitate, quã me iam diu cõplexus es, te tuãeq̃ dignitati
amplificatione praepotẽti Deo meis precibus cõmendo. Vale. oxon. Idib. octob
1575 ?

tibi tuisq̃ deditissimus

Robertus Dorsett

Specimen of Robert Dorsett's handwriting

Two days after you left, our friend Wotton arrived here and brought me a very kind letter from Master Walsingham. I see that your countrymen have begun to have some suspicions about your piety because you lived in Venice too intimately with those who profess a faith hostile to yours. I shall write Master Walsingham about this, and if he has formed any such opinion of you I shall take pains to disabuse him of it. And I hope that my letter will carry so much weight with him that he not only will believe that what I write him about you is true, but will also take pains to convince the others of this. In the meantime I advise you to form acquaintances with the learned and sagacious French preachers where you are, to offer them invitations, and to attend their sermons, and to do the same at Heidelberg and Strasbourg. Yet do not be troubled at what I say; for I am sure that you do not doubt my affection and are aware that persons of high position take care to avoid not only guilt but the suspicion of guilt.

Languet mapped out Sidney's future contacts with his friends along the projected route to Paris. Dr. Zacharias Ursinus had been another pupil of Melanchthon and was one of the most influential theologian-statesmen in the Palatinate.[13] Ludwig, Count of Sayn-Wittgenstein (1532–1605) had recently received the appointment to his eminent post.

At Heidelberg pay your respects to Dr. Ursinus, an excellent man, to whom I have written about you. Within a few days I shall send you a letter for Count Ludwig von Wittgenstein, majordomo of the Palatine court, to give you the opportunity of forming a friendship with him, for he is a distinguished man. At Strasbourg you will find our friend Lobbet; he is very fond of you, and you can avail yourself of his advice in your planning. But it seems best for you to go from Strasbourg into Burgundy, and from there to make directly for Paris. In Switzerland the roads are rough and rutted, so I fear that if you go there your horses will not stand the strain of so long and hard a journey. Further, I do not know whether it would be very safe, if you are going to the French court, to spend much time with religious refugees from France.

13. See K. Sudhoff, *C. Olevianus und Z. Ursinus, Leben und Schriften der Vater . . . der reformirten Kirche*, vol. 8 (Elberfeld, 1857).

Advice follows concerning Sidney's conduct on reaching England. In view of the fact that Sidney had already spent hundreds of hours with Languet and had known Burghley and Walsingham for years, Languet's admonitions seem totally unnecessary.

> When you arrive in England, take care to cultivate Cecil, who is fond of you and will make everything easier for you. And surely, nothing will enable you to earn his favour more than befriending his children, or at least pretending to do so. But remember that a shrewd old man, and one with long experience in affairs, readily detects a young man's pretences.
>
> It will also do you honour to cultivate the friendship of Master Walsingham. You remember what you have often heard from me about my friend Beale's talent and learning. Men usually have an excellent opinion of youths whom they notice seeking the company of wise men.
>
> I write you these things as you are about to take up life at court, a sort of life in which you will encounter greater problems than have your contemporaries who have already entered into their patrimonies. In other words, it would not be seemly for you to pursue a life of ease while you are still a son and heir.
>
> To put it in a word, one who wishes to live free of scorn in the courts of mighty kings must govern his emotions, swallow many vexations, very carefully avoid all motives of controversy, and cultivate those men in whose hands supreme power lies. But I shall not trouble you further, since you understand all those things better than I.

These mildly Machiavellian hints reveal the extent to which Languet, though a Reformation man, also lived in the Renaissance.

Languet's concluding paragraph descends to the practical problem of Sidney's financial position. With characteristic generosity Languet was writing to friends to arrange for them to advance Sidney more money if he should need it.

> I am glad that your friend Wotton is joining you, so that you may have a companion who is pleasant, loyal, and fond of you to relieve the tedium of your journey. I wish my countryman, Master Jacques Gons, were your companion. I do not know why you wanted Wotton to witness the promissory note which you left with me. You

wrong me if you think that I trust anyone more than you. Do not worry if you should be unable to do as you wish with regard to the money you have borrowed from me, and do not imagine that my affection for you will diminish at all on this account. In fact, I am writing Dr. von Glauburg and Welchel to give you travelling money on my credit if you should not have enough to complete your journey.

I shall write again in three days. Farewell, my very dear son. Prague, March 10, 1575.

The Frenchman, Jacques Gons, remains unidentified. Dr. Johann von Glauburg (1529–1609), member of a leading Calvinist family in Frankfurt, had in hand money belonging to Languet. Languet's letter to von Glauburg has been preserved, and the portion on Sidney reads as follows:

There will presently come to you an illustrious and noble English youth, Master Philip Sidney, son of a most worthy father who is now Lord Deputy of Ireland. His mother is the sister of the Earl of Warwick, and of Robert Earl of Leicester; and he is their heir-presumptive, as they are both childless. I do not consider this splendour of birth and fortune so much to be admired as his wit and his zeal for virtue, which he pursues with the greatest assiduity. Such great ornaments, I believe, will make you wish to oblige him; but if my prayers have any influence with you, assist him, I beg you, that you may deserve his favour in other matters: for his friendship may be useful to you and your friends in the future, since he will surely be given great authority in his own country, if God grants him long life. If he needs money, I wish you would give him as much as he asks for, out of what you owe me.[14]

This description closely parallels one Languet wrote in the same week to Ludwig, Count Wittgenstein, mentioned earlier in Languet's letter.[15] One sentence may be quoted from it, since it helps to complete our knowledge of Languet's observations on Sidney. "I admire ... the force and dis-

14. This letter, now at Harvard, was edited, translated, and well explained by William H. Bond in "A Letter of Languet about Sidney," *Harvard Library Bulletin*, 9 (Winter, 1955): 105–09. The passage quoted appears on p. 107.

15. In the article cited above Bond accepted the heading in the 1646 edition of Languet's letters that this introduction was addressed to the diplomat Achille de Harlay in Paris. Charles Levy argues convincingly that it was addressed not to de Harlay but to von Wittgenstein; see Levy, pp. 244–45.

position of his spirit, which not only displays flowers that give us hope of virtue, but has already produced fruits which you may find by no means unripe." [16]

Languet's concern for Sidney's probable future power and influence, like his advice on dealing with Cecil, has raised questions about the sincerity of his possessive interest in the young English aristocrat. If he emphasized these worldly considerations in his letters of introduction, how large did they loom in his attitude towards Sidney? The answer is that Languet was writing to practical men, asking favours of them for a young friend. To have said that Sidney was a bright and charming youth was not adequate excuse for asking eminent men to go out of their way for him: since these men understood position and potential political power which Sidney possessed in plenty, Languet stressed these factors. Sidney himself, like any young man sufficiently mature to understand his status and potential, must have recognized his role and accepted it.

However practical-minded Languet was at first, he soon discerned Sidney's intellectual powers, personal attractiveness, and a maturity of judgement far beyond his years. With the vision of a Protestant League capable of crushing the forces of the papacy burning in his own mind, Languet saw Sidney as the future leader of such a crusade: the young man possessed all the qualities necessary to become its leader. He himself had been impressed with Sidney's status before discovering that, quite apart from these family advantages, Sidney was one of the most brilliant young men ever to cross his path. In writing letters of introduction Languet now wished to have Sidney warmly received, knowing that the young man's abilities and charm would be discovered as extra virtues.

Three days after he sent the letter that prompted this digression, Languet wrote again. In this letter, dated March 13, he chafes at the fact that he still had to sit in Prague waiting for the document which would permit him to leave the Emperor's court and catch up with Sidney's party, now receding into the west. Languet explains his situation in this paragraph:

> I have now given up almost all hope of seeing you in the future, because I have not received a letter from our court; but what in fact distresses me no less is that I hear nothing about you, though I suppose you arrived in Dresden a week ago and received a letter and that you have written to me from there. If within three or four days

16. *Langueti Epistolae*, p. 178; the letter is dated Mar. 12, 1575.

I should receive permission to join you, I would still take to the road, since I hope that you will hardly be leaving Frankfurt before the end of this month.

After this beginning Languet gave detailed accounts of the reception of the envoy, Maximilian's trouble with a kidney stone, and the conflict over the religious question. Here again he commented with a touch of bitterness on the need for compromise of conscience to achieve political success. "Not only those who aspire to command must learn to dissemble, but similarly persons who wish to serve princes in such a way that they may benefit adequately from their efforts; this Thaddeus [Dr. Hájek] and I have not so far learned to do."

In concluding, Languet listed prominent persons to whom Sidney should become known; of these the first of the two not previously mentioned was Odoard Biset, Sire de Charloys, a Protestant living in Basle. Languet also named a "Master de Harlay," who may have been Achille de Harlay, a diplomat in Paris, or perhaps his brother Charles, whom Sidney had known in Venice and who later succeeded Jean de Vulcob as French ambassador in Vienna.

> I am sending you a letter addressed to his Excellency Count Ludwig von Wittgenstein, an outstanding man, in order that you may have the occasion to present yourself to him. As I suggested before, in Heidelberg pay your respects also to Dr. Ursinus. I shall arrange that when you do he will have received an appropriate letter from me; similarly with Lobbet at Strasbourg.
>
> If you go to Basle, extend an invitation to Master Biset, a good and sagacious man, and one dear to me. Please pay your respects to Master de Harlay, and see to it that you make friends with him. You will, I hope, hear many things from him which you will find neither unpleasant nor useless to know. I am writing to him, but I have reasons for preferring that the letter be delivered by someone other than you.
>
> I am sending you a list, compiled at random, of several writers, to which you will add or subtract according to your own judgement. Write to Master de Vulcob. And write me diligently, I beg you, of your activities, of how you plan your journey, and of the news you have of English affairs; and please take care of the letter which I wrote to Master Walsingham. Do not trouble yourself greatly over my money. In fact, as I wrote before, if you should lack travelling

money, go to Dr. von Glauburg or to Wechel, whom I have asked to pay you in my name as much as you need.

Pay my respects to Master Wotton and to Griffin, your trusty servant. I hear that our Marseille intends to demand her ancient freedom back. All this in haste. Farewell, my very dear son. Prague, March 13, 1575.

Once Sidney was well established in Frankfurt he received a friendly letter from Lobbet, the principal purpose of which was to remind Sidney how welcome he would be when he reached Strasbourg. It was carried by Hubert de la Rose, Sidney's host on the previous visit. Apart from a description of Sidney's travelling companion, Lenormand, it adds little new information.

Sir,

In your last letter, dated the sixth of last month, you told me that you were intending to visit these parts. It is for this reason that I did not write earlier, fearing that had I done otherwise my letter might have been lost or at any rate temporarily misdirected. I have since received a letter from Master Languet dated the sixth of this month, telling me that you left Prague on the third of this month (you can imagine how sad your departure made him), accompanied by a certain Master Lenormand whom I used to know at the French court, and who is known as a very excellent, wise, and intelligent gentleman. Master Languet also writes that you will travel through the states of Meissen, Thuringia, and Hessen, and attend the Easter Fair at Frankfurt. Although he has also told me that you would be coming to this town, yet I did not wish to fail to meet you, if not physically, then at least with this letter which will speak for me.

Do not, I beg you however, expect much news from me: for you have so much of it from all sides that you must be overstocked and at a loss what to do with it all. The Frankfurt Fair is like a garden where all sorts of herbs grow. I would certainly not maintain that that they are all good and healthy, but you are so good a herbalist that you will recognize them and distinguish between them. But, God willing, we will speak more of this and other matters when you are here.

It is splendid that you can come and stay here with Master Hubert de la Rose, your host: he is as excellent company as before. I am giving him this letter with the request to give it to you: for this once you will find in it little save the promise of any service I can do you whenever it should be convenient to you.

I imagine you will be seeing the Count of Hanau, Philip Louis: if so, please let him read in this letter my most humble respects to his benevolence—and do not forget Master Welsperg. I hope to see them soon, having recently missed an opportunity of doing so: not through any fault of mine, but because I did not have the time and the leisure. I should also like you to pay my respects to Master Wechel, but I do not dare ask. Here I shall end and present my humble respects to your benevolence, praying God,

Sir, to keep you in His own. From Strasbourg this seventeenth of March, 1575.

Your humble servant,
J. Lobbet

Just before Easter Sunday (April 3) Sidney also had a letter from Dr. Crato von Crafftheim, written from Prague on March 20. Brief and very friendly, it asks one favour, that after reaching England Sidney send the second volume of a book on botany. This request seems definitely to refer to *Stirpium adversaria nova, perfacilis vestigatio* (*STC* 19595) by Pierre Pena and Matthias de l'Obel, published in two volumes (1570–71) by Thomas Purfoot, with a promise that the second part would soon appear.[17] More importantly, Crato's letter shows that Languet had finally obtained permission to leave the Imperial Court and join Sidney at Frankfurt.

Most noble Master Philip,

Our excellent friend Master Languet has persuaded me that my letter will not be unwelcome to you. I can scarcely imagine this to be true, as I have neither matter nor manner that could possibly be agreeable to a reader, and lack the time to write with any due attention. However, remembering your great kindness, and spurred on by that part of me that admires your remarkable qualities, I suddenly decided to pen these few lines, so that Hubert could take them when he leaves. For I desire, and that most earnestly, to give you some sign of my devotion to your excellence; and beg your Excellency to

17. Evidently Purfoot was disappointed by the lack of sales, for he disposed of eight hundred sets of sheets to Christopher Plantin, the eminent printer in Antwerp. Plantin then issued the completed work in 1576 under the title *Plantarum seu Stirpium Historia*, with the new section filling the first volume and the purchased sheets making up the second.

realize that, if there is any more concrete way to show my zeal than in a letter and you will let me have but the slightest word, I shall consider it a great favour to be of service.

I shall not give you any news of us nor of public affairs, as you have Master Hubert to tell you. If I hear that this nonsense of mine has been welcome to you, I shall write to you whenever I can manage it.

Although I certainly deserve no kindness, and would not dare ask anything of you, yet if the second volume of *Plants*, by the two doctors, has been published in England, I should be very grateful if it could be sent to me, so that it may join the first volume, which I already have. In return there is no wish of your Excellency's which I shall not be happy to satisfy. Farewell, most noble Sir. Prague, March 20, 1575.

Yours with devotion to your Excellency,
Johannes Crato von Crafftheim

When Languet reached Frankfurt we do not know, but the four hundred miles from Prague via Dresden was a long way on horseback for a man approaching sixty. Probably he did not arrive until shortly before Easter Sunday, though there can be no doubt about the cordiality of the reunion of the two friends when Languet dismounted at Wechel's doorstep. Once they had a chance to sit down to talk, Sidney would promptly have told Languet his important news: instructions had come from the Earl of Leicester for Sidney to return directly to England via Antwerp. This meant a change in plans; he could neither visit Lobbet in Strasbourg nor take the route through Burgundy and Paris.

CHAPTER 16

The sudden change in Sidney's plans is revealed in a letter written on the Wednesday after Easter (Lobbet to Sidney on April 6, 1575, in the newly recovered series), thus the young man must have received his instructions to return promptly to England at the height of the holy season. Lobbet's letter is very specific but does not provide the name of Leicester's emissary.

Sir,

I wrote to you last on the seventeenth of last month, addressing the letter to Frankfurt. I trust it was delivered to you. Since then I have lived in continual hope that you would visit this town: partly because you wrote that you would, and also because I was told so by Master Languet. I was confirmed in my hope by Master Hubert de la Rose, who has returned here.

However, Master Mentetheus, a learned man who recently spoke with you at Frankfurt, arrived here yesterday and put me in some doubt about your coming. For, although he admits having found you well disposed to come, he told me that on his way through Heidelberg he spoke to an English secretary who told him that he had been commanded by the Earl of Leicester to bring you back directly to England with the greatest possible speed, indeed without even going through France.

This, Sir, is the reason why I am writing to you, taking the opportunity offered by the passage of one of your servants who is on his way to you: to ask you (in case you might not wish to come and see us) to take the trouble to write me a brief note, informing me of your departure. Also, please tell me what should be done with the young son of Doctor Thaddeus, who has been awaiting you and is still doing so, with all respect and great devotion. So far as I am concerned, Sir, you may dispose of me as of one who bears you the greatest affection and is entirely at your service: and rest assured that your absence has in no way diminished my humble affection for you but has, on the contrary, increased it incomparably. I present my humble respects to your benevolence, and pray God,

Sir, to keep you in His own. From Strasbourg, this sixth of April,
1575.

Your humble servant,

J. L.

Although the "English secretary" is not named, undoubtedly he was
Thomas Wilkes, Clerk of the Council, who had been selected by Elizabeth's government to go to Heidelberg and negotiate agreements with
Frederick III, the Elector Palatine, for a loan to assist the Huguenots under
the Prince of Condé. The instructions given to Wilkes ended with the
official excuse which he was to make for his presence in Heidelberg, in
order to conceal his true mission:

> As the Queen would have this matter as secretly used as may be,
> she would have the occasion of his journey known to be for the meet-
> ing with Philip Sidney; yet when he shall come to the Count Palatine
> he shall require him to let it be understood that his coming is about a
> certain horrid damnable book lately made in Germany, entitled
> against Moses, Christ, and Muhomet, and to require him that the
> same may be condemned and punished as so unspeakable and devilish
> attempt may be vanquished and suppressed.[1]

Sidney, Languet, and other eminent friends understood the true purpose
of Wilkes's errand and also that Sidney had instructions from Leicester to
accompany Wilkes back to England, but they would not have known that
Sidney was formally named in Burghley's official instructions to Wilkes.
Nor have previous writers on Sidney shown an awareness of this circumstance. Wilkes's first dispatch from Heidelberg is dated March 30, which
fits the time of Lobbet's report almost exactly. Wilkes expected to complete
his mission in time to depart on April 7.[2] Accordingly, Sidney bade
farewell to Languet, Wechel, de Banos, and other intimate friends in
Frankfurt and hastened at once to join Wilkes in Heidelberg.

Information on Sidney's movements occurs in Lobbet's next letter,
written on April 7.

Sir,

I wrote to you yesterday, the sixth of this month, and despatched
the letter to Master Mont. Since then—today—I received a letter

1. *CSPF2*, p. 17. The book was *De tribus impostoribus*, and attributed to one J. M.
Lucas.
2. *CSPF2*, p. 38.

from Master Languet dated the third of this month. He tells me that
you are not passing by here as you are obliged to return directly to
England, without going much out of your way. You can imagine how
chagrined I am, and how sad it makes me. For if ever I wished for
something, it was to see you again and to place myself at your service,
as well as to converse with you on divers matters which are difficult
to treat in letters. One of the things I intended to ask you was how—
if it so pleased you—we could write to each other, i.e. where you
would be living. But as your pressing business renders it inconvenient
to you to come here, and as my affairs make me unable to come and
meet you (which I would have been delighted to do), I shall have to
be patient and leave the rest to God.

Fortunately, Languet's letter to Lobbet had solved the problem of what he
was to do with young Johannes Hájek, whom Sidney had generously
offered to take to England under his protection. Lobbet's relief is manifest.

Master Languet sent me twenty écus to defray the expenses incurred here by the son of Doctor Hájek, and told me to send the boy
to you at once, either by boat to Master Wechel at Frankfurt, or, if
there is no boat, by hired horse to Heidelberg. The letter was only
delivered to me at 10 A.M. today. He told me that you would be at
Heidelberg all this week until next Sunday. Things were somewhat
awkward because time was so short: everything had to be done at
once. However, one must make a virtue of necessity: I did the
best, or the least bad, I could.

I was unable to find a boat going to Frankfurt, so I thought I
would send him straight to you at Heidelberg, directing him (in
accordance with Master Languet's instructions) to Doctor Ursinus,
professor of theology at the University there. And as the shortness of
the time did not let me furnish him with a carriage or even a horse,
I found him a messenger, a citizen of this town, who will gently
take him to Heidelberg on foot. I have made a bargain with the said
messenger, and have paid him in full or will do so. I have also given
the boy twenty golden florins and one florin in change for the journey.

For the rest, Sir, I commend the child to your care as best I can,
and pray you, for his father's sake, to have him well instructed in
letters and manners. He has a promising nature, and it is to be hoped
that in time he will be able to be of service to you. I present my
humble respects to your benevolence, and pray God,

Sir, to keep you in his own. From Strasbourg this seventh of April, 1575. Please forgive haste.

Your humble servant,

J. Lobbet

Of Sidney's activities during his brief visit in Heidelberg little is known. Judging from Lobbet's instructions to address him care of Dr. Ursinus. Sidney may have stayed with that learned man, but Ursinus may merely have been someone who would certainly know where Sidney could be found. After his arrival, Sidney wrote a letter back to de Banos in Frankfurt, sending him a gift, presumably of money. De Banos replied at once.

I expected, most excellent sir, that you would return to us for a short while, so that I should once more be granted the opportunity to enjoy your highly delightful and learned conversation. For while it is true that your letter is as the image of the absent man, yet the wisdom of the present man, when heard from his own lips, fires us with an amazing love for you and declares that, though endowed with all the trappings of nobility, you yourself are nobler still. For a noble name without virtue is a cloak for duplicity, but joined to virtue it is an ornament for the inner as well as for the outer man.

Indeed, it is the recollection of that virtue in you, as well as of your wisdom, which ensures that, while I should have cherished you had you come, I shall never cease to love and honour you in your absence. However, my very pen blushes at the bounty of your present. For what comes to mind is not so much the saying concerning the philosopher's refusal of Alexander's wealth, but rather the one about it being more blessed to give than to receive! Yet your singular benevolence impels me to concentrate on manifest gratitude rather than on mere bashfulness, and I accept this kindness of yours as a token of your love for me.

In return de Banos sent Sidney a ring. He also reiterated his promise to dedicate to Sidney the important volume he was preparing for the press, *Petri Rami Commentariorum de Religione Christiana Libri Quatuor*. Like most authors and editors, de Banos was overly optimistic about when his work would be published, for instead of its being in the hands of the public in the autumn of 1575 the volume appeared in the following spring.

In return I beg you to accept and keep by you this ring from your friend Théophile, as a token of his eternal esteem. With regard to the

Commentaries I shall fulfill my promise and see to it that, with your approval (for that is best) they are ready by the time of the next Fair. Farewell, most admirable Sidney, and may you live long and happily for the good of Christ's Church and the State of England. From Frankfurt, the fourteenth of April, 1575.

Yours most respectfully,
Théophile de Banos

Two days later de Banos wrote again; this time he took the precaution of sending his letter to Cologne, through which Sidney and Wilkes would pass on their way to Antwerp. With it he sent a book, apparently the octavo titled *La Déclaration et protestation de Monseigneur de Dampville . . . avec la protestation des églises refformées de France, assemblées à Millau en Ronvergue, sur les troubles de presant* (Strasbourg, 1575). Presumably the earlier work of the same author was *La response faicte par le Mareschal de Montmorency . . .* (Paris, 1565).

I fear, most excellent sir, that this letter may reach you later or at a less convenient time than I could wish: however, I had rather face that danger than in any way neglect my duty of friendship. And so please accept Master Dampville's new work, greatly like the first in that it pertains to the cause of unity, but in some things new and in a few, different.

News from Paris follows: Henry III was trying to hold on to the throne of Poland despite his accession to that of France.

The ambassadors of peace sent by Condé to the King, sixty horsemen in German apparel, entered Paris on April sixth not without the admiration and clamour of the populace. Marshal Bellegarde, who, with Pibrac, will travel through Germany to the Polish Diet, is being sent to justify the absence of the King, who is excessively occupied with the French troubles; but he [i.e. the King] is promising on oath to hasten to Cracow as soon as the quarrels among his people are settled.

De Banos then mentions a pamphlet by Pierre Charpentier (d. 1612), *Pium et christianum de armis consilium*, which had been published at Lyons in 1575. Finally, he provides early confirmation that Edward Wotton, Sidney's intimate friend since the winter together in Vienna, was travelling with him.

In the meantime, a pamphlet in Latin has been published by Charpentier, the slave and flatterer of the Queen Mother, which clearly shows what hopes the French may henceforth have of a Valois peace. It would have given me great pleasure to send it to you: but as the nobleman who gave it to me to read was on his way to the court of the Emperor, he could not spare it. If it can be bought I shall take care to have it sent to you before you leave Antwerp. Farewell: and may you and your noble travelling companions, especially Master Wotton, enjoy a long and happy life. Frankfurt-am-Main, the sixteenth of April, 1575.

Yours most respectfully,
Théophile de Banos

Once the travellers reached Antwerp Sidney had leisure to write letters, though only one is known to have survived. Addressed to his close friend the Count of Hanau, it reveals the surprising possibility that while in Frankfurt Sidney may not have seen him, though his seat at Hanau was only twelve miles away. Indeed Sidney and his entourage must have passed through Hanau on their route from Dresden to Frankfurt, but apparently they did not halt for a visit with his Lordship. Nor is there any indication that the Count came into Frankfurt during the Easter Fair. Sidney's letter is dated May third.

Sir,

Since on my way back I did not, as I had promised, visit your Highness, I earnestly entreat you to excuse me; I was compelled to travel with such haste, by the command of my Queen and my family, that not only could I by no means perform this particular duty that I owe you, but I could not even allow for the illness with which I was severely afflicted. Therefore I beg you, as earnestly as I can, to understand that my feelings towards you, either because of your virtues or because of a certain quality of your mind, are so strong that I would not only have performed this duty gladly, and indeed would have considered it a pleasure rather than an obligation due to your rank, but also I would have found no task whatsoever so arduous that I would not joyfully have done it out of love for you.

Tomorrow I leave for England, where if you should wish to judge any work I could do for you worthy, as it were, of your service, or useful in any way, then I will at last believe that you are fully returning to me the love I have for you. There is no news here, except (and this is not new) that the Prince of Orange carries on his administration with the greatest circumspection in all things. The chances of peace are minimal. You see how hurriedly I write: I hope you will forgive me. I pray fervently to the Lord God that he will long keep your Highness from harm. Antwerp, May 3, 1575.

Your Highness' most devoted servant,

Philip Sidney

If I had had enough time I would have written to A. Welsperg; I would be grateful if you could be so kind as to make my excuses to him on these grounds and give him my warmest greetings.

For some reason Sidney and his party did not sail as planned on May 4. Unfavourable winds could have postponed departure for a day or two, but their delay of three weeks must have had another cause. That illness was not the reason we learn from one of Lobbet's Strasbourg friends, Georg Zölcher, an agent of the Elector Palatine. Sidney sent greetings to Lobbet through Zölcher, who reported that Sidney seemed to be in good health. The party did not sail until late in May, for Sidney used the words "ultimo Maii" to describe the date of his arrival in England, though he made no complaint about the delay. The letter Sidney wrote containing this information was also addressed to the Count of Hanau. Dated June 12, it reads:

Excellent Sir:

On my return to my country, my first duty is to acquaint your Excellency of the fact without delay. I have received such strong indications of your regard for me that I am glad to believe you will be pleased to hear of any good that may befall me. On the last day of May, a fair wind wafted me to this our island nest, where I found all my family well, and the Queen, though somewhat advanced in years, yet hitherto vigorous in her health, which (as it is God's will that our safety should hang on so frail a thread), is with good reason earnestly commended to the care of Almighty God in the prayers of our people. She is to us a Meleager's brand; when it perishes, farewell to all our quietness.

But to pass from this subject, I most earnestly assure you that, wherever I may be, I am unchanged in the strong and faithful affection with which I regard you. I will no longer detain your Excellency, for I have no news to communicate. I only beg that I may be heartily commended to that good and wise gentleman, Paul von Welsperg;

and although I know that his worth and your good sense render this unnecessary, yet I must ask permission to recommend him to your regard, Farewell.

Your most devoted,
Philip Sidney

London, June 12, 1575.

To his Excellency, Philip Louis, Count of Hanau, my much respected friend at Frankfurt.

No doubt Sidney's report that he found his family well understated the rapture that his parents, his brother Robert, and his sister Mary felt at welcoming him back after three eventful years. His letters to them must have shown the same growth in maturity and comprehension which shine from those which have been preserved. His own health, judging from Zölcher's report from Antwerp and Sidney's flurry of epistolary energy immediately after his return, must have reassured his family that their worries over his recent illnesses could now be dismissed.

Sidney's father, Sir Henry, stood like a rock of reliability, despite the waves which buffeted any man who accepted great responsibilities under the Queen. In 1571 he had escaped from his post as Lord Deputy of Ireland, and, since then, he had merely administered the government of Wales in his capacity as Lord President. For four years Sir Henry had been a relatively happy man, only relatively happy, however, for his position required a drain on his personal funds to supplement those supplied by her Majesty's government. This fitted Elizabeth's usual practice of milking the resources of her loyal career men, and Sir Henry's sacrifices contrasted sharply with the rewards granted to Leicester and other court favourites.

Yet Sir Henry found the inhabitants of Wales willing to cooperate, a welcome change from the ever turbulent factions in Ireland. This cooperation led to successful, efficient, and just government, which yielded Sir Henry the pride of accomplishment. As he wrote of Wales to Walsingham some years later, "A happy place of government it is, for a better people to govern, or better subjects to their sovereign, Europe holdeth not."[3]

Aside from the pleasure of watching her two sons and her older daughter Mary become adults of whom the Dudley family could justly be proud

---

3. Sir Henry Sidney to Walsingham, Mar. 1, 1583; and quoted also by Wallace, p. 149.

(their Sidney blood gave them stability and sustained intellectual powers), Lady Sidney seems to have spent her life weathering a succession of sad experiences. She had seen her father follow his father to the Tower and to the block; a brother and a sister-in-law (Lady Jane Grey) had also died on the scaffold. Her husband, the model of loyalty, quiet ability, and dedicated service to the state, had never received compensation to equal his out-of-pocket expenses. When Elizabeth had finally offered Sir Henry a mere barony, Lady Sidney, the daughter of the Duke who once controlled England, had to write the letter declining this meagre honour on the practical ground that they could not afford the title without lands to support it.

In addition to their lack of appreciation for Sir Henry's efforts, the Queen and her officials did not seem to value Lady Sidney's services at the court. True, the Queen had visited her when she was convalescing from the smallpox, but court officials assigned inadequate rooms to her, and income for her duties dwindled to a trickle. At least, so Lady Sidney's letters, still preserved among state papers, set forth. The strain on family finances was a source of grief for the Sidneys but an even greater sorrow was the death at Ludlow in February of their youngest child, Ambrosia, then in her tenth year. That sad event prompted Queen Elizabeth to write Sir Henry a genuinely touching letter of condolence, in which personal compassion seems to have prompted her to change the original salutation, "Right trusty and well beloved," to the simple "Good Sidney." Elizabeth's letter deserves repeating here.

> Good Sidney:
>
> Although we are well assured that by your wisdom and great experience of worldly chances and necessities, nothing can happen unto you so heavy but you can and will bear them as they ought to be rightly taken, and, namely, such as happen by the special appointment and work of Almighty God which He hath lately showed by taking unto Him from your company a daughter of yours, yet, forasmuch as we conceive the grief you yet feel thereby, as in such cases natural parents are accustomed, we would not have you ignorant (to ease your sorrow as much as may be) how we take part of your grief upon us, whereof these our letters unto you are witness, and will use no further persuasions to confirm you respecting the good counsel yourself can take of yourself but to consider that God doth nothing evil, to whose holy will all is subject and must yield at times to us uncertain.

He hath yet left unto you the comfort of one daughter of very good hope, whom, if you shall think good to remove from those parts of unpleasant air (if it be so) into better in these parts, and will send her unto us before Easter, or when you shall think good, assure yourself that we will have a special care of her, not doubting but as you are well persuaded of our favour toward yourself, so will we make further demonstration thereof in her, if you will send her unto us.

And so comforting you for the one, and leaving this our offer of our goodwill to your own consideration for the other, we commit you to Almighty God.[4]

Philip's only surviving sister was fourteen years old, Mary, later Countess of Pembroke, who inspired the *Arcadia* and the literary creations of many other young men. From the time of her appearance at court in response to this invitation from the Queen, Mary Sidney's beauty and fresh spirit were widely praised. The Sidneys also had reason to be proud of Philip's younger brother Robert, who was then only eleven. Sir Henry and his wife were already planning Robert's further education, for in that era able boys of his age were ready to be sent off to Oxford or Cambridge. The question of where Robert would study was deferred until Philip's return, so that he could be consulted about whether or not his brother should follow him to Christ Church, Oxford.

The subject was promptly discussed with Philip, and soon after arriving in London he wrote a letter to his former tutor Dr. Robert Dorsett,[5] now a canon of Christ Church. Sidney sent the faithful Griffin Madox to deliver the letter in which, besides commending his younger brother's character and love of study, he recommended two other prospective pupils, the first being his young cousin, Edward Montagu,[6] who had been chosen to be Robert's companion in education. The other young man was Sidney's special charge, the Czech Johannes Hájek. Sidney had become

4. State Papers Domestic, Warrantbook, 1 : 83, Public Record Office.

5. After taking his B.A. degree in Feb., 1564/5, Dorsett became a canon in 1572 and rector of Ewelme in 1574. In 1579 he became Dean of Chester, but died in the following year.

6. Born in 1562, the second son of Sir Edward Montagu of Boughton Castle, Northants, he received his B.A. on Mar. 14, 1578/9. Created first Baron Montagu of Boughton in 1621, he served for many years as Lord-lieutenant of Northamptonshire and as a member of Parliament. A devoted Royalist, he had several brushes with the Parliamentary forces before his death in 1644. Ringler (p. 538) has described a manuscript copy of *Astrophil and Stella* bearing the arms of Baron Montagu of Boughton, and he now suggests that Montagu may have obtained it with the help of Robert Sidney.

his sponsor both because of innate generosity and out of admiration for the boy's eminent father, Dr. Thaddeus Hájek.

Our knowledge of Sidney's letter, written about June 1, derives from Dorsett's answer of June 3. Written in the Ciceronian and often exaggerated style which Sidney had now come to deprecate, Dorsett's letter begins with this effusive passage:

> Upon your return in splendour, most noble and even more beloved Philip, I have a double duty: to thank you and to offer you my congratulations. The gratitude that overcame me is witnessed by my prayers to almighty God, in which I revere Him for your well-being and high rank, and which will not cease in my mind to encompass you till my dying day. The congratulations, which would need several rather than one of my letters to contain them, must wait until a time more suited to their contemplation: I should have preferred to express them in person, so that you might have seen the love and honour I felt for you not only in my words—which may perhaps have been overcome with joy and thus be less accurate—but also in my mien, my eyes, and countenance.

Although Dorsett continues in the same vein, he does reveal that Sidney had already made an appearance at court where he had been given a warm reception.

> Indeed, when I received that most excellent news (which your Griffin was the first to bring me) of your well-received and honoured entrance at court, believe me, I was transported with delight. For why should I not glory in the fact that you have been restored to me—you, with whom my spirit has been bound up all my life, and will be until the end; you, to whose great goodness I not only confess but rejoice to be quite devoted? But such things can wait.

Evidently Sidney had asked Dorsett to take charge of the three young men, and Dorsett had prudently brought in his colleague, John Buste,[7] also well known to Sidney. Buste seems to have been a reliable but rather pedestrian person, who could easily take on day-to-day responsibility for the three well-born young men.

---

7. Buste had been Dorsett's schoolmate, matriculating with him and taking his degree in the same year. He served as proctor in 1574.

Now I come to your brother, whom in your remarkable letter you commend to me; I shall cherish him, because he is your brother, because he is worthy of you, and because I cannot but love him for his dedication to integrity and to the study of letters. And therefore, since you are turning him and your other kinsman over to my tutelage, I shall surely take great pains to do all that is in my power to teach him, in fulfilment of your wishes: and in this matter I will always be guided by your advice.

Your friend Buste, who last year served as a remarkable proctor of this University (where, considering the resources available, he managed the finances in no mean way), is joining me in taking charge of this teaching business: he has confirmed my previous experience of his trustworthiness in all things.

Because the financial decisions about Robert would have to be made by his father, Dorsett had written directly to Sir Henry about them; perhaps he expected him to pass the information along to Montagu's father also. But Hájek was Philip's liability, and Philip seems to have been unaware of the financial requirements at Oxford. Indeed, Sidney's blithe assumptions about monetary facts of life are one of his most engaging characteristics, though a source of frequent miscalculation during his short lifetime.

The rest I have written to your most noble father, and told your man Griffin, so that he may let you know in person. As regards that other lad, the German, he is most welcome for your sake, and I shall make sure that all such funds as you consider necessary are spent on him. Please let me know, therefore, if you have a moment (either by letter or message) what his position among us should be. For as regards the allowance you so earnestly desire him to be given: Griffin will tell you how difficult a matter this is unless you send more funds—he will explain more clearly.

Dorsett, constantly active in academic politics, now seized the opportunity to try to get high-level support for his candidate for the Deanship, the chief office at Christ Church. Tobias Matthew, who maintained his canon's stall there even though he had become President of its affiliate, St. John's College, had been nominated. An attractive person and eloquent preacher, Matthew had come to the attention of Queen Elizabeth, who appointed him one of her chaplains-in-ordinary and granted him various cathedral offices. Other canons at Christ Church looked with distaste on the prospect of Matthew's becoming their Dean, for they saw him as a "shameless if reverend place seeker."[8] Their candidate, another Christ Church man, was Dr. William James, then Master of University College. Dorsett now tried to get Sidney to influence Leicester.

> Matthew's appointment to the Deanship is not yet finally decided. For this reason he is earnestly collecting friendships at court. On his home ground, however, I know he is not getting the votes of the prebendaries and students: and if my brother and I had not sought to keep the peace in this business, our whole House would long since have devoted its energies to a contrary petition in favour of your friend James. He, I make bold to say, is bettered by Matthew neither in age, nor in rank, nor in experience, knowledge of leadership, erudition, labour expended in the spreading of the Gospel, services to our most noble Lord the Earl, goodwill among the University or our House, nor finally in integrity or purity of life; he is exceeded by him only in fluency, in the art of currying favour, and consequently in strength of support. If, therefore, you would let us know what you think you could do in this matter, we will surely add to your opinion and effort the moral support and testimony of all of us.
>
> Master Piers[9] also, our present Dean, who has asked me to greet you warmly from him, urgently requests that, when you have been to court, you will further advise him; so that (as he promises) he may help you as far as he can to strike, if possible, a blow against that "safe" petition. I know that among noble men and women you will find many who favour James. However, if you act for us, God will see to that.

How much Sidney tried to help Dr. James we do not know; Tobias Matthew became the new Dean and held the position for nine years until he left for higher offices in the church which culminated in his elevation to the Archbishopric of York. Then the turn of Dr. James finally came, and in 1584 he was elected Matthew's successor. He also became chaplain to the Earl of Leicester, so Sidney's recommendation may have worked to James's ultimate benefit.

Sidney's answer to Dorsett has not been preserved, though Dorsett's reply reveals that Sidney reported being ill during the middle of June.

8. Sir John Neale, *Essays in Elizabethan History* (London, 1958), p. 64.

9. John Piers left this position at Christ Church when elevated to the Bishopric of Rochester in 1576.

Meanwhile, Robert Sidney and Edward Montagu had arrived at Oxford, and Dorsett's remarks on them occupy most of his letter dated June 21.

> The greatness of the power of brotherly love, most noble Philip, is shown by the recent letter you so carefully and kindly wrote me. However, I consider us most fortunate in having your most excellent brother with us: for while we must needs have loved him no matter what kind of person he was, now he has joined us we find him to be one whom it is a pleasure to receive with every affection. For together with a quite polished mind he shows such gentle and moderate ways, combined with a remarkable spirit and such delicate courtesy, that it would clearly require a stony heart not to welcome such a balanced, gentle, and tender nature. Therefore I declare and promise you that I will take the greatest care to cultivate in him such a spirit as you would wish to see, and as he should have: indeed, I shall not depart an inch from your judgement and counsel.
>
> Although Montagu seems to you a little less polished, yet if in the very short time I have known him his modest bearing, his voice, and his face may prompt a guess, he has no wildness in him, either by nature or by habit: and I do not doubt that, if Christ favours our undertaking, we will so apply our efforts, care, and industry to both, that you will consider your desire, their interests, and the office we promised to perform and were entrusted with to have been fulfilled in rich abundance.

At Sidney's request Dorsett had prodded young Robert into writing him. Of special interest is the fact that at Philip's explicit urging Robert and Edward Montagu were given supervised training in physical exercises, such as throwing the javelin.

> In the meantime we will keep you informed of our news from day to day, in such a way that your own energetic presence may seem to prompt our labours. I enclose a letter from your brother, because you wanted one; it is unmistakably his. Judge it indulgently: practice will make future ones more fluent.
>
> For the time being hopes of physical improvement will have to be moderate: later, when there is an opportunity, they will throw the javelin more often. The rest of the precepts in your letter we shall diligently follow.

Dorsett closes with copious compliments and promises to send another letter by the hand of an unidentified dignitary who will soon be coming to the court.

> For your recovery from illness we thank God our Governor, as we clearly should; and we pray humbly and modestly that He may be favourable towards you, in this as in all matters—which I shall tell you plainly in my next letter, when our Master ——— comes to court. However, because you communicate your love and remarkable benevolence to me on so many occasions, I do indeed return all I received before, so that I may be able to respond to a great part of your kindness towards me by presenting, or at least feeling, my necessary gratitude. And it will give me the greatest pleasure some time to see an occasion on which, in return for your most ample benefits to me, I shall be able to help you and yours with all the zeal and effort at my command.
>
> I do not want to trouble you longer; meanwhile, accept the greetings of my brother, James, Buste, and many others. And so, farewell: and I hope that we shall see you there, as you will see us here. Oxford, June 21, 1575.
>
> Yours in utmost devotion to your name,
>
> Robert Dorsett

For the rest of June little evidence exists of how Sidney may have occupied himself. That he was warmly received at court he himself testified in letters to friends on the Continent, and doubtless he spent much time there, basking in the attention which a recent arrival receives from the seekers of news and novelty. Probably he had sessions with both Burghley and Walsingham, his host in Paris after the horrors of St. Bartholomew's Day. Walsingham would have been eager for reports on Languet and other friends. Indeed, Walsingham hoped so strongly for a Protestant League that he would have questioned Sidney closely on affairs in Saxony, Prague, Frankfurt, and Heidelberg. The manner in which Sidney had matured and blossomed both socially and intellectually should have pleased Walsingham, to whom Sidney had been recommended three years earlier as "young and raw," one who would "find those countries and the demeanours of the people somewhat strange." Philip's opinions and experiences were now of interest to men in high places.

Sometime during this month Sidney received letters from friends abroad. One came from Lobbet who had written on May 31. It begins with

Lobbet's pleasure at having heard news of Sidney at Antwerp and his relief that Johannes Hájek was now safely in Sidney's charge.

> Sir,
>
> I waited with my answer to the letter you were pleased to write to me from Heidelberg on the tenth of last month, until you should finish your journey. This I hope you have by now done and have, with God's help, safely arrived in London. Mr. Zölcher, a citizen of this town, told me he had seen you at Antwerp in excellent health and humour, which greatly pleased me: as did also the kind greeting you sent me via him, which I received with such joy and humility that I shall always be delighted to be able to be of service to you.
>
> To reply to your letter, I most humbly thank you for having so kindly received the son of Master Thaddeus and for your kind willingness to have him learn virtue and all good things. I have let his father know, who will naturally be most grateful to you. I beg you, Sir, to continue this intention and to put it into practice. I am writing a brief letter of credentials for the boy, which I beg you to let him have.

Lobbet continues by proposing that they maintain a correspondence. The practicalities of such an exchange had to be worked out.

> For the rest, Sir, when I think that you have returned to England without my having had the good fortune to see you, I can scarcely contain my chagrin. However, to lessen the pain I have found this device: I shall occasionally, if it please you, greet you by letter. And until I know your will in regard to this, I shall not presume to write to you frequently. If you like it this way, and if you are pleased with the letters which I can write to you often, sending them will not be difficult. All that is needed is for you to let me know to whom you wish me to despatch the letters in Antwerp that they may be sent to you.
>
> I have a friend at Brussels called Doctor Rana, a well-known German, to whom I shall send my letters, and who will have them taken to Antwerp and delivered to whomever you name. And on your side, when you are pleased to write to me in return, you should tell your man in Antwerp to send your letter to the said Doctor Rana at Brussels: this will not be difficult for him, as at Antwerp there are many German merchants who know the said Rana.

You might also let me know in which language you prefer me to write to you: in Latin, French, or Italian. Finally would you put on a piece of paper for me the title by which I should address you and your address in London.

Lobbet's account of affairs in France reveals that the unfortunate Guy du Faur, Sire of Pibrac, was having troubles on his errand to the Diet of Stezyca in Poland.

I am not sending you any news of France, nor of the Netherlands, as you are nearer to its sources than I am. M. de Pibrac who was sent to Poland by the King together with the Marshal de Bellegarde (who has left for Italy) was robbed near Montbelliard, and two of his men killed, by a certain Captain Brissac. This man took his money and his letters of attorney, and then let him go. Pibrac reequipped himself with all he needed and is now on his way again, making haste to be in Poland in time for the Diet about to be held there. It is being said that at that Diet there will be more to discuss than was previously thought. The Turk is said not to be treating his subjects so kindly as had been hoped. A few days ago it was said that he was dead. "Je ne le crois pas."

In Genoa quarrels had again broken out between the old and the new nobility. This situation afforded a beneficial opportunity for outside powers, so Philip of Spain ordered Don John to go there. The Pope in turn sent his veteran troubleshooter Cardinal Giovanni Morone to make peace between the factions. The topic recurs repeatedly in reports from the Continent, including those to Sidney from his friends.

The late troubles among the Genoese are in no way diminished as yet. There are plenty of windfalls for the papal ambassador. Near Augsburg two or three regiments of Lansquenets are being fitted out to be sent to Italy. Part of this force might be employed for these troubles. Don John of Austria was being awaited in Italy.

Further, the most dreadful ill omens are being seen. I was told that at Genoa there have been three earth tremors in one day, viz. the twenty-fourth of last month: in the evening at ten, eleven, and twelve o'clock, and after that fiery shapes were seen above the town. At Würzburg (which in Latin is called Herbipolita [sic]—it is a diocesan city in Franconia) on the sixth of this month three suns were seen, of which the main one was the colour of blood; also a [illegible] was seen in the air, much shaken and agitated; also a headless bishop spurting great streams of blood from his torso; also many Turkish hats or turbans, all of fire. One might philosophize endlessly on it all, but that I shall leave to those who are wiser than I.

I present my humble respects to your benevolence, and pray God, Sir, to keep you in His own. From Strasbourg, this last day of May, 1575.

> Your humble servant,
> J. Lobbet

Another letter came to Sidney from Théophile de Banos. Written from Cologne on May 26, it reveals that before leaving Frankfurt he had heard from Sidney.

I received your last letter, most noble Sir, on the very day that I intended to leave Frankfurt for Cologne; but before leaving I saw to it that it would be delivered to the Count of Hanau and Master Languet as soon as possible, and I know that it will have brought them great happiness. For the latter had written a short time before to ask me, should I have any news of you, not to fail to send it to him; and the former was surprised that you had not written. We were all afraid that you might have passed away. So it is with great pleasure that I give thanks to God who watched over your journey and your health: and I pray that He will long preserve you among your family and friends.

De Banos was suffering as a result of the religious troubles in France. Once he had sent his *Commentaries* to the printer, he attempted to visit his family there, but was prevented by new religious oppressions.

As far as I am concerned, there is only the following. I had decided to leave for France, to go and greet my family and survey my affairs. (For as an exile of Christ I have already tolerated—not to use worse terms—the German way of life for nearly seven years.) But today I heard that the ambassadors of the Prince of Condé and of the Churches have gone home empty-handed and that the war in France is flaring up again, far worse than before: and so, disappointed, I am staying here and do not know what to do—only that I refuse to start on a dubious journey and to plunge foolhardily into the midst of armed hosts. Tomorrow I am leaving for Aix-la-Chapelle, and I will travel as far as Antwerp to find out what I can; but if more is impossible I shall return to Frankfurt, commending myself and my affairs to God.

Before I left there, I had given the *Commentaries* of Peter Ramus to Wechel, the printer, to have them printed at my own expense. I have prefaced it with a life of that illustrious man, in which I describe his philosophical studies, his habits (of body and soul), the dangers he suffered for his religion, and finally his noble death; and I am dedicating it to your Excellency. I hope by the time of the next Fair to send quite a few copies to England, but first of all to yourself in whose name they are being published.

The rest of the letter is taken up with political events.

There is almost no news to give you. In Germany all is peaceful and calm. There is this: the date for the Frankfurt Diet to elect a King of the Romans has been set for the end of July. But it seems there are various hindrances, and many think that the Diet will be put off until the winter.

Matters French are (no doubt) reaching you more quickly and surely than I could relay them. This one thing I will add: the Duke of Lorraine has left for Paris with three hundred horse, to marry the widow of the late King. The Prince of Orange is marrying the daughter of Montpensier, who is staying at Heidelberg with the [Elector] Palatine because of her religion, and will shortly pass through here on his way to Holland.

Farewell, most noble Sir, and love me as hitherto. From Cologne, May 26, 1575.

Yours most respectfully,
Théophile de Banos

To my most honoured master, the noble and illustrious Philip Sidney, of the great family of the Earls of Warwick, at London.

Towards the end of June Sidney received a very full account of Continental news from Languet, in a fat letter written on June 12 in Prague. The personal passages in the letter are also ample. Languet begins by describing the pain he felt at parting from Sidney in Frankfurt.

I seek relief from whatever source I can for the great distress which your departure has caused me; but the remedies I apply aggravate rather than soothe it. Whenever I think how very kind you were to endure all the annoyances you had to suffer while we lived together, for you did not receive the consideration you deserved, I am entirely overcome with distress, knowing that your goodwill toward me is what subjected you to these annoyances.

I made my recent journey to Frankfurt to offer you my humble services, since I was afraid that your people would not take enough thought for you, but no opportunity presented itself there of doing anything to please you. I of course fed my soul with my last look at you, and I took the greatest pleasure in that opportunity; however, the same thing happened to me as usually happens to one who eagerly drinks cold water when he is burning with fever, for that brief pleasure very greatly aggravated my distress, and made it more incurable.

Languet then discusses the nature of their correspondence and openly admits that his purpose had been to foster the habit of writing in Sidney. Their future exchanges must have a different basis.

There remained to me a slight hope of some relief in your parting promise that you would arrange with someone at Antwerp to take charge of sending your letters on to me, or mine to you, and that you would let me know his name. But I see that I am bereft even of hope, for I have not received a letter from you besides the brief one you sent me from Heidelberg. Perhaps you were afraid that I would belabour you with frequent letters and too insistently demand an-swers to them, as I used to do while you were living in Italy. I was playing with you at that time, in order to stimulate you to write, since I thought that the habit of writing would greatly benefit your studies.

But now you are leading a far different sort of life. I know that the court is not at all a thrifty steward of time. I know that you will have to accommodate yourself to friends and relatives, who wish to enjoy your delightful company, and that you will have to wait upon those whom it is customary for young men to wait upon because of their age and rank. Therefore, since I know that you were not greatly charmed by letter writing while you had more leisure, I am sure that these frequent interruptions by friends will readily succeed in making you write either seldom or never.

That Sidney was consciously preparing himself for a future career in statecraft may be glimpsed in his thirst for knowledge about European politics.

Of course, I do not wish to write you so frequently, or send you idle and teasing letters, as I did formerly. Instead, I had decided to write you about public affairs and hoped that letters on this subject would not displease you, for I realized that you have an unusual desire for information on the nations with which we have some contact, and on the changes occurring there. And since this desire is most praiseworthy, and quite necessary to those who are to take up statecraft, no one will easily convince me that you have wholly divested yourself of it.

If you had replied: "I have received your letter," "I am enjoying good health," "I shall shortly take a wife," or something of the sort, I would have thought I had been given ample satisfaction. Or if you had not been disposed to do even this, it would have been enough to tell your Griffin to write me these things. But, although I am committing this letter of mine to so uncertain a fate that I scarcely may hope it will reach you, I shall nevertheless write you something about Polish affairs, since I know that the minds of a great many people are intent upon their outcome.

After these personal remarks Languet launches into a long account of affairs in Poland, followed by another about the Emperor Maximilian's lack of cordiality towards the Moravian Brethren's proposals. The letter ends with another paragraph of personal comment.

But no one will prevail upon you, now that you have returned across the sea, to entrust yourself once again to the deep. The sirens of your homeland will not permit these thoughts to occur to you, even in a dream—for I do not doubt that you now shudder all over whenever you think once more of the discourtesy with which we treated you. Even though I scarcely hope that this letter of mine will reach you, I still could not restrain myself from pouring into it these foolish moods of mine, and from abusing your courtesy in my fashion. But since I can do nothing else for you, I pray almighty God that he allow you long to enjoy the prosperity of your native land, and her your virtue. Farewell, Prague, the day of the solstice 1575.

In early June, Sidney had written to Languet (as a later letter from Languet reveals) reporting his arrival in England. He also revealed that his plans for the summer had already been determined. He had been invited to accompany the court on Queen Elizabeth's "progress" and so warned

Languet not to expect any letters during the time the court was on the move. The rest of the month scarcely seemed long enough for the visits to tailors and all the other tasks necessary to refurbish the wardrobe of a young man just returned from three years on the Continent.[10]

Besides the excitement promised by the successive entertainments in the great houses to be visited by the Queen and her court, Sidney had a special pleasure in store. Now after a three-year absence he could be with his family. Sir Henry, Lady Sidney and his sister Mary were all commanded to accompany her Majesty, and Robert could join them for most of the time. Since Sir Henry had been talked into resuming the administration of Ireland as Lord Deputy, the Sidney family knew that they would not soon again enjoy the opportunity of being together.

10. For an account of Sidney's expenditures for shoes and apparel see Zouch, p. 333, and Wallace, p. 158.

CHAPTER 17

Since myriad details had to be arranged for Queen Elizabeth's progress from one great house to another, plans for her route and entertainment during the summer of 1575 were being discussed months before Sidney reached England. The Queen's visits were a mixed blessing for her hosts. That a noble's hospitality would be welcomed by her Majesty markedly raised the lucky courtier's prestige, but at the same time he knew that the food, drink, and entertainment he offered would be subject to close comparison with that provided by his peers.

The host's minimal obligation was to turn his house over to the royal party, since the Queen's household was expected to pay for the provisions and even to supply necessary furnishings. But the host's standing and subsequent place in the Queen's favour could be influenced by his contributions above this minimum. Hence a nobleman recognized the royal visit as an expensive honour, indeed as an investment in his future and that of his family which could pay off handsomely in position, power, and financial favours. Such thoughts lay behind the jewelled and elegant gifts presented to her Majesty. Little wonder that as much as £1,000 spent on entertaining the Queen and her court was considered a justifiable investment.

On her progresses in previous years Elizabeth had been attended by Leicester in his function as Master of the Horse. In this role he was responsible for requisitioning horses and carts to transport the chattels of the royal party; thus he was thoroughly experienced in the mechanics, the routine, and the standards of these migrations. The Queen had visited Leicester at Kenilworth twice since giving him the estate in 1565. In 1568 she had made an "unlooked for" stop there and in August 1572 had made a brief excursion to Kenilworth, leaving her train at Warwick. This summer Kenilworth had been chosen as a major location and Leicester resolved to outshine any of her previous hosts. By happy chance written reports by two participants in the fabulous visit have been preserved, each of which confirms and complements the other.

The first account was written by Robert Laneham (or Langham), a London mercer serving on Leicester's staff. Published later in 1575, it bears the title *A Letter Wherein part of the entertainment vntoo the Queen at*

Kenilworth Castl is signified (*STC* 15191)[1] and is addressed "Unto my good Freend, Master Humphrey Martin, Mercer." It contains some of the most delightful descriptions of the Elizabethan scene in contemporary literature. Laneham had taken careful notes of the events during the first two weeks of the Queen's visit and described them with zest and flavour. Ever since John Nichols reprinted Laneham's pages in *The Progresses of Queen Elizabeth* (1788), writers from Sir Walter Scott to the present have made use of his breezy style and amusing details in accounts of Elizabeth and Leicester.

Laneham himself seems to have been a choice character. After St. Paul's School and apprenticeship to a London mercer, he had spent some time on business in France and Flanders where his flair for languages had opportunity to develop. After his return he came to the attention of Leicester who seems to have been amused by Laneham's gusto, linguistic skills, and jolly personality. Leicester had him made Doorkeeper of the Council Chamber and bestowed other favours such as a licence to import beans free of charges. Here is Laneham's report of his conduct as Doorkeeper:

> Noow, syr, if the Councell sit, I am at hand, wait an inch, I warrant yoo. If any make babling, "peas!" (say I) "woot ye whear ye ar?" if I take a lystenar, or a priar in at the chinks or at the lokhole, I am by & by in the bones of him; but now they keep good order; they kno me well inough; If a be a freend, or such one az I lyke, I make him sit dooun by me on a foorm, or a cheast: let the rest walk, a God's name![2]

Leicester's favours elevated the Doorkeeper's status considerably, an obligation which Laneham took pleasure in acknowledging:

> It pleazed his honor to beare me good wil at fyrst, & so too continu. To haue giuen m' apparail, eeuen from hiz bak, to get me allowauns in the stabl, too aduauns me vntoo this worshipfull office, so neer the most honorabl Councell, to help me in my licens of Beanz (though indeed I do not so much vze it, for I thank God I need not), to permit my good Father to serue the stabl. Whearby I go

1. Edited in 1871 for The Ballad Society by F. J. Furnivall as *Captain Cox, his Ballads and Books, or Robert Laneham's Letter.* I have quoted from the original text, changing only the punctuation.
2. Laneham, *Letter*, p. 83.

Robert Dudley, Earl of Leicester

noow in my sylks, that else might ruffl in my cut canues: I ryde now a hors bak, that els many timez mighte mannage it a foot: am knoen to their honors, & taken foorth with the best, that els might be bidden to stand bak my self. . . . What say ye, my good freend Humfrey? shoold I not for euer honor, extol him, al the weyz I can? Yes, by your leaue, while God lends me poour to vtter my minde! And (hauing az good cauz of his honor, az *Virgil* had of *Augustus Cezar,*) wil I poet it a littl with *Virgill,* and say . . .

> For he shallbe a god to me, till death my life consumez:
> His auters will I sacrifice with incens and parfumez.[3]

Because Kenilworth did not have adequate facilities, most of the Queen's retinue had to be lodged five and a half miles away in Warwick, thus causing a constant stream of horse and cart service in both directions over the road between the towns. That Lady Sidney was housed in Kenilworth Castle (probably with her daughter Mary, as well as Sir Henry and Philip) we learn from the ebullient Laneham, whom Leicester had assigned to serve his sister.

In afternoons & a nights, sumtime am I . . . at my good Lady Sidneis chamber, a Noblwooman that I am az mooch boound vntoo, as ony poore man may bee vnto so gracyous a Lady: And sumtime in sum oother place; But alwayez among the Gentlwemen by my good will (O, yee kno that cum alweyez of a gentle spirite); & when I see cumpany according, than can I be az lyuely to; sumtyme I foote it with daunsing: noow with my Gittern, and els with my Cittern, then at the Virgynalz:—Ye kno nothing cums amisse to mee—then carroll I vp a song withall, that by and by they com flocking about me lyke beez too hunny: and euer they cry, "anoother, good Langham, anoother!" Shall I tell you? When I see Misterz— (A! see a madde knaue! I had almost tollde all!) that shee gyuez onz but an ey or an ear: why then, man, am I blest! my grace, my corage, my cunning iz doobled: She sayz sumtime she likez it, & then I like it mooch the better; it dooth me good to heer hoow well I can doo. And, too say truth: what, with myne eyz, az I can amoroously gloit it, with my Spanish sospires, my French heighes, mine Italian dulcets, my Dutch houez, my doobl releas, my hy reachez, my fine feyning, my deep diapason, my wanton warblz, my running, my

3. Ibid., pp. 80–81.

tyming, my tuning, and my twynkling, I can gracify the matters az
well az the prowdest of them; and waz yet neuer staynd, I thank God.
By my troth, cuntreman, it iz sumtim by midnight ear I can get
from them. And thus haue I told ye most of my trade, al the leeue
long daye: what will ye more? God saue the Queene and my
Lord![4]

The second participant in the festivities at Kenilworth who left a
detailed account of the entertainment was an equally colourful individual,
the poet George Gascoigne. Now in his mid-thirties, Gascoigne had led
a checkered career ever since his days at Trinity College, Cambridge.
Early years of extravagance at the Middle Temple and Gray's Inn were
followed by election to Parliament at the beginning of Elizabeth's reign.
Still unable to settle down, Gascoigne applied himself to translating and
adapting the plays of ancient authors.[5] In 1572, having earlier married a
prosperous widow, he again stood successfully for Parliament, though his
election was challenged by unsatisfied debtors who charged him with
atheism, manslaughter, and being "a common rymer and a devisor of
slanderous pasquils against divers persons of great calling."[6] The next
few years found Gascoigne in Holland serving as a Captain of the English
forces at Middelburg and elsewhere. He was captured by the Spaniards
and suffered four months' imprisonment.

By the autumn of 1574 he was back in England, where he issued *The
Posies of George Gascoigne Corrected and Augmented*, dated "from my poore
house at Walthamstow in the forest, 2 Feb. 1575."[7] Thus Gascoigne was
available to help write the speeches for the pageants being planned to
entertain the Queen during her three weeks as Leicester's guest. Gascoigne
wrote an account of those weeks, *The Princely Pleasures at the Courte at
Kenelwoorth. That is to saye, The Copies of all such Verses, Proses, or poetical
inuentions, and Other Deuices of Pleasure, as were there deuised, and presented
by sundry Gentlemen, before the Quene's Majestie, in the yeare* 1575.[8]

4. Ibid., pp. 84–85.
5. *The Supposes*, based on Ariosto's *Gli Suppositi*, and *Jocasta*, adapted from Euripides'
Phoenissae. Both were performed in 1566 and published in *A Hundreth Sundrie Flowers,
bounde vp in One Small Posie* (1573), *STC* 11635.
6. *Gentleman's Magazine* (1851), 2:241–44.
7. *STC* 11636. This corrected the 1573 volume issued by some of his friends during his
absence.
8. This pamphlet was "Imprinted at London by Richard Ihones, and [is] to be solde
without Newgate, ouer against St. Sepulchres Church, 1576," but only one copy of this
separate printing has ever come to light, and it was destroyed in a fire in 1879(J. W. Cunliffe,

From the reports of Laneham and Gascoigne a fairly full description of the events on each day of Elizabeth's visit can be reconstructed. Leicester was to welcome the Queen and her followers at Long Ichington, a town belonging to Leicester, ten miles southeast of Kenilworth. After travelling by way of Woodstock and Banbury the royal party reached the great marquee Leicester had had erected on his property there. Dinner was served the Queen and her attendants before they set out for Kenilworth. According to Laneham, the riders indulged in "pleasant pastime in hunting by the wey" in the ten-mile journey before they reached the gates of Kenilworth Castle about eight o'clock.

As they arrived at the tilt-yard in front of Mortimer's Tower, the weary riders had to pause for the first of the allegorical performances that were to continue daily for the next three weeks. A sibyl draped in white silk stepped out of an arbour and pronounced sixteen lines in poulter's measure. From Gascoigne we learn that "This device was invented, and the verses also written, by M. Hunneys, Master of her Majesties Chappell."[9] After this edifying pause, the Queen entered the tilt-yard where six trumpeters garbed in Arthurian costumes eight feet high greeted her with a fanfare of "huge and monstrous trompettes." Next a giant porter dressed like Hercules and carrying an enormous club and great keys stopped her Majesty; after fourteen more lines of poulter's measure he surrendered club and keys to the "soveraigne Goddess." This contribution was "devised and pronounced by Master Badger, of Oxenforde, Maister of Arte, and Bedle in the same Universitie."

But the Queen and her retinue were still not allowed to dismount and refresh themselves. On the lower lake three nymphs now appeared on a raft disguised as an island and outlined by blazing torches. One nymph who represented the Arthurian "Ladie of the Lake" addressed the Queen in seven stanzas of iambics, a welcome change from the pedestrian poulter's measure of the other speakers. "These verses were devised and penned by M. Ferrers, sometime Lord of Misrule." They ended with a misstep, the Lady of the Lake's concluding couplet: "Passe on, Madame, you need no longer stand; / The Lake, the Lodge, the Lord, are yours for to command." Laneham recorded Elizabeth's tart response: "We had

---

ed., *Complete Works of George Gascoigne*, vol. 2 [Cambridge, 1910], p. v). The text appears in the 1587 edition of Gascoigne's *Whoole Works*. For Gascoigne's part in the Kenilworth entertainments see Charles T. Prouty's *George Gascoigne, Elizabethan Courtier, Soldier, and Poet* (New York, 1942), pp. 87–90.

9. William Hunnis, Armiger (d. 1597), Master of the Children. See Nichols, 1:487–89.

thought indeed the Lake had been oours, and doo you call it yourz noow? Wel, we will heerin common more with yoo heerafter." [10]

Now, to the accompaniment of "looud muzik" played by cornets, hautboys, and shawms, the Queen and her attendants were permitted to ride across the seventy-foot-long bridge, each ten-foot section of which was lined with gifts successively symbolizing Sylvanus, Pomona, Ceres, Bacchus, Neptune, Mars, and Phoebus. But the royal party also had to hear nine lines of Latin verse [11] read by a poet, appropriately dressed in a long blue garment over a crimson silk doublet. The Queen finally entered the inner court, where she dismounted from her palfrey to the sound of "drummes, fifes, and trumpets" and entered her lodgings. Now the roar of cannon and discharge of fireworks celebrated her presence. Laneham testifies that "the noiz and flame wear heard and seene a twenty myle of." [12]

Although there is no record of Sidney's reactions to these events or of his part in them, he doubtless enjoyed them as much as any person present. Because he had been in Paris during the masques, fireworks, and great bonfires that preceded the marriage of Henry of Navarre and Marguerite of Valois, Sidney could judge the masques and revels, sports and "shewes," as well as the pyrotechnic displays, with a fuller basis for comparison than most members of the court who had not attended similar functions on the Continent. Fortunately the elegant entertainments offered by Leicester avoided the extremes Sidney had witnessed in Paris; no live cats were dropped into raging flames.

The second day, a Sunday, began quietly with services in the parish church. The afternoon offered "excelent muzik of sundry swet instruments" followed by "dauncing of Lordes and Ladiez . . . with . . . liuely agilitee & commendabl grace." [13] This gave Sidney an opportunity both to demonstrate any steps he may have learned on the Continent and to wear some of the handsome new shoes made since his return to England. The evening's entertainment consisted of more fireworks, louder and brighter than those of the previous night.

Monday, July 11, proved to be hot, so it was just as well that no events were planned until five in the afternoon when the Queen and her party rode to hounds. A hart with a splendid spread of antlers had been produced,

10. Laneham, *Letter*, pp. 10–11.
11. Written by Dr. Richard Mulcaster, Master of Merchant Taylor's School.
12. Laneham, *Letter*, p. 15.
13. Ibid.

and the pursuit provided "pastime delectabl" according to Laneham, with "the swiftness of the Deer, the running of footmen, the galloping of horsez, the blasting of hornz, the halloing and hewing of the huntsmen, with the excellent Echoz between whilez from the woods and waters in valleiz resounding."[14] The finish was even more spectacular; the hart plunged into the lake, "the stately cariage of hiz head in hiz swimmyng, spred . . . lyke the sail of a ship, the hoounds harroing after."[15]

At about nine o'clock when Elizabeth returned from the chase surrounded by torch bearers, George Gascoigne had another opportunity to display his literary and histrionic abilities. He now appeared before the Queen as an "*Hombre Saluagio*, with an oken plant pluct vp by the roots in hiz hande," dressed "all in moss and Iuy."[16] Accompanied by Fauns, Satyres, Nymphs, and Dryads, all of whom proved speechless, he engaged in a long dialogue with an accomplice dressed as Echo. Gascoigne's verses were not improved by the fact that he had devised them "upon a great sudden," or by the fact that he had inserted a transparent personal plea for the Queen's bounty.

The only dramatic part of Gascoine's contribution occurred unintentionally. Here is Laneham's description:

> As thiz Sauage, for the more submission, brake hiz tree a sunder, kest [cast] the top from him, it had allmost light vpon her highnes hors head; whereat he startld, and the gentlman mooch dismayd. See the benignitee of the Prins; as the foot men lookt well too the hors . . . "no hurt, no hurt!" quoth her highnes, which words I promis yoo wee wear all glad to heer; and took them too be the best part of the play.[17]

Tuesday was a day of rest and of business too, for this gathering offered a welcome opportunity for the nobles and gentry of nearby counties to talk to one another and to members of the court. A favoured few even had a chance to appear before the Queen. At least five knighthoods were conferred, including one upon Burghley's son Thomas. On Wednesday another hart was produced so that the hunt could be repeated. This one

14. Ibid., p. 17.
15. Ibid.
16. Ibid., p. 18. This "shew" device, centuries old, had been used in court revels in the winter of 1573–74. See Prouty, *Gascoigne*, p. 180.
17. Laneham, *Letter*, pp. 20–21. Gascoigne's published text of this "shew" describes it in full detail. Accordingly the text is of considerable historical importance.

quickly took refuge in the lake and was rewarded by the Queen's command to spare his life, though "he lost his earz for a raundsum," a strange degree of royal compassion

The sheer physical problem of providing food and drink for the assembled throng staggers the modern reader. Laneham reports "in lyttl more then a three dayz space, 72 tunn of Ale and Beer was pyept vp quite . . . in devoout drinking allwey." The supply ran out and when the situation became known "my Lord's good neighboourz, cam thear in a too dayz space, from sundry friendz, a releef of a xl tunn, till a nu supply waz gotten agayn, and then too oour drinking a freshe az fast az euer we did."[18]

On Thursday the program called for more entertainment. It began with bearbaiting, which occupied much of the afternoon. The evening brought another round of fireworks, broken periodically by the roar of cannon, which lasted for about two hours. Once the noise subsided an Italian gymnastic dancer put on a show to the marvel of the Queen and her attendants. Laneham, who could not get over the Italian's limber turns and leapings, concluded that his spine must have been like that of "a lamprey, that haz no bone, but a lyne like a Lute string."[19]

Friday and Saturday were free days, rather fortunately, for the cold, wet weather discouraged outdoor activities. Sunday proved a fine day, and that afternoon a rustic wedding was celebrated in the tilt-yard, followed by a morris dance. After this came a quintain, a village variation of tilting. Country youths on horseback hit the target end of a pivoted crossbar and tried to speed past in time to avoid a bag of sand swinging from the other end. The gentlemen and ladies enjoyed watching these provincial amusements. Laneham summarized the fun with these words: "twaz a lively pastime; I believe it would have moved some man to a right merry mood, though had it be toold him hiz wife lay a dying." The afternoon's entertainment was capped with a historical pageant performed "by certain good-harted men of Coventree," depicting the defeat of the Danes by the English. Then, after a banquet, the company enjoyed a masque by actors in rich and costly costumes. When the masque ended even Laneham found the hour rather late.

As usual, the fine air of Sunday (July 17) was succeeded by a hot Monday, and the Queen stayed inside the castle until late afternoon when she

18. Laneham, *Letter*, pp. 60–61.
19. Ibid., p. 25.

again followed the hounds in pursuit of a stag. On returning to the bridge across the lake the Queen and her party were treated to another aquatic pageant. A mermaid "that from top too tayl waz an eyghteen foot long" appeared, followed by Neptune himself. The Lady of the Lake made her second appearance and bewailed the distress caused by the "cruel Knight, one sir Bruse sauns pitee, a mortall enemy untoo Ladiez of estate," in three stanzas provided by Master Hunnes.[20] The music for the songs was especially praised by Laneham and led him to exclaim, "muzik iz a noble art!"

The Coventry players gave another performance on Tuesday the nineteenth of July, the only event recorded for that date. The royal party had expected to spend the evening of the following day at the Queen's estate of Wedgnock Park, just three miles west of Kenilworth, but the weather caused plans to be cancelled. This change aroused consternation among the catering staff and disappointed the actors who were to appear as nymphs and goddesses in Gascoigne's "Devise" written for the evening's entertainment.

Laneham's narrative stops here, so details of the Queen's last week at Kenilworth are lacking. Doubtless time for rest and court business was more than welcome. How much Sidney participated in the hunts and how he may have responded to the protracted masques, pageants, and other entertainment we have no way of knowing. As Leicester's nephew he had every opportunity of being well placed at the various dinners and entertainments. Perhaps he valued even more the chance to be with his own family on such an occasion.

During the visit Sidney received various letters from his Continental friends. Evidently the first to arrive came from Théophile de Banos at Antwerp, written on June 30 and addressed to Sidney care of the Earl of Warwick. De Banos begins with news of German politics; squabbles between the Lutherans and the Calvinists were boiling like a vat of acid.

> Sir,
>
> I have not written to you since I was at Cologne, for the reasons I mentioned in my last letter to Master Wotton. I imagine he will have told you about them, so I need not repeat them here. I plan to leave tomorrow for Frankfurt, where the Imperial Diet may be held in the autumn after the Fair. It is being delayed by the Elector of Saxony: no one knows why, but several people believe that his Excellency is

20. See Gascoigne's account in Nichols, I :491.

not pleased with the marriage which the Emperor proposed to him between the Emperor's son and the Elector's daughter. Before agreeing to his [i.e. the Elector's son's] election as King of the Romans, they think, he intends to make sure in other ways.

Some believe that at this Diet the matter of religion will be brought up; and the Elector Palatine has already been warned to make adequate preparations to defend himself on this point. He has also been requested by the Elector of Saxony promptly to expel the Calvinists from his territory. In a proclamation on a triumphal arch the Elector of Saxony had erected at Dresden the last time the Emperor was there, he is promising to exterminate them completely. Reiter companies are being raised in several parts of Germany: though it is said that this is for the King of France and the Prince of Condé, it would none the less seem that such considerable forces must be intended for some other purpose.

Next de Banos sends the bad news from the Netherlands, where the Spanish armies were threatening various cities.

So far as news from the Netherlands is concerned, Buren has been taken by the Spaniards, and the Prince's garrisons have pulled back to the manor where they are apparently holding well. They [the Spanish] have also taken the island of Hille: and acts of war are taking place daily, although they are still holding out hope of peace to the common people. Eighteen warships have left here, and the goings-on here are much as if the enemy was at the gates. The worst is that neither one's life nor one's property is safe, since the crowd has got the idea of a massacre. This is more to be feared than to be avoided unless the good Lord takes a hand.

The situation in strife-torn France follows that of neighbouring states:

The church at Besançon in Burgundy, beautiful and populous, has been sacked by the Papists: they have been celebrating St. Bartholomew's Eve in their town with such cruelty that they did not even spare little children nursing at their mothers' breasts. These examples, and the conspiracies of certain mutineers here, make one fear that we have not seen the last of such things. If peace does not come soon it looks as if there may be great rebellions or at least intolerable tyranny.

I had intended to spend several months here [Antwerp], awaiting the outcome of peace negotiations; but apart from this situation the inconvenience I have suffered prevents me. I shall return to the peace and security of Germany although the corruption and factions there foretell some change in her condition. I believe that if France had a spell of peace, the Reiters would soon try to wreak the havoc of war on their own native land, which they would plunder with their insatiable avarice, being no longer able to put the blame for their chronic madness on their neighbours.

De Banos next sends rumours of various personalities who were reported to be suffering divers afflictions.

I shall not give you more news of France except that, according to rumours, M. Damville has been poisoned and Marshal de Montmorency has since been placed under close arrest. If this is so, the war will be fought to the death. The Prince of Condé is still at Basle and is well.

As for the rest: I imagine you will have heard of the wedding of the Prince of Orange and Madame de Bourbon, the daughter of M. de Montpensier. The latter sent a gentleman posthaste to prevent it, but he arrived too late. My Lord of Pembroke left here on the twenty-seventh: the Commander received him splendidly. Prince Casimir is as good as widowed: but his wife left him on the pretext of going to see her family in Saxony, then wrote to her husband that she could not square it with her conscience to live with him unless he changed his religion. *Quod precor tibi sit in aurem dictum* [i.e. keep this confidential] until I tell you more about it when I am there. For if the efforts made to bring her back fail, the whole business will soon be public property in England.

And so I will make an end. Sir: I pray the good Lord to extend to you His holy benevolence, and commend myself humbly to your own. From Antwerp, June thirtieth, 1575.

Your most humble servant,
Théophile de Banos

At the end of the letter de Banos appended a lengthy postscript.

Sir,

Since I wrote this letter the Commander has had news that the Manor of Buren has been taken: it was surrendered on terms of compromise. The Commander says he is having a census made of all the arms possessed by private persons and that he is going to have them all collected in a public place. Moreover he says he has concentrated on finding out which of the possessors are Catholics and which are not. It is strange to see the people here afraid to say much, or to do anything. We have had news that several towns in France have revolted, but I dare not name them, for fear of being mistaken. Moreover I feel sure you are better informed where you are. I beg you to present my humble respects to Master Wotton. Adieu.

About a week later a letter came from Dr. Lobbet in Strasbourg. Not unexpectedly Lobbet touched on some of the same topics mentioned by de Banos. But first he attempted to establish how Sidney should send his replies to Strasbourg.

> Sir,
>
> I wrote to you last on the last day of last May; and in that letter I told you the method I intended to use in sending you my letters: viz. that I would send them to Brussels to a certain Doctor Rana, a German who is the agent for the imperial cities, and well known to all the German merchants at Antwerp. He despatches my letters to Antwerp, to have them sent to London: and the last one I wrote to you was despatched by him to a certain Master Edouard Chastellin, the factor of an English merchant at Antwerp. I am telling you this again so that, should you at some time be pleased to write to me, you may be able to tell the merchant to whom you send your letters to Antwerp to have them sent to Brussels to the said Dr. Rana whose address all the German merchants can give him.

Lobbet enclosed a letter for Johannes Hájek, and he also reported having recently received one from Languet written on June 12. To Lobbet Languet showed more concern than he had to Sidney about plans to elect a new King of Poland. The Russians were attempting to gain the title for their Czar, while the Turks supported Stephen Báthory of Transylvania. Because of this struggle the Warsaw Diet was postponed a number of times and did not convene until October 3. The election took place on November 7, though the votes were not counted until November 22.

> With my last I sent you a letter for your young Bohemian. In this packet you will find another from a friend of his, which I pray you to let him have.

M. Languet is still in Prague, and in good health, thank God. He sends you his love and the honour you deserve. I had a letter from him dated the twelfth of last month. It was being said at Prague that the Polish Diet had been put off until the twenty-ninth of next August. Nevertheless, various items of news are coming in from other places, and it is said that there will be a new royal election: but I have not heard for certain who will be elected. There will be plenty of rivals, and the Poles will in all probability be hard pressed, intimidated as they are by the Turk on one side and by the Muscovite on the other. We had best let them carry on, as neither you nor I are in a position to influence matters.

Lobbet next turned to the news of events nearer to his home city.

So far as matters French are concerned, we are awaiting the time for the Protestant and other delegates to return to court: this will be about the twentieth of this month. Then we shall know whether it is to be peace or war. There are some who have high hopes for peace, but others are not prepared to believe in it so soon, and prefer to wait and see. In all truth, the poor kingdom could do with a breathing space, and with a sincere peace. May God vouchsafe it, as also in Flanders. Rumours here have been saying that the Marshall Damville had been poisoned, but it is now said that nothing came of it, although apparently there was an attempt to do so. There is also a rumour that the Vicomte de Touraine has attached himself to the said Marshal Damville with three thousand infantry harquebusiers and five hundred horse; and also that the Count de Ruffec[21] was defeated in Poitou by M. de La Noue. I do not know if all that is said is true.

The bloodshed in Besançon, which de Banos had mentioned, resulted in a retaliatory raid by the Huguenots, a total failure which led to further massacres.

On the twenty-first of last month, those who had been banished from Besançon in Burgundy on account of their Protestantism put into effect a plan to reestablish themselves in their town and to raise their standard there. And they did in fact find a way of entering by

---

21. Philippe de Volvire, Baron (later Marquis) de Ruffec (d. 1586), Lieutenant-general for Brittany.

managing to open one of the gates, at about three A.M. Then they ran through the city fighting (for the inhabitants had heard the noise, rung the alarm, and were defending themselves) and held out until ten or eleven A.M. Finally they saw that the help they had hoped for was not forthcoming—viz. that they were joined by very few of the city's inhabitants—and were forced to withdraw, having lost five men and having killed fifteen or sixteen of the citizens. And so their undertaking went up in smoke, and the suspected citizens will be in great trouble.

Lobbet ended with a miscellaneous bag of news items:

Two German bishops have died, almost at the same time: the Bishops of Augsburg and Basle.

We have the Fair here in town at the moment. I am sending you for your home (and isn't it a pretty present?) the portrait of Amurathes [Murad III], the new Turkish Emperor. He is a great lord but will cost you nothing to entertain, as indeed he has cost me virtually nothing. He was made in Venice. I beg you to accept him as he is and to regard rather my great and humble affection for you than the quality of the gift.

M. de Montbrun, the old commander of the Protestants in [the Dauphine], is said to have defeated the Swiss who were there for the King under the command of M. des Gordes; and there have been messages that M. des Gordes has since been captured.

On the fourteenth of last month the old Duchess of Ferrara, the daughter of King Louis XII, died at Montargis: she is mourned by many. In a letter of the twenty-first of last month I am notified that the Duke of Lorraine, M. de Vaudemont, the father-in-law of the King, has arrived at court.

And here I shall end by presenting my humble respects to your benevolence and praying God,

Sir, to keep you in His own. From Strasbourg, this fifth of July, 1575.

Your humble servant,

J. Lobbet

About the same time Sidney received another long letter from Wolfgang Zündelin in Venice. It was brought to him by Lodowick Bryskett who had returned to Venice while Sidney headed back to England. (The purpose of Bryskett's trip to Venice is unknown: he may have been on business for Sir Henry Sidney, or for Leicester, or he may simply have gone for a farewell visit to his brother Sebastian.) Because the letter was carried by Bryskett no penalty would be invoked by its weight, so Zündelin's words flowed over four folio pages.

When last night, most noble sir, I happened upon your man Lodowick in the square of St. Mark's, and he told me that he was returning to England today, I did not wish to fail to send you a short letter, to congratulate you on your return to your own country. When, hastening elsewhere, he told me briefly of that return, I was flooded with unspeakable joy: for at that moment I was freed from the anxiety that had held me in suspense about the uncertain outcome of your journey; and I was filled with singular happiness to think of the great and perpetual pleasure you would afford your most delightful parents and your country. And the more this pleasure is combined with praise and glory of your name, the better I shall be pleased, because of my exceeding love and friendship for you.

Sidney's last letter had not reached Zündelin, even though he had heard it was coming. Zündelin's concern over it seems to go beyond mere politeness.

Only one thing has slightly troubled me: through the fault of some unknown person I have not received your most excellent letter, which I understand you have written to me. For the same Lodowick told me that you had ordered the letter you wrote to him to be included in the packet addressed to me. I, however, my most excellent Philip, have seen no trace of any letter since the one you sent me when you left Vienna; and I am totally perplexed as to who would have dared thus to open that packet, simultaneously robbing me of your much-hoped-for letter and, I imagine, doing you something of a disservice too.

A month ago, also, a certain German told me that he had met an Englishman who had shown him a letter addressed to me, which he wished to deliver to me, but that he had been unable to do so through press of affairs. Because I thought that that letter came from you, I have inquired diligently of Master Lodowick and of him who spoke of it, but so far I have found nothing. Nevertheless, I thank you eternally for having been pleased to testify to your most constant love for me with the witness of your letter—not necessary indeed, but certainly most exquisitely welcome to me. May it reach me yet —even after a long wandering—so that in it I may recognize and honour the likeness of that kindness, talent, and most excellent spirit of yours which, though it is so deeply impressed on my mind that I carry it about with me everywhere, nonetheless I seek daily to renew by thinking of you. May nothing succeed in obscuring or erasing it! But enough of this, which I think it would be better for me to recite privately than to talk to you about.

In my situation, since I gave my last letter to your servant, scarcely anything has changed. I am up to the neck in the same morass, with little prospect of emerging soon unless something very different occurs. So if at some time you should have the leisure in your kindness to write something to me, please address it to the Black Eagle Inn, whence it will be brought to me as soon as possible.

After all this persiflage (perhaps the result of having so much blank paper before him) Zündelin finally offers news about Sidney's friends and comments on the political situation.

Our friend Perrot left here about six weeks ago to visit his daughter in Sedan, where she has decided to live. He has often spoken to me about you in such a way as became one by whom you were greatly, and deservedly, loved. We, however, have been left with an incredible longing for that splendid man, our friend Wacker. It is now more than a month since he once again left for Rome etc., to collect the maximum amount of those Jubilee Year indulgences.

The German Lutherans in Rome live a fairly unfettered life. For the Pope, out of gratitude to the Duke of Saxony, has decided not to persecute them with fire and sword for the time being, but rather to treat them with all kindness and clemency, perhaps in order to coax them into being his allies and to rouse them more fiercely against the Calvinists. He has even sent agents into Germany to attempt, by secret ways, to fan the flames of that fire in which he sees his enemies on both sides being consumed. What grounds the Duke of Saxony is giving for this (together with a certain number of the major Saxon cities which praise him to the skies for his severity toward the Calvinists) you will hear more correctly from other sources. A friend has already written twice to tell me that our friend Languet is in some danger—I hope this is quite untrue.

Cardinal Hosius has offered many copies of a pamphlet by a certain Quadrantinus (a German Lutheran who defected to the Papists), via the great Prior of that England of yours, to certain Protestant German noblemen, amongst whom were the two Barons of Liechtenstein. When he came to the house of Count Solms to offer him a copy too, he was informed that the Count was still in bed; so, with his mission uncompleted, he departed, and has not yet, as far as I have heard, returned. The elder Liechtenstein is at present at home, the younger has left for Lake Geneva because of his health; both are most kindly disposed toward you, as they have often shown in their talk.

Besides reporting present calamities Zündelin found on every side predictions of portending troubles and future woes.

For political news you have your Lodowick. Everywhere there is abundant evidence of great upheavals and changes. The Italian astrologers—though I do not greatly credit their fallacious pronouncements—threaten Italy this year either with unusual sickness and plagues, or with dreadful wars. Diseases are feared because the spring was made very humid by the floods, and because of the subsequent heat wave. The commotions of the Genoese would afford an opportunity for war in Italy to any stronger power willing to take advantage of it; but as you will have heard about this already, and will moreover hear the news Lodowick is bringing, I shall not go into it.

Zündelin reported that the two power centres, Turkey and Spain, were well occupied with each other, though the Turk held the initiative.

The Turk is quiet this year, so that next year he may with all his strength attack Italy or Africa—or Sicily, or Malta? How dangerously Italy will be threatened whichever of these areas he attacks you will understand without comment from me. John of Austria, who recently strengthened his forces by adding five thousand Spanish recruits and who moreover has raised two legions in Germany and one in Milan, mentions (and, indeed, openly declares) that when Genoa has been restored to order he will go to Naples and thence to Africa: to recapture Tunis and raze it to the ground, to supply Bizerta with more equipment and garrison troops, and to block up and destroy the port of Farina so that it will never be any use to the Turks again.

For he fears that, if the Turk can flaunt his troops at Spain from the nearest coast, without hindrance and whenever he pleases, those old seeds of sedition will combine with certain new ones to increase their strength, so that he himself will face a highly dangerous contest with a very powerful enemy with his forces split and divided. It is thought that this may well occur unless he has the courage to act sharply and promptly against the Genoese, who might otherwise (as often happens to desperate men), despairing of any remedy, bring down destruction on themselves.[22]

France was the mystery: which way would the French turn now that their own territories had been largely pacified?

It is amazing how widely people are convincing themselves that peace has been made in France and that the King of France will send vast troops of cavalry and infantry to Italy, in order to use the Genoese affair to pursue his own ends there. Those who know the King better do not expect any such thing from him or his . . . [illegible] mother, and certainly not a peace which could properly be called a peace: whatever he may pretend to prepare or begin. He has written to Venice in the last few days, magnificently confirming that he is very far from peace. But that is nothing new: he has done so many times before. The Venetians, deprived of all foreign troops, do not cease to exhort him to conclude such a peace, and he (as I said) lavishes promises on them to that effect.

On the other hand, however, he is promising the Pope that whatever he does will be aimed at the downfall of the Huguenots. The Pope himself is working to this end spurred on by the King of Spain, who has him completely in his pocket, hoping permanently to drive the French out of Italy. He is very much afraid that with the religious war the [general] upheaval may spread, to the ultimate downfall of the Roman See. A certain astrologer here boldly asserts that the French King has at most three years left to reign and predicts all manner of great good fortune for his brother Alençon. Certain others of the same ilk warn us that the King of Spain will die this year and that the Empire will be greatly diminished. But to what lengths does the love of conversing with you drive me that I should even mention such things!

22. Part of the MS torn away; *ipsius* has been emended to *ipsos*.

Zündelin would probably have continued in this vein a good deal longer, but he found himself getting low on the fourth page.

Certain quite important people here attest that before the month is out we shall see some very great and unexpected events in Italy: beyond small hints they offer no further information. There is much that comes to mind, which nevertheless I shall not go into; for I fear that with all the above I am already troubling you more than is proper.

I should not have decided to write it all, but (as I said) my singular love of conversing with you has made me continue longer than I should have done. Forgive me in your kindness: and, I beseech you, continue to love me as I shall not cease to honour you. Farewell, illustrious and most noble sir; from Venice, the twentieth of June, 1575.

> Yours, with all love and respect,
> most devotedly,
> W. Z.

These letters gave Sidney material for well-informed conversation as he sat with other members of Elizabeth's court. Indeed, some of Sidney's seniors may have been impressed with his understanding of the political structure of Europe and the characters on the political stage. There cannot have been many young men (Sidney was still only twenty) who could grasp the trends and the consequences of the events then happening or impending. The testimony of his friends shows that Sidney's intellect and understanding were widely recognized. Doubtless his uncles Leicester and Warwick applauded his abilities and his remarkable development from the "raw" youth who had left for Paris with Lord Lincoln's party three years earlier. It is even possible that Elizabeth also noticed, for the Queen was alert to rising merit among her courtiers. For the moment, however, she showed no signs of recognizing Sidney's abilities, aside from her cordial welcome when he appeared at court.

CHAPTER 18

As the visit at Kenilworth drew to a close, Elizabeth and Leicester were distracted from the round of entertainments by other matters. One in particular appears to have been the presence of the beautiful Laetitia Devereux, Countess of Essex; her husband Walter, recently created first Earl, was absent in Ireland. Leicester had been having a closely guarded affair with Lettice, as she was known to family and friends, an affair which he naturally wished to keep from the Queen.[1] Although Elizabeth had decided against marrying Leicester herself, she had rewarded him well for remaining at her beck and call and insisted on absolute primacy in his attentions. Because of indications that the Queen considered leaving Kenilworth precipitately on Wednesday, July 20, Elizabeth Jenkins has suggested that the Queen learned of their affair (or at least began to suspect it) and reacted with a characteristic burst of temper.[2]

If this crisis did occur, Leicester succeeded in calming her. A marriage without Elizabeth's permission would have been unforgivable (as it indeed proved to be four years later), but the Queen could not expect a man of Leicester's virility to remain continent indefinitely. Furthermore, the Countess was scheduled to be the Queen's hostess at Chartley, the Essex estate in Staffordshire, soon after the visit at Kenilworth. Any disruption of the carefully planned itinerary would upset the progress, since the forty members of the royal court with all their retainers could not be left to fend or forage for themselves. In any case, the progress continued on schedule.

After leaving Kenilworth on Wednesday, July 27, the Queen and her party proceeded north some thirty miles to the ancient cathedral city of Lichfield, where they remained for a week. Details of the entertainment

1. Five months later the Spanish resident in London, Antonio de Guaras, reported to Secretary Gabriel de Zayas in Madrid, "As the thing is publicly talked about in the streets there is no objection to my writing openly about the great enmity which exists between the earl of Leicester and the earl of Essex, in consequence, it is said, of the fact that while Essex was in Ireland his wife had two children by Leicester. She is the daughter of Sir Francis Knollys, a near relative of the Queen, and a member of the Council, and great discord is expected in consequence" (*CSPS*2, p. 511).

2. *Elizabeth and Leicester* (London, 1961), pp. 210–11. Ringler, however, doubts the accuracy of the Spanish report in the absence of collaborative evidence.

there offer little information except that Elizabeth "enjoyed a grand musical treat by attending divine service in that noble Cathedral."[3] The town had few centres of activity besides the Cathedral to divert the Queen and her train, including the Sidney family. Account books show that a scaffold had been erected for the royal visit, the guildhall had been painted and mended, and one James Oliver provided a bear for baiting at a charge of twelve shillings.[4] The Queen may have been pleased with this relatively quiet week after the succession of opulent entertainments at Kenilworth, but young bloods like Sidney would be left with time on their hands. At least he could relax with his adoring sister Mary and his mother.

On the other hand Sir Henry Sidney was very busy, for he was deep in preparations for his return to Ireland. This was his last opportunity to talk over the problems awaiting him with Burghley, Leicester, and the Queen herself. Not only was he returning to Ireland, but he had also been elevated to the Privy Council and had been duly sworn on July 31 at Lichfield. On August 2 he received letters patent appointing him Lord Deputy of Ireland as well as his written instructions. The following day he attended a meeting of the Council.

After leaving Lichfield the next stop for Elizabeth and her entourage was Chartley Park, about a dozen miles to the northwest in the rich valley of the Trent. Like other early castles, Chartley had been built with two massive round towers on top of an artificial hill. Later the de Ferrers family, finding the old fortress inconvenient, built a half-timbered mansion a short distance below it, carved and battlemented in the medieval style. The surrounding park was approximately eight miles in circumference and thus could offer hunting to a Queen's taste. No doubt Leicester had a large part in the arrangements. Although Lettice Devereux was the Queen's cousin, they were not close in affection or interests. Eleven years younger, Lettice had formerly been in Elizabeth's favour but as she grew older her tastes and interests became quite different. Elizabeth had been cast by fortune into a grim and dominating status, whereas the beautiful and voluptuous Lettice early found herself to be very attractive to men. Since her latest conquest was the favourite of the Queen, this visit to her home by both Elizabeth and Leicester created the classic triangle situation. So far as we know all three principals played their parts with formal dignity.

3. Nichols, 1:529.
4. Ibid.

Some of Sidney's biographers have given a great deal of attention to the supposition that here Sidney first saw Lady Essex's daughter Penelope, who was then only thirteen but already showing her inherited blond beauty and bewitching charm. According to this theory Sidney, fresh from the courts of Europe, scarcely noticed the girl, a fact he later lamented in Astrophil's lines on Stella: "And yet could not, by rising morn foresee / How fair a day was near. Oh, punished eyes!" Unfortunately for this romantic notion, Penelope may not have been at Chartley on this occasion. Rooms for the Queen's party would tax the capacity of the castle; more-over, when the Queen deigned to stay in a country house younger members of the host's family were often expected to move out.[5] It would still have been possible, however, for Penelope to have been present during some or all of the entertainments at Chartley. Indeed, the Countess may have welcomed the chance to have the members of the court see her daughter's budding beauty, now that Penelope would soon be ready for the marriage market.

From Chartley the Queen moved on about half a dozen miles to Stafford where she stayed in the castle then occupied by Edward, Lord Stafford. In the register of St. Mary's Church this memorandum of the royal visit is preserved.

> Mem. That the viii daie of August 1575 Our Soverign Ladie Queene Elizabethe came from Chartley in progresse to Stafford Castle, and was Received upon the poole dam without the East gate by the Bayliffs and burgesses with an oracion made by Mr. Launde the Schoole maister in the name of the Towne and the bay-liffs delivered to her majestie a goodlie large standing cup of sylver and gilt of xxx li price which her hyghnes cheerefullie and thank-fullie Received and so shee passed through the Eastgate streete the markett place the Crobury lane, and the broad eye, and there over the River to Stafford parke.[6]

The only other detail known is that the Queen inquired why the town had fallen into such a decayed condition; on being told that this resulted

---

5. On p. 437 Ringler calls attention to such instructions in Nichols, 2:412. In a private letter he comments that evidence of the visit to Chartley is surprisingly meagre.

6. W. Beresford, *Memorials of Old Staffordshire* (London, 1909), p. 22. We also learn that in Stafford the youngest child, not the eldest, inherited property. This was explained by the fact that the lord of the manor exercised his seigniory on local brides, so that the eldest child was often illegitimate.

from the removal of the assizes formerly held in Stafford, her Majesty promised to restore them.

The royal party now turned south to Chillington Hall where they were the guests of John Giffard Esq., who had recently served as High Sheriff of Staffordshire. They entered the park by an oak-lined avenue over a mile long. To the south Chillington Hall looked down on a lovely lake, also over a mile in length. Elizabeth's choosing to stop here was unusual in that her host's family, the Giffards, and the tenants on the estate were Catholics.

From Chillington the progress continued to Dudley Castle which was situated on the summit of a conical hill north of the town of Dudley and looked out over Staffordshire, Worcestershire, and Warwickshire. Although Dudley Castle had been in the Sutton/Dudley family since the fourteenth century, it had been seized by the Crown during the Marian troubles and had recently been restored to Sir John Sutton, later fourth Baron Dudley. Perhaps the distant cousinship of the present family with Leicester, Warwick, and Lady Sidney was involved in the selection of Dudley Castle for the royal progress. After leaving these lofty battlements the Queen and her court continued south to Worcester, arriving at Hartlebury Castle on August 12.

The time had now come for the Sidney family to leave the Queen and her entourage. Mary may have stayed on but Sir Henry, Philip, and possibly Lady Sidney said farewell at Dudley Castle just before her Majesty's departure. Lady Sidney's name is not listed among the Ladies of Honour attending the Queen at Worcester;[7] nor is that of her daughter. Philip and Sir Henry went to Shrewsbury and probably visited the school where the boy had passed several happy years. The corporation of the city responded to the presence of the Lord President and his son by holding a reception in their honour. It is recorded in the corporation accounts with the entry: "Spent and given to Mr. Philip Sidney at his coming to this town with the Lord President, his father, in wine and cakes and other things—7s. 2d."[8]

Sir Henry now set about ordering his affairs, as was proper before returning to Ireland. One task he undertook was to make a new will. It was ready for signing on Saturday, August 20, and Philip's name appears

---

7. Nichols, 1:544–45.
8. See the account of this visit in H. Owen and J. B. Blakeway, *A History of Shrewsbury* (London, 1825), 2:360.

among the signatures of the eight witnesses.[9] How long Sidney stayed with Sir Henry, and whether he accompanied him to the port of embarkation, is not known. Wallace, Sidney's able biographer, wrote with confidence, "We may be sure that Philip did not take leave of his father until immediately before the latter set sail."[10] This would have been during the first week in September, for Sir Henry landed in Ireland on Thursday the eighth. Wallace's evidence, however, is merely based on Languet's response[11] to Sidney's excuse that he had accompanied his father after leaving the royal progress. But the distance from Shrewsbury to whichever port Sir Henry had selected would require several days' travel time, and it would be about a week before Philip could rejoin family or friends. It seems equally probable that Philip bade farewell when Sir Henry left Shrewsbury and then returned to the court at Woodstock, where the progress made its penultimate stop early in September. Certainly Mary Sidney was there, for in one of the entertainments a poet addressed this compliment to her:

> Tho yonge in yeares, yet olde in wit, a gest dew to your race,
> If you holde on as you begine, who ist youle not deface?"[12]

Furthermore, at this time Robert Sidney, accompanied by Griffin Madox, hired horses to go from Oxford "to the Courte,"[13] so that he could enjoy a reunion with his sister Mary and any other members of the family who were near at hand.

Sometime after leaving Kenilworth, Sidney received another batch of letters from his friends on the Continent. Shrewsbury would have been a likely forwarding address, though postal arrangements were so uncertain that the letters could have been waiting for him when he returned to London, presumably late in September. The steadfast Languet had written from Prague on July 16, so the letter probably came too late to be sent to Kenilworth. The letter consists almost entirely of a report on

---

9. *Historical Manuscripts Commission; Third Report*, p. 199. The manuscript is at Longleat, where it was kindly transcribed by Mr. Archibald Elias. Among the witnesses were William Blunt, who had charge of some of Sir Henry's finances, and Sir Edward Montagu (d. 1602) of Boughton, Northants, a close friend whose son Edward was Robert Sidney's companion at Christ Church.

10. Wallace, p. 157.

11. See Languet's letter of Dec. 3, 1575 in chap. 19, below.

12. First pointed out by J. W. Cunliffe in "The Queenes Majesties Entertainment at Woodstocke," *PMLA* 26 (1911):100.

13. *HMC De L'Isle*, 1:269.

the Polish Diet, but it begins with Languet's complaint about Sidney's failure to respond, especially his neglecting to suggest an intermediary who would forward letters to England.

> If you had kept your promise to arrange with someone at Antwerp to take charge of our letters, I would not now be forced to send this one via Hamburg. Indeed, it may never reach you, or come after such delay that all the pleasure you might gain from the news I am sending about Polish affairs will be lost. I went to much trouble to collect the information; and if it should be forwarded to you promptly it may counter the various reports already invented about the Slezyca Diet. These reports will probably reach you since they are being widely circulated.

Languet's Hamburg intermediary was an eminent man Sidney had met in Austria.

> I have given this letter to Dr. Joachim Möller, who stayed in the same lodging house with you in Vienna a year ago. He is a learned and devout man, well informed about German affairs. Should her Majesty the Queen need someone to take charge of her business in Saxony, Möller would be more than suitable. He is thoroughly experienced in such matters and personally known to the princes, being very influential with most of them. (His brother serves as Councillor of the Republic of Hamburg.) Dr. Möller offers his humble duty to her Majesty the Queen if he should be able to serve her in any way. He asked me to write you about this, and to send you his courteous respects. I recommend him as an old friend.

Möller took the occasion of this introduction to enclose a letter to Sidney which is now preserved in the British Museum.

Languet's next letter, that of August 13, probably awaited Sidney on his return to Leicester House. The personal passage with which it begins shows that the letter Sidney had written before setting out for Kenilworth had reached Languet about a month later.

> The anxiety I feel during your absence was greatly relieved by your letter written from London in June, in which you reported that you had surmounted the usual dangers of a journey and also that you are almost completely restored to health. Further, it contains such evidence of your affection for me and is written so gracefully and

wittily that it could easily have enticed me to love and admire you, had not your pleasant manners, sound judgement, and surprisingly mature experience in political affairs already done so.

Nevertheless Languet felt he should resume the role of preceptor and so continued with schoolmasterly advice.

I know that it may seem absurd to ask that, surrounded by the bustle of the court and so many temptations to waste time, you do not fail entirely to practise your Latin. Because your letter shows the great progress you have made in this skill and your proficiency in writing whenever you wish to apply your mind to it, should you drop your interest in Latin style I scarcely shall be able to restrain myself from accusing you of laziness and spiritual weakness. Thus you observe how I reward you for a very welcome letter: by attempting to persuade you to value those accomplishments which make men of your status sometimes seem, in the eyes of most, lacking in practical sense, if they pursue such tastes. Now I shall stop bothering you with trifles of this sort.

The remaining pages of Languet's letter are devoted to informing Sidney about political and military affairs in Hungary, Bohemia, and Poland, as well as the activities of the Turks and Muscovites. At the end comes some personal news with a delicate hint.

May God grant that excellent young man, Wotton, full success in his new marriage plans. He is giving an example for you to follow, though I believe you are making haste on your own and do not require an instructor. You see how I have carried on in my desire to trifle with you, which scarcely permits me to stop writing.

The letter from Joachim Möller, which accompanied Languet's letter of July 16, is a handsome example of Italic calligraphy. It begins, "Greetings, illustrious, noble, and honourable Sir," and continues in stately style.

When, a few days ago, I was once more at the Emperor's court on business and met our friend Master Hubert Languet, it was both my duty and my pleasure to inquire about your Excellency's position and well-being. It was indeed a great delight not only to see your picture at his house, and to renew the memory of the great kindness with which you treated me last year in Vienna, but also to hear that you, who were born of the highest rank, have been granted a place worthy of your great virtues at the court of the most honoured Queen of England. I pray wholeheartedly that you may adorn this station to the glory of God and the benefit of the Christian Commonwealth.

Because you have fired me with amazing love and admiration for you, when our friend Languet sent me this letter from Hamburg to send on to you I could not help adding my own, albeit uncouth, testimony of the perpetual honour and respect I feel for you. And I should like you to know that I shall always be indebted to you; that among those who respect and honour you I shall to the best of my ability strive for a high, if not the principal, place; and that nothing, however difficult, will be other than easy for me, so it be undertaken for your sake.

Now Dr. Möller comes to the real purpose of his letter, already described by Languet, his wish for a position as salaried agent of the Queen's government, preferably in Saxony.

Therefore, if there is anything I can do for you, you have but to command. I shall strive not to be found wanting in my duty and devotion to you. And indeed, if you feel that any effort of mine could possibly be of use to the most honoured Queen of England (either in discharging her affairs with neighbouring princes or states in Saxony, with others farther away, or at imperial assemblies; or whenever the journey's difficulties or other reasons make it awkward to send ambassadors from England), it would be a great joy for me to be able to show her Majesty my loyalty, devotion, and zeal.

A few years ago also, at the command of Duke Adolph of Holstein, I transmitted his orders to certain Saxonian princes and estates: and on that occasion I believe that I failed neither his Majesty's will nor my duty. I am close to Duke Otto of Brunswick and Lüneburg who is devoted to her Majesty, and I live six miles from Hamburg, where my brother Eberhardt is councillor. To him, should the occasion call for it, any letters can easily be sent.

No letter from a European court would be complete without some political news, so Möller inserts a few items before his concluding compliments.

Of political matters I have no doubt that Hubert is writing to you at length. The Emperor is calling a Diet here in Prague with the Bohemians, where the subject will be the selection of his successor— especially since the Emperor is by no means in good health. The Bohemians are demanding freedom of worship before they will reply. We shall see what happens.

The Imperial Diet with the German Princes is set for September twenty-sixth at Regensburg. The purpose is to begin talks about a successor to the imperial crown: let us hope God will guide their counsels. Perhaps, because of the spreading plague epidemic at Regensburg, Nuremberg will be selected for the meeting. The Elector of Saxony is still holding the theologians as if they were prisoners.

Farewell, and all health and happiness to you, noble Sir, most worthy as you are of the best life has to offer; and continue, as you did last year, to consider me worthy of your love, as I honour and cherish you. From Prague.

Devotedly your Excellency's,
Dr. Joachim Möller

Whatever Sidney may have done to pass on Dr. Möller's application, whether to Burghley, Walsingham, or Leicester, nothing appears to have come of it. None of the published volumes of state papers carries a single reference to his name. Perhaps Möller's age handicapped him; he was fifty-five, an age at which a man was considered past his prime. More probably there was no opening for such an agent at that time.

Another letter awaiting Sidney came from Dr. Lobbet in Strasbourg. Dated July 25, it begins in a businesslike fashion with a personal note and then plunges into current news.

Sir,

This is the third time that I am writing to you since your arrival in England. Besides the present moment, I wrote to you on the last day of last May, and on the fifth of this month. If my letters or my assiduity in writing them displeases you, you might let me know: similarly I should like to know if they do gratify you, for I shall try to follow your wishes. In the meantime, I beg you not to be offended at my boldness in writing to you, but rather to ascribe it to my respect and reverence for you.

This present letter is to let you know that life in general is fairly quiet here: except that several gentlemen and other Frenchmen, Protestants as well as malcontents, have assembled here from various places, both on foot and horse, and armed. At first we thought they meant to go and join M. de Montbrun who is said to be winning in the Dauphiné, but they took another route and are said to have made for Burgundy and Champagne. There is evidently something going on that not everyone knows about. Time will tell. M. de Méru is said to have arrived at Heidelberg with the son of the late count of Montgomery: I believe they are going to make for Basle, where Monsieur the Prince of Condé is still residing.

Lobbet next mentions a riot in Paris on July 4 when fifteen hundred students demonstrated against the widely disliked Florentine group (the Dukes of Retz and Nevers and their followers) who seemed to dominate the court under the sponsorship of Catherine de Médicis. Other news items follow:

We have heard rumours of some student riot in Paris, of which you will probably have more recent news. We are daily awaiting news of the accomplishments of the peace delegates at court. Polish affairs are not stable, and there are very disparate reports of their King. M. de Pibrac is still there, and I believe Marshal de Bellegarde must also have arrived there by now. Rumour has it that the Lithuanians wish for a duke of their own. We do not know whether the Turk has made any move either by land or by sea. Italy is quiet, and the Genoans are said to have been pacified or paid off. I am sending you a small treatise which will tell you the history of their quarrels. The Emperor is still at Prague, and I have heard no mention of any speeding-up of affairs. M. Languet is there, and is well, thank God.

From Lobbet we also learn that another of Sidney's bachelor friends, the Count of Hanau, had announced plans for his forthcoming marriage to Magdalen, daughter of Samuel (not Philip), Count of Waldeck. The ceremony took place on February 5, 1576.

Our friend the Count of Hanau, whom you knew at the court of the Emperor, is about to enter the estate of holy matrimony (so Master Welsperg writes). He is marrying the daughter of Philip Count of Waldeck; her mother is of the house of the Counts of Neuburg and is related to the Elector of Cologne. I was pleased to hear this news and wanted to let you know, as I realize that you too would be so because of your friendship with him. Truly he is a gentleman whose virtues deserve all good fortune: and however much good may befall him, I wish him yet more. I hope shortly to hear that you have entered the same order: when I do, I shall not fail to congratulate you on that estate, to which I myself have not aspired, any more than has M. Languet. *Non omnia possumus omnes.*

I beg you to present my humble respects to Master Walsingham and to let me know how your young Bohemian [Hájek] is behaving so that I can let his father have some news.

It is reported that on the twenty-sixth of September next there will be a Diet at Regensburg for the election of a King of the Romans.

And here I shall present my humblest respects to your benevolence, and pray God,

Sir, to keep you in His own. From Strasbourg, this twenty-fifth of July, 1575.

> Your humble servant,
> J. Lobbet

A month later the familiar French hand of Dr. Lobbet again appeared in a letter dated August 30. Most of it deals with equally familiar topics: Sidney's failure to write and news of strife in Poland, Transylvania, Hungary, and France, as well as of various friends of Sidney.

Sir,

I wrote to you last on the twenty-sixth [*sic*] of last month. From you I have received nothing at all since you left Heidelberg.

The Emperor has been somewhat ill, but now, thank God, his Majesty is feeling better; he is still in Prague, awaiting the Diet which will be held at Regensburg on the twenty-sixth of next month for the election of the King of the Romans. The Poles have planned their Diet [of Slezyca] for the third of next October at Warsaw.

The Muscovite is fighting in Livonia, and it is said that he has taken a town called Bernau. The Transylvanian war is over, because he [Békesy] who was the cause of it has been defeated. At the present moment the Turks are fighting in Hungary: apart from the Blaustein Castle, which they had already captured, they have conquered three or four other fortresses. This is why the Emperor is sending infantry and cavalry to Silesia, Moravia, and Austria.

In Italy the Genoans are on their guard because of the troops the King of Spain has there: these, it is said however, will be taken to Barbary. Don John of Austria is in Naples, and it is said that he has been demanding extortionate amounts of money.

They say that Duke Eric of Brunswick is collecting large numbers of Reiters to take to France in aid of the King. The others are considering what to do. Apparently M. de Torré will shortly take two thousand Reiters to his brother M. Damville in Languedoc. The Prince of Condé is making no move as yet: I believe he is waiting for another opportunity. It is said that M. de Montbrun, who was imprisoned at Grenoble, has been beheaded there. M. de Chastillon, the elder son of the late Admiral, is taking his place in the Dauphiné.

A young Bohemian gentleman on his way back to Bohemia entrusted the enclosed letter to me for your young Bohemian [Hájek], to whom I pray you to have it given. M. Languet is well, as is also M. de Vulcob. They write to me every week. The Count of Hanau has celebrated his engagement. The wedding has been put off until around next Lent.

I present my humble respects to your benevolence, and pray God, Sir, to keep you in His own. From Strasbourg, this thirtieth of August, 1575.

Your humble servant,

J. L.

Besides these letters from Continental friends, one other received from a young Scot has been preserved. Its survival appears to be accidental; probably because it is written in French Sidney's secretary or some similar person placed it with the letters from across the Channel. It was written by Sir John Seton (d. 1594), later Lord Barns, who became Master of the Stable to the young James VI of Scotland and in 1581 a member of the Privy Council and an Extraordinary Lord of Session.

Sir,

The great courtesy you showed me has moved me to trouble you with this letter, in the assurance that you will take it in good part. Although my style is far too uncouth for your deserving, yet I know your kindness to be such that you will interpret everything in the best spirit.

Sir, I have presented your respects to our King, and I have conveyed to his Majesty the great desire you have to be of service to him and to kiss his hand. This, I assure you, was very well received, and his Majesty thanked you several times. I can assure you, Sir, that if you intend to travel here to see his Majesty, and let me know, I shall come and meet you halfway: for this, I think, would be the very least I should do, considering the great favour you and yours have shown me. This favour I attribute a thousand times more to their courtesy than to my deserving: but should God ever grant me the grace to be of some useful service to my Lord your uncle, my Lord the Earl of Leicester, this would make me happier than anything else in this world could do. For I feel myself to be so indebted to your Lordship that I can scarcely believe that I or mine could ever repay you.

Sir, I fear that I am troubling you with too long a letter: so I shall end, praying God the Creator to vouchsafe you fulfilment of all your good desires, and assuring you, as before, that I remain your faithful friend and servant as long as I live. Given at Setoun, this second of September, 1575.

In perpetual readiness to serve you,

Jehan Setoun

This letter shows that Philip Sidney was an apt student of politics. Evidently Seton and Sidney had met at court[14] and Sidney had gone out of his way to be cordial to the young Scot. He knew that Seton's young King, the nine-year-old son of Mary Stuart, was second in the line of succession to the throne of England, and so early began to keep his political avenues in repair.

When Sidney returned to London around mid-September 1575, he found still more letters from his friends in central Europe. One he received from the hand of a messenger, Georg Zölcher of Strasbourg, whom Sidney had met in Antwerp four months earlier. Zölcher had come on an errand: to obtain cloth for Count John Casimir of the Palatinate for use in his own household.[15] With him from Strasbourg he brought a letter from Dr. Lobbet, dated September 5, which begins with Lobbet's reason for writing.

Sir,

So little time has passed since I wrote to you (for my last letter was

14. On Sept. 6 Lord Seton wrote to the Queen thanking her for favours shown to his son during this visit to her court (*CSPF2*, p. 125).

15. *CSPD1*, p. 510.

dated the thirtieth of last month) that I have no pressing reason to write to you at this moment: the more so since I have not even received a single letter from you since you returned to England. However, Master Zölcher whom you know, and who is himself his own best recommendation, asked me not to let him leave for England without giving him my letters. This is the reason, Sir, for this letter, in which you will not find any views of what is happening here, since the bearer can tell you personally what he has seen and heard.

Lobbet devoted the rest of his space to reporting other news, most of it concerning the Emperor's problems.

You are also sufficiently well informed about events in the Netherlands and in France: so I shall not mention them, but rather tell you that the Turks are continuing the war in Hungary and creating as much havoc as they can. They are taking one town after another and though they have not yet seized any cities of major importance, the Christians are nevertheless having difficulty getting supplies through to the most important towns. Moreover, the place where those pretty little ducats grow could be in danger. Recently they have taken a town called Samosky, and since then they have been besieging another called St. Andrew.

On the eighteenth of last month the Emperor put his proposal before the Bohemian Diet in Prague. It contained the same articles which he put forward six months ago, except that his Majesty has added the article concerning the succession and coronation of his son to the Kingdom of Bohemia. And as for the Bohemian proposal concerning their religion, his Majesty was to reply to this on the twenty-first or twenty-second of the same month.

Dispatches from Italy had brought news of the Pucci conspiracy, a new topic in Sidney's correspondence. Orazio Pucci, seeking revenge for the execution of his father by Cosimo de' Médici, had fomented a plot against the present Grand Duke, Francesco. The conspiracy failed, but before Pucci was arrested he wounded himself in order to give the others time to escape. Francesco used the plot to justify a purge of the Florentine nobility which embittered his enemies for years afterward.

The Genoese are said to have recommenced their former quarrels, and it is reported that at Florence several citizens have been conspiring against their Duke. The principal conspirators are named as

Capponi, Ridolfi, and Pucci (these are their surnames, I do not know their Christian names). The business was discovered, and Pucci has been arrested, while Capponi and Ridolfi have escaped. But their goods have been confiscated, which are said to be estimated at six hundred florins, viz. six hundred thousand écus. There is scarcely any talk of Poland: we must await their Diet on the third of October next.

I present my humble respects to your benevolence, and pray God, Sir, to keep you in His own. From Strasbourg, this fifth of September, 1575.

Your humble servant,
J. L.

By coincidence another friend from abroad turned up in London about the same time, Thomas Lenormand, with whom Sidney had travelled from Dresden to Frankfurt during the spring. Afterwards Lenormand had continued on to Paris, whence he had written Sidney a letter that would have been tardy in reaching his hands.

Sir,

I beg you to excuse me for not having written by the messenger with whom I travelled from Paris to this city, but time and opportunity would not allow a letter of sufficient length and thoroughness. Nevertheless I have asked him to present my humble respects to you and to offer my services. I believe you will have received my letter of the sixth of last August, which I sent via a servant of M. de la Motte, who left Paris on the eighth of that month.

It is somewhat strange to the modern reader that in announcing his presence in London Lenormand devotes most of his letter to the latest news from France. His doing so indicates how important *les dernières nouvelles* was among courtiers, and possibly that Lenormand thought his news might whet Sidney's appetite to learn more.

These brief lines are just to let you know what is happening in our poor France, which is more ravaged than ever a poor country was: and, unless God takes a hand, I do not think there was ever such a cruel war as this one will be. M. de Guise left Court to go to the camp which is being assembled in Burgundy, near Langres, on the fifth of last August, and a few days later the Duke of Maine, M. D'Aumale, the Marquis Delboeuf, and several other gentlemen left

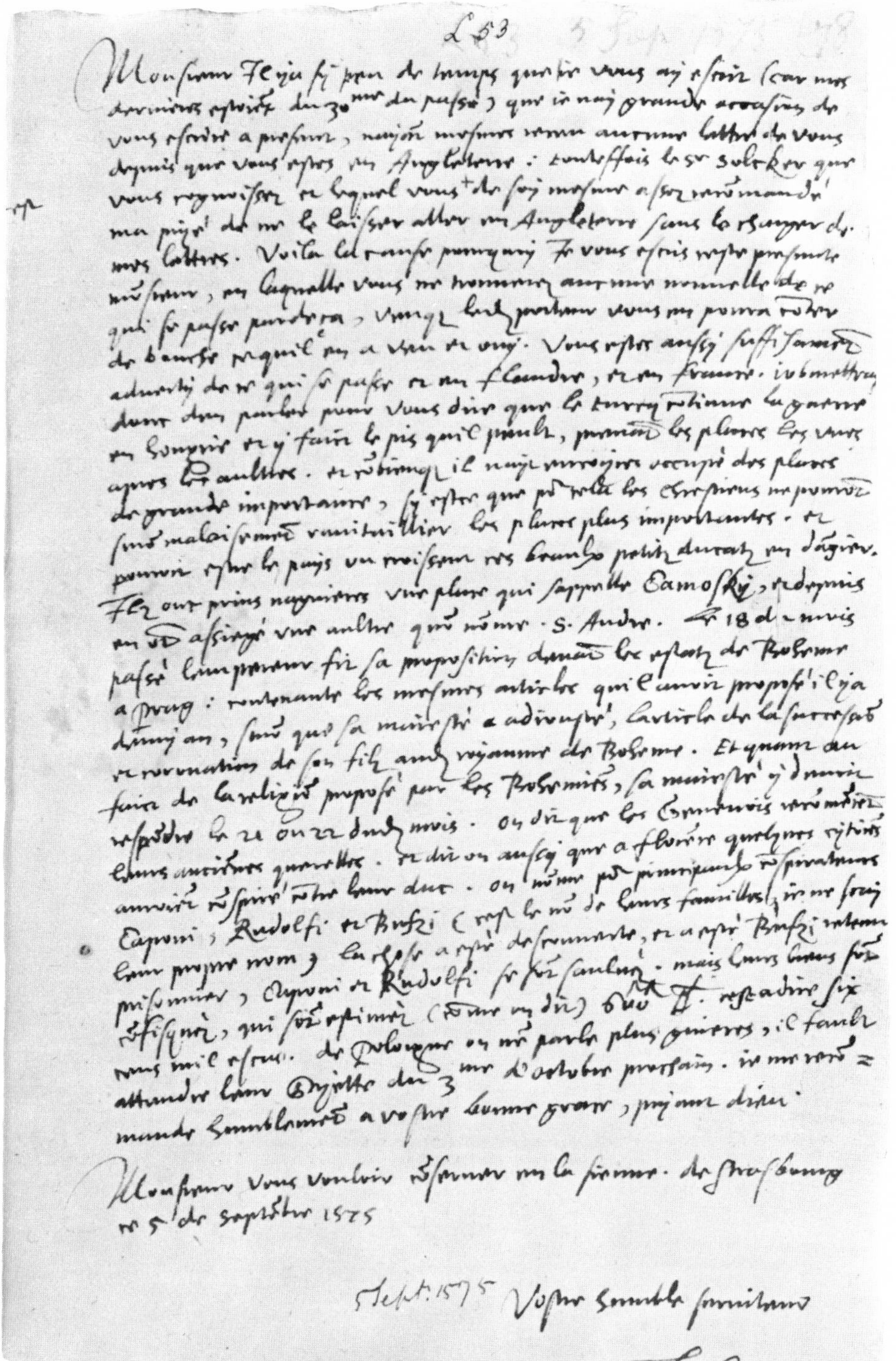

Specimen of François Lobbet's handwriting

also. Last Tuesday, the thirteenth, M. de Guise sent one of his gentlemen to the King to beg urgently for men and money and to say that
he could not possibly await the enemy with so few men. For where
they expected ten or twelve thousand men he found fewer than
five thousand. The Queen Mother and Chancellor Birague have no
more to contribute. The King is hiring twelve thousand Reiters.

The Prince of Condé already has two thousand Reiters on the
borders of Lorraine, with one thousand French cavalry and four
thousand infantry led by M. de Clermont; and it is thought certain
that Duke Casimir and the Prince of Condé will march as soon as
possible with eight thousand more Reiters. The King is in such doubt
and fear as never poor prince has been, and never leaves Paris. Last
Saturday, the tenth, two doors of the Louvre were closed and blocked
up, so that now there is only one door to enter by. On the same day
more than fifteen gentlemen were arrested and imprisoned: no one
knows why, unless they were suspected of being, or having been,
Protestants.

The house where Lenormand lodged was that of Thomas Randolph
(1523–90) who had been Postmaster General since 1566 despite a diplomatic career that sent him to Russia on an embassy in 1568 and to Paris
in 1573 and again in 1576. His house was at St. Peter's Hill, near Thames
Street.

> I hope that, with God's help, I shall visit you soon and tell you
> more personally. I would have come at the same time as the mes-
> senger I came with, only between here and Dover I fell from my
> horse and hurt one leg rather badly: however, I hope it is nothing.
> In this city I am staying with the Master of the Posts, who is your
> most affectionate servant.

In concluding Lenormand could not refrain from interjecting a bit more
news. Presumably Sidney arranged for him to call, but no record of any
such meeting is known.

> As for news of Germany, I believe you will have heard that the
> Emperor left on August twenty-seventh for Regensburg, where the
> Diet is to be held. The King of Hungary has been very ill—but he is
> now doing quite well. You may also have heard that the Turks had
> assembled quite a number of men to invade Transylvania, but the
> Prince of Transylvania has defeated them entirely and they have

retreated. On the fifth the Turks captured three small towns on the Hungarian border—I cannot tell you their names. Poor Master Rüber lost more than three hundred men.

Since for the time being I have nothing else worth writing I shall end, and pray the Creator our God to grant you,
Sir, good health and a long and happy life, as well as the fulfilment of your desires. From London, this nineteenth of September, 1575.

Affectionately yours in perpetual
obedience and service,
T. Lenormand

The month of October 1575 brought Sidney more letters from abroad. After a three month interval de Banos wrote from Frankfurt to report that the commentaries of Ramus, which he was paying to have printed, had been delayed because of Wechel's illness. Here we learn that Sidney, properly sensitive about the fact that in England he was just plain "Mr.," had taken the precaution to write to Wechel to make sure de Banos did not address him as the "Baron de Sidenay" or by any other title of his own devising.

My Lord,

Although there is no pressing reason for me to write, this letter is to let you know that the Ramus *Commentaries* have not appeared in time for this Fair because I have been away for four months, as I wrote to you before.

Master Wechel has been ill and was thus unable to fulfil the promise he made me when I left here. Had I been here I would have had them printed even if it had cost me a hundred écus more; and, if by God's will I live, I hope to be able to let you have them by next year at the latest. I have seen a letter which Master Wechel received from you in which you ask him to tell me not to give you any title of honour in my dedicatory epistle to you. As that is how you wish it I shall do it: I hope, however, that you will not take it amiss if I mention in passing such things as I could not honestly pass over in silence.

Following his usual order, de Banos reports the news from the German states.

As for the rest, I think you will be sufficiently well informed about the Emperor's journey: he is headed for Regensburg where the

Bishop of Cologne has already arrived; but apparently the other Electors are not in such a hurry. The Emperor is still in Prague where he has granted the Bohemians the right of public exercise of the true Religion: he had various motives for this which I think you must have heard. The same Lord has recently been hard pressed by the Turks, who have relieved him of several important cities on a pretext of war afforded then by a certain gentleman called Bequze. The latter has been at the court of the said Prince and has since openly waged war against his master, the King of Translyvania. But since he has been defeated in battle and taken prisoner, the Turks are blaming the Emperor for his enterprise. The Emperor is trying to justify himself, and I believe he has already bought peace, but with considerable shame and loss. The result of this imperial journey will enable us to judge the condition of Germany, which seems to be uniting itself internally: it is to be feared that those of its neighbours who mock at it will end up being mocked themselves.

Next come the events in France, where the bankrupt King stood helpless because he lacked money to hire mercenaries.

As for France, you will be better informed [than we]: I shall just tell you what we know here. M. de Thoré, one of the sons of the late Connetable, has left with twelve hundred Frenchmen and two thousand Reiters to join his brother, Marshal D' Ampuille; but M. de Guise has sworn that they will pass only over his dead body and is on the border with all his troops to prevent them: it looks as if they will be fighting before this reaches you. The Prince of Condé, with the Lords of his retinue, will soon follow with their force of six thousand horse. The King, meanwhile, is doing what he can to obtain aid as soon as possible, but he is lodged at the sign of the Empty Coffers: and without cash no Reiter will march a yard.

Finally de Banos includes reports from the Mediterranean and the Bosporus whence the news was dire, as usual.

From Italy we hear that John of Austria is sailing on the Mediterranean and that he is making for Marseilles with eight thousand Italians. I have nothing else to write: except that at Constantinople they have burned one of the preachers of the great Lord for having maintained the pure doctrine of the Gospel; and when he had been put in the fire, several others voluntarily accompanied him and were

burned with him. Some say they did it because of the great friendship they had for this preacher: others think that, as their ideas and
their faith were the same as his, they bore the same witness to the
steadfastness thereof. Thus does the Gospel, having run its course in
the West, appear to be returning to the East whence it came. I pray
God to have mercy on His Church, and to vouchsafe you increase,
Sir, of His holy benevolence, and present my humble respects to
your own. From Frankfurt-am-Main, this nineteenth of September,
1575.

For the duration of this Fair we have been seeing the Count of Hanau
with his fiancée: jollier and more cheerful than usual.

Your most humble servant,
Théophile de Banos

On the heels of this letter from Frankfurt came another from Languet,
still in Prague on September 18. It begins on a note of affectionate remon-
stration.

I have decided to criticize you for your constancy, a paradox intended to make you defend your honour by replying. About the
beginning of June you sent me a letter, and none ever pleased me
more. In it you seemed to surpass yourself in skill and sagacity. There
I first learned that you had returned safely to your family and friends
and had also been restored to good health. That I found the greatest
gratification in this report I believe you will not doubt. You also
said that you will be away from London for some time and that
during this period you would not send me any letters, a promise
you conscientiously fulfilled.

Languet had little idea of the scale of the royal progress, or of the
number of lengthy visits with which the Queen was wont to favour the
luckless hosts whose invitations she deigned to accept. Being "away for
August" was already a pattern for Englishmen who had the means.
Languet continues with his playful chiding:

By now I fear that you have long ago returned to London, and
yet you still do not write to me. It is this constancy with which I
find fault. What else can I suppose than that the lone letter which
you sent me from your homeland, written with such ease and care,
represented your last exertion of diligence born of the trials you en-

dured while with us, a diligence which perceived that it must succumb to the allurements of the pleasures that assailed your wavering spirit?

Perhaps you will think that I treat you unfairly in persuading you to neglect the pleasures of friendships at hand for the vexations of writing. I even fear that my letters will ultimately cease to please you because they adulterate, however slightly, the sweets of leisure. My noble Sidney, you must shun that sordid Siren, Idleness! We also are your friends, and though we do not doubt your love for us, yet we should like our love to bear some fruit. Our harvest is richest when you report good health and the success in your undertakings which your virtue merits and which we wish for you.

The problem involved in forwarding letters safely from the coast of Europe to England and from England to Continental destinations still remained unsolved, but Languet now proposed a promising solution. The de Tassis (or Taxis) family of Brussels, ever since leaving their original home in Italy, had for generations specialized in the imperial postal service. Currently Giovanni Battista de Tassis held the office of Master of the Posts, in addition to his supervisory responsibilities over the Spanish forces in the Netherlands.[16] Languet planned to enlist his help.

If you have not irretrievably decided to stop writing letters, I suggest that you send one to Giovanni Battista de Tassis who is in charge of the stage horses in the Low Countries. Recently he wrote to our friend de l'Ecluse that he regretted not having met you in Antwerp, for he is very eager to serve you. Because this seems the best way of sending letters to you, I shall write him and try to develop his friendship. Now I shall stop pestering you, even though it brings some annoyance on myself. Indeed, if I wished to please myself, I would never stop finding fault with you!

Languet next launched into the political and military news: developments at the Imperial Court, the Emperor's irritation at the French for circulating the story that the Turks had invaded Hungary at his own instigation, and the Polish election. One of Languet's points may well have struck home to Sidney:

I fear nothing more than that the Turks will abandon their ambitions towards Italy and turn their power upon us [Christian

16. Another member of the family, Rudijer von Taxis, served as Imperial Postmaster in Venice.

central Europe]: for I hear that the Spanish are negotiating a truce with them and, indeed, not without hope of obtaining it. Should that happen, woe unto us! and unto you [the English] who are watching the destruction of the Low Countries undisturbed.

The English policy makers were not undisturbed for long. The situation in the Netherlands had deteriorated so badly that the Dutch began to feel desperate. The Spanish yoke became ever more oppressive, and some leaders were seriously considering accepting Catholic dominance as their fate if only they could be left relatively free politically and economically. One faction favoured yielding the country to the French crown if this submission would result in the French driving out the Spaniards.[17] Another party thought their salvation would come by offering submission to Elizabeth of England if she would place the Netherlands under her protection. Indeed, the request for Elizabeth to become Protectrix was made during this month, October 1575. Elizabeth, however, was still disposed to regard Spain as an ally and a counterweight against the threat of France. Despite her pragmatism, she failed to realize that Philip of Spain had placed the extermination of the Protestant heresy high among his priorities.

The Dutch leaders became so despondent that they now decided to offer Elizabeth the crown. To legalize the proposal, emphasis was placed on the genealogical fact that Elizabeth was descended from Philippa, Queen to Edward III and daughter of William, Count of Holland, Zeeland, and Friesland; hence Elizabeth had some Dutch blood. Accordingly, envoys were selected and dispatched to London in November when the nature of their mission became widely known. The court buzzed with speculation and Sidney's special interest in the Netherlands seems to have taken root at this time. His "very greatest friend" from Venetian days, Robert Corbett, was deep in the negotiations. He was designated to go to Requesens, the Spanish governor, on a special embassy for which he left at the end of October. Corbett's mission was to sound out Requesens on accepting Elizabeth as mediator between the Dutch and the Spanish, on the grounds that if the French accepted the crown of the Netherlands Elizabeth would step in to help the Dutch resistance party.

To return to Languet's recommendation that Sidney employ de Tassis as agent for forwarding his letters, it may be observed that Languet took

17. *CSPF2*, no. 424, p. 167.

the step of sending the letter for Sidney with a covering note to de Tassis. The latter then forwarded Languet's packet to Sidney accompanied by a letter in Italian offering his services. Dated October 15, it reads:

> Illustrious and most honoured Sir,
>
> Since I have received the enclosed for your Excellency, very highly recommended by Master Languet, I wished to discharge my obligation by accompanying it with these few brief lines.
>
> I always count myself happy whenever I have an opportunity to be of some useful service to your Excellency, but I should consider myself even more fortunate if you would deign to let me have your orders and commands in any matter in which you judge I could be of service to you. Further, I can assure you that you will find me always a most ready servant to obey you. I shall therefore beg your Excellency to grant me the grace and favour of employing me in everything I can perform. If my ability is not great enough, good-will and readiness to serve you will supply the deficiency.
>
> And thus I shall end, sending you my most affectionate respects, and praying our Lord God to keep your Excellency in health and such good fortune as you may desire. From Antwerp, the fifteenth of October, 1575.
>
> > Always your Excellency's most devoted servant,
> > > Giovanni Battista de Tassis

The connection was exactly the sort that Sidney had been seeking, and it proved mutually beneficial.

Two other letters from the Continent arrived about this time. Sidney's friend from the University of Padua, Baron Slavata, wrote from Paris on October 8, the first letter since they had parted a year and a half earlier. Slavata explains why:

> Greetings, illustrious and noble Master Sidney.
>
> I owed it to our friendship (to which I attained by your singular kindness and the exceptional fame of your virtue and learning, but certainly not through any merits of mine) to confirm and fortify it by assiduity in writing and by perpetual respect for you. But since the time when we parted in Italy I have found no sufficient opportunity to declare my respect and affection for you. For you went

directly to Vienna, but my friend Baron Dohna and I went to the Dauphiné[18] together.

There, by an unhappy stroke of fortune, I was laid low with an illness so serious and so lengthy that it not only severely afflicted all parts of my body, but also completely deprived me of that basic human faculty, the power to write to one's friends. Moreover, I was unsure whether you were living in Vienna or in Poland. Now, however, I can no longer put off this duty, if I wish to make use of these most noble youths (who told me that you are well and have received much honour) to greet you respectfully in this clumsy letter of mine, and at the same time to testify to my constant and perpetual affection for you.

When I had recovered from my illness, I thought it a good idea to restore my vitality and at the same time see the area by travelling to France. This was done as planned, and after a journey full of both pleasure and hardship I reached Paris. It was like a safe port, far from the tumults of war: and I thought to enjoy this tranquillity for a long time. But as happens in kingdoms prone to fatal upheavals, trouble begets trouble, and there is a continual succession of cataclysms.

Baron Slavata now touched on the event that a few weeks earlier had staggered the French court. The King's younger brother, Alençon, the favourite of Catherine de Médicis but Henry III's rival, was being kept in restricted quarters to prevent him from causing trouble. Alençon, who had taken a liberal attitude towards the Huguenots, became the favourite of other dissident groups. The Flemings had indicated that they would like him to become their king, a prospect that perturbed the governments of Elizabeth and Philip, not to mention Henry of France. Alençon still hoped to marry Elizabeth, whose power and treasury were more to his liking. In mid-September he managed to escape to join the Prince de Condé and began to add to his signature "Gouverneur Général pour le Roy et protecteur de la liberté et bien publique de France."

The consternation he caused at court was described by Dr. Valentine Dale, English ambassador in Paris, in a dispatch on September 21.

18. The Latin text reads "ad Allobroges," a people who lived between the Rhône and the Isère.

The King tormented himself upon his bed; the Queen Mother sat much dismayed and lamenting . . . [she] was determined to go to Monsieur to persuade him, but now she is better advised. . . . The King is in a marvellous perplexity; he considers if he should use force against his brother and send any other man against him no other man should be obeyed, and if he should go himself he doubts lest he might be forsaken, neither has he means to levy an army or money to maintain it.[19]

Catherine de Médicis did in fact travel as far as Chambourg "to hearken of his doings, and to induce him to treaty."[20] The King was reported willing to cede Normandy and Brittany to Alençon to appease him; Henry feared that Catherine would join his younger brother. Here is Slavata's report:

The departure of the Duke of Alençon, which to many looked very like flight, greatly endangered French affairs, since many noblemen with a love for revolution joined him and vast amounts of troops from Germany and France (the latter said to be Huguenots) flocked to his standard. Indeed, about three thousand German cavalry have entered France in spite of the Duke of Guise's vain attempts to stop them. The Queen Mother has followed her son, both to please him and to try to bring him back to the path of duty. So far she has had little success. Marshal Montmorency and Cossé were released from prison on October fourth. What a series of upheavals! That is what comes of the counsels of cruelty and tyranny. But more than enough of this: you will doubtless be better informed.

Slavata ends with news about Germany and some of Sidney's friends there.

As for German affairs, I have no news worth writing. The Imperial Diet will be held this month at Regensburg, unless it is delayed by the plague epidemic which is said to be spreading rapidly in that area. What the outcome of the Prague meeting was I have not heard for certain. The Princes have long refused to elevate Rudolph to the crown unless he would grant them freedom of religion.

19. *CSPF2*, no. 365, p. 141.
20. Ibid., no. 374, p. 144.

Our friend Hubert is following the Imperial Court: it is a long time since I had a letter from him. The Count of Hanau is still single, but is contemplating marriage. I have decided that, when spring comes, I shall (D.V.) come to England, where I shall be able to talk with you personally about this and other matters and present my respects in person.

It will be a mark of kindness and singular benevolence towards me on your part if you will accept this letter in a friendly spirit, and rest assured that I remain constant in my love for you and my respect for your dignity. I shall never suffer you to find me wanting in courtesy towards one for whom I have the greatest affection. Farewell, and live in happiness. Given the eighth of October, 1575, at Paris.

Michael Slavata, Baron of Chlum and Cossumberg

A short note from de Banos arrived a few days later.

My Lord,

I wrote to you only recently to tell you what news we had here: nevertheless I have taken advantage of the coming of the bearer of this to send you my greetings, and to have him inform you orally of what he has learned here. The Emperor's voyage is continuing to Regensburg: it was thought that he would break it off because of the plague, which is rampant in the area, and because of a fierce fire which raged in the city to such an extent that more than forty houses were burned down.

My Lord the Prince of Condé is in Strasbourg, and I believe that within the next month he will go and pay quite a close visit to the gates of Paris. The rest you will hear from the bearer of this. I pray God,

Sir, to vouchsafe you His holy benevolence, and present my humble respects to your own. From Frankfurt-am-Main, this seventeenth of October, 1575.

Your most humble servant,
Théophile de Banos

During the last fortnight of this month several letters passed between Sidney and Robert Dorsett at Christ Church. Although Sidney's side of the correspondence has not been preserved, the contents of his letters can be reconstructed from Dorsett's replies. Dorsett's first letter probably reminded Sidney of his own undergraduate experience of having to flee from Oxford when the plague broke out there.

> The suspicion of a plague epidemic that recently reached us is now heralding open danger. The plague is slowly spreading throughout the city and threatening us all; hence the greater part of the University men has fled. Your "flower of youth," to use the poet's expression, and Edward Montagu were summoned by Sir Edward Montagu, with Buste and their two servants Griffin and Hobson, and, after spending a few days at the house of Kellaway, left for Northamptonshire. There, unless you wish otherwise, they will stay until God with greater favour will release the city from the plague.
>
> For the other two, Johannes [Hájek] and [Rowland] White, who are living with me, I will determine which of the two places is more suitable, unless you decide otherwise. I have done what I could to see to the commissions of Master Fulke Greville: but the Latin version of Xenophon's Cyrus I cannot find.
>
> I shall not be too long: so I thank you most sincerely for the immense goodness with which you have long favoured me, and commend yourself and the advancement of your position to almighty God in my prayers. Farewell. Oxford, October 15, 1575.
>
> In greatest devotion to you and yours,
> Robert Dorsett

Sidney's request for the book for Fulke Greville adds special interest to this letter. Rowland White, who may have been a nephew or other relation of Sidney's man Harry White, later became a trusted henchman of Robert Sidney after he became Earl of Leicester.

The next letter, written on October 24, asks Sidney to help Dorsett get some advancement in the church. However much Sidney pushed the matter no success occurred until 1579 when Dorsett was made Dean of Chester.

> If the final phase of my office were not already approaching, most noble Sir, I should most certainly have come to be present at the controversy which I hear is now raging at court: not to start some new drive or request, but to see how each pursues his point. However, though I am not all that well furnished with life's necessities, I shall not strive for anything lest I seem to fall a prey to ambition,

which I have always feared as a stain on any virtuous life. Should there, however, be anything of which, on the recommendation of Dr. Piers, you might find me worthy, I should indeed accept your favour with the greatest pleasure and gratitude.

There is nothing else to tell you; your brother Robert, who recently wrote to me, is in excellent health. May God keep you well and favour your career. Farewell. Oxford, October 24, 1575.

Yours wholeheartedly,
Robert Dorsett

The third letter was written on Monday, October 31. Again the contents require little explanation. Dorsett's reference to November 18 as the day "appointed for our meeting" probably refers to the date on which Robert and the other boys were expected to return to Oxford.

Your man White gave me your letter, of which the first point was that you want your brother Robert, with Johannes and Rowland White, to leave for court; at the end, however, you say that, though you are seized with a great desire to see your brother, you think he is very well established in every way where he is now, and that you wish both Rowland and Johannes to be sent to join him. Whether you decide that he is to come to you, or otherwise, your Excellency will, in my opinion, do well to arrange his journey so as to fall on November eighteenth. For that day has been appointed for our meeting; and I have given that date in my letter to Buste, if the plague epidemic now raging can be brought under control.

As is fitting, I am referring this matter to your judgement: but as they will have so little time to return, I do not think you will find it necessary for Johannes and Rowland to go and join him. Meanwhile lest I do not seem sufficiently obedient to your wish, I am sending this messenger so that I may know your opinion—if only in a single word—at once.

Here there is no news, except that Daniel Bernard—of whom, with his old father, I cannot omit a complimentary mention—is arousing admiration of all by having been granted our next prebend by letter patent from the crown. I am appalled that such a good and learned man should have had no one's support for his candidacy and his hopes; yet I count myself happy in that this office should have gone to one who is by no means a stranger to us.

Farewell, my most noble Sir; and may God not cease to adorn you with His gifts. Oxford, October 31, 1575.

Yours in all devotion to yourself and your name,

Robert Dorsett

On the last Thursday of October Sidney took part in a colourful ceremony at Westminster Abbey along with his uncle the Earl of Leicester and his aunt the Countess of Warwick. The occasion was the christening of a child born to one of Lady Sidney's closest friends, the former Elizabeth Cooke who, eight years after the death of her first husband, the able Sir Thomas Hoby, married John, Baron Russell, second son of Francis, Earl of Bedford. After Sir Thomas's death Queen Elizabeth had written to his widow and in gratitude for her late husband's service as ambassador promised "whereinsoever we may conveniently do you pleasure, you may be thereof assured." Now, nine years later Lady Russell, brought to bed of a daughter, asked her Majesty to serve as godmother for the child, who would be named for her.

The Queen consented and designated the Countess of Warwick as her deputy. The cathedral was decked out for the occasion with crimson taffeta and a great baptismal basin with flowers around the brim. At ten o'clock the participants emerged from the dean's lodging and walked through the cloister and into the cathedral; the men, arranged by rank, came first, followed by the Earl of Leicester as godfather. Next came the midwife holding the baby, caparisoned "in a mantle of crimson velvet, guarded with two wrought laces of gold, having also over the face a lawn, striped with bone lace of gold overthwart, and powdered with gold flowers and white wrote thereon." Then came the Countess of Sussex, one godmother, and the Countess of Warwick as deputy, her train borne by Lady Russell's sisters, Lady Burghley and Lady Bacon.

The dean now had his innings, but when he ended Leicester and the Queen's deputy proceeded to the font where the Countess christened the baby with the Queen's name. Once they had finished "Mr. Philip Sidney came out of the chapel called St. Edward's shrine, having a towel on his left shoulder." The Queen's deputy now came forward and while Sidney and a colleague knelt she washed her hands. Once the ceremony had concluded the attendants marched out of the choir in the same order they had entered and in due course enjoyed "a stately and costly delicate banquet."[21] Thus during the five months after Sidney reached English

21. These details come from Hargreave MS. no. 497, printed by J. H. Wiffen in *Memoirs of the House of Russell* (London, 1833), I : 501–04.

soil he found himself in a succession of official ceremonies in court, castle, and cathedral. Some were entertaining, others strictly formal. He probably relished every minute of it, for as his twenty-first birthday approached he was now enjoying the status for which his heritage and his education at home and abroad had prepared him.

CHAPTER 19

Most of what we know about Sidney during the remaining months of 1575 must be gleaned from the letters his friends wrote to him. On Saturday, November 5, Dorsett made another request about a Christ Church matter. He did so at the prompting of a brother canon, Thomas Thornton, whose candidacy for a vacant stall in the Cathedral Sidney had endorsed in a letter to Cecil at the tender age of fourteen.[1] Now Thornton was seeking to help a Student of Christ Church who had been involved in an "affray at the house of William Noble" during the past June.[2] A year or more of travel seemed in order for the young man, so the governing body of Christ Church turned to Sidney, whose experience and position made his advice valuable and his potential sponsorship invaluable.

> My brother Thornton wrote to your Excellency when you were at Kenilworth to ask you to take under your wing Thomas Hickson, who has an exceptionally ardent desire to see the world. Him I also commend to your goodness: not to trouble you in any way, but so that under your authority he may be kept safe from all harm. He now awaits whatever decision as it may please you to make.
>
> A few days ago you wanted to get in touch with Thomas Alland, the companion of your undergraduate days. He is ready to do whatever you wish, if you would send him word of your desire within the next few days.
>
> That is all I wanted to write for now; more later. May the Lord God grant you all honour. Farewell. Oxford, November 5, 1575.
>
> Yours most devotedly,
Robert Dorsett

Concerning Hickson the records reveal only that he entered from Westminster school in 1565 and proceeded B.A. in 1569 and M.A. in 1572. Nothing further can be learned about William Noble except that he was not a university man. Thomas Alland also remains obscure, since neither his name nor one similar in any way occurs in the university records or in the incomplete buttery-books of Christ Church. One

1. See chap. 1 above.
2. *CSPD*1, p. 498.

mention of this unusual name occurs among the "Diverse necessaries and extra ordinary charges" in the Sidney accounts, "charges of a pardon for Richard Alland, 20th June 1569, £4 15s. 0d."[3] This entry would indicate that Alland was some sort of dependent of Sir Henry.

Only one other note came from Dorsett during the rest of the year. Dated December 1, its purpose is directly stated.

> Most noble Sir,
>
> Apart from thanking you most sincerely—as with all my life and talents I should—for your extreme goodness towards me, there is only one thing with which I need delay the haste of this messenger: i.e. to tell you that your brother Robert with his company will shortly come to Ewelme, where I have a house, albeit a sparsely equipped one. For Master Edward Montagu is thinking of going from Boughton to London with his family at the beginning of next week. He asks you earnestly to call the boys to court. I enclose the letter he wrote me about this: please let me know, if only by a word, your decision on the matter.
>
> The messenger is ready to go, so I must end. Farewell. Oxford, December 1, 1575.
>
> Entirely yours,
> Robert Dorsett

Doubtless Sidney complied. In passing it may be remarked that "Master" Edward Montagu named his seventh son Sidney in honour of his friendship with Sir Henry's family.

Meanwhile, letters from the Continent continued to flow in. Lodowick Bryskett returned from Italy bringing some from various friends, among them two in the thick handwriting of Zündelin. Only the second has been preserved;[4] it consists mainly of compliments.

> It has been two months, most noble sir, since I gave a letter to your Master Lodowick, who was on his way back to you. He, however, was detained by his business until now; and by his unexpected return after such a long interval he has given me an opportunity, not only to write to you again, but also to offer you my sincerest congratulations. For he told me (and because of my incredible love for

3. HMC De L'Isle, 1:244.
4. Possibly Zündelin's memory played a trick on him and he had in mind the letter he wrote not two but four months earlier, that of June 20.

you it was the most delightful news he could have given me) that
you had returned safe and sound to your family and, what is even
more wonderful, that you are enjoying the highest favour of the
greatest and only Queen in the world, as well as being highly appreciated by the best and most important men of your realm.

Zündelin now turned his compliments into a broad hint that he would
like an invitation to visit Sidney. How Sidney responded we do not know.
Before he had returned to England he invited many friends to visit him.
Several of them did so, including Baron Slavata, Lenormand, and Languet.

And while I knew that you would be so, and had previously heard
all the splendid rumours of your Queen's amazing benevolence to
others like you: yet I cannot help rejoicing most heartily that in your
case all this has been more than soundly confirmed both on behalf
of yourself and of your country. For I believe the latter will reap the
most rich and abounding harvest from all the praise and glory accorded your name; and I am wonderfully happy to be able—instructed by your case—to think that there is in this world a place to be
preferred to all others, for this reason: that there virtue and upright-
ness are accorded the honour due to them, and debts are paid with
interest. And while I wanted to see that place before, I am now
positively aflame to do so and desire nothing so much as to see first
the wonder of the world, your Queen, and then yourself: and with
all due modesty to embrace you. I pray to God that some day I shall
be able to realize this wish.

The letter ends with more compliments. It also reveals that Zündelin had
received no letters from Sidney, a lot which he shared with others now
that Sidney had returned to the whirl of life at Elizabeth's court.

I beg that you will continue to love me and to rest assured that I
shall be constant in my respect and honour for you. I shall waste no
more words to this end, as I know that you fulfil both these requests
abundantly. What, in fact, I should wish above all I dare not ask of
you, deterred by my bashfulness and your magnificence: that, when
your affairs allow it, you would write to me. But if you should
write, you will inspire me to reply and add as it were a bonus to the
many letters with which you have testified to your goodwill towards
me.

I am told that you wrote to me after your departure, and I grieve the more that, through what must be the fault of some stranger, that most longed-for letter has gone astray. I would have written and told you the news from here, but the bearer of this will be worth all the letters in the world to you in that respect. Farewell, most noble sir. From Venice, the twenty-third of October, 1575.

> Yours most devotedly,
> with all honour and respect,
> Wolfgang Zündelin

A second letter carried by Bryskett came from Cesare Carrafa. From it we learn that Sidney had written Bryskett from Lichfield on August 2, the day his father had received the letters patent which appointed him Lord Deputy of Ireland. We also learn that in Venice Sidney had become a friend of Giovanni Grimani (ca. 1500–93), Patriarch of Aquileia (the title of the Bishop of Venice). A member of one of the foremost families of Venice, Grimani built the Palazzo which bears his name. In 1570 he had contributed a large sum to aid the campaign against the Turks in Cyprus. Because the Inquisition considered him too lenient towards the Reformation his efforts to obtain a red hat by offering proof of his orthodoxy were thwarted. Doubtless Sidney became acquainted with the Patriarch in the company of Carrafa and Lord Windsor.

Most noble and honoured Sir,

I have grieved for many months that your Excellency did not reply to two letters I wrote you. I discussed it with Master Lodowick, the bearer of this, and together we came to the conclusion that you must have written to me but that the letter was lost. This plainly appears from a letter your Excellency wrote to Master Lodowick on August second. That letter has been out of Venice for a month with the most noble Monsignor Grimani, the Patriarch, and so was not shown to me until this morning. I was very sorry to read what your Excellency told him to say to me. I swear I never received your letter, or I should have answered you at once: the more so since it contained something important, as you write to my most honoured friend Bryskett. This makes me regret all the more the letter's loss. I beg you to write again. In my letters I offered to serve you as you desire and deserve.

I thank you most kindly for your news (in Master Lodowick's letter) that her Majesty your Queen is well. May God bless her and grant her a long life. Quite a while ago I wrote two letters to her

Majesty, commending to her the children of my friend Edward Windsor. In those letters I told her Majesty that had you been there, you would have testified to my great desire to serve her Majesty. I should be very glad to hear if my letters ever reached her Majesty; and if the request is not presumptuous, I beseech you to inquire of her Majesty whether they did or no. Also I ask you to offer her, in my name, most humble duty and service, begging her to make use of me here in any matter that may befall, to the service of her Majesty.

I spoke at length with Master Lodowick and told him that, because of the duty I owe your Excellency both for your rich deserving and for your high degree, I am yours freely to command. And if I should have occasion to write to you, I shall hope to send you such news as is worth writing. This I will do with pleasure, so your Excellency love me and regard me as your servant.

You will do well to keep your eyes wide open in the service of your Queen where you are, for all that glitters is not gold—*qui habet aures audiendi audiet.*

And so let me end with my most respectful greetings to yourself, to your most noble father, to Master . . . Robert [Corbett] and to your most excellent lady mother. From Venice, October 22, [15]75.

Your Excellency's most affectionate servant,

Don Cesare Carrafa

The most noble Monsignor the Patriarch greets you warmly.

Bryskett also brought a letter from a friend whose identity is otherwise unknown, Johann Conrad Brüning. The letter contains many personal details, the only available information about Brüning. Considering that Sidney had known him at Paris in 1572, and later at Strasbourg and Padua, the absence of other references is surprising. The letter begins with the customary compliments.

Having found an opportunity to write to you, noble and illustrious Lord, and feeling myself strengthened both by your goodwill towards me and my own respect for you, I could not restrain myself from inscribing this letter to you—brief indeed, yet the product of a heart so full of honour and love for you that it desires nothing but to renew (for we are now so very far apart) your memory of us via this letter of mine.

For I have conceived such an opinion of your noble and excellent nature and of your amazing and well-nigh diurnal virtue that, however much the very high degree and rank your parents hold in the realm of England may have aided your rise to the highest honours among your own people, yet I do not doubt that you will shortly rise to the greatest dignities by your own virtue. And as I hear that you have already found at the English court an ample field to exercise that virtue, I congratulate not only you but myself as well: you, because such things are befalling you as your virtue deserves, but myself because I can already see the very opinion I previously conceived of you being confirmed by the events themselves.

Brüning next described the difficult situation in which he now found himself. (Investigations in Naples have failed to produce any record of the incident.)

After my return from Germany last year, I set out with my friends the Barons [Lichtenstein] on a journey through Italy, visiting Rome and Naples. In this latter city I was accosted by a certain German nobleman in a most unbecoming manner and assailed with many atrocious insults such as no gentleman should be subjected to. Then, taking the matter from words to deeds and indeed to blows, he laid hands on me and attacked me with such violence that he almost severed two fingers of my right hand.

Because, from the gravity of my wound, I could no longer (according to the German custom) defend myself with the edge of my sword, I was forced to repulse his attack with the point. At which my adversary, having sustained but one thrust in the chest, succumbed and died. Your wisdom will be able to judge the calamities and hardships into which this matter has precipitated me. However, by the will of Almighty God and the help of good men, I was able to escape from the realm of Naples, so that (apart from private vendettas) I have no more to fear in this region.

Because, however, his father is in a position of some authority among the German nobility and is greatly incensed with me for having killed his son, I cannot yet return to Germany in safety, and will not be able to do so until affairs have been settled with the dead man's family. My parents, indeed, are omitting nothing that might help a settlement, and many great men (chief among them Master Schwendi) have interceded for me, but my adversaries are being so difficult about it that neither my parents' efforts nor the counsels and authority of those who are interceding for me have been able to accomplish anything. My last hope is the Emperor: if that fails, I shall count as lost any expectation of a return home.

The solution to his problem, in Brüning's opinion, lay in his migrating to England where his friend Sidney could open the doors to opportunity.

I have therefore decided that, although one's native land must needs be dear to one, should the state of my affairs prohibit a safe return to my country and I be forced to seek my fortune abroad, I shall—never yet having seen the flowering realm of England—within a year at most travel via France to England and remain there until my affairs in Germany are settled and I shall have a prospect of a safer return to my ancestral hearth.

As, however, my means will not permit me, when I arrive, to live in unoccupied idleness, need itself will drive me to look for some patron to whom I can dedicate my efforts and energies. And, if, of the many who might advance my cause, one were to be chosen, there would be none who could compare with yourself: for, apart from the fact that we have known each other in Paris, Strasbourg, and here in Padua, I am also quite sure that the high authority you hold in your country could be of great help to me when I am there.

So that I need not trouble you with a longer letter, I shall let you hear the rest from Bryskett. Our friend Septimus[5] sends you his friendliest greetings. Henricus, however, left four months ago to join the Imperial Court. Farewell: may you always live in safety and happiness. You may be sure that I am full of love and honour towards you and would willingly take up arms in your defence should an occasion present itself. From Padua, the thirty-first of October, 1575.

Yours with all respect and honour,

Johann Conrad Brüning

Quite different from these letters was one Sidney received about the same time from the Calvinist theologian Dr. Ursinus at Heidelberg. Written on November 5, it plunges into unhappy news.

5. Baron Johann Septimus and his brother Baron Hartmann ("Henricus") of Lichtenstein. The latter became the founder of the princely house of Liechtenstein (note altered spelling), and Septimus achieved distinction as a humanist. Hartmann visited England in midsummer 1577 when Sidney entertained him (Sidney to Languet, Oct. 10, 1577).

Greetings.

I would not dare to write to your Excellency if I knew that our friend Master Hubert Languet had recently written to you. As, however, I am in doubt about this, especially in these times and those places in which letters have become the target of such well-aimed and dangerous ambushes, and as I am sure that you would nevertheless like to have some news of how that best and kindest of men is, I trust that you will ascribe the sending of this letter not to any boldness or impudence of mine, but rather to my wish to satisfy your desire to the best of my present ability.

So far as I can tell from letters, by him and others, received some days ago, our friend Languet is still at the court of the Emperor, which he has followed to Regensburg. With his prince he is in ill favour, and in great peril. He cannot obtain access to his friends without immediate danger, nor dare he enter the presence of his master: yet because of his virtue and honesty, neither will he take precautions to protect himself instead. And so he remains, and lives out of the public eye, in great perturbation of spirit. Let us at least hope that he will be dismissed, whether with bad grace or good. Great is the hatred the hypocrites bear him; and we always considered his master's tolerance towards him suspect—not without reason. Let us pray God to protect him. I shall wait anxiously to see what becomes of him after the close of the Regensburg Diet.

We can easily imagine how upset Sidney must have been at this news and how worried he remained until a reassuring letter arrived from Languet himself about three weeks later. Lutheran sympathizers among the Saxonian delegation at the Regensburg Diet apparently thought the time was ripe to remove the Calvinist Frenchman from his position of influence. Fortunately for Languet the Elector Augustus still valued his services and did not give way to the Lutheran cabal.
Other news of the unsuccessful gathering follows:

It is thought, however, that the Princes have either already left Regensburg, or will leave soon, as the son of the Emperor, the King of Hungary and Bohemia, Rudolph, was elected King of the Romans on the twenty-fourth of October and crowned on the last day of that same month. This is said in letters by several correspondents, while a public messenger is expected hourly. Our Prince [the Elector Palatine] did not go, whether because of his health or for other reasons, and sent ambassadors instead. The other Electors were all present.

The Elector of Saxony is showing the most vehement indignation towards us because of our doctrine of the Eucharist. He is also said to have been offended by the divorce and remarriage of the Prince of Orange and by the expedition that his son-in-law John Casimir is preparing to make to France with eight thousand German horsemen. So far it is being said that he himself will go with the army, but I am not yet certain of that. I pray to God that everything will work out well—there seems to be no lack of danger and fear. The minds of many are wavering as to what is to be done: much is involved in the religious issue that has no bearing on it. Actions are being begun and carried through on plans often lacking in vigour and with assistance which is of doubtful efficiency and questionable probity.

Turmoil continued to characterize the situations in both Hungary and Poland. In his analysis of the Polish election Dr. Ursinus showed a great deal of perspicacity, as events proved after Stephen Báthory became king of that strife-torn country.

In Hungary the Turks are assembled: they have already taken several towns and threaten for next year a war for which we are ill equipped. So an Imperial Diet is expected in early spring. The Poles are already meeting at Warsaw about the election of a new king: many think it will be Stephen Báthory, Voivode of Transylvania. For since the Hungarian troubles there is more enthusiasm for him than for the Austrian. About eighty thousand Tartars have invaded Poland, laying waste many regions: on the Podolian border there are about one hundred and twenty thousand Turks, and Tartars who fight for the Turks. But we believe the Poles may yet be spared all this if Báthory becomes king: he has a peace treaty with the Turks, and they are among those who have sponsored him and recommended him to the Poles.

Ursinus now leaves political confusions for comments on theological ones. Because the names of the theologians he mentions are unfamiliar, a brief explanation is in order. Dr. Caspar Peucer was a physician and mathematician and a son-in-law to Melanchthon. A professor of medicine at Wittenberg since 1559, his brilliant mind had won him high favour at the court of Saxony, but recently his close friendship with Languet had been held against him. In 1574 Peucer was imprisoned on the charge that he had written a Zwinglian treatise on the Eucharist, and he languished in jail for twelve years. The fiery Tillemann Heshus, a Lutheran theologian, became Bishop of Prussia in 1573. Johann Wigand, another Lutheran, had been appointed Professor of Theology at Jena in 1569. Expelled by the Elector Augustus after the death of the Duke of Weimar in 1573, he became Bishop of Pomerania. The theologian Heinrich Bullinger had succeeded Zwingli at Zürich.

> In Meissen our coreligionists are not being any better treated. The theologians are still under house arrest, such as Master Peucer, since the death of Cracovius who was killed in prison: I hear, however, that they are bearing their fate with equanimity. The new theologians at Wittenberg are being dreadfully persecuted with the most abusive literature by Heshus and Wigand, the Bishops of Prussia and Pomerania, because they dared to assert that Philip's [i.e. Melanchthon's] opinions on the Eucharist coincided with Luther's: in fact they conclusively prove the opposite. Thus does evil destroy itself. That Master Heinrich Bullinger has died at Zürich, and that he has been succeeded by Master Rudolph Walter, you doubtless know already.
>
> May the Lord Jesus guide and protect your Excellency and grant to your virtue and piety such rewards as may increase the glory of His name and the well-being of his Church. Farewell. Given at Heidelberg, the fifth day of November, 1575.
>
> With all honour and reverence to your Excellency,
>
> Zacharias Ursinus,
> Professor at the Heidelberg College of Theology

Understandably these troubles vexed Dr. Ursinus more than they did Sidney's other correspondents. In addition to being worried about his dear friend Languet as a Calvinist, Ursinus belonged to the group under attack.

The next letter from across the Channel to reach Sidney appears to be that from Lobbet, dated November 22. It answers one Sidney had written from Windsor where he had been with the court on October 28.

> It is a long time since I wrote to you, my lord Sidney, and if my memory does not fail me, I have sent you no letter since our friend Zölcher left for England about three months ago. The sole reason for my lapse is that you have not vouchsafed me a single reply to all the letters I sent you earlier. To tell the truth, I was certainly surprised at

this; yet so well do I know your kindness and good nature that it would not enter my mind that you might despise my letters.

Yet I did not know what else to think. I feared that you were either ill or had left England for other parts. Because I thought this I remained silent, until I should at any rate hear some news of you from others. Yet all my doubts were dispelled by your extremely charming letter from Windsor dated the twenty-eighth of last month, in which you give a perfectly adequate reason for your silence. I for my part accept this excuse in good part as both just and legitimate.

I have conveyed your greetings to your host Hubert de la Rose; the good man has been bedridden now for a full three months, almost completely paralysed. He welcomed your greeting and asked me to present to you his respects and his apologies for not writing himself. Mont also presents his respects to you. What you write about taking pleasure in my letters is most welcome to me, and I shall take pains that you may not find me wanting in diligence.

Sidney had been so pleased at the arrangement he had made at Languet's suggestion to have de Tassis at Antwerp forward his letters, that he had suggested Lobbet should use the same agent.

The only thing we have still to find is a way of sending our letters back and forth that will operate smoothly and silently. I do not know what you think but I do not wish in this single matter to bother de Tassis, the Master of Posts at Antwerp. There is no point in doing in a complicated way things that can be done simply. What need is there to trouble de Tassis for one simple letter?

And so (if you agree) you can do it this way. In London there are many merchants who trade with Antwerp. You might, therefore, strike up an acquaintance with some suitable London merchant who could include your letters to me in the packet he sends to Antwerp, and have someone in Antwerp give them to some German merchant who would despatch them to Doctor Rana at Brussels. I, on the other hand, would send my letters for you to the same Doctor Rana, who would despatch them to London via whatever Antwerp merchant you would suggest to me.

If you think this route too long and that we could send our letters back and forth without the aid of Doctor Rana and without going via Brussels, I should understand, as otherwise the letters might be delayed at Brussels. But I see no reason why they should be. If you

> could find a method in London whereby your letters could be sent directly via Antwerp here to Strasbourg, and to some merchant here, that would be good. For the merchant here could give me your letters, and I could give him mine.
>
> Sometime we shall find a method which will save us trouble and expense, but the chief aim is to further our acquaintance and (as they say) "good correspondence." I have been rather long in explaining this, but have done so on purpose as, if you would like us to correspond more frequently and regularly, we must lay a few foundations. But I will await your opinion on this. Meanwhile I shall send this letter to Doctor Rana, so that he can despatch it to London.

To judge from the documents themselves, Sidney preferred to have letters directed to Leicester House. Evidently he was indifferent about whether they were written in Latin or French; Lobbet's subsequent letters are about equally divided between the two languages.

Lobbet now relates the latest news in Strasbourg, much of it long known to Sidney, though he may have welcomed confirmation.

> There is something else I should like to ask you: whether you approve of the way I address my letters to you, or whether it should be different. I usually send them to the house of the noble lord the Earl of Leicester. I shall await your verdict as to whether this is all right. I should also like to know whether you had rather that I write in Latin than in French, or vice versa. Whichever of these languages I use, I shall write without pomp and circumstance and, drawing my inspiration from some plain Minerva, shall try to take myself intelligible to you.
>
> I should like to know how our young Bohemian friend [Hájek] is getting on; I also wish that he would write to me, so that I can give his father some news of him.
>
> We have not yet heard that a king has been created: yet some think that one will be elected before the end of the Diet which is being held by the Estates of Poland. For they do not think that the Poles can remain kingless much longer without clear detriment to themselves. At present there are many thousands of Tartars, enlisted at great cost by the Turkish Emperor, uncomfortably close to them.
>
> As for the Turkish Emperor himself, he is said to be preparing to join the French war by land and by sea. At Constantinople the red banner has been publicly raised: this is the sign of a major military

expedition which must be attended and led by the Turkish Emperor. Such things are greatly troubling the minds of Christians.

The eldest son of our Emperor, Rudolph, who before was King of Hungary and Bohemia, has been made King of the Romans. His coronation was celebrated at Regensburg on the second of this month. That Diet at Regensburg is finally over. Some proposal about the religious question was made there, but its discussion has been deferred until the coming Imperial Diet which, it is said, will begin next February at Worms or Augsburg.

As for matters French, you will have as much, and as trustworthy, news of them as we do here. The Prince of Condé is making major military preparations: he has conscripted many thousands of men (some say nine to ten thousand)—German cavalry, and Swiss and German infantry. Everyone is saying that he is ready for battle now; I do not know whether the cease-fire that the Duke of Alençon is said to be arranging in France will delay the expedition.

The Duke of Wittenberg celebrated his wedding on the seventh of this month with the daughter of the Marquis of Baden. It is said there will be a marriage shortly between Eric, Duke of Brunswick, and Dorothea, the younger sister of the Duke of Lorraine. At the Wittenberg wedding, during the jousting, Albert Count of Hohenlohe was killed by the thrust of a lance.

Finally, Lobbet reported about several friends. Probably Sidney already knew William Lewin (d. 1598); he had been the tutor of Anne Cecil whom Sidney nearly married in 1569. Lewin served as proctor and public orator at Cambridge University and became a judge of the prerogative court of Canterbury. He was a friend and correspondent of Dr. Sturm, which explains why he had visited Strasbourg. His wife was a daughter of Sir Francis Goldsmith of Crayford, Kent.

Such is the state of the world. Our friend Languet has left Regensburg for Vienna with the Emperor. Our friend the Count of Hanau will celebrate his wedding next February. But I am going on longer than I expected. I beg you to give my humble greetings to my lord of Walsingham, the First Secretary of your realm. I should also like to convey my greetings to a certain most excellent man who recently visited Master Sturmius in this [city]—his name is William Lewin. He lives in the house of the noble Francis Goldsmith in Colman Square, London.

I wish you a happy life, noble lord Sidney, and send you my respects.
Given at Strasbourg, the twenty-second of November, 1575.

Yours most respectfully,

J. Lobbet

Early in December Sidney received a letter from a Venetian literary
man hitherto not known to have been one of his friends. Cesare Pavese
had been born in Aquila but spent most of his life in Venice. He numbered
the Tasso family among his friends, corresponded with Bernardo, the
father of Torquato Tasso, and is mentioned with respect in the preface to
Torquato's *Rinaldo* (1562). Pavese's own chief publication appeared in
1569 under the pseudonym "Pietro Tarza"; it bore the title, *Cento e
cinquanta Favole tratte da diversi autori antichi e ridotte in versi e rime*. In the
next twenty years it went through four editions. Besides other verses
which appeared in miscellaneous publications, Pavese also wrote the
preface and notes to an Italian translation of Statius's *Thebais*, published in
Venice in 1570.

In the absence of other traces of the friendship between Sidney and
Pavese, the two letters among the newly recovered group are the basis
for any facts or inferences. Because he speaks familiarly of Robert Corbett
and George Lewknor, Pavese evidently counted most of the travelling
Englishmen among his friends. George Lewknor himself is something of a
mystery man. He appears to have been a Catholic and an intimate of Lord
Windsor, since he paid for the latter's elaborate monument. In the early
summer of 1574 Lewknor had travelled across Europe with Robert
Parsons, an Oxford don who later became a Catholic priest.[6] Parsons and
his friends took a house in Padua, which they furnished with "apparell"
formerly belonging to Lord Windsor, shortly after his death.[7] Written
in Italian, Pavese's first letter speaks for itself:

Most Illustrious Sir and honoured Patron,
As you will have heard I left Venice at the beginning of May, and
the journey as well as my stay in Rome together took about six
months; I returned here on the first of this month. When I returned
I heard that Master Bryskett had left here six days before, which I

6. Parsons's *Autobiography*, published by the Catholic Record Society in their *Miscellanea*
(London, 1906), 2 : 23.
7. Ibid., p. 24.

greatly regretted as it deprived me of the opportunity to pay my due respects to you. Then there arrived here Master George Lewknor, who told me that Bryskett had urgently asked for me to deliver some request of your Excellency's: but, though I looked most diligently I could not find any clearer order left by him than the standing one I have to send on letters or parcels for you: I hope I have correctly guessed the rest.

This letter, therefore is to present to your Excellency and to Master Corbett the affectionate respect which I owe both of you as your customary servant in all places, and particularly here in Venice, as I have plenty of time here which I dedicate to God, as much as shall please him, and to those who are my masters among whom your Excellency takes pride of place. You will, accordingly, be obeyed if you will be so kind as to favour me with a letter to let me know exactly in what way I can be of service to you, so that I do not by some mischance make the wrong guess.

Also I should be grateful if you would let me know to whom I can give your letters that they may not fail to arrive, or indeed (which would be even better) to whom I should send them in Antwerp— someone who would not fail to send them to you, so that they are certain to reach you. I will then do this, and anything else that would be of service to you, gladly and with all my heart, as experience, and results, will tell you.

The remainder of Pavese's page is a halfhearted summary of foreign news, apparently included because convention called for it.

The main news here is that, after long debates, the Genoese troubles are said to be settled: but as for me, I think this unity is not going to be achieved soon or easily and that, when it does occur, it will not be successful for long. From the Levant we hear that in spite of the famine and the plague there the Sultan is making incredible preparations for next year: and we here are by no means so secure as people believe. We have plenty of reasons for not being particularly confident, and for being troubled and anxious.

As for Germany and France, I have no news for your Excellency, since I know that you are much better informed than we are—perhaps even about what I mentioned above. Therefore I shall tread lightly this time: and I shall wish, and pray to the Lord God, that you may have the greatest happiness. I greet you with the highest affection and present you my best respects, as also to my friend Master Robert. From Venice, the nineteenth of November [15]75.

> Your Excellency's most affectionate servant,
>
> Cesare Pavese

In December after an interval of more than two months, two letters arrived from Languet. Sidney must have been eager to receive them after Dr. Ursinus's worried letter about their friend's position at the Elector's court. Languet's report supplied reassurance that rumours proved worse than the facts behind them. He begins, however, by acknowledging that Sidney had foreseen the situation long in advance.

> You hit the nail on the head in your letter from Antwerp: I have indeed devoted myself too long to ungrateful Sparta. Indeed at Regensburg I found this to be more true than ever. There many men with whom I have passed a good part of my life, men who previously appeared to show me goodwill, avoided me as if we were adversaries in a contest. Moreover, they did so without indicating that I had given cause for grievance, but rather to show off to the onlookers, thinking that they could gain favour with those persons whom they wished to flatter.
>
> At first their behaviour bothered me, but later I paid no attention to these persons and their foolish actions. This was made easy for me because many eminent men who were unshaken in their friendship flocked there from various places, and I could enjoy their company. Nevertheless I complained directly to his Excellency my prince about their discourtesies and deliberately stated the matter in writing, a note which I gave him just the day before his departure, in order to forestall further slanders.
>
> Later it turned out that he did not then read my note because he was so busy bidding farewell to the Emperor and the other princes. Yet, when he had gone only one day's journey beyond Regensburg he sent me a letter full of kindness in which he stated that my only fault was not to have informed him of these matters sooner. In addition he then demonstrated by his generous attitude to me that the rude conduct of the others did not please him in the least.

Trained rhetorician that he was, Languet now turned this recent experience into a device to chide Sidney for not writing more often.

The ingratitude of men whom I believed to be my friends disturbed me . . . but your persistent silence troubles me far more. . . .
Indeed, I fear that I have somehow done something to alienate you
from me. . . . Not only have I always felt an extraordinary fondness
for you, but I have also among friends admired greatly the remarkable mental gifts which God has generously bestowed upon you.

And so on. For us special interest attaches to Languet's continued praise of
Sidney's intellectual powers, a quality unlikely to be mentioned in flatter-
ing a man who had other attractions of personality, manners, supposed
affluence, and connections with the politically powerful. Clearly Languet's
repeated references to Sidney's unusual mind explain why he considered
him worth every possible attention. In Sidney he saw the potential for a
great leader of the Protestant cause, a man capable of heading a united
Protestant front.

The balance of the letter is filled with political news of the reported
movements of the Muscovite, the Turk, the Emperor, and lesser forces on
the European chessboard. Later in the week Languet wrote again, and the
two letters may well have arrived together. Perhaps Sidney even opened
the second one first. The tone was very different, for a letter from Sidney
had finally arrived. It begins with rather full comment on Sidney's pages
and is thus more directly personal than usual.

Five or six days ago I sent you a letter written in a slightly more
imperious tone than perhaps I now wish I had done, though I am
not very apologetic for my fervour: since in that letter you may see
how ill I endure being unjustly treated. Though a letter from you
arrived yesterday, it does not convince me that I was unjust in finding
fault with your negligence, because a full five months have passed
since you last wrote. You offer as excuse for your idleness attendence
on the progress of the court and your accompanying his Excellency
your father, Yet when Caesar wrote his *Commentaries* in camp he was
far busier than you. I beg you, please ponder the implications of not
having wished in all that time to devote one hour to the friends who
love you dearly and worry more about you than they do about themselves. You could have more than satisfied us merely by giving up one
dance a month. A year ago you were with us for only three or four
months. Recall how many excellent writers you read through in that
short time and the profit you gained by reading them.

From another viewpoint, you may reason that, because you learned from these books so much about the proper ordering of life, this should not prevent you now from immersing yourself in pleasures from top to toe.

Possibly, of course, I am reproaching you unjustly and you have not lost any of your former diligence (I pray that this is so). Yet, your neglect in writing to us convinces me otherwise; indeed, this neglect arouses the fear that your exceptionally brilliant mind will be encrusted in rust if you fail to exercise it. Never allow yourself to think that God gave you so fine a mind merely for you to let it decay from misuse. Instead, know that He demands more from you than from others to whom He has been less bountiful. Moreover, should you get accustomed to continued idleness, even if tempestuous events clear idle habits away, you will find their violence more difficult to overcome than if you were more accustomed to coping with trials and troubles.

This is advice straight from the shoulder and intended to be man-to-man; it is touched with enough master-to-pupil and Calvinist morality that Sidney was unlikely to have been offended. His English friends were equally conscious of the gifts nature had bestowed upon him and of his high seriousness in regard to his mission in life. From our vantage point in time, Sidney would seem to have earned both a holiday from his reading program and an opportunity to find his way as a young man at court. More than that, he deserved the chance to enjoy being young and attractive in the ruling class to which he had been born. To give stern Languet his due, he knew the world, he understood human nature and temptation, and he had studied Sidney's mind and personality with concentrated devotion. Posterity can be grateful for this sustained dedication. Equally, we may be grateful that this human story can be so well documented.

Conscious that he had been heavily didactic, Languet now adopted a milder tone:

> Note how discourteous I am to repay you in this manner for your courteous letter. Thus do I try to prevent you, as far as I can, from fulfilling the joys which you doubtless feel in the pleasant company of so many friends. I never questioned that you would prove highly congenial and very dear to your family and to good men everywhere. Hence you report nothing about your reception among them which I had not previously anticipated. Nevertheless I was delighted to have confirmation from your letter and found high pleasure in it.

Other details of Sidney's letter are reflected in Languet's response to them. Because of Sidney's posthumous image as the superb mind in a perfect body, a man who was supreme at all sports,[8] Languet's concern about the state of his health seems curious. During his years on the Continent, a hazardous enough place for most but especially so for a roving youth, his health probably did suffer from periodic infections and imbalances. With maturity he seems to have escaped these earlier afflictions. Whatever Sidney wrote Languet on the subject, here is the latter's reply:

> I am distressed that at your age your health is causing problems. Perhaps you suffer from the fact that you are living so high, since abroad, when you lived more moderately, you enjoyed good health except for the illness you suffered shortly before leaving us. Do take care not to bring it on again by excessive exercise or in any other way.

Languet next reverted to a favourite theme, Sidney's marriage plans. His motives are quite understandable, for he wished Sidney to enter a settled life and enjoyed thinking of Philip's making a match with some great family which would aid his career. Moreover, since Sidney was the eldest male in his generation of the Sidney and Dudley lines, Languet wished him to marry early enough to propagate his family.

> What you write jokingly about a wife I take quite seriously. Do not overestimate your firmness, for men more cautious than you have been ensnared. For my part, I wish you were already in the bonds, so that for your country's sake you might produce children like yourself. Whatever eventuates in this matter, I pray God that the results may be fortunate and prosperous. You observe how courageously Wotton has borne that ordeal; his bravery seems to accuse you of timidity. Fate has a strong sway in such matters, so you have no cause for thinking that by foresight you can control your destiny to be happy in every particular, or that you may achieve all the success you desire.

8. For example, Spenser's elegiac description in "Astrophel," ll. 73–78:

> In wrestling nimble, and in renning swift,
> In shooting steddie, and in swimming strong:
> Well made to strike, to throw, to leape, to lift,
> And all the sports that shepheards are emong.
> In euery one he vanquisht euery one,
> He vanquisht all, and vanquisht was of none.

Most of the rest of Languet's letter was given to the current news on events or rumoured developments in Poland, Hungary, Italy, Turkey, France, and Spain. At the end, however, Languet added greetings from friends.

> Wacker returned from Italy a month or two ago and will write reporting his activities. He is a very fine man and much attached to you. Please give my courteous regards to Master Wotton, who, I trust, thrives. Give my respects also to Master Corbett and to my other friends. Hereafter do not blame Priscian [a grammarian, fl. 500 A.D., whom Sidney evidently had cited] for your negligence. I shall procure indulgences from him for many years so that you may slaughter him whenever you wish.
>
> Farewell, and remember that you are involved with a man who does not easily endure being cheated! Vienna, December 3, 1575.
>
> My host [Lingelsheim] and his entire household send you their regards, as does Monau, who left here yesterday. I have not yet given your greetings to Crato.

Languet's reference to Wacker shows that he was unaware that Wacker had written to Sidney two days earlier. His letter is unique among the Sidney correspondence in two particulars, the first being that Wacker sends fulsome apologies for having failed to answer Sidney's last letter to him, a notable contrast to the usual complaints of Sidney's neglect. Wacker clearly had a good excuse for not writing, since he had undergone a siege of ill health. His report suggests that he still suffered a verbal diarrhea:

> Your most excellent kindness and virtue in all things appears in this letter which, a few days ago, you sent to our friend Languet. Not that it was new and unknown to me: yet it was pleasing and most welcome—I would say "delightful," had a not daily and most vexing sickness made that word something of a mockery to me. And not only was it so for the reason you might perhaps suspect (i.e. because in the paragraph referring to me you spoke of me with kindness and honour), but also because you have been pleased not to let that abundant silence of mine, which I do not know whether in my guilt I should even mention, in any way diminish your former benevolence towards me. For though I believe I had the best of reasons for that silence, yet I have long had such affection for you

that, even with an honest and appropriate reason, I should think myself boorish if I neglected even the smallest part of my friendly duty to you.

Yet fortunately, my most noble Sidney, you are not given to evil opinions about the loyalty of your friends, while I have found an opportune occasion for doing penance in the letter of our friend Languet. For that I have written to you less frequently than I should have, and than was due to your kindness, was in no way due to my forgetting you—indeed, nothing is sweeter and more lasting to me than your memory—but in part because of my ill health (which, however, seems at last to be slowly improving), and in part because I was far from any place where I might know someone who was travelling your way.

However, after that last letter I sent to you in Frankfurt I have written again and again to our friend Languet. In those letters I would not only append respectfully the greeting I owed you, but I would also assure him at some length that the association we had begun always had, and would continue to have, my heartfelt enthusiasm. And the main point of my speeches was this: that among my desires none was greater, or had been so for a long time, than the wish that I too might hasten to come to you as soon as possible, in order once more for a while to enjoy your most sweet and delightful company.

Yet, as in the past many things have prevented the fulfilment of my wishes, so now a long illness is frustrating it to the extent of holding me involuntarily where, of all places, I could at this moment least wish to be. Yet we must obey the law imposed by necessity and not (as the saying goes) wish to kick against the pricks. If by the divine mercy, however, it be vouchsafed me at some stage to recover somewhat and to be so restored to strength as to be able to travel, I shall not fail to pursue this goal: that at last I may with these infinitely yearning eyes behold you. If, that is, our friend Languet remains of the same mind as he is at present; and if you will not, because of the lateness of my coming, have suffered any of your love for me to die.

Meanwhile, until at some time I can present you with the completion of what alone occupies my prayers and hopes, embrace me perpetually with your former innate goodwill, and in return rest assured that I shall be at pains to undertake anything which I understand will be in the least welcome to you, wherever in the world I may be: so that, though there are many others who would join me in doing so, I shall strive in such matters to be the first of them all. Farewell, From Vienna, Austria, the first of December in the year of the last age, 1575.

Yours with singular honour and respect,
Matthaeus Wacker of Constanz

At the end Wacker added a postscript. It gives his letter its second claim to uniqueness, for the long Latin hymn he appended is the only original poem known to have been sent to Sidney during these years. It is written in the hendecasyllabic metre named after the Alexandrian poet Phalaecus. The metre is too complicated to attempt in translation, so the poem is here loosely rendered in lines of four stresses each.

> As there was a page left over and I knew that—which is the height of your kindness—you take pleasure in my work, I have made free to append (out of a great collection) these Phalaecians, which were wrung from me by grief in my sickness. It was not Apollo who dictated them: read them, therefore, as the slight verses, not of an excellent poet, but of a little friend languishing in sickness.

To God

Although thou refusest me thy merciful ear
These three months, awful Father of all,
While I plague thee ever with my complaints:
Yet thou doest it not so that, suddenly robbed
Of all hope and broken, I should trip and fall:
Thine anger, long and almost too lasting,
Has taught me never, in day or night,
To cease to call on thee, ever more
And ever more, as Father and Lord.
Nay rather, the less I see that thou wishest
To listen to my complaints, the more,
Ever more, will I plague thee with my complaints;
With constricted throat I will say thy name
Again and again and again: I shall cry
My prayers till at last, forced by my sighing,
Though against thy will, thou wilt lighten the grief
Of a wretched man, and return me my health.
O King, O Father, O awful Father,
What end wilt thou make to this my pain?

What bounds wilt thou set to this my pain?
Within what space wilt thou confine my pain?
Or wilt thou drown me in endless pain?
    And yet a gentle Father we call thee,
Mild, and gracious, and good we call thee:
And gentle to the wretched, and most benign
To the afflicted, and kind to one and all.
    So whither has that thy goodness departed?
Whither have thy mercy and favour departed?
Whither has that soon-turned anger departed?
Or wilt thou refuse to me alone
What with grace and gentleness thou failest not
Liberally to grant to all the world?
    Ah merciful Father: ah, Father benign,
Turn in thy kindness thy merciful eyes
And thy face benign unto thy servant.
Let thy mercy and the vast favour of thy justice
Swiftly deck me—broken with a sick
Body and prostrated by helpless limbs—
With my old vigour: let my pains, trembling,
Be expelled from these wretched powers of mine.
And in thy gentle goodness grant me once more
A body endowed with my former health.
    Then will I hymn thee, Eternal One,
With my songs and my lyre, nor will any night
Or day discover me forgetful of thy name:
Until the Moon gives us perpetual night,
And Phoebus shines in eternal day.

Another letter written about this time came from Carrafa. Apparently it was carried by one Thomas Sans, perhaps the future Sir Thomas Sondes (or Sands), Deputy Lieutenant of East Kent whose family intermarried with the Sidney family's friends, the Montagus of Boughton.

My very noble Sir,
    I wrote your Excellency a long letter via Master Lodowick Bryskett; and such is my desire to be of service to you that I did not wish to let pass the occasion, offered by the departure of Master Thomas Sans, to discharge my obligation. I have asked him to greet

your Excellency warmly in my name, and to tell you how much I love and honour you.

A servant of the Earl of Oxford arrived here, who I thought would bring a letter from your Excellency. From him I heard that you are well, in great favour with her noble Majesty your Queen, and beloved of all the court, all of which has made me extremely happy. This week great things have been said about England, but the Ambassador of Spain says that they are untrue and that what the merchants write is false. They said that her Majesty had intercepted the fleet my Sovereign had sent to Flanders, had impounded one hundred thousand ducats, and captured an ambassador my lord had sent to the King.

The Genoese troubles have apparently been settled, and already the inhabitants have dismissed everyone. From France we hear that a six months' truce has been concluded, with great disadvantage to the King. From Constantinople there is news that a great fleet is being prepared. Here we live under a peace of Octavian—under the excellent and prudent government of our present Signori, compounded with the prospect of plague, we are fairly well.

Please greet your most noble father and my lord of Oxford most reverently from me, and give my respects to the most honourable Master Lodowick Bryskett. And may our Saviour grant your Excellency the fulfilment of all your desires. Venice, December 2, 1575.

I pray you most humbly and reverently to greet her Majesty in my name and assure her of my devotion in recognition of her great favour.

Your Excellency's most affectionate servant,
Don Cesare Carrafa

Two points in the letter are of interest, the first being that the Earl of Oxford's servant was well informed about Sidney's health and affairs. The other is the confirmation from an independent source that Queen Elizabeth had bestowed "great favour" on Sidney, who was "beloved of all the court." The only tangible favour seems to have been his appointment as one of Queen Elizabeth's cupbearers some time soon after his return to England.[9] The rising sun promised a great career for the young

---

9. As Ringler has shown (p. xxiv) this was less an honour than the transfer of a sinecure from Sir Henry to his son to assure him an official place at court. The accounts of Sir

man who seemed to have all personal and educational advantages necessary for a distinguished career in the Queen's service.

Henry's receiver-general, Robert Walker, gent., show that £100 was paid between 1575
and 1578 for "the fee of the cupbearer for three years" (*HMC De L'Isle*, 1:249).

The original acquittance for one half-year's fee from the Exchequer, dated May 10, 1576
and signed by Sidney, is now in the Folger Shakespeare Library. Formerly it belonged to the
great Elizabethan scholar, Edmond Malone, from whom it passed to James Boswell the
younger. At the Boswell sale in 1825, as lot 3128, it was purchased for three guineas.

CHAPTER 20

Sidney's far-flung network of friends continued writing as the year 1576 opened. Many began their letters with mild but pointed complaints about not having had replies to previous letters, but that deficiency did not seem to diminish their faithfulness. From Vienna came a reply from Charles de l'Écluse with welcome news about the circle of friends in whose company Sidney had found such high pleasure.

> Sir,
>
> I was delighted to learn from your letter of October twenty-eighth that you are well; and I am most grateful for the kind remembrance you have of your humble servants. I have never doubted that, in one of your high degree, this would afford me every virtue and courtesy.
>
> Since the Emperor has returned to this city, Master Languet and Master Vulcob, from whom you may not have heard for some time, have been restored to us. I enclose a letter from Master Languet which will doubtless inform you of events here. I also enclose one from Dr. Purkircher, who has been staying here this week.

News from Poland continued to report the unhappy state of that headless kingdom.

> The Poles are dithering about their royal election. They have, however, suffered a crippling raid by the Tartars: if such attacks are redoubled, they may hasten the deliberations. This Tartar expedition has greatly harmed the kingdom, and the Cracovians were so frightened that they thought of razing the city and seeking salvation in headlong flight. But there is a common saying, "It is an ill wind that blows nobody good." The fear of the Canons of Cracow has profited Laski: they have elected him their leader and voted him vast sums for troop levies to counter such sudden Tartar raids. This is most convenient for Laski who, as you know, had reached the bottom of his purse.
>
> The court will leave for Bratislava in a few days' time, and when affairs there are settled I shall make a trip to Regensburg, where the court will stay for a time. And I so pray God, Sir, to grant you good

health, a long life, all happiness and fulfilment, and I commend myself humbly to your benevolence. If perchance you should meet Master Wotton, I pray you to give him my affectionate respects. From Vienna, December 4, 1575.

Your humble servant,
Charles de l'Écluse

For the modern reader the chief interest in this letter comes from the postscript, for it sheds some light on a problem in Sidney portraiture.

Master Abondio also commends himself humbly to your benevolence. He told me he will finish your portrait as soon as he recovers from a sickness that has laid him low all summer, and will send it to Master Languet to be conveyed to you. And if he can serve you in any other way you will always find him most ready to do so.

Thus, ten months after Sidney left Vienna, Antonio Abondio had not yet finished this second portrait. Furthermore, it was being made for Sidney himself, and not for one of his Viennese friends. Probably a medallion or bas-relief, the portrait remains a mystery beyond these references to it while it was still in the artist's studio.

On December 27 Lobbet wrote from Strasbourg, sending the news current at that moment. First he reports on the mustering of the Huguenot forces.

Sir,

I wrote to you last on the twenty-second of last month, proposing a method by which we could send our letters to and fro without addressing ourselves at once to the master of the posts at Antwerp. I hope you have considered it. I am writing to you now to let you know that the Prince of Condé and Duke Casimir have pitched their camp in the bishopric of Metz: all the soldiery is assembled, infantry as well as cavalry.

The Swiss were the last to arrive. They number sixteen standards but are extremely well equipped. Some Cantons have tried to get them to return and have sent envoys to summon them, but in spite of that they have continued to march. The general inspection was to take place these last few days, and soon afterward they were to go into France. The poor kingdom, so long afflicted, truly had no need of these guests, but such, I see, is destiny. It is reported that the King intends to establish a great encampment in their way which is being set up at Langres, and that his Majesty's Reiter colonels are said to be assembled at Metz for recruitment.

Lobbet gives the remainder of his letter to the latest intelligence from Poland, where the situation was becoming more complicated as the royal election dragged from one intrigue and postponement to the next.

> The rumour, these last few days, has been that the Emperor was King of Poland beyond doubt because, it was said, his Majesty received thirty-six out of forty-five votes. However the letter from the Imperial Court dated the eleventh of this month does not say so, but reports that the Poles have postponed a royal election until after Epiphany. There will be problems with this election. A correspondent from Wroclaw (the capital of Silesia) writes that in Poland an harquebus shot wounded a German gentleman who was standing next to the imperial ambassador. A remarkable incident: not the way to get free elections.
>
> I have seen a copy of a letter in German which the Turkish Emperor, Murad, apparently wrote to the Polish parliament. Its opening goes as follows: "Murad, God of the Earth, Emperor of the Entire World, Staff of God and Guard of Paradise, Faithful Minister of the Great Prophet Mohammed, to the noble and excellent senators of the Polish commonalty, greetings." After that, he goes on in his letter to complain that the Poles have not retained the King of France as their King, and says that it was their behaviour that caused that King to leave them; after which he presents the Voivode of Transylvania as his candidate for the royal election. Finally he greatly threatens them in case they should choose a king who is an enemy of his.
>
> I present my humble respects to your benevolence and wish you a good and happy new year, praying God,
> Sir, to keep you in His own. From Strasbourg this twenty-seventh of December, 1575.
>
> > Your humble servant,
> > J. Lobbet

In Vienna the faithful Languet began the new year by writing to Sidney, just four weeks after last doing so. In his letter of January 1 he goes more deeply into the complexities of the Polish election, but not until after he obliquely chides his protégé for dilatory habits in answering letters.

> I shall now judge myself strictly and penalize myself: in my agitation I reprimanded you too severely, in my recent letter, for

casting aside the memory of your friends so quickly. In fact, they never gather without delighting each other with the happy memory of your company here.

At that time they discerned your innate courtesy; so they find it difficult to believe that you agree with the theory that affection cannot bind persons separated by great distances. Never, even in dreams, did it occur to your friends that the fondness you showed for them here was feigned.

The fine I have now decided to pay you is an account of recent events in Poland. Though I expect that rumours of the Emperor's election have already winged their way to your ear, I doubt whether you have had an authentic account of the background of what has happened.

Languet's lengthy letter was written while the Emperor Maximilian seemed to be winning the Polish crown for the Hapsburgs. Thus he ends with the prophecy that both France and England would someday fall beneath Maximilian's sway, perhaps Languet's wildest prediction. At the court of England the chief threat was judged to be Philip of Spain, and properly so.

I believe it is the destiny of his family [the Hapsburgs] to gain control both over us [the French] and ultimately over you. With our folly and fratricidal slaughter we hasten this destiny. You [English] aim at almost the same goal with your Machiavellian thinking, for you are now attacking the Gueux on whose welfare your prosperity depends.

Languet was also wide of the mark about a Huguenot minister, Pierre l'Oyseleur, Sire de Villiers, who had fled to England in 1573 and became chaplain to William of Orange in 1575.

I hear Villiers now serves as pastor of the French church in London, so recommend that you become acquainted with him. Because he is such a learned, eloquent, and highly talented man I hope very much that you can gain both pleasure and profit from conversing with him.

I pray to almighty God that the year which begins today will bring you good fortune and prosperity and that you will remember your friends more frequently than you did last year. Vienna, January 1, 1576.

For some reason, perhaps the frigid weather of January, Languet's letter travelled more slowly across Europe than usual. It took three weeks to reach Antwerp, a fact we learn from a letter written by de Tassis on January 22 and forwarded along with Languet's from Vienna. Sidney would not have received the two letters until some days later.

Illustrious and most honoured Sir,

Having received some letters from Master Languet of Vienna, among which was one for yourself, I wished to accompany it with these three little words, although I have received so much better. In the first place to present myself to you as one who is always at your service, and secondly to offer you all that it is in my power to do. Your Excellency will find me a most devoted servant in deed rather than merely in word.

Here there is little news of any importance. May God grant the present parliament success to the benefit of all. The differences between the Paladins in Poland about the recent election have been appeased; and his Majesty the Emperor will soon go to receive the crown of that kingdom. It is said also that he did not want to accept the crown until an agreement was reached. The truce of eight years with the Turks has been renewed, and there are rumours of a marriage between the son of the Muscovite and a daughter of the Emperor. May God grant the Christian princes concord in the face of the common enemy.

And here I must end. I honour your Excellency immensely and pray God to keep you and grant you all the good fortune that you desire. From Antwerp, the twenty-second of January, 1576.

Your Illustrious Excellency's affectionate servant,

Giovanni Battista de Tassis

On Thursday, January 5, Théophile de Banos sent a message he had been eager to dispatch for some time. The printers at Wechel's had finally produced the sheets for his edition of Ramus's *Commentaries*, preceded by his biographical account of Ramus. The whole volume was too large to send by the post, so he dispatched only the biographical preface with this letter.

Sir,

I enclose the biography of the late Master Ramus, which I have dedicated to you along with his *Commentaries* on the Christian religion. I hope you are pleased with the result. I greatly regret I cannot send you the *Commentaries* by the same messenger, but no one I can trust will take them, because of their subject and bulk: however, if I cannot find a friend to take them, I will send a man specially to Master Harvey[1] in Antwerp, so that you will safely receive them.

Moreover, we have recovered most of Master Ramus's books, of which I write at the end of his biography; and I hope that the others which have disappeared will be recovered in time. If I have your permission to dedicate to you any hitherto unpublished works of his that may turn up, kindly let me know in your next letter: I shall take pains to satisfy you and honour you in any way I can, in accordance with your piety and virtue. I am sending you the memorable story of Sancerre translated into Latin: but I beg you not to let it fall into the hands of printers over there, so that the edition printed here, but not yet published, can be sold without loss.

The rest of the sheet contains the latest news to reach Frankfurt from the troubled areas of eastern Europe and France.

As for news, I think you will have heard how the bishops and great lords of Poland chose the Emperor to be their King: but the rest of the nobility elected the Transylvanian king. At that point, Laski seized Cracow, although it is not clear in whose name. However, the Emperor is raising eight thousand Reiters to consolidate his election by force, these being mainly paid for by the Duke of Saxony and the Marquis of Brandenburg. The Turk on the other hand favours the Voivode, whose arrival is expected any day now so that he may be crowned and marry the Infanta as he has promised. However, the Muscovite is taking the part of the Emperor and, with his Tartars, has begun laying waste the borders of Lithuania. The Imperial Diet has been rescheduled for the fifteenth of next month at Regensburg.

I shall not write anything about France, as you will be more reliably and regularly informed about it than we are here. However, from the enclosed German document you will see the plans for a second raising of Reiters, to be recruited and commanded by the Duke of Liegnitz[2] if need be.

1. Buxton suggests that this may be the merchant James Harvey.
2. Apparently Heinrich XI (1539–88) rather than his brother Friedrich IV (1552–96).

Sir, I pray God to vouchsafe you increase of His holy benevolence and pay my humble respects to your own. From Frankfurt, January 5, 1576.

Your most humble servant,
Théophile de Banos

From Dresden came a letter written by Dr. Andreas Paull with whom Sidney had exchanged compliments for about two years, though they did not actually meet until Sidney stopped in Dresden on his journey back to England through Bohemia and Germany. As with so many other eminent men, Sidney owed this friendship to Languet, a fact Dr. Paull acknowledges at the beginning of his letter.

Greetings.

I have always loved our friend Languet, that best of men, and have had frequent experience of his benevolence and kindness towards me, as well as various kind services he has done me: but never has he done me a greater service than by being the author and mediator of our friendship. Yet, while I am indeed indebted most of all to him, I am most grateful to you also (and will be as long as I live) for having begun to love me without having seen me, simply out of faith in his judgement.

Yet whenever I think of the great kindness which you later showed me when you came here and of your wise conversation about exalted matters which at that time I enjoyed, I am deeply grieved that I was unable to converse further with you, and indeed to live in your proximity, and I sincerely hope that sometime I will be given another opportunity to do so. I have the more hope of this, as we are already being treated in such a way that I imagine we will in the end be forced to move. Should anything like that occur, I should certainly not go anywhere else than to your most lovely England which, through the admirable wisdom of its renowned Queen, is far more wisely and successfully governed than any of the other kingdoms of Europe.

Dr. Paull then launched into the news, first about some changes in the Elector Augustus's own court. Doubtless these troubles were of more interest to persons dependent on the Elector than to Sidney.

Master Zeschius was, on account of the religious issue you know of, on the fifteenth of July deprived by his Prince of all his offices and banished to his estate at Buchana. It is said that even the Chancellor will be removed from his office as soon as they have another with whom they can easily replace him. What hope there is for me you can easily imagine. But I do not want to bother with an account of our troubles, particularly because, as I said, you will perhaps hear it all from me in person sometime.

Next Dr. Paull once again gives accounts of the Emperor's court, of the Polish election, and of the peace arranged between Hungary and the Turks.

The rest of the news that has any bearing on politics I believe you will have heard already. Rudolph of Austria, the King of Hungary and Bohemia, was elected King of the Romans at Regensburg on October 27 by the vote of the Electors, and was crowned there on the first of November. The debate on that subject presented no trouble, as the entire business had been settled before the Electors even met. The Elector Palatine did not attend this Diet, but his son Louis acted as his deputy. The Emperor and the King of Spain complained loudly about him to the other Electors: about the gunpowder he exploded two years ago, and about the aid he has given to what they call the Dutch rebels. Although it is said that there are some who would like to see him overthrown, yet so far nothing has been decided against him—because, I think, they were afraid that it might create greater anxiety in Germany.

In Poland, the Diet of Warsaw that was held in November resulted in our Emperor being proclaimed King of Poland on December twelfth—may it prove a happy and fortunate choice. However, a few days later the Zborovians (who, as you know, are not over-friendly to the Austrians) seceded with several others and proclaimed as King the Voivode of Transylvania, Stephen Báthory: saying that he should marry the sister of the late King, known as the Infanta of Poland, and acquire the kingdom together with her. Some think that Báthory will give way to the Emperor because it is said that the aforesaid royal sister shrinks from the thought of marrying him. But I do not think this likely: I consider it much more probable that the fate of Poland will be, doubtless, to perish in the same fire which a few years ago consumed Hungary.

An Imperial Diet has been planned, again at Regensburg, for the fifteenth of February. While there will as usual be copious debates, it is to be feared that in the meantime opportunities for action will be missed. The Turk has concluded a five years' peace treaty with Hungary, which he will honour with the same integrity he is accustomed to show in his dealing with us. And yet the Emperor's courtiers still think they can attempt great things.

Paull concludes with another reference to Languet, now under the roof of Lingelsheim, so familiar to Sidney.

Our friend Languet has returned from Regensburg to Vienna with the Emperor, and is again living there, as usual, with his friend Lingelsheim. I wanted to write you this letter, my most noble Master Sidney, as a token of my perpetual esteem and most hearty affection for you; and I beg you most sincerely to accept my respects and to continue to love me as you have begun—which, in view of your great kindness, I have no doubt you will do. Farewell. You are respectfully greeted by Master Cancellarius and Costicius. From Dresden, the sixth of January, 1576—and I pray God that the year may bring you prosperity and happiness. Farewell again.

Yours with the utmost respect and love,

Andreas Paull

About this time the second letter came from Cesare Pavese in Venice. Pavese did not have much to say except that he was afraid Sidney might not know that he had never received the message which Lodowick Bryskett had tried to deliver.

Most Illustrious Sir and most honoured Patron,

If I were certain that the letter I sent you after my return from Rome by Signor Pasquale Spinola had reached you, I would not trouble you now with this second one: as, in the first, I sufficiently and wholeheartedly paid my respect to you. But as I am in some doubt about this, having received no reply from you for so long, I thought better to repeat what I said before; I hope that your Excellency will take this as a sign of affection and of a desire to serve you, rather than as a wish to trouble you, which indeed it is not.

When I arrived here I heard that Master Lodowick Bryskett, on the point of leaving, had urgently asked for me, to give me some request from your Illustrious Excellency: but since he had left no order I let you know that I had arrived in this city so that you might avail yourself of me and give me any commission you might have, and that, as I would have to remain here for some time, I should have ample opportunity, as well as a wholehearted desire, to fulfil your orders. It is to confirm this that I am sending you this second letter: for the rest I refer you to my previous letter, which I do hope you received.

And so I wish, both for your Illustrious Excellency and for my friend Master Corbett, the accomplishment of all your excellent desires; I send you both my warmest greetings and present my respects to my friend Master Bryskett. From Venice, this tenth of January, [15]76.

Your affectionate servant,
Cesare Pavese

This brief note does at least name the messenger who had carried Pavese's previous letter of November 19, Pasquale Spinola. Apparently he belonged to the Genoese trading family of which Benedict, the well-known merchant-banker, was the London representative.[3]

Another note to reach Sidney later in January came from Canon Dorsett in Oxford. Evidently young Hájek was becoming something of a problem.

> Although there is no news with us, yet I do not want to let my letter to you wait any longer. For I should prefer to be thought excessively importunate than to be considered too little mindful of my duty. You will, I think, have understood from my previous letter that we have met again at Oxford, thank God; we have prayed daily that, as He seems to have removed hence all danger of plague, so He would keep us safe and well from all sickness and disease.
>
> Your Robert is taking to his books with great pleasure, much to his own benefit, and Montagu is equally devoted to them; Johannes however now thinks of nothing but the court, and has become quite estranged from all study. He thinks that the best thing he could do for himself would be to get himself called to court as quickly as possible.
>
> We, your friends here, greet you as is indeed most fitting, and pray and beseech you with what art we can muster to let some messenger on his way to Ireland stop at Oxford, so that he can take

3. See frequent references in the *CSPF*; of Benedict Leicester wrote to Walsingham, Nov. 2, 1572, "he is my dear friend and the best Italian I know in England."

some letters of ours to your most honoured father—for it is many months since we wrote to him. Farewell. Oxford, January 23, 1575 [i.e. 1576].

Yours entirely at your desire,
Robert Dorsett

Of the letters which reached Sidney in February only three have been preserved. Two came from de Banos, the earlier of which accompanied the text of Ramus's *Commentaries*.

Sir,

I sent you recently the biography of the late Master Ramus printed as a preface to his *Commentaries*. These last I am now sending you, by special messenger as far as Antwerp, so that from there on they may reach you safely by the ordinary post. I hope you will be pleased with the result; and should there be any other occasion when I can honour you I am yours to command.

I wrote in my last letter but one that the Duke of Liegnitz has passed through here on his return from escorting Prince Casimir, whom he left with his army near Dijon in good shape. If a peace is negotiated there, as we hear has been agreed by the King and the Duke, the new raising of Reiters may be put off, and even cancelled; but while England is said to attach great importance to the peace negotiations, preparations for war are increasing in Germany, mainly on the part of the King, whose standard is daily joined by multitudes of Reiters. The Imperial Diet has been put off until April.

I have nothing else to write except, Sir, that I pray the good Lord to vouchsafe you increase of His holy benevolence, as I humbly pay my respects to your own. From Frankfurt, January 28, 1576.

Your most humble servant,
Théophile de Banos

The second letter, written on February 10, arrived a fortnight later. Besides political news it brought Sidney some details of the persons who attended the marriage of his close friend, the Count of Hanau.

Sir,

I pray you to let me have a word to tell me if you have received the *Commentaries* by Master Ramus that I sent you. I sincerely hope they have reached you safely, thus fulfilling my promise to you and testifying to my determination to honour and serve you.

Today, February tenth, marks the end of Count Hanau's wedding, and most of the gentlemen who attended have left. Among them were ambassadors of the Elector Palatine, the Electors of Mainz and Cologne, Duke Richard (the brother of the Elector Palatine), the Duke of Liegnitz, and several counts and great lords. It all went off very well and very quietly.

As for other parts of the world: the Emperor has left for Poland, accompanied by Duke August and the Marquis of Brandenburg, to take possession of the kingdom. It is believed that his Majesty has arrived at a compromise with the Voivode on the matter. Be this as it may, twelve great lords from that country have come to Vienna to escort his Majesty to Cracow.

Concerning the French armies, the Prince of Condé and the Duke of Alençon joined up at Roanne near Lyon on the twenty-ninth of January. Since then we have no reliable news that I can tell you. I am sure you are kept well informed from other sources.

And so I shall pray God, Sir, to vouchsafe you increase of His holy benevolence, and present my humble respects to your own.

Your most humble servant,
Théophile de Banos

In contrast to these short letters devoted to personal messages, one crammed with news arrived about a week later from Lobbet in Strasbourg. His opening sentences show once again the patience with which Sidney's devoted friends had to bear his silence. Despite this silence, his friends were still writing to him a year after he had vowed at parting to be a faithful correspondent.

Sir,

I wrote to you last on the twenty-seventh of last December. I have not written to you since because you do not reply to my letters. For after your return to England, during which time I have written to you quite frequently, I have only received a single letter from you, dated the twenty-eighth of last October. From that letter I hoped to learn how the son of Doctor Hájek was doing, whom I sent to you at Heidelberg last year, but you do not mention him at all. It depends upon your convenience and pleasure: nevertheless I beg you to let me have some news, as I have urged before.

Lobbet's report of recent events in France adds many details to the accounts in earlier letters.

> I shall not send you any news about the war in France, as I think you will be better informed over there than we are here. For since the camp of the Prince of Condé and Duke Casimir has been removed from here we have scarcely heard anything, at least little that is to the point. You will have heard of the poisoning of Monsieur the King's brother [Alençon] and of M. de Thoré and several others, and how they managed to survive thanks to good medicines and remedies. You will probably also have heard that when the King heard of this he sent the president of Paris and a councillor to Monsieur to find out about the matter.
>
> The said M. Alençon, the King's brother, is reported to be going up the Loire to join the Prince of Condé, Duke Casimir, and Marshal Damville. To concentrate all their forces for this affair, the Prince of Condé and Duke Casimir are said to have started out through Burgundy on their way to La Charité or Roanne on the Loire, where Marshal Damville apparently is also. It is said, however, that the Château de Paigny (which was a Burgundian house of the late Marshal Tavannes) has been taken by the Prince of Condé on the way, and that four cannon were found there. The château has been demolished and razed to the ground.
>
> It is also reported that the fortified Abbey of Lourdon in Burgundy has been taken and a garrison installed. Six thousand Swiss are ready to march for the King. The Reiters supposed to join the King have not yet crossed the Rhine; their numbers are said to be smaller than expected, as several German princes are raising troops in their territories to accompany the Emperor to Poland.

Next comes news of persons better known to Sidney and of the latest developments concerning the crown of Poland.

> The wedding of Eric of Brunswick with Princess Dorothea, the sister of the Duke of Lorraine, was celebrated about five weeks ago. Speaking of weddings, the Count of Hanau, whom you know, celebrated his wedding on the fifth of this month. Your host here, Master Hubert de la Rose, is still ill and cannot use his limbs.
>
> You know that our Emperor was legitimately elected King of Poland by a majority of votes. The Polish ambassadors have come to

Vienna to congratulate his Majesty on his new crown. Their leader is elector Laski, the same who was in France when the French King was elected King of Poland. These ambassadors are urging his Imperial Majesty to lose no time in taking possession of the realm of Poland, the more so since there are electors who did not agree to the aforesaid election and are therefore opposed to it; the chief of them being the Elector of Cracow. These have been protesting and have voted the Voivode of Transylvania to be their king, on condition that he marries the sister of the late Polish King Sigismund.

Because of this his Majesty does not intend to go to Poland except with an army; and indeed the Electors of Saxony and Brandenburg are making great military preparations to accompany his Majesty, as also are the Duke of Pomerania and the Marquis of Ansbach. The Emperor is also raising a large number of troops in his lands and territories, and it is thought that he will start out as soon as possible. Some are afraid that the Turks will take a hand, although they have concluded an eight years' peace treaty with his Majesty concerning Hungary.

The situation in Italy remained quiet, though the Turk always loomed beyond the eastern horizon.

In Italy the Turks are feared, and no one knows from which side they will attack first: it is thought they will go for Malta. The quarrels of the Genoese are said to have been settled, but I do not know the terms of the settlement. The Genoese on both sides have taken hostages as security: some of these have been sent to the Pope, others to the Duchy of Milan (in the care of the King of Spain), and still others to Venice.

Lobbet's letter ends with more news of personal interest to Sidney and with the mention of a gift which probably accompanied the letter.

Master Languet is well, thank God, and is still at the court of the Emperor. Neither of us is married yet! I beg you to present my humble respects to Master Walsingham, to whom I wrote on the twenty-seventh of December; also to Master William Lewin, who lives in London, in Colman Square, in the house of Master Francis Goldsmith; also to your Master Bryskett. I am sending you, by way of new year's gift, an almanack for this year of 1576, printed in Cracow and calculated by a Polish mathematician. The type is somewhat crude. Of the prophesies you can judge for yourself, and time will tell. Indeed the Poles could do with a good prophet, to know the future, for even guesswork can tell that they are in for some problems.

I have this minute had a letter from Master Languet, written at Vienna on the twenty-second of last month. He tells me they are laying out the red carpet for the Polish ambassadors. Apparently elector Laski spoke in Polish, to which the Emperor replied in Czech, and that with considerable elegance and without the slightest hesitation. And here I shall end by presenting my humble respects to your benevolence and praying God,
Sir, to keep you in His own. From Strasbourg, this fourteenth of February, 1576.

Your humble servant,
J. Lobbet

A rumour is beginning to spread that the King of Navarre has left the King's court to join the Prince of Condé.

About the middle of March Sidney's friend Baron Slavata arrived in England. This we learn from the letter that Achille de Harlay (1536–1615), an eminent figure at the French court, wrote from Paris to Walsingham on March 3. De Harlay commended Slavata as "a Baron of Bohemia, who, having travelled over the greater part of Europe, is desirous of visiting England and Scotland."[4] Undoubtedly Sidney enjoyed Slavata's company, entertained him well, and introduced him to various friends. The only other evidence of their reunion indicates that Sidney lent him some money which he later had difficulty collecting.

Indeed, Sidney sent Slavata's note to Languet hoping he could arrange to collect the debt. Languet left the document with a bookseller in Prague. During Sidney's visit to Prague in the spring of 1577 he talked to the bookseller about it, and received back the note from him, or so the latter claimed. Sidney appears to have mislaid the paper, and as the matter dragged on into late summer Languet wrote Sidney asking what the next step should be.

> After your return from the Imperial Court I wrote to ask if you had released Baron Slavata from paying the money which you lent him a year ago. You answered "No." Therefore I concluded that

4. *CSPF*2, no. 647.

the payment ought to be demanded from him, which is what you had earlier written to ask me to do. Hence, I wrote to him saying that I was surprised that he should forget so soon the kindness you showed him in London. At the same time I wrote our friend Dr. Jordan asking him to remind the Baron of his obligation.

When I wrote these letters I thought that his promissory note was still in the keeping of the Prague bookseller into whose hands I had given it before I left Prague. He has since written that he gave it to you. Thus I should be glad to learn what you wish done next in this matter, especially whether I should take his money if Slavata offers it. I scarcely expect he will do so, especially if he learns that his note is not in our possession so that we cannot force him to pay.[5]

How the matter ended is not known. Either Baron Slavata tardily repaid the debt, or Sidney learned by hard experience that this friend of Padua days was a sponger. At least the incident shows Sidney had been generous to Slavata on his visit to England in the spring of 1576.

To return to March of that year, towards the end of the month Sidney received letters from two other friends in the Rhineland. Lobbet wrote from Strasbourg on March 13.

Greetings.

I wrote to you a month ago, noble and most admirable Master Sidney, and included with my letter the Polish Almanack for this year 1576 into which we are now making headway. Yesterday, however, I received your letter of the first of last month, from which I perceive that while you were writing it you were in merry mood. Evidently you were affected by the breezes approaching spring. Indeed, in the very opening your sprightly wit was at once apparent, in your calling me "your best Lobbet" because you know no Lobbet better than me. I am glad that you are merry, and such jokes make me all the more fond of you.

In attempting to answer Sidney's wit with wit, Lobbet now introduces a term then current in scholastic logic, *baroco*. This word is a mnemonic to help students remember the combination of the symbols A (an affirmative premise), O (a particular negative premise), followed by O (a negative conclusion). Hence the word "bArOcO." None of Lobbet's examples of spurious syllogisms fits this pattern, however, which suggests that he

5. Languet to Sidney, Aug. 12, 1577.

intended them as parodies of the excesses then current in scholastic philosophy.[6]

Yet, if Languet now (who is still in Vienna and very well) had to pronounce judgement on your argument, he would find fault with your conclusion, especially in *baroco*. First of all, because one only uses "best" in comparison to other things: yet you have seen no other. Secondly, there is a non sequitur in the assumption that, because you have seen no Lobbet better than me, therefore I am the best. For if there were many Lobbets and all were bad, how could I be called the best? Thirdly, no one but God is good, let alone best. Your reply to such an argument of Languet's might be that he could with more truth call you the one-and-only: first because he has never, so far as I know, seen another Sidney, and secondly on account of the general opinion of your virtues, of which I would say more if I were writing to someone other than yourself.

This learned joking over, Lobbet now passes on to political news, especially the latest report on the vexatious Polish question.

Polish affairs are going badly. The Transylvanian ruler [Báthory] has for quite some time now been preparing for his journey to Poland. A day was appointed for his coronation: the fourth of this month. At the same time the Infanta of Poland, the sister of the late king, was to be crowned: a spinster of far from tender years who (I am told) used to have great influence over the mother of your queen. The zealots in the Transylvanian's party have managed to expel from Cracow all those siding with the Emperor. It is to be feared that that cursed Poland will give everyone a lot of trouble. The Turkish Emperor is said to be willing to support the Transylvanian to the limit of his ability. The Emperor had not yet replied to the Polish ambassadors by the twentieth of last month, so even then the Poles had no idea whether the Emperor was willing to accept the Polish crown or not.

The widowed queen of France, the Emperor's daughter, reached Vienna safely on the fifteenth of last month, having been accompanied on her journey there by Wilhelm, Duke of Bavaria.

6. The excesses indulged in by Renaissance logicians prompted the adoption of the term as a description of architectural extravagance, i.e. *baroque*. See the studies by Karl Borinski and Benedetto Croce cited by René Wellek, *Concepts of Criticism* (New Haven, 1963), p. 69.

The letter ends with a few personal notes. Lobbet was obviously annoyed that Sidney had not sent reports about Johannes Hájek. Perhaps he suspected that the boy had failed to become a serious student.

> I have by now asked you repeatedly to give me news of the activities and general well-being of that Bohemian lad whom I turned over to you last year, so that I can in turn write and tell his father something. The lad himself might have written to me. [Marginal note:] Nota bene and do not forget!
>
> I am sending you the "Pope's Jubilee," so that you may be reminded to be devout in the midst of the court. Farewell, and rest assured of my great devotion to you. Strasbourg, the thirteenth of March, 1576.
>
> Yours most respectfully,
>
> J. L.
>
> Your host at Strasbourg, Hubert de la Rose, is beginning to recover, thank God. Give my respectful greetings to my lord of Walsingham, the Great Secretary of England.

Hájek's career at Oxford actually had come to an end. This is made clear in a letter from Canon Dorsett. It was brought from Oxford by Robert Sidney, who was travelling under the watchful eye of his Christ Church tutor, John Buste.

> Here, with this letter, is your "little soul-mate" Robert, whom I may truly call your mother's golden offshoot; and I have no doubt that, if he gets sufficient leisure from other activities to unfold the riches of his mind, it will bear some rich and rare fruits. Buste moreover (who since their arrival has always accompanied them, not only with a most dutiful spirit, but with singular affection and a watchful eye) decided that, although quite weighty causes existed to detain him here, yet as regards this journey of theirs he could not well put off the duty he had been requested to discharge. And I, who know you well, have no doubt that, should a time come when you can help him in any way, you will repay his tremendous zeal, care, and effort with an uncommon reward.
>
> It would be best, in my opinion, if you could either obtain Johannes a place at court, which is what he is hoping for, or admit him to your retinue: for, at a guess, I should say nature had not intended him for the discipline of higher learning. White is by far the more enthusiastic

for the study of letters: he is even getting to the stage where he tries somewhat too strenuously to do the same work as your brother.

What you write about Greek and about a philosopher I do not know whether I can manage. I have three people principally in mind: I shall find out their inclination and let you know.

May God keep you long in health and well-being, for His own sake and for ours. Farewell. Oxford, March 21, 1575 [i.e. 1576].

Ever yours truly,
Robert Dorsett

Sidney's inquiry "about Greek and about a philosopher" suggests that he had asked Dorsett to propose someone to teach Greek and another to instruct philosophy. Presumably these teachers would be engaged to introduce Robert to these disciplines. Yet it is possible that Sidney himself wished to extend his education in these fields, despite Languet's former disapproval.

Early in April Sidney received another letter from de Banos. It answers Sidney's response to the dedication in de Banos's edition of Ramus's *Commentaries*. Evidently Sidney considered the dedication too lavish in its reference to his Dudley lineage and too meagre with regard to the Sidney family.

Most noble Sidney,

When I returned from church I received your two letters: the first of February twenty-eighth, the second written on the second of March. I should like to reply to them briefly, as the bearer is leaving almost at once. I am so glad you received my biography of Peter Ramus which I dedicated to you: but I am extremely surprised that Ramus's *Commentaries* which, if I remember rightly, I sent to you on February first, do not yet seem to have reached you. So I beg you to let me know about this in your next.

As for your request to change the dedication: although it is impossible to do a complete job, as two thousand copies of the *Commentaries* have already been printed, yet Wechel and I will see to it that, at my expense, your wish may, if possible, be fulfilled at least in the other copies. Admonished by the letter you wrote me last July, I did indeed leave out many praises of your nobility, so as to comply with your wish. The words I did use, however, were not published at my own impulse, but on the advice of Master Languet, who considered that nothing more modest could be said than to mention that noble gentleman, Philip Sidney, as belonging to the illustrious family of the Earls of Warwick. However, had I known earlier that you would have preferred the English style about which you write, I would have used that title—than which nothing could be more fitted to your fame, and clear and splendid to the praise of your family's virtue.

For I love and honour you, and shall not cease to love you in the future for the great gifts of piety and virtue which it has pleased the Lord to bestow upon you in such liberal measure. I shall pray Him continually to vouchsafe you increase of His Spirit, to the glory of His name and the good of His Church. Farewell; Frankfurt, March 19, 1576.

> Yours most devotedly,
> Théophile de Banos

Considering that Sidney had raised the issue, it seems somewhat odd that de Banos addressed the letter to "Monseigneur Philippe Comte de Sidné en Angleterre, a Londres," a nonexistent title. Indeed, Sidney seems to have discouraged the use in England of "Baron," the title bestowed upon him by Charles IX of unhappy memory. If de Banos altered the dedication, no copy of the new version is known to exist.

Another letter Sidney received about this time came from Languet in Vienna. Dated March 17, it begins with the usual reproof.

> I should write you more frequently if I did not infer from your continued silence that our letters either do not please you or that you pay scant attention to them. We realize that our friendship can be of no profit to you. Yet it is unlike your courteous manners to forget so soon the memory of those who, as your earlier conduct indicated, did not displease you, those who love you dearly and esteem you very highly.
>
> Nor should you imagine that I am speaking only for myself, for other men whose friendship you earned here in Germany by your virtuous qualities and gentle manners feel just the way I do. Whenever they write to me they complain that you unexpectedly spurn their friendship, which they had reason to hope would be lasting.

Languet had proper cause for his annoyance as later letters show. Having relieved himself of this complaint, he devoted the body of his letter to reporting that Maximilian had found the conditions attached to the crown of Poland to be unjust and unacceptable. Accordingly, Stephen Báthory, who was prepared to accept the conditions, was getting ready to leave Transylvania for Warsaw.

Languet's letter came in a packet sent by Charles de l'Écluse which enclosed a copy of the botanist's latest publication, C. *Clusii rarorum aliquot stirpium per Hispanias observatorum historia, libris duobus expressa* (1576), recently issued from the distinguished press of Christopher Plantin in Antwerp. The covering letter from de l'Écluse is self-explanatory.

Sir,

I could think of nothing that was in my power to send you, by which I could show you the noble desire that I have to be your humble servant, except this little book that I have compiled on the subject of the rarest of the plants that I saw in my journey to Spain. I did not wish to miss the opportunity of sending you a copy via the Postmaster of Antwerp, in the hope that you would receive it as kindly as you would the more magnificent gift which would certainly have been given you by someone richer than I. I beg that you should be willing to do this, and also that you should believe of me that I will always remain your humble servant, in whatever it will please you to ask of me.

It has been a long time since we have heard any news of you, and Monsieur Languet has often complained about this to me; he tells me you have grown idle. I am sure he will not have forgotten to reproach you about this in the letter which he has written to you, which will be enclosed with this one. You will send him your answer when it is convenient, but I would be glad if you would do this at the first opportunity, in order to dissuade him from that idea. It only remains for me to pray God to give you,

Sir, a long and healthy life, with all happiness and contentment; and I commend myself to your good favour, as does my host Doctor Aichholtz. From Vienna, March 19, 1576.

> Your very humble servant,
> Charles de l'Écluse

The Ambassador sent to the Emperor was granted an audience yesterday afternoon; or rather, he came to give his credentials to the Emperor. It is believed that he was sent to tell his Majesty not to rid himself of the affairs of Poland.

Inside the cover de l'Écluse inserted a page of errata, prefaced by this head-note:

> Sir, since the printers were not so observant as to notice all of the errata, I am sending you a list of those which I noticed whilst reading the printed leaves sent to me here by the Seigneur Plantin, just in case he does not print them on the last leaf, as he has promised me he would do once I have sent him a list of the mistakes from here. You should therefore correct the following: [a list of errata follows].

Languet's letter of March 17 spurred Sidney to reply on April 21, the day before Easter. Languet's chiding seems to have stung him, for he defended himself with warmth and at length in a letter hitherto unknown to Sidney's biographers.

> I wonder what you can be thinking of, that you should put to such torment the friend who loves you more than himself. Has your heart hardened so suddenly, my friend? I would never have thought that our friendship, of which the deepest, indeed, the only foundations have been love of virtue and my admiration for you, could have degenerated to such an extent that one of us could reproach the other with bad faith. One may condemn a friend for indolence, even without hearing his defence, or for carelessness, but to cast doubt on his constancy—that is, if there is any good in him at all—what is this but to announce that you wish to terminate our sacred friendship?
>
> But you not only accuse me of inconstancy towards you and of forgetting you, to which evils God forbid I should stoop, you also clearly imply, in all seriousness, that you suspect me of deceit and ingratitude. My friend, if you do not know me, I myself do not know what kind of promises I can make to defend myself; I can under no circumstances be led to believe that your hopes of me have weakened to such an extent that you imagine sins of this enormity could find any room in my heart—and yet you cannot deny that you have behaved too harshly towards a friend by heaping misery upon misery in this way. For let it be sufficient torment that I am denied your company; but now you have also deprived me of your delightful letters. You have long been punishing me in full measure by writing so rarely; but what kind of cruelty is this, that you should insult the misfortunes of a friend and at the same time add to them?

The reason for Sidney's warm rejoinder was that after the turn of the year he had written Languet a letter which the latter denied having received.

> I wrote to you on the first of February, quite cheerfully, in keeping with my frame of mind then; I am surprised that you did not get my letter, for de Tassis claims he sent it on faithfully and, on this occasion, wrote that he conjectured that that letter of yours and that of de l'Écluse were in reply to the one which I had sent him two months before. Both of those I wrote to de l'Écluse and Wacker have been answered. This being so, I must ask you to write and tell me if you have received my letter yet, for I would not like it to have fallen into other hands.
>
> My friend, so may God be good to me as there is no other human being for whom my love is more heartfelt than for you, and by whom I have a greater wish to be loved. So I beg you, do not torture me any further with these suspicions. As far as I am concerned, you may do anything else so long as you consent to write: say that I am lazy, idle, even stupid, if you wish; but as to my love for you, not a word!—unless you want to stir up this hornet's nest again. You knew that I am easily provoked; if fact, I would have answered you in the high tragic style, had my vocabulary not been deficient. For this you can thank life at court, which has driven all my Latin into exile. However, I have said more than enough on this contentious topic.

Life at the English court was palling on Sidney; he had begun to yearn for a return to the Continent where opportunities for military action beckoned. A letter from Thomas Lenormand, his travelling companion from Prague to Frankfurt in 1575, had especially tempted Sidney.

> We are doing nothing here. I long to live in your part of the world again. D'Alençon has very kindly invited me through Lenormand. I sincerely hope I will be able to get together the means to return to you, especially if war should break out between your side and the Turks. I would prefer to fight my first campaign in that kind of conflict, rather than involve myself in a civil war.
>
> Lenormand has had a good reception from the Duc d'Alençon, and has notably cleared himself of the crime of treachery, of which he had been suspected by Villerius and several others of your church. We have Baron Slavata here; I have done my best to make him wel-

come, and I could have shown him even greater kindness had he not been, as it seemed, anxious to shun the more crowded places.

I would never end this letter were I not compelled to write because the courier is in a hurry. My greetings to all of our friends. I hear that Master Vulcob has returned to France—I am surprised that you did not mention him in your letter. Farewell, Languet, best and dearest of friends. London, April 21, 1576.

Yours in deepest friendship,

Philip Sidney

A postscript sends greetings to other friends in Vienna and reports further disappointment over the light-headed young Hájek.

I hope that eventually you will grant me the favour of a visit here; then at last I will consider myself fortunate. I have written about the above-mentioned matters and I await your answer daily. I hope also that I will hear from Wacker. Give my greetings to those worthy men Lingelsheim and Purkircher, and I drink their health in good French wine. The son of Dr. Thaddeus is well, but his mind is highly unsuited to scholarship. As far as money is concerned Wechel [should select] those books which please him most, and if I remember, I will send him more money for the next bookfair.[7]

This letter, probably because the courier for de Tassis was delayed, remained in Sidney's hands for a number of days. Thus he had a chance to add the following post-postscript:

A week ago the letters I had written to you three months ago were returned; they had been intercepted by the Dutch and mislaid for some time. Once more, farewell.

Lacking the evidence in this letter, Sidney's biographers have known of Alençon's invitation only from a letter Languet wrote on May 28: "Nor . . . would it be unpleasant for you to be with Alençon, now that you report that he has courteously invited you to spend several months in France to study the manners and characters of his and my countrymen, just as you have observed those of the Germans and the Italians." The invitation was not in a letter addressed by Alençon to Sidney, but came at second hand through Lenormand. Doubtless the latter had highly praised his English friend to Alençon, who welcomed any support in his rebellion

7. Three words are illegible, but the general sense is clear.

against his brother, Henry III, and asked Lenormand to invite Sidney to join him.

Alençon was encamped with his army of Huguenots and mercenaries near the Loire; but his revolt had lost momentum. The King's army did not force a battle, and a truce had been arranged. A division of French territory between the discordant parties was proposed but, as the truce continued, Alençon began to run out of money. In plans discussed for a permanent settlement he asked only "some country where he may have absolute government," his standing army of three thousand men to be paid from the King's revenues.[8]

Simultaneously, Alençon was carrying on his negotiations with Elizabeth for a loan to keep his forces in the field, for if he could strengthen his military threat the King would have to concede larger territories in the proposed settlement. After the agreement Alençon could renew his suit for Elizabeth's hand, the ultimate prize. Catherine de Médicis also considered the marriage a consummation devoutly to be wished. It would provide her favourite son with a throne and resolve the fraternal rivalry that was tearing France asunder.

Alençon's actual motives for inviting Sidney are beyond recapture, but we may speculate. Sidney was already recognized as a young man to whom an eminent career in statecraft lay open. As the heir presumptive of both Leicester and Warwick he already had access to the ears of the great. The Queen herself had smiled on him since his return to court. Alençon, himself heir apparent to the throne of France and now leader of the Huguenots, saw Sidney as a future leader with whom it would be profitable to build a friendship. Someday, in one of his ambitious plans, Alençon could hope to turn such a friend to good use.

8. *CSPF2*, p. 287.

An͠o d͠m 1573
Ætatis suæ 44

Sir Henry Sidney

CHAPTER 21

Sidney had now begun to be a court figure in his own right, though neither he nor men of affairs at court would deny that family connections remained the dominant factor in his status. Early in the winter his father's comrade-in-arms from Ireland, Walter Devereux, Earl of Essex, returned from that island of blood and tears, and Sidney found himself frequently in the Earl's company. Although Sir Henry now distrusted Essex, the Earl had looked with favour on Philip during his days at Shrewsbury when he had provided Philip with a horse to carry him to Oxford for Queen Elizabeth's visit of 1566.

Probably they met rarely, if at all, during the intervening years. From 1568 on, Essex had carried out various assignments for the Queen. First he stood guard over Mary Queen of Scots, and then he engaged in active service as High Marshal of the Field under Warwick in suppressing the rebellion of the Northern Earls. Finally he became the Queen's partner in an expedition to conquer and settle Ulster. In Ireland Essex proved himself a bold and courageous soldier, though his enthusiasm was often irrational and he frequently lacked foresight. The bloody purges he ordered, and the deceit he practised in these slaughters, have stained his name ever since. Now that the Ulster scheme was a failure and his fortune had evaporated, he returned in October, deeply in debt to the Crown, for a brief visit. Even this journey proved disastrous, for during the passage a storm scattered his ships and much of his baggage was lost.

Worse yet, Essex returned broken in health, though still a young man in his thirty-fifth year. At first the Queen was petulant, but gradually she took pity on him; she wrote him a letter of encouragement, granted him two large estates in Ireland, and agreed to make him Earl Marshal of Ireland for life. During this winter of misery Essex and Philip Sidney appear to have renewed their friendship on a more equal basis now that Sidney had become a man, though he was thirteen years younger than the Earl. Knowing that his father suspected Essex of duplicity, Philip may have responded to the Earl's friendship partly for diplomatic reasons. Essex found that the attractive boy he had known had now become an able and promising courtier, established in the Queen's favour and well informed about political events on the Continent. The more he saw of Philip, the more he admired him. Sir Henry's letters to Walsingham continued to support Essex, an attitude that Philip would have seconded. Essex seemed to be particularly pleased with Sir Henry's letter to the Council on February 27 asking for his return. He defended it briskly to Leicester and began to call Philip his son by adoption.[1]

In mid-July 1576 Essex set out again; he reached Dublin on the twenty-third of that month. Available evidence, though meagre, indicates that Sidney may have accompanied him.[2] Because Essex paused en route at Chartley Hall for several days, Sidney may have stayed there with him. Here he would have seen a Chartley very different from the one he had visited a year earlier during Elizabeth's progress. As the Earl bade farewell to his children, of whom he was extremely fond, Philip may have noted how much Penelope had blossomed during the intervening year. She was now thirteen, and her father began to entertain the thought that she and his son "by adoption" might be married. This thought reflects both his high opinion of Sidney and the strong affection that he felt for his daughter.

During the late spring and early summer letters from friends abroad continued to reach Sidney. Two days after Easter de Banos again wrote from Frankfurt, sending a sample page of the corrected dedication to the Ramus volume. To his delight the book had sold well during the recent Frankfurt Fair.

> Most noble Sir,
>
> From the enclosed page you will gather that your wish has been completely fulfilled. If there is anything else I can do to honour and praise you, I am yours to command. The *Commentaries* of Peter Ramus, now in print and dedicated to you, is being bought by everyone at the present Fair, and especially by Germans—a better omen than I had hoped. We are sending a few copies to England which, because of your patronage, I have no doubt will be gladly received by the English who hold your virtue and piety in such high esteem.

The remainder of de Banos's report consists of current events or rumoured developments.

---

1. Sir Henry's letter is printed in Collins, 1 :96. The reactions of Leicester and Essex were reported by Edward Waterhouse to Sir Henry on Mar. 21 (ibid., p. 168). For examples of Sir Henry's support see *CSPI*2, pp. 90, 93.

2. Wallace (p. 166) says it was "highly probable," but the coincidence that they both went to Ireland at that time is the only tangible evidence.

As for other matters: in my last letter but one I wrote that the most illustrious Prince Palatine was gravely ill—from this, by the grace of God, he has now recovered, to the extreme joy of all the faithful. The Poles conferred the title of king upon the Emperor at Vienna on March twenty-fourth—although the Voivode was acclaimed as king on the eighth of that month! The Emperor has begun the troublesome journey through Moldavia and Podolia, making for Cracow: but the Muscovite is preventing him from going any further. The Turk, however, is warning the Emperor sternly, through his ambassadors, not to interfere in Polish affairs. The Emperor has set the date for the Regensburg Diet at the first of May. The Swiss are preparing a delegation to the Imperial Diet, either to have the censure of the Fifteen changed, or to prevent the adoption of any secret resolutions against the Churches' Confession. Farewell. Frankfurt, April 24, 1576.

Yours most devotedly,
Théophile de Banos

Most noble Sir, do, I beg you, let me know if you have received the *Commentaries*: for I am afraid to tackle the merchant to whom I gave them to send on to you. This, for many reasons, would be most awkward for me.[3]

Early in May Sidney thought seriously about making a visit to his friends at Christ Church in Oxford. His brother Robert was now back at his studies after an interval at court. Dorsett responded to the hint of Sidney's visit by inviting him to stay in his house, rather than in college.

If now at last your plan for your visit to us, of which rumour recently reached me, is certain, most noble Sir, I rejoice first of all because you now have the opportunity you had hoped for: someday to revisit the place where you spent a part of your life in the study of letters—I think I can say to your true pleasure as well as your benefit. And secondly, I consider myself happy because it has been vouchsafed me to see you flourishing there where you formerly laid the shining foundations of your whole life and career, while I looked on and wished you the very best of fortune.

---

3. The address of this letter avoids the noble title used previously; it reads "*Illustri et generoso domino Philippo Sidneio Proregis Hyberniae filio, Comitum Warwici, et Lycestriae nepoti. Domino mihi plurimum observando.*"

In addition, I should like to ask you the favour to let me do for you what you have often most magnificently done for me: that, whenever you do arrive, you will take the time to visit my house, which I should in truth call yours; for though it is ill equipped to receive your Excellency, yet I have no doubt that you will gladly accept the devoted goodwill of its master. This is what I wanted to send and tell you via our friend Argall, that most opportune messenger.

Your Robert is well, as are we, and we most earnestly wish you all good health and a life full of the adornments of God's grace and eternal fame, as well as the fulfilment of all your wishes. Farewell. Ewelme, May 17, 1576.

Yours as may please you,
Robert Dorsett

About this time Sidney probably received a short letter from Lobbet. The letter does not fit neatly into any of the earlier years, nor does it seem to belong to a later year. It opens by referring to Lobbet's letter of March 13, one already quoted—unless by coincidence he wrote on this same date a few years later. The simplest explanation is that Lobbet became annoyed because Sidney had not responded promptly. Then, shortly after sending this letter, he received Sidney's warm and witty reply of April 21.

Here is the text of the brief undated letter.

Sir,

I must apologize for not having written to you since the thirteenth of last March, and for thus having waited for two whole months before writing to you again. You must not attribute this to negligence on my part: it was due to the fact that you did not reply to several letters of mine, and I was not sure whether you had received them. Since you now ask me in your letter to write to you often, I will, if you like, write to you every week or every fortnight—whichever you prefer—and give you some news of what is going on both here and in other lands, in Latin or French, quite simply and brusquely, without pomp or much Pindarising: in fact just a simple account of what I may have heard.

I am proposing this because I know that a knowledge of what is going on elsewhere is not only a good thing but indeed most essential to lords and great men who are occupied, or will be occupied, with the running of important matters and affairs of state. I am not going to give you my opinion of your natural talents in this field and of the promise they show, because this letter is addressed to you!

Please let me know your pleasure, and I shall await your opinion and your command. Subject to your wishes, I shall address my letters merely to "Master Sidney, at etc."; and as I think you know my handwriting well enough, I shall not sign myself in full, but just J. L. You can do as you wish.[4]

A proper long letter from Lobbet arrived at the end of May, written after he had received Sidney's reply to the banter about the technicalities of logic. Evidently Sidney had again been in a witty mood on the Easter Saturday when he answered Lobbet's playful letter.

Greetings.

I have received, noble Master Sidney, your letter dated the twenty-first of last April, which was full of most amusing pleasantries and subtle urbanity. I am speechless and dare not gape further, let alone speak of Baroco or Bocardo [another term in logic], for I should be afraid that you would again receive me as you did before. Whether I deserved that I do not know, but I do know that, even though you are separated from me by a great distance, you have washed my head in the most remarkable way!

Lobbet then returns to the most frequent topic in these letters, the complaint that Sidney had encouraged his correspondent to write often but did not himself reciprocate or even indicate what letters he had received.

You ask me to write to you frequently, a matter in which I will gladly comply with your wishes if you will only undertake to give some reply to my letters. I ask you this, not to bother you or to distract you from more important affairs, but solely in order to know whether you have received my letter. For if I do not know that, it is as good as lost. To facilitate this, and so that I may know whether all your letters to me have been delivered to me, you might make a habit of beginning your letters thus: "My dear Lobbet, I wrote to you last on such-and-such a day; since then I have received yours dated on such-and-such a day," etc. These phrases will confirm the number of letters received.

---

4. Written in French on a half sheet, the MS is bound at the beginning of the newly recovered volume of letters, indicating that its placing puzzled an earlier owner.

This method I have from the merchants, whose better ways we should not be ashamed to learn. Because if you should say "Who could remember the days?" I reply: memory would be helped if one made a little book in which, as in a journal, one noted down what letters one writes and what letters one receives. I consider this to be not only useful but essential to those commonly engaged in business and the conduct of affairs. I know that few educated men bother much about this, but (with all due respect to them) the reason why they do not do this is not greatly to their credit. But I fear that in my flight from Baroco and Bocardo I shall come up against your censure, for being so presumptuous as to presume that I could teach you anything. But may your easy courtesy easily forgive me, in the assurance that I do not act out of any malice.

An invitation from Sidney asking Lobbet to visit him in England provided an occasion for more banter. Lobbet followed this with comments on two persons with whom Sidney and he had been concerned. Evidently Sidney had reported that young Johannes Hájek had allowed the visit to Elizabeth's court to go to his head, to the subsequent neglect of his studies.

I am most grateful to you for so kindly inviting me to England with Master Languet. I greatly prize your invitation (as I have indicated to Languet), but I shall attempt never to abuse any kind impulse of yours. In addition, Amurathes [Murad] the Emperor of the Turks is not yet so close that I have to resort to flight. What! Do you consider us here so weak and effeminate that in this city we could not withstand an attack from that tyrant? Or do you consider Strasbourg inferior to Vienna? But comparisons are odious: God grant that we do not experience such pressing times. I certainly hope that the seer (whoever he may be) who predicted that the Turks would reach Cologne will be proved wrong in that—if so, as far as I am concerned, his other predictions can all come true.

I shall convey your greetings to Mont and Hubert [de la Rose]. That Hubert, who was formerly your host, is a little better than before, but he is clearly not yet recovered. There is one thing that in my opinion is affecting his health, viz. that he takes "syrup of vine"— or, as the French call it, "purée de Septembre"—more frequently than he should.

Lobbet reacted predictably to the not unexpected news that young Hájek's mind had become filled with notions of a glamorous career at court, instead of with his studies at Oxford. He responded as follows:

I am grieved that Johannes Hájek is not proving a satisfactory student. I am sending him quite a serious warning—I send you the letter unsealed, so that you may read it first. It is no great matter that his spirit shuns [the study of] letters: one should rather aim to stop him shunning it. For boys at that age cannot judge what is useful to them: they must have watchful instructors who ask what is necessary. But you have certainly honoured him with so many favours already (which he himself in his letters to me praises greatly and deservedly) that his father is very much indebted to you on his behalf.

Sidney's weakness as a correspondent extended beyond the infrequency of his letters to their lack of political news, the chief function of most such exchanges.

You give me no news from England in your letter. I do not know whether to be more liberal: I know that, in money matters, it does not become a poor man to equal a great lord in magnificence or liberality, still less to surpass him. But in this field I may perhaps be granted some indulgence if, by increasing my efforts, I can contribute something to your peace and quiet: so let me give you these few items of news. It is said that this year two things are preventing the Turk from launching a naval attack on the Christians: the plague and the poor harvest. This will not be unwelcome to the Pope and the King of Spain. But it is to be feared that what he cannot accomplish by sea he will more than make up for by land.

It is said that the Transylvanian [Báthory] is already in Poland (thus by his speed anticipating the Emperor). When he arrived there he had a retinue of two thousand Hungarian horsemen. Rumour has it that the day appointed for his coronation was a Sunday, namely the twenty-ninth of last April, on which day he was to wed that old maid the Infanta of Poland. By now he must be saying, "Blessed are those in possession." Certainly it would have been easier to deny him entry than it will be to remove him, as he has the support of such a great and powerful patron [the Turkish Emperor]. The Imperial Diet is scheduled to begin on the fifteenth of this month. At the same time the Bohemian Diet will be held at Prague, presided over by the King of the Romans. It is said that there has been a fire in Prague (whether or not it was an accident is not known) in which 120 houses were burnt down.

What may yet happen in France, and what the state of affairs in the Netherlands may be, I shall not go into, as I believe you will know. John of Austria has not so far launched any attack: he has been awaiting funds and orders from the King of Spain. The Genoese troubles have been settled by bargaining, but not so lulled that the results of the former quarrel are not somehow promptly serving [to start] a new one. In this area and in the neighbouring countryside all the vines have been largely spoiled by cold and blight. This has caused great distress to everyone, and most of all to those who enjoy the rights to the grapes. But I shall stop lest I go on too long. Farewell, noble master Sidney, and accept my respects. Dated Strasbourg, May 15, 1576.

Yours with respect and affection,

J. L.

Clearly Sidney realized that he had fallen far behind in his personal correspondence, and so he spent much of Holy Week at his writing desk. Besides replying to Lobbet on April 21, he also dispatched a letter to Languet enclosed in one to Charles de l'Écluse in Vienna. The learned botanist answered on May 28.

Sir,

I was very happy to hear from your letters of April twenty-first that you received the copy of my book which I had had sent to you, but even more so that you liked it. I, for my part, could not do less than to let you know by that gift, however small, the obligation I feel towards you, and my wish always to remain your humble servant.

The rest of the letter consists of news about friends in Vienna.

I gave Master Languet the letter for him: he told me he would repay you in your own coin! You know that Burgundians are usually stubborn, like Picardese, and that they do not like to be defeated. So if you attack him, you will have to give way in the end for the sake of peace. Shortly after we wrote the letters that accompanied my book, he received your letter and the one for Master Wacker, which you feared was lost. There was none for me. I believe Wacker had gone to Wroclaw at that time to see his pupil, whom he afterwards took to the city on Lake Geneva. At any rate, Master Languet sent on your letter to him to Breslau, where he was staying for some time before setting out on his journey.

I shall soon be losing the splendid brotherly company of Master Languet, as the Emperor is leaving shortly for Regensburg. But I console myself with the hope of his speedy return (as I do not believe the Emperor will be there long, since there is not one Elector at the Diet), unless he should have to accompany the Emperor to Poland, should the affairs of that kingdom require his presence.

Three weeks ago Dr. Thaddeus [Hájek] left here, escorting the King of the Romans to Prague, where he had previously sent his whole family. I have conveyed your respects to him in my letters, and to Dr. Aichholtz orally. The latter thanks you greatly for your kind remembrance of him and asks me to give you his respects.

At which point, I shall pray God to grant you, Sir, good health and a long life with all honour and fulfilment: and pay my humble respects to your benevolence. Vienna, May 28, 1576.

Your humble servant,
Charles de l'Écluse

Lobbet wrote again on June fifth. Sidney's Basle correspondent, Jacques Le Goulx, remains unidentified, this being the only time his name occurs. The treaty of Beaulieu, granting most of Alençon's demands on Henry III, was concluded in April and published on May 6. Other references in Lobbet's letter are largely self-explanatory.

Sir,

I wrote to you last on the fifteenth of last month and did not plan to write again until you had replied, as I feared I should importune you if I wrote so frequently. Nevertheless I shall send you these few brief lines to accompany a letter which Master Jacques Le Goulx sent me from Basle for you.

You will know that peace has been concluded in France, and I am sure you must have seen the treaty with its sixty-three articles. One hears varying opinions and judgements on it from people of both faiths, and I believe it must be the same over there. So far as I am concerned, the subject is above my head, and I should not know what to say about it. But I will say that I am greatly annoyed that because of these troubles the kingdom is going to be drained of a lot of money that would have been better used to pay our debts.

It is thought quite certain that the Voivode of Transylvania has been crowned King of Poland and that he has married the Infanta of that country. Whether there is, or later will be, a movement to oust him I could not say: God knows, and if we live time will tell.

The general rumour is that the Emperor would leave Vienna on the first of this month to go to Regensburg for the Imperial Diet to be held there. Meanwhile the Bohemian Diet is being held at Prague, with the King of the Romans presiding: he has brought along Archduke Ernest his brother.

It is a fortnight since I had a letter from Master Languet: at that time he was well, thank God, and was still in the retinue of the Emperor's court, preparing to go the Regensburg Diet. Master Vulcob was preparing to go to France and was awaiting a successor called M. de Harlay, who was to raise the siege. That is all I have to write for the time being. I present my humble respects to your benevolence, and pray God,

Sir, to keep you in His own. From Strasbourg, this fifth of June, 1576.

Your humble servant,

J. Lobbet

During the early summer Sidney received three letters from friends in Vienna, the first being a very long one from Languet dated May 28. Fortunately much of it is personal, prompted by the letter Sidney had written him on Holy Saturday. Sidney evidently had responded heatedly to the hint Languet made in his letter of January first that friends in Vienna were beginning to wonder whether Sidney's professions of friendship had been insincere.

However it happened that I lured (or rather beat) a letter out of you, I am happy that I succeeded, since letters are now the chief benefit I can gain from your friendship. Of course I realize that I have aroused your anger, but in turn I am relishing the pleasure which reading any letter of yours gives me. Indeed it is more enjoyable because I feel that it is the fruit of my own labour. Certainly if I had not written you stinging letters my work would have been fruitless, for I could not have prodded an answer from you.

In truth it is no small accomplishment to have aroused a friend. Yet, as the poet [Ovid] says, "a noble mind is easily subject to passions," though persons easily so aroused are usually pacified with equal ease. Some sages have gone so far as to describe a quick temper as the whetstone of virtue and have called anger the greatest enemy of idleness, a trait of which I by no means entirely acquit you.

Other shortcomings for which I reproached you in my letters were, however, mentioned only in jest, hoping to prompt you to write. Could you believe that I could have entertained the slightest doubt about the purity of your heart? As Erasmus wrote of your [Thomas] More, I know that it is whiter than snow. Beyond this, do you realize how much importance I place on the fact that though you were born to so high a rank yet "your noble spirit does exceed your birth" and that, though you are endowed with judgement so acute and knowledge of affairs so wide that before I knew you I did not believe such qualities could belong to a person of your age, yet you did not spurn my friendship.

Further (allowing myself some tactlessness and boasting) I am convinced that my presence was not the least of the reasons that prompted you to return here from Italy and to endure many trials with us. Oh, my noble Sidney, if you understood how much value I place on this favour and how much I owe you for it! Accordingly, cease to reproach me as you did in this letter. Had this occurred to me even in a dream I should consider myself deserving of any punishment. Please believe that what I wrote you was sent teasingly in order to force you to answer, even against your will.

This rhetorical exercise concluded, Languet speaks more directly from the heart. Clearly he had developed a deep love for Sidney, almost amounting to adoration. Besides believing that Sidney was the ideal pupil and recipient for the outpourings of his wisdom and experience, and besides seeing in Sidney the future leader of a Protestant League, Languet yearned to be in his presence. His affection was clearly the profound avuncular love of an older man for his brilliant, virtuous protégé. Languet pinned his hopes of a reunion on the possibility that should a war break out Sidney might return to serve under Marshal von Schwendi in order to study the military art.

Your departure caused me so much torment that our friends are affected by observing my distress. It is so far from diminishing that I now carry my longing for you much less patiently than I did at the time of your leaving. Thus I must satisfy my yearning by seeing you again, unless death should deprive me of the opportunity. If some war should break out hereabouts to bring you back (for you seem to give us such a hope in your last letter) I should consider myself greatly indebted to that war, even though I should prefer to share your company in a peaceful setting.

As a further possibility, Languet thought that he might even return to France, his native country, painful though the experience would be, if Sidney were soon to be there. Sidney's letter had reported the invitation from Alençon to make such a journey.

Oh, that you should be seized by a wish to visit the ruins of miserable France! Or that you may still have the keen desire, which you formerly did, to tread the soil where four hundred years ago your ancestors first rose to public eminence! If that were to happen I certainly should count myself fortunate and should somehow extricate myself from my present situation and hasten to meet you. Nor, for that matter, would it be unpleasant for you to be with Alençon, now that you report that he has courteously invited you to spend several months in France to study the manners and characters of his and my countrymen, just as you have observed those of the Germans and the Italians. The unhappy conditions you encountered on your previous visit to France did not permit any of this.

Yet this is a wish rather than a hope: I was not born under such a star that I can expect this good luck to befall me. I fear that you must shudder whenever you think of the discomforts which must be endured by persons forced to live abroad. Furthermore I do not doubt that the reception on your return home, when you experienced everyone's goodwill, has so melted your heart that you will remain where you are forever, as if bound by chains of steel. Henceforward you will think nothing sufficiently important to let yourself to be torn away from your dear native land.

In his letter Sidney had evidently asked Languet to send a portrait of himself. Accordingly, Languet had tried to retrieve one which had been retained by an artist or dealer who, however, thwarted his attempts.

I have taken every possible step to acquire the portrait you say you would like to have, and to this purpose I have used the help of our friend de l'Écluse, whom I asked to buy it in his name from the owner, since I knew that on no account would that rascal sell it to me. He [the owner] realizes that he has received gifts from me whose value greatly exceeds the price of the painting. It is not customary for a man of that type to return a favour so received. He answered de l'Écluse's offer by saying that he intended it for our friend Jordan and had already promised it to him. Since then the painting has not been seen in his rooms.

All he said about Jordan is mere fiction. Indeed, he was not satisfied by having reciprocated in this way the favours received; after my return from Regensburg he imposed on me shamelessly in another matter. Yet as the proverb tells us, a man shipwrecked a second time will reproach Neptune in vain. Accordingly, I blame this latest incident on my own folly. I report these things so that you can understand how delightfully some supposed friends here conduct themselves.

Only after these personal concerns does Languet turn to political news. A review of the situations in Cyprus, Poland, Hungary, Italy, and Turkey follows. But Languet concludes with additional personal items.

I have received the letters you sent me on February 1 and April 21. The letter from young Hájek I have forwarded to his father Dr. Thaddaus at Prague, where he has gone with the King of the Romans. The son is harming his own interests by not applying himself to his studies, for he cannot expect much help from his parents.

With the letter you sent on February first there was no letter enclosed for de l'Écluse as you later reported to him; instead, there was one for Wacker, which I forwarded to him since he has left us. Master de Vulcob awaits the arrival of his successor, Charles de Harlay, who paid his respects to you in Venice. Bochetel also asks me to add his compliments. I anticipate that we shall leave here in seven or eight days, so if you wish to reply you should address your letter to Regensburg.

Farewell, and please pay my respects to Master Wotton. Vienna, May 28, 1576.

The two other letters from Vienna came from Dr. Purkircher, who had arrived there from Bratislava on a brief visit, and from Charles de l'Écluse. While dining together these eminent men had raised a glass of wine to toast Sidney, which inspired them to demonstrate their regard by writing to him. Purkircher's pages are largely taken up by the report of a strange phenomenon at Tömesvar, a fortified town on the Bega River in western Rumania, then a part of Hungary and under the heel of the Turks. Although these two letters did not reach Sidney until they had been forwarded to Ireland,[5] they fit best here in the narrative. Purkircher's letter is dated June 6.

Greetings.

When I came here to Vienna to visit my friends, I found your letter, in which I saw that you still retain a pleasant memory of me: and so that you should not be able to call me ungrateful, I preferred to inscribe this epistle rather than incur such blame.

In Hungary things are now fairly quiet. The Turks are ready for battle, and whenever they see us stirring up any trouble in Poland they at once invade the wretched remnants of Hungary. The only piece of Hungarian news worth writing is the following:

A few months ago, word came that a castle near the Transylvanian border, which we Hungarians call Tömesvar, had been razed to the ground by fire and artillery bombardment. At that same time a vast flood erupted from the earth. While Bassa [Hassan Pasha] wanted to surround the Tömesvarians with rocks and earth, he lost both time and trouble trying to fill this gulf: everything they threw in was spewed out again. Bassa who was anxious to rebuild the castle—the place is of crucial importance for its proximity to both Hungary and Transylvania—consulted his astrologers and seers for a way by which [illegible], yet first of all the powerful flood must be brought under control [illegible].

The astrologers consulted their books and replied that the remedy was to put a Christian into a barrel, fill up the barrel with stones, seal it, and throw it into the whirlpool, which would thus be stopped. Bassa at once had his men fill a man from Rascia [Serbia] with wine, put him in a barrel with stones, and throw him into the gulf from the ruins of the castle. By this sacrifice the flood is said to have been stopped so effectively that there is not a drop of water left, and already materials for a new castle are being brought up. The story was told by the Hungarian farmers who filled in the pit to their master Simon Forgách, who is our Commander-in-Chief: and you can believe that it is true. So much for news from Hungary: about Polish affairs I

5. Both are docketed by Sidney's secretary, "*Recue a Galway le 16 Septemb. 1576.*"

believe you have been told in the letters of others. According to de l'Écluse's letter you have toasted me in French wine: I shall reply here, for the time being, in Viennese wine and toast you, when I get home, in Hungarian. You are also greeted by my fellow drinkers: Masters Padius,[6] Lingelshiem, Blotius, Languet—and myself—who pray that all that is happy and fortunate may befall you. From Vienna, before . . . the sixth of June [15]76.

The companion piece by de l'Écluse was written two days later, though it was not given to a carrier until June 9. A mixture of news about friends and political gossip, the letter shows the ease and charm of the writer's epistolary style.

Sir,

I would not have written to you at this moment, except to accompany Dr. Purkircher's letter: partly because I have nothing much to tell you, and also because of my grief at the departure of M. Languet, my oldest and most faithful friend, who leaves tomorrow to follow the Emperor to Regensburg. God grant him a good journey and a speedy return. Of this latter I have little hope, unless something turns up to make the Emperor go to Poland, where there is plenty of trouble. M. de Vulcob is leaving today or tomorrow, but he is going via Prague, to present his respects to the King of the Romans; and thence he will go and join the Emperor at Regensburg where, trusty as ever, he will await his successor, M. de Harlay—who would have done him a great favour had he arrived before the Emperor's departure.

This week a messenger returned from Constantinople, who says he saw the arrival at Constantinople of an ambassador from the King of Persia. He was received with great splendour: many galleys and other vessels had been sent out to escort him in. After his arrival, the messenger said, all sorts of things were suddenly very cheap in Constantinople, which had previously been very expensive, especially food; but he thinks that once the ambassador has left everything will go back to its former price level, and maybe even higher.

6. Unidentified. For the names which appear in square brackets in this letter I am indebted to Dr. Paul Cernovolena of the Historical Institute, the Romanian Academy, Bucharest. He reports that this incident of human sacrifice is not recorded in the chronicles of Turkey, Hungary, or Romania.

Dr. Purkircher was here for a few days and the night before last sent me the enclosed to be forwarded to you. We had dinner together, since he was leaving yesterday morning, and he toasted you in excellent Austrian wine, saying that when he got home he would do it again in even better Hungarian wine. M. Languet and Dr. Blotius were also among the company: they present their humble respects—as do I, praying God, Sir, to grant you health, long life, and the fulfilment of your best desires. Vienna, June 8, 1576.

Your humble servant,
Charles de l'Écluse

M. de Vulcob left yesterday about 5 P.M., and M. Languet today. He told me he would write you from Regensburg (the ninth).

Sidney's movements for the next few weeks are difficult to trace precisely. When he wrote Languet on June 21 he mentioned nothing about a visit to Ireland, though such an expedition may have been under discussion. That Sidney found himself too busy to make the projected excursion to Oxford we learn from Canon Dorsett's letter of June 23. It was carried by one Christopher Buste, probably a relative of John, the tutor and guide to Robert Sidney and his companions at Christ Church.

Our letters are so winged, as the poet says, that they will find you wherever you are; and they will tell you of the grief we feel at your untimely haste. For what is it that thwarts your visit to us, which we have often awaited long and eagerly, and cheats men wholly devoted to you of their hope? But of this we shall hope to speak personally at some time: for nothing can repair this loss but your presence.

The only object of this letter is to ask you to extend to its bearer, Chr. Buste, your goodwill, which has never been refused to any in a good cause. The name of Buste, in fact, and the services with which he has honoured your respected father, so recommend him as to render any words of mine superfluous.

So I shall not trouble you further, but recommend the man and his business most sincerely to you, and yourself to Almighty God—adding also the greetings of Dr. James, which he sends you personally. Farewell. Oxford, June 23, 1576.

Yours entirely at your desire,
Robert Dorsett

At the end of the letter the Master of University College, formerly of Christ Church, added a note.

> I would write more if time and space allowed it; meanwhile I hope you will accept this as a token.
>
> William James

What kind of favour Buste sought from Sidney can only be guessed, possibly some advancement in the church. But Sidney was now pre-occupied with plans for going to Ireland. We can be certain that Sir Henry was delighted when he heard definitely that his able and attractive elder son would soon be with him; Philip would be a companion on his travels around the island and a confidant with whom he could discuss the problems which he faced daily.

When Essex and his party arrived in Dublin on July 23, Sir Henry was on a tour of duty in the west of Ireland: on the twenty-ninth he was still at Limerick and on August sixth at Kilkenny. Somewhere along the road word reached him that Philip and Essex had arrived. He sent word of his proposed route of return and Essex set out to meet him. The actual meeting occurred on August 10, twenty-eight miles from Dublin, prob-ably at the village of Kilcullen. They returned to Dublin where Sir Henry had rooms in the castle.

This month found Sir Henry Sidney at the height of reputation and favour with the Queen and her advisers. On July 10 the Privy Council wrote sending him their "most hearty thanks . . . for his diligence and execution of justice in all places."[7] The following day Chancellor Gerrard in a letter to Walsingham praised Sir Henry's "success in suppressing the rebels."[8] On July 24 Walsingham reported to Sidney, "your verry Enemyes can not but commende you."[9] Once settled in Dublin Castle, Sir Henry reported to the Council that except for one area, the whole of Ireland could be considered pacified.[10]

The relations between the Lord Deputy and his newly arrived Earl Marshal were also at their most cordial. On July 17, just before Essex left England Walsingham wrote to Sir Henry.

7. *CSPI*2, p. 97.
8. Ibid.
9. Collins, 1 : 124.
10. Ibid., p. 126.

> I perceyve, by your Lordships Letters, the good Disposytyon you
> have to use the Earle of *Essex* well, whoe, I doe assure my selfe wyll
> recompence the same, by well Deservying any Kyndnes and Favour
> he shall receyve at your Handes. Before his Departure hence, I dyd
> laye before him the Inconvenience that would ensue, as well for the
> publycke Servyce, as his owne pryvat, in Case ther should not be
> good Agrement betwen you: Whoe protested unto me, that,
> thowghe he hopethe to receyve at your Handes all kynde Dealyng,
> yet, in Case you shoold mynister unto him very hard Measure, he
> would swallowe up any Injurye, rather then breake out into any
> Disagreement: So that I hope, consydering bothe your resolute
> Determynatyons, to contynewe good Frendeship betwene you.[11]

The admiration and friendship which Essex felt for Philip reinforced his
desire to ally himself with the Lord Deputy. Considering the financial
difficulties and precarious health which were handicapping him, Essex
had every reason to support Sir Henry in his program to achieve tranquillity and reform in troubled Ireland.

Sir Henry and Philip remained at Dublin Castle for a fortnight; then
as the month ended, they set out for the west, reaching Athlone by
September 4, whence Sir Henry wrote a long letter to Queen Elizabeth.
By September 16 Sir Henry had reached Galway on the west coast.
Three days later he sent a long report to the Council, describing the
guerrilla warfare in which he was ensnared.

> I have bene still occupied, as presentlye I am, in a Kinde of actuall
> Warre, and contynuall Searche for the Rebells; sometymes dispers-
> inge one Parte of my Forces into one Parte of the Countrey, and some-
> tymes into another, as I was directed by the best Intelligence where
> theire Haunte was. . . . I hope to make an Ende of the Matter, but
> if I cannot, whyles I shall remayne here, by Reason of their often
> Flittinge from Place to Place, in soch secrete Sorte, as I cannot have
> trewe Intelligence of theim, and where they lurcke.

Thus any military experience which Philip gained in Ireland would have
been in the futile pursuit of guerrillas, and not in regular military engagements or in the storming of fortresses that he would have observed
had he joined General von Schwendi in Germany.

11. Ibid., p. 123.

Sir Henry's letter to the Council concludes with plans to go as far north as Sligo on the west coast and Carrickfergus on the east before returning to Dublin, "beinge not a little weried with the toylesome Travall of this werisome Iorney, in tracinge and searchinge the Rebells from Place to Place, and the ill Successe I have to light vpon theim." [12] On the same day Sir Henry also wrote to Burghley. In describing his activities he remarked, "I pray your Lordship in the rest of Ireland for this time give credit to Ph. Sidney." [13] This means that Philip was returning to England, where he could verbally supplement Sir Henry's written report.

The Sidneys' stay in Galway coincided with a visit by the renowned amazon of the ocean, Grania O'Malley, whose name is still celebrated in Ireland. She was the wife of the sea rover Sir Richard Burke an iarain (In Iron), a member of the MacWilliam sept, who held the baronies of Carrowe, Owle and Irryes in County Mayo. Her name (the English equivalent is Grace) appears in the records in various forms, such as Graine and Grany. Like her husband she commanded a ship, sometimes several of them, and she engaged more often in privateering and smuggling than in commerce. Years later Sir Henry recalled vividly the encounter at Galway where as Lord Deputy he granted Burke a knighthood after they formed an alliance.

> There came to me also a most famous feminine sea captain, called Granny O'Malley, and offered her services unto me wheresoever I would command her, with three galleys and two hundred fighting men, either in Ireland or Scotland. She brought with her her husband, for she was as well by sea as by land more than master's mate with him. He was of the nether Burkes . . . called by the nickname Richard the Iron. This was a notorious woman in all the coast of Ireland. This woman did Sir Philip Sidney see and speak with. He can more at large inform you of her.

Both Grania and her husband refused to pay taxes or to stop engaging in piracy. They avoided penalty for a while because of the remoteness of their home port but were finally forced to submit. [14]

12. Ibid., p. 130.
13. This letter is listed as no. 32 in vol. 56, *CSPI*2, p. 99.
14. Sir Henry's letter was written from Ludlow on Mar. 1, 1583, during the arrangements for Philip's marriage to Frances Walsingham. (*CSPD*2, p. 98; here quoted from Wallace, pp. 167–68.)

Meanwhile, back in Dublin the Earl of Essex had been fighting for his life, a victim of the epidemic of virulent dysentery that was sweeping Ireland.[15] Essex became "sorely vexed with the flux" on August 30, though he still thought of returning to England on September 11. Three days later the Archbishop of Dublin, Adam Loftus, wrote Walsingham that the Earl's condition had become desperate. "Having every day and night no less than twenty, thirty, or sometimes forty stools, through which being sore weakened and natural strength diminished" he saw the hand of death beckoning to him.[16]

Other letters mention Essex's decline and his death on Saturday, September 22: "Between 11 and 12 o'clock of the forenoon he fell asleep as meekly as a lamb."[17] News of the severity of his attack reached the Sidneys in Galway, as Sir Henry recalled later. "Here heard we first of the extreme and hopeless sickness of the Earl of Essex, by whom Sir Philip being often most lovingly and earnestly wished and written for, he with all the speed he could make went to him, but found him dead before his coming, in the castle at Dublin."[18] On reaching Dublin Sidney found that the enfeebled Essex had left a message for the young man whom he had come to admire and to love. "Tell him I send him nothing, but I wish him well, and so well, that if God do move both their hearts, I wish that he might match with my daughter. I call him son; he is so wise, so virtuous, and godly; and if he go on in the course he hath begun, he will be as famous and worthy a gentleman as ever England bred."[19]

Because, in the Renaissance tradition, such a relentless illness with severe intestinal pains suggested poison, this charge was promptly bruited about. Postmortem examination produced no supporting evidence, and the attending physicians concurred that the Earl's death had resulted from natural causes. Within a fortnight his body was sent back to England, accompanied by his page. Probably Sidney had gone on before, though

15. The Earl of Ormonde complained from Kilkenny on Sept. 6, "I have had a Toche of the lose Diseas, that trobleth manye in this Land." Collins, 1:128. Sir Henry Sidney later testified that members of his household suffered severely from "a mere Flux, a Dysease apropryated to thys Cuntry, and whearof thear dyed many in the later Part of the last Year, and sum out of myne one Household" (ibid., p. 88).

16. W. B. Devereux, *Lives and Letters of the Devereux, Earls of Essex* (London, 1853) p. 139.

17. *CSPI2*, p. 99.

18. Letter to Walsingham, Mar. 1, 1583, from Ludlow, *CSPI2*, p. 432 (here quoted from Wallace, p. 168).

19. Devereux, *Lives*, pp. 139–40.

he may also have travelled on this melancholy mission. Once the corpse reached England, Essex's agent, Edward Waterhouse, who had been present at the deathbed, took charge of burial arrangements and settling the Essex estate. When Sir Henry returned to Dublin Castle on October 13 his first task was preparing a report for Walsingham to refute the rumour that Essex had died of poison.[20]

Before Philip left Dublin he arranged to purchase ten Irish horses. They followed a month later, as a letter from him to Robert Walker, another of his father's agents, makes clear. It suggests that the ship bearing the horses sailed around southern England into the Thames, probably the simplest way of transporting them to Kent or London.

> Good Mr Walker.
>
> I pray yow in any cace make with as muche speede as may be possible for me, provision of a stable, and hay and provender for halfe a score of horses which are comminge owt of Irelande withein this ten dayes I loke for them they shall not stay there above a monthe but this I must needes have done as yow will any way pleasur me. From Grenewiche. This 4 of November 1576.
>
> Yowr lovinge frende,
Philippe Sidney
>
> To my lovinge frende and servante Mr Roberte Walker, or in his absence to Thomas Smallman keeper of Otforde.[21]

Later in the month Sidney paid his last respects to Walter Devereux, first Earl of Essex and Knight of the Most Noble Order of the Garter. Evidently he also journeyed to Chartley and assisted Waterhouse with the Earl's estate problems, for Waterhouse wrote to Sir Henry from there on November 14 that, if confirmation of Philip's assiduity was required, "I stand to the Report of Sir *Phillip Sidney*, above enie other." [22] He also testified to the widespread approval of the Earl's deathbed wish that Philip and Lady Penelope might marry. He wholeheartedly supported the proposed match, going far beyond his station to do so.

> And all thes Lords that wishe well to the Children, and, I suppose, all the best Sort of the *Englishe* Lords besides, doe expect what will

---

20. Dated Oct. 20 and printed in Collins, 1 : 140–42.
21. Feuillerat, 3 : 103.
22. Collins, 1 : 147. The anachronism "Sir" may have been a slip by Collins in transcribing "Mr."

become of the Treaty betwene Mr. *Phillip*, and my Lady *Penelope*.
Truly, my Lord, I must saie to your Lordship, as I have said to my
Lord of *Lecester*, and Mr. *Phillip*, the Breaking of from this Match,
if the Default be on your Parts, will turne to more Dishonour, then
can be repaired with eny other Mariage in *England*.[23]

Leicester certainly showed no warmth at the suggestion even though
Penelope's mother, the widowed Countess, had already caught his eye.
Not only did Leicester (who himself had made an impulsive marriage)
wish to avoid complications, but Philip, as prospective heir to the estates
of Leicester, Warwick, and Sir Henry, was too valuable a commodity
to let go so cheaply. Approaches had been made by other families for
their daughters, but without avail.[24] Needless to say, Philip himself had
little to do with the choice of his wife, the usual situation then for a youth
of his position. All we know for certain about Astrophil's early relationship with his Stella is that Sidney later lamented in sonnet thirty-three his
failure to recognize her beauty when he might have won her:

> But to my self myselfe did give the blow,
> While too much wit (forsooth) so troubled me,
> That I respects for both our sakes must show:
> And yet could not by rising Morne foresee
>   How faire a day was neare, ô punisht eyes,
>   That I had been more foolish or more wise.

23. Ibid. The letter is now BM MS. Cotton Vitellius C, xviii, fol. 370.
24. See D. E. Baughan, "Sir Philip Sidney and the Matchmakers," *MLR* 33 (1938):
506–19.

CHAPTER 22

Some time after his hasty return from Ireland Sidney received two letters from Languet; the first is dated August 13, 1576, from Regensburg where an Imperial Diet was in session. Fortunately much of it consists of personal passages, beginning with one discussing Sidney's departure for Ireland.

> From your letter of June 21 sent from London I infer that you did not intend to inform me of your Irish expedition unless you received a letter from me on the eve of departure. Yet you had earlier written detailed plans of the journey to other friends who told me about them: though when you wrote me you were already well prepared for the expedition. Perhaps you feared I should not wish you success and considered the goodwill of others towards you to be stronger than mine. Since my complaints on other occasions caused you to feel this way about me, I shall henceforth refrain from offering them, and instead reproach my ill fortune.
>
> I laud your filial piety for not allowing his Excellency your father to miss the sight of you any longer, as well as for showing no fear of the dangers and difficulties of so long a journey. But you must also give him the high pleasure which he will experience on seeing you adorned with those virtues which wise men wish for their children, though they dare not expect them.
>
> Of course I also praise you for your high determination; but when I turn my mind to the rugged mountains of Wales, to the stormy Irish Sea, and to the consistently unhealthy autumn season I feel unusual concern about you. Hence, by the love which you once felt for me, I beg you earnestly to report that you are safe once you have reached the happy haven of your court: thus relieving me of the anxiety that, as the ancient poet [Ennius] says, "torments and agitates me deep within my breast." Doubtless you will write to us punctiliously describing the Irish miracles and will send specimens of the birds which reportedly grow on trees there.

Having baited Sidney with these tongue-in-cheek comments, Languet next offers news of the Imperial Diet where such questions were being debated as how to drive back the Turks, whether to invade Poland, and whether to make a treaty with the Muscovites "who have sent envoys here so filthy in appearance and manners that the Turks could seem polished and elegant compared to these savages." Indecision, lack of money, and arguments about religion paralysed their deliberations. Next Languet reported the attempt of a court clique to persuade the Emperor to dismiss him. This situation had diverted Languet from his regular correspondence.

Here is the news about my personal affairs: since your departure, and particularly since the beginning of last winter, I have experienced unbelievable discourtesy, and even treachery, at the hands of certain men who had formerly pretended to be my friends. For although I did not provoke them by any wrongs, they have not only forsaken my friendship but also attempted to ruin me, and they have still not stopped trying. But God has so far kept me safe from their plots, and will do so as long as seems right to Him in His mercy.

Hence, do not be surprised that these troubles of mine have kept me from writing as often as usual. But I find compensatory pleasure in the company of Dr. Andreas Paull with whom I am living, as well as that of other friends here of whom I have found a good number. So would you, had you made the journey here and thus enabled yourself to enjoy the conversation of many outstanding men (especially Lazarus von Schwendi) among whom you are often mentioned. Count Solms and Baron Dohna, both of whom are very fond of you, send their compliments.

I am forwarding the treatise on Persian affairs mentioned in my last letter; when you have read it you will understand why we hold no high opinion of that nation's power. . . . I am sending you another account of Spanish affairs and trust that you will find it neither unpleasant nor useless. Farewell.

Languet next wrote on September 8, again from Regensburg. The letter had been sent by Dr. Joachim Möller, sometime secretary to Melanchthon, to his brother Eberhardt at Hamburg, whence it was forwarded to London. Dr. Möller, it will be remembered, had written in August 1575 asking Sidney to offer his services to the Queen's government, an offer which appears to have gone unheeded.

Last month I wrote you and, with my letter, sent certain reports on the affairs in Persia and in Spain, which perhaps you found not uninteresting. The packet I gave to Dr. Joachim Möller; he forwarded it to his brother who is a magistrate in Hamburg, and who will probably have it sent on to you. Dr. Andreas Paull, who greatly admires you, has enclosed his letter with mine.

The remainder of Languet's letter is filled with details of the frustrations and indecisions of the Diet of Regensburg; because of Maximilian's illness, the situation became even more complicated only a few days after the letter reached Sidney. The Emperor had been suffering badly for about a fortnight:

Four days ago he passed a stone as big as the pit of a large olive. Since then he has begun to feel somewhat better, but he has not yet regained his health, for he had other illnesses as well as the stone.

Languet concluded in his old vein of spurring Sidney to write him more frequently.

I trust that this letter will find you safely back in London from Ireland, and enjoying the luxurious ease of your court which after the troubles and trials of a laborious journey will seem more delicious to you than ever. Yet you are already negligent in answering letters, and I fear that it will make you more negligent still.

The death of Maximilian, news of which reached England at the end of October, proved to be a turning point in Sidney's career. By coincidence, another leader in central European politics, Frederick, the Elector Palatine, died within the same week. Thus the statesmen in central Europe now faced uncertainty and change. Maximilian, with all his limitations, had set a standard of enlightenment and relative tolerance well ahead of his era. His son Rudolph, though still to be proven by adversity, showed authoritarian tendencies consistent with his Spanish upbringing and near-domination by others. Clearly the benevolent neutrality practised by Maximilian could no longer be counted on by the Protestant states of Europe.

In the Palatinate the staunch Calvinist Frederick was succeeded by his elder son Count Ludwig who was known to favour the Lutheran tenets of his neighbours to the south and east. His brother, the exuberant John Casimir, held to Calvinism just as strongly as his father had done. Each

brother had his band of supporters, both at home and in nearby princi-
palities. Now that the settlement of the crown had brought stability to
Poland, uncertainties began to cloud the banks of the Danube and the
Rhine.

The situation in the Low Countries also changed from bad to worse.
The unpaid Spanish mercenaries overthrew all authority and became an
army of brigands. After sacking and burning several smaller cities, they
converged on Antwerp, then the richest city in the world. The warehouses of Antwerp's merchants bulged; its tall houses were full of rich
silks and tapestries, works of art, and plate of gold and silver. During the
first week of November Antwerp fell to the marauders. They looted
shops and warehouses, despoiled mansions of their treasures, and tortured
citizens to force them to disclose their secret hoards of wealth. Simultaneously the torch was systematically applied to the high, half-timbered
houses, and the Gothic glory of the Hôtel de Ville went up in flames.
Before the ashes had cooled, over eight thousand defenders and civilians
had been murdered, far more than the number of victims on St. Bartholomew's Day in Paris four years earlier.

News of this bloody holocaust greeted the new Governor-general who
had just arrived in Luxemburg. Don John of Austria, the hero of Lepanto
and romantic symbol of victory, had hoped to recoup his recent losses in
this new assignment. Instead he arrived to find his army had become a
great band of outlaws; they served under elected commanders, and their
ruthless and undisciplined behaviour was now the cause of hostility from
Catholic and Protestant alike throughout the Low Countries. Through
no fault of his own, Don John found his mouth filled with ashes. The
situation augured ill for the tasks before him.

Elizabeth and her advisers perceived that the changed state of European
affairs required careful reassessment. The balance of power had become
uncertain, both in the Low Countries and among the German states. The
creation of a third force was now desirable, so Walsingham finally had an
opportunity to again propose a Protestant League. The idea had existed
from the time of Queen Mary and seemed an obvious counterpoise to
the Holy League sponsored by the Vatican which had led to the victory
of Lepanto. But Walsingham's last previous chance to urge it strongly
had been in August 1571, after the Anjou proposals to marry Elizabeth
were recognized as a failure.

The first step in such a plan, obviously, would be to send an exploratory
mission to the German courts and to William of Orange, who had now

emerged as the leader which the Netherlands had lacked for so many years. Probably Walsingham proposed that Philip Sidney head such a mission, for the matter belonged under his jurisdiction even though he would need the Queen's approval and that of Burghley, Leicester, and other influential members of the Council. Sidney, though only just past his twenty-second birthday, had the prerequisite experience in the courts and knowledge of the personalities involved, especially the influential Protestant advisors at various courts—men such as Languet at the Imperial Court, Andreas Paull in Saxony, and Zacharias Ursinus in Heidelberg. Further, Sidney was an excellent linguist, a polished courtier, and a well-grounded student of foreign politics; he also carried the prestige of a noble family.

The discussions dragged on for weeks, though no detailed record of them exists. Elizabeth, abetted by the indecisive Burghley, possessed an unrivalled ability to hesitate, vacillate, and postpone decisions, especially about new ventures. The only step she seems to have taken before the end of 1576 was to write the Emperor Rudolph to announce that he had been created a Knight of the Garter and that she was sending him the insignia by the hand of the Earl of Sussex.[1] But in the matter of naming Sidney as special ambassador there is no indication that he was even apprised of the possibility. Elizabeth maintained her insistence that the people of the Low Countries recognize Philip of Spain as their sovereign: she would support their rights to their ancient laws, liberties, and privileges, but they must be obedient to their sovereign and accept the state religion of his choice.[2]

The only record of Sidney's affairs during these months at the turn of the year occurs for January 16, 1577, in the diary of Dr. John Dee, the mathematician, astrologer, alchemist, and student of the occult. On this day Dee was visited at his house in Mortlake by a group of eminent men which included Leicester, Philip Sidney, and the latter's close friend, Edward Dyer. It has been suggested that the purpose of this visit was to ask Dr. Dee to determine the date or circumstances when Sidney's departure might be "under good auspices,"[3] but the little evidence available indicates that the decision to dispatch the embassy to Germany had not yet been reached. Dr. Dee and his collection of books and instruments were considered among the curiosities of England. He was consulted as

1. CSPF2, no. 1149.
2. CSPF2, nos. 1166, 1178.
3. See, e.g., Wallace, p. 173.

a scientist, mathematician, and astrologer, but he was also visited as one of the colourful eccentrics of the age.

Finally, about the beginning of February, the decision was made to send Sidney as head of a special embassy to the Emperor and to have him visit several other heads of state on the journey thither and back. The ostensible purpose of his trip was to carry Elizabeth's letters of condolence to Rudolph as well as to Count Ludwig and Count Casimir of the Palatinate. Sidney's real objective, however, was to explore the possibilities of forming a Protestant League to oppose future aggression by the Pope and the Kings of Spain and France. For obvious reasons, this ulterior purpose is not mentioned in the Queen's instructions to Sidney, dated February 7. Because these have never been printed in any biography of Sidney they will be found in appendix 3.

The days following the official decision to send Sidney back to the German courts were filled with hectic preparation for him and the members of his ambassadorial party. Tailors, shoemakers, and other craftsmen were pressed into extra service. Quite properly, considering Sidney's youth, two older experienced men were to go with him, Sir Henry Lee and Sir Jerome Bowes. Sir Henry, "the model knight," was forty-five and still rode in the Accession Day tilts as Queen's Champion. He also served as Master of the Leash and had fought in Scotland as Regent Marshal. In addition, he had been on a mission to the Netherlands and the Rhineland in 1568.[4] Sir Jerome had been a member of Lord Lincoln's embassy to Paris in 1572, when the "young and raw" Philip had travelled to France. A third experienced diplomat in the party was Richard Allen, later envoy to the King of Denmark. Besides another friend, Gervase Cressy, the company also included Mr. Basset, Mr. Bouker, and Mr. Stanhope, probably the Michael Stanhope who ultimately became a Gentleman of her Majesty's Privy Chamber.

Sidney was also allowed to take two of his intimate friends, his old schoolfellow Fulke Greville and another companion at court, Edward Dyer. In later years when he had leisure for poetical studies, Greville and Dyer were two of his closest friends, and in his will Sidney directed that his library be divided between them. On this expedition, however, Greville was a working member, albeit the most congenial to Sidney among the whole group.

Before leaving for Dover and Flanders Sidney had a few business

---

4. Sir Henry Lee to the Earl of Leicester, July 3, 1568, in *HMC Pepys*, p. 119.

matters to arrange. The day after he received official instructions he wrote to Burghley concerning a financial transaction for his father.

Righte honorable my singular good Lorde.

Sir Nicholas Bagnoll dothe requeste my humble lettres to yowr Lordeship for the somm of to hundred pownde owt of the treasure, which he for his necessities dothe desyre to receave here and to pay at his comminge into Irelande.

I do take it that there is as muche due unto him, and besydes I know the creddit my father hathe in him, dothe stretche to a matter of greater importance, so that thus furr these few lynes shall only serve, humbly to advertise yowr Lordeship that I holde it for assured my father will be very well satisfied withe it. Furdre I can not proceede, but referringe it holy to yowr Lordeships goodnes humbly leave yowr Lordeship to the protection of the Allmightie. Frome Leyster howse. This 8th of Februarie. 1576[-7].

Yowr Lordeships moste humbly at commawndement,

Philippe Sidney

To the righte honorable my very good Lorde, the Lorde Burghley. Lorde Hy Treasorer of England.[5]

The second brief letter was addressed two weeks later to Robert Walker, paying agent for Sir Henry Sidney, and is still among the Sidney papers at Penshurst.

Servante Walker.

I pray yow that yow will owt of the money yow receive of my fathers lett my sisters olde governes, Mrs Anne Mantell have the summe of twentie powndes which is dew unto her for her wages my father gives her. If yow possibly may I pray yow doe this and yow shall doe me a greate pleasure, and so farewell. This 22th of Februarie. 1576[-7].

Yowr lovinge frende

Philippe Sidney

To my lovinge frende Mr Roberte Walker. etc.[6]

The letter carries the endorsement, "Received £10 in part of payment. Robert Mantell."[7]

5. Feuillerat, 3 : 104.
6. Ibid. Mrs. Mantell (usually called Jane), wife of Robert Mantell, one of the Sidney household staff, had also been nurse in 1560–61 to Philip himself. *HMC De L'Isle*, 1 : 240.
7. Wallace, p. 164.

Sidney's departure was delayed at least one more day while he waited for a letter of introduction from Queen Elizabeth to Don John of Austria. It is written in her formal, rather ornate French which is here translated.

Cousin,

Since it has pleased God to call unto himself our good brother and cousin, the late Emperor Maximilian, and in his stead to elevate to Imperial dignity his son Rudolph; and since it is the worthy custom of all princes, linked in alliance and careful of their friendships, to visit the new prince and observe such courtesies as are proper to the occasion; we have to this end determined to send the gentleman who bears this letter, Master Sidney, a Gentleman of our Chamber, unto the new Emperor.

We do believe that, since this gentleman travels as our representative through such countries as are our good friends and allies, and on a peaceful mission (of which he can show good proof), he will not be hindered in any way. We have nevertheless decided to send you these few words, to beseech you that, should Master Sidney decide to pass through, or close to, the place where you are, and should he require it, you will furnish and equip him with your safe-conduct and recommendation; so that, under your aegis, he may the more safely traverse the peoples, lands, and jurisdictions of our well-beloved brother the Catholic King. We beg you also to furnish him with anything he may require upon reasonable payment: which, in similar case, we shall not fail to perform likewise unto such as may pass through our jurisdictions, lands, and kingdoms, bearing the recommendation of the said King our brother or of yourself. This indeed is known unto Almighty God, to whom we pray to grant you, Cousin, good health and a long and excellent life.

From our palace at Westminster, February 23, 1576[-7]; the nineteenth year of our reign.[8]

Another member of Sidney's entourage, according to the unsupported statement of the Dutch scholar, J. A. van Dorsten, was Daniel Rogers, one of Walsingham's most valuable men in the foreign service.[9] In his

8. Lettenhove, 9:215-16.

9. The thick manuscript volume of Rogers's Latin poems, formerly owned by the Marquess of Hertford, was purchased at Sotheby's on June 23, 1969 (lot 169) by the Henry E. Huntington Library. It has been carefully studied by Dr. van Dorsten and others, especially

penetrating study of Rogers, van Dorsten states unequivocally, "During his [Sidney's] first week in Flanders he was accompanied by Rogers."[10] If so, Rogers probably crossed the Channel with Sidney's party, though the chronology involves some very quick movements to make this possible. But Rogers was in Westminster on February 28, and Sidney's entourage arrived in Brussels no later than March 4 and probably a day earlier.[11] Because they travelled through Ghent, Sidney and his company apparently landed at Ostend. The most rapid schedule would have required a full day from London to the port of embarkation, a second day to cross the Channel (assuming no waiting for favourable winds), and two more days from Ostend to Brussels, thus covering a full four days. Hence it is difficult to place Sidney's party still in London any later than Tuesday, February 27. If Rogers did travel with Sidney's entourage, his experience and knowledge of Flemish and of the facilities along the road would have been a great help.

The English ambassador at Brussels, Dr. Thomas Wilson, welcomed Sidney and his companions and promptly made plans for the visit to Don John. The Spanish Governor had been settled for a week at Louvain, seventeen miles east of Brussels. Wilson's chief concern was not that Don John might be unfriendly, but that the rabble of English and Scottish exiles who surrounded him might cause trouble. These fugitives were assiduously paying court to Don John because their hopes for freeing Mary Queen of Scots were now anchored on a scheme involving an invasion of England by Don John. He was to free Mary and marry her, thus becoming king of England. The exiles included the Earl of Westmorland, the Countess of Northumberland, Sir Francis Englefield, and sundry others. They faded discreetly into the background when Sidney's party appeared.

Fulke Greville has left a memorable picture of the meeting between the two symbols of chivalry: Don John, the glamorous knight of the Roman Catholic world, only thirty despite his now somewhat faded

by Professor James E. Phillips who is preparing an edition of many of the poems. See his discussion in the William Andrews Clark Memorial Library Seminar Paper, *Neo-Latin Poetry in the Sixteenth and Seventeenth Centuries* (Los Angeles, 1964).

10. *Poets, Patrons, and Professors: Sir Philip Sidney, Daniel Rogers and the Leiden Humanists* (Oxford/Leiden, 1962), p. 49.

11. Rogers's letter to Buchanan is dated Feb. 28; see Thomas Ruddiman, ed., *Georgii Buchanani opera omnia* (Edinburgh, 1715), 1: xx. See also Dr. Thomas Wilson to Walsingham, Mar. 5, 1577, *CSPF2*, no. 1319; the full text appears in Lettenhove, 9:232.

fame, and Sidney, the budding hero of the Protestant courts. In the glow of memory Greville somewhat overpaints the interview.

> Again, that gallant Prince *Don John de Austria*, Vice-Roy in the Low Countries for *Spain*, when this Gentleman [Sidney] in his Embassage to the Emperor came to kiss his hand, though at the first, in his Spanish haughture, he gave him access as by descent to a youth, of grace as to a stranger, and in particular competition (as he conceived) to an enemy; yet after a while that he had taken his just altitude, he found himself so stricken with this extraordinary Planet, that the beholders wondered to see what ingenuous tribute that brave, and high minded Prince paid to his worth, giving more honour and respect to this hopefull young Gentleman than to the Embassadors of mighty Princes.[12]

Unfortunately Greville's account seems somewhat tinted by hagiography. Don John was only eight years senior to Sidney. The latter was not only the ambassador of a mighty prince, but himself ranked as a prince since he was "*Proregis Hibernici filius.*" As van Dorsten has pointed out, this title was more than mere protocol, for it allowed Sidney to treat with the princes of Europe on equal terms.[13]

Further, despite Don John's military fame, he was soon discovered "to bee a man of smale discourse and litle experience," in which he resembled most Spaniards "who seeme to knowe moche by their pryde and stowtenesse, and yet are verie ignorant in political governement."[14] His fondness for repetition in conversation did not suggest an agile mind. As Don John, shorn of genuine power, lingered on to preside over the liquidation of mercenaries and the repatriation of Spanish personnel, diplomatic dispatches described his conduct towards the Netherlanders as almost excessively sweet. Sidney's charm undoubtedly made a gentle response easier, but Don John was prepared in any case to meet him with smiles and soft answers. Dr. Wilson's report to Walsingham on March 10 (as calendared) confirms this: "He and Mr. Sidney had audience the sixth with Don John at Louvain, and notwithstanding his [Sidney's] plain

---

12. Greville, p. 37.

13. *Poets, Patrons, and Professors*, p. 49.

14. Lettenhove, 9:221. Dr. Wilson to Queen Elizabeth, quoting the opinion of M. Champagny.

Don John of Austria

speech had fair and sweet answers, which being performed in very deed then is he satisfied."[15]

Sidney's "plain speech" concerned the English and Scottish traitors hanging about Don John's court, a great annoyance to Elizabeth and her advisers. The Spanish Governor answered her Majesty the day after Sidney's visit. The calendar summary of his letter of March 7 reads as follows:

> Thanks her for her letter of congratulation on the peace [the Pacification of Ghent], and assures her of his intention to govern the country peaceably and well and in friendship with England. Denies that he has, as she says, encouraged her rebels, for when certain came to him he ordered them to depart, and they went on the morrow. No one is more desirous of preserving the friendship between England and the house of Burgundy than he.[16]

But Wilson saw through these fair words. Three days later he wrote to Burghley giving his analysis; undoubtedly Sidney had taken part in the discussions.

> Don John uses such courtesy and familiarity to all that come to him that he wins credit greatly with them of least understanding, and shows himself to him [Wilson] so well disposed with such "dolce" and good words that he doubts him more than others trust him, for his deeds are contrary to his words, using conference in secresy with her Majesty's rebels. . . . Don John has secretly charged all rebels and fugitives to absent themselves, and yet he gives order for their pensions, and tells him [Wilson] they are all banished.[17]

Sidney could not linger to follow this cat-and-mouse game, for he had his own duties to perform. Leaving Brussels, he and his party journeyed to the Rhine and proceeded upstream to Heidelberg where the next incident in his embassy was to occur.

The journey to Heidelberg probably took most of a week. Once there, however, the young ambassador went promptly about his business.

---

15. *CSPF2*, no. 1326.

16. *CSPF2*, no. 1322. Elizabeth's reply to Don John, written on Mar. 18, confirms her annoyance at his encouragement of the rebels and names specifically Stukeley and the Earl of Westmorland; Lettenhove, 9:224–25.

17. *CSPF2*, no. 1325.

By the end of another week he was ready to write a long report for Walsingham on the results accomplished to date. The letter, dated March 22, 1577, begins as follows:

Right Honorable.

I received in commandement from hir Majesties that in my waye to the Emperor, I should deliver her Majesties letters to the brethren Palatins, and withall give them to understand how greatly, and in what good respectes her Majestie was sorry for the death of the late Elector, and yet withall somewhat comforted by the assured expectation her Majestie had of their succeeding unto him in all his vertues, I should according as I sawe cause perswade them to brotherly love necessary for the publique weale, and their owne preservation.

Afterwards to Casimire in particular I should so much the more expresse her Majesties good favor towards him, as he was the son most deere unto his father, and had allready given very good shew of his princely vertues. Lastly I should learne of him, whether the mony delivered, were as yet received, which her Majestie would be content to leave there in some place of that country in deposite.

For the first I could not yet doe it, but only to Prince Casimir, the Electour being at a towne of his in the upper Palatinate called Amberg, whether I meane to goe unto him, being not much out of the way for Prage, where the Emperour lyes, if I doe not meete him by the way, as it is thought I shall, but to Prince Casimire I said according to mine Instructions, and to that purpose so much more, as the course of speech, and the framing of the time did give occasion.

Count Casimir's answer began with the usual compliments and reciprocal courtesies.

His answer was that her Majestie in deed had great reason to be sorry for the losse of his father, having bene in truth so trew a friend and servant unto her, of his other good partes he left to be wittnessed by the things he hath done in the advancement of vertue and Religion. For himselfe he could not thinke himselfe bound enough to her Majestie for this signification of her goodnes towards him, and in the vertues of his father, there was none he would seeke more to follow, then his duty and good will to her Majestie. This he did in very good termes, and with a countenance well witnissing it came from his hart.

The split between the brothers, caused by Ludwig's turning from the Calvinism of his father to Lutheranism, seemed to Casimir, who still was faithful to the Geneva beliefs, a gulf too wide to bridge. Casimir viewed with special alarm Ludwig's antagonism towards Dr. Ursinus and other Calvinist theologians, who had long been part of the court and university at Heidelberg.

> For the second I founde no cause to perswade him to unity with his brother, he being as he saith, fully perswaded so to embrace it as nothing more, yet found I in him great miscontentment that his brother beginnes to make alteration in Religion, for having two principall gover[n]ments the upper Palatinate which lyes in Bavaria, and this which they calle the nether by the Rhine, the Elector hath allready in the upper established Lutheranisme, and as it is feared, is comming shortly to doe the like here.
>
> He hath used great perswasions to his brother in it, and of late hath sett out in print his fathers confession in his owne name, to the end as I pe[r]ceive by him to avoyde all suspicion, that either flattery in his fathers time or feare now did or may move him either to embrace or leave that which concernes his conscience. This confession he hath sent to all the Electors, and most part of the Princes of Germany. He is resolved if his brother doe drive away from him the learned men of the true profession, that he will receive to him, and hereof something may breed gall betwixt them if any doe, but the best is to be hoped, considering Prince Lodovick is of a soft nature, ledde to these things only thorough conscience, and Prince Casimir wise, that can temper well with the others weaknes.

On the more practical matter of Elizabeth's loan to pay the Reiters, how Casimir had used it and when he would repay it, Casimir's answers were far from satisfactory. Yet Sidney concluded with the optimistic prediction that the loans would be redeemed within the following two years.

> For the third which was to shew her Majesties speciall good liking of Prince Casimir, I did it with the first, and his answere was the same protestation of his good harte as before I wratte.
>
> In the last touching her Majesties money his answer was the King of France had falsefied his promise, and therefore neither her Majestie nor the Ritters who doe greatly cry for it, could as yet have their dew. I told him it would be a cause to make her Majestie withdraw

from like loanes, as the well paying would give her cause to doe it in greater sommes. He was greeved with my urging of him, and assured me, that if he could gett the payement, he wolde rather dye then not see her Majestie honorably satisfied.

Then I pressed him for certeine jewells and ostages, I had learned he had in pawne of the King, he told me, they were allready the rittreses, but if her Majestie would buy any of them she might have a good bargaine.

In fyne this I find that of nyne monthes was dew to the soldiers they are paied but to and an halfe, for other the Duke of Lorrayne and Vaudemont are bound of which they make perfect account.

Their Jewells and ostages they valew a little more then at halfe a moneths paye, so that there is due unto them yet foure moneths pay, which according to their gentle allowance comes to above a million of frankes: untill most part of this be payed I doe not think her Majestie can receive her dew. The best is a thing well employed is halfe paied, and yet truly by that I find in the Prince, I doe hold my selfe in good beleefe, that her Majestie within a yeare or two shalbe honorably answered it.

Sidney next reported Casimir's opinions on the political and economic situation at the Emperor's court and in the rest of central Europe. None of Casimir's responses gave much ground for encouragement.

Now touching the particularities her Majestie willed me to learne of him, as of the Emperors both in matters of State and Religion how the Princes of Germany are affected in French and Low Country matters, what forces there are preparing here, and what he himselfe meanes to be.

For the Emperor he knowes very little of him, but such generall pointes every where knowen, of his papistry or Spanish gravity. But this I understand by men of good judgement, that he is left poore, the division with his brethern not yet made, warres with the Turke feared, and yet his peace little better, considering the great tributes he paies, and the continuall spoiles his subjectes suffer uppon the Frontiers.

The other Princes of Germany have no care but how to grow riche and to please their senses; the Duke of Saxony so carried away with the ubiquity, that he growes bitter to the true Lutherians.

The rest are of the same mould, thinking they should be safe, though all the world were on fire about them, except it be the Landgrave William, and his brethern, and this Prince Casimire, who wisheth very earnestly, that her Majestie would writte of purpose unto the Landgrave, being a Prince both religious, wise, and very much addicted to her Majestie.

Finally, Casimir had discussed briefly the military and political picture in France, Don John's ambitions, and the prospects for forming a Protestant League.

Forces there are none publiquely preparing. Casimir the only man, the Ritters and soldiors doe looke and depend uppon him, he temporises a little staying till he gathers of the King of France and King of Navarre 3 months paye for such an army, as he will bring, and then in deed he saith, I shall heare, that he is dead, or that he hath left a miserable France of the papishe syde. I have sent the Princes confession in Dutch. The Prince did give of a meaning Don John should have to marry the Quene of Scotts, and so to sturr troubles in England.

There is none of the Princes like to enter into any League (and that rather as it were to serve the Queen than any way ells) but the Prince Casimir, the Landgrave, and the Duke of Brunswick.

The Bohemians which were earnest in Maximilians time to have Churches of the true Religion granted them doe now grow cold only being content to have the freedome in their houses. I will not furder trouble you, but with my humble commendations unto you leave you to the Eternall. From Heidelberg this 22 of Marche 1576 [-7].

Yours to doe you any service

Phillipp Sydney[18]

Tact required that Sidney also write to Burghley, so after finishing his long report to Walsingham he wrote a short note of greeting to the Lord Treasurer. Both letters were carried by one Woodall, evidently a courier in Walsingham's service.

Righte honorable my very good Lord only to give yowr Lordeshippe to undrestande that I do not forgett the dutie I beare to yowr Lordeshippe I am bolde in haste and parting to wryte these few

18. Feuillerat, 3 : 105–08.

wordes unto yow. For otherwise neither is there matter worthy the sendinge unto yow, and suche as this my journey breedes I have at large writtne it to Mr Secretary. Therefore it shall suffise me to give yowr Lordeshippe humbly to undrestande that I am in helthe and in deede, as I have greate cawse, reddy to do yowr Lordeshippe any service. I beseeche yowr Lordeshippe to take these few lynes in good parte which I will ende withe my humble praier to the Allmightie to sende yowr Lordeshippe longe lyfe in helthe and prosperitie.

Frome Heidelberg this 22th of Marche 1576[-7].

Yowr Lordeshippes humbly at commawndement.

Philippe Sidney

Before Woodall departed Sidney received a long letter full of political news from a friend at the Emperor's court in Prague. Accordingly, he added a lengthy footnote to his letter.

Thus muche I thoughte yowr Lordeshippe woolde be contente if I did adde to these former lynes. that as yet the division betwixte the Palatins is not perfittly made, allthoughe the fathers will be sett downe, in so muche that there is some feare there will some jar fall betwixte them that beinge on with the diversitie of their religions. Lodowick hathe hetherto kept Casimirs subjectes frome swearing unto him, and at this very present, gives owt it is in respect he will bring his brother from Calvinisme.

Lifland [i.e. Latvia] hathe givne them selves to the Moscovite, and Dansick warr sorely begonne againe. Of the other syde the Emperour feares revolte in Hungary to the same king of Poland. These news becaws I newly receaved them from a very honest gentleman at Prage, I am bolde to sende them thus scribblingly to yowr Lordeshippe.

To the righte honorable my singular good Lord the Lord Burghley Lord Hyghe Threasorer of England and Knight of the most noble ordre.[19]

A week later the ambassadorial troop had reached Nuremberg. Whatever impression the city of Hans Sachs made upon Sidney, he was distracted by news that Languet would not be in Prague to greet him. Grieved by the hard-line Lutheranism followed by the Elector of Saxony, Languet had decided to retire from his service. After some delay Augustus

19. Ibid., pp. 108–09.

granted the request, and on March 8 Languet took leave of the Emperor and his court at Prague and made plans to return to the hospitable house of Andreas Wechel in Frankfurt. That Sidney had heard of Languet's intended visit is clear from the postscript of a letter he sent from Nuremberg to the Count of Hanau.

Sir,

There is nothing in which I consider myself happier than to be acquainted with you as a friend, as you have graciously allowed me to be; nothing, that is, except the great favours I have received from this friendship. On my part I have not the slightest doubt or anxiety, Sir, that I will one day be able to prove to you by my actions how much I feel myself to be in your debt for the great kindness with which you have been pleased to treat me.

However I know that you are not infatuated with mere words, and I in any case have none ready to use; nonetheless I know you will be happy to continue in the good opinion you once formed of me without my trying to improve it by any other means than by my humble service, which will always be ready when you think it suitable to take advantage of it.

After I have returned from the court of the Emperor I hope to come and kiss your hands, and I will put off until then all the other things I have to say, apart from this: that I beg you to keep me in your favour. With that I shall make an end, asking God, Sir, to give you a long, healthy, and happy life. From Nuremberg, March 30, 1577.

Your humble and affectionate friend, always ready to serve you,

Philip Sidney

I beg, Sir, that you will pass on to Monsieur Welsperg my most affectionate desire for his good favour; I beg also, Sir, that you will greet Monsieur Hubert Languet for me, because I have seen nothing of him for a long time.

CHAPTER 23

After almost a week of hard travel Sidney and his entourage reached Prague on April 4, Maundy Thursday. The travellers and the court rested quietly during the remaining days of Holy Week. Once Sidney had celebrated Easter Sunday, he wrote a letter to his close friend in Vienna, Charles de l'Écluse, the eminent botanist.

> Sir,
>
> It is a great grief to me, you may be sure, that having travelled into these parts with a good chance of finding you here, I find myself frustrated not only in that, but in any hope at all of being able to see you before I return.
>
> However, since there is no solution to this problem, there is no point in discussing it. This gentleman is a very near relation of mine, and since he has a great desire to see your beautiful city of Vienna, I gave him these few words to take with him, as much to refresh your memory of me as to make this demand on our friendship: would you be so kind as to show him the memorable parts of the city, and, much more important, to let him make your acquaintance, a thing he greatly desires? I have no wish to trouble you further, except to assure you that I am indebted to you, and that there is no man in the world who holds you in greater affection, or is more ready to do as you please or as you will than I. With that I will make an end. I ask God,
> Sir, to give you a long, happy, and healthy life. From Prague, April 8, 1577.
>
> Your very good friend to command,
Philip Sidney

He also wishes to kiss the hands of the Archduke Ernest; I have also written about this to Baron Prainer. All in all, Sir, he is a very worthy gentleman, to whom all courtesy is due. I must ask you to give warm greetings in my name to that excellent man Doctor Angelius, my very good friend and host, and do the same, if you would, to the renowned Raccolsius.

Neither the last named nor Sidney's "near relative" can be identified.

Friedrich, Baron Prainer (of Stübing, Fladnitz, and Rabenstein) served Archduke Ernest as Chamberlain and Councillor. Petro de Angelis 1517–96), who may be the Dr. Angelius mentioned by Sidney, was a Tuscan scholar of Greek manuscripts who spent part of his life in Vienna.[1]

Following the Easter holiday an audience with the Emperor was arranged for Monday, April 8. A newsletter from Prague dated April 13 reported, "The Queen of England's ambassador had audience of his Majesty, who received him very graciously, and on the following day caused such arrangements to be made as that he should be at no expense; and it is said he will soon be taking his departure."[2] The following issue a week later added, "The English ambassador is making ready to return home; and it is believed that the Emperor will make him some beautiful present, after the very gracious reception which he has accorded him."[3] The present was the usual chain of gold, a gift which could easily be turned into cash but was more tactful than mere money. The chain for Sidney was large enough to merit the description "great."

On April 12 Rudolph wrote to Elizabeth, thanking her for the letter of condolence which Sidney had brought, and expressing appropriate hope "that the friendly relations between the two crowns will be maintained."[4] Sidney did not attempt to write a detailed description of the Emperor and his government until he had returned safely to Heidelberg early in May. Besides his formal audience with Rudolph, Sidney also paid visits to the Dowager-empress and to her daughter, the widowed Queen of Charles IX of France.

During his two weeks in Prague Sidney enjoyed a reunion with various old friends whom he had not seen since leaving the Continent in the spring of 1575. To his delight he found that Languet had postponed his departure to await Sidney's ambassadorial visit to the Emperor. On Sidney's arrival Languet made the most of the opportunity to be with his former pupil. The joy with which the friends embraced is easily imagined, as are the happy hours they spent catching up on each other's affairs. The room where they met must have buzzed with their confidential news and opinions about the chief actors on the stage of Europe. Now their positions were reversed, for Languet had been living in seclusion

1. These identifications were kindly supplied by Dr. Gertraud Leitner of Vienna.
2. *CSPR*, p. 301. This newsletter states that the meeting took place on Tuesday, but in his own report (see p. 469) Sidney says that the meeting was on Monday.
3. *CSPR*, p. 301.
4. *CSPF2*, no. 1386.

for more than a month while Sidney had been moving from court to court. Languet remained with Sidney for a month, travelling with him back to the Rhine.

The only record of a reunion was preserved by Philip Camerarius of Nuremberg; Sidney had doubtless been introduced to him by Languet. The account of Sidney's talk is rather long, which may explain why it has never been printed in full in any book on Sidney.[5] Ironically, considering Sidney's fame as "poet, soldier, statesman," this is the only recorded example of his conversation.

Sir Philip *Sydney*, sonne to the Lord Deputie of Ireland, a most worthy knight, discended of the noble house of the Earles of Warwicke, and called by *William Camden, The great hope of men, the liuely picture of vertue, the delights of learned men,* . . . He being sent Embassador by the most excellent Queene of England, to the Emperors maiestie, as one day he talked priuatly with me and some others, he entertained vs with very memorable discourses.

And as we fell vpon the speech, Whether it were true (as the Ancients say, and the Moderne beleeue) that England cannot indure wolues, either bred in the country, or brought thither out of other places; and whether the same proceed of some hidden propertie and naturall antipathie, as we see some other countries cannot indure rats, mise, serpents, or other venemous beastes: he deliuered vnto vs the true reason thereof in good and proper termes, the which, because it is not (for ought I know) spoken of any where else, I haue thought good to deliuer in this chapter.

It is a meere tale (*said Sidney*) that the reason why our kingdome of England hath no wolues, proceedeth of some naturall and knowne propertie: for in diuers places of the countrey there are of them to bee seene in parks of great lords, who send for them out of Ireland and other places, to make a shew of them as of some rare beast: but it is forbidden vpon grieuous penalties to let them escape out of their enclosure. And as touching that England hath been cleane rid of them a long time since, and is so still at this day, the wisdome of our kings hath effected that. For it is well knowne, that this rauenous

5. First printed in Philip Camerarius, *Operae Historiarum Subcisivarum* (Frankfurt, 1591); quoted here from the English version, entitled *The Living Librarie*, trans. J. Molle (London, 1621), pp. 98–99. To aid the reader, it has been divided into paragraphs and the pages of italic type replaced by roman.

and cruell beast was in times past as common in England, as in Germanie and other neighbour countries, and did much harme to sheepe, which England aboundeth with, and of the great flocks whereof there be great reuenues made euery yeare, as appeareth by the good and great store of clothes that are made of their wooll, and that are so much spoken of among all nations.

Now albeit that England is had in estimation for her dogs, which are strong and of a noble kind, and being armed with their collars according to their custome, are not afraid of a whole herd of wolues, but doe brauely set vpon them, and if they kill them not, yet doe they giue them the chase: Notwithstanding, for all that euer could be done, this trecherous beast hath sometimes done much hurt to flockes of sheepe, both by night and by day, as well in their stalles, as abroad. Therefore there was an Ordinance made by the king a great while since, that such persons as not of set purpose, but vnwittingly had committed an offence deseruing any grieuous punishment (saue the forfeiture of their liues) should be thus punished, namely, That they should stand banisht and discredited vntil they had brought the tongues and heads of some wolues by them slaine, in a greater or lesse number, according to the sentence of the Iudges.

This amends was imposed upon them, and this tribute they payed for their heads. Which law hauing lasted a long space of time, the wickednesse of men, and the number of guilties alwayes increasing, the fugitiues betooke themselues to seeke so narrowly for wolues and for their young, that in the end there were more hunters then wolues: whereby it came, that there was neither brake, bush, nor any couert but was void of such harmefull beasts: so as at length the race of them was vtterly extinguished.

And for that England is of all sides enuironed with the sea, save where it bordereth vpon Scotland, and it was very sharply forbidden to bring or to fetch wolues from any other countries that might store England againe with the vermin of which it had beene deliuered: there was never any feare of them since, so as after that time the kingdom was rid of them, whereupon ensued the rest and safetie of the cattell. And so now flocks of sheepe and other beasts feed in quiet without shepherd, both day and night, here and there, both vpon hils, and in plaine fields.

For which cause, the penaltie also inuented for the destruction of wolues (for as much as there are no more of them to be found, either in the mountaines, or in forrests, or in dennes) hath been abolished. For in latter ages, the Banditoes hunting in vaine after that which cannot be found, are forced to abide all their life in exile, which to them is a kind of death.

Touching Scotland, it cannot be denied but it hath some wolues: but because it ioyneth to England by a little necke of land which is hemd in of each side with a continual ebbing and flowing of the Ocean, and with some deepe riuers that discharge themselues into the sea, and that this little between-space of land being the bounder of the two kingdoms, is kept by mightie garrisons in certain strong places, where be great store of dogs: it is not to be feared that the wolues will hazard to passe out of Scotland into England, and we haue no opinion of any such thing.

This discourse of Sydneys, accompanied with other memorable speeches touching Ireland, where his father gouerned; and of Saint *Patricks* Hole, much esteemed when time was (at this day little set by) was verie pleasing to the companie that sate at table with him, and no man would make any question thereof, especially when we saw it approved by *Hubert Languet*, a man of most exquisit iudgment, and exceeding wel trauelled in the knowledge of things, and in the affairs of the world.

One other well-documented session, paradoxically, took place with the brilliant English Jesuit Edmund Campion. Because Campion had been conspicuous for his eloquence at Oxford for more than a decade, Sidney's biographers have strained to swallow the statement of Campion's biograper, Robert Simpson, that Sidney had known Campion during his Oxford days. Actually, their Oxford careers overlapped by only a year and a half. Sidney arrived at Christ Church in February 1568, when he was only thirteen. Campion was fourteen years older than Sidney; after serving as Junior Proctor despite the fact that he was a devout and convinced Roman Catholic, he left England in August 1569. The two lived in quite different worlds. At Christ Church the thirteen-year-old boy was swathed with the attention of the dons when he was not exercising or sporting with his classmates, while Campion, at St. Johns, would have been arguing fine points of philosophy and theology with his peers in the Common Room or in hall.

True enough, in 1566 during Queen Elizabeth's visit, Campion had been chosen to welcome her Majesty in the name of the University, and his brilliantly eloquent performance had been warmly received by Elizabeth. Sidney probably witnessed the ceremony. At the Queen's request Leicester extended his patronage to Campion, but this does not imply a welcome into the Dudley family circle. Similarly in 1570, when Campion went to Ireland expecting to become head of the new Dublin University, he found Sir Henry Sidney in favour of the scheme (it came to nothing). However, Philip was still at Oxford. Sir Henry saved Campion's life in 1571, but the only connection with Sir Henry's son that can be established with even modest likelihood is that Philip saw Campion at Oxford, heard him dispute or preach, and knew of his reputation for piety, eloquence, and intelligence. Campion, in turn, probably knew that the Chancellor's nephew was enrolled at Christ Church and may have known him by sight.

Once Sidney had completed his official audience with Rudolph and his calls on the Dowager-empress and Charles IX's widow, his time in Prague was largely at his own disposal. He learned that an Englishman was then resident in Bohemia; the man was Edmund Campion. He had joined the Society of Jesus in Rome five years earlier and was now completing his novitiate in Prague. (Not till the following year did he proceed to the priesthood.) Sidney probably remembered Campion's reputation at Oxford and sought him out. From his years with Languet and the Calvinist theologians, Sidney knew how to stimulate Campion's mental powers, and so gave him a chance to demonstate his Jesuit training. Apparently Sidney was so tactful that Campion did not realize that, though enthralled by his performance, his listener was unconvinced by it. By the time Sidney left Campion considered him prime material for conversion.

This reconstruction of the Prague interview comes from the only direct evidence preserved, a letter Campion wrote the following summer to his old tutor in Rome, Dr. John Bavand.

A few months ago Philip Sidney came from England to Prague as ambassador, magnificently provided. He had much conversation with me, I hope not in vain, for to all appearance he was most eager. I commend him to your sacrifices, for he asked the prayers of all good men, and at the same time put into my hands some alms to be distributed to the poor for him, which I have done. Tell this to Dr. Nicholas Sanders, because if any one of the labourers sent into the vineyard from the Douai seminary has an opportunity of watering this plant, he may watch the occasion for helping a poor wavering soul. If this young man, so wonderfully beloved and admired by his countrymen, chances to be converted, he will astonish his noble father, the Deputy of Ireland, his uncles the Dudleys, and all the young courtiers, and Cecil himself. Let it be kept secret.

Campion's biographer, Richard Simpson, fictionalized his account following Father Parson's version written two decades after Sidney and Campion met.

> Sir [sic] Philip was afraid of so many spies set and sent about him by the English Council; but he managed to have divers large and secret conferences with his old friend [sic]. After much argument, he professed himself convinced, but said it was necessary for him to hold on the course which he had hitherto followed; yet he promised never to hurt or injure any Catholic, which for the most part he performed.[6]

Simpson clearly knew his own audience and told them what they wished to hear.

Sidney's official duties were now accomplished and his party well rested. After a final banquet given by the Emperor they made their farewells to friends and left Prague on Saturday, April 20. Sidney's departure was reported by the papal nuncio to the Cardinal of Como at Rome: "The English ambassador, after being feasted by his Majesty, has departed today, taking with him most honorific gifts."[7] The party returned to Heidelberg on Tuesday, April 30, in time for Sidney to have an audience with the Elector Ludwig on the following day.

Sidney's next order of business was to write a long report to Walsingham about his sessions at Prague and Heidelberg and the response to the Queen's letters. Dated May 3, his report covers so many topics that it is best digested one section at a time. Like many other documents in the Cotton Collection, one margin is badly damaged; plausible additions have been supplied in square brackets. Sidney begins with a succinct exposition of how he followed each step called for his instructions. His highly developed sense of structure in thinking and writing are evident throughout.

---

6. Richard Simpson, *Edmund Campion* (London, 1896), pp. 123, 115.

7. John Delfino, Bishop of Torcello, to Ptolemy Galli, Cardinal of Como, in *CSPR*, p. 301.

Righte honorable.

The nexte day I dispatched away Woodall be[ing the] 22 of Marche, I departed frome Heidelberge, and not findinge the [Elector] at Amberg as I hoped to have done came to Prage uppon Maun[dy Thursday] uppon Easter Monday afterwardes I had Audience, where accor[ding to] her Majesties commawndemente, I was to make knowne unto him, h[ow] greatly Her Majestie was grieved withe the losse of so worthy a [Prince] the Emperour his father was, her Majestie havinge so greate cawse [for sorrow] as bothe the publicke losse of suche a prince (the fruites of whose [Royal] governement were well fownde, bothe in the mainteining the empir[e] and staying the Turkes invasion) and the particular goodwill [which stood] ever betwixte Her Majestie and him, coolde not but greatly g[rieve] her.

Secondly Her Majesties good hope of him, that he woolde seconde his fath[er] in his vertues and the manner of his governemente.

And [thirdly] her Majesties cownsaile unto him to avoide the turbulente cowncells, of [men] guyded withe pryvate passions whereof the issue is uncertaine [the bene]fittes none and the harmes manifeste.

Besides these as ocasion shoolde serve I shoolde give him to undres[tande how] nobly Her Majestie had proceeded in the Low Contrey matters and upp[on what] good growndes. The .3. firste I did declare together unto him [and also] other reasons as bothe the instructions did more largely specify, and [the occasion] it selfe did ministre.

Next, the account of the Emperor's reply. The first decision Sidney had to make was how to reply fully to some of Rudolph's rather vague remarks.

He awnswered me in Latin withe very few wordes, to the first, [that he did] persuade him selfe so of her Majestie as it pleased her to signify unt[o him], for which signification he gave her Serenitie (for that was the tearme he [used,)] very greate thankes. And therewithall added a certaine speeche o[f thanks for] the praises her Majestie gave his father he saide he woolde not stande [silent] becawse he mighte seeme to deryve parte of the glory to him selfe [to speak] his goodwill towardes her Majestie of which he was lefte very good wi[tness] havinge by many meanes knowne his fathers minde therein.

To the seconde and thirde he awnswered together, that as God had pr[ovided him] of the Empire, so he woolde provyde him withe cownceile how to [govern] it, but that he did in most gratefull manner accepte her Majesti[es advice] and that the rule he woolde follow chiefly, shoolde be his fathers imit[ation.]

[And] after that he fell into dyverse other particuler demandes and speeches [that be] to longe to recyte, but that I uppon ocasion of Don Jhon D'Austri[che thought] twise or thryse to give him to undrestande how her Majestie had pr[ovided of] those thinges, but his allowance thereof was so generall that I coolde [let the] tyme passe no furdre.

On Tuesday, April 9, Sidney had made the other calls required by protocol, and had delivered the letters of condolence from Queen Elizabeth to the two widowed queens of the Imperial Court.

The nexte day I delivered her Majesties lettres to the Empresse, withe the singular signification of her Majesties greate good will unto her, and her Majesties wisshinge of her to advise her son to a wyse and peaceable governemente. Of the Emperour deceassed I used but few wordes, becawse in trothe I saw it bredd some troble unto her, to heere him mentioned in that kinde. She awnswered me withe many cowrteowse speeches, and greate acknowledginge of her owne beholdingenes to her Majestie. And for her son she saide she hoped he woolde do well, but that for her owne parte she saide she had given her selfe frome the worlde and woolde not greatly sturr frome thence forwarde in it. Then did I deliver the queene of Frawnces letter, she standinge by the Empresse, usinge suche speeches as I thought were fitt for her double sorrow, and her Majesties good will unto her, confirmed by her wyse and noble governinge of her selfe in the tyme of her beinge in Frawnce. Her awnswere was full of humblenes but she spake so low that I coolde not undrestande many of her wordes. Frome them I wente to the yonge princes, and paste of eache syde certaine complementes, which I will leave becawse I feare me I have allreddy bene over longe therein.

These official audiences out of the way, Sidney had devoted the remaining days in Prague to gathering information which would aid Walsingham and other members of the Council in future decisions concerning central Europe.

The reste of the daies that I lay there I enfourmed my selfe as well as I coold of suche particularities as I receaved in my enstructions, as of the 1. Emperours disposicion and his brethren. 2. By whose Advise he is directed. 3. When it is lykely he shall marry. 4. What princes in Jermany are moste affected to him. 5. In what state he is lefte for revenews. 6. What good agreement there is betwixte him and his brethren. 7. And what partage they have. In these thinges I shall at my returne more largely be hable and with more leysure to declare it now only thus muche I will troble yow withe.

In his analysis of Rudolph's character and personality Sidney relied on his own observation during the formal audience, supplemented by the evaluations of friends in the Emperor's court. Rudolph was clearly trying to carry out the role of Emperor as he had been trained to do.

1.   That the Emperour is holy by his inclination givne to the warres, few of wordes, sullein of disposition, very secrete and resolute, nothinge the manner his father had in winninge men in his behavior, but yet consta[nt] in keepinge them. And suche a one as thoughe he promise not muche owtwardly, hathe as the Latines say *Aliquid in Recessu.*

Sidney's reading of Rudolph is fair enough for the time when he talked with him. Later, however, Rudolph turned from his interest in wars and in the other "business of being an Emperor" and gave himself more and more to moody contemplation and inaction. A modern scholar has described this development:

He was a gentle character, benevolent, and a friend of the arts and sciences. But it was especially the secret arts of astrology and alchemy that ensnared his spirit, and in the study of the constellations and the search for the Philosopher's Stone he forgot realm and government. Added to this was a penchant for solitary brooding and a languid distaste for affairs which accorded perfectly with his strange pastimes and studies, but very ill with his princely position. And so Rudolph soon became the plaything of the forces surrounding him.[8]

Sidney's account of the Emperor's five brothers is equally succinct. The fact that their mother was a Bourbon, the sister of Philip II of Spain, strongly influenced their characters and careers.

8. J. F. A. Gillet, *Crato von Crafftheim und seine Freunde* (Frankfurt, 1860), 2:208.

His Brother Earnest, muche lyke him in disposition, but that he is more franke and forwarde, which perchawnce the necessity of his fortune dryves him to. Bothe extreemely Spaniolated. Matthias and Maximilian lykew[ise] broughte upp togeather, but in Jermany, and in their behaviour fram[ed] of them selves to the lykinge of this contrey people, especially Maximilian who seemes in deede to promise some greate worthines, but their yowthe, and education as yet under governement makes the judge[ment[the harder.

Albertus and Wenceslaus are in Spaine. Albertus of late made Car[dinal] of the beste witt of them all, and uppon him it is thoughte t[he See] of Toledo shall be bestowed. Wenceslaus is of very quick spr[ite, but] as yet very yonge, and made putt on a Spanishe gravity. [They were brought] upp to be servantes to the pope, and that is lyke to be their h[ighest] Ambition.

In a similar vein, the answer Sidney found for his second question, "By whose advice is Rudolph directed?" stresses the dominance of Spanish and papal interests. Adam, Baron von Dietrichstein, at one time Maximilian's ambassador to the court of Spain and later majordomo of his household, became a collaborator of the Jesuits and the scourge of the Protestants who had been welcomed by Maximilian in earlier, enlightened days.

2.   The Emperour is most governed by one Die[trichstein the] greate Master of his howse, beares the redd crosse of Spaine and [is] a professed servante to that crowne and inquisitors governemente.

The nuntio of the Pope that is now there is lykewise great [influence] and followed by him, so that what cownceills suche authors give m[ay be] easily imagined, thoughe the effectes be longe in bringing forthe [the consequences.]

Spanish influence also hung over the marriage plans of the Emperor. These promised a genetic pattern familiar to fanciers of pedigreed animals, but confined chiefly among humans to members of royal houses and inhabitants of isolated valleys.

3.   He dothe kepe him unmaried till the Daughter of Spaine be [of age. Since she] is now eleaven yeere olde, there was lyke to have growne some [delay] becawse the kinge of Spaine seemed rather to have lyked of the k[inge of] Portugall, but it is now hoped that that kinge will have the Da[ughter of] Frawnce, and so the Emperour to

strengthen the holinesse of [his kinship] muche the more, will become bothe son, brother, nephew, and [cousin of] the kinge of Spaine.

Sidney found the answer to his fourth question too full and too complicated for this written report.

4. How the princes of Jermany are affect[ed to] him, and what authority the howse of Austriche dothe daily g[ive unto] them by their carelesnes, and whylst as yow wrate they are [now] in securitie, I will if it please yow referr till my returne. [For] thereuppon hanges dyverse thinges, and I have allreddy bene [over-long.]

The economy of the Holy Roman Empire Sidney also found too involved to describe in the brief space available.

5. His revenews are greate, but his enemy the Turke so muche ab[ove him in] greatnes, that he can not turne muche of them to other use [elsewhere.] The Empire of late at the Dyet of Ratisbone did grawnte his fa[ther a loan] of six million of florins to be paide in six yeere. He hat[h had] nothinge of [it] as yet, but makes perfitt accompte not only to [obtain] it but to continew it, which if it be so will be a matter of greate [wonder] consideringe he is bounde to no other thinge for it but the defenc[e of his] owne patrimony. I will bringe yow a particular of his revenews [and lar]gesse in a thinge yeerly allmoste changinge may suffer.

In Sidney's answer to "What good agreement is between Rudolph and his brothers?" so many gaps occur in the manuscript that it cannot be reconstructed to satisfy both syntax and sense.

6. The brethren do agree very well and so certainly are lyke to doe [for the] suttlety of the worlde is conspyred to unite them, and more a greate [fear of] that sorte, to some terrible ende. This is certaine that none is loked [for from her] Majestie, and the poore reliques of Frawnce and Flawndres, as the [suppliants] to her state, for as for Jermany I assure yow they make accown[t consideringe] them in effecte allreddy at leaste hurtlesse enemies.

Even more difficulty occurs in his comments on the division of property and position among the brothers, for about two dozen words are missing entirely.

7.   Their pa[rtage is not] as yet made, Austriche is the only thinge
that can be divyded. I am of [the opinion that they] will be contented
withe Pensions. Earnestus especially having as h[is share] absolute
governemente of Hungary and Austriche the Emperour will keepe
hi[s control of the Empire and Bohemia, and of his other territories]
in [the states of Germany.]

Well aware of the length to which his letter had grown, Sidney now
briefly summarized the ceremony which marked his departure from
Prague and his reception by the Elector Ludwig back in Heidelberg.[9]

I am ashamed I have trobled yow so long. But I will leave the
Emperours acceptacion of the Low Contrey matters till I may my
selfe it unto yow, and so his speeches at my farewell which I am
afraide I was in the beginninge of these scribbles to longe in. Hether
I came the laste of Aprill, and had Audience the nexte day. I had
frome her Majestie to condole with him and to perswade him to
unitie withe his brother, he made his vizchancelour to awnswere
me, whiche he did in a very longe speeche, withe thanke[s] to her
Majestie and prayses of the worthy prince that is dead, the pointe of
concorde with his brother he thanked her Majestie for remembringe,
and fell into a common place of the necessitie of brothers love, but
descended nothinge into his owne particularitie or what he thoughte
of him.

Sidney had then tackled Ludwig on the main purpose of his mission, to
investigate the possibilities of uniting the German princes in a Protestant
League. He was hampered by the fact that the Elector had to be addressed
in German; this involved using Ludwig's Vice-Chancellor as interpreter,
a man Sidney felt would give his words a prejudiced twist. By stringing
out the interview Sidney managed to outlast the Vice-Chancellor and to
repeat his plea that Ludwig support such a League.

One thinge I was bolde to adde in my speeche, to desyre him in
her Majesties name to have mercyfull consideration of the churche
of the religion, so notably established by his father as in all Jermany

9. Count Ludwig's reply, thanking Elizabeth for the letter Sidney had delivered to him,
is dated May 1 (*CSPF*2, no. 1420). It was written "In Castro Novo," which the clerk who
calendared this letter identified as Neustadt. Because Sidney reports that Ludwig had
"gone to the bathes for the last remedy of his infirmity," Ludwig's letter undoubtedly was
written at Baden, while he was staying in the New Castle there.

there is not suche a nomber of excellente learned men, and truly woolde rue any man to see the desolation of them. I laied before him as well as I coolde the dangers of the mightiest princes of Christendome by entrying into lyke vyolente changes, the wronge he shoolde doe his worthy father utterly to abolishe that he had instituted and so as it were condemne him, besydes the example he shoolde give his posterity to handle him the lyke.

This I emboldened my selfe to doe seinge as me thoughte greate cawse for it either to move him at least to have some regarde for her Majesties sake, or if that followed not, yet to leave that publicke testimony with the churche of Jermany that her Majestie was carefull of them, besydes that I learned Prince Casimir had used her Majesties authoritie in perswadinge his brother from it. This I hope will be takne for sufficiente cawse therein, of my boldenes.

My awnswere was at firste none, so longe as Mr vizchanceilour stode by: after I had an other interpretour he made me this awnswere that for her Majesties sake he woolde doe muche, he mislyked not of the men, but must be constrained to doe as the other princes of the Empyre. In the mea[n] time he is gone to the bathes for the laste remedy of his infirmity.

Sidney felt a wave of discouragement after the interview, as well he might. His one resource was to discuss the matter with Count Casimir and William, Landgrave of Hesse. On this note he ended his fat letter.

How his brother and he stande I will lykewyse referr till my returne and that I have spokne withe Prince Casimir. Frome who[m] so to ende this longe troblinge of yow, I meane to goe with her Majesties lett[er] to the Langrave who is the only prince Casimir makes accownte of. What I shall fynde amonge these princes truly I know not till I have spokne with Prince Casimir. I go to morrow to Caisarlautar, but I see their proceedinges suche that my ho[pe] dothe every day grow lesse and lesse. I beseeche yow pardon me for my longe troblinge of yow. I most humbly recommende my selfe unto yow, and leave yow to the Eternalls most happy protection. Frome Heidelberg, this 3^d of May. 1577.

Yowrs humbly at commawndem[ent]

Philipp Sidney

The day before he wrote this report, Sidney was joined in Heidelberg by

Languet who doubtless read it over and listened eagerly while Sidney related the steps taken so far towards a Protestant League, one of Languet's fondest hopes.

On the first of the month Sidney had told the envoys of the Landgrave of Hesse of his plans to visit him. He intended to deliver a letter from Queen Elizabeth and to sound him out on the project for a Protestant League. This expedition would have been a double pleasure, because Languet would have been able to accompany him. But their preparations were suddenly interrupted. A letter arrived from England with instructions for Sidney to return promptly and report to the Queen and her advisers on the situation. Evidence of this occurs in the letter Sidney wrote to the Landgrave on May 13.

> Most Illustrious Prince,
>
> Twelve days ago I met your Highness's envoys at Heidelberg and told them that my most gracious mistress her Majesty the Queen of England had ordered me to discuss certain matters with your Highness. This was all the more pleasant for me since it afforded me an opportunity to meet and become acquainted with your Highness, of whose virtue and wisdom I had heard much from others. But as I was girding myself for that journey I received a letter from her Majesty the Queen, ordering me to hasten my return to England. Since I have been thus forced to change my previous plan, I now send your Highness her Majesty's letter via this noble gentleman Master Richard Allen, one of her Majesty's Gentlemen of the Bedchamber.

With this explanation out of the way Sidney then launched into the formal compliments preliminary to stating the immediate purpose of his mission.

> These were the matters which I was ordered to discuss with your Highness:
>
> Her Majesty the Queen is most desirous to establish with your Highness, or rather (since it is already established) to maintain, that close friendship with which her father King Henry, of most happy memory, and indeed she herself, formed such a strong bond between themselves and that most noble Prince, your Highness's father. She hopes to maintain a tradition of mutual service, and to discuss such things as concern the welfare of a Christian nation.

Now Sidney presents the case for a Protestant League. One of his most effective points is the distinction between accepting a sovereignty which permits freedom of religion and resisting the tyranny of religious persecution, a distinction which Queen Elizabeth consistently made concerning both France and Spain in the Netherlands.

> One of these matters is how you may together repulse the designs of the Bishop of Rome who seeks with all his might to destroy those who have cast off the yoke he had laid upon the necks of our forefathers, and who now maintain themselves in such liberty as enables them rightly and devoutly to worship God and to work out their own salvation. To achieve these ends, however, the Pope is attempting to join such Kings and Princes as are still bound in his tyranny in alliances that are to destroy us in concert. This, in their view, will be easy unless we also join together, to repel the harm they will try to inflict on us.
>
> Such an effort on our part would be irreproachable, since it is noble and virtuous to defend not only oneself but also those who cannot shield themselves from unjust force. That the Pope's league is aimed at our destruction, however, is made plain by the wars that have raged so long in France and the Netherlands. For in those lands there is no one who would not be the most obedient of his Prince's subjects, if he were allowed to worship God in the true religion; but the Pope has so spellbound those monarchs that for many years they have practised every kind of cruelty upon their subjects in order to settle his tyranny more firmly on themselves and their peoples.

Sidney then brings the situation home to Germany:

> Furthermore, in recent years he has greatly harmed Germany by the fact that several states which had formerly freed themselves and professed the true religion have been brought back under his sway. How arrogant this has made his supporters I have heard at length, and indeed last summer's Regensburg Diet plainly showed it.
>
> But these matters need no rehearsing, and I shall leave them: they are sufficiently known to your Highness, and, moreover, I have recently discussed them at length with that most noble Prince, my lord John Casimir Palatine of the Rhine. I doubt not that he has already written extensively to your Highness of them, or will shortly do so. I merely beg your Highness that these things, which I have

said in good part, will be by you similarly pondered and that you will deign to send Her Gracious Majesty such reply as may please her and show her that your Highness is minded steadfastly to tread in the footsteps of your most noble father.

For myself, I wish your Highness and all your most noble family every happiness and beg your Highness to remember that I shall ever be greatly desirous of serving you whenever an opportunity offers. From Frankfurt-am-Main, May 13. 1577.

Your most illustrious Highness's greatly devoted,

Philip Sidney[10]

That Sidney was justified in citing the attitude of Count Casimir is confirmed in a letter Casimir sent to the Privy Council on May 8, a few days before Sidney wrote to the Landgrave.[11] The Count promised to join the Protestant League and to try to induce the Landgrave and other relations to join. He backed this up by stating his willingness to contribute one hundred thousand dollars in currency to advance the common cause, and he asked, in turn, how far Queen Elizabeth was prepared to support the League. Further, Casimir reported that he had discussed at length with Sidney a general agreement which all reformed churches could be asked to sign. He wrote also that he planned to communicate with these churches in the Netherlands, in Switzerland, in France, and even in Poland. Hence Casimir asked the Queen to endorse the good work with her authority. In support of Casimir the Landgrave answered Sidney's letter with one to Elizabeth dated May 20, professing his own zeal in the cause.[12]

In the meantime, Sidney and his attendants left Frankfurt and headed north for the Channel, presumably for Ostend. Languet accompanied Sidney as far as Cologne. In the course of their journey, Languet had carried out a request of some friends. "At the mouth of the Main," that is, at Mainz, he had told Sidney that these friends were prepared to arrange a marriage for him with a German princess. Probably she was Ursula, sister of Count Casimir, an identification first proposed by Lord Hailes in

10. Feuillerat, 3 : 114–15, the Latin text. The Landgrave replied on May 20; he regretted that his court would not see Sidney's intelligence and courtliness in action, since they had so often heard it commended, and pleaded his devotion to "the common cause" of Protestant unity (Staatsarchiv, Marburg). It reached Sidney after his return to England, so his acknowledgement from Elizabeth's court was dated June 30 (ibid.).

11. *CSPF2*, no. 1425.

12. *CSPF2*, no. 1437.

1776. This identification fits all the ascertainable facts, especially Languet's part in the proposal, for he served as both intermediary and advocate. We know that the princess was willing, and so rejected the suit of the Elector of Brandenburg while awaiting a definite answer from Sidney. One "Monsieur Ley," who is unidentified, knew of the secret discussions. Sidney seems to have fancied the plan but realized that he was "the son of a family," and so could not make the decision alone. Equally important, Queen Elizabeth looked with disfavour on marriages between her subjects and noble families on the Continent. As time dragged on, Languet's letters alluded again and again to the proposal which did not expire until the end of the year.[13]

Sidney's reunion with Languet had been shorter than anticipated but was sweet while it lasted, even though Languet regretted a liberty taken in jesting with Pietro Bizari who then happened to be in Cologne. The pleasures Languet enjoyed in Sidney's company are distilled in his comment, "I felt an incredible satisfaction from being together for so many days, but have had the experience of a man who drinks avidly and deeply of cold water when he is heated, and by doing so, brings on a fever."[14] Languet was both proud and gratified at the maturity, judgement, and air of command displayed by his former pupil. This was exactly what he had expected ever since becoming acquainted with Sidney's qualities of mind and character. Before they parted at Cologne Sidney exacted a promise from Languet that he would visit him in England.[15]

When Sidney and "the other noble and most courteous gentlemen who were the faithful and agreeable companions of your journey," as Languet described them,[16] had almost reached Ostend, a message from Queen Elizabeth altered their plans. She now advised Sidney to turn back and visit William of Orange. The nominal purpose was for Philip to represent his uncle, the Earl of Leicester, as godfather at the christening of the Prince's second daughter who was to be named Elizabeth after England's Queen. Sidney retraced his route from Bruges to Ghent and thence to Antwerp. Leaving there on May 27 he went on to Breda and Geertruidenberg where William and his Princess were in residence.[17]

13. See Languet's letters of June 14, July 15, Sept. 23, Oct. 9, and Nov. 28 (also, Sidney to Languet, Oct. 9), all in 1577.
14. *Langueti Epistolae*, p. 269.
15. Feuillerat, 3 :116.
16. In his letter of June 14, 1577.
17. *CSPF2*, no. 1440.

No change of plans could have made Sidney happier. He had originally intended to return to England through Zeeland in order to meet William and to represent Leicester at the christening. But Elizabeth's first letter ordering his return had altered this plan. Evidently Leicester had since then convinced her Majesty that a visit to the Prince by Sidney would be desirable, though the counterorder did not reach Sidney's hands until the eve of embarkation.[18] Languet had noted that after his recall Sidney was tempted to make a detour through the Netherlands on his return journey, but Languet had warned Philip against offending the Queen. He saw that Sidney was "burning to be presented to Orange, and form an acquaintance with him."[19]

William the Silent well deserved Sidney's admiration. His soubriquet derived from the self-discipline and experience he had gained in the rough school of politics where he had learned to listen much and speak little. William knew how and when to be silent, for he remembered the dictum that a word uttered is a thought surrendered. Although he was high-principled and had firm objectives, qualities that ordinary citizens recognized and valued, he had early learned the necessity in politics to tack according to the wind. Hence his opponents accused him of zigging and zagging, of being a weathercock. He was frequently misunderstood through envy, malice, or myopia. Despite his detractors, William's integrity and political skill carried him past shoals and through cross-currents that would have wrecked the career of a lesser man. His leadership in the Low Countries had now become so preeminent that diplomats described the Prince as "the only man Don John fears."[20]

Sidney had every reason to be happy at this sudden opportunity to meet William, who was now at the height of his career. All factions in the seventeen provinces—town officials, churchmen, and the leaders of the usually jealous noble families—realized the need for unity against the mutinous and uncontrolled Spanish soldiers, now subject only to the weak authority of Don John. These leaders recognized that the only man who could bring about effective unity was William. He was the one nobleman with a large private fortune (the wealthiest in the Netherlands) who had shown the necessary moral courage and ability to meet succes-

18. See Leicester's letter to the Prince of Orange dated from Greenwich, May 8, 1577: in Lettenhove, 9:294.

19. Languet's letter of June 14, 1577, in Pears, p. 107.

20. *CSPF2*, no. 1370. For an authoritative account of Orange see H. L. T. de Beaufort, *Willem de Zwyger* (Rotterdam, 1950).

sive challenges. With these qualities he combined good judgement, and thus did not attempt to exceed his limited powers while maintaining his duties and responsibilities. Thomas Wilson summarized William's sterling qualities in a report from Brussels to Leicester: "And no dowbt the Prynce is a rare man, of greate authoritie, universallie beloved, verie wyse, resolute in al thynges and voyde of covetousenes, and that which worthie of especial prayse in hym, he is not dismayed with any losse or adversitie, his state beeinge better now than ever it was."[21]

Sidney probably remained with the Prince and his wife, Charlotte de Bourbon, from May 28 until May 30. In Geertruidenberg he stayed with Philip Marnix, Lord of St. Aldegonde; they had known each other during the winter of 1575–76 when Marnix led the fruitless Netherlands mission to London in the attempt to gain Elizabeth's active help in driving out the Spaniards. Elizabeth had been offered sovereignty over some of the provinces, but she had rejected the proposal because she feared sparking a full-scale war with Spain. Instead she preferred to follow her theoretical policy of maintaining the balance of power. Theoretical rather than real, because Elizabeth rationalized instead of thinking and followed her predilections for procrastination and prevarication. Abetted by the shilly-shallying of her treasurer Burghley, she ignored the hard-minded recommendations of her foreign-affairs expert, Walsingham. Recent historical opinion has emphasized the weakness of her handling of this area in England's affairs, her "strange and tortuous dealings with the Low Countries" which caused some of her officials to wonder "whether their royal mistress was entirely sane."[22] As for Elizabeth's theory of the balance of power, her "fear of France, like her reverence for Spain, was rooted more in superstition than in reason."[23]

Faithful to method and to his responsibilities as the Queen's ambassador, Sidney devoted most of a day after his visit with William to making a detailed summary of their conversations. He covered both the specific points and conditions of proposed agreements and also his own observations on the Prince's sources of strength in the Lowlands. The report is titled "Certain notes concerning the present state of the Prince of Orange, and the

21. Dated Dec. 3, 1576, in Lettenhove, 9:68.
22. Wilson, p. 70.
23. Ibid., p. 127. The same critic adds "Conservatism, parsimony, snobbery, distrust: these explain her refusal to commit herself down to 1585 . . . on each occasion when the moment of decision arrived, she suffered one of her characteristic last-minute black-outs" (pp. 128–29).

provinces of Holland and Zeeland, as they were in the month of May
1577."[24] All available evidence points to Sidney's authorship of this document, though it has never been included, or even mentioned, in a book
on Sidney. However, the text was printed in Brussels in 1890 by Baron
Kervyn de Lettenhove in volume 9 (pp. 310–14) of his monumental *Relations politiques des Pays-Bas et de L'Angleterre, sous le règne de Philippe II.*
In order to facilitate comment on it here, each section of "Certain Notes"
is given seriatim.

The opening section concerns the territories and power base on which
Prince William could depend in his relations with the Spaniards, with
England, and with the various provinces into which the Netherlands
were then fragmented. These provinces were independent and jealous of
each other, united in little but their opposition to foreign rule and their
belief in independence. They differed even in religion. Approximately
half of the citizens were Roman Catholic; the other half was divided
among reformed sects. William's greatest accomplishment was his skilful
leadership in bringing the provinces together in several common causes.
As Sidney's report shows, William was aware that commerce was the
lifeblood of the citizens of the Netherlands. The provinces guarded it
enviously, often seeming to put profit above abstract patriotism.

*Certain notes concerning the present state of the Prince of Orange, and
the provinces of Holland and Zeeland, as they were in the month of
May 1577.*

The Prince of Orange hath at this present all Holland and Zeeland
with the Province of Utrecht under his government; for, as concerning Amsterdam, the case is altered, the Prince being able to
annoy and pleasure them, whereas they of the town are in that case
that they can neither profit the Prince and much less hinder or en-
damage him. In such sort that the Prince is better able than ever he
was to withstand all force which may be prepared against him, and
hath greater means than he had to annoy such as shall be his enemies.

Besides the Province of Utrecht, which is returned to the Prince's
government, Gelders, Friesland, and Groningerland are wholly bent
to embrace the Hollanders' and Zeelanders' side, and to follow the
Prince of Orange his directions if war be renewed against him; for

24. For a detailed examination of the case for Sidney's authorship and the extant texts
see appendix 5.

that they shall lose all traffic (unless they join themselves with the Prince), by which means they especially maintain themselves. Wherefore the Prince of Orange assureth himself that the rest of the Estates of the Low Countries will not be very hasty in renewing war against him, especially now that the Spaniards be departed out of the country.

The chief opponent to Prince William's plans was Don John, thus it was necessary to assess both his knowledge of William's position and the nature of their relationship. Recently Don John had sent Dr. Elbertus Leoninus of Louvain to William for an exploratory session, and Leoninus had revealed what great and even desperate gambles Don John was prepared to take.

Don Juan is not ignorant of the Prince's strength; he knoweth that he fortifieth daily and easily forseeth that the Provinces of Gelders, Utrecht, Friesland, and Groningerland will take part with him in case war be renewed: as Doctor Leoninus, being sent in April last unto the Prince from Don Juan, when the Prince asked of him what might be the cause that Don Juan made so great promises unto him, confessed that he knew that four of five Provinces would take his part more than during the last war was done. Therefore Don Juan useth all gentle and amiable ways to assure him of his goodwill; by which means he trusteth either to win the Prince or to deceive and circumvent him. He willeth the Prince to set down in writing his demands and he will accord them; yea, he caused Leoninus to tell him that, in case the King of Spain would not maintain the Pacification made with him, he would fight against the King for him. He thinketh that the Prince is of himself not so hard to be won and putteth all the fault in the Councillors; wherein he is deceived.

The Prince nourisheth Don Juan his humour, and maketh him believe that he shall find him tractable, and travaileth to persuade them which come from Don Juan that there shall be no fault in him. When Leoninus was last with him and declared unto him what great goodwill Don Juan bore towards him, he answered that Don Juan either meant sincerely or used dissimulation. If he dealt covertly with him, the effect would declare it and fall ⌐out⌐[25] unto his dishonour. If he meant sincerely, then were he like to offend the King. He said

25. Texts X and Y.

he knew not his meaning, but peradventure he went about, knowing the King to be mortal, to establish his estate in the Low Countries, and to make him master of them. If he so were bent, he willed Leoninus to declare unto him that he would further his endeavours. And here he desired to know her Majesty's opinion: what her Majesty would judge of him if he went about to reduce the Low Countries into the form of a kingdom and made Don Juan the first King thereof. He added ⌐that⌐26 if her Majesty did like well of it he knew the means how to compass it, and thought to bind the ⌐new⌐27 King unto such conditions that he would think her Majesty should take her profit of it, for that by this means the King of Spain his authority should be diminished and power separated, which being united unto the Low Countries is to be feared.

In the meanwhile, to satisfy Don Juan, who requireth him to declare what he would demand for his assurance, he answereth that his particular estate is so joined with the welfare of the commonwealth that, if the commonwealth be well assured, he shall be well assured. Wherefore, to the intent he may understand what he requireth, he proposed these demands to Doctor Leoninus ⌐and willed him to declare them unto Don Juan:⌐28

Prince William's demands then follow. William wished to build the strength of the Estates General, repatriate the German mercenaries, eliminate potential strongholds for rebels, and repossess some of his own territories and guard forces. These proposals had been made to Don John just a fortnight before.

> First, he requireth that the General Estates of the Low Countries, according unto their privileges, may not be subject unto the Council of Estate, but rather that it may be lawful for the General Estates to deprive such of the Council of Estate and to put in other, as often as the General Estates shall think good; and that Don Juan would do nothing without their advice; so that he desireth the authority of the General Estates to be maintained for the government jointly with Don Juan, which form of government is according unto the privileges of the countries.

26. Text X.
27. Texts X and Y.
28. Texts X and Y.

Secondly, he requireth that all the Almans soldiers be licenced and sent away, which in great number are as yet in Antwerp, Barrow, Bolduc, Breda, Grave, and Luxembourg.

Thirdly, that the citadels and castles, which stand not upon the frontiers of strange countries, be razed, as Utrecht, Antwerp, Vallenciennes, Ghent, etc.

Fourthly, he requireth that the General Estates may be assembled together in such manner as was before Charles the Fifth his time, and that they may call themselves together as often as they shall think good.

Fifthly, he requireth ⌐that¬[29] according unto the Pacification, he be restored unto all his dignities and lands, as well in Burgundy as in other places; and, to the intent he may perceive in effect Don Juan his goodwill towards him, to procure that his son, the Count of Buren [held hostage in Spain], be restored unto him ⌐shortly.¬[30]

Sixthly, for that he hath understood that Berlaymont and D'Asson-[le]ville are returned unto the Council of Estate, which is against the Pacification, he requireth that they may be excluded from thence until the General Estates be assembled, and then rather to be deprived as evil councillors then to be admitted again.

⌐And because that in the Pacification many things are reserved unto the assembly of General Estates, the Prince, trusting that by them many things may be redressed, especially being called together with due liberty, he in any case travaileth that they may be assembled; and as for the matter of Religion which many think would be by the General Estates condemned, the Prince sayeth that the rest of the Provinces cannot condemn one other province if the said one province hold out with one consent; the example thereof was lately seen in the month of January at Brussels when the rest of the Estates had consented to new impositions for the maintenance of war against the Spaniards: they of Artois refused to do it, neither could the rest of the Provinces by right condemn them of Artois. Which yet at the last by intercession were persuaded to do as the other.¬[31]

Last of all, he desireth Don Juan and the rest of the Estates to give and entertain him his old company of the hundred men of arms,

29. Text Y.
30. Texts X and Y.
31. Text X.

even as he had before the troubles, and, for so much as he hath made great debts for the recoverment of the welfare of the country, in so much that he oweth eighteen hundred thousand florins, he desireth the General Estates to discharge him of the said debt, as made for the commonwealth.

Unto these things Don Juan and the Estates have not as yet answered, but the Duke of Arskott was appointed as the 16 of May[32] to go from Don Juan with Doctor Leoninus unto the Prince, as the Estates sent from them the Count of Lalaing and certain others, the 10th[33] of this present, to go towards the Prince for to satisfy him in these points.

While negotiations were being carried on, Prince William continued to strengthen his outposts. Companies of troops were being raised by the Estates. Evidence about Don John constantly reveals his habit of double-talk.

In the meanwhile the Prince fortifieth in Brabant at Sevenberch for to assure his island of Chlondron, *alias* Rügen, as also at Workum over against Gorinchem. *Item* he maketh battering pieces in every town, buyeth powder and munition with all diligence, calleth the Estates of Holland, Zeeland, and Utrecht together, to provide with them if war should be renewed against them.

The Estates ⌜of Holland and Zeeland⌝[34] have already promised him to entertain forty-five ensigns in North Holland and South Holland, and to stand unto the defence of ⌜the⌝[35] religion which they presently profess. Yea, Don Juan (as the Prince is assured) will permit Holland and Zeeland the use of the reformed religion, so that in other things they show him all obedience. *In summa* he understandeth very well all the subtleties of Don Juan and provideth duly for them. The wiser sort of men well perceive, by the very effect, that Don Juan lacketh but opportunities to break the Pacification, for as yet he hath not restored unto the Prince Breda and his lands in Burgundy, besides he hath travailled as much as he could to take the government of Utrecht from him, ⌜which things are directly against the Pacifi-

32. 18 in texts X and Y.
33. 16th in texts X and Y.
34. Text X.
35. Text Y.

William of Orange

cation;[136] and whereas he wrote him a fair letter, the 25 of April, containing great promises and goodwill towards the Prince, the same day he called him rebel twenty times in one hour unto Mr. Doctor Wilson, her Majesty's ambassador.

Now Sidney comes to the major issue facing Elizabeth and her Council, Prince William's proposal that the Queen and he sign a secret treaty of mutual benefit, in which he hoped other provinces would later join.

Seeing therefore the Prince is thus provided with both ⌐hability of forces,[137] strong places, and good counsel, he persuadeth himself that the Estates will not easily enter into war again against him. Yet nevertheless, for that he assureth himself that the King of Spain will never cease until he have revenged himself upon the Prince, the Hollanders, and Zeelanders; and because he well knoweth that the King will never permit the reformed religion long in the said countries, to assure both his estate and the safety of the religion he must provide for war; for that the [Prince] knoweth th[ey will] return unto it. And therefore providing against the worse in best manner, he thinketh it necessary both for Holland and Zeeland and himself, as also very expedient and good for the realm of England, that England, Holland, Zeeland, and such other Provinces as shall follow the Prince's side, may be linked together in greater amity for their mutual defence and ⌐the[138] assurance of the religion; and to the intent this amity may be kept secret and the be[   ] made, the Prince of Orange told me her Majesty might first [   ] hit with him; a few of the Hollanders, as Paul Buys, and D[   ] might be made privy of this amity, which might consist upon [these] or the like conditions.

Next William outlined some of the very tangible advantages which England would gain by the treaty. He urged that the domino theory be kept realistically in mind: once resistance in the Netherlands were crushed by Spain, England would be the next target.

First he said, he would think what service or pleasure he [   ] Hollanders and Zeelanders might show unto her Majesty and her dominations and having thought thereupon he said that whereas her Majesty as also her subjects had always to do upon the seas, where

36. Texts X and Y.
37. Texts X and Y.
38. Texts X and Y.

the winds commanded, the havens of Holland and Zeeland could not but serve very commodiously unto her Majesty; which heretofore, as he was of the King's council, were oftentimes shut against England, and express commandment given that no harness or other arms, as likewise no hops, and other commodities serving the realm of England should be carried out of them for England; which havens now, by this amity, should be as open unto her Majesty and her subjects as her own havens.

Secondly, whereas Holland and Zeeland is very well provided with all sorts of ships and a great number of mariners, her Majesty should lack none of them in case her Majesty should demand either shipping or mariners.

Thirdly, whereas neither the King of Spain, neither yet the French King, is able to make war upon the realm of England if England, Holland, and Zeeland be linked together in amity, her Majesty should be assured that of the goodwill of these provinces, in case any war were made by the aforesaid kings against her Majesty, and by these means her Majesty should not only save many men's lives, but also notable sums of money; for neither the French, neither the Spaniards, should as much have, as masts, cables, pitch and other things, necessary for the making of ships. If there be any other things her Majesty would demand of the Hollanders and Zeelanders, if he might understand it, he would them, he said, unto her Majesty's request.

In return for these concessions and privileges Prince William asked comparatively little. His main request was that Elizabeth would lend his government money in case of a long and devastating war, a matter of contingency only.

On the other part, thinking what he would require of the Queen's most excellent Majesty, he said, he would require in this amity to be made, first that her Majesty would not permit the Spaniards to enter into her havens with any Armada or navy which might come out of Spain or Portugal against Holland or Zeeland; which thing, as he demanded for his own commodity, so thought he, it would be good for England; in no case to hurt the Spaniards so much, as to give them leave to come unto her Majesty's havens with any demand. He affirmed that he knew both the Spaniard and their counsels, and how they were affectionated towards England, as well as any stranger might know.

Secondly that her Majesty would maintain the traffic according unto the intercourses made with the House of Burgundy, in such manner that the Hollanders, Zeelanders, and other Provinces, which were to take part with them, might traffic with England as they do presently, and that her Majesty would forbid her subjects to traffic with their enemies; which would not hinder the vent of England's commodities, for that Flanders itself would join with the Prince, in case war were renewed.

Thirdly that it might please her Majesty, in case the war should be extreme and dure so long as last it did, (which [thing] he thinketh cannot happen) that [   ] as to lend Holland and Zeeland fifty thousand pound yearly; the Estates of both countries, and their Provinces which would follow them [   ] providing assurances for the repayment to be made [   ] unto her Majesty.

These things, the Prince affirmed, he proposed as well for the welfare of England as of Holland and Zeeland; for that as [this] amity will confirm the minds of the Hollanders and Zeelanders to be constant in maintaining the reformed religion and their privileges, so will it assure England that neither the King of Spain neither the French King shall attempt any thing against the realm to any effect.

To show his goodwill William now reconfirmed that Philip of Spain had definite plans for "sharp war" against England.

And because the Prince hath of long time been a counsellor unto the King of Spain and the Low Countries, and hath good occasion to be well acquainted with the Spaniards' [   ] designs, he beseecheth her Majesty to assure her estate and welfare against the Spaniards; he said, for that his particular state tendeth to some repose, because of the Pacification, he would now the bolder declare that which before he kept unto himself, for that he knew if during war he had made mention of the Spaniards' counsels against her Majesty, it would have been thought he did it for to serve his purpose in animating the Queen against the King of Spain his enemy, and not for a zeal he had unto her Majesty or to declare the truth.

He affirmeth that six years past, after the victory of the Spaniards against the Turk, the King was resolved to execute two things, first to make sharp war upon England, and at the same time to become master of the Rhine, by [sur?]prendring the city of Cologne;

which then was easily to be compassed; for ⌜to⌝[39] both these enterprises they lacked neither men, neither yet favour; for that the French King was privy of this counsel against England, and great factions the Spaniards had in England. The best friends the King had wrote unto him of these matters, for that they thought he was not so hot in religion, but would accommodate himself unto their purpose. He said he had hindered both these the King's practices; but he desireth her Majesty and my lords of the Council to be persuaded that, as the Spaniards are slack in resolving, so they are most stubbornly bent to accomplish that which once they have concluded.

He willed me likewise to give her Majesty to understand that the King had renewed of late the league made at Bayonne with the French King.

Finally, Prince William wished the Queen success in her projected league with the German states, even though he considered that as allies the Hanseatic cities would be more effective. In any attempt to deal with these cities, he offered his experience and services.

Furthermore he declared that he had understood her Majesty went about to confederate herself with the German Princes; he said it was wisely done, and especially counselled her Majesty to enter into league with the Hansteads, for that they could serve the Queen's turn better than any Princes of Germany. He added that no Princes did know what the Hansteads could do, and, because he knew how to deal with them, if he knew her Majesty's pleasure, he would employ himself willingly for her Majesty to the making of a farther amity with them. He said Don Juan began to hearken unto such a motion, as for to make a league with them, and that it would be good to prevent him.

On June 2 William wrote directly to Elizabeth in order to confirm by the tone of his letter what Sidney would report directly. He assured her that he was joined by other officials in Holland and Zeeland in his desire to serve her. He had "requested Mr. Sidney, her ambassador with the Emperor, to more particularly declare to her" the details of the proposed agreement.[40]

39. Texts X and Y.
40. *CSPF2*, no. 1450.

This report does not mention a topic which William must have raised privately in his talks with Sidney. To him, whom William saw as the rising star of England and the Protestant cause, he offered in marriage his beloved eldest daughter, "demoiselle Marie" of Nassau, who was then about twenty. According to rumours which ultimately reached Bernardino de Mendoza, the Spanish ambassador in London, Prince William "promises as a dowry to make him lord of Holland and Zealand,"[41] a proposition that certainly would have given Sidney pause, coming so soon after the suggestion of his marriage to a German princess. Because of the advantages it would bring to English trade, an alliance with the house of Nassau would be much more acceptable to Queen Elizabeth than one with a more distant principality in central Europe. Still, such a marriage would carry with it negative factors, such as repercussions in Spain. Indeed, the Sidney family, Leicester, and Warwick might also have disapproved, for Philip remained the heir to all three fortunes, and he was now at the beginning of a highly promising career.

The marriage proposal demonstrates William's high opinion of Sidney's character, conduct, intellect, and future prospects. If William could strengthen the bond between his country and England through this match, he felt he could both help his own nation and advance the Protestant cause. Although the marriage plans fell through, William maintained his warm opinion of the brilliant young Englishman and two years later sent a message to the Queen through Fulke Greville. After describing his involvement with and knowledge of the leaders of Europe since the time of Charles V, William praised Sidney.

> In all which series of time, multitude of things and persons, he protested unto mee and for her service that if he could judge, her Majesty had one of the ripest, and greatest Counsellors of Estate in Sir *Philip Sidney*, that at this day lived in *Europe*: to the triall of which

41. *CSPS2*, no. 488, dated Apr. 12, 1578. William must have been considering this proposal even before Sidney's visit. As early as June 1, 1577, Antonio de Guaras, a Spanish merchant and intelligence agent in London, wrote to Don John: "[Philip Sidney] is busy arranging a secret marriage with the Prince of Orange's daughter by his first wife ... [The Prince] will give him as dowry the government of the provinces of Holland and Zealand" (Lettenhove, 9:316). Mendoza mistakenly reported that a sister, not a daughter, of Prince William was the prospective bride. The possibility of the marriage between Sidney and Maria probably was behind William's letter of June 18, 1577 asking his brother, John of Nassau, to send Maria to him "pour certains affaires que j'ay à communicquer avecq elle." *Archives de la Maison d'Orange-Nassau*, ed. G. Groen van Prinsterer (Leiden, 1839), 6:100.

hee was pleased to leave his own credit engaged, untill her Majesty might please to employ this Gentleman, either amongst her friends or enemies.[42]

A recent biographer has suggested that Sidney's recall was prompted by Queen Elizabeth's fear that "her young diplomat intended to commit England to a policy she and Burghley could not approve of."[43] In consequence Sidney supposedly considered his embassy an "evident failure," as indicated by Languet's remark about Sidney's "low spirits" before they parted at Cologne.[44] Such a reaction could have accompanied the end of his official responsibilities besides being part of the ritual of *amicitia*. Moreover, the evidence against his having considered his mission a failure seems overwhelming. Sidney's long report on his talk with Prince William gives no indication that he felt his wings had been clipped in any way. Indeed, the report offers the prospect of a far-reaching alliance. Only a week before the Queen dispatched her letter of recall, Walsingham had written to Sturm in Strasbourg asking his opinion about the feasibility of a Protestant League.[45] The strongest evidence that Sidney's embassy was considered a success occurs in the State Papers (Foreign). Soon after he returned to England and reported in person to the Queen and the Council, the outline for a proposed Protestant League was drawn up. The document covering the proposed League, dated June 1577, reads in summary as follows:

HEADS of a TREATY between the QUEEN OF ENGLAND
and the PROTESTANT PRINCES OF GERMANY

1. That all such Princes as make profession of the Gospel, as well those of the Augustan confession as others being willing to enter into a league defensive against the Pope and his adherents, shall give order for the suppressing of such as seek by preaching or otherwise to breed any contention upon points of religion until such time as by conference the said matters may in peaceable sort be drawn to some reconciliation.

2. Each prince shall lay in a convenient portion of money in deposits for the sustentation of such forces as shall be employed in the general defence of the common cause of religion.

42. Greville, p. 31.
43. Howell, p. 40.
44. Pears, p. 108.
45. *Zürich Letters*, p. 286.

3. The said money to be delivered into the hands of some sufficient merchants at some reasonable interest.
4. That the interest shall be employed by way of pension to some of the principal ritmasters [commanders of mercenaries] of Germany.
5. That the Princes Associate shall support one another in case of being assailed for the cause of religion.
6. That those Princes who join first the association shall seek by all good means to draw other princes, as also the free towns and cantons of the Swiss into the said association.[46]

Sidney's return had been made with minimum delay. He probably reached England on Saturday, June 8, and promptly went to the court which was then at Greenwich Palace. Within the next two days he appeared before Walsingham and the Queen; presumably Burghley, Leicester, and some other Lords of the Council were present. Two reports sent to Sir Henry Sidney on Monday, June 10, testify to the warm approbation with which he was received and his successes hailed. The first is from the hand of Edward Waterhouse.

> *It may please your Lordship,*
> The things that may minister you the greatest Comfort is, that Mr. *Sidney* is returnid safe into *England*, with great good Acceptacion of his Service at her Majesties Hands; allowed of by all the Lords to have bene handled with great Judgement and Discretion, and hath bene honorid Abrode in all the Princes Courts with much extraordinary Favour. The Emperour gave him a great Chaine, the Princesse of *Orange* another with a fair Jewell. The rest I will leave to Mr. Secretary his Report, and to Mr. *Phillips* owne Letters. God blessid him so, that nether Man, Boy, or Horsse failid him, or was sick in this Journey; only *Folke Grevill* had an Ague in his Returne at *Rochester*.[47]

This enthusiastic account might be discounted on the ground that Waterhouse was closely involved with Sir Henry and was thus prejudiced in the family's behalf. The second report, also written from the court at Greenwich, came from Walsingham. His fondness for both Sir Henry and Philip was cautiously limited by his position as Principal Secretary to her Majesty. His letter exudes admiration for what the

46. *CSPF2*, no. 1509.
47. Collins, 1:193.

young man had achieved and for his presentation of the business when he appeared before Queen Elizabeth and her closest advisers.

> I am to impart vnto you the Returne of the yonge Gentleman, Mr. *Sidney*, your Sonne, whose Message verie sufficientlie performed, and the Relatinge therof, is no lesse gratfullye received, and well liked of her Majestie, then the honorable Opinion he hathe left behinde him, with all the Princes with whome he had to negotiate, hathe left a most sweet Savor and gratfull Remembraunce of his Name in those Parts. The Gentleman hathe given no small Arguments of great Hope, the Fruits wherof I doubt not but your Lordship shall reape, as the Benefitts of the good Parts which ar in him, and wherof he hathe given some Tast in this Voyage, is to redounde to more then your Lordship and him self. There hathe not ben any Gentleman, I am sure these many Yeres, that hathe gon throughe so honorable a Charge with as great Comendacions as he: In Consideracion wherof, I could not but comunicate this Part of my Joy with your Lordship, beinge no lesse a Refreshinge vnto me, in these my troublesome Business, then the Soile is to the chased Stagge. And so wishinge the Increase of his good Parts, to your Lordships Comfort, and the Seruice of her Majestie and his Countrie, I humblie take my Leave.[48]

The Queen and her Council were so impressed with Sidney's report that they immediately decided to send the experienced negotiator, Daniel Rogers, to turn the proposed League into an actuality. Her Majesty wrote letters to the Prince of Orange and to Count Casimir, thanking them for their kindness to Sidney and for their support of the common cause. To Casimir she explained why she was sending Rogers. The State Papers report: "This negotiation might seem to demand a person of more con-sequence than Rogers, but she thinks it better to send him so that the matter may be arranged the more secretly."[49] The promptness with which Elizabeth followed up Sidney's embassy suggests that the reason for his recall was her wish to lose no time in forming the Protestant League.

Sidney's star now stood high in its ascendant. He appeared at court in triumph from an embassy which would have crowned the career of a diplomat twice his age. Besides this, he shone as the model of chivalry,

48. Ibid.
49. *CSPF2*, no. 1486.

the ideal courtier, the exemplar of an educated aristocrat—learned beyond his contemporaries at court, master of exposition and style, the observed of all observers. Young Philip, heir presumptive of the Dudleys, stood waiting to take over their influence, to inherit their fortunes, to culminate and crown their fame. His parents, his powerful uncles, and the other leaders of England (even the Dudleys' enemies) could not fail to wonder what the next step in the career of dazzling young Philip Sidney would be.[50]

50. Sidney's success as a diplomat was promptly hailed by the grandiloquent Pietro Bizari in his next book, *Senatus Populique Genuensis Rerum Domi Forisque Gestarum Historiae* (Antwerp, 1579), p. 569. A translation of the relevant passage follows:

Nor indeed do I here speak from gratitude or adulation, since it is now obvious to every observer from new and abundant evidence that he [Sidney] at this early stage of his life has performed such outstanding service to both his sovereign and his whole nation that from his first diplomatic assignment, the rude beginnings of greater events, results of the highest significance may be expected. . . . in that most splendid and honourable Embassy to the newly elected Holy Roman Emperor which he led almost two years ago in order to congratulate him in the name of his queen he [Sidney] was so clearly the exemplar of the heroic spirit and the prudent, well-educated young man, that almost anyone could anticipate where his precocious and unique talent might direct him.

Six years later Alberico Gentili, whom Sidney and his family had encouraged, dedicated his *De Legationibus* to Sidney and cited him as the ideal ambassador.

CHAPTER 24. EPILOGUE

Sidney's triumph did not last long. As Elizabeth pondered William's proposals her suspicions began to stir. She noted that William (the richest nobleman in the world's most prosperous economy) to strengthen his line had offered his daughter's hand to Sidney, together with appropriate territories and titles. William's desire to obtain this promising young man as father of his future heirs dovetailed with his need to train a future commander of his army. Other leaders in the Low Countries would welcome a hero around whom they could rally, a commander who could help Protestant and Catholic alike to throw off the yoke of Spain. This prospect conflicted with a theory to which Elizabeth was committed, that no anointed sovereign should contest the legal status of a fellow sovereign. She held to this despite the evidence that Philip of Spain had more than once encouraged rebels in England and had even plotted her own death.

Elizabeth's attitude comes through clearly in her instructions to Daniel Rogers when she sent an answer to the proposed treaty which Sidney had presented in "Certain Notes." Dated June 22 and probably dictated by the Queen herself, these instructions contain the following passage:

> We have in all our former actions, in theis their late troubles, sought by all meanes to bringe the provinces of the Lowe-Countrye that weare at discord and divided, to an unitye. Yf nowe, after such a coorse taken, we should, without further offence geven, seeke to dismember the body and plucke th'one parte thereof from th'other, by withdrawing the subject from the Soveraigne, we should enter a matter which should much towche us in honnour and might be an evill precedent for us even in our owne case. For we could not like that any forreyn prince should enter into any such secreat combination with our President of Wales or Deputye of Ireland or any other governor under us, which might any waye estraunge him from th'obedience he oweth us.[1]

Besides the specific statement that she wished to avoid challenging Philip's sovereignty, the example Elizabeth chose would not have passed

1. Lettenhove, p. 357.

496

unnoticed: Sir Henry Sidney, Lord Deputy of Ireland, was now serving his eighteenth year as Lord President of Wales. It would seem that behind the negotiations with the Prince of Orange Elizabeth may have smelled a plot of the Dudley faction. If Philip became Lord Governor of Holland and Zeeland he could emerge from the Dutch wars as a leader on whom the Lowlanders could ultimately bestow sovereignty. He could then become the Dudley candidate for Elizabeth's own throne. Such a possibility should be nipped in the bud. Though the only evidence to support this speculation is Elizabeth's singling out of Sir Henry in the instructions for Rogers, it would help to explain her neglect of Philip so promptly after she "well liked" his report on June 10. Indeed, from now on she seems to have disliked him, an attitude in which Burghley apparently concurred.[2]

Historians now view this moment as one of the fateful crossroads in the path of the western world,

> a political and military watershed in European history. What was at stake was not merely the future of a sizeable territory and the most advanced economy of the contemporary world: it was the future of Europe itself for the next three centuries. For the preservation or destruction of the unity of the Netherlands was a key to the major problems of international relations in Europe—the relations of Spain and the great powers in the sixteenth and seventeenth centuries, of France and the great powers in the seventeenth and eighteenth centuries, even of Germany and the great powers in the nineteenth and twentieth centuries.[3]

Elizabeth followed the advice not of the tough-minded Walsingham, but of the indecisive Burghley. Together they shut their eyes to the possibilities of a united Netherlands, the creation of a third force on the Continent, a chance that disappeared when the southern provinces were separated from the northern three years later. If Elizabeth could conceive of such great possibilities she did not rise to the opportunity. Personal policy and personal diplomacy were her method, not to mention personal pique at times. The causes behind her dislike of Sidney, especially her attitude that he was too ambitious, are difficult to establish, though

2. Wilson, p. 88.
3. Ibid., p. 43.

clearly the attempt by the Prince of Orange to install the *lumen familiae* of the Dudleys in his own family displeased England's Queen.

As the summer wore on, Sidney's roseate hopes for a Protestant League dimmed. About the first of August a report received from Daniel Rogers indicated that instead of a Protestant League Prince William preferred the union of England with Holland and Zeeland; he thought it was impossible to achieve effective unity among the German states.[4] In mid-August Leicester found the French ambassador disturbed at the prospect of the League, a reaction which the Earl promptly passed on to Queen Elizabeth.[5] At the end of the month Rogers enjoyed a cordial talk with Count Casimir, who concurred on the proposed terms of organization but confessed that quarrels between the Lutherans and the Calvinists remained a great stumbling block. Late in September Rogers reported his conversations with the Elector Palatine and with the Landgrave of Hesse at Ems, where he had been accompanied by Languet.[6]

Rogers's letters now began to sound a new note, that of retreat. The Landgrave told him frankly that he thought a League would be impossible because of "certain mad divines," the Lutheran theologians whose "ubiquitarian zeal" was strongly supported by the Elector of Saxony. On October 11, Rogers wrote Walsingham that the Elector Palatine had come out in opposition to the League on the ground that he disapproved of the Queen of England's meddling in German affairs. Casimir still hoped to put life into the project by bringing in the rulers of some minor German states. The reaction in England was prompt: on October 31 Walsingham informed Rogers that Queen Elizabeth had decided to drop the plan.[7]

At this moment Sidney was far from the court. His charming and intelligent sister Mary, with whom he felt an extremely close understanding, had married Henry Herbert, second Earl of Pembroke, on April 21 while Sidney was abroad. In August Philip had gone down to the Pembroke estate at Wilton in Wiltshire, where he remained for September. Then, after a few weeks with his mother at Penshurst, he returned to Wilton for November. During the next few years he spent many months there with his sister. Her company provided solace for his

4. *CSPF2*, nos. 38, 41. Rogers also wrote that his Highness mentioned "Mr. Sidney (of whom he had conceived a great opinion)."

5. *CSPF2*, nos. 100, 109, 114.

6. *CSPF2*, nos. 138, 249.

7. *CSPF2*, nos. 323, 392.

frustration as he waited for another appointment worthy of his status and proven abilities.

The causes of Philip's frustration were many and various. First of all was the clash between his conviction that the support of Continental Protestantism should rank high in England's foreign policy and Queen Elizabeth's view that it would cost more than it could justify. All summer long she procrastinated while Count Casimir begged for the troops and the money needed to build an effective Protestant army. He also asked that Sidney be sent as joint commander. As time passed the gulf widened between what Sidney wished and what actually took place. In the end Sidney stood as a Protestant "ultra" in politics; he was a hero to those of his beliefs but was viewed with misgivings by politique contemporaries.

Secondly, Philip was Sir Henry's son, and Sir Henry no longer enjoyed her Majesty's favour. He had become identified with the impossible situation in Ireland, to which neither Elizabeth nor any of her successors was to find a solution, despite the ever-increasing bloodlettings. Sir Henry's steady insistence that more money was needed blinded Elizabeth to his merits and to the realities of the occupation.

During 1577 the backbiting of English landowners in Ireland had become especially troublesome to Sir Henry. In the absence of money from the Queen's treasury to pay wages and quartering for his troops Sir Henry imposed a property tax known as the cess. The Earl of Ormonde wished to be exempted and appealed to Elizabeth. His protests rose to such a clamour that some defence of Sir Henry's course of action seemed called for. At court Philip indignantly refused to talk to Ormonde and then decided to defend his father's policy and conduct in a tract. On September 30 Edward Waterhouse reported this plan to Sir Henry in Dublin. "Mr. *Philip* had gatherid a Collection of all the Articlis, which have bene enviously objectid to your Government, wherunto he hath fraimid an Answer in Way of Discours, the most excellently (if I have eny Judgement) that ever I red in my Lief; . . . But let no Man compare with Mr. *Philips* Pen."[8]

The result was the *Discourse on Irish Affairs*, written in seven sections. It was not intended for publication, and a copy of the last four sections in Philip's hand is the only surviving text. The tract probably reached Burghley and Walsingham, and it may even have been seen by Queen Elizabeth. All would have recognized it as a son's special pleading and

8. Collins, I :228.

discounted it as such. By the end of the year Elizabeth had determined to recall Sir Henry. The official order was dispatched in February 1578, but, frail in body and beaten in spirit, Henry did not land at Chester until September.

A third factor in Philip's frustration was the disparity between his expected inheritance, the ample estates of his two uncles and the lesser properties of Sir Henry, and his immediate lack of money. The two things were constantly in opposition: Sidney ran up bills and handed out bounties as his position at court or in the Queen's service required. As a result he carried an inordinate burden of debt which his allowance and other sources of income never managed to equal. Further, he speculated beyond his means in the voyages of maritime adventurers, notoriously in those of Martin Frobisher, who claimed to have found Arctic islands of the purest gold. The two hundred tons of ore that Frobisher brought back proved to be iron pyrites or fool's gold, a foreshadowing of what would happen to Sidney's prospects of inheriting the properties of Leicester and Warwick.

In fact, the tide of Dudley fortune had now begun to ebb. Warwick's health was failing, and he became increasingly less prominent except on formal occasions. Leicester continued to be eminent, influential, and active, but his *affaires de coeur* and errors of judgement were beginning to stretch severely Elizabeth's loyalty and indulgence. Sad and sick, Sir Henry Sidney was soon to join his bitterly disappointed wife, no longer solaced by Dudley pride and privilege. And Philip Sidney, the heir of the Dudley fame and fortune, now began to experience the same ebb tide.

Finally, some of those qualities which have appealed so strongly to later generations were liabilities to Sidney at the sycophantic court of Elizabeth. He was too direct and uncompromising in written argument (and doubtless also in speech) to avoid causing occasional resentment. Philip was the glass of fashion and the mould of form at court, but he lacked the agility, adaptability, and capacity to accept what was possible in place of what was desirable, qualities necessary for continuing success in court politics. Duplicity, the standard practice at court, was not one of Sidney's skills. As an administrator his ambitions exceeded his means to attain them. His extensive travels, linguistic skills, and friendships with learned foreign diplomats did not gain him a foothold in the councils of state. Here he had several other handicaps: he was too young for a major appointment, he had overestimated the possibilities of a Protestant League, and Elizabeth had somehow acquired the opinion that he was too ambitious.

Under these circumstances Sidney soon wearied of the court and was happy to linger with Mary at Wilton. During the long winter weeks he began to find the art of poetry both a solace and a challenge. To amuse Mary he began to write a long romance, "a trifle, triflinglie handled," written on "loose sheetes of paper," usually while sitting in her company. He called it the *Arcadia*, and as it grew from sheet to sheet he began to insert passages of verse. The more verse he wrote, the more he began to experiment. The process began slowly, and the romance was put down and picked up several times during the next three years. How gradually Sidney began to develop skill in rhyming becomes apparent in his first dateable verses, three short sets embedded in a prose masque created for performance before the Queen in Leicester's gardens at Wanstead, near the royal palace at Greenwich. This masque, *The Lady of May*, was composed in May 1578; it is a highly conventional pastoral drama, and the ten scattered stanzas show little promise of the poetical powers which Sidney developed later.

The rest of 1578 brought few events pleasing to Sidney and many which were discouraging. Sir Henry's recall and his arrival in September, shaken in body and spirit, cast a pall over most of that year. Moreover, after a gap of two years the Queen now revived marriage negotiations with the mercurial Alençon, a depressing threat to the anti-French and strongly Protestant group with which Leicester, Walsingham, and Sidney were affiliated.

Philip grew more restless and weary as the year progressed. He confessed as much to Languet, who counselled him against getting involved in any of the rash projects which seemed to offer escape from the boredom of court routine: joining Count Casimir's army which now faced Don John's forces in Belgium, or rushing off on a voyage to *terra incognita*, or singeing the beard of Sidney's godfather, Philip of Spain. Languet also mentions a new honour bestowed on Sidney by Queen Elizabeth; it meant that he was no longer his own master but henceforward must always place his country's foreign policy above private desire or inclination.[9] The Queen and her ministers had decided to give Sidney a post in the Admiralty, as an act of the Privy Council taken on June 5 reveals: "To Mr. Phillipp Sydney that where her Majestie intendeth forthewith to sett certeine of her shippes to the seas wherin his service is to be used, he is therefore required immediatlie to make his repaire to the Court

9. See Languet's letter of July 16, 1578.

with all expedicion, to receive such charge as shall be committed unto him in that behalf."[10] This intended appointment, about which Sidney's biographers have been silent, appears to have fallen through; it would seem that once again the Queen changed her mind.

Soon after the end of the Christmas festivities Sidney's spirits were lifted by the sudden news that Count Casimir was to pay an unexpected visit to England. He had been at Ghent and, on the spur of the moment, decided that since he was so near the coast he would cross the Channel. The wavering support he had received from the Queen may have prompted him to try personal persuasion. Elizabeth commissioned Sir Henry and Philip to meet Casimir's party (the Count was travelling disguised as a merchant) on their arrival in London. The surprise was capped when Sidney discovered that on two days' notice Languet had impulsively joined Casimir. The festivities continued until the Count's departure on February 14; meanwhile he had offered the Queen a large area of the Belgian coast, including Dunkirk, Nieuport, and Bruges. In return she created him a Knight of the Garter and herself placed the Garter on his leg.

Sidney and his father were kept fully occupied by their charge, even though Leicester and Walsingham conducted the negotiations. But Sidney and Languet enjoyed their reunion, and Philip's special friends Edward Dyer and Fulke Greville shared it with them. Sir Henry and Languet had their first opportunity to express the admiration each felt for the other, and as a parting gift Sir Henry gave his son's mentor a gold chain which cost £45. Fulke Greville accompanied Languet on the return journey, as did Robert Sidney whose travels were to begin with a season of study under the famous Dr. Sturm at Strasbourg. Languet had been disappointed to find that Sidney's mode of life did not measure up to the high standards he had set for his protégé. After several months of reflection he wrote,

> It was a delight to me last winter to see you high in favour and enjoying the esteem of all your countrymen; but to speak plainly, the habits of your court seemed to me somewhat less manly than I could have wished, and most of your noblemen appeared to me to seek for a reputation more by a kind of affected courtesy than by those virtues which are wholesome to the state, and which are most becoming to generous spirits and to men of high birth. I was sorry

10. *Acts of the Privy Council*, 10:240.

therefore, and so were other friends of yours, to see you wasting the flower of your life on such things, and I feared lest that noble nature of yours should be dulled, and lest from habit you should be brought to take pleasure in pursuits which only enervate the mind.[11]

Events did not allow Sidney to languish long. Casimir's visit coincided with the arrival of Alençon's agent, Simier, who had come to negotiate the proposed marriage with Elizabeth. To the consternation of most members of her Council, her Majesty seemed disposed to accept Alençon, though she still turned like a weathercock with each day's breeze. Leicester stood firm among those in opposition, but suddenly his own indiscretion in marriage sent him tumbling out of the Queen's favour. Simier had learned of Leicester's secret marriage, but he kept this information from Elizabeth until the right moment. Early in August 1579, when Alençon's expected arrival prompted Leicester to eleventh-hour obstructive tactics, Simier played his trump. How could her Majesty trust Leicester, Simier asked, when he had deceived her even about his own marriage? In her fury Elizabeth ordered Leicester's arrest and almost sent him to the Tower. When her rage abated somewhat, she isolated him in a less sinister tower in Greenwich Park. But her cousin, who was now recognized as Countess of Leicester, was banned from ever coming into the royal presence again. At this time Leicester's sister, Lady Sidney, gave up her small apartment at court, a coincidence noted by the Spanish ambassador Mendoza.

About the middle of August the contrite Earl met with Sir Henry Sidney and other friends of the anti-Alençon group at the Earl of Pembroke's house, Baynard's Castle, in London. Those assembled, who probably included Walsingham, Sir Christopher Hatton, and Philip Sidney, sketched out a brief of the arguments against the marriage and, recognizing that no pen could compare with Mr. Philip's, asked him to turn this brief into a formal letter to the Queen. The resulting discourse, extending to about forty-five hundred words, of which a score of manuscript copies still exist, was presented to Elizabeth late in August. Oddly enough, there is no record of any response, negative or otherwise. (Alençon, whom she finally rejected, never forgave Sidney.) Once again Sidney appeared as the author of a direct, overly frank statement of principle, a bold dose of medicine offered when sugared remedies had failed.

11. Pears, p. 167.

During these tense days Sidney also suffered a personal insult when the spoiled and conceited young Edward de Vere, Earl of Oxford, an intimate admirer of Alençon, ordered him off the tennis court while the French visitors were in the gallery. When Sidney refused, Oxford insolently addressed him as "puppy." Sidney stood on his honour, and a duel was avoided only by the Queen's order. Yet Elizabeth saw fit to remind Sidney that he and De Vere were of different rank and that inferiors owe respect to their superiors. These events put Sidney under a cloud for the following year, much of which he passed in the country at Wilton with Mary. She was expecting her first child, who was born early the following April.

In his frustration Sidney pondered possible courses of action, for example, to employ himself abroad since no constructive assignment seemed likely to be forthcoming at home. Languet urged him to join the Prince of Orange with whom he would gain military experience. Sidney finally settled for the congenial company of his sister and their friends at Wilton. To relieve his enforced inactivity he returned to the *Arcadia*, the continuation and completion of which occupied the winter months during his sister's pregnancy. The study of poetry, especially poetic techniques, renewed its fascination. He and his friends Dyer and Spenser (whom Sidney met this autumn) had begun to ask why English poetry could not be as fresh and various in rhythm and form as the verse written in Italian, French, and other Continental languages. They set out to free English poetry from its "balde Rymers" and succeeded in doing so. The golden phase of Elizabethan poetry grew out of these sessions, in which Philip Sidney was the leader. Seldom has political frustration yielded such a glorious harvest, one of the happiest paradoxes of cultural history.

From Wilton on Whitsunday (May 22) Sidney wrote the only letter containing a direct reference to his poems, a letter which also shows the wide range of Sidney's reading. Addressed to his friend Edward Denny, who was then about to depart for Ireland with Baron Grey (Sir Henry Sidney's successor as Lord Deputy), the letter lists a series of books for Denny to read. Besides recommending this heavy course of study, Sidney advises Denny to "remember with your good voyce, to sing my songes, for they will well become an other" (see appendix 5).

Apparently Sidney did not return to court until the autumn of 1580. His friends had begun to wonder at his acceptance of rustic retirement, as Languet reported when the summer drew to an end.

They fear that others who are not aware of your steadiness may suspect that you have wearied of the troublesome path that leads to virtue, which previously you followed with such assiduity. Similarly, they fear that the sweet pleasures of lengthy retirement may to some degree relax the vigour with which you formerly rose to noble enterprises, and that a love of ease, which once you despised, may by degrees creep over your spirit.[12]

Aside from a long letter of advice to his brother Robert on how to make the most of his travels and another to a friend in Paris, Sidney's life during the balance of 1580 is a relatively blank page. He seems to have been in low spirits, which were acerbated by the lack of proper employment and a shortage of money.

In a step to get back into government affairs Sidney agreed to serve as a member of the parliament which convened on January 16, 1581. He sat on various committees and took part in other routine business without achieving any prominence. After the session ended he became involved in a grand entertainment which was being prepared for the French ambassadors then expected in London. They were coming to conclude the marriage contract between the Queen and Alençon, whom Elizabeth had decided to accept now that he had been offered the sovereignty of the Netherlands. Sidney, Greville, and two noble lords agreed to appear together in a tournament. After several postponements it took place on Whit Monday, May 15. Including numerous attendants, their brilliantly costumed group numbered about two hundred. The plot required that Sidney and his three companions suffer defeat from superior numbers, but his reputation as horseman and swordsman was enhanced. Sidney may also have contributed a sonnet spoken by his group and the answering sonnet; they were printed in a contemporary description of the tournament, and if written by Sidney would be the only verses from his pen which were printed during his lifetime.

It is also highly probable that one of the spectators at this tournament was Lady Penelope Devereux. Since the death in 1576 of her father, the Earl of Essex, she had been under the wing of the Countess of Huntingdon, who did not bring her to court until January, 1581, when she was eighteen.[13] Her guardian's purpose, of course, was to find her a wealthy husband. Within a month one appeared, the appropriately named Lord

12. Languet to Sidney, Sept. 24, 1580.
13. Established by Ringler, p. 438.

Rich whose father died late in February. The new heir found Lady
Penelope to his liking, and the marriage took place on the first day of
November.

Just when the dark-eyed, golden-haired Penelope began to attract
Philip Sidney cannot be determined precisely. When he celebrates her
and their love in *Astrophil and Stella*, he says only that when he first encountered her he "loved not" (sonnet no. 2) and that he did not begin to
respond to her beauty for some little time. Not until the twenty-fourth
sonnet does he identify her, and in the thirty-third he reveals that when
he might have possessed her he "would not." He tells us, however, that
he failed to realize the force of his love for Stella until after she had become
Lady Rich. This clearly indicates that nearly all of the sonnets were
written after Stella's marriage.[14] Their long flirtation helped to pass the
time and inspired the first great sonnet sequence in the English language.
Its passing seems to have left no scars on the heart of Stella but evidently
Sidney remembered her tenderly to his deathbed. George Gifford, the
chaplain who ministered to him, reports Sidney's confession: "There
came to my remembrance a Vanitie wherein I had taken delight, whereof
I had not ridd myselfe. It was my Ladie Rich. But I ridd myselfe of it,
and presentlie my Ioy and Comfort returned within a few howers."[15]

Sidney's concentration on writing verse produced another golden off-
spring, his best and longest prose essay, *The Defence of Poesie*. Whether it
was written before or after *Astrophil and Stella* has never been determined;
a number of the same ideas and illustrations appear in both the sonnets
and in the *Defence*. An equally good case could be made for Sidney's
writing the critical treatise at the very time he was engaged in putting
his theories into practice in his verses. *The Defence of Poesie* remains a
landmark of literary criticism and a marvelous projection of Sidney's
brilliant mind and personality.

The year 1581 also found Sidney's finances at a low point, "beinge
growen almost to the bottome of my pursse." He was forced to ask the
Queen for money. Letters to Leicester, to Burghley, and to the Vice-
Chamberlain, Sir Christopher Hatton, beg their help in his appeal. In
mid-November he wrote to Hatton, "If you finde, you can not prevaile
[with the Queen] I beseeche you lett me knowe it as sone as may be, for

14. See Ringler, p. 438.

15. Quoted by Jean Robertson, "Sir Philip Sidney and Lady Penelope Rich," *RES* 15
(1964):296–97, from *The Manner of Sir Philip Sidneyes Death*, ed. H. J. Davis and B. Juel-
Jensen (Oxford [privately printed], 1959).

I will even shamelessly once in my lief, bringe it her majestie my self: neede obays no lawe, and forgetts blusshinge." The appeal succeeded to the extent that Elizabeth agreed to turn over a sum from "the forfeyture of papistes goodes." Sidney responded by accepting her decision (he had asked for £3000), though he commented to Leicester, "Truly I lyke not their persons and much less their religions, but I think my fortune very hard that my reward must be built upon other mens punishments."

Lest this give the impression that Sidney was a rabid antipapist, it should be noted that although Sidney was dedicated to defeating the designs of the Holy League, he had many friends who were practising Catholics, men he had known in Venice and Vienna, Carrafa and Lord Windsor, Bochetel and Vulcob. Indeed, during his Italian sojourn Walsingham had heard rumours that Sidney had become "soft on Catholicism" and in 1577 Campion had hoped for his conversion. A year and a half after Sidney wrote the passage quoted above he acted as intermediary in the purchase of three million acres in America from Sir Humphrey Gilbert's "Commonwealth," land he then sold to Sir George Peckham, a prominent Catholic. This transaction, which had Walsingham's blessing, was to enable Peckham, Sir Thomas Gerrard, and others to establish a colony in America where members of their faith could find refuge and freedom to practise their religion.

Whether the money came from the forfeited property of Catholics or from other sources, Sidney apparently received it in due course. His financial plight was due to two circumstances: his habit of spending more than a member of "so yongli a fortuned famili as the Sidneis" could afford, and the fact that Queen Elizabeth did not see fit to employ his services. Various small errands were assigned to him, such as attending Antonio, the bastard pretender to the Portuguese throne who was preparing ships for an invasion to establish his title in September 1581. As Sidney wrote to Hatton from Dover, "The Quene means, I thinck, that I should go over with hym, which at this present mighte hinder me greatlie, and nothing avail the kinge for any service, I should be able to doo hym." Sidney's appeal to Hatton attained the desired end; the ships sailed without him and soon he was back in London.

A few months later, apparently after Sidney had received the royal grant he needed so desperately, the Queen named him among the large contingent which was to escort Alençon back across the Channel. Even with Alençon in England expecting marriage almost daily, Elizabeth continued to postpone the nuptials. She finally realized that her prospective husband did not wish to leave the island before the event was celebrated. Finally she succeeded in dislodging him and, accompanied by six hundred persons in fifteen ships, he crossed to Antwerp on February 1, where farewell festivities lasted for a fortnight. Among such a great crowd of Englishmen Alençon's grudge against him could scarcely poison the occasion for Sidney.

During the remaining months of 1582 Sidney flitted from one possibility of "employment" to another. In April, a few weeks after returning from Alençon's farewell party, his name was mentioned as prospective leader of a cavalry troup to be sent to the Netherlands. Nothing materialized. A fortnight later several high officials, confronted by renewed rebellion and bloodletting in Ireland, contemplated asking Sir Henry Sidney to take charge there once again with Philip as his right-hand man, and Sir Henry indicated his willingness if his terms were met. He felt that his personal sacrifice would be justified provided it would open up a career for Philip. Once again the proposals fell through. In July Philip prodded his father's London agent Edmund Molyneux to approach Burghley and Sir Christopher Hatton to get him appointed to the Council for Wales, again without success.

With a career in Ireland or Wales no longer possible, Sidney now turned to the far-off worlds which waited to be conquered. Frobisher's voyages had inflamed his imagination, even though his cargo of two hundred tons of gold had proved worthless except as ballast. The recent return of Sir Francis Drake from his voyage around the world ignited new enthusiasm for maritime adventures. In 1582 Richard Hakluyt, Sidney's fellow undergraduate at Christ Church, published *Diverse Voyages touching the Discoverie of America and the Ilands Adjacent unto the Same*, and the notion of England's manifest destiny—expansion into the new world—began to stir. Hakluyt's dedication records Sidney's "favour towards these godly and honourable discoveries," as well as his other kindnesses. But, whatever Sidney's hopes were for a leading part in the westward expansion of English power, destiny did not accommodate him.

Despite the continued emptiness of his purse Sidney paid his usual tribute to Queen Elizabeth with a New Year's gift. Records of the occasion describe his offering: "a juell of golde like a castell, garnished with small diamonds on th[e] one side, being a pott to set flowers in." Just a week later, though not in consequence of this annual tax which Elizabeth expected from her courtiers, Sidney received his knighthood and became

Sir Philip Sidney of Penshurst. Even this honour was an empty one, since it was not awarded because of Sidney's own achievements, or his services as ambassador, or his merits as a member of the court. The situation was simply that Count Casimir was now to be officially installed as a member of the Order of the Garter. Since he could not return to England for the ceremony, he nominated Sidney as his proxy. Protocol required that a proxy hold a rank not lower than knighthood, so Sidney was awarded the title. Thus did Sir Philip participate for the first and last time with his father and uncles in the proceedings of England's most noble order.

In the succeeding weeks of 1583 the quest for a suitable appointment for Sir Philip continued, much as it had for Mr. Philip. In March rumours circulated widely that he would become the new Captain of the Isle of Wight. Once again the reports proved disappointing. Meanwhile, towards the end of January Lord Warwick had requested the Queen to appoint Philip his partner as joint Master of the Ordnance. Sidney was eager for the appointment and solicited Burghley's help. The application dragged on until midsummer when Sidney was given a subordinate appointment under Warwick; he did not achieve joint responsibility until two years afterwards.

This year, 1583, also brought marriage to Sir Philip. His status as a desirable match had been greatly altered at the beginning of 1581 when Lettice, Lady Leicester, produced a son. The child immediately became heir to both Leicester and Warwick, so that Philip now had only the "yongli" fortune of the Sidneys as his inheritance. His bride was Frances Walsingham, daughter of Sir Francis and Lady Walsingham, who loved and admired him as much as he did them. Their intimacy had begun eleven years earlier after St. Bartholomew's Day in Paris, when Sidney found refuge in Walsingham's embassy. Little Frances was then five years old and she could scarcely have appeared to Philip as a prospective bride. Now she was an attractive girl of sixteen, and she seems to have become a devoted and much-loved wife.

Even so, the nuptials were not an occasion of unalloyed bliss. Despite the marriage settlement of Sidney lands, Philip was deeply in debt. Accordingly, Walsingham had to agree to pay off £1,500 of his son-in-law's obligations at the time of the wedding and to permit the young couple to live in his house without charge. Further difficulty arose when Queen Elizabeth raised the petty objection that she had not been consulted before the marriage plans were announced. The long-suffering Walsingham was forced to write a letter of humble apology, saying that he did not consider his daughter and a free gentleman high enough in rank to be worthy of asking the Queen's permission. Although Elizabeth agreed to overlook the offence, she did so rather rudely, exhibiting the captious attitude she had developed towards the Sidneys. The marriage took place on September 21; Sir Philip and his bride promptly moved into the Walsingham house at Barn Elms, Surrey, only six miles from London.

As the year 1583 ended, storm clouds rose over the Protestant cause abroad and at home; soon lightning began to strike. Alençon's false character became apparent. Instead of proving to be the unifying leader of the Netherlands, he practised such duplicity that the Protestant forces were thrown into disarray. The Spanish soldiers rallied and recaptured city after city. Finally, in May 1584, Alençon died. Elizabeth and her Council now began to prepare for a Spanish attempt to invade England. In June William of Orange fell to the bullet of an assassin, a tragedy that sent shivers through Protestant leaders everywhere. In the autumn, discovery of the Throckmorton plot alarmed the government even more. Sir Philip took an active part in the preparations to defend England against invasion, both as an officer of the Ordnance and as a representative of his father, the Lord President of Wales.

By midsummer the situation in the Low Countries had become so desperate that Elizabeth realized immediate relief could come only from French intervention to counteract the Spanish forces. She hoped that Alençon's status as sovereign of the Netherlands might make Catherine de Médicis wish to perpetuate French hegemony there. So once again she asked Sir Philip to go as her special ambassador, ostensibly to express bereavement at Alençon's death, but with the unofficial purpose of persuading the French King and the Queen Mother to send forces to oppose the Spanish troops. Sidney accepted the mission as a duty, but he was too knowledgeable to expect success. By now he and his advisors realized that in Paris Elizabeth was recognized as a wily player in the game of diplomacy whose word could no longer be trusted. For years she had been trying to get France to pull England's chestnuts from the fire in the Netherlands, and this new round would repeat the old pattern. Fortunately, at this juncture Henry III decided on a jaunt to Lyons, so Elizabeth called Sidney back from Gravesend where his ships were being prepared. Thus once again Sidney's opportunity for a state appointment came to naught. His seat in Parliament with its committee work and his duties in the Ordance provided his only official employment in affairs of state.

As 1585 opened Sidney's convictions about the most effective way of defending England against Spanish aggression began to change. For years he had believed that the best place to curb Spain was the Netherlands, but Elizabeth's balance-of-power theory had thwarted this course of action. Now Sidney came to believe that a shift from defensive manoeuvres to offensive tactics was necessary. As he saw it, Spain's greatest weakness lay in its dependence on shipping, both to bring supplies and treasure from overseas and to support the far-flung Spanish armies. Sidney now wished to carry war "to the very bowels of Spain," and the method should be to develop a large and well-organized fleet. English ships could then control the Channel and other narrow seas and also attack Spanish vessels in those parts or at the most distant sources of supplies or wealth.

Such an expanded fleet would open up a new career for Sidney, and opportunities soon began to appear. Early in 1585 he was deeply involved in plans to organize and command a combined fleet of English and Dutch ships against Spanish shipping and settlements. In August a letter from Ralph Lane, governor of the new colony of Virginia, urged him to accept command of the forces needed to seize Spanish outposts and treasure in that area. Meanwhile Sir Philip was thoroughly occupied with his responsibilities in the Ordnance. In discussing the preparations against invasion he told her Majesty quite directly that supplies were deficient and that the Earl of Warwick should not be blamed for it. The situation alarmed Elizabeth so much that in July a patent created Sir Philip Master of the Ordnance jointly with Warwick, the position he had sought two years earlier.

These administrative responsibilities, much as Sidney had desired them, seemed tame now that the prospect of fighting beckoned. An expeditionary force of five-thousand foot soldiers and one thousand horse was being raised to be sent to Zeeland under the command of Leicester. The second highest position would be governor of the forces at Flushing, which was situated at the entrance to the Schelde and controlled traffic to and from Antwerp. Sidney's name had been prominently mentioned for the post, but again the Queen dallied and seemed to favour another candidate. Sidney yearned for active service. Instead of eating out his heart in waiting he decided to plunge into an expedition with Sir Francis Drake, who was then on the eve of departure from Plymouth. In fact the voyage had been Sidney's brainchild; the ships were officially fitted out under Drake's name but with supplies obtained on Sidney's credit. Once the ships had cleared port, Sidney and Drake were to exercise command jointly. A letter from Walsingham to William Davison, English ambassador to the Netherlands, dated September 13, explains the situation.

> Sir Philip hath taken a very hard resolution to accompany Sir Francis Drake in this voyage, moved thereto for that he saw her Majesty disposed to commit the charge of Flushing unto some other; which he reputed would fall out greatly to his disgrace, to see another preferred before him, both for birth and judgment inferior unto him. The despair thereof and the disgrace that he doubted [not] he should receive have carried him into a different course.[16]

Elizabeth responded promptly by having Sir Christopher Hatton send three letters. In the first she ordered Sidney's immediate return; the others were addressed to Drake and to the Mayor of Plymouth. In this way Sidney learned he would be Governor of Flushing.

Sidney now threw his energies into preparing for the expedition to Zeeland. His ships sailed on November 16 and anchored two days later. With him were his brother Robert and a few other intimates, but the company of two hundred soldiers did not reach full strength for another month. The dilatory tactics of Queen Elizabeth once again produced too little, too late. Sidney was shocked by the condition of the garrison at Flushing. Many in his undermanned companies were sick, their living conditions "loathsome." Some of the ramparts and barriers were so dilapidated that they had fallen to the ground, and morale was correspondingly low. Sidney set about repairing the fortifications and revitalizing the troops and soon won the admiration of both the soldiers and the burghers of Flushing.

Leicester did not arrive until three weeks later, in all the pomp of a visiting potentate. His splendour so impressed the leaderless Netherlanders that they offered him the position of Governor-general. A month after his arrival Leicester accepted the offer, thus violating Queen Elizabeth's specific instructions. When the Queen learned of his action, she erupted in fury. Not unexpectedly, she included Sidney in her anger, blaming him for persuading Leicester to disobey her orders. In the uproar Sidney was threatened with recall, but Elizabeth's rage subsided before such a step was taken.

16. Wallace, p. 331.

Sidney put his heart into his responsibilities as few could have done under such discouraging conditions. Because of its control over commerce on the Schelde and other North Sea traffic, Flushing was a key to the Netherlands. He struggled to get pay and proper barracks for his English troops, refusing to believe that Elizabeth could abandon them, but fearing mutiny from the miserable, sick, undersupplied, and unpaid men. The crucible of this experience further refined the metal in Sidney's character. Under fire he developed new capacities and ripened in judgement and command. His letters show this growth in maturity and reveal his strong resolution to cope with the grim realities of the situation.

Perhaps the finest letter Sidney ever wrote was addressed to Walsingham on March 24, 1586. Telling his father-in-law not to worry about the difficulties surrounding him in Flushing, Sidney continued:

I had before cast my count of dang[er] want and disgrace, and before God Sir it is trew [that] in my hart the love of the caws doth so far over-ballance then all that with Gods grace thei shall never make me weery of my resolution. If her Majesty wear the fowntain I woold fear considring what I daily fynd that we shold wax dry, but she is but a means whom God useth and I know not whether I am deceaved but I am faithfully persuaded that if she shold withdraw her self other springes woold ryse to help this action. For me thinkes I see the great work indeed in hand, against the abusers of the world, wherein it is no greater fault to have confidence in mans power, then it is to hastily to despair of Gods work. I think a wyse and constant man ought never to greev whyle he doth plai as a man mai sai his own part truly though others be out but if him self leav his hold becaws other marrin[ers] will be ydle he will hardli forg[ive] him self his own fault. For me I can not promis of my own cource no nor of the my[   ] becaws I know there is a hyer power that must uphold me or els I shall fall, but certainly I trust, I shall not by other mens wantes be drawn from my self.

Therefore good Sir to whome for my particular I am more bownd then to all men besydes, be not troubled with my trouble for I have seen the worst in my judgment before hand, and wors then that can not bee. If the queen pai not her souldiours she must loos her garrisons there is no dout thereof.

But no man living shall be hable to sai the fault is in me. What releef I can do them I will. I will spare no danger if ocasion serv I am sure no creature shall be hable to lai injustice to my charge, and for furdre doutes truly I stand not uppon them. I have written by Adams to the Cownceil plainli thereof lett them determin. It hath been a costly beginning unto me this war, by reason I had no thing proportioned unto it my servantes unexperienced and my self every wai unfurnished, and no helpes, but heerafter if the war continew I shall pas much better thorow with it. For Bergen up Zome I delighted in it I confess becaws it was neer the enemy, but especially having a very fair hows in it and an excellent air I destenied it for my wyfe, but fynding how yow deal there [a]nd that ill paiment in my absence thens might bring foorth som mischeef and considering how apt the Queen is to interpret every thing to my disadvantage, I have resigned it to my Lord Willowghby my very frend and in deed a vaillant and frank gentleman, and fitt for that place. Therefore I pray yow know that so much of my regality is faln. I understand I am called very ambitious and prowd at home, but certainly if thei knew my ha[rt] thei woold not altogether so judg me.

Sidney's manifest honesty, his resignation to divine will, and his dedication to the high purpose of his mission contrast sharply with the treatment that the Queen returned to him and his comrades-in-arms. Their needs were now neglected, and even Sidney's motives were suspected. He bore this ill-usage and neglect with Christian patience and simple dignity.

Nor were his trials to diminish. In May he learned of the death of his beloved father, and three months later Lady Sidney followed her husband to the tomb in the family church at Penshurst. Sir Philip's request to be allowed to return to deal with estate problems was promptly denied. At least his sweet wife Frances was allowed to join him in Flushing where she arrived late in June. She was again pregnant, and the possible birth of a son provided one future event in which their hopes combined.

Another trial now afflicted Sidney and his soldiers; evidence mounted that Leicester lacked the qualities necessary in a commander, for he proved to be timid and incompetent. His chief officers split into factions and indulged in drunken quarrels and other displays of jealousy which he could not control. Sir Philip succeeded in bringing together some of the dissidents and by his own example inspired them to bravery in combat. Accounts of his feats speak of his skill and fierce courage; he excelled as much in planning the forays and attacks as he did with his sword in hand. The capture of the walled city of Axel on July 6 was spectacular: his forces slaughtered the defenders without losing a single man, the first important blow struck by the English and their local allies. The description in Stow's *Annals* tells of Sidney's gathering his men before the attack and addressing them in terms similar to King Henry's before the walls of Harfleur: "Which oration of his did so link the minds of the people that they desired to die in that service than to live in the contrary."[17]

Elizabeth somehow took these achievements for granted. She found Sidney's reports about deficient funds and short supplies too direct and blunt. He wrote to the Council in bald terms that he doubted if Flushing could be held against a full-scale attack and pointed out that it was the keystone of defence of the Low Countries. In his judgement strengthening Flushing was the most effective way to prevent an invasion of England, an invasion which would surely follow if the English forces were forced to withdraw from the Continent. But the Queen had soured against him and such direct speaking offended her. As Walsingham sadly wrote to Leicester, "I see her majesty very apt upon every light occasion to find fault with him."[18]

Her occasions to find fault with Sidney soon came to an abrupt end. On September 22 he led a cavalry attack on an overwhelmingly larger force of Spaniards and, after a full afternoon of heroic fighting, was hit by a musket ball which shattered the femur above his left knee. The scene has been described scores of times, but despite its familiar details the most indurate heart will melt at Fulke Greville's account of the scene which he witnessed:

> Being thirstie with excess of bleeding, he called for drink which was presently brought him; but as he was putting the bottle to his mouth, he saw a poor souldier carred along . . . gastly casting up his eyes at the bottle. Which Sir Philip perceiving, took it from his head, before he drank, and delivered it to the poor man, with these words, *Thy necessity is yet greater than mine.*[19]

For a time the surgeons maintained that his wound would heal, but Sidney himself had no such delusion. He lingered on with his wife at his bedside for four weeks but lost weight so rapidly that his shoulder blades

17. John Stow, *The Annals of England* (London, 1592), pp. 1244–45.
18. *Correspondence of Robert Dudley, Earl of Leicester . . . 1585 and 1586*, ed. John Bruce (London, 1844).
19. Greville, p. 145.

cut through the skin. Blood poisoning set in and soon his death was expected daily, to the grief of his friends and the garrison alike. As a devoutly religious man he faced the end peacefully, filled with anticipation of future bliss. When news of his death reached England his family and admirers were numbed. Poor, long-suffering Walsingham, who had loved Philip since their first intimacy in Paris, could only write, "Her Majesty hath lost a rare servant, and the realm a worthy member."[20] He had also lost the brilliant son-in-law of his choice. Walsingham spent most of his remaining years paying off Philip's debts, for the Sidney estate was so encumbered by money spent in her Majesty's service by Sir Henry and Sir Philip that the properties failed to cover them.

Upon hearing the news of Sidney's death Elizabeth uttered the proper sentiments and may even have regretted that his talents were no longer available for her service. Walsingham ordered the most splendid funeral ever given to anyone below the rank of royalty, an occasion on such scale and accompanied by such a demonstration of national grief that it remained unrivalled for a commoner until the death of Sir Winston Churchill. And the sense of loss extended far beyond the shores of Sidney's native land. The paragon of Protestant chivalry was dead.

20. Lansdowne MS. 982, fol. 69.

APPENDIX 1

SIDNEY'S HOROSCOPE

This document, titled "Genitura Philippi Sydnei Nati," now Bodleian MS. Ashmole 356(5), extends to 62 pages, most of which contain nothing of biographical value. A few passages, however, do yield information, a circumstance which results from the fact that the horoscope was cast not at Sidney's birth, but when he was a youth of sixteen. At that age half of Sidney's life already lay behind him, a fact of which the astrologer was, of course, ignorant. The circumstance, however, permitted the compiler of the horoscope to use an alternative method of determining "the true time of birth," and his procedure explains the slight disparity between the hour and day he fixed on and those recorded by Sir Henry.

The beginning paragraphs of the horoscope, headed "De Vero Geniturae tempore," describe the astrologer's attempt to rectify Sidney's nativity. Of the three accepted methods for establishing the true hour of birth, he rejected the first two called the "Trutine of Hermes" and the "Animodar of Ptolemy." Instead he applied the third method described as the "Accidents of the Native." John Gadbury, the famous English astrologer, explained this system as follows: "Collect and gather from the Native the time of as many remarkable accidents as have hapned unto him; by which you will be guided to finde the proper Significators and Promiters of such accidents, be they good or evil." [1]

In nontechnical language this method allowed the astrologer to use a few established events in the past life of the "Native" as if they were points on a graph. From them he proceeded to create a curve and this curve was then projected back so that "the moment of Birth will be found out exactly." Similarly, the curve was projected into the future to predict events in the individual's later life. This method was considered superior to using the alleged hour of birth, if recorded, since this was subject to the inaccuracy of clocks, confusion over latitude or longitude, and human fallibility.

For the scholar the significance of Sidney's horoscope lies principally in the "remarkable accidents" which the sixteen-year-old "Native" reported to the astrologer, a man with whom he had conversed several times. [2] The identity of the learned mathematician who cast the horoscope may be suggested with

1. *Doctrine of Nativities* (London, 1658), p. 30.
2. Ashmole MS. 174, fol. 145 contains a copy of the diagram of Sidney's nativity. On the reverse is a list of the "Accedents by which the Nativity was Rectified." It appears to be derived from Ashmole MS. 356(5) and adds nothing.

high probability. Thomas Allen (1542–1632) matches all the known qualifications.[3] According to Anthony Wood, Allen was considered "the very soul and sun of all the mathematicians of his time."[4] In 1570, the year Sidney's horoscope was cast, Allen had resigned his fellowship at Trinity College, Oxford, because he refused to take orders. He passed the remainder of his life at Gloucester Hall, now Worcester College. Wood also testifies that Sidney's uncle, "Robert earl of Leicester, chancellor of this university, and the grand favourite in queen Elizabeth's reign did also before that time entertain him." Further, "The truth is that earl did highly value him, and no person was more familiar with him than Mr. Allen and [Dr. John] Dee."

From a study of this neglected manuscript five incidents in Sidney's early life emerge; four of them are otherwise unknown. As "accidents" Gadbury particularly recommended illnesses and honours received from the state; Sidney's astrologer lists three illnesses and two instances of recognition by the Queen. The earliest illness occurred during his first year. "Primo statim anno quo in Lucem exieras gravissima febri cruciabaris, quod de vita tua vix quisque cogitaret" (During the very first year in which you saw the light of day you were tormented by a most serious fever, so that scarcely anyone hoped for your life).

The second illness is more specific: "Nono aetatis tuae anno currente scabie et foeda per totum corpus spurcitie perinde ac potionatus esses laborabas" (In the course of the ninth year of your life you suffered from scabs and foul uncleanness throughout your body, just as if you had been poisoned). Since 1562 was the year of the great smallpox epidemic, the explanation seems clear. As mentioned in chapter one, in October of that year Lady Sidney had nursed Queen Elizabeth through a severe attack of smallpox and had herself become badly marked. Young Philip seems to have escaped disfigurement, but this childhood illness could explain Ben Jonson's description of his appearance: "S[ir] P[hilip] was no pleasant man in countenance, his face being spoiled with Pimples."[5] Objection has been made to this statement on the grounds that Jonson was no older than fourteen when he could have seen Sidney and that Sidney's portraits do not reveal even the slightest disfigurements. But painters ordinarily put the best face forward. In later life Jonson enjoyed a close friendship with Sidney's daughter Elizabeth, Countess of Rutland, so his description may well represent family tradition. That Sidney's complexion was marred

3. This identification was proposed independently by Miss Mary Ellen Bowden of Yale University and Hugh R. Dick of the University of California at Los Angeles, both of whom made other helpful suggestions.

4. This and other quotations are from *Athenae Oxonienses*, ed. P. Bliss (Oxford, 1815), vol. 2, col. 542.

5. Conversations with William Drummond of Hawthornden, *Works*, ed. C. H. Herford and P. Simpson (Oxford, 1925) 1:138–39.

by this illness is confirmed by Dr. Moffet in his *Nobilis: sive Vitae Mortisque Sydniadis Synopsis*, written six years after Sidney's death. Moffet knew Sidney well during the years after his marriage. Accordingly, his medical comments are authentic though his chronology is questionable.

> When he had scarce completed six years of life, measles and smallpox laid waste, as with little mines, the excellence and the fashion of his beauty; and yet not in such wise that the residue was unbecoming to him; and by the same token it showed, moreover, that the flower of beauty ought not to be held in price but that grace of soul ought, rather, to be esteemed—which neither the tooth of the most furious wind will ravish nor the malice of any sickness subdue.[6]

"Six years" should read "eight years" to accord with the date of the smallpox epidemic as well as the astrologer's careful calculations.

The third illness occurred in Sidney's fourteenth and fifteenth years, apparently the winter of 1568–69. It is described as "calidis oculorum fluxionibus et lippitudine," hot discharges from the eyes and inflammation. This sounds as if Sidney had conjunctivitis in some form, perhaps pink eye or possibly trachoma. The fact that Sidney suffered another serious illness in the spring of 1571, unmentioned in this horoscope, confirms that it was cast before that affliction. Dr. Moffet supplies no dates or details about these illnesses, but simply reports that "it twice occurred that, overstimulated by his prolonged studies in early adolescence [i.e. his fourteenth year and after] he fell ill of a fever attended by the greatest peril; and he was forced to slacken the reins in sports, until, the breakdown in his health having been repaired, more fit and more active he returned to the Muses."[7]

The other two incidents cited by the astrologer were boyhood appearances before the Queen. The first is placed in 1566, when Sidney was eleven: "11° vero anno oratorem egisti apud serenissimam Principem Elizabetham." Doubtless Sidney appeared before Elizabeth in August 1566 when the Queen visited Oxford on her summer progress, and Philip and a group of schoolfellows from Shrewsbury were brought to the university city to witness the reception (see p. 15 above). His second appearance involved another "oration" two years later when he was an undergraduate at Christ Church. The astrologer, who was a member of the university, has underlined the last portion for emphasis.

> Norunt fateor omnes qui in nostra Achademia sunt Oxoniensi quam praeclara semina tibi a Natura ad bonas artes capessendas insita fuerint, quantosque progressus feceris summa cum aetatis tuae admiratione et

6. Moffet, p. 71.
7. Ibid., p. 73.

audientium applausu cum *coram sereniss. principe orationem habueris & ornatam vix annum aetatis tuae 13. egressus.* (See p. 16 above.)

No other details of this occasion in 1568 are known. Because Elizabeth did not visit Oxford that year, Sidney's appearance before her probably took place at court, sometime after Sir Henry's return from Ireland late in 1567. The success of Philip's performance then could well have been reported at Oxford.

The passage just quoted continues with further testimony to Sidney's precocity. In the process it reveals that the astrologer was a mathematician whose retirement from teaching prevented him from having Sidney as his pupil.

> Potuissent sine metuis scire qui grammatica Rhetorica Dialectica Naturali Philosophia, & Ethica te erudierunt apud nos qui nobis celebritate & reipsa Iuuenes literatissimi et essent et existimarentur. Expertus & essem ego indolem tuam vere liberam et ingenuam in Mathematum studiis ac disciplinis nisi me temporis iniuria tibi proripuisset, vel te mihi iniqua sortis conditio potius praeclusisset. Doleo ego Adolescentem tantae spei futurum qui a Natura ad Mathematum studia conformatus & celestem philosophiam discendam natus, acumine felici, ingenio diuino menteque ad altissima quaeque a terris remota spectante in reliquis profecerit, in Vrania vero haud ita multum laborant. Quod hic multa referam, animaduerti propensionem tuam in Astronomiam quam studiosa & ardens fuerit cum te inuiserem et adirem sermoque multus inter nos vltro citroque haberetur de Mathesi, quam tunc prudenter de illis rebus dissecueris mecum ipse in recessu plus doloris quam in aditu amoris concipiendo & pensitando quod exceperam bene conscius sum. At vt inde quo digressa est eo se referat oratio felicis ingenii haec accipe testimonia. (See p. 18 above.)

Once again, confirmation may be found in Dr. Moffet's *Nobilis* of Sidney's assiduous application to his studies. In contrast to the astrologer's narrow concerns with mathematics, though, Moffet stressed Sidney's all-round abilities:

> For, when barely ten years old, to whom did he yield in reputation for and knowledge of grammar? A little later whom did he fear in the matter of rhetorical principles? And, on going on, was he surpassed by any of his schoolmates in mathematical exercises (which often tease, or indeed harass, adult minds)? Also, did he not put other boys of his age to blush and to shame because of his reputation for a knowledge of many languages? In fine, he was to such a degree tenacious and desirous of esteem gained through any learning, that he would sooner allow much to be taken away from his life than a tittle withdrawn from his studious pursuits.[8]

8. Ibid.

Moffet, however, reports that Sidney had little interest in the casting of horoscopes. Indeed, Moffet—who knew Sidney in his years of maturity— writes that he strongly disapproved of what Kepler called "the foolish daughter" of astronomy.

> Astrology alone (which only chance and vanity have made an art) he could never be so far misled as to taste, even with the tip of his tongue. Nay, he seemed purposely to slight it, among all accepted sciences, even with a certain innate loathing.[9]

Dr. Moffet is a formidable witness, so his testimony poses the problem of how to reconcile his description of Sidney's loathing of astrology with the horo-scope-maker's statement about Sidney's eager propensity for the study of the stars. Doubtless Sidney displayed an intelligent interest in the subject, and the astrologer, obviously prejudiced in favour of his arcane art, may have hoped that Sidney might be lured into pursuit of the celestial craft. Perhaps he was misled by Sidney's polite response as well, just as years later in Prague Father Campion mistook Sidney's politeness for an indication that he might be ripe for conversion to the Roman church.

But Sidney's purported loathing for astrology must also be reconciled with the contents of sonnet twenty-six of *Astrophil and Stella:* "Though dustie wits dare scorn Astrologie . . ." This sonnet, we should remember, was just one of 108 in a series in celebration of Sidney's love for "Stella." Despite the dominant image of this pseudonym, we find a scant sprinkling of astrological allusions in the 2,267 lines of the sonnet sequence. Indeed, apart from this single sonnet, the words "star" or "stars" appear only four times. A check of sixty other astrological terms (e.g. ascendant, retrograde, aspect, conjunction, opposition, trigon, quartile, sextile, Zodiac, phase, nativity, etc.) reveals only single instances of four such words: planet, influences, signs, and zenith. In contrast, astrological words appear fifteen times in Shakespeare's sonnets and eight times in Spenser's. Furthermore, sonnet twenty-six's evidence is weakened by the fact that most of the lines echo a passage from du Bartas's *La Semaine*, as Ringler points out. As we know from various sources, Sidney made a translation, now lost, of this poem. In summary, then, the evidence indicates that with maturity Sidney rejected judicial astrology as a believable system, though he did not disdain to employ its imagery for poetic purposes, albeit less frequently than the domi-nant metaphor of "Stella" would seem to call for.

Two other sections of Sidney's horoscope may be cited here, despite the fact that they do not reveal much specific information about the sixteen-year-old youth. The first concerns his fortune:

9. Ibid., p. 75.

Si libeat commemorare anteactae aetatis tuae annos, experiere per 15 et 16 annum fortunae inaequalitatem primum ... ex martialibus, contumeliosis seditiosis, praedonibus, furibus, per contentiones nixas et in affinibus & societate.

[If I may remind you of the years of your life now past, you experienced your first piece of ill-fortune in your 15th and 16th years through losses from war, insolent treachery, robbers, thieves, and through disputes among relatives and friends.]

What experiences Sidney could have reported to the astrologer to prompt such a description cannot be determined. Aside from his illnesses, and the health and financial problems of his parents, no such instances are now known; none of them can properly be considered due to war, treachery, robbers, thieves, or family quarrels.

During the specified years, the proposed marriage between Sidney and Anne Cecil, the daughter of Lord Burghley, was broken off by the Cecils, but that scarcely would fit the descriptions of Philip's ill-fortune. The incident does seem to be reflected, however, in a passage titled "De Coniugio"; here, again, the last sentence was underlined for emphasis.

... & nisi id tempus tibi assumpseris Philippe quo annum 16 egeris vix immo ne vix quidem tempus dabitur *usque ad 26 annum Maxima tamen* (ni fallat me coniectandi ratio) *inclinatio fuit tibi & propensio 16 exacto & iam lapso aetatis tuae anno.*

[... unless you seize that time, Philip, in which you are sixteen years old, there will be scarcely (no, not even scarcely) any time available until your twenty-sixth year. Unless my method of forecasting deceives me, *you had the strongest possible inclination and propensity to marriage now that sixteen years are passed and gone.*]

There is no indication that Sidney took this analysis seriously, for not until his twenty-ninth year, 1583, was marriage arranged for him with Frances, daughter of Sir Francis Walsingham. Indeed, there is no evidence that once the horoscope had been completed Sidney ever paid the slightest attention to its predictions.[10]

10. For a more detailed account of Sidney and astrology, see James M. Osborn, "Mica, Mica, Parva Stella," in *TLS*, Jan. 1, 1971, pp. 17–18.

APPENDIX 2

SIDNEY'S PATENT TO BEAR ARMS IN ITALY

[Documents in the Venetian archives]

29 aprile 1574

L'Illustre Signor Filippo Sidnei figliolo dell'Illustrissimo Signor Henrico Governatore della Provincia di Gales si ritrova qui in Venetia, et vol partir per Padoa, dove dissegna fermarsi qualche tempo allo studio. Desidera non esser molestato Lui, né un suo gentil-huomo con tre servitori per il portar dell'armi, et però si supplicano le eccellentissime etc. [Signorie vostre etc.] Il nome del gentil-huomo e il Signor Lodovico Bruschetto li servitori sono

> Harrigo Vita
> Grifone Appiano
> Gio. [Giovanni] Fisher
> [Consiglio dei Dieci, Parti Comuni, R. 31, c. 127 r.]

30 Aprile 1574   *Patentes*

Universis et singulis, Rectoribus quarúcunq; civitatum, praesertim Padua^r, terrarum et locorum nostrorum, Magistratibus huius urbis nostra^r Venetiarum, officialibus, et ministris nostris quibuscunq; tam praesentibus quam futuris signi-ficamus, heri in cons°. nostro Decem captam fuisse partem tenoris infrascripti vz. che al Signor Filippo Sidnei Inglese figliolo dell' Ill. S$^{or.}$ Henrico Sidnei govern-ator della provincia di Gales, che si ritruova qui per andar a Padoa, ove disegna fermarsi per studiar, sia concessa licentia di portar le armi si in questa citta di Venetia come in ogni altra città, terra, et luogo del Dni͡o nostro, con un suo gentil'huomo appresso di lui nominato Lodovico Bruschetto, et con tre servitori, li nome d'i quali siano notati in questa città nell' officio d'i capi diquesto cons°. et di fuori, nelle cancellarie delli luoghi, ovi si ritroverà, giurando, che stiano in casa sua, et a sui spese. Quare auctoritate sopradicti consilii mandamus vobis, ut supradictam concessionem observetis, et ab omnibus observari faciatis. Dat, Die 30. Aprilis 1574.

> Vigore partio captae in cons°. X
> Die 29. Aprilis 1574.
> > [Archivio di Stato: Venezia
> > Capi del Consiglio dei Dieci: Lettere. fil. 75.]

APPENDIX 3

INSTRUCTIONS FOR SIDNEY'S EMBASSY, FEBRUARY 7, 1576/77

Instructions geuen to Phillipp sidney esquier: beinge sent Ambassadore to Rodulphe the .2. Emperore & His Mother ye Empresse, to Condole the Deathe of ye Emperor Maximillian his father: and withall he was Directed to take in his way. the twoe Counte Palatines, & to Condole also the Deathe of theire father, then latelie Dead,

Dated the vij of February ano. 1576.

We thinke it verie Convenient in your way to the Emperore that you visit the two sonnes of the late Counte Pallatine, Frederike and Cassimire whom you shall lett vnderstand howe muche we lamente the death of theire late father a prince aswell affected to the Cause of Religeon. soe carefull for the conservac̄on of the libertie of the Empire and so good & faithfull a freinde towardes vs which respectes might greatli increase our greefe were it not that we see the Empire soe happie to haue two so noble princes of soe great towardlines as they are, soe well disposed to follow the good steppes of theire father to succead and supplie his place whereof if the Empire shall reape the Comoditie by havinge such worthie members directed by soe good a paterne: soe they them selves by houldinge so good a Course shall wine to them selues both reputacon and suretie and as herein noe doubte many of those princes who were well afected to theire good fathere will reioyce soe non more then ourselues beinge so greatlye devoted to that famelie as we weare: these and the like kinde of Speches we thinke it meete in generalletie to be deliuered vnto the two Brothers.

And in case you shall heare that they live together in good and brotherlie amitie as we are informed they doe: then shall you perswade them to the Continvaunce of the same by puttinge them in minde of the great benefite that will growe both perticulerlie to themselves and generallie to the Empire by their good Concorde and agreement: on the other side if you shall heare of any disagreement betweene the[m] then shall you laye before them the perill that maye followe therof to both theire Ruins especially in this tyme when it behvoveth those princes that make profession of the Gospell to Combine and knitte them selues in perfecte Amitie at the inwarde greefes removed: This pointe you may delate accordinglie as you shall see them inclined either to good agreement or to the Contrarie not forgettinge to pute them in Minde of the

frenche Kinges determinacon resolued in this assemblie of the states, as also
what is to be looked for of don John de Austrias proceedinges in the Lowe
Countries in case his designes maye take place: After theis generall speeches
deliuered vnto both the bretheren you shall perticullerlie let Casimire vnderstande that as we doe assure our selfe greatly of his good affectione and devotion
towardes vs soe may he on the other make full assurance of our freindlie inclina-
con towardes him, aswell in respecte of the princelie partes that are in him, as
that he was one whome the Prince his father did soe dearlie loue which Cannot
but yeild augmentacon of our affeccon towardes him.

These Compleaments beinge done you shall informe your selfe at his handes
whether the money deliuered vnto his father be allreadie receaved to the ende
that we may accordinglie dispose there of which we meane shall remaine in some
place of that Countrye in deposition vntill such tyme as we shall see what will
become of those newe fieres nowe in kindelinge.

Further you shall learne of him the state of the Empire what opinion they
haue of the Emperores sonne. Whether he be like to incline to warre or to Peace,
how he standeth disposed to make him selfe a partie againste those of the
Religeon or no, how the Princes of the Country are affected towards him and
what mariag he is towarde, and with whom, moreouer how the princes of
Germanie are seuerallie bent and affected toward the states of the Lowe Coun-
tryes and to the Princes of the Religeon in Fraunce what forces ther are pre-
paringe either for the one side or for the other whether he him selfe meane to
be a dealer and for whom, After informaco receaved from him of these particularities you shall dispatch one from thence with aduertisements to vs and
soe proceed in your voyage. And at your Accesse to the Emperore after the
deliuerie of our lettres you shall lett him vnderstand how much we were greeved
with the losse of so worthie a prince that Germanye might haue soe evell
spared that had maintayned the same in soe good Peace within it selfe and lefte
them in some staye or soarte of agreement with the great enemye to Christendome the Turke a thinge most necessarie in this tyme; Consideringe the inwarde
divisiones amongest our selues that Carie the name and Tytle of Christian
Princes, and therefore a greate argument of his singuler foresight and wisdome
and besides this Cause of Greefe which is Come to vs with the reste of the Princes
of Christendome you shall declare vnto him that perticulerlie we had Cause
to lament his death havinge there by loste a freinde in whome we reposed so
greate Trust, and at whose handes we had receaved soe greate honore: in
Consideration where of, as also for the desire we haue to linke our selfe in
frendshippe with him: we Coulde doe no lesse then performe all frendlie
offices towards the sonne of such a father by sendinge you to visitt him.

And therefore in respecte of the loue we beare him aswell for his fathers sake
as the place he is Called too beinge the Cheefe potentate in Christendome,
vpon the direccon of whose gouernement dependeth the well doinge or Ruine

of Christendom we Cannot but wishe him to followe the Course and steppes of the provident Prince his Father: which was to embrace peace both at home and abroade, and to beware as a moste perilous thinge both for his owne state perticulerlye and for the whole Empire, that hee give noe eare to such violent Counsell as some martiall and turbulent sperites are apte to give to yonge Princes who respecte more theire Ambitiones and privat passiones then foresee the mischeefes that moste Comonly accompanye warres whereof the issue is vncertaine, the benefites non and the harmes manyfeste.

Which Aduise you shall assure him in our name we were moued to give him not for any Curiositie or desire we haue to intrude our selfe into others Councelles but only for the loue we beare him, and the benefyte we haue receaved our selfe by a peaceable gouernement beinge Comonly accompanyed with sundrie blessinges of god, for warres are not to be vsed but as in procuringe the health of the bodie cuttinge and searinge are; which are neuer Admitted but in Case of greate perrill and great necessetie.

And for that it may be vpon some sinister informačon given vnto him touchinge our proceedinges with the states of the Lowe Countries he may enter into some speech thereof, for the betere iustefyinge of our proceeding therein you shall receave informačon before your departure, from our Secretarie in that behalfe.

After the complements done to the yonge prince then you shall visitt the Empresse and vse some such speeche of Condolinge as by you shall be thought meete for that purpose and also lett her vnderstande, how greatly we esteeme and honor her for the greate good reporte we have heard of her vertues, and that we are sorie that in respecte of our qualletie and the fare distaunce of place we are devided from so good happe to enioye the Companye of soe vertuous a princesse beinge no lesse reverenced for her vertues then for her degree, that the loue we beare to her and her Children in respecte of the honor we receaved of the Emperore her Husband hathe moued vs to Aduise her sonne, vpon whom the gouernement of the Empire is Caste to followe the steppes of his father by Continuinge a peaceable kinde of gouernement and therefor cannot but wishe her as one who shall reape most comforte of his well doinge to aduise him therevnto in respecte of the perill that may ensue otherwise both to him selfe and to the whole estate of Christendom, & amongest other thinges to aduise him to flie the Authors of violent Counselles who comonly insinuate them selues into younge princes bosomes: These Complements done to her ye shall in our name visete the rest of her Chilldren vsinge such speeches as to their Ages & persones may be thought meete.

And during the tyme of your beinge there, you shall informe your selfe of the younge Emperors disposityon and his bretheren, whether he bee martially enclined or otherwise, by whose advise he is directed: when it is likelie he shall marrie: what Princes in Germany are most affected towardes him: In what state hee is left for revenewes: what good agreement there is betweene him and his bretheren: what partage they haue, and how they are enclined.

After you shall haue accomplished these thinges, and other good offices there vnto incident for our honor and receaved such Answere as our said good brother the Emperore shall make vnto you to be deliuered vnto vs: you shall take your leave of him, And the Emperisse and her Children, and make your repaire home to our presence with convenient speede.

[Harley MS. 36, fols. 295–98]

APPENDIX 4

THE CASE FOR SIDNEY'S AUTHORSHIP OF "CERTAIN NOTES"

Because no author's name appears on the three contemporary manuscript copies of "Certain Notes," the complex evidence for attributing the report to Sidney requires orderly examination. When studied this evidence points convincingly to Sidney's authorship. Details of chronology fit neatly, the style resembles that of the report he wrote to Walsingham on May 3 (it is intentionally different from the style he used when addressing a literary audience), and Daniel Rogers, the only other diplomat involved in the delicate negotiations, was back in England at this time.

Rogers was so intimately involved that scrutiny of his actions is imperative. During part of April and May 1577 he was with the Prince of Orange at Dordrecht. This we know from Rogers's own account in a letter dated July 20 to Walsingham describing a second visit to Orange made in June and July 1577. Rogers tells Walsingham that on the later occasion he reminded Orange of his earlier visit:

> This being donne I desired His Excellency to call to mynde the conditions of the offre which he desired me, as I was with hym in apryll and may last at Dordrecht, to propose unto Her Majesty, to th'entent he might understand the better what Her Majesty answered. I repeted therefore unto him the talke which then he had with me, and gave him to understande that I had declared from him unto Her Majesty how . . .[1]

Here Rogers repeats what appears at first sight to be, with some variations, a condensation of eight paragraphs (17–24) of "Certain Notes," delineating terms of the treaty of union which Orange wished the Queen to enter into with him. (That Rogers could not have written "Certain Notes" will be demonstrated later.) In this letter he refers, however, not to "Certain Notes" but to a document entitled "Certaine conditions which the Prince of Orange proposeth unto Your most excellent Majestie for the makinge of a farther amity betwixt the realme of Inglande and the countries of Hollande and Zellande."[2] Indeed, he calls it "certain conditions which from him I had deliuered unto Her Majestie," thus repeating the two most important words of the title.

1. Lettenhove, pp. 406–07. See also Rogers's letter to Leicester of the same date, in which he repeats the contents of this letter almost word by word.
2. Lettenhove, pp. 344–45.

Similarity in title tends to compound the confusion in the content. "Certain Conditions" is in fact a condensed version, with some variations, of paragraphs 17–24 of "Certain Notes"; moreover, on collating "Certain Conditions" with the "conditions of the offre" Rogers gives in this letter, we find that, allowing for lapses in Roger's otherwise remarkable memory, the two agree in differing from "Certain Notes" in a very large number of verbal details.[3] This textual evidence is sufficiently strong to offset the problem that "Certain Conditions" was not calendared as having been received at the court at Greenwich until June 12.[4]

The treaty conditions, then, were first communicated to the Queen via Rogers at the beginning of May. Rogers left the Low Countries some time before May 11, as we know from a letter from Wilson, Ambassador in the Low Countries, to Walsingham in London—a letter which contains the clause "as I did write to yow, by Mr. Rogers."[5] There is no evidence that Rogers returned to visit Orange until the mission of June and July, which he describes in his letter of July 20 quoted above.

In this letter, Rogers goes on to say that when he had recounted the treaty conditions, and the Queen's response to them, the Prince reacted as follows:

> All which thinges he hard very attentively, and, perceaving I had made an ende, he beganne to aunswere me in such order as I proposed Her Majesties meaning. . . . Than he came to the artycles of the unyon and amity, which from him I had proposed to her Majestie, which he saied I had well remembered, and thancked me hartely for my endevours, affirming that I concurred with his discourse, which he had sent since my being with him, by Monsieur Sydney in writing.

Thus we also learn that the details of this treaty had been sent to Elizabeth by the hand of Philip Sidney.

Sidney's audience with Orange took place at the end of May. He had left Antwerp on May 27 for Geertruidenberg, where the Prince was in residence,[6] and after the meeting he left for England on or after June 2, carrying a letter from

---

3. For instance, Rogers's letter states the last clause to be a request for "an yerely support" in case the war "should endure long tyme." "Certain Conditions" asks for "a certain somme of mony specified in this amity to releeve them yearely." But in "Certain Notes" the amount of money is clearly given: it is a loan of "fifty thousand pound yearly." It seems as if Rogers had not even seen "Certain Notes," since he is ignorant of this exact sum.

4. *CSPF2*, no. 1475.

5. Lettenhove, p. 298. Rogers probably left on May 8. Wilson wrote to Walsingham on May 6 that he was "myndinge to send Mr. Rogers shortlie after." A letter of May 8 from Wilson to Walsingham is extant (Lettenhove, p. 291).

6. See above, p. 479.

Orange to the Queen written on this date.[7] The Prince wrote: "Nous avons supplie tous ensemble Monsieur de Sedenay, ambassadeur de Vostre Majeste vers l'Empereur, de nous faire cest honneur de declarer plus particulierement a icelle ce qu'il a cogneu de nos bonnes volontes et aussi l'estat en quoi il nous a laisses."

Although Orange had already proposed the conditions of the treaty via Rogers, he was now giving Sidney a written version. From this letter we learn that he also asked Sidney to declare more particularly to the Queen "what he has understood of our good wishes and also of the state in which he left us." In other words, "Certaine notes concerninge the present estate of the Prince of Orenge, and the provinces of Hollande and Zelande, as they were in the mounth of May, 1577." This document contains an expanded version of "Certain Conditions," together with Sidney's analysis of the state of the three provinces at that time.

Other evidence corroborates the attribution of "Certain Notes" to Sidney. The latest date mentioned in the report is May 16. As we have seen, Rogers, the only other diplomat known to have been involved in this important transaction, was in England by then. On June 23 Elizabeth wrote a reply to William which began: "Monsieur mon Cousin, Par nostre serviteur le Sr. Philippe de Sidney avons receu vostre lettre laquelle et ce qu'il nous a raccompté en vostre endroict nous ont faict ample tesmoignage de vostre syncère et dévote affection envers nous."[8] She refers to "Certain Notes." Elizabeth then goes on to mention "le Sieur Danyel Rogers, nostre serviteur, présent porteur, lequel il nous a semblé bon de depescher devers vous pour de nostre part vous communicquer nostre resolution sur les choses, lesquelles de vostre part par luy nous ont esté proposées." Here she designates "Certain Conditions."

The foregoing evidence, then, takes into account and explains all of the available information, with the exception of the date when "Certain Conditions" was calendared by the clerk. It is therefore very probable, within the limits of current knowledge, that Sidney was the author of "Certain Notes." Until new and conclusively contradictory information comes to light, "Certain Notes" should be accepted into the canon of Sidney's prose works.

THE TEXTS

The three extant manuscript texts may be designated as follows:
   X: in the Public Record Office (State Papers, vol. 70/145, no. 1225).

---

7. Lettenhove, p. 322. We know that this letter was entrusted to Sidney to carry over because of Elizabeth's answer of June 23, 1577, quoted below.
8. Lettenhove, p. 363.

Y: in the Public Record Office (State Papers, vol. 70/145, no. 1226); this text was printed by Lettenhove.

G: in the British Museum (Galba MS. C. VI, i, 52).

Manuscript X contains one paragraph not found in either of the other texts. Otherwise it agrees closely with Y, though in a few instances it agrees with the reading of G, or provides unique readings. G also agrees closely with Y, though it deviates from Y slightly more often than X does. But in seven successive paragraphs G differs considerably from both X and Y, paragraphs where X and Y agree closely with each other. The substance of these seven paragraphs, however, is very much the same in all three.

Of the variant readings scarcely any are manifest errors. Usually they are alternative phrasings which mean more or less the same thing. In some cases X and G expand the slightly more condensed text of Y, or to some degree explain the meaning. Notably, both X and G offer information available only to the author, details not found in the other manuscript. Therefore these variants are more than mere scribal interpolations.

In paragraph 13 of "Certain Notes," two dates are given: "The Duke of Arskott was appointed as the 16 of May to go from Don Juan with Doctor Leoninus to the Prince, as the Estates sent from them the Count of Lalaing and certain others, the 10th of this present, to go towards the Prince for to satisfy him in these points." For these dates both X and Y read "18" for Arskott's appointment and "16th" for the other date. The latter cannot be verified with certainty, but Wilson wrote to Leicester on May 18, 1577, "The Duke of Arschot, Monsr. de Hierges, Monsr. de Resinghen, Monsr. de Villervalle and others were sent by Don John and the States to deale with the Prynce the 16th of this monthe."9 This vindication of G's reading indicates at least that G's copyist was more accurate.

Because each of the three manuscripts has some unique readings, none of them is clearly descended from one of the others. Indeed, all three manuscripts offer apparently authorial though variant readings. The foregoing characteristics suggest that Sidney made three different reports, perhaps intended for three different recipients. In summary, then, the three texts are:

Y: a condensed and summary account containing the basic details of the proposed treaty.

X: a similarly condensed account, which adds one paragraph not found in either of the others.

G: a more discursive account, offering fuller details of what William actually said.

There is no evidence to indicate which text was made first.

In consideration of these points, manuscript G has been taken as the copy-text.

9. Lettenhove, pp. 301–02.

Substantive additions from X or Y have been inserted in half-brackets when they add to the sense; the source is given in a note. Variant readings, as opposed to additions not found in other copies, are not here recorded. The spelling has been modernized because the spelling habits of the copyists differ, and occasionally the punctuation has been altered for the convenience of the reader. Some future editor of Sidney's writings may prefer a fuller textual apparatus, but this should be adequate for present purposes.

APPENDIX 5

SIDNEY'S LETTER TO EDWARD DENNY

This important letter was unknown until a nearly contemporary transcript of it was offered for sale at Sotheby's on June 15, 1971. There it was purchased by the Bodleian Library. The letter covered three pages in a volume labelled "Miscellanies relating to Cambridge," which had been purchased by Sir Thomas Phillipps from Thorpe in 1836 (Phillipps MS. 9014), now sold by the Robinson Trust. While cataloguing the volume for Sotheby's, Peter J. Croft noticed the copy of Sidney's letter. He removed it from the volume (lot 1412) and described it separately as lot 1660.

Mr. Croft identified the handwriting as that of John Mansell of Lincolnshire (d. 1631). Mansell had entered Queens' College, Cambridge, in 1594 and graduated B.A. in 1598; he eventually became President of Queens' in 1622. The Sidney letter appears among some university exercises written when Mansell was an undergraduate. Because the subscription and signature appear to be a conscious attempt to imitate Sidney's hand, Mr. Croft suggests that Mansell copied it directly from the original.

The recipient of the letter, Edward Denny (1547–99), had been orphaned in early childhood. His education included several years at Merton College, Oxford. Being seven years senior to Sidney, he probably did not know him well before 1573. In that year, during which Sidney lived in Frankfurt, Vienna, and northern Italy, Denny accompanied the Earl of Essex on his ill-fated expedition to Ireland. In 1575, after Sidney's return to the English court, the friendship of the two men had an opportunity to develop. Several references show that by the early summer of 1580 Sidney and Ned Denny had become close friends.

The new letter, written before Denny again left for Ireland and dated May 22, 1580, is the earliest evidence of their intimacy. Four months later Sir Henry Sidney sent his greetings "to my Gouerner and deere Frend Mr. *Edward Denny*" in a letter to Lord Grey.[1] Denny's stay in Ireland ended before the new year, and in January 1581 he was back in England, participating with Sidney in a tournament in response to the challenge against the field issued by the Earl of Arundel and Sir William Drury.[2] Denny's biographer, the Reverend H. L. L. Denny, cites two letters of Denny's which testify to his great

1. Collins, 1:282.
2. Sir W. Segar, *The Booke of Honor and Armes* (1590), STC 22164, pp. 95–96.

admiration for Sidney. The first, written in Dublin to his cousin, Sir Francis Walsingham, and dated July 16, 1581, contains the following commendation: "Above all things, Sir, geve me leve to remember you to love Mr. Sidne, for I know that at your hands he is best worthy love." A few weeks later, writing to Walsingham from Powerscourt, Denny referred to "Mr. Sidney, the most worthy young man in the world."[3] In the following October Sidney wrote to Sir Christopher Hatton in support of Denny's claim to an estate in Ireland.[4]

Denny had evidently asked Sidney to suggest some reading for his stay in Ireland, and this newly recovered letter is Sidney's reply. Besides revealing the extent of Sidney's knowledge of historical and other literature, the letter provides information on several points of interest:

1. Sidney openly chafed at his lack of employment in affairs of state: ". . . since the vnnoble constitution of our tyme doth keepe vs from fitte imployments. . . ." Fulke Greville also emphasizes Sidney's lack of employment, for example, "the impossibility for Sir *Phillip* to win the Queen . . . to dispense with an employment for him."[5] This evidence shows that both Sidney and his friends considered the situation to be notorious. As early as July 1, 1578, Sidney had complained to Languet, "For to what purpose should our thoughts be directed to various kinds of knowledge, unless room be afforded for putting it into practice, so that public advantage may be the result, which in a corrupt age we cannot hope for?"[6]

2. Sidney had already written songs which he assumed Denny would know: "Remember *with* your good voyce, to singe my songes for they will one well become an other." Indeed, he may have heard Denny sing them already. Ringler pointed out that eight of the *Certain Sonnets* "derive their stanzaic structure and rhythms from contemporary tunes";[7] this indicates that Sidney intended that they should be sung rather than read.

3. As Mr. Croft pointed out, Sidney apparently referred to Edmund Spenser in the following passage: "Good will carries mee on to this impudence to write my councell to him, that (to say nothing of your selfe) hath my Lord Grayes company." Ringler suggests that Sidney may have helped Spenser gain his position as secretary to Lord Grey.[8] The appointment followed the brief period of less than six months during which the two poets had occasional meetings. In December 1579,

---

3. "Biography of Sir Edward Denny," *Transactions* of the East Herts Archaeological Society for 1904, p. 251.

4. Feuillerat, 3:157.

5. Greville, p. 82.

6. Pears, p. 143.

7. Ringler, p. xliii.

8. Ibid., p. xxxiii.

Spenser's *Shepheardes Calendar* appeared, dedicated "To The Noble and Vertuous Gentleman most worthy of all titles both of learning and cheualrie M Philip Sidney"; Sidney's response may have been to recommend Spenser to Lord Grey.

4. The program of study outlined for Edward Denny reveals what Sidney, the beau ideal of "learning and cheualrie," considered essential. Sidney lists the ancient and modern writers whom Denny should read, and he characterizes many of them. Similarly, he advises Denny to read the Scriptures and recommends that special study should also be given to geography, military art, style in writing, draftsmanship, and mathematics. He urges Denny to follow a methodical plan of study and to outline the contents of books as he reads them, doubtless the same program Sidney had followed during his own days of study in Italy and elsewhere.

The text of the letter has kindly been made available for publication by the Bodleian authorities. Most of the authors and books cited are obvious enough, though some, such as Ortelius, do not appear in Sidney's other writings. "Langeai in french" refers to Languet's *Harangue au roy Charles IX*, printed in the first volume of *Memoires de l'Estat de France* in 1578, for his other published writings at this date were in Latin.

To my welbeloved friend Mr Edward Denny

My Ned. that you love me is no newes vnto me, havinge received so notable proofs of it, but yet is the remembrance alwayes exceedinge gratefull. And very willingly doe I beare the preferringe of the noble Lord Gray; since so I preferre him to my selfe, as I will ever be most glad to doe him service with affectionate honor, which truly I am but to very fewe. And if you should doe otherwise, in steade of thankinge you I should doute you might in like sorte dispence with your selfe to sett me behinde some other of lesse bothe acqueintance & worthe. Honour him therfore still, and as you matche me with him, soe therein will I matche my selfe with you. And continewe my good Edward in lovinge of me, or else I shall bee a looser by you. You will me to tell you my minde of the directinge your studyes. I will doe it as well as the hast of your boy, and my little Judgement will hable me. But first let me reioyse with you, that since the vnnoble constitution of our tyme, doth keepe vs from fitte imployments, you doe yet keepe your selfe awake, with the delight of knowledge; one of the notablest effects of that, which makes vs differ from beasts. Resolve therfore vpon that still, & resolve thus that when so ever you may iustly say to your selfe you loose your tyme, you doe indeed loose so much of your life: since of lyfe (though the materiall description of it be the body

& soule) the consideration and markinge of it stands only in tyme. Neither
let vs leave of, because perchance the right pryce of these things is not had
without we shoold wishe our selves Asses because some folks knowe not
what a man meanes. But to your purpose I must say this; If I should generally discourse of knowledge what it is? how many kindes? which worthy,
which not? I might build vpon a large ground, and yet perchaunse leave
you vnsatisfied, & my selfe wander beyond myne owne reach. This no
doubt is trewe, that such is to humane mindes the infinitenes of them, that
to swallow them vp is impossible. Well may a man be swallowed in them,
and fruitelesly, if he have not the better lyne to guide him in the Laberinthe.
This consideration therfore must must [sic] be particular, and particularly
bent to your selfe, for one thinge is fitte to be knowne by a scoller that
will reed in the scools and an other by Ned Denny: and even in Ned
Denny one way to have been begone if you weare a child, and an other of
this age you nowe pass in. If you were younge surely the toungs of Latine
& Greek (which be as it were the tresure howses of learninge) & the art
of Logick (which indeed helps much to try the valew of eche thinge) were
exactly to be desired. And such lyke which nowe without a miraculous
witte, & blessinge of God, woold bring forth as vayne a labourer, as if a
man that must fight to morowe, would only studdy howe to sende for a
good sworde into spaigne. To my Nedd Denny therfore, and even soe to
my [selfe], (for I doe in this with you, as we doe one to an other in horsemanship; teach before wee have well learned) this I think may be the course,
to knowe, what it is we desire to knowe. And that I thinke to be double,
the one as concerninge our selves, the other an outward application of our
selves. The knowledge of our selves no doubte ought to be most pretious
vnto vs; and therein the holy scriptures, if not the only, are certainly the
incomperable lanterne in this fleshly darkness of ours: For (alas) what is all
knowledge? if in the end of this litle and weerisome pilgrimage, Hell
become our scoolmaster. They therfore are diligently, to be redd. To them
if you will adde as to the helpe of the second table (I meane that which
contaynes the love of thy neighbour, & dealing betwixt man & man)
some parts of morall philosophy, I thinke you shall doe very wisely. For
in trothe oftentymes wee erre, thinkinge we doe well, as longe as we meane
well; where indeed want of knowledge, may make vs doe as much
wickedness (though not soe wickedly) as they which, even pretensedly
commit all naughtiness. Thereout therfore may we seeke what is is [sic] to
be truly iuste, truly vallyant, rightly temperate, & rightly friendly, with
their annexed quallityes and contraryes. And therof are many bookes
written; but to my pleasing Aristotles Ethickes passe; but he is somethinge
darke and hath need of a Logicall examination, Tullyes offices next if not
equall, & truly for you & my selfe beyond any. With him you may ioyne

some of Plutarcks discourses, as of Refreining anger, of curiosity, of the
Tranquillity of the minde, of the Flatterer, & the Friende, of Morall vertew,
and soe by peeces as your leysure serves. But let Tully be for that mater
your foundation, next to the foundation of foundations, and wisdome of
wisdomes, I meane the holy scripture. And when you have redd these, we
will conferre further. The second parte consists as it were in the trade of
our lives. For a physician must studdy one thinge, and a Lawyer an other,
but to you that with good reason bend your selfe to souldiery, what bookes
can deliver, stands in the books that profess the arte, & in historyes. The
firste shewes what should be done, the other what hath bene done. Of the
first sorte is Langeai in french, and Machiavell in Italian, and many other
wherof I will not take vpon me to iudge, but this I thinke if you will
studdy them, it shall be necessary for you to exercise your hande in setting
downe what you reed, as in descriptions of battaillons, camps, and marches,
with some practise of Arithmetike, which sportingly you may exercise.
Of them I will say noe further, for I am witness of myne owne ignoraunce.
For historicall maters, I woold wish you before you began to reed a litle
of Sacroboscus Sphaere, & the Geography of some moderne writer,
wherof there are many & is a very easy and delightfull studdy. You have
allready very good iudgement of the Sea mappes, which will make the
other much the easier; and provide your selfe of an Ortelius, that when
you reed of any place, you may finde it out, & have it, as it were before
your eyes; For it doth exceedingly confirme, both the iudgement, &
memory. Soe muche of this, as I account necessary for you is to be [do]ne
in a monethe space, or litle more, for I doe not wish an artificers wadinge
into it. Then for the historyes them selves gladly I would wish you shoold
reed the Greek & Romane writers, for they were the wisest, and fullest of
excellent examples, both of discipline & stratagemes, and then woold I
tell you, you shoold begin with Phillip Melanthons Chronology, so to
Justine, then to Herodotus, Thucidides, Xenophon, Diodorus Siculus,
Quintus Curtius, Polybius, Lyvy, Dionisius, Salust, Ca'sar, Dion, Tacitus,
& then the Emperours lyves, gathered together in a volume by Henricus
Stephanus. Then to take Zonaras, & Nicetas, for the Greek parts, &
Procopius; and from thence to fall lower, to the particular chronicles of
eche country, as Paulus Aemilius for France, Polidore for Englande, and
soe of the rest. But because this might seeme too longe, though in deed not
soe longe, as a man woold thinke, my councell to you is even to begin
with our english Cronicle, sett out by Hollinshead; which you shoold reed
thorow till you came to Edwarde the thirdes lyfe, then to take Froyssart,
after him Anguerard of Monstrelett, written in old frenche, after him
Philip de Comines, & then Guicciardin who reacheth almost to our tyme.
And these will serve your turne for historicall matters. But nowe may you

aske me: what shall I doe first? Truly in my opinion, an hower to your Testament, & a peece of one to Tullyes offices, & that with studdy. Plutarkes discourses you may reede with more ease. For the other maters allott your selfe an other howre for Sacroboscus, & Valerius, or any other of Geography, and when you have satisfied your selfe in that, take your history of England, & your Ortelius to knowe the places you reed of; and soe in my conceite, you shall pass both pleasantly and profitably. Your books of the Art of Souldiery must have an other hower, but before you goe to them you shall doe well to vse your hande, in drawing of a plotte, & practise of Arithmetike. Whether nowe you will doe these by peece-meale, all in a day, or first goe thorow with one, yow must be your owne iudge, as you finde your memory best serve. To me, the variety rather delights me, then confounds me. Thus not as a generall doctrine, but as I thinke it best for thee my owne Ned, have I spent more lynes then I thought to have done words. but good will carries mee on to this impudence to write my councell to him, that (to say nothing of your selfe) hath my Lord Grayes company; which nowe I will end with these 2 remembrances; 1. that you forget not to note what you conceave of that you reed. And 2. that you remember with your good voyce, to singe my songes for they will one well become an other. My Lord of Pembrook, my sister, & your charge thanke you with many thankes, and your cakes are reserved against all the parrish come to dinner. Remember your last promise, & Farewell from my heart. At Wilton This Whitsondai. 1580.

> Yowre master in name but trew
> Frend in deede. Philip Sidnei.

LOBBET TO PHILIP SIDNEY, OCTOBER 1, 1581

This letter, dated three years after the central events described in this book, is preserved with the other new letters to Sidney now in the Osborn Collection. Because the subject matter speaks for itself and most of the persons named, especially Lobbet himself, are already familiar, little comment is required.

Languet had arranged for Robert to live in the house of Dr. Sturm at Strasbourg, but Lobbet was in general charge of him. The young man with Robert Sidney was the fifteen-year-old son of Baron Johannes Žerotin, Charles Žerotin, a youth highly praised for his intellect and polished manners. Philip had met him six years earlier in Brno (see the letter dated May 24, 1579, from Languet to Robert Sidney, cited in chap. 15).

Sturm had been in a theological controversy on the side of the university against the pastors of Strasbourg for several years. On June 29 he had been unjustly condemned by the magistrates without even the formality of a hearing. On December 7 following he was deposed as rector of the academy. Daniel Rogers's disaster consisted of sitting in prison in Germany where he had been seized by Baron Von Anholt at the request of Philip of Spain in the autumn of 1580. He did not gain release until 1584.

Greetings.

Although I have received no letter from you, illustrious and noble Master Sidney, I do not think it will be unwelcome to you if I send you my greetings via this brief epistle: in which I wanted to tell you that the illustrious and noble Master Robert, your brother (who after his return from England stayed with us for a few weeks) left here on the twenty-sixth of last month, to begin his journey to Paris. I hope that, with God for guide and angels for company, he will have reached Paris in comfort and safety. It would certainly make me very happy if this were so, and to find out I am writing to him today, asking him to write and tell me about the outcome of his journey. I gave him a letter, when he left here, which I wrote to some friends of mine in Paris, so that they may be able to do anything they can for him. I hope that will not be a burden to them. Certainly his [pleasant] nature and good manners make him worthy to be treated with courtesy and respect. Indeed, his virtues have attached me to him in the strongest possible way.

Added to this, when he left he gave me (who was expecting nothing of the kind) an exquisitely crafted ring adorned with various jewels; I did not want to conceal this from you. It was a gift I accepted unwillingly: for I am not of the sort that covets rewards, nor is it my custom to proffer courtesies in the hope of recompense. Because of this, I almost refused that "modest" gift, and would have done so, had I not perceived his enthusiasm and feared lest he should think that I despised his generosity. So, with some hesitation, I accepted the gift, and thanked him most warmly—as I do you also: and I declare, now and for the future, that it has left me deeply indebted to both of you. Indeed, I shall strive—should an occasion present itself—to show you that no one is more ready and willing to show you all deference.

He left behind here that German lad who has accompanied him for about six years, and took his leave of him very graciously; dismissing him with such generosity that he has no more to wish for, and only respect and praise. This youth is thinking of finishing the course of studies to which he seems born: his father is instructing him to do so, he himself wants it, and his affairs require it. It was for this reason that he could not take up a career at court or in the army. If, however, in the progress of his studies, he should at any time be able to be of service to you or your family, I am certain that he would try anything, with alacrity and with all the energy he has.

I am not writing any news, as we have little that is worth writing. The good Sturmius, for making the choice you know of, is being greatly hounded by the theologians who believe that, whether he stays or goes, they can easily get him accused here. Since, therefore, the good old man will have to be publicly defended at a trial, it is only fair that good people should aid and support him. So I commend him to you; and you can, should you have an opportunity, commend him to your queen. Farewell and live in happiness, illustrious and noble lord, and accept my respects. From Strasbourg, October 1, 1581.

Yours most respectfully,
Jo. Lobbetius

My greetings, with all due reverence, to Master Walsingham, Master Beale, and (if only one could get them to him) to Rogers, whose disaster I grieve for.

INDEX